TEACHERS, SCHOOLS, AND SOCIETY

TEACHERS, SCHOOLS, AND SOCIETY

EIGHTH EDITION

DAVID MILLER SADKER

American University

MYRA POLLACK SADKER

Late Professor, American University

KAREN R. ZITTLEMAN

American University

Boston   Burr Ridge, IL   Dubuque, IA   Madison, WI   New York   San Francisco   St. Louis
Bangkok   Bogotá   Caracas   Kuala Lumpur   Lisbon   London   Madrid   Mexico City
Milan   Montreal   New Delhi   Santiago   Seoul   Singapore   Sydney   Taipei   Toronto

Higher Education

TEACHERS, SCHOOLS, AND SOCIETY
Published by McGraw-Hill, a business unit of The McGraw-Hill Companies, Inc., 1221 Avenue of the Americas, New York, NY, 10020. Copyright © 2008, 2005, 2003, 2000, 1997, 1994, 1991, 1988 by The McGraw-Hill Companies, Inc. All rights reserved. No part of this publication may be reproduced or distributed in any form or by any means, or stored in a database or retrieval system, without the prior written consent of The McGraw-Hill Companies, Inc., including, but not limited to, in any network or other electronic storage or transmission, or broadcast for distance learning.

Some ancillaries, including electronic and print components, may not be available to customers outside the United States.

This book is printed on acid-free paper.

1 2 3 4 5 6 7 8 9 0 DOW/DOW 0 9 8 7 6

ISBN: 978-0-07-352590-7
MHID: 0-07-352590-1
AIE ISBN: 978-0-07-326215-4
AIE MHID: 0-07-326215-3

Vice President and Editor-in-Chief: *Emily Barrosse*
Publisher: *Beth Mejia*
Senior Sponsoring Editor: *Allison McNamara*
Senior Developmental Editor: *Cara Harvey Labell*
Executive Marketing Manager: *Sarah Martin*
Permissions Coordinator: *Marty Moga*
Managing Editor: *Jean Dal Porto*
Lead Project Manager: *Susan Trentacosti*
Art Director: *Jeanne Schreiber*
Art Manager: *Robin Mouat*
Designer: *Srdjan Savanovic*
Lead Photo Research Coordinator: *Alexandra Ambrose*
Photo Researcher: *Robin Samper*
Lead Media Producer: *Jocelyn Spielberger*
Media Project Manager: *Magdalena Corona*
Senior Production Supervisor: *Janean A. Utley*
Composition: *9/12 Stone Serif, by Techbooks*
Printing: *45# Pub Matte, R. R. Donnelley*

Cover: © *Royalty-Free/Corbis*

Credits: The credits section for this book begins on page C–1 and is considered an extension of the copyright page.

Library of Congress Control Number: 2006937408

The Internet addresses listed in the text were accurate at the time of publication. The inclusion of a Web site does not indicate an endorsement by the authors or McGraw-Hill, and McGraw-Hill does not guarantee the accuracy of the information presented at these sites.
www.mhhe.com

ABOUT THE AUTHORS

David Sadker

Dr. Sadker has taught in middle and senior high schools, as well as at the college level, and has been a professor at American University (Washington, DC) for more than three decades. He and his late wife Myra Sadker, gained a national reputation for research and publications concerning the impact of gender in schools. (To learn more about Myra's life and work, visit www.sadker.org.) Dr. Sadker has degrees from the City College of New York, Harvard University, and the University of Massachusetts. He has written several books and numerous articles in both professional and popular journals. He coauthored *Failing at Fairness: How Our Schools Cheat Girls,* published by Touchstone Press in 1995, and his research has been reported in hundreds of newspapers and magazines including *USA Today, USA Weekend, Parade Magazine, BusinessWeek, The Washington Post, The London Times, The New York Times, Time,* and *Newsweek.* He has appeared on local and national television and radio shows such as *The Today Show, Good Morning America, The Oprah Winfrey Show,* Phil Donahue's *The Human Animal,* National Public Radio's *All Things Considered* and *Talk of the Nation,* and twice on *Dateline: NBC* with Jane Pauley. The Sadkers received the American Educational Research Association's award for the best review of research published in the United States in 1991, their professional service award in 1995, and their Willystine Goodsell award in 2004. The Sadkers were recognized with the Eleanor Roosevelt Award from The American Association of University Women in 1995, and the Gender Architect Award from the American Association of Colleges of Teacher Education in 2001. David Sadker has received two honorary doctorates.

Myra Sadker

Myra Sadker was a professor and Dean of the School of Education at American University (Washington, DC). Her pioneering work in gender bias included one of the first books on the topic, *Sexism in School and Society* (Harper and Row, 1973), as well as a popular trade book, *Failing at Fairness* (Scribner, 1994), which documented gender bias from pre-school through professional school. She grew up in Maine (a state of endless beauty) and graduated from Boston University, Harvard University, and the University of Massachusetts. Her numerous publications appeared in both the professional and popular press. Myra's many awards testify to the power of her life as an educator, but the reward she most cherished was connecting with the lives of students. Myra coauthored many of the early editions of this book, and this text reflects her unwavering commitment to a student-friendly teacher education textbook. She remains the inspiration behind *Teachers, Schools, and Society.*

Myra died in 1995 while undergoing treatment for breast cancer. For more information on her life, visit www.sadker.org.

Karen R. Zittleman

Dr. Zittleman attended the University of Wisconsin for her bachelor's degree, and American University for her master's degree and doctorate. She teaches at American University's School of Education and has been a virtual teacher for several courses offered online through the Women's Educational Equity Act. Her articles about gender, Title IX, and teacher education appear in the *Journal of Teacher Education, Educational Leadership, Phi Delta Kappan, Principal,* and other professional journals. She is a contributing author to *Gender in the Classroom: Foundations, Skills, Methods and Strategies Across the Curriculum* published by Lawrence Erlbaum and has created several equity Web sites. Karen has also authored *Making Public Schools Great for Every Girl and Boy,* an instructional guide on promoting equity in math and science instruction published by the National Educational Association, and educational film guides for *A Hero for Daisy* and *Apple Pie: Raising Champions.* She is project manager for Myra Sadker Advocates. Karen's research interests have focused on educational equity, foundations of education, teacher preparation, and spirituality in education.

BRIEF CONTENTS

CONTENTS

PART II
SCHOOLS AND CURRICULUM

Chapter 4
Schools: Choices and Challenges 126

Chapter 5
Student Life in School and at Home 169

Contents

Chapter 10
School Law and Ethics *381*

PART IV
YOUR CLASSROOM

Chapter 11
Teacher Effectiveness *428*

Chapter 12
Your First Classroom *467*

The readings, case studies, and classroom observations listed below are available on the CD-ROM inside the booklet packaged with your new text.

PART IV
YOUR CLASSROOM

If you think that *Teachers, Schools, and Society* was written to introduce you to the world of teaching, you are only half right. This book also reflects our excitement about a life in the classroom and is intended to spark your own fascination about working with children. The basic premise for this text has not changed through all the previous editions: write a book students want to read, not have to read. While we continue to work hard to provide you with information that is both current and concise, we work even harder to create an engaging book—one that will give you a sense of the wonderful possibilities found in a career in the classroom.

To help you determine if teaching is right for you, and to learn more about education in general, you will find reflection questions throughout the text. These questions will put you right into the center of these issues, a personal connection that encourages your thoughtful deliberation. While the text has been designed to engage you, we also devised an absorbing "electronic-option," the Web site resources. The text's Web resources are accessible through www.mhhe. com/sadker8e. Here you can choose to go into the Online Learning Center that houses the student study guide, and activities and resources to help you practice with and further explore concepts introduced in the text. Throughout the text you will see links to the activities and study resources found on the Online Learning Center. Each link includes a brief explanation of what you will find online. Now it is time for your first reflection question: How can you discover this wonder trove of electronic treasures? Easy. We have blue "hot link" type whenever there is a Web site connection. Visit us in our cyber-classroom at www.mhhe. com/sadker8e.

To help you discover and use all of these new interactive opportunities, we have created a key of useful icons. Look for the following as you read this book:

REFLECTION: Wh
of these reasons fc   highlights reflection questions.

www.mhhe.com/
sadker8e   indicates that you should go to the Online Learning Center for more information or to do an activity.

Now, join us for a tour of the special features of the text.

Class Acts

Each of the four part openers includes a *Class Act*—a story from a current or future teacher about his or her involvement in education. You can find additional Class Acts submitted by your classmates nationwide on the Online Learning Center. Have you had a teacher who made a difference in your life? We want to hear about that teacher, and perhaps include your story in the next edition of the text. Please submit your own story!

Chapter Opener

The chapter opener page includes Focus Questions and a Chapter Preview to prime you for the content that will follow. At the end of the chapter, the summary will be framed by these very same focus questions. The page also includes an online *What Do You Think?* poll. Answer the questions and then, via the Internet, find out how your peers responded. It's an opportunity to participate in our national survey system and is only one of the activities that you will find on the Online Learning Center.

CLASS ACT

At this time of year, graduates may feel a little lost. We have been students for SO long, and now suddenly things are changing. At such time of transition, we need a larger purpose to guide us—why have we chosen these careers as educators? It certainly wasn't for the money! I would like to share some words that I have turned to for a sense of purpose.

Over thirty years ago, W.E.B. DuBois, the great African American writer and activist, said from his death bed: "One thing alone I charge you: As you live, believe in life! Always human beings will live and progress to greater, broader, and fuller life. The only possible death is to lose belief in this truth . . . ."

Despite all the injustice he experienced, DuBois died believing that the future will be ever brighter. In our line of work, it is not always easy to believe in progress. Apparently, DuBois never tried to get licensed at the New York City Board of Ed.! I have had many discussions with other students, wondering how to tackle problems such as glaring educational inequity based on race and class, negative or indifferent attitudes toward bilingual and special education, international disparities in the quality of education, and a general lack of respect in this country for the work

that we do. What impact can I have as one individual educator? True, one person alone cannot change society. But each of us does have the power to change other people, and collectively we are an impressive force. For example, think of a teacher or family member who has passed on a legacy to you.

I am imagining two people up here with me: my mother's mother and my father's father. My grandmother, Mercy Oduro, was a West African woman who touched hundreds as a teacher and headmistress of an elementary school. It's a testament to her life's work that, although she died six years ago, I am still called "Teacher Mercy's granddaughter" when I go back to Ghana. To me, she has passed on a flair for celebration and an unshakeable belief in her students, and I will pass these on to my own students.

My American grandfather, William Steel, 83 years old, is a retired teacher, but STILL tutoring daily at his local school. His legacy is so strong that on his eightieth birthday he got letters from people he taught over fifty years ago, acknowledging his influence on them. To me, he has passed on a fantastic curiosity about the world and a playful sense of humor, and I will pass these on when I teach.

Imagine now that all the people we will reach ARE crowded in this room today—hundreds, thousands of them. In each of these people there is a piece of one of us, continuing the legacy of those who came before. Look around. Can you see the ocean of possibility flowing from us here today? Together, how can we NOT create DuBois' vision of greater, broader, and fuller life? Let me tell you, we are powerful: We are educators.

Melissa Steel
Teachers College Graduation Speech
Columbia University

www.mhhe.com/
sadker
Read more Class Acts on the Online Learning Center.

427

Culturally Responsive Teaching

3

CHAPTER

FOCUS QUESTIONS

1. In what ways are American schools failing culturally diverse students?
2. How do deficit, expectation, and cultural difference theories explain different academic performance among various racial, ethnic, and cultural groups?
3. How do metaphors like "melting pot" and "tossed salad" both capture and mask American identity?
4. What are the political and instructional issues surrounding bilingual education?
5. What are the purposes and approaches of multicultural education?
6. Why is culturally responsive teaching important?
7. How can teachers use culturally responsive teaching strategies?

www.mhhe.com/
sadker
WHAT DO YOU THINK? Cultural diversity of students. Estimate the racial, ethnic, and social class backgrounds of today's students.

CHAPTER PREVIEW

America has just experienced the greatest immigration surge in its history. In the past few decades, newly minted Americans have arrived mainly from Latin America and Asia, but also from the Caribbean, the Middle East, Africa, and Eastern Europe. Today, about one in ten Americans is foreign born, and the native language of well over 30 million Americans is a language other than English. By 2030, half of all school children will be of color. These demographics create a remarkable and formidable challenge for the nation's schools.[1] Some advocate a multicultural approach to education that

recognizes and incorporates this growing student diversity into teaching and the curriculum. Others fret that disassembling our Eurocentric curriculum and traditional approaches to education may harm our American culture. For many teachers, the struggle is to teach students with backgrounds different from their own. How to best do this is a tough question, and one that this chapter addresses directly not only with breath-taking information and some astute (we hope) insights, but with practical suggestions as well.

67

You Be the Judge

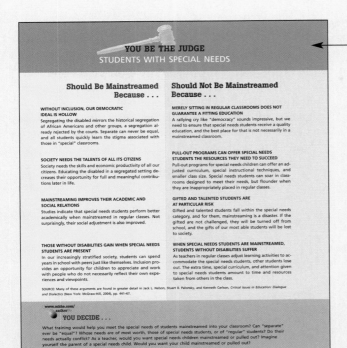

YOU BE THE JUDGE
STUDENTS WITH SPECIAL NEEDS

Should Be Mainstreamed Because . . .

WITHOUT INCLUSION, OUR DEMOCRATIC IDEAL IS HOLLOW
Segregating the disabled mirrors the historical segregation of African Americans and other groups, a segregation already rejected by the courts. Separate can never be equal, and all students quickly learn the stigma associated with those in "special" classrooms.

SOCIETY NEEDS THE TALENTS OF ALL ITS CITIZENS
Society needs the skills and economic productivity of all our citizens. Educating the disabled in a segregated setting decreases their opportunity for full and meaningful contributions later in life.

MAINSTREAMING IMPROVES THEIR ACADEMIC AND SOCIAL RELATIONS
Studies indicate that special needs students perform better academically when mainstreamed in regular classes. Not surprisingly, their social adjustment is also improved.

THOSE WITHOUT DISABILITIES GAIN WHEN SPECIAL NEEDS STUDENTS ARE PRESENT
In our increasingly stratified society, students can spend years in school with peers just like themselves. Inclusion provides an opportunity for children to appreciate and work with people who do not necessarily reflect their own experiences and viewpoints.

Should Not Be Mainstreamed Because . . .

MERELY SITTING IN REGULAR CLASSROOMS DOES NOT GUARANTEE A FITTING EDUCATION
A rallying cry like "democracy" sounds impressive, but we need to ensure that special needs students receive a quality education, and the best place for that is not necessarily in a mainstreamed classroom.

PULL-OUT PROGRAMS CAN OFFER SPECIAL NEEDS STUDENTS THE RESOURCES THEY NEED TO SUCCEED
Pull-out programs for special needs children can offer an adjusted curriculum, special instructional techniques, and smaller class size. Special needs students can soar in classrooms designed to meet their needs, but flounder when they are inappropriately placed in regular classes.

GIFTED AND TALENTED STUDENTS ARE AT PARTICULAR RISK
Gifted and talented students fall within the special needs category, and for them, mainstreaming is a disaster. If the gifted are not challenged, they will be turned off from school, and the gifts of our most able students will be lost to society.

WHEN SPECIAL NEEDS STUDENTS ARE MAINSTREAMED, STUDENTS WITHOUT DISABILITIES SUFFER
As teachers in regular classes adjust learning activities to accommodate the special needs students, other students lose out. The extra time, special curriculum, and attention given to special needs students amount to time and resources taken from others in the class.

SOURCE: Many of these arguments are found in greater detail in Jack L. Nelson, Stuart B. Palonsky, and Kenneth Carlson, *Critical Issues in Education: Dialogue and Dialectics* (New York: McGraw-Hill, 2004), pp. 441–67.

www.mhhe.com/sadker
YOU DECIDE . . .
What training would help you meet the special needs of students mainstreamed into your classroom? Can "separate" ever be "equal"? Whose needs are of most worth, those of special needs students, or of "regular" students? Do their needs actually conflict? As a teacher, would you want special needs children mainstreamed or pulled out? Imagine yourself the parent of a special needs child. Would you want your child mainstreamed or pulled out?

You Be the Judge provides two sides of an argument so you can consider different points of view, and not just ours. Then we ask you to be the judge (law school not required), by responding to the reflection questions following the arguments. You can also do this on the Online Learning Center and either e-mail your response to your instructor, or save your response for your portfolio.

Profile in Education

Teaching is all about people—it's a very human connection. The people we profile are teachers, teacher educators, social activists working for children, and educational researchers. Each was chosen for an important contribution to education. And to follow up the text descriptions, you can visit the Online Learning Center to find out more about the profiled educator.

PROFILE IN EDUCATION — Jane Roland Martin

"Domephobia," the fear of things domestic, is Jane Roland Martin's word for gender bias in schools and in society. She coined the term when she compared the distinct educations Jean-Jacques Rousseau designed for his fictitious students Emile and Sophie. Martin was frustrated that while the boy, Emile, was said to revel in intellectual exploration, Sophie was to receive second-rate training—to be a wife and mother.

Martin deplores the disconnect between intellectual development and the development of abilities to love and care for a family. She recognizes that today's schools continue to craft different expectations for males and females. In fact, she knows this inequity firsthand. Teaching philosophy at the University of Massachusetts at Boston for over thirty years, Martin found herself fighting to have her intellectual voice heard in a traditional male discipline. Her experience of bias fueled her anger that equal opportunity education is still so far from reality.

Yet, Jane Roland Martin knows "women are barometers of change." Feminism today, like Sophie's education 300 years ago, gives men and women a special gift—a new perspective on gender roles. At the dawn of a new millennium, women's roles at work and in the family are indeed changing. Not only are women wives and mothers, they are corporate CEOs, medal-winning soccer players, and Supreme Court justices. Yet even as

society may champion the greater earning power and talents of women, we are seeing a backlash against the more liberated roles of women. The trouble? The changes have cast as fiction the rosy Norman Rockwell portrait of the American family: More than half of all mothers work outside the home and single-parent homes number 1 in 5. These numbers stir concern that day care is bad, working mothers are neglectful and the well-being of the nation's children is threatened.

What society may see as problematic, Jane Roland Martin envisions as opportunity. Historically the physical, emotional, and social needs of children have been met by family, primarily mothers. Today, women are drawn by economic need and personal desire to enter the workforce. Martin sees these changes as a defining moment for schools, a chance to recreate within schools the nurturing tasks traditionally performed at home.

Martin's critics say no, schools should focus only on intellectual development. Not Martin. A social reconstructionist, she challenges schools to open their doors to what she calls the 3Cs—caring, concern, and connection. As more children are cared for outside the home, she fears the 3C curriculum is in danger of being lost. And American society has paid a heavy price for ignoring such domestic needs. Social inequalities continue and children are often the victims. Martin has an antidote: transform schoolhouses into "schoolhomes."

The schoolhome is far different from traditional "factory-model" schooling which views children as raw material, teachers as workers who process their students before sending them on to the next station on the assembly line, [and] curriculum as the machinery that forges America's young into marketable products."[1] Instead, Martin's schoolhome focuses on students' individual emotional and cognitive needs. It

embraces the experience of all learners and welcomes racial, cultural, and gender diversity. Martin's vision of schools reflects her vision of American society as everyone's home:

Instead of focusing our gaze on abstract norms, standardized tests, generalized rates of success and uniform outcomes, the ideas of the schoolhome direct action to actual educational practice. Of course a schoolhome will teach the 3Rs. But it will give equal emphasis to the 3Cs—not by designating formal courses in these but by being a domestic environment characterized by safety, security, nurturance and love. In the schoolhome, mind and body, thought and action, reason and emotion are all educated.[2]

The schoolhome will incorporate the 3Cs into our very definition of what it means for males and females to be educated. Creating such nurturing and equitable schools will require "acts of both great and small, strategic and utterly outrageous. The cause demands no less, not one whit less."[3]

[1] Jane Roland Martin, *The Schoolhome: Rethinking Schools for Changing Families* (Cambridge, MA: Harvard University Press, 1992), p. 41.
[2] Jane Roland Martin, "Women, School, and Cultural Wealth." In Connie Titone and Karen Maloney (eds.), *Thinking Through Our Mothers: Women's Philosophies of Education* (Upper Saddle River, NJ: Merrill, 1999), pp. 161–62.
[3] Jane Roland Martin, *Coming of Age in Academe: Rekindling Women's Hopes and Reforming the Academy* (New York: Routledge, 2000), p. 182.

REFLECTION: Do you agree with Jane Roland Martin that the 3Cs should be an integral part of the curriculum? Explain. Describe what a 3C curriculum might look like in schools today.

www.mhhe.com/sadker

To learn more about Jane Roland Martin, click on *Profiles in Education.*

328

xix

Photo-Synthesis

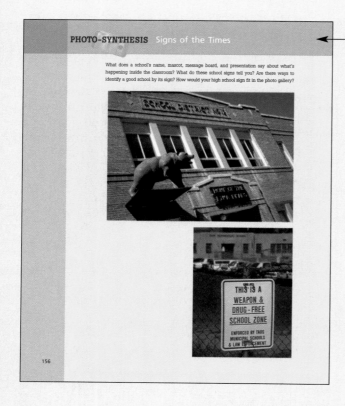

What does a school's name, mascot, message board, and presentation say about what's happening inside the classroom? What do these school signs tell you? Are there ways to identify a good school by its sign? How would your high school sign fit in the photo gallery?

156

Most of us enjoy "seeing" theoretical concepts come to life. In fact, some people are more visual than verbal and greatly benefit from photographs and illustrations. That's why we developed *Photo-Synthesis*—photo collages that encourage analysis. And if you need a thoughtful boost, one or more questions help you focus your inquiry.

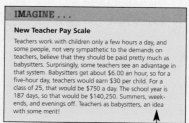

IMAGINE . . .

New Teacher Pay Scale

Teachers work with children only a few hours a day, and some people, not very sympathetic to the demands on teachers, believe that they should be paid pretty much as babysitters. Surprisingly, some teachers see an advantage in that system. Babysitters get about $6.00 an hour, so for a five-hour day, teachers would earn $30 per child. For a class of 25, that would be $750 a day. The school year is 187 days, so that would be $140,250. Summers, weekends, and evenings off. Teachers as babysitters, an idea with some merit!

Imagine . . .

Throughout the chapters you will find brief overviews of education-related news items. We selected these items because we found them funny, poignant, or particularly relevant to the chapter content. The *Imagine . . .* items also provide a sense of currency to the issues and topics discussed in the text.

Frame of Reference

These boxes take a closer look at important topics. They provide research updates, further information about an issue, or even suggestions for classroom use.

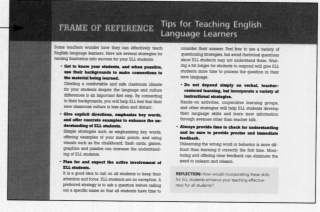

FRAME OF REFERENCE Tips for Teaching English Language Learners

Some teachers wonder how they can effectively teach English language learners. Here are several strategies for turning frustration into success for your ELL students.

- **Get to know your students, and when possible, use their backgrounds to make connections to the material being learned.**
  Creating a comfortable and safe classroom climate for your students despite the language and culture differences is an important first step. By connecting to their backgrounds, you will help ELL feel that their new classroom culture is less alien and distant.

- **Give explicit directions, emphasize key words, and offer concrete examples to enhance the understanding of ELL students.**
  Simple strategies such as emphasizing key words, offering examples of your main points, and using visuals such as the chalkboard, flash cards, games, graphics and puzzles can increase the understanding of ELL students.

- **Plan for and expect the active involvement of ELL students.**
  It is a good idea to call on all students to keep their attention and focus. ELL students are no exception. A preferred strategy is to ask a question before calling out a specific name so that all students have time to

consider their answer. Feel free to use a variety of questioning strategies, but avoid rhetorical questions since ELL students may not understand them. Waiting a bit longer for students to respond will give ELL students more time to process the question in their new language.

- **Do not depend simply on verbal, teacher-centered learning, but incorporate a variety of instructional strategies.**
  Hands-on activities, cooperative learning groups, and other strategies will help ELL students develop their language skills and learn new information through avenues other than teacher talk.

- **Always provide time to check for understanding and be sure to provide precise and immediate feedback.**
  Unlearning the wrong word or behavior is more difficult than learning it correctly the first time. Monitoring and offering clear feedback can eliminate the need to unlearn and relearn.

REFLECTION: How would incorporating these skills for ELL students enhance your teaching effectiveness for all students?

teachers provide variety in both content and process. In elementary ty in content can involve moving from one subject area to another. y instruction, the move might be in the same subject area, such as the memorizing vocabulary to analyzing symbols in a short story.

avvy teacher knows, student interest can be maintained by moving from to another during a single lesson. For example, a 60-minute lesson on the evolution might begin with a 10-minute overview providing the structure , then move into a 15-minute question-and-answer session, then change ute video, and conclude with a 10-minute discussion and closure. Another to vary content and process in teaching is to accommodate different ning styles. Some students might miss what is said in a lecture (not being

www.mhhe.com/
sadker 5e

INTERACTIVE ACTIVITY
Create a Course Schedule
What do you think your students' week should consist of?

Interactive Activities

Interactive Activities are listed in the margin and can be found on the Online Learning Center under the corresponding chapter. The activities are designed to allow you to apply what you are learning in an interactive environment.

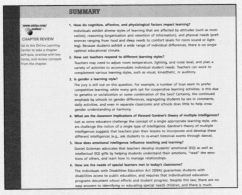

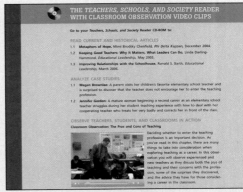

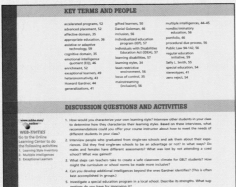

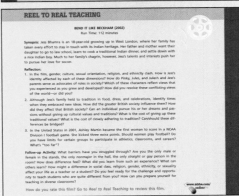

Chapter-Ending Spread

The material at the end of the chapter is designed to structure your review of the content and help you make sure you understand key ideas. Here's what you'll find there:

- A *Chapter Review* link reminds you to go to the Online Learning Center to take a quiz, practice with key terms, and review key ideas from the chapter.

- The *Summary* is organized by the Focus Questions at the start of the chapter.

- *The* Teachers, Schools, and Society *Reader* section lists the readings, case studies, and classroom observation video clips that accompany the chapter.

- *Key Terms and People* will help you identify and remember the critical terminology and influential individuals discussed in the chapter. Page references next to each entry guide you to the place that each is discussed in the chapter.

- The *Discussion Questions and Activities* are designed to promote deeper analysis, further investigation, and even an evaluation of the controversial issues discussed in the chapter. Also included are the Internet-based *WEB-tivities* you can find on the Online Learning Center.

- *Reel to Real Teaching* summarizes a popular movie, usually available on videotape or DVD, that will add to your appreciation of the information included in this chapter. We believe that Hollywood can actually enhance your education, and movies can both deepen your understanding of the chapter an offer a richer educational context. The *Reel to Real* feature provides questions and follow-up activities that guide you through the movie and the issues described in the text. Go to the Online Learning Center to rate the movie.

- *For Further Reading* includes an annotated list of recent and influential books related to the chapter.

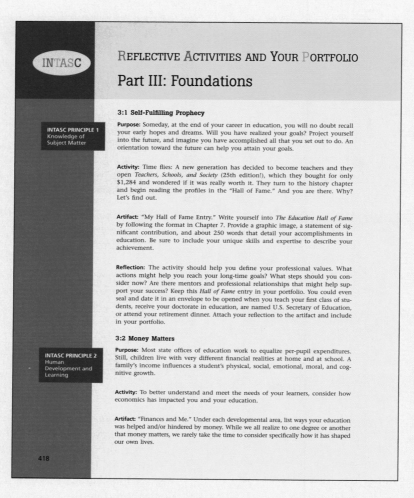

REFLECTIVE ACTIVITIES AND YOUR PORTFOLIO

Part III: Foundations

INTASC

INTASC PRINCIPLE 1
Knowledge of
Subject Matter

3:1 Self-Fulfilling Prophecy

Purpose: Someday, at the end of your career in education, you will no doubt recall your early hopes and dreams. Will you have realized your goals? Project yourself into the future, and imagine you have accomplished all that you set out to do. An orientation toward the future can help you attain your goals.

Activity: Time flies: A new generation has decided to become teachers and they open *Teachers, Schools, and Society* (25th edition!), which they bought for only $1,284 and wondered if it was really worth it. They turn to the history chapter and begin reading the profiles in the "Hall of Fame." And you are there. Why? Let's find out.

Artifact: "My Hall of Fame Entry." Write yourself into *The Education Hall of Fame* by following the format in Chapter 7. Provide a graphic image, a statement of significant contribution, and about 250 words that detail your accomplishments in education. Be sure to include your unique skills and expertise to describe your achievement.

Reflection: The activity should help you define your professional values. What actions might help you reach your long-time goals? What steps should you consider now? Are there mentors and professional relationships that might help support your success? Keep this *Hall of Fame* entry in your portfolio. You could even seal and date it in an envelope to be opened when you teach your first class of students, receive your doctorate in education, are named U.S. Secretary of Education, or attend your retirement dinner. Attach your reflection to the artifact and include in your portfolio.

3:2 Money Matters

INTASC PRINCIPLE 2
Human
Development and
Learning

Purpose: Most state offices of education work to equalize per-pupil expenditures. Still, children live with very different financial realities at home and at school. A family's income influences a student's physical, social, emotional, moral, and cognitive growth.

Activity: To better understand and meet the needs of your learners, consider how economics has impacted you and your education.

Artifact: "Finances and Me." Under each developmental area, list ways your education was helped and/or hindered by money. While we all realize to one degree or another that money matters, we rarely take the time to consider specifically how it has shaped our own lives.

418

Reflective Activities and Your Portfolio

Reflective Activities and Your Portfolio, what we like to refer to as *RAPs,* give you a chance to explore your role as an educator by carefully considering what you have just read, and tying it to your own experiences. *RAPs* are intended to help you decide if teaching is right for you. And if it is right, these very same *RAPs* will give you direction as you prepare for a career in teaching. For those of you who want to start a portfolio, the RAPs will be your first step.

RAPs follow and connect to each of the four sections of the textbook. Each *RAP* includes:

- *Purpose*—explains why this activity is useful, and what it is intended to accomplish.
- *Activity*—allows you to apply your readings through observations, interviews, teaching, and action research.
- *Artifact*—challenges you to collect and manage the items you will find useful for developing your portfolio.
- *Reflection*—helps you think deeply and realistically about education and your place in it.

Student Resources

In addition to writing a text that broadens your understanding of the teaching profession, we created a supplements program designed to allow you to confirm your understanding of key concepts, practice and apply what you are learning, and extend the information in the text.

Online Learning Center

The Online Learning Center is your study guide. It includes:

www.mhhe.com/ sadker8e

- Focus Questions
- Chapter Summaries
- Key Terms
- Flash Cards

News, Articles, and Links

- Web Links
- *Profiles in Education*

Quizzes

- Multiple-Choice quizzes with feedback
- True/False quizzes with feedback

Interactive Exercises

- *What Do You Think?* surveys referenced in the text

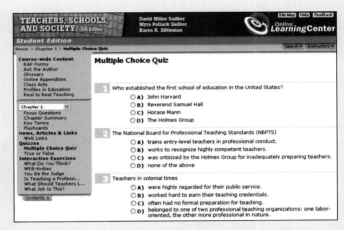

- *Web-tivities*
- The *You Be the Judge* response area
- The Interactive Activities referenced in the text

Resources

- RAP Forms
- *Ask the Authors* Link
- The Glossary
- Online Appendices
- More *Class Acts*
- *Profiles in Education*
- *Reel to Real Teaching* resources

The Teachers, Schools, and Society *Reader*

The Teachers, Schools, and Society *Reader* that accompanies this eighth edition is an electronic reader designed to expand coverage of important topics first introduced in the text. The reader, housed on the CD-ROM in the Reader booklet, includes:

- 35 Readings from both contemporary and classic sources. Each reading includes an introduction and analysis questions.

- 23 Case Studies that provide you with the opportunity to read about how issues introduced in the text may play-out in a K–12 classroom. Each case study is followed by analysis questions.

- 19 Classroom Observation video clips that allow you to see teachers, students, and classrooms in action. Each observation is followed by analysis questions.

For a full listing of the readings and cases, go to page xiv.

The Reader is packaged for free with new copies of the text. If you purchased a used copy of this text, you can purchase a copy of the Reader from your bookstore or by calling McGraw-Hill Customer Service at 1–800–338–3987.

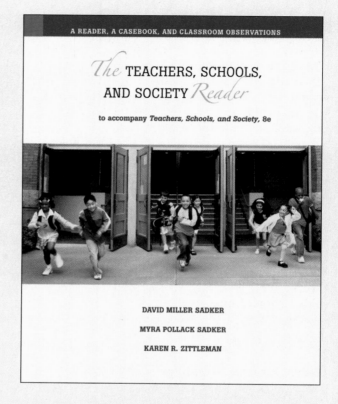

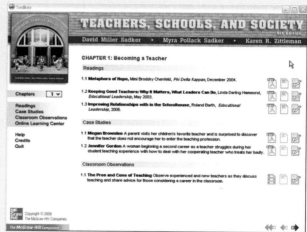

TEACHERS, SCHOOLS, AND SOCIETY

PART I

Teachers and Students

CLASS ACT

Every December I watch *It's a Wonderful Life.* I was 13 years old when I first saw George Bailey scramble down the Main Street of Bedford Falls, waving his arms and screaming at the top of his lungs, rejoicing in the beauty of life, love and friendship. As an adult who savors this film, I feel the bittersweet pang of watching a man who is reborn, glowing in the recognition that he has made a difference in the world. In the final act, as George stands in his living room surrounded by family and friends celebrating his life, I always develop that painful lump in my throat—you know the one. It stings and makes it nearly impossible to swallow. I love this film, and I always want to say that I know a George Bailey. The thing is I do—he's my dad.

My father has been teaching English and Dramatic Arts at the same high school in Massachusetts for the last thirty years. His journey has been one similar to George Bailey's—he has settled down in a small town, a teacher, committed to his family and profession, but at times frustrated. He has seen thousands of students come and go, some moving on to big and exciting things, others staying in the very same town. From time to time growing up, I'd see a glimmer in his eyes wondering, "What if . . . ? What if I'd quit teaching, what if I'd gone off traveling around the world?" These moments of wonder were not full of anger or resentment, only seconds of reflection, and perhaps a little regret for not "doing more with his life." But he always returned to teaching with a positive spirit, endless patience, and astounding energy.

Over the years my dad and I have shared lots of travels together. It was a family joke that no matter where we went, we always ran into one of my father's former students. More often than not, the run-in went beyond a courteous hello and how are you. These former students, now adults with children of their own, embrace my dad, literally and figuratively. We could be standing at a light waiting to cross, sitting in a restaurant—we inevitably ran into these joyful faces who recognize the sparkling eyes, full beard and unmistakable energy of my dad. As a young child, I was somewhat bored by the endless stories recounted by these strangers. The older I got, the more I realized that these spontaneous reunions were quite special. These people were paying tribute to someone who touched their lives. It wasn't a grand parade or a front-page article or a million dollar salary bonus. They were simple yet beautifully sincere words—"You inspired me . . . You gave me the courage to try . . . You were the only one who believed in me . . ."

This may sound like a tribute to a father from an adoring daughter, and to some degree it is. But it is also recognition of something more. Just like George Bailey, my dad has a wonderful life. Through teaching he is able to reach that troubled kid who sits in the back making wisecracks and give him a reason to care about school. He has taken the shy girl who doesn't speak, put her up on the stage and helped her find her voice and confidence. He has acted as adviser and inspiration for countless young people, giving them the opportunity to learn, grow and succeed. Although I've never been a student in his class, my dad has inspired me as well. As I begin my pursuit of a Masters in Teaching, I see just how unique my father's gifts are. This year when I watched *It's a Wonderful Life,* I couldn't help but think of my father. I still got that lump in my throat—and loved it.

Amanda Helfen
American University

www.mhhe.com/
sadker8e

Read more *Class Acts* on the Online Learning Center.

3

CHAPTER 1

Becoming a Teacher

FOCUS QUESTIONS

1. What are the advantages and disadvantages of being a teacher?
2. What are the satisfactions—and complaints—of today's teachers?
3. Can we consider teaching to be a profession?
4. How has teacher preparation changed over the years?
5. What traits and characteristics are needed for successful teaching?
6. Is teaching a "good fit" for you?
7. What steps can you take now on the road to becoming a teacher?

www.mhhe.com/
sadker8e

WHAT DO YOU THINK? Why do you want to be a teacher? Rate the factors influencing your decision whether to become a teacher, and see how other students have rated these factors.

CHAPTER PREVIEW

This chapter looks at classroom life through the teacher's eyes. You may be thinking: I have spent years in a classroom, watching teachers and what they do. If there is one thing I know, it is teachers and teaching! But during your years in the classroom, you have looked at teaching through "student-colored glasses," a unique but somewhat distorted view, like looking through a telescope from the lens that makes everything tiny instead of large. This chapter offers you a teacher's perspective. We give you an opportunity to consider both the pros and cons of a teaching career. Then we turn to another question: Will you and teaching be a good match?

We love teaching, but not everything about teaching is wonderful. In the past, teachers were often considered second-class citizens, pressured to conform to strict moral and social codes while being paid meager wages. Today, teaching is center stage, a common topic in the media and in political debates. Your study of education comes at a propitious time, a period of ferment and change as teachers strive for a more professional, more influential role in U.S. society. What role might you play in tomorrow's classrooms?

The chapter is also about "us." Yes, us. We are now a team, this textbook, the authors, and you. When your authors were students, we did not much like our textbooks. They were far from exciting to read. By extension, we feared that we might not like teaching. In the end, we loved teaching—but still hated our textbooks. We want this textbook to be different—to be not only informative, but also enjoyable. This first chapter offers us the opportunity to introduce the textbook, and in a sense, to introduce ourselves.

Welcome to our classroom.

Do Teachers Like Teaching?

In a "Peanuts" cartoon, Linus comments that "no problem is so big or complicated that it can't be run away from." Charles Schulz succinctly highlighted a human frailty shared by most of us—the tendency to put aside our problems or critical questions in favor of day-to-day routine. In fact, it is amazing how little care and consideration many of us give to choosing a career. It is always easier to catch a movie, surf the net, or even study for the next exam than it is to reflect on and plan for the future. This may be one reason why questions such as: "What are you going to be when you grow up?" and "What's your next career move?" make so many of us uneasy. The big question facing many readers of this text: Is teaching right for me? Some of you are in college or university programs and will be teaching in the next few years. Others of you may already be in a classroom, teaching as you work toward your license in one of several alternative teacher certification programs. For some of you, teaching may become a decades-long career filled with joy and satisfaction. For others, teaching may be limited to only a few years spent in the classroom, one of several careers you explore during your working years. And, still others may reach an equally useful and important realization: Teaching is not the ideal match for your interests or skills. We'd like to help you decide whether you and teaching are a good fit.

Throughout this text, we pose a variety of questions for you to consider. We have devised a feature called *You Be the Judge,* which presents several sides of an issue, and encourages you to sort out where you stand. When the authors have a strong opinion about these or any of the issues in the text, we will not hide it from you. For example, we told you that we love teaching, but there are drawbacks, so you know pretty much where we stand. But our opinion is just our opinion, and we want you to form your own ideas. To that end, we will work hard to be fair, to present more than one side of the issue, and to help you form an independent point of view. *You Be the Judge* is one way that we hope to spark your interest and thinking on critical issues.

In the first *You Be the Judge,* where we highlight the joys and concerns of a career in the classroom (see pp. 6–8), we include comments by teachers themselves that reveal their perceptions and feelings about their work. A more structured attempt to assess teachers' views on their careers was carried out by the National Education Association (NEA). Teachers from around the nation were asked why they decided to become teachers, and why they choose to stay in teaching.[1] Teachers elect a career in the classroom for the intrinsic rewards that make teaching pretty unique, including a desire to work with young people, the significance of education generally, and even the love of a particular subject—not a bad bunch to have as colleagues (see Figure 1.1 on page 9).

And once in the classroom, most teachers report that they like what they are doing. In the NEA survey, the vast majority of the teachers, more than 80 percent, reported that they were satisfied with their jobs, collegial relationships, the intellectual challenge of their work, their job security, and their autonomy in the classroom. The teachers also gave high scores to supervisors, with solid majorities viewing their school principals as supportive and encouraging leaders who were able to communicate their expectations and to enforce school rules. When asked about the adequacy of resources, such as textbooks, supplies, and copying machines, the majority of teachers agreed that the materials were available as needed. But not everything surveyed was rosy.

The Good News . . .

YOU ARE NOT WORKING ALONE, STARING AT A COMPUTER SCREEN OR SHUFFLING PAPERS

If you enjoy being in contact with others, particularly young people, teaching could be the right job for you. Almost the entire working day is spent in human interaction. Young people are so often funny, fresh, and spontaneous. Your discussions may range from adding fractions to feeding pet snakes, from an analysis of *The Catcher in the Rye* to advice on applying to colleges. As America's students become increasingly diverse, you will find yourself learning about different cultures and different life experiences. Your life will be enriched by the varied worlds of different children— black, white, Hispanic, Asian, blended—all kinds of children. The children will make you laugh and make you cry, but always they will make you feel needed. "I still can't get used to how much my heart soars with every student's success, and how a piece of my heart is plucked away when any student slips away."[2]

THE SMELL OF THE CHALKBOARD, THE ROAR OF THE CROWD

You spend several days researching and planning your lesson on social protest literature for your eleventh-grade English class. You collect many fine poems and statements to share; you bring your favorite CDs and videos of social protest songs into the classroom; you prepare an excellent PowerPoint presentation to highlight the key labor figures and issues of the time; and you punctuate your lesson with thoughtful discussion questions and creative follow-up activities. Wow, what a lesson! The students are spellbound. They ask many questions and make plans for doing their own research on social protest. One group even decides to meet after school to create an MTV-type video of a social protest song about the destruction of the natural environment. Their animated discussion continues as the bell signals their passage to the next classroom.

When you have taught well, your students will let you know it. On special occasions, they will come up to you after class or at the end of the year to tell you "This class is awesome." At younger grade levels, they may write you notes (often anonymous), thanking you for a good class or a good year.

I'M PROUD TO BE A TEACHER

Although teacher status took a battering in public opinion in the early 1980s, the public is once again acknowledging

The Bad News . . .

STOP THE CROWD—I WANT TO GET AWAY

Right in the middle of a language arts lesson, when fifteen kids have their hands in the air, you may feel like saying, "Stop, everybody. I feel like being alone for the next fifteen minutes. I'm going to Starbucks." For the major part of each day, your job demands that you be involved with people in a fast-paced and intense way—whether you feel like it or not. Researchers report that you will be involved in as many as one thousand verbal exchanges in a single day, almost all of them with children, which could impact behavior beyond school. One kindergarten teacher warned her 40-year-old brother "to be sure and put on his galoshes. Wow! Did he give me a strange look."[3] And as America's classrooms become more multicultural, teacher interactions will become more challenging, as teachers stretch beyond their own background to connect with a diverse student population.

IS ANYBODY THERE?

After teaching your fantastic lesson on social protest literature, you want to share your elation with your colleagues, so you head for the teachers' room and begin to talk about the lesson. But it is hard to capture the magic of what went on in the classroom. You can sense that your description is falling flat. Besides, people are beginning to give you that "What kind of superstar do you think you are?" look. You decide you had better cut your description short and talk about CDF (Casual Dress Friday).

It is rare to have another adult spend even ten minutes observing you at work in your classroom. Once you have obtained tenure, classroom observation becomes incredibly infrequent. Often, the evaluation is little more than perfunctory. Some teachers feel they and their students share a "secret life," off-limits to others. Most of your colleagues will have only a general impression of your teaching competence. The word may leak out—through students, parents, or even the custodian—if you are doing a really fine job; however, on the whole, when you call out, "Hello, I'm here, I'm a teacher. How am I doing?" there will be little cheering from anyone outside your classroom.

I DON'T GET NO RESPECT

While many Americans value teaching, many others don't. One reason for this inconsistency is sexism. Occupations

The Good News . . .

the importance of teachers. Nine out of ten students give their teachers a passing grade.[4] When you become a teacher, many people will accord you respect, because they admire teachers. You will be someone whose specialized training and skills are used to benefit others. Mark Twain once wrote, "To be good is noble, but to teach others how to be good is nobler." Which would have summed up this point perfectly, except, being Mark Twain, he added: "—and less trouble."

AS A TEACHER, YOU ARE CONSTANTLY INVOLVED IN INTELLECTUAL MATTERS

You may have become very interested in a particular subject. Perhaps you love a foreign language or mathematics, or maybe you are intrigued by contemporary social issues. If you decide you want to share this excitement and stimulation with others, teaching offers a natural channel for doing so. As one teacher put it: "I want them to be exposed to what I love and what I teach. I want them to know somebody, even if they think I'm crazy, who's genuinely excited about history."[5]

Using your extended vacation times to continue your education can further advance your intellectual stimulation and growth. The Internet is a great source for finding creative teaching ideas, and staying on top of emerging developments in your field. Other helpful sources are journals, weekly educational newspapers, conferences and meetings sponsored by school districts and professional education associations. You have ready access to the intellectual community.

PORTRAIT OF THE TEACHER AS AN ARTIST

You can construct everything from original simulation games to videotapes, from multimedia programs to educational software. Even the development of a superb lesson plan is an exercise in creativity, as you strive to meet the needs of the diverse children who come into your classroom each day. Some people draw clear parallels between teachers and artists and highlight the creativity that is essential to both:

> I love to teach as a painter loves to paint, as a musician loves to play, as a singer loves to sing, as a strong man rejoices to run a race. Teaching is an art—an art so great and so difficult to master that a man [or woman] can spend a long life at it without realizing much more than his [or her] limitations and mistakes, and his [or her] distance from the ideal. But the main aim of my happy days has been to become a good teacher. Just as every architect wishes to be a good architect and every professional poet strives toward perfection.[6]

The Bad News . . .

with large numbers of women generally face prestige problems, and teaching is no exception. (There may come a day when we will not have to mention this issue, but, for the time being, prejudice still exists.) Unfortunately, in our materialistic society, people's work is frequently measured by the size of the paycheck—and most teachers' wallets are modestly endowed. Despite the resurgence of support for teachers, when it comes to the game of impressing people, teachers are still not collecting a large pile of status chips.

THE SAME MATTERS YEAR AFTER YEAR AFTER YEAR

Yes, you will be continually involved in academic subject matter—but the word continually is a double-edged sword. Teaching, like most other jobs, entails a lot of repetition. You may tire of teaching the same subject matter to a new crop of students every September. If this happens, boredom and a feeling that you are getting intellectually stale may replace excitement. For some, working with students who seem unmoved by the ideas that excite you can be frustrating and disillusioning. You may turn to your colleagues for intellectual stimulation, only to find that they are more concerned about the cost of auto repair and TV shows than the latest genetic decoding breakthrough or the intricacies of current government policy.

Since you are just embarking on your teaching career, you may find it difficult to imagine yourself becoming bored with the world of education. However, as you teach class after class on the same subject, interest can wane.

THE BOG OF MINDLESS ROUTINE

Much is said about the creativity of teaching, but, under close inspection, the job breaks down into a lot of mindless routine as well. A large percentage of the day is consumed by clerical work, child control, housekeeping, announcements, and participation in ceremonies. Although there is opportunity for ingenuity and inventiveness, most of the day is spent in the three Rs of ritual, repetition, and routine. As one disgruntled sixth-grade teacher in Los Angeles said,

> Paper work, paper work. The nurse wants the health cards, so you have to stop and get them. Another teacher wants one of your report cards. The principal wants to know how many social science books you have. Somebody else wants to know if you can come to a meeting on such and such a day. Forms to fill out, those crazy forms: Would you please give a breakdown of boys and girls in the class; would you please say how many children you have in reading grade such and such. Forms, messengers—all day long.[7]

continued

The Good News . . .

The Bad News . . .

TO TOUCH A LIFE, TO MAKE A DIFFERENCE

Teaching is more than helping a child master phonics or discover meaning in seemingly lifeless history facts. Each classroom is a composite of the anguish and joy of all its students. You can feel the pain of the child in the fourth seat who always knows the answer, but is too shy to speak. Then there is the rambunctious one who spills all over the classroom in a million random ways, unable to focus on any one task or project. Or that physically unattractive victim, who inspires taunts and abuse from usually well-mannered classmates. You can be the one who makes a difference in their lives:

> I am happy that I found a profession that combines my belief in social justice with my zeal for intellectual excellence. My career choice has meant much anxiety, anger, and disappointment. But it has also produced profound joy. I have spent my work life committed to a just cause: the education of Boston high school students. Welcome to our noble teaching profession and our enduring cause.[8]

BETTER SALARIES, LONGER VACATIONS

In the last two decades, the average teacher salary rose about 20 percent, from the $30,000 to the $40,000 bracket, though salaries vary enormously from one community to another. The average teacher in South Dakota earns only in the low $30,000 range, while California teachers average mid $50,000. Additional salary can be earned by working in the summer or accepting extra faculty responsibilities. Occupational benefits, such as health and retirement, are generally excellent. You will enjoy long vacations. A few school districts provide teachers with an opportunity to study, travel, or engage in other forms of professional improvement through an extended leave or sabbatical program. All of these considerations make for a more relaxed and varied lifestyle, one that gives you time for yourself as well as your family. Whether you use your "free time" to be with your family, to travel, or to make extra money, time flexibility is a definite plus.

THE TARNISHED IDEALIST

We all hope to be that special teacher, the one students remember and talk about long after they graduate. But too often, idealistic goals give way to survival—simply making it through from one day to the next. New teachers find themselves judged on their ability to maintain a quiet, orderly room. Idealistic young teachers find the worship of control incompatible with their humanistic goals. Likewise, they feel betrayed if a student naively mistakes their offer of friendship as a sign of weakness or vulnerability. As a result, many learn the trade secret—"don't smile until Christmas" (or Chanukah, Kwanzaa, or Ramadan, depending on your community)—and adopt it quickly. Even veteran teachers throw up their hands in despair and too often leave teaching. Teacher-student conflict can lead to lost idealism, and worse. Some teachers are concerned with the increase in discipline problems, and a decrease in support from parents and others. How can teachers stay inspired when their classrooms lack basic supplies?[9] Trying to make a difference may result in more frustration than satisfaction.

BUT SALARIES STILL HAVE A LONG WAY TO GO

Although teachers' salaries have improved, they still lag behind what most people would call a good income. Teachers ages 22 to 28 earn about $9,000 less per year than other college-educated adults of the same age. The gap is three times greater for teachers 44 to 50, who earn approximately $25,000 less than their counterparts in other occupations, such as engineers, accountants, and lawyers.[10] A history teacher says, "It's really difficult to maintain a family . . . I'm not sure I could have done it then except for a wife who's not demanding or pushy. She's completely comfortable with the things we have, and we don't have a great deal."[11] And the following comment comes from a well-to-do suburban community: "You can always tell the difference between the teachers' and the students' parking lots. The students' lot is the one with all the new cars in it."[12] The long vacations are nice—but they are also long periods without income.

www.mhhe.com/
sadker8e

YOU DECIDE . . .

Which of these arguments and issues are most influential in determining if teaching is a good fit for you? Is there a particular point that is most persuasive, pro or con? What does that tell you about yourself? On a scale from 1 to 10, where 10 is "really committed" to teaching, and 1 is "I want no part of that job," what number are you? Remember that number as you read the text and go through this course—and see if you change that rating in the pages and weeks ahead.

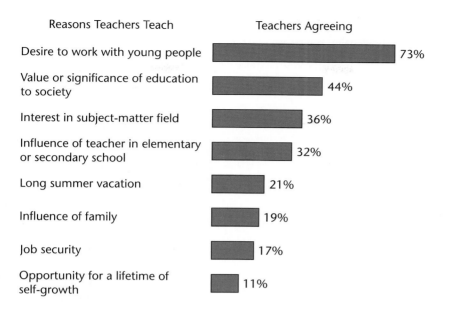

FIGURE 1.1
Why teach?

SOURCE: National Education Association, *Status of the American Public School Teacher*, 2003.

REFLECTION: Which of these reasons for teaching speak to you? Can you suggest others?

High on the teachers' "Top Ten List of Things I'd Like to Change about My Job" was salary, with about four out of ten teachers registering their dissatisfaction. Salaries, although better today than they have been historically, are still considered inadequate (see Figure 1.2). But salaries are not the only concern. Incremental obstacles pile up and wear down a teacher. One in five teachers focus their complaints on poor working conditions, heavy workloads, and extra responsibilities. Discipline issues, negative attitudes expressed by students, unresponsive school administrators, and lack of support from parents also steal teachers' enthusiasm. Parental support, like most of these factors, varies dramatically from school to school. If you are interested in a teaching position with a high level of parental support and involvement, you would be well advised to begin your search in suburban public schools, private schools, and at the elementary level.

Despite the common perception that teachers are disillusioned, more than 90 percent of new teachers report that they love teaching, and a majority would choose to teach again (see Figure 1.3). Yet, nearly one-half of new teachers exit the classroom within five years. This rapid turnover of teachers, as well as continuing teacher shortages, underscores the need for greater improvement in the quality of their working lives.[13]

 ## Professionalism at the Crossroads

What noble employment is more valuable to the state than that of the man who instructs the rising generation?

(Cicero)

Education makes a people easy to lead, but difficult to drive; easy to govern but impossible to enslave.

(Lord Brougham)

I shou'd think it as glorius [sic] employment to instruct poor children as to teach the children of the greatest monarch.

(Elizabeth Elstob)

FIGURE 1.2

Average and beginning teacher salaries in 2003–2004 ranked by average salary within region.

State	Average Salary	Beginning Salary	State	Average Salary	Beginning Salary
NEW ENGLAND			**SOUTHEAST**		
Connecticut	$56,516	$34,462	Georgia	$45,848	$35,116
Rhode Island	54,809	32,902	Virginia	43,936	32,437
Massachusetts	53,274	34,041	North Carolina	43,211	27,572
Vermont	43,009	25,819	South Carolina	41,162	27,883
New Hampshire	42,689	27,367	Florida	40,598	30,969
Maine	39,864	25,901	Tennessee	40,318	30,449
			Kentucky	39,831	28,416
MID-ATLANTIC			Arkansas	39,226	26,129
New York	$55,181	$36,400	West Virginia	38,496	26,692
New Jersey	53,663	37,061	Alabama	38,282	30,973
Pennsylvania	52,640	34,140	Louisiana	37,123	29,655
Delaware	51,122	34,566	Mississippi	36,217	28,106
Maryland	50,303	33,760			
			ROCKY MOUNTAINS		
GREAT LAKES			Colorado	$43,318	$31,296
Michigan	$54,474	$34,377	Idaho	40,111	25,908
Illinois	53,820	35,114	Wyoming	39,537	28,900
Ohio	47,791	28,692	Utah	38,976	26,130
Indiana	45,791	29,784	Montana	37,184	24,032
Minnesota	45,010	30,772			
Wisconsin	41,687	23,952	**FAR WEST**		
			California	$56,444	$35,135
PLAINS			Alaska	51,136	40,027
Nebraska	$39,635	$28,527	Oregon	47,829	33,396
Kansas	38,622	28,530	Hawaii	45,456	37,615
Iowa	38,381	26,967	Washington	45,437	30,159
Missouri	38,247	28,938	Nevada	43,211	27,942
North Dakota	35,411	24,108			
South Dakota	33,236	25,504	**U.S. Average**	**$46,597**	**$31,704**
SOUTHWEST					
Arizona	$42,324	$28,236			
Texas	40,476	32,741			
New Mexico	38,469	31,920			
Oklahoma	35,061	29,473			

SOURCE: American Federation of Teachers, annual survey of state departments of education, 2005.

REFLECTION: How do states and regions differ in teacher salaries? What are some of the reasons for these disparities? Why do you believe that private schools can attract teachers, while generally paying less salary?

We must view young people not as empty bottles to be filled, but as candles to be lit.

(Robert Schaffer)

I touch the future; I teach.

(Christa McAuliffe)

Literature, philosophy, and history are replete with such flowery tributes to teaching. In many minds, in some of our greatest minds, teaching is considered the noblest of professions. But the realities of the job do not always mesh with such

Percent of Teachers Who Say

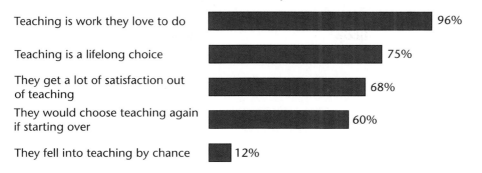

Teaching is work they love to do — 96%

Teaching is a lifelong choice — 75%

They get a lot of satisfaction out of teaching — 68%

They would choose teaching again if starting over — 60%

They fell into teaching by chance — 12%

FIGURE 1.3

New teacher satisfaction and willingness to enter teaching again.

SOURCE: National Education Association "Status of the American Public School Teacher," 2000–2001 © 2003.

REFLECTION: Why do you believe that there is a gap between the popular image of disillusioned teachers and the results of this survey? This survey data comes from those who have been teaching for five years or less. How might more experienced teachers respond?

admirable appraisals, resulting in a painful clash between noble ideals and practical realities. In the preface to *Goodbye, Mr. Chips*, James Hilton writes that his portrait of the lovable schoolmaster is a "tribute to a great profession." But an article in the *NEA Today*, a teacher's magazine, is entitled: "Are You Treated Like a Professional? Or a Tall Child?" For many teachers, the "Tall Child" analogy is closer to the truth. Says English teacher Carol Davis:

> We're told when to get here, when to leave, what to teach, what to want, what not to want, and how to think. . . . I'm trained in how to teach English, but I'm rarely asked for my opinion. If I were to be "promoted out of my classroom" my opinion would be more respected immediately. The irony would be that I'd no longer be teaching children.[14]

Many teachers feel that the satisfaction they realize inside the classroom is too often jeopardized by forces beyond the classroom: politicians mandating numerous standardized tests, demanding parents offering little support, and textbook publishers determining course content. Teachers desire more autonomy and control over their careers, and like all of us, want to be treated with more respect. Teachers increasingly see themselves as reflective decision makers, selecting objectives and teaching procedures to meet the needs of different learners.[15] They must know their subject matter, learning theory, research on various teaching methodologies, and techniques for curriculum development.[16] Some believe that the problems confronting teachers stem from the more pervasive issue of professional status and competence. Are teachers professionals? What does it take to be a professional, anyway? *Educating a Profession*, a publication of the American Association of Colleges for Teacher Education (AACTE), lists twelve criteria for a **profession.** We have

Collectively, teachers struggle to empower their profession; individually, they struggle to empower their students.

shortened these criteria below, and ask you to consider each one and decide if you believe that teaching meets these criteria. After marking your reactions in the appropriate column, compare your reactions with those of your classmates.

Criteria for a Profession	True for Teaching	Not True for Teaching	Don't Know
1. Professions provide essential services to the individual and society.	_____	_____	_____
2. Each profession is concerned with an identified area of need or function (e.g., maintenance of physical and emotional health).	_____	_____	_____
3. The profession possesses a unique body of knowledge and skills (professional culture).	_____	_____	_____
4. Professional decisions are made in accordance with valid knowledge, principles, and theories.	_____	_____	_____
5. The profession is based on undergirding disciplines from which it builds its own applied knowledge and skills.	_____	_____	_____
6. Professional associations control the actual work and conditions of the profession (e.g., admissions, standards, licensing).	_____	_____	_____
7. There are performance standards for admission to and continuance in the profession.	_____	_____	_____
8. Preparation for and induction into the profession requires a protracted preparation program, usually in a college or university professional school.	_____	_____	_____
9. There is a high level of public trust and confidence in the profession and in the skills and competence of its members.	_____	_____	_____
10. Individual practitioners are characterized by a strong service motivation and lifetime commitment to competence.	_____	_____	_____
11. The profession itself determines individual competence.	_____	_____	_____
12. There is relative freedom from direct or public job supervision of the individual practitioner. The professional accepts this responsibility and is accountable through his or her profession to the society.[17]	_____	_____	_____

www.mhhe.com/ sadker8e

INTERACTIVE ACTIVITY

Is Teaching a Profession? Do this exercise online. See how other students responded to each statement.

Do not be surprised if you find some criteria that do not apply to teaching. In fact, even the occupations that spring to mind when you hear the word *professional*— doctor, lawyer, clergy, college professor—do not completely measure up to all these criteria.

Those who developed these twelve criteria for a profession also listed another twelve criteria that would describe a **semiprofession.** Read these items carefully, and compare them with the characteristics that define a profession. Consider each item separately. Does it accurately describe teaching, or does it sell teaching short? After you have considered all the items and have marked your reactions in the appropriate column, decide whether you think teaching is actually a profession, or whether it would more accurately be termed a semiprofession.

Criteria for a Semiprofession	True for Teaching	Not True for Teaching	Don't Know
1. Lower in occupational status	_____	_____	_____
2. Shorter training periods	_____	_____	_____
3. Lack of societal acceptance that the nature of the service and/or the level of expertise justifies the autonomy that is granted to the professions	_____	_____	_____
4. A less specialized and less highly developed body of knowledge and skills	_____	_____	_____
5. Markedly less emphasis on theoretical and conceptual bases for practice	_____	_____	_____
6. A tendency for the individual to identify with the employment institution more and with the profession less	_____	_____	_____
7. More subject to administrative and supervisory surveillance and control	_____	_____	_____
8. Less autonomy in professional decision making, with accountability to superiors rather than to the profession	_____	_____	_____
9. Management by persons who have themselves been prepared and served in that semiprofession	_____	_____	_____
10. A preponderance of women	_____	_____	_____
11. Absence of the right of privileged communication between client and professional	_____	_____	_____
12. Little or no involvement in matters of life and death[18]	_____	_____	_____

Where do you place teaching? If you had a tough time deciding, you are not alone. Many people feel that teaching falls somewhere between professional and semiprofessional in status. Perhaps we should think of it as an "emerging" profession. Or perhaps teaching is, and will remain, a "submerged" profession. Either way, teachers find themselves in a career with both potential and frustration.

Why does all this "profession talk" matter? You may be more concerned with *real* questions: Will I be good at teaching? Do I want to work with children? What age level is best for me? Will the salary be enough to give me the quality of life that I want for myself and my family? You may be thinking, Why should I split hairs over whether I belong to a profession? Who cares? The issue of professionalism may not matter to you now or even during your first year or two of teaching, when

IMAGINE . . .

New Teacher Pay Scale

Teachers work with children only a few hours a day, and some people, not very sympathetic to the demands on teachers, believe that they should be paid pretty much as babysitters. Surprisingly, some teachers see an advantage in that system. Babysitters get about $6.00 an hour, so for a five-hour day, teachers would earn $30 per child. For a class of 25, that would be $750 a day. The school year is 187 days, so that would be $140,250. Summers, week-ends, and evenings off. Teachers as babysitters, an idea with some merit!

FIGURE 1.4

America's priorities.

SOURCE: Public Agenda, 2005.

REFLECTION: Why do you think Americans place such a high priority on education? Do you believe that this strong support contributes to building a teacher profession? Why or why not?

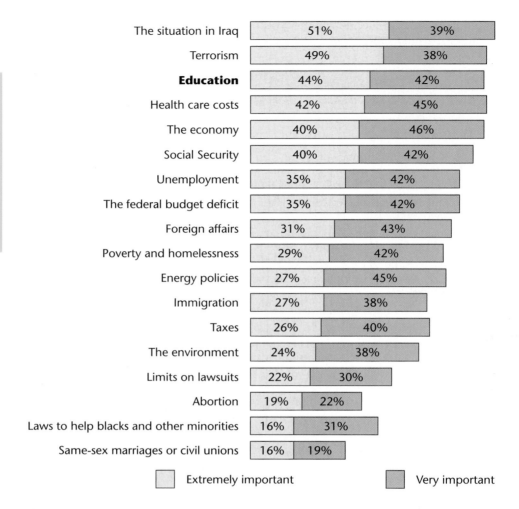

	Extremely important	Very important
The situation in Iraq	51%	39%
Terrorism	49%	38%
Education	44%	42%
Health care costs	42%	45%
The economy	40%	46%
Social Security	40%	42%
Unemployment	35%	42%
The federal budget deficit	35%	42%
Foreign affairs	31%	43%
Poverty and homelessness	29%	42%
Energy policies	27%	45%
Immigration	27%	38%
Taxes	26%	40%
The environment	24%	38%
Limits on lawsuits	22%	30%
Abortion	19%	22%
Laws to help blacks and other minorities	16%	31%
Same-sex marriages or civil unions	16%	19%

classroom survival and performance have top priority. But if you stay in teaching, this idea of professionalism will grow in significance, perhaps becoming one of the most important issues you face. Even now, as a student, you can become more reflective in your views of teaching and learning; you can begin to refine your own professional behaviors and outlooks. Beyond your personal decisions, you will confront a difficult question faced by so many teachers through time: Is teaching a genuine profession? Or does teaching languish in semiprofessional status? The issue remains at a crossroads, but the importance of education to the nation is clear (see Figure 1.4).

From Normal Schools to Board-Certified Teachers

Basic to any discussion of professionalism is the question of how its members are prepared. As you read this brief history of teacher preparation, think about whether teachers are prepared in a way commensurate with belonging to a profession.

From colonial America into the twentieth century, teacher education scarcely existed. More often than not, teachers in colonial America received no formal preparation at all. Most elementary teachers never even attended a secondary school. Some learned their craft by serving as apprentices to master teachers, a continuation of the medieval guild system. Others were indentured servants paying for their passage to America by teaching for a fixed number of years. Many belonged to the "sink-or-swim" school of teaching, and the education of an untold number of students undoubtedly sank with them.

The smaller number of teachers working at the secondary level—in academies or Latin grammar schools and as private tutors—had usually received some college education, more often in Europe than in America. Some knowledge of the subject matter was considered desirable, but no particular aptitude for teaching or knowledge of teaching skills was considered necessary. Teaching was viewed not as a career but as temporary employment. Many of those who entered teaching, especially at the elementary level, were teenagers who taught for only a year or two. Others were of dubious character, and early records reveal a number of teachers fired for drinking or stealing.

From this humble beginning there slowly emerged a more professional program for teacher education. In 1823, the **Reverend Samuel Hall** established a **normal school** (derived from the French *école normale,* a school that establishes model standards) in Concord, Vermont. This private school provided elementary school graduates with formal training in teaching skills. Reverend Hall's modest normal school marked the beginning of teacher education in America. Sixteen years later, in 1839, **Horace Mann** was instrumental in establishing the first state-supported normal school in Lexington, Massachusetts. Normal schools typically

Many of today's noted universities began as normal schools a century ago and were established to prepare teachers.

MICHIGAN STATE NORMAL SCHOOL,

provided a two-year teacher training program, consisting of academic subjects as well as teaching methodology. Some students came directly from elementary school; others had completed a secondary education. Into the 1900s, the normal school was the backbone of teacher education. The lack of rigorous professional training contributed to the less than professional treatment afforded teachers. The following is a teacher contract from the 1920s, a contract that offers a poignant insight into how teachers were seen . . . and treated.

Teaching Contract

Miss _____ agrees:

1. Not to get married. This contract becomes null and void immediately if the teacher marries.

2. Not to keep company with men.

3. To be home between the hours of 8 P.M. and 6 A.M. unless in attendance at a school function.

4. Not to loiter downtown in ice-cream parlors.

5. Not to leave town at any time without the permission of the Chairman of the Trustees.

6. Not to smoke cigarettes. This contract becomes null and void immediately if the teacher is found smoking.

7. Not to drink beer, wine, or whiskey. This contract becomes null and void immediately if the teacher is found drinking beer, wine, or whiskey.

8. Not to ride in a carriage or automobile with any man except her brother or father.

9. Not to dress in bright colors.

10. Not to dye her hair.

11. Not to wear less than two petticoats.

12. Not to wear dresses shorter than two inches above the ankles.

13. To keep the schoolroom clean:

    a. To sweep the classroom floor at least once daily.

    b. To scrub the classroom floor at least once weekly with soap and hot water.

    c. To clean the blackboard at least once daily.

    d. To start the fire at 7 A.M. so that the room will be warm by 8 A.M. when the children arrive.

14. Not to wear face powder, mascara, or to paint the lips.

(Reprinted courtesy of the *Chicago Tribune,* September 28, 1975, Section 1.)

As the contract indicates, by the 1900s, teaching was becoming a female occupation. Both female workers and teaching being held in low regard, the reward for the austere dedication detailed in this contract was an unimpressive $75 a month. But as the twentieth century progressed, professional teacher training gained wider acceptance. Enrollments in elementary schools climbed and secondary education gained in popularity, and so did the demand for more and better-trained teachers. Many private colleges and universities initiated teacher education programs, and normal schools expanded to three- and four-year programs, gradually evolving into state teachers' colleges. Interestingly, as attendance grew, these teachers' colleges expanded their programs and began offering courses and career preparation in fields other than teaching. By the 1950s, many of the state teachers' colleges had evolved into state colleges. In fact, some of today's leading universities were originally chartered as normal schools.

The 1980s marked the beginning of the modern effort to reshape education. A number of education reform reports fanned the flames of controversy regarding professionalism and teacher preparation, including one written by a group of prominent education deans. The Holmes Group, named for former Harvard Education Dean Henry H. Holmes, debated the teacher preparation issue for several years before releasing its report, entitled **Tomorrow's Teachers** (1986).[19] The same year, the Carnegie Forum also issued a highly publicized report, **A Nation Prepared.**[20] Both reports called for higher standards and increased professionalism for the nation's teachers. The Carnegie report also called for an end to the undergraduate teaching major, to be replaced by master's-level degrees in teaching. While some universities followed this recommendation and created fifth-year teacher education programs (bachelor's and master's degrees required for teacher education candidates), other colleges continued their undergraduate education programs. Teacher education remains a hodgepodge of approaches. Some critics place much of the blame on universities themselves, for failing to adequately fund and support schools of education.[21]

But not all of the attention has been on initial teacher education. In the 1990s, the Carnegie Forum was influential in creating the **National Board for Professional Teaching Standards (NBPTS).** The goal of the NBPTS is to recognize extraordinary teachers, those whose skills and knowledge indicate their high level of achievement. This is a significant departure from simply licensing new teachers who reach minimal standards. During its first years of operation, the NBPTS developed assessment procedures to identify highly competent teachers, teachers who would be designated **board-certified.** Like medicine, teaching now had not just an entry license—a standard teaching license—but advanced recognition of a higher level of skills and competencies. Thousands of educators annually compile professional portfolios (including videotaped examples of their teaching), and undergo assessment tests and interviews en route to becoming board-certified teachers. As you might imagine, the board assessment is not inexpensive, with a price tag of several thousand dollars. Fewer than half the states and a handful of school districts now pay for their teachers to prepare for board certification.

As teachers aspire to board certification, states and communities are developing ways to recognize their accomplishments. Many teachers who become board-certified receive stipends or are placed on a higher salary scale. Others are given release time to work with new teachers. To date, less than 2 percent of teachers are board-certified.[22] Will new responsibilities be found for board-certified teachers? Are we developing a new cadre of educational leaders, "lead" or "principal" teachers? Will board certification evolve into a sort of national merit pay? Or will board certification simply become another failed attempt to transform what some view as a semiprofession into a true profession?[23] These and other pivotal questions will likely be answered during your time as a classroom teacher.

How Teachers Are Prepared Today

Even as educators strive toward professional status, there is no consensus on how best to prepare teachers. The two teacher education approaches that currently dominate the landscape can be categorized as traditional and alternative. The traditional teacher education path is a preservice program in which students study the science of teaching and the subject matter, and then do a clinical teaching experience. These programs lead to either a B.A. or an M.A., or may simply involve a fifth year of study for those who want to obtain a teacher's license. Traditional programs graduate about five times as many students as the second, more controversial approach, which emphasizes on-the-job training rather than preservice preparation. Students in these alternative teacher education programs seek licensure through a structured apprenticeship, an untraditional route to obtaining a teacher's license that is now possible in virtually all states. These alternative programs assume that beginning teachers already know their subject matter, and with some time in the classroom, can acquire and refine their teaching skills. The extent of training and support given to new teachers in alternative programs varies greatly, and this has become a point of contention. Imagine yourself in one of the nation's most challenging classrooms, and feeling less than well trained. This is the challenge facing programs like Teach for America (TFA). Although relatively small in size, TFA has enjoyed great success in recruiting highly motivated and talented recruits who find themselves in very distressed schools. Supporters of the program point out that many of these volunteers become excellent teachers, and that the proportion of teachers of color is higher in Teach for America than in traditional teacher education programs. Moreover, many of the challenging schools where these teachers are assigned have a difficult time finding any teachers, and eagerly welcome these new recruits. Defenders of such fast track training programs argue that "on-the-job-training" is not new, and can be quite effective.

Not very long ago, lawyers and doctors were prepared for their professions through similar apprenticeships. But many educators see such programs as the height of irresponsibility, quite the opposite of profession building.[24] Teach for America critics like Linda Darling-Hammond argue that today's classroom challenges require more thorough career preparation, and that even when teachers are in short supply, professional standards must be maintained.[25] Some detractors argue that students in alternative programs learn less[26] and are more likely to leave teaching after only a few years.[27] How can teaching ever become a real profession, they ask, if we train and license teachers in such "quickie" teacher education programs?

Research is not yet conclusive on the relative effectiveness of either approach, and it would not be a stretch to conclude that strong and weak programs can be found within each model. In fact, comparing these two models may not be as productive as finding the answers to some critical questions, questions that can be asked of any teacher education program: Do the candidates have a strong background in their subject matter? Have they received effective pedagogical training? Has there been a carefully planned and implemented clinical experience?[28] As you begin your own teacher education program, whatever type it is, you may want to consider these questions and think about the specific content and skills you would find most useful.

Views of Teacher Education

As you begin to consider your ideal teacher education program, you may want to pick the brains of those whose job it is to prepare teachers. Education professors have some clear ideas on what kind of teachers they want to prepare in the classroom.[29] (While

PHOTO-SYNTHESIS   A Teaching Legacy

Meet Sarah, Amy and Claudia, representing a three-generation teaching family. Sarah started in 1948 when the average annual salary was under _____. Her daughter Claudia, a recently retired principal, began teaching in 1969, when the salaries had climbed to _____. When Amy entered the field in 2003, the nation's teaching wage averaged _____. Moving beyond salary, what other differences might have characterized teaching in 1948, 1969, and 2003? If you could interview these three educators, what questions might you ask?

Answers: 1948—$3,000; 1969—$8,626; 2003—$46,597.

SOURCE: American Federation of Teachers www.aft.org/.

there is no guarantee that your instructor in this course agrees with his or her colleagues, it may be fun to ask and find out.) Education professors want to prepare:

- Teachers who are themselves lifelong learners and are constantly updating their skills.
- Teachers committed to teaching children to be active learners.
- Teachers who have high expectations of all their students.
- Teachers who are deeply knowledgeable about the content of the specific subjects they will be teaching.

Are these goals similar to the ones you hold? Or do you agree more with the general public who worries less about teacher knowledge of subject matter and instead prefers teachers who focus on discipline and control; emphasize traditional

19

values such as punctuality, honesty, and politeness; and create learning experiences that inspire children, including competitive teaching strategies?[30] What do first-year teachers consider most beneficial from their teacher training programs? Preparation in lesson planning, using a range of instructional methods, practical classroom management techniques, and student assessment top the list. Importantly, and not too surprising, teachers who feel significantly prepared plan to stay longer than those who do not.[31] Whichever views are more to your liking, it is time to think of yourself as a consumer of teacher education—because in a very real sense, you are.

> **REFLECTION:** If you were to design a teacher education program, what would it look like?

Urban Legends about Teaching

While sensible people may disagree about how best to prepare teachers, not all views are sensible. In fact, several bizarre ideas are so popular that they qualify as urban legends: "Teachers are born, not made," or "To be a good teacher, all you really need to know is the subject you are teaching." Like the urban legend of alligators cavorting in the New York City sewer system, these teaching myths have taken on a life of their own and deserve a moment of our time to clear the air and dispel the myths.

Teachers are born, not made: It is certainly true that some students enter a teacher education program with impressive instructional skills, yet training and practice is what is needed to transform a strong teacher into a gifted one. Teaching is far from unique in this. When a group of Olympians and their coaches were asked what it takes to become a champion, none of the answers suggested that they were "born" champions. On the contrary, the athletes credited well-designed practices and good coaching. Accomplished musicians attribute their performance to hours of focused practice, as do master chess players. So too, superior teachers are trained, not born.

All you really need to know is the subject you are teaching: While it is true that subject mastery is critical in effective teaching, research reveals that teachers skilled in **pedagogy,** the art and science of teaching, especially teaching methods and strategies, outperform teachers with superior subject area knowledge. Clearly, the most successful teachers do not view this as an either/or proposition. Effective teaching requires both knowledge of the subject and instructional skills.[32]

Teacher education students are less talented than other college majors: This popular canard lives on despite very mixed evidence. On the one hand, education majors are less likely to score in the top 25 percent on the SATs than the general population. On the other hand, adult literacy surveys (see Figure 1.5) show that teachers attain scores similar to those of physicians, writers, engineers, and social workers.[33]

These urban legends aside, it is certainly true that teacher education programs are stronger today than they have been in years. And the public holds high expectations for such programs. More than two-thirds of the public believe that good teachers are best prepared through an accredited teacher training program, and four out of five Americans want these programs to prepare teachers to pass a national competency exam.[34] Yet far more can be done. Universities typically spend less on teacher education students than those enrolled in other professional schools. Only a handful of states actually measure teacher performance in the classroom, and as long as some alternative licensure programs place relatively untrained teachers in

www.mhhe.com/ sadker8e

INTERACTIVE ACTIVITY

What Should Teachers Learn? Create your own teacher education curriculum based on what you think teachers need to know.

FIGURE 1.5

Adult prose literacy scores by selected occupations.

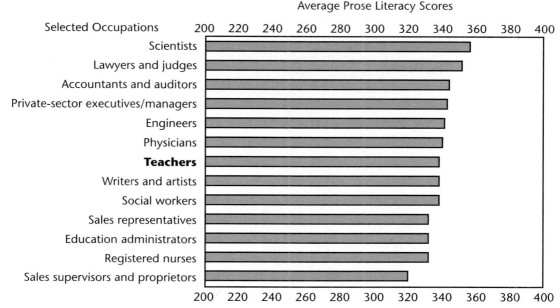

SOURCE: David C. Berliner, "A Personal Response to Those Who Bash Teacher Education," *Journal of Teacher Education* 51, no. 5, November/December 2000.

REFLECTION: Why is there a popular perception of low teacher competence, despite their strong scores on tests like this one? Which of these occupations that score close to teaching do you find particularly surprising?

the classroom, teacher education will continue to be far less than it could and should be.[35]

Some teacher preparation programs emphasize current research as well as practical classroom skills, often working in close collaboration with local schools. Many teacher education students are studying at the graduate level, bringing more of life's experiences to the classroom than did their predecessors, all signs of positive changes in teacher preparation.

Quality professional preparation suggests not only increased professional status, but also the responsibility that goes with that training. This translates into teacher influence over school policies, procedures, schedules, and curriculum. Yet, teachers are frequently kept far from policy-making circles. When Andy Baumgartner, National Teacher of the Year in 2000, criticized the lack of significant teacher representation on a commission to reform education in his home state of Georgia, he quickly became *persona non grata*. The governor would not have his photo taken with him, and several politicians roundly criticized him for his audacity.[36]

In the traditional "top-down" organization of schools, teachers find themselves with little influence over education policy, and little say in how schools operate. Yet other organizations do not lack imagination in how they view or treat employees. In fact, we need only look skyward to find an innovative example of employee influence.

Southwest Airlines and Teaching

The first time we flew on Southwest Airlines, we really did not know what to expect. We knew that we paid less for the ticket than other airlines charge, and that made us nervous. We had been advised to eat before the flight, since the airline cuisine consisted of a bag of nuts. Since everything was on a first come, first served basis, we were given firm instructions: "Get to the airport early if you want a good seat." We boarded the plane, found a seat, and buckled up.

As we began the takeoff, an amazing sound reverberated through the cabin. It sounded like a whistle, a railroad whistle. Dumbstruck, we wondered: what are they using to power the engines? Is there such a thing as a steam plane? Panic turned to relief as we discovered that the flight attendant was blowing into a toy train whistle. By the time we lifted off, most of the passengers were either laughing or joining the flight attendant with their own versions of train sounds. Once airborne, the flight attendants organized a contest. Each passenger willing to tell a joke on the public address system would receive a $50 voucher. The passengers, by their applause, would choose the best jokester, and that person would receive a $100 voucher (a bit higher than the price of the ticket). Someone would fly for fun *and* profit.

If you have ever flown with Southwest, perhaps you have noticed their flight attendants as they walk through an airport. They are the ones wearing shorts and polo shirts instead of traditional uniforms and suits, strolling about in sneakers instead of wingtips or heels, and smiling, if not laughing. Southwest employees look like they are going on vacation instead of going to work. Not only are they more comfortable than many passengers, they seem happier too! So what's going on at Southwest?

In a book called *Nuts!*, Kevin and Jackie Freiberg write about how Southwest Airline's founders rejected a fundamental tenet in American business, the belief that the customer is always right. At Southwest, there are things more important than the customer, even more important than making money. One of those is the happiness of employees. Yes, employees. Employee happiness creates customer happiness. Southwest prides itself on its egalitarian corporate culture, one in which the head of the company explores options and policies with *all* employees, including those with the lowest paychecks. The president visits employees during meals and at work, seeking their ideas for improvements. Meeting employee needs is a top priority. One thing they need, according to Southwest, are celebrations. Yes, celebrations. Personal and corporate accomplishments and milestones are reasons for employees to be honored and for all involved to celebrate and party. Sound strange? Southwest believes that creating a contented, even joyful workforce does more than improve employee self-esteem and create a caring corporate culture; it also sparks innovative suggestions for improved performance. Celebrations break work routines, a necessary prerequisite for viewing work in a different way, and this leads to new and creative ideas for improving performance. The company's mission is not simply to make money. The kind of motivated employees that the company wants to attract need more than a corporate profit mission to spark their commitment. Southwest's mission is somewhat egalitarian and idealistic: to open air travel to people with limited means. "It is not a job, it is a crusade," is the company motto, a crusade that keeps ticket prices incredibly low.

Have we motivated you to buy some stock? (Don't look for it to be listed under a typical three-letter code like *SWA.* The company is listed under *LUV.*) How does the stock do? Even as many airlines descend into bankruptcy or get "absorbed" in corporate takeovers, Southwest has remained independent and its stock price has soared for three decades. The company may seem iconoclastic, but the bottom line has been all green. Its workforce is considered to be the most efficient in the industry, serving twice the usual number of passengers per employee. Southwest has few delays, and one of the best on-time records of any airline. Its safety procedures are more rigorous than the government requires, and it has been voted the safest airline in the sky. All of this comes from the cheapest airfares around.

Before you run off to buy some *LUV* stock, remember that nothing lasts forever, and despite its remarkable progress, Southwest may very well suffer some reverses in the years ahead. But the first three decades at Southwest have been amazing, and they merit a closer look. What has been the formula for the company's success? Many experts say it is the confidence that the executives placed in Southwest employees. As a result, the company attracted inspired employees and created a model workplace. But before we go any further with our airline industry story, this may be a good time to remind ourselves that we are really interested in teaching and schools (thought we forgot, right?), so let's broaden this discussion and also ask: What traits and characteristics are needed for successful teaching? How do these two sets of characteristics compare?

Here's your challenge: Sort out which of the following job attributes are listed by Southwest, and which have been drawn from the literature on effective teaching. (We did alter a few words to avoid any obvious reference to either occupation.) Put a mark in the appropriate columns to indicate which career attributes you believe are sought by Southwest, and which are drawn from teacher education sources. You certainly can check both columns, if that seems to be appropriate.

The final column is for you. Put a check in the last column if you feel that you are being described by that attribute. After you have marked your columns (but before you race off to apply for a position at either a school or an airline), we will look at the lists, and their meaning.

We Are Hiring for a New Position, and Invite You to Apply. To Succeed in this Career, You Should:[37]	Southwest Airlines	Teacher Education	Does This Describe Me?
1. Have a passion for the job (a purpose you are crazy about)	_____	_____	_____
2. Enjoy and appreciate other people	_____	_____	_____
3. Have a strong work ethic	_____	_____	_____
4. Possess a solid knowledge base	_____	_____	_____
5. Believe in continuous self-improvement	_____	_____	_____
6. Work effectively with people	_____	_____	_____
7. Be a positive member of the community	_____	_____	_____
8. Successfully respond to people's different needs	_____	_____	_____
9. Develop caring and trusting relationships with people	_____	_____	_____
10. Have a sense of humor	_____	_____	_____
11. Maintain your curiosity in life and work	_____	_____	_____
12. Not take yourself too seriously	_____	_____	_____

continued

We Are Hiring for a New Position, and Invite You to Apply. To Succeed in this Career, You Should:[37]	Southwest Airlines	Teacher Education	Does This Describe Me?
13. Not "hide" yourself: Be authentic	_____	_____	_____
14. Dare to be different and experiment	_____	_____	_____
15. Pursue "love" and caring over "techniques"	_____	_____	_____
16. Choose service over self-interest	_____	_____	_____
17. Be committed to unleashing the human spirit, yours and others	_____	_____	_____

Have you sorted out which items come from teacher education literature, and which from Southwest Airlines? The first item, having a passion for your job, actually appears on both lists. (Did you check both columns?) In fact, the first ten items are tied to teacher effectiveness. In addition to the first statement, items 11 through 17 are from Southwest Airlines. At the core, to be effective and successful in either job requires a passion or spirit as well as strong interpersonal skills.

Why are we drawing this comparison between the attributes needed to be successful at Southwest and at teaching? We are not being paid for the plug, nor do we own stock in Southwest. We make the comparison because we believe that Southwest offers lessons for all of us. Although a stream of headlines and news stories call for improvement in the nation's schools, there is little agreement on just how to accomplish this. While some school critics demand higher standards and more testing, others believe that technology and computers hold the key to more effective schools. Still others believe that increased competition, parent choice, and school vouchers will create stronger schools.

www.mhhe.com/ sadker8e

INTERACTIVE ACTIVITY
What Job Is This?
Match job titles to Education-related job descriptions.

If you are not familiar with these arguments and approaches, worry not. In this text, you will learn about all of these and more. You will also learn that few if any of these education critics do what Southwest did: look to career professionals for answers. What would schools be like if teachers were more autonomous, if they were responsible for the curricular, instructional, and testing decisions? How could we design schools to be happier places, where learning is a joyful experience? How can we reward teachers for going that extra mile? (These are not rhetorical questions. How do you think schools would be different if communities were committed to making teachers happy, and giving them meaningful decision-making powers?) Although the personal qualities sought by Southwest and by schools are remarkably similar, few headlines or news stories, few pundits or commentators talk about doing in schools what Southwest did in the airline industry: improving the quality of teachers' lives as a starting point to improving the education of students.

IMAGINE . . .

The $100,000 Teacher

Brian Crosby not only teaches at Hoover High just outside Los Angeles, he also knows how to push a button or two. That's what he did in his book, *The $100,000 Teacher*. Crosby argues that the top 5 percent of teachers be paid six-figure salaries, that bonuses be given for teachers in critical areas like science and math, and that weak teachers be forced to find employment elsewhere. He believes that pay should be tied to classroom performance, and urges teachers "to trade job security for professional integrity."

SOURCE: *The Baltimore Sun,* 2003.

This Southwest story tells you something about us, the authors of this book: we love teaching, but want to love it more. We believe that although teaching is a wonderful career, teachers deserve more than they get, both in money and psychic rewards. We have taught in many different settings, from the military to overseas, from elementary school to the university, and while each position gave us joy, we always thought of ways to make those teaching positions better. Like so many careers, teaching has both assets and liabilities, and you would do well to consider both as you look to your own future.

 ## We Like Questions

Education is a dynamic field, rife with controversies, misperceptions, surprises, and constant change. Throughout this book, we will work hard to immerse you in that excitement, and to tweak your interest. (OK, so it's not a Stephen King *Fright Night at the School Prom* novel for that rainy day at the beach. But we do want this text to be more exciting and interesting than most, to mirror the enthusiasm that we feel about education.) Issues discussed in this text may well spark questions. A sage once said that the only dumb question is the one not asked. (While this particular sage might have been overrated, we concur with that premise.) This text is all about answering questions. In fact, at the end of the text, we list a number of questions that students typically ask: How do I get a teacher's license? Where are salaries and working conditions the best? What's on the Praxis exam? We not only ask these questions, we try our best to answer them. What if *your* question is not listed? Responding to your questions is one of the purposes of the Web site that accompanies this book. (Have you visited the Online Learning Center at www.mhhe.com/sadker8e yet?) In addition to attracting and answering student questions, the Web site is filled with useful Web links, study hints, sample test questions covering each of the chapters in this text, and suggested student activities. We invite you to submit your questions through the text Web site, and we will try to answer them. In fact, we like questions so much that we will start the questioning ourselves. The following question is a good one to ask first, because if you are interested in becoming a teacher, there is no time like the present to begin.

What steps can I take between now and graduation to make myself an attractive teaching candidate?

Become informed about the job market.
Begin gathering current information about the job market and search out those particular content areas and skills that will increase your marketability. This information will help you select appropriate courses and extracurricular activities. Geography plays a role, as some local communities face critical teacher shortages, and others have an ample number. Special education and bilingual skills are often in demand, and demographics plays a big role as well. The nation's growing population of students of color is not matched by an adequate number of teachers of color, so there is a great need to attract African Americans, Hispanics, and Asian Americans into the teaching ranks. There are also too few male candidates for elementary teaching positions, and too few female teachers in physics and technology programs, so gender is yet another consideration. To find out more about the teaching job market, you can check educational associations and state departments of education, many of which are listed in the appendix of this text or found on our Web site. The National Teacher Recruitment Clearinghouse—www.recruitingteachers.org—is

Actor James Edwards Olmos with Jaime Escalante

For four years, Jaime Escalante had been struggling to build a strong advanced placement (AP) calculus program at Garfield High, a troubled East Los Angeles school with a poor academic history. Finally the program seemed to blossom with 18 students, almost double the number from the year before. Every one of them passed the difficult and prestigious AP examination.

During the summer, however, a controversy developed. The Educational Testing Service (ETS), which administers the AP exam, told 14 of the students that a high correspondence in their answers suggested cheating. They would either have to retake the test or have their scores nullified. Escalante, the students, and others protested. There had been no cheating, they argued. It seemed to be just another example of the experts underestimating the potential of students who are poor and Latino. But the ETS would not budge, so a retest was arranged. Even after a summer away from the theorems and formulas, all of the students passed the test again, many with higher scores than the first time.

After that, Escalante's calculus program took off, and encouraged other Garfield teachers to add and expand AP classes in history, English, biology, and other subjects. By 1987, Garfield had become known as one of the best public schools in the country.[1]

How does Escalante account for his achievements? He sums up much of his teaching as the pursuit of *ganas*, a Spanish word meaning "the will to succeed."

> Really it's not just the knowledge of math. Because to have knowledge is one thing, and to use that knowledge is another, and to know how to teach or how to motivate these kids is the combination of both. My skills are really to motivate these kids, to make them learn, to give them *ganas*—desire to do something—to make them believe they can learn. Anybody, any kid can learn if he or she has the desire to do it. That's what *ganas* is about.[2]

Escalante's own life story demonstrates *ganas*. When he emigrated from Bolivia with his wife and young family to the United States in 1963 because of sociopolitical unrest, he had already been teaching math and physics for 11 years, gaining a reputation as one of the finest teachers in La Paz. Yet, as a newcomer to the United States, Escalante faced a decade of adjustment as he learned English, worked as a bus boy and cook, and attended college. Upon graduation, he dabbled in the computer industry, yet once again his heart called to teaching. Honoring his own *ganas*, Escalante earned a California teaching license in his free time and headed to Garfield High.

While "Kimo," as Mr. Escalante was nicknamed, could be a charming, colorful character, latecomers and those with incomplete assignments often found themselves interrogated, hounded by calls to parents, and threatened with a transfer to a less effective school a very long bus ride away. Using rewards, taunts, afternoon study sessions, or even mild bribery, Escalante refused to allow students to give up. He set high standards and skillfully adopted the carrot-and-stick approach: the carrot was college and the world of opportunities higher education could offer; the stick was his commitment to challenge all students. Escalante was a tide turner, setting into motion the idea that poor and immigrant students can indeed achieve great intellectual accomplishments when given high expectations, demanding curricula, and committed teachers.

> The teacher has to have the energy of the hottest volcano, the memory of an elephant, and the diplomacy of an ambassador. . . . Really, a teacher has to possess love and knowledge and then has to use this combined passion to help kids accomplish something.[3]

Nearly two decades after the movie *Stand and Deliver* catapulted this math teacher and Garfield High into the pantheon of education stardom, Escalante is now retired from active teaching and lives in his native Bolivia. Will Escalante ever return to teaching in American schools? Unlikely, "unless officials get serious about supporting public education."[4]

[1] Jay Matthews, *Escalante: The Best Teacher in America* (New York: Henry Holt, 1988). [2] Quoted in Anne Meek, "On Creating Ganas: A Conversation with Jaime Escalante," *Educational Leadership* 46, no. 5 (February 1989), pp. 46–47.
[3] Ibid. [4] Jerry Jesness, "Still Standing," *Education Week* 17, no. 4 (January 1, 2006), pp. 12–13.

REFLECTION: How does Jaime Escalante's philosophy and teaching style compare to the positive and negative points about a teaching career discussed in this chapter's *You Be the Judge*? Do you think *ganas* can be taught (to teachers or students) in the classroom, or is it something that you are born with?

www.mhhe.com/ sadker8e

To learn more about Jaime Escalante, Click on *Profiles in Education*.

also a terrific resource for prospective teachers seeking jobs—and for school districts and states seeking qualified teachers. A central feature of the Clearinghouse is the unique gateway to job banks nationwide.

For additional sources of information, check with your university's placement office. You may want to begin reading professional education journals that include information about the employment picture. Web sites are often the best source of up-to-date information, so you may want to visit sites sponsored by school districts, professional associations, placement services, or your university. You can also visit real sites, such as job fairs sponsored by school districts. Knowledge about the employment picture and the kind of candidate that is in demand can give you a powerful start on your teaching career.

Make sure your coursework is planned carefully.

Your first concern should be to enroll in courses that fulfill your certification and licensure requirements. We will explore certification and licensure in some depth later in the text, but for now it is worth remembering that, in addition to earning your degree, you want to leave your program licensed to teach. A second consideration is to make yourself more marketable by going beyond minimum course requirements. For example, technology and special education skills are often in demand by schools, as are elementary teachers with special competence in math or any teacher with a proficiency in a second language. Plan to develop a transcript of courses that will reflect a unique, competent, and relevant academic background. Your transcript will be an important part of your overall candidacy for a teaching position.

Do not underestimate the importance of extracurricular activities.

Employers are likely looking for candidates whose background reflects interest and experience in working with children. A day care center or summer camp job may pay less than the local car wash, bank, or restaurant, but these career-related jobs may offer bigger dividends later on. Think about offering your services to a local public school or community youth group. Try to make your volunteer situation parallel the future job you would like to have. You want to build an inventory of relevant skills and experiences as well as personal contacts.

Begin networking.

Through both your coursework and your extracurricular activities, you will come into contact with teachers, administrators, and other school personnel. You should be aware that these people can function as an informal network for information about the local employment picture, as can your professors and even your class-mates. Go out of your way to let these people know of your interests, your special skills, and your commitment to teaching. This does not mean that you should become such a nuisance that people will duck behind their desks when they see you coming. It does mean that, at the right times and in the right places, you can let them know what jobs you are looking for and your skills and experiences that qualify you for those jobs.

Begin collecting recommendations now.

Studies reveal that letters of recommendation greatly influence employment deci-sions. Even if you find it difficult to request such letters, do not wait until you are student teaching to begin collecting them. Extracurricular activities, coursework, part-time employment, and volunteer work can all provide you with valuable recommendations. Your university placement office may be able to begin a placement folder for you, maintaining these recommendations and forwarding copies to potential employers at the appropriate time.

Ask for letters of recommendation while you are in a job or course or immediately after leaving it. Professors, teachers, and past employers may move or retire, and, believe it or not, they may even forget you and just how competent and talented you are. You may be asked to help by drafting key points. Anything you can do to lighten the burden will be appreciated. Collecting letters of recommendation should be a continual process, not one that begins in the last semester of your teacher education program.

Develop a résumé and portfolio.

Traditionally, a résumé has been a central document considered during job applications, typically including a specific career objective and summarizing education, work experience, memberships, awards, and special skills. For example, a résumé might target a social studies teaching position in a particular area as your career objective, and it might report membership in the student NEA, an office held in school government, fluency in Spanish, experience with a student newspaper, honors you have won, and any relevant jobs, such as summer camp counselor or aid in a day care center. Many software packages have résumé templates, there are scores of books and Web sites devoted to résumé writing, and advisers and counselors at your school should be able to assist.

Today, many colleges and school districts are moving beyond résumés and toward **portfolios,** a more comprehensive reflection of a candidate's skills. If you would like to do something a bit more innovative than simply preparing a dynamite résumé and providing sparkling letters of recommendation, or if your teacher education program is promoting more authentic and creative assessment strategies, then you might want to consider developing a portfolio. This text will help you in that process. You will find, cleverly placed between the major sections of this book, a special feature called *Reflective Activities and Your Portfolio (RAP)*. The *RAP* activities will encourage you to reflect on your reading, undertake some interesting observations and activities, and begin collecting relevant materials for your portfolio. Even if you decide not to develop a portfolio, these *RAP* activities will be useful for developing professional materials that you can use in many different ways.

Make good first, second, third, and fourth impressions.

In many education courses, you will be asked to participate in local school activities. This participation may take the form of observing or of being a teacher's aide or student teacher. (You may find the Observation Handbook in the Online Learning Center of this book particularly useful for school visits.) Recording and thinking about your impressions can be a useful step in deciding on the kind of position you want. In each case, you will be making an impression on the school faculty and administration. Good impressions can lead to future job offers. Poor impressions can result in your name being filed in the *persona non grata* drawer of people's needs.

Consider every visit to a school as an informal interview. Dress and act accordingly. Demonstrate your commitment and enthusiasm in ways that are helpful to school personnel. If you are viewed as a valuable and useful prospective member of the school community, you are a candidate with a head start for a current or future teaching position. Remember, known quantities are nearly always preferred to unknown quantities.

SUMMARY

1. **What are the advantages and disadvantages of being a teacher?**

   In the *You Be the Judge* feature, we consider both advantages and disadvantages of teaching. Routine, lack of respect, student apathy, and bureaucracy can wear teachers down, while the joy of working with children, caring colleagues, and intellectual stimulation motivate teachers.

2. **What are the satisfactions—and complaints—of today's teachers?**

   Although the vast majority of teachers are satisfied, many teachers believe that their pay is inadequate and their workloads heavy, and teachers generally desire fewer discipline problems and more parental and administrative support.

3. **Can we consider teaching to be a profession?**

   There are trends to make teaching more "professional" (five years of training, growing research base, qualifying exams, and the recognition of board-certified teachers), and countertrends that question the status of teachers (alternative certification and lack of teacher influence over licensure and curricular standards). Some claim teaching is, at best, a semiprofession.

4. **How has teacher preparation changed over the years?**

   In the early 19th century, normal schools were established to train future teachers. While some recent reform reports, including *Tomorrow's Teachers* and *A Nation Prepared,* urge higher standards, increased professionalism for teacher preparation, and recognition of superior performance through board certification, other programs emphasize alternative certification, a type of apprenticeship not unlike what was practiced in colonial America.

5. **What traits and characteristics are needed for successful teaching?**

   Successful teachers enjoy working with children, managing and motivating people, working well with the community, and are often found to have a pretty good sense of humor. A strong work ethic, intellectual curiosity, and a commitment to lifelong learning are also associated with success in the classroom. Many of these skills are also useful in other people-oriented occupations. While organizations like Southwest Airlines have developed corporate cultures that focus on employee satisfaction and autonomy, schools have yet to mirror that level of confidence in teachers.

6. **Is teaching a "good fit" for you?**

   In reviewing characteristics and traits related to effective teaching, we ask you to evaluate yourself. How do you rate on these skills and traits? In fact, a major purpose of this text is to help you connect with teaching and assess if teaching is the right career for you.

7. **What steps can you take now on the road to becoming a teacher?**

   You are invited to use the RAP activities, further suggested readings, and online activities in this text to clarify your thoughts about teaching. We try to anticipate your questions and get you actively involved in this book, but we invite you to send additional questions to us, either through snail mail or e-mail at **www.mhhe.com/sadker8e**. If you are pretty sure that teaching is for you, we can help you reach that goal. You may also want to begin preparing our résumé and portfolio, soliciting recommendations, and staying informed about the job market. It may be early, but it is not too early.

CHAPTER REVIEW

Go to the Online Learning Center to take a chapter self-quiz, practice with key terms, and review concepts from the chapter.

THE *TEACHERS, SCHOOLS, AND SOCIETY* READER WITH CLASSROOM OBSERVATION VIDEO CLIPS

Go to your *Teachers, Schools, and Society* Reader CD-ROM to:

READ CURRENT AND HISTORICAL ARTICLES

1.1 **Metaphors of Hope,** Mimi Brodsky Chenfield, *Phi Delta Kappan,* December 2004.

1.2 **Keeping Good Teachers: Why It Matters, What Leaders Can Do,** Linda Darling-Hammond, *Educational Leadership,* May 2003.

1.3 **Improving Relationships with the Schoolhouse,** Ronald S. Barth, *Educational Leadership,* March 2006.

ANALYZE CASE STUDIES

1.1 **Megan Brownlee:** A parent visits her children's favorite elementary school teacher and is surprised to discover that the teacher does not encourage her to enter the teaching profession.

1.2 **Jennifer Gordon:** A mature woman beginning a second career as an elementary school teacher struggles during her student teaching experience with how to deal with her cooperating teacher who treats her very badly and corrects her in front of the class.

OBSERVE TEACHERS, STUDENTS, AND CLASSROOMS IN ACTION

Classroom Observation: The Pros and Cons of Teaching

Deciding whether to enter the teaching profession is an important decision. As you've read in this chapter, there are many things to take into consideration when exploring teaching as a career. In this observation you will observe experienced and new teachers as they discuss both the joys of teaching and their concerns with the profession, some of the surprises they discovered, and the advice they have for those considering a career in the classroom.

KEY TERMS AND PEOPLE

DISCUSSION QUESTIONS AND ACTIVITIES

1. This chapter introduces you to the importance of well-thought-out career decision making. You can read further on this decision-making process in one of the many career books now available. For example, Richard N. Bolles' *What Color Is Your Parachute?* contains many exercises that should help you clarify your commitment to teaching. Or you may want to visit Bolles' Web site at www.jobhuntersbible.com/. These resources, or a visit to your career center, can help you determine what other careers present viable options for you.

2. Interview teachers and students at different grade levels to determine what they think are the positive and negative aspects of teaching. Share those interview responses with your classmates.

3. Suppose you could write an open letter to students, telling them about yourself and why you want to teach. What would you want them to know? When you attempt to explain yourself to others, you often gain greater self-knowledge. You might want to share your letter with classmates and to hear what they have to say in their letters. Perhaps your instructor could also try this exercise and share his or her open letter with you.

4. Check out teacher-related Web sites on the Internet. Schools and school districts, professional teacher organizations, and all sorts of interest groups sponsor not only Web sites but also listservs, chat groups, and other Internet activities. Seek out opportunities to interview practicing classroom teachers about their own classroom experiences. (Check out our Web site at www.mhhe.com/sadker8e for related Web links.)

5. Imagine that you are taking part in a career fair. Someone asks why you are exploring teaching. Briefly frame your answer.

WEB-*TIVITIES*
Go to the Online Learning Center to do the following activities:
1. The Advantages and Disadvantages of Being a Teacher
2. A Closer Look at Teach for America
3. Why Become a Teacher?

REEL TO REAL TEACHING

Movies with an education theme are a valuable and, yes, fun tool for learning about teachers, schools, and society. The Reel to Real Teaching feature gives you an opportunity to apply your understanding of key concepts explored in each chapter while appreciating the art and power of film. The Reflection provides connections between the chapter, the film, and you, while the Follow-up Activity can build on your understanding of the film. You may also want to visit the Web site's Critics Corner and share your thoughts with your future colleagues.

STAND AND DELIVER (1988)
Run Time: 105 Minutes

Synopsis: Convinced that his students have potential, mathematics teacher Jaime Escalante employs unconventional teaching methods to motivate a class of low-achieving, inner-city Hispanic students. Escalante teaches his students how to stretch beyond their limited horizons, and how to stand up when the world tries to crush their hopes.

Reflection:

1. Have your teachers ever shared with you their reasons for teaching? Did some teachers tell you through words and others through actions? What were they?

2. Most careers offer both satisfaction and sacrifice. Consider the professional and personal sacrifices made by Escalante. Would you be willing to make the same? Why or why not?

You may wish to revisit the *You Be the Judge* feature in the chapter when contemplating the joys and sacrifices of teaching.

3. Consider how viewing *Stand and Deliver* might influence your answer to the question, "Why teach?"

Follow-up Activity: It's movie night for your campus student education association (e.g., Kappa Delta Pi, Phi Delta Kappa, Student NEA). *Stand and Deliver* is the feature flick and your task is to create a media announcement for the event. Develop a flyer, a newspaper announcement, radio advertisement, a blurb for a Web site, or create your own idea that really inspires your membership to attend this film.

www.mhhe.com/ sadker8e

How do you rate this film? Go to *Reel to Real Teaching* to review this film.

FOR FURTHER READING

Primary Teacher's Stress, by Geoff Troman and Peter Woods (2001). This book looks at the causes of teacher stress, asks why thousands of teachers are leaving the profession every year due to stress, and suggests ways of coping with and preventing stress.

Stories of the Courage to Teach: Honoring the Teacher's Heart, by Sam Intrator (2002). This collection of essays, written by teachers at every level of practice, honors the hearts of all teachers who struggle to connect with the source of their vocation. Their warm, practical, funny, and wise stories will provide inspiration, companionship, and hope to teachers who strive to discover the courage to teach.

Touching Eternity: The Enduring Outcomes of Teaching, by Tom Barone (2001). This case study of a high school art teacher and his former students explores the long-term impact teachers make on the lives of students.

What Keeps Teachers Going? by Sonia Nieto (2003). What helps great public school teachers persevere? To find out, Sonia Nieto, a renowned teacher educator, collaborates with experienced urban school teachers who effectively and enthusiastically work with students of culturally and linguistically diverse backgrounds—students who are among the most marginalized in our public schools.

What the Kids Said Today: Using Classroom Conversations to Become a Better Teacher, by Daniel Gartrell (2000). Each story includes an account of a teacher's conversation with children, as well as reflections on how each conversation can help build a stimulating and nurturing classroom.

Different Ways of Learning

FOCUS QUESTIONS

1. How do cognitive, affective, and physiological factors impact learning?
2. How can teachers respond to different learning styles?
3. Is gender a learning style?
4. What are the classroom implications of Howard Gardner's theory of multiple intelligences?
5. How does emotional intelligence influence teaching and learning?
6. How are the needs of special learners met in today's classrooms?

www.mhhe.com/
sadker8e

WHAT DO YOU THINK? Different ways of learning. Vote on the eight-point proposal presented on page 34 and see what the *Teachers, Schools, and Society* results are.

CHAPTER PREVIEW

At the dawn of the twenty-first century, basic educational concepts are being re-defined, re-examined, and expanded. What does "intelligence" really mean? How many kinds of intelligences are there? What is EQ (emotional intelligence quotient), and is it a better predictor of success than IQ (intelligence quotient)? How should classrooms best be organized to meet the needs of different learning styles?

Gender issues are an issue in schools as some argue that girls' and boys' learning differences create the need for separate schools. Are single-sex schools a good idea? Do girls and boys learn differently? In exploring these questions, we introduce you to the distinctions between stereotypes and generalizations. In the next chapter, you will find generalizations useful as you consider how to teach students with different backgrounds. We want you to begin thinking about how teachers can recognize group differences while avoiding the dangers of stereotypic thinking, and the current gender debate is a good place to begin.

Another educational transformation is the increasing numbers of school children now identified as exceptional learners—students with learning disabilities, physical disabilities, mental retardation, and emotional disturbances—all of whom deserve appropriate educational strategies and materials. Students with gifts and talents represent another population with special needs too often lost in the current educational system.

This chapter will broaden your ideas of how students learn, and, based on this, how teachers should teach.

CHAPTER 2

Learning Styles

Imagine you are on a committee of teachers that has been asked to offer recommendations to the school board regarding academic climates to increase the academic performance of the district's students. It is an awesome responsibility. Here is the first draft of an eight-point proposal. Take a moment and indicate your reaction to each of the points.[1]

	Strongly Agree	Agree	Disagree
1. Schools and classrooms should be quiet places to promote thinking and learning.	_____	_____	_____
2. All classrooms and libraries should be well lighted to reduce eye strain.	_____	_____	_____
3. Difficult subjects, such as math, should be offered in the morning, when students are fresh and alert.	_____	_____	_____
4. School thermostats should be set at 68 to 72 degrees Fahrenheit to establish a comfortable learning environment.	_____	_____	_____
5. Eating and drinking in classrooms should be prohibited.	_____	_____	_____
6. Classroom periods should run between forty-five and fifty-five minutes to ensure adequate time to investigate significant issues and practice important skills.	_____	_____	_____
7. Students must be provided with adequate work areas, including chairs and desks, where they can sit quietly for the major part of their learning and study.	_____	_____	_____
8. Emphasis should be placed on reading textbooks and listening to lectures, for this is how students learn best.	_____	_____	_____

You might find that these points seem to make a lot of sense. And, for many students, these eight recommendations may lead to higher academic achievement—for many, but not all. Ironically, for a significant number of students, these recommendations can lead to poorer performance, even academic failure. The reason is that students have different **learning styles**—diverse ways of learning, comprehending, and knowing.

Did you notice these different learning styles in your own elementary and secondary school experience? Perhaps you see them now in college or graduate school. Some students do their best work late at night, while others set an early alarm because they are most alert in the morning. Many students seek a quiet place in the library to prepare for finals; others learn best in a crowd of people with a radio blaring; still others study most effectively in a state of perpetual motion, constantly walking in circles to help their concentration. Some students seem unable to study without eating and drinking. Simultaneously imbibing

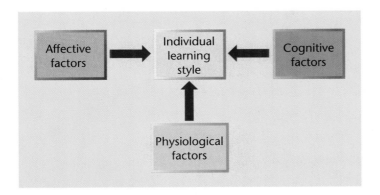

FIGURE 2.1
Factors contributing to
learning styles.

REFLECTION: Describe your own learning style by identifying at least one factor under the affective, physiological and cognitive domains.

calories and knowledge, they all but move into the refrigerator when preparing for tests. (These differences really strike home if you and your roommate clash because of conflicting learning styles.)

We are a population of incredibly diverse learners. Intriguing new research focusing on the ways students learn suggests that learning styles may be as unique as handwriting. The challenge for educators is to diagnose these styles and to shape instruction to meet individual student needs.

At least three types of factors—as diagrammed in Figure 2.1—contribute to each student's individual learning style:

1. *Cognitive (information processing).* Individuals have different ways of perceiving, organizing, and retaining information, all components of the **cognitive domain.** Some students prefer to learn by reading and looking at material, while others need to listen and hear information spoken aloud. Still others learn best kinesthetically, by whole body movement and participation. Some learners focus attention narrowly and with great intensity; others pay attention to many things at once. While some learners are quick to respond, others rely on a slower approach.

2. *Affective (attitudes).* Individuals bring different levels of motivation to learning, and the intensity level of this motivation is a critical determinant of learning style. Other aspects of the **affective domain** include attitudes, values and emotions, factors that influence curiosity, the ability to tolerate and overcome frustration, and the willingness to take risks. A fascinating aspect of the affective domain is a concept termed **locus of control.** Some learners attribute success or failure to external factors ("Those problems were confusing," "The teacher didn't review the material well," or "My score was high because I made some lucky guesses"). These learners have an external locus of control. Simply stated, they do not take responsibility for their behavior. Others attribute performance to internal factors ("I didn't study enough" or "I didn't read the directions carefully"). These students have an internal locus of control because they have the sense that they control their fate, that they can improve their performance.

Students exhibit a wide array of learning styles. Which one of these photos is closest to your style? How can schools best be organized to respond to different learning styles and even help students develop new styles?

37

3. *Physiology.* Clearly, a student who is hungry and tired will not learn as effectively as a well-nourished and rested child. Other physiological factors are less obvious. Different body rhythms cause some students to learn better in the day, while others are night owls. Some students can sit still for long periods of time, while others need to get up and move around. Light, sound, and temperature are yet other factors to which students respond differently based on their physiological development.[2]

With this introduction to learning styles, you now know that the committee's eight recommendations will not create a productive learning climate for all students. The following section paraphrases the original recommendations, explodes myths, and provides research concerning diverse learning styles.[3]

www.mhhe.com/
sadker8e

INTERACTIVE ACTIVITY
**Learning Styles
Assessment** Take a
learning styles
assessment to determine
your own learning style.

Myth	*Fact*
Students learn best in quiet surroundings.	Many students learn best when studying to music or other background noise. Others need so much silence that only ear plugs will suffice.
Students learn best in well-lighted areas.	Some students are actually disturbed by bright light and become hyperactive and less focused in their thinking. For them, dimmer light is more effective.
Difficult subjects are best taught in the morning, when students are most alert.	Peak learning times differ. Some students are at their best in the morning, while others function most effectively in the afternoon or evening.
Room temperature should be maintained at a comfortable 68 to 72 degrees Fahrenheit to promote learning.	Room temperature preferences vary greatly from individual to individual, and no single range pleases all. What chills one learner may provide the perfect climate for another.
Eating or drinking while learning should be prohibited.	Some students learn better and score higher on tests if they are allowed to eat or drink during these times. Banning such activities may penalize these individuals unfairly.
The most appropriate length of time for a class is forty-five to fifty-five minutes.	This period of time may be too long for some and too brief for others. The comfort time zone of the student rather than a predetermined block of hours or minutes is the factor critical to effective learning.
Students should be provided with appropriate work areas, including chairs and desks, where they spend most of their classroom time.	A substantial number of students need to move about to learn. For these learners, sitting at a desk or a computer terminal for long periods of time can actually hinder academic performance.

Many educators believe that students have preferred learning styles and that teaching to these preferred styles will increase educational success. Following are three learning styles frequently mentioned in the literature. (Do you recognize yourself in any of these categories?) Since all of these students are typically in class at the same time, as a teacher you will be called on to use a variety of instructional approaches to reach all of them.

VISUAL LEARNERS

About half of the student population learns best by *seeing* information. They are termed visual learners.

Teaching Tips

- Textbooks, charts, course outlines, and graphs are useful instructional aids.
- Ask these students to write down information, even rewriting or highlighting key points.
- Ask students to preview chapters by looking at subheadings and illustrations before they read each chapter.
- Seat these students up front, away from windows and doors (to avoid distractions).
- Encourage them to ask for comments or directions to be repeated if they did not understand directions the first time.
- Use overheads and flip charts.

KINESTHETIC LEARNERS

This is another popular learning style, which is also called *haptic* (Greek for "moving and doing") or *tactile*. These are "hands on" learners, students who learn best by doing.

Teaching Tips

- Try to plan for student movement in class presentation, as well as independent study time.
- Movement should be planned to avoid distracting others.

- Memorizing information can be enhanced if these learners are encouraged to physically move about the room.
- Providing students with a colored desk blotter or a colored transparency to read a book is called "color grounding" and can help focus their attention.
- Ask them to take notes and encourage them to underline key points as they read.
- Encourage them to take frequent but short breaks.
- Try to use skits and role-plays to help make instructional points.

AUDITORY LEARNERS

This is a style used less frequently than the previous two. These students learn best by hearing; they can remember the details of conversations and lectures, and many have strong language skills.

Teaching Tips

- Provide the opportunity for auditory learners to recite the main points of a book or lecture.
- Encourage these students to study with a friend, so they can talk through the main points.
- Audiotapes of classroom activities can be helpful.
- Suggest that they read class notes into a tape.
- Encourage them to read the textbook out loud.
- It can be helpful for these students to say out loud the meaning of the illustrations and main subject headings, and to recite any new vocabulary words.
- Group work can be a useful class activity for auditory learners.

REFLECTION: Choose a subject or topic that you want to teach. Describe three learning activities (visual, kinesthetic, auditory) that you can use to reach students with different learning styles. Which of these learning styles appeals to you? Why?

Reading a textbook or listening to a lecture way to learn.

Diverse students learn through a variety of modes, not only through reading or listening. While many students rely on these two perceptual modes, they are less effective for others. Some learn best through touch (for example, learning to read by tracing sandpaper letters), while others rely on kinesthetic movement, including creative drama, role-play, and field-based experiences.

Is Gender a Learning Style?

If your flying saucer arrived on earth from another world, landed in a schoolyard, and you peeked through the schoolhouse windows (using your invisible shield, of course), you might observe the following:

- In a kindergarten class, students practice math skills by taking attendance: A girl counts the number of girls present each day and places that number of female paper dolls on a wall chart. A boy does the same with paper boy dolls.
- In another class, the teacher decides to put a girl between two boys in order to "calm them down."
- Throughout the school, you sense the excitement as the students talk about the championship spelling bee, the one that will decide if the girls or the boys are the better spellers.
- Outside, the boys have three basketball games in progress, while the girls are off to the side talking.
- Over the public address system, the leader of the school (called the principal) announces: "Good morning boys and girls."

It is all so obvious. You radio back to your home base: "Planet earth dominated by two tribes: boys and girls. Will investigate further."

Teachers' comments and behaviors often blindly reinforce this gender divide, yet if applied to race, religion, or ethnicity, teachers would quickly regain their vision. You will search long and hard to find a teacher who announces: "We will have a spelling bee today to see who will be the champion spellers, Jews or Christians!" Or imagine, "Good morning blacks and whites." How about, "You two Hispanics are causing too much disruption, so I am placing a Native American between you!" Although sensitive to religious, ethnic, or racial affronts, we seem rather oblivious to gender comments. This is a situation with serious consequences.

Constant references to gender lead children to believe that teachers are *intentionally* signaling important differences between boys and girls. What are these

What are the assumptions inherent in boy-versus-girl competitions? Why are gender competitions still used, while school competitions based on race, religion, or ethnicity are seen as destructive?

differences? Most people see males as physically stronger, and often more aggressive; better in math, science, and technology; and more frequently involved in discipline problems than girls. Some consider the competitive and action orientation of males to be a learning style. Girls, on the other hand, are seen as nurturing and intuitive; preferring to personalize knowledge; more successful in the arts and languages; and more compliant than boys. This cooperative and personal approach to learning has been termed a female learning style. Some contend that genetics determine how males and females learn best, while others believe that these behaviors simply reflect socialization: girls are praised for cooperation and compliance, while boys are rewarded for activity and competition. Do you see these as genetic learning styles, as socialization, or as somewhere between the two? If you are not certain, then you are in good company, for this question is still debated. But finding an answer may be less crucial than effectively using the information that some boys and some girls approach learning differently. How important are these gender differences? Some believe important enough to build schools around them. (See the *Frame of Reference:* Single-Sex Education: Reform or a Step Backward?)

Generalizations and Stereotypes about Gender Learning

While many girls prefer to personalize learning and enjoy cooperative learning, and some boys seem to thrive in active, competitive learning environments, many educators believe that building schools with instruction based on such premises reflects stereotypic thinking. **Stereotypes** are absolute statements applied to all members of a group, suggesting that members of a group have a fixed, often inherited set of characteristics. Stereotypes ignore individual differences. Many believe that building schools based on perceived gender differences is stereotypic thinking, and may actually exaggerate gender differences and reinforce stereotypes.

The idea that many females prefer to learn one way, and many males another, does suggest a potentially useful generalization. **Generalizations** offer information,

Single-sex education is gaining popularity, but the research on the effectiveness of this approach is far from clear.

Single-Sex Education: Reform or a Step Backward?

Between 1991 and 2005, there was a 23 percent increase in all-girls' private schools, an increase in single-sex public high schools from 5 schools to 30, a more modest increase in all-boys' schools, and a new creation: single-sex classrooms within coed schools.[1]

Why this resurgence? A major cause is disappointment in coeducational public schools. Boys continue to struggle and girls continue to be stereotyped into sexist behaviors and careers.[2] Some believe that removing the other sex from the classroom will help reduce the "hormonal interference"—the male-female relationship dynamics that keep students from focusing on academics. Others advance a genetic argument: boys' brains and girls' brains are "hard-wired" differently, genetic differences that require separate schools.[3] Still others are impressed by the reputations of prestigious single-sex private schools and believe all students, not just the wealthy, should have the right to choose high-quality single-sex schools.[4] At first glance there seems to be no shortage of reasons for separating the sexes. But these appealing arguments become less convincing under a more careful examination.

1. *The Failures of Coeducational Schools.* Critics argue that creating single-sex schools only avoids the problem, and that resources used to create single-sex schools would be better spent eliminating sexism in coed schools.

2. *Brain Differences and Biology.* Research on the psychology of gender differences has long argued that males and females are ultimately more alike than different, and the small sex differences that do exist are malleable and increased or decreased by socialization and education.[5]

3. *Distraction-Free Learning.* While the raging hormone argument for choosing single-sex schooling is quite popular, it completely discounts the fact that students are quite capable of distracting each other in many creative ways.[6]

Critics point out that successful single-sex schools may succeed because they are simply excellent schools that just happen to be single-sex. Rather than gender learning styles or lack of hormonal distractions, these students do well because they learn in small classes with dedicated teachers, and have a desire to attend the best college possible. One major national study evaluated private single-sex secondary schools only to find "no consistent pattern of effects for attending either single-sex or coeducational independent schools for either girls or boys."[7]

The lack of supporting research has not inhibited public schools from trying this approach. In the late 1990s, California created several all-boys' and all-girls' high schools under the premise that boys and girls learn differently and should be taught differently. The schools were not successful and within a few years all but one were gone. Why did they fail? Educators point to few resources, little teacher training, increased gender stereotyping, and lack of a clear purpose. The all-boys' schools actually experienced an increase in discipline problems. Simply creating schools based on assumptions about gender learning styles of girls and boys may not be the best plan.

NOTES:
[1] Rosemary C. Salomone, *Same, Different, Equal* (New Haven: Yale University Press, 2003); Mary Leach, "Shelby Considers Same-Sex Classes," *The Birmingham News*, November 21, 2005, retrieved on November 24, 2005, www.al.com/news/birminghamnews/.
[2] *Title IX at Thirty* (Washington, DC: National Coalition of Women and Girls in Education, 2002); Myra Sadker and David Sadker, *Failing at Fairness: How Our Schools Cheat Girls* (New York: Touchstone, 1995).
[3] Michael Gurian and Kathy Stevens, *The Minds of Boys: Saving Our Sons from Falling behind in School and Life* (San Francisco: Jossey Bass, 2005); Leonard Sax, *Why Gender Matters: What Parents and Teachers Need to Know about the Emerging Science of Sex Differences* (New York: Doubleday, 2005).
[4] National Coalition of Girls Schools (October 2005), *Report on Single-Sex Education Finds High Satisfaction Levels: 90% of Alumnae Would Choose Girls' School Again,* retrieved on November 25, 2005, www.ncgs.org/pressview.php?aid=52.
[5] Sadker and Sadker, *Failing at Fairness.*
[6] Amanda Datnow and Lea Hubbard (eds.), *Gender in Policy and Practice: Perspectives on Single-Sex and Coeducational Schooling* (New York, RoutledgeFalmer, 2002).
[7] Kathryn Herr and Emily Arms, "The Intersection of Educational Reforms: Single-Gender Academies in a Public Middle School," in Amanda Datnow & Lea Hubbard (Eds.) *Gender in Policy and Practice: Perspectives on Single-Sex and Coeducational Schooling* (New York: RoutledgeFalmer, 2002).

REFLECTION: How do you view the pros and cons of single-sex schooling? If you attended a single-sex school, do you believe that your education would have been superior, the same, or less effective than at a coeducation school?

clues about groups that can help you as a teacher plan more effectively. Based on what you know about different learning styles, you should plan to include both competitive and cooperative activities, both personal connections and active learning in your teaching to appeal to all students. By including this variety, you are enabling each student to engage not only in a learning style he or she may find comfortable, but also to grow through experiencing new styles.

Unlike stereotypes, generalizations recognize exceptions. Not all boys or all girls prefer to learn in the "predictable" way. Some girls love competition, and some boys love cooperative activities. Some fear that when schools are built on the notion of gender different learning styles, the boys who prefer personalized learning in a cooperative setting will lose out, as will girls who prefer to work alone or in a competitive mode.

Some single-sex schooling advocates make other assumptions. One is that both girls and boys are distracted by the presence of the other sex. But this assumes that everyone is heterosexual, and that gender identities match physical sex. "Hormonal distractions," for example, are not decreased for gay or lesbian students in single-sex classes, and not every student's sexual makeup (biology) corresponds to their gender role (how they feel and see themselves). Viewing the world as heterosexual, rendering lesbian, gay, bisexual and transgender students invisible, is called **heteronormativity.**

Gay, Lesbian, Bisexual, and Transgender Students (GLBT)

Being gay, lesbian, bisexual, or straight refers to a person's sexual orientation, an innate characteristic that determines who one is attracted to sexually and romantically. Being transgender refers to a person's gender identity—a person's innate sense of being male, female, or somewhere in-between. Many school practices assume that all people are heterosexual and either male or female. A typical curriculum reflects this assumption in subtle and not so subtle ways. Literature like *Romeo and Juliet*, math word problems like "David bought Julie one dozen roses . . .", or electing a homecoming king and queen are obvious examples of assumed heterosexuality for all. However, some schools are altering these practices: inviting same sex couples to the prom, providing gender-neutral or individual bathrooms and locker rooms for transgender students, and including GLBT people and perspectives in the curriculum.[4]

These different responses to GLBT students reflect our national division. A number of states have laws preventing teachers from even mentioning the word "homosexual," or mandating that homosexuality be presented in exclusively negative terms in the classroom.[5] Other school districts recognize GLBT people in their nondiscrimination policies, sending a clear message that no student, parent, or school employee will be discriminated against because of their sexual orientation or gender identity. There are more than 3,000 Gay-Straight Alliances (GSAs), student clubs that provide a safe space for GLBT students and their allies.[6] GSAs sometimes engender controversy, but the 1984 Federal Equal Access Act states that if schools allow any noncurricular clubs then they have to allow them all.

Depending on where you teach, you may or may not be able to include GLBT in your teaching. But wherever you teach, you can ensure democratic norms of

This sign can be found outside classrooms and school offices to announce a safe zone for GLBT students.

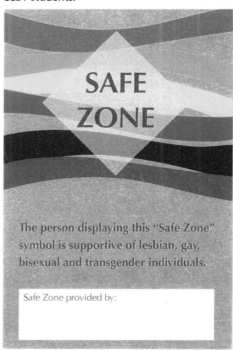

The person displaying this "Safe Zone" symbol is supportive of lesbian, gay, bisexual and transgender individuals.

Safe Zone provided by:

equality are followed, and that all students are respected regardless of individual differences. Students do not have to agree "It's okay to be gay," but they should understand that "It's not okay to discriminate against those who they are gay." By providing a safe place for all students to learn, teachers can create nurturing classrooms where every child can learn and every family is welcome.

What Does the Gender Debate Teach Us?

The ongoing debate about gender learning styles offers valuable lessons. One is that simplistic stereotypes about girls and boys short-circuit our thinking, but generalizations about how different groups may approach learning can help teachers plan different lessons to meet different needs. One does not have to accept the notion of gender as a learning style to appreciate that individuals arrive at school with different ways of learning and different ways of viewing the world. The successful teacher honors these differences with a variety of teaching strategies. There is no one-size-fits-all teaching style, and as we are about to learn, there is not one-size-fits-all intelligence either.

Multiple Intelligences

INTERACTIVE ACTIVITY

Multiple Intelligences
Label descriptions of different intelligences.

Intelligence Quotient, called IQ, was developed early in the twentieth century, to measure a person's innate intelligence, with a score of 100 defined as normal, or average. The higher the score, the brighter the person. Some of us grew up in communities where IQ was barely mentioned. In many cases this lack of knowledge might have been a blessing. Others of us grew up with "IQ envy," in communities where IQ scores were a big part of our culture. Since the score is considered a fixed, permanent measure of intellect, like a person's physical height, the scores engendered strong feelings. Friends who scored 150 or 160 or higher on an IQ test had a secret weapon, a mysteriously wonderful brain. We were impressed. But then our friend, the "genius," was stumped trying to unpack and plug in a toaster oven or got hopelessly lost trying to follow the simplest driving directions. How could this person have such a high IQ? We may have been equally puzzled when another friend, who scored horribly low on an IQ test, went on to fame and riches (and promptly forgot that we were ever their friends). What is this IQ score supposed to mean?

Puzzled by these contradictions raised by IQ scores was Harvard professor **Howard Gardner.** Concerned about the traditional assessment of intelligence, with such a heavy emphasis on language and mathematical-logical skills, he broadened the concept to define *intelligence* as "the capacity to solve problems or to fashion products that are valued in one or more cultural settings."[7]

Gardner identified eight kinds of intelligence, not all of which are commonly recognized in school settings, yet Gardner believes that his theory of **multiple**

intelligences more accurately captures the diverse nature of human capability. Consider Gardner's eight intelligences:

The ability to perform intricate and extended physical maneuvers is a distinct form of intelligence.

1. *Logical-mathematical.* Skills related to mathematical manipulations and discerning and solving logical problems (*related careers:* scientist, mathematician)

2. *Linguistic.* Sensitivity to the meanings, sounds, and rhythms of words, as well as to the function of language as a whole (*related careers:* poet, journalist, author)

3. *Bodily-kinesthetic.* Ability to excel physically and to handle objects skillfully (*related careers:* athlete, dancer, surgeon)

4. *Musical.* Ability to produce pitch and rhythm, as well as to appreciate various forms of musical expression (*related careers:* musician, composer)

5. *Spatial.* Ability to form a mental model of the spatial world and to maneuver and operate using that model (*related careers:* sculptor, navigator, engineer, painter)

6. *Interpersonal.* Ability to analyze and respond to the motivations, moods, and desires of other people (*related careers:* psychology, sales, teaching)

7. *Intrapersonal.* Knowledge of one's feelings, needs, strengths, and weaknesses; ability to use this knowledge to guide behavior (*related benefit:* accurate self-awareness)

8. *Naturalist.* (Gardner's most recently defined intelligence) Ability to discriminate among living things, to classify plants, animals, and minerals; a sensitivity to the natural world (*related careers:* botanist, environmentalist, chef, other science- and even consumer-related careers.)[8]

Gardner and his colleagues continue to conduct research, and this list is still growing. A possible ninth intelligence being explored by Gardner concerns an *existential intelligence,* the human inclination to formulate fundamental questions about who we are, where we come from, why we die, and the like. Gardner believes that we have yet to discover many more intelligences. (Can you can think of some?)

The theory of multiple intelligences goes a long way in explaining why the quality of an individual's performance may vary greatly in different activities, rather than reflect a single standard of performance as indicated by an IQ score. Gardner also points out that what is considered *intelligence* may differ, depending on cultural values. Thus, in the Pacific Islands, intelligence is the ability to navigate among the islands. For many Muslims, the ability to memorize the Koran is a mark of intelligence. Intelligence in Balinese social life is demonstrated by physical grace.

Gardner's theory has sparked the imaginations of many educators, some of whom are redesigning their curricula to respond to differing student intelligences. Teachers are refining their approaches in response to such questions as[9]

- How can I use music to emphasize key points?
- How can I promote hand and bodily movements and experiences to enhance learning?

- How can I incorporate sharing and interpersonal interactions into my lessons?
- How can I encourage students to think more deeply about their feelings and memories?
- How can I use visual organizers and visual aids to promote understanding?
- How can I encourage students to classify and appreciate the world around them?

Instructional Technology

Instructional technologies can open a wide door to the multiple intelligences. For instance, authoring tools such as PowerPoint enable students to create projects that incorporate text, animation, graphics, video, and sound, integrating several intelligences. The computer allows students to compose music, or model art and science projects that enhance spatial learning. A physical education or dance teacher can videotape and then coach students on their techniques. Gardner suggests improving interpersonal intelligence by "recording tense interactions on video and having students choose the best human(e) means of reducing the tension; by involving students in chat rooms or discussion forums that include opportunities for helpfulness or deceit; or by creating cartoon simulations or virtual reality scenarios of human dilemmas where the student has options to interact in different ways."[10] While Howard Gardner is impressed with the potential marriage of technology with his multiple intelligences approach, he has also voiced concern about teachers who get enamored with the technological wizardry, and lose sight of the educational goal.

Assessment

As instruction undergoes re-examination, so does evaluation. The old pencil-and-paper tests used to assess linguistic, math, and logical intelligences seem much less appropriate for measuring these new areas identified by Gardner.[11] The **portfolio** approach, as found in the *RAP*s in this text, is an example of a more comprehensive assessment, which includes student artifacts (papers, projects, videotapes, exhibits) that offers tangible examples of student learning. Some schools ask students to assemble portfolios that reflect progress in Gardner's various intelligences. In other cases, rather than As and Bs or 80s and 90s, schools are using descriptions to report student competence. In music, for example, such descriptions might include "The student often listens to music," "She plays the piano with technical competence," "She is able to compose scores that other students and faculty enjoy," and so on. Whether the school is exploring portfolios, descriptive assessment, or another evaluation method, Gardner's multiple intelligences theory is reshaping many current assessment practices.[12]

 ## Emotional Intelligence

While the theory of multiple intelligences raises fundamental questions about instruction and assessment, EQ may be even more revolutionary. **EQ,** or the **emotional intelligence quotient,** is described by **Daniel Goleman** in his book *Emotional Intelligence.* Goleman argues that when it comes to predicting success in

Giants, Wizards, and Dwarfs was the game to play.

Being left in charge of about eighty children seven to ten years old, while their parents were off doing parent things, I mustered my troops in the church social hall and explained the game. It's a large-scale version of Rock, Paper, and Scissors, and involves some intellectual decision making. But the real purpose of the game is to make a lot of noise and run around chasing people until nobody knows which side you are on or who won.

Organizing a roomful of wired-up grade schoolers into two teams, explaining the rudiments of the game, achieving consensus on group identity—all of this is no mean accomplishment, but we did it with a right good will and were ready to go.

The excitement of the chase had reached a critical mass. I yelled out: "You have to decide *now* which you are—a GIANT, a WIZARD, or a DWARF!"

While the groups huddled in frenzied, whispered consultation, a tug came at my pants leg. A small child stands there looking up, and asks in a small concerned voice, "Where do the Mermaids stand?"

A long pause: A *very* long pause. "Where do the Mermaids stand?" says I.

"Yes. You see, I am a Mermaid."

"There are no such things as Mermaids."

"Oh, yes, I am one!"

She did not relate to being a Giant, a Wizard, or a Dwarf. She knew her category, Mermaid, and was not about to leave the game and go over and stand against the wall where a loser would stand. She intended to participate, wherever Mermaids fit into the scheme of things. Without giving up dignity or identity. She took it for granted that there was a place for Mermaids and that I would know just where.

Well, where DO the Mermaids stand? All the "Mermaids"—all those who are different, who do not fit the norm and who do not accept the available boxes and pigeonholes?

Answer that question and you can build a school, a nation, or a world on it.

What was my answer at the moment? Every once in a while I say the right thing. "The Mermaid stands right here by the King of the Sea!" (Yes, right here by the King's Fool, I thought to myself.)

So we stood there hand in hand, reviewing the troops of Wizards and Giants and Dwarfs as they rolled by in wild disarray.

It is not true, by the way, that Mermaids do not exist. I know at least one personally. I have held her hand.

SOURCE: Robert Fulghum, *All I Really Need to Know I Learned in Kindergarten* (New York: Villard Books, 1989), pp. 81–83.

REFLECTION: Was there ever a time when you did not fit neatly into a category—were you ever a mermaid? When and why? How will you make room for mermaids in your class?

life, EQ may be a better predictor than IQ. How does EQ work? The "marshmallow story" may help you understand:

A researcher explains to a 4-year-old that he/she needs to run off to do an errand, but there is a marshmallow for the youngster to enjoy. The youngster can choose to eat the marshmallow immediately. But, if the 4-year-old can wait and *not* eat the marshmallow right away, then an extra marshmallow will be given when the researcher returns. Eat one now, or hold off and get twice the reward.

What do you think you would have done as a 4-year-old? According to the social scientists who conducted the marshmallow experiment, decisions even at this age foreshadow an emotional disposition characteristic of a successful (or less successful) adult. By the time the children in the study reached high school, the now 14-year-olds were described by teachers and parents in a way that suggested their marshmallow behaviors predicted some significant differences. Students who

IMAGINE . . .

Class Act

The Stuttgart, Arkansas, Junior High School varsity football team all shaved their heads so they could look more like teammate Stuart H., who lost most of his hair while undergoing chemotherapy. The coach explained: *They got together so he wouldn't feel weird, so they would all look weird together.*

SOURCE: *The American School Board Journal*, December 1997.

Like Daniel Goleman, Yale psychologist Peter Salovey works with emotional intelligence issues, and he identifies five elements of emotional intelligence. How would you rate yourself on each of these dimensions?

KNOWING EMOTIONS

The foundation of one's emotional intelligence is self-awareness. A person's ability to recognize a feeling as it happens is the essential first step in understanding the place and power of emotions. People who do not know when they are angry, jealous, or in love are at the mercy of their emotions.

Self-Rating on Knowing My Emotions *Always aware of my emotions__Usually aware__Sometimes aware__Out of touch, clueless.__*

MANAGING EMOTIONS

A person who can control and manage emotions can handle bad times as well as the good, shake off depression, bounce back from life's setbacks, and avoid irritability. In one study, up to half of the youngsters who at age 6 were disruptive and unable to get along with others were classified as delinquents by the time they were teenagers.

Self-Rating on Managing My Emotions *Always manage my emotions__Usually manage__Sometimes manage__ My emotions manage me.__*

MOTIVATING ONESELF

Productive individuals are able to focus energy, confidence, and concentration on achieving a goal and avoid anxiety, anger, and depression. One study of 36,000 people found that "worriers" have poorer academic performance than nonworriers. (A load off your mind, no doubt!)

Self-Rating on Motivation and Focus *Always self-motivated/focused__Usually self-motivated/focused__ Sometimes self-motivated/focused__I can't focus on when I was last focused (and I don't care).__*

RECOGNIZING EMOTIONS IN OTHERS

This skill is the core of empathy, the ability to pick up subtle signs of what other people need or want. Such a person always seems to "get it," even before the words are spoken.

Self-Rating on Empathy *Always empathetic__Usually empathetic__Sometimes empathetic__I rarely "get it."__*

HANDLING RELATIONSHIPS

People whose EQ is high are the kind of people you want to be around. They are popular, are good leaders, and make you feel comfortable and connected. Children who lack social skills are often distracted from learning, and the dropout rate for children who are rejected by their peers can be two to eight times higher than for children who have friends.

Self-Rating on Relationships *I am rich in friendship and am often asked to lead activities and events.__I have many friends.__I have a few friends.__Actually, I'm pretty desperate for friends.__*

RATINGS

Give 4 points for each time you selected the first choice, 3 points for the "usual" or "many" second option, 2 points for the "sometimes" selection, and 1 point for the last choice.

18–20 points: A grade—WOW! Impressive!
14–17 points: B grade—You have considerable skills and talents.
10–13 points: C grade—Feel free to read further on this topic.
5–9 points: D grade—This may be a perfect subject to investigate in greater detail. Do you have a topic for your term project yet?

REFLECTION: Are you satisfied with your rating? If you earned a high rating, to what do you attribute your high EQ? If your rating was lower than you liked, how can you work on increasing your EQ?

ten years earlier were able to delay their gratification, to wait a while and garner a second marshmallow, were reported to be better adjusted, more popular, more adventurous, and more confident in adolescence than the group who ten years earlier had gobbled down their marshmallows. The children who gave in to temptation, ate the marshmallow, and abandoned their chances for a second one, were more likely to be described as stubborn, easily frustrated, and lonely teenagers. In addition to the differences between the gobblers and waiters as described by parents and teachers, there was also a significant SAT scoring gap. The students who, ten years earlier, could wait for the second marshmallow scored 210 points higher than did the gobblers. Reasoning and control, "the regulation of emotion in a way that enhances living,"[13] might be new, and perhaps better, measures of what we call smart, or intelligent.

Emotional intelligence "is a type of social intelligence that involves the ability to monitor one's own and others' emotions, to discriminate among them, and to use the information to guide one's thinking and actions."[14] Goleman suggests that EQ taps into the heart, as well as the head, and introduces a new gateway for measuring intelligence, for children and adults.[15] By the way, how would you rate your EQ?

Goleman and Gardner are toppling educational traditions, stretching our understanding of what schools are about. In a sense, they are increasing the range and diversity of educational ideas. The students you will teach will learn in diverse ways, and a single IQ or even EQ score is unlikely to capture the range of their abilities and skills. But these are not the only differences students bring to school. We will end this chapter with a close look at teaching exceptional learners, from students with disabilities to gifted learners. Inclusion of these students may further broaden different learning styles and the range of skills you will need.

www.mhhe.com/
sadker8e

INTERACTIVE ACTIVITY
Emotional Intelligence Quotient Quiz Take an EQ quiz to determine your own emotional intelligence quotient.

Exceptional Learners

In a typical classroom, a teacher faces students with a great range of abilities, from students reading years behind grade level to students reading years ahead. Both these groups of students are described by the same broad term: **exceptional learners.** Integrating exceptional learners into the regular classroom adds further challenge to the job of teaching diverse students.

Typically, exceptional learners are categorized as follows:

- Students with mental retardation
- Students with learning disabilities
- Students with emotional disturbance or behavior disorders
- Students with hearing and language impairments
- Students with visual impairments
- Students with attention deficit hyperactivity disorder
- Students with other health and physical impairments
- Students with severe and multiple disabilities
- Gifted and talented students[16]

Teaching exceptional learners, from students with disabilities to gifted and talented learners, offers teachers the opportunity to stretch their imagination and creativity. Let's begin with a group many people believed deserve little, if any, special attention. How wrong they are.

The Gifted and Talented

Misha is a 10-year-old eighth grader who reads up to six books a month, plays violin and piano, and asks so many questions that her teachers sometimes get angry at her. Driven by an insatiable curiosity, she wants to be a brain surgeon. Her parents expect her to have a bachelor's degree by the time she is 14 and a medical degree soon after. The pace will be wholly dependent upon her teachers' abilities to feed an intellect that often goes wanting. She is eager for challenge and excitement in the classroom, rather than disappointment and isolation. By next fall, Misha may have her chance. She has applied to the Davidson Academy of Nevada, a newly formed public school at the University of Nevada, Reno for profoundly gifted children, those whose test scores and evaluations place them in the 99th percentile. It is a rare opportunity.

In Westchester County, a suburb of New York City, a 2½-year-old boy already emulates the language abilities of his parents. He speaks and reads English, French, Hebrew, Spanish, and Yiddish, and he has mastered some Danish. He is studying music theory and is conducting scientific experiments. The parents, however, are unable to find any educational facility willing and able to educate their young, gifted child. A member of their local school board told them: "It is not the responsibility or function of public schools to deal with such children." As a result, the parents considered moving to Washington state, where there was an experimental preschool program for the gifted.[17]

If you are like most Americans, you may find it difficult to consider gifted and talented children to be in any way disadvantaged. After all, **gifted learners** are the lucky ones who master subject matter with ease. They are the ones who shout out the solution before most of us have a chance to write down the problem. Others may have perfect musical pitch, are athletic superstars, become the class leaders who inspire us, or demonstrate insights that amaze and inform us. Many exhibit endless curiosity, creativity, and energy. Small wonder that there is relatively little national support for extra funds or programs targeted at these gifted students, the ones who make the rest of us feel somewhat uncomfortable, inadequate, and sometimes just plain envious.

Defining *giftedness* invites controversy. To some, the traditional definition of *giftedness* includes those with an IQ of 130 or higher; to others, the label *giftedness* is reserved for those with an IQ score of 160 or higher. The National Association for Gifted Children defines five elements of giftedness: artistic and creative talents, intellectual and academic abilities, and leadership skills. (See Figure 2.2) Noted psychologist Robert Sternberg has suggested that a new area be included: wisdom. After years of researching what it means to be gifted, Sternberg now believes that giftedness is not just about how analytical and insightful you are, but how you use such skills. A clever business executive who uses his intelligence to earn a fortune, only to leave the company and stockholders in bankruptcy, may have been quite bright, but Sternberg argues that he should not be considered gifted. "The world is getting too dangerous. We have to train kids not just to be smart but to be wise."[18] Sternberg looks to Gandhi and Martin Luther King, Jr. as examples of wisdom too often ignored in current definitions.

While definitions of *giftedness* vary, only a small percentage of our population possesses this high degree of ability, creativity, motivation, pragmatic talent, or wisdom—making for a very exclusive club. Exclusivity can invite hostility. Since most people are, by definition, excluded from this highly select group, few believe that the gifted merit any special educational attention. To many Americans, it seems downright undemocratic to provide special services to children who already enjoy an advantage. While many parents of gifted children are strong advocates for their children, some parents of the gifted have shown reluctance to request additional educational resources.

Many gifted students do not succeed on their own. Highly talented young people suffer boredom and negative peer pressure when kept in regular classroom settings.[19] Instead of thriving in school, they drop out. The picture is especially

FIGURE 2.2
Characteristics of giftedness.

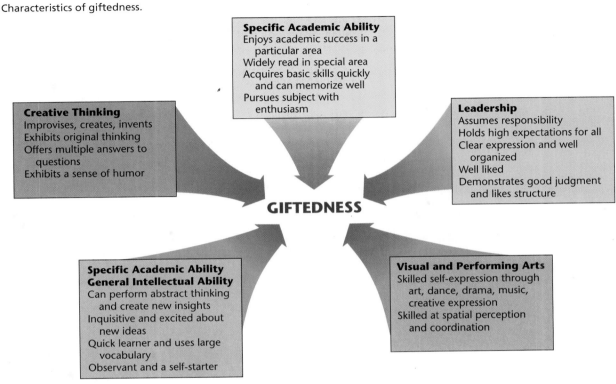

Specific Academic Ability
Enjoys academic success in a
   particular area
Widely read in special area
Acquires basic skills quickly
   and can memorize well
Pursues subject with
   enthusiasm

Creative Thinking
Improvises, creates, invents
Exhibits original thinking
Offers multiple answers to
   questions
Exhibits a sense of humor

Leadership
Assumes responsibility
Holds high expectations for all
Clear expression and well
   organized
Well liked
Demonstrates good judgment
   and likes structure

GIFTEDNESS

Specific Academic Ability
General Intellectual Ability
Can perform abstract thinking
   and create new insights
Inquisitive and excited about
   new ideas
Quick learner and uses large
   vocabulary
Observant and a self-starter

Visual and Performing Arts
Skilled self-expression through
   art, dance, drama, music,
   creative expression
Skilled at spatial perception
   and coordination

REFLECTION: Would you include Sternberg's concept of wisdom in this definition? How do these areas relate to Gardner's multiple intelligences?

dismal for females, children of color, and English language learners who are identified as gifted, and once identified, are more likely to drop out than gifted white males. The result is that many of our nation's brightest and most competent students are lost to neglect and apathy, and some of our most talented youth have not always succeeded at school.

Research shows that a significant number of gifted students contemplate suicide. Gifted students may be haunted by a sense of isolation and loneliness, pressure to achieve, and fear of failure.[20] Talent, giftedness, and creativity set adolescents apart at a time when the push is for conformity, for being "normal" and "like everybody else." Gifted students most often talk about their feelings of isolation:

> I feel as though I'll never fit in any place, no matter how hard I try. Basically, the challenge in my schooling has not been academic, but having to conform—to be just like everyone else in order to be accepted. I hate it when people use you. For example, if you have an incredible vocabulary and someone wants your help writing a speech, and then later they tell you to get lost.[21]

Even in school districts that recognize the special needs of gifted children, opposition to providing special programs and educational opportunities continues. Some object to special programs for the gifted because they see it as a form of tracking, an undemocratic strategy that separates the gifted from the rest of the population. In some cases, funds are lacking; in others, little interest and commitment to the gifted may be the problem. Struggling with shrinking revenues and federal mandates that focus on improving the test scores of the lowest-achieving pupils, many school districts across the country are cutting programs for their most promising students.[22] *No Child Left Behind* is silent on the education of gifted children. The law offers no rewards for raising the scores of high achievers, or punishment if their progress lags—potentially leaving gifted students behind.

How do teachers develop an instructional plan that will be challenging, enlightening, and intriguing to students of different abilities, and still maintain a sense of community within the classroom? This is the central question for educators as they begin the quest of bringing sound instruction to gifted students in regular classroom settings. The regular classroom can be a major instructional resource by providing **enrichment** activities such as independent projects, small-group inquiry and investigations, academic competitions, and learning centers that provide in-depth and challenging content beyond regular grade-level lessons.[23] A gifted student might also spend most of the day in a regular class and be pulled out for a part of the day, perhaps an hour or so, to receive special instruction. At the secondary level, comprehensive high schools have augmented their offerings with challenging courses of study, such as the International Baccalaureate (IB) program, an internationally recognized degree program that includes rigorous science, math, and foreign language requirements. Special high schools, such as the Bronx High School of Science and the North Carolina School for Mathematics and Science, have long and distinguished histories of providing educational opportunities for intellectually gifted students. Other special schools have focused on programs in acting, music, and dance. Yet many believe that we need to do a better job of "gifted inclusion," by designing regular class activities that are more responsive to the needs of the gifted.[24]

Some school districts go beyond their own resources in order to meet the needs of gifted students. For instance, one such program connects gifted high school students with the local college or community college. These students spend part of their day enrolled in college-level courses, being intellectually challenged and receiving college credit while still enrolled in high school. Still other gifted students receive additional instruction through summer camps or even special year-long programs that augment their regular courses. Johns Hopkins University, for example, has been sponsoring the Center for Talented Youth (CTY) in different parts of the nation for several decades.

Many of these college programs are termed **accelerated programs,** for they allow gifted students to skip grades or receive college credit early. **Advanced placement** courses and exams (the APs), provide similar acceleration opportunities, permitting students to graduate before their chronological peers. While many Americans accept the notion of enrichment for the gifted, acceleration runs into stronger opposition. The common belief that the negative social consequences of acceleration outweigh the intellectual benefits represents an obstacle to implementing such programs for the gifted.

Whereas social maladjustment due to acceleration may indeed be a problem for some gifted children, others claim they feel just as comfortable, both academically and socially, with their intellectual peers as they do with their chronological peers. Yet, not accelerating gifted children may lead to boredom, apathy, frustration, and even ridicule. Several studies confirm the value of acceleration, from early admission to elementary school to early admission to college. Grade-accelerated students surpass their classmates in academic achievement and complete higher levels of education. While research suggests that grade acceleration does not cause problems in social and emotional adjustment, cases of students who found acceleration to be a disaster are also plentiful.[25] No single program is likely to meet the needs of all gifted students.

The qualities of effective gifted programs include a mastery dimension that allows students to move through the curriculum at their own pace; in-depth and independent learning; field study; and an interdisciplinary dimension that allows for the exploration of theories and issues across the curriculum. Moreover, an important but often overlooked advantage of these programs is the sense of community they offer, the opportunity for gifted students to connect with others like themselves. This is an important step in reducing student anxiety and alienation. When gifted students are placed in appropriate programs, they are often empowered to realize their full potential. One student was relieved to find that "there are lots of people like me and I'm not a weirdo after all." As one 12-year-old girl said,

> My heart is full of gratitude for my teacher who first wanted to have me tested for the gifted program. I'm not trying to brag, but I'm really glad there's a class for people like me. We may seem peculiar or odd, but at least we have fun and we respect each other's talents.[26]

In the final analysis, it is not only the gifted who have suffered from our national neglect and apathy; it is all of us. How many works of art will never be enjoyed? How many medical breakthroughs and how many inventions have been lost because of our insensitivity to the gifted?

Special Education

Perhaps you have read the book *Karen*. It is the story of a child with cerebral palsy, a child who persevered despite devastating obstacles. A formidable obstacle was an educational system that had no room for children with disabilities. The book was written by Karen's mother, who, like her daughter, refused the rejection of a hostile school and society. She wrote of her attempts to gain educational rights for her daughter and other children with disabilities:

> We constantly sought a remedy for this appalling situation which deprived so many of an education, and eventually we found a few doctors and educators who had made strides in developing valid testing methods for handicapped children. On one occasion, when I voiced a plea for the education of the handicapped, a leading state official retorted, "It would be a waste of the state's money. They'll never get jobs."
> We were frequently discouraged and not a little frightened as many of our "learned" men [sic] felt the same way.[27]

Such disparaging attitudes were common in our society for years and resulted in inadequate educational programs for millions of exceptional children. Today, the educational rights of these children have been mandated by courts of law and are being put into practice in classrooms across the nation.

Before the Revolutionary War, the most that was offered to exceptional children was protective care in asylums. The asylums made little effort to help these children develop their physical, intellectual, and social skills. Following the American Revolution, however, the ideals of democracy and the development of human potential swept the nation. Within this humanist social context, procedures were

A FEW OF THE PEOPLE IDENTIFIED WITH PHYSICAL, LEARNING, AND SPEECH DISABILITIES:

Moses, Aesop, Cotton Mather, Benjamin Franklin, Clara Barton, Harriet Tubman, Charles Darwin, Jane Addams, Franklin Delano Roosevelt, Congresswoman Carolyn McCarthy, Cher, Charles Schwab, Arctic explorer Anne Bancroft, and James Earl Jones.

THE FOLLOWING INDIVIDUALS WERE ASKED TO LEAVE SCHOOL, DROPPED OUT, OR FOUND ALTERNATIVES TO THE ADOLESCENT SCHOOL SCENE:

Salvador Dali, Whoopi Goldberg, Beryl Markham, Edgar Allan Poe, George Bernard Shaw, Percy Bysshe Shelley, James Whistler, and Frank Lloyd Wright.

REFLECTION: Do you know accomplished individuals who did not do well in school? How could education respond to the unique needs of these individuals? (You may want to research the learning issues of these well-known people.)

devised for teaching the blind and the deaf. Then, in the early 1800s, attempts were made to educate the "idiotic" and the "insane" children who today would be called "mentally retarded" or "emotionally disturbed."

For many years, the legal system mirrored society's judgment that the best policy toward those with disabilities was "out of sight, out of mind." The courts typically saw education as a privilege rather than a right, and they ruled that children with disabilities should be excluded from schools. The notion was that the majority of children needed to be protected from those with disabilities: from the disruptions they might precipitate, from the excessive demands they might make, and from the discomfort their presence in classrooms might cause.

The years following World War II brought renewed hope and promise. Such pioneers as Grace Fernald, Marianne Frostig, and Heinz Werner—to name but a few—conducted research, developed programs, and gave new impetus to the field of **special education.** Their work was aided by the emergence of new disciplines, such as psychology, sociology, and social work. Parents also continued their struggle, individually and collectively, to obtain educational opportunities for children with disabilities. They took their cause to both the schools and the courts. Special education has broken away from the isolation and institutionalization so common in the late nineteenth century and has moved to mainstream exceptional children, as much as possible, into typical school settings.

By the 1970s, court decisions and federal law had established five critical principles of special education:

1. **Zero reject.** The principle of zero reject asserts that no child with disabilities may be denied a free, appropriate public education. Representatives of the disabled have asserted that excluding children with disabilities from public schools violates the constitutional interpretation behind the Supreme Court's *Brown* v. *Board of Education* (1954) decision, which put an end to claims of "separate but equal" schooling. The courts have responded with landmark decisions in Pennsylvania (*Pennsylvania Association for Retarded Children* v. *Commonwealth*) and in Washington, DC (*Mill* v. *D.C. Board of Education*) that mandate public schools in those jurisdictions to provide a free, appropriate education to all children with disabilities. Other federal and state decisions have followed suit.

PROFILE IN EDUCATION Sally L. Smith

Would you rather go to school, or join a Secret Agents Club? Want to do both? Look no further than The Lab School of Washington and its colorful leader Sally L. Smith, who started this "school modeled after a party" more than 40 years ago. The school offers innovative programs for children and adults with learning disabilities, emphasizing experiential learning and the arts. Explains Smith, "I am in the business of saving lives." She started with her youngest son.

Gary Smith was born with severe learning disabilities. By the first grade, he struggled with the alphabet and math, yet easily solved puzzles and expounded on the similarities between Greek myths and Navajo rain dances. School officials quickly decided that Gary could not be taught. So Smith drew upon her background in psychology and cultural anthropology to create new approaches to teaching her son and tapping into his talents. Children's birthday parties provided initial clues.

> When I had birthday parties for the kids, I always picked a theme, whether it was Indians or secret agents or the Civil War. We made costumes, castles and tents, festive feasts; all were concrete activities with focused involvement. Suddenly it dawned on me that this kid couldn't tell you two plus two is four but through everything we did at birthday parties, he was learning. So I thought, what am I doing in these parties that is working?[1]

Her answer: "Total immersion of the senses." Smith discovered that children with learning disabilities are often visual thinkers and hands-on learners. The central nervous system of children with learning disabilities often scrambles information and impairs the orderly acquisition of knowledge. Smith calls it the "hidden handicap." While students with learning disabilities struggle in learning environments focused on language and conformity, they can thrive in settings that use the arts as a gateway to learning.

In the summer of 1967, Smith received a telegram from a long-time friend and educator suggesting she start a school. She had 25 days to find volunteers, create a curriculum, and hire teachers. Recalls Smith, "I had the audacity, and perhaps naïveté, to design and direct a school for my son and others like him, when there was no such thing available." The seeds of the Lab School were sown. And after 40 years, Smith remains a tireless champion of arts-based learning.

> The arts demand involvement. They counteract passivity. The arts ignite the whole learning process. The arts help organize knowledge. Our experience is that the arts hold children's attention and deal constantly with sequence and order—areas that cause the learning disabled so much trouble. The arts provide connections, linkages, and often clarify relationships.[2]

Smith designed the Academic Club Method, which encourages exploration and deep learning of academic content while building knowledge, language fluency, and critical thinking. The rigorous academic model combines various educational methods, including multisensory learning, cooperative education, discovery and project learning, and authentic assessment. Students study great thinkers, works of art, and literature in rooms decorated like ancient Egypt, a prehistoric cave, or a Renaissance hall.

Students role-play to learn the various stages of evolution. The Academic Clubs help students learn how to learn, not merely master facts.

Many students with learning disabilities are not comfortable in the world of words and are called stupid or lazy.

> They may look typical, but they don't learn typically. They are visual thinkers. They see shapes, forms, contours, colors, textures, movement. When imparting knowledge we need to paint pictures in their minds through hands-on-project learning and active learning. We see astonishing successes when we honor their different styles of learning.[3]

Yet, for many years, Sally Smith encountered doubts and derision. "Here comes the arts and crafts lady" the friendliest doubters said with a sneer. She didn't waver. Today her students' achievements speak volumes: Over 90 percent of Lab School students go on to college. And the success is spreading. Smith recently opened arts-based schools in Baltimore and Philadelphia for students with learning disabilities. Our understanding of diverse ways of knowing continues to advance, in no small part due to the work and talents of Sally Smith.

[1] Sally Smith, *No Easy Answers* (Bantam Books, 1995). [2] Sally Smith, *Learn It, Live It* (Brookes Publishing, 2005). [3] Ibid, p. 21.

REFLECTION: Describe how the Academic Club Method could be used in regular classrooms. Do you believe that arts-based learning has a place in our standardized testing culture? Why or why not?

www.mhhe.com/ sadker8e

To learn more about Sally L. Smith, click on *Profiles in Education.*

2. **Nondiscriminatory education.** The principle of nondiscriminatory education, based on the Fifth and Fourteenth Amendments of the U.S. Constitution, mandates that children with disabilities be fairly assessed, so that they can be protected from inappropriate classification and tracking. Much of the court activity in this area has centered on the disproportionate number of children of color assigned to special education classes, a situation that some claim is the result of biased testing. In one case, a court ruled that IQ tests could not be used for placing or tracking students. Other courts have forbidden the use of tests that are culturally biased, and still others have ordered that testing take place in the children's native language.

3. **Appropriate education.** While the principle of zero reject ensures that children with disabilities will receive an appropriate public education, it is important to recognize that this principle goes beyond simply allowing children with disabilities to pass through the schoolhouse door. The term "appropriate education" implies that these children have the right to an education involving the accurate diagnosis of individual needs, as well as responsive programs keyed to those needs.

4. **Least-restrictive environment.** The least-restrictive environment protects children with disabilities from being inappropriately segregated. Court decisions have urged that special needs students be educated in a setting that most closely resembles a regular school environment while meeting their special needs. **Mainstreaming** has traditionally referred to placing special needs students in regular classroom settings for at least part of the day. The more recent term, **inclusion,** sometimes called *full inclusion,* reflects an even stronger commitment to educate each student in a least-restrictive environment to the maximum degree possible. Separate classes and schools are to be avoided unless a child's disabilities are such that education in a regular classroom, even with the aid of special materials and supportive services, cannot be achieved. When to include and when to separate is a source of constant debate.

School learning environments in the future must accommodate a wide variety of individual and cultural learning styles.

5. **Procedural due process.** The principle of procedural due process upholds the right of students with disabilities to protest a school's decisions about their education. Due process entails the right of children with disabilities and their parents to be notified of school actions and decisions; to challenge those decisions before an impartial tribunal, using counsel and expert witnesses; to examine the school records on which a decision is based; and to appeal whatever decision is reached.

These five principles of special education law are encompassed in landmark federal legislation passed in 1975, **Public Law 94-142,** the Education for All Handicapped Children Act. This law offers states financial support to make a free and appropriate public education available to every child with disabilities. It was replaced and expanded in 1991 by the **Individuals with Disabilities Education Act (IDEA),** which not only provided a more sensitive description of the act's purpose but also extended the act's coverage to all disabled learners between the ages of 3 and 21, including individuals with autism or traumatic brain injuries. IDEA also provided for rehabilitation and social work services. IDEA requires that each child with disabilities "have access to the program best suited to that child's special needs which is as close as possible to a normal child's educational program."[28] Classroom teachers shoulder the responsibilities of monitoring the needs of each child with disabilities placed in their classrooms and of using constructive procedures to meet their needs. The law further states that an **individualized education program (IEP)** be developed to provide a written record of those needs and procedures. The law states that an IEP must be written for each child who receives special education services. The IEP must include:

- A statement of the student's current performance, including long-term (annual) goals and short-term objectives

- A description of the nature and duration of the instructional services designed to meet the prescribed goals

- An overview of the methods of evaluation that will be used to monitor the child's progress and to determine whether the goals and objectives have been met

There is no specific IEP form that must be used, as long as goals, objectives, services, and evaluation are accurately reflected. In fact, hundreds of different IEP forms are currently in use; some run as long as twenty pages; others are only two or three pages. New teachers should learn about their school district's norms and procedures for writing IEPs when they begin teaching. Remember, it is not the format that is important but, rather, whether or not the IEP accurately describes the educational needs and the related remedial plans. While writing these IEPs will undoubtedly consume a great deal of a teacher's time and energy, it often leads to better communication among the school staff, as well as between teachers and parents. Also, the practice of preparing IEPs will likely lead to more effective individualization of instruction for all children, not just those with disabilities.

IDEA has been one of the most thoroughly litigated federal laws in history. Parents whose children qualify for special education services can and do sue the school district if they believe their children's needs are not being met. Local courts agreeing with parents' views have ordered public schools to hire extra teachers or specialized personnel or to spend additional dollars to provide an appropriate education. When judges believe that a school is unable to meet the special needs of a child, even with these additional resources, they can and have ordered the public school to pay the tuition so that the student can attend a private school. However, parents will likely find it more difficult to demand better special education services for their children. The Supreme Court recently ruled that parents who disagree with a school's IEP for their child have the legal burden of proving that the plan will not provide the appropriate education. Disability advocates worry that school districts will now have little incentive to address parents' complaints, or even worse, to provide quality special education services.[29]

Today, about one in every eight students is special needs, a number that has risen 30 percent since 1990.[30] In a few areas, like autism, growth has sky-rocketed tenfold in only two decades.[31] (See Figure 2.3.) **Learning disabilities** comprises the largest group of special needs students. Students with learning disabilities have

FIGURE 2.3

Distribution of students served under IDEA (rounded to nearest percent).

SOURCE: U.S. Department of Education, Office of Special Education Programs, 25th Annual Report to Congress (2003), Table 1-5.

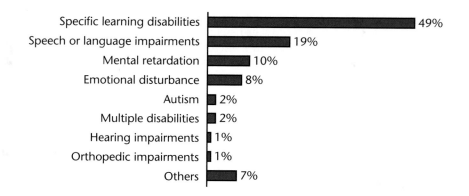

Specific learning disabilities	49%
Speech or language impairments	19%
Mental retardation	10%
Emotional disturbance	8%
Autism	2%
Multiple disabilities	2%
Hearing impairments	1%
Orthopedic impairments	1%
Others	7%

REFLECTION: This distribution offers an insight into which special needs students teachers are most likely to have in regular classrooms. What are some of the accommodations a classroom teacher might consider for each of these special needs?

difficulties with listening, speaking, reading, writing, reasoning or mathematical skills. A student with a learning disability might perform poorly in one area, but extremely well in another. Uneven performance, hyperactivity, disorganization, and lack of follow-through are typical problems for these students. Educational literature reflects more than 50 terms to describe students with learning disabilities.

Meeting the needs of special needs students has strained education budgets nationwide.[32] Why the upsurge? The reasons are complex—and troubling. Some believe environmental pollutants increase children's disabilities. Others argue that special needs have always been common, but in past years went undiagnosed. Some critics wonder if today we are over-diagnosing the problem. They point to affluent communities where parents hire private psychologists to ensure that their children are identified as having a learning disability. Why would they do this? In wealthy communities such labels attract additional educational resources, smaller class size, and even extended time for taking high-risk tests like the SATs.

But if special education means special privileges for the wealthy, the same diagnosis can mean fewer resources for the poor. Studies indicate that African American and Latino special education students are twice as likely to be educated in a more restrictive and separate setting than wealthier students. Poor parents struggle to make certain that the special education label is *not* attached to their children. In addition to poverty, cultural misunderstanding, low expectations, and the desire to remove "difficult" students from the classroom contribute to the high rate of African American students identified as mentally retarded or emotionally disturbed.[33] And then there is gender. While boys' behavior gets noticed, girls are quieter in class, less likely to cause discipline concerns, and more likely to turn inwardly with problems and anxieties. As a result, their special education needs often go undetected and untreated.[34] So behind the growing numbers of special education students is a disturbing imbalance as boys, students of color, and wealthy students may be over-identified, while females are under-identified.

Once identified, attention focuses on how best to educate these students.[35] Students with mild disabilities typically attend regular classrooms for part of the day, and leave for a period of time to receive special instruction in a resource room. These "pullout" programs have been criticized for stigmatizing students while failing to improve their academic performance. This concern has fueled the **regular education initiative,** which encourages schools to provide special services *within* the regular classroom and encourages close collaboration between classroom teachers and special educators. Today, about half of the students with disabilities spend 80 percent or more of the school day in a regular classroom.[36]

Regular classroom teachers often express concerns about their ability to handle a mainstreamed classroom:

> They want us all to be super teachers, but I've got 33 kids in my class and it's really a job to take care of them without also having to deal with special needs kids too. I'm not complaining really—I wouldn't want to do anything other than what I'm doing—but it is demanding.[37]

Although classroom teachers are expected to meet many of society's obligations, including the education of special needs students, they are not always given adequate resources for the task. Frustration is often the result. To succeed, teachers need additional planning time, appropriate curricular materials, ongoing staff development programs, and sometimes, extra classroom assistance.

Assistive Technology

Technology-based devices for students with special needs, called **assistive or adaptive technology,** can provide a real boost for students in and beyond the classroom. Assistive technologies include wheelchairs, switches that respond to voice commands, and computer programs that read material for blind students. For example, blind students and their teachers can use Braille software that provides easy-to-use print-to-Braille and Braille-to-print translations. Students with visual or

Technological advances have created new and exciting learning possibilities.

Should Be Mainstreamed Because . . .

WITHOUT INCLUSION, OUR DEMOCRATIC IDEAL IS HOLLOW

Segregating the disabled mirrors the historical segregation of African Americans and other groups, a segregation already rejected by the courts. Separate can never be equal, and all students quickly learn the stigma associated with those in "special" classrooms.

SOCIETY NEEDS THE TALENTS OF ALL ITS CITIZENS

Society needs the skills and economic productivity of all our citizens. Educating the disabled in a segregated setting decreases their opportunity for full and meaningful contributions later in life.

MAINSTREAMING IMPROVES THEIR ACADEMIC AND SOCIAL RELATIONS

Studies indicate that special needs students perform better academically when mainstreamed in regular classes. Not surprisingly, their social adjustment is also improved.

THOSE WITHOUT DISABILITIES GAIN WHEN SPECIAL NEEDS STUDENTS ARE PRESENT

In our increasingly stratified society, students can spend years in school with peers just like themselves. Inclusion provides an opportunity for children to appreciate and work with people who do not necessarily reflect their own experiences and viewpoints.

Should Not Be Mainstreamed Because . . .

MERELY SITTING IN REGULAR CLASSROOMS DOES NOT GUARANTEE A FITTING EDUCATION

A rallying cry like "democracy" sounds impressive, but we need to ensure that special needs students receive a quality education, and the best place for that is not necessarily in a mainstreamed classroom.

PULL-OUT PROGRAMS CAN OFFER SPECIAL NEEDS STUDENTS THE RESOURCES THEY NEED TO SUCCEED

Pull-out programs for special needs children can offer an adjusted curriculum, special instructional techniques, and smaller class size. Special needs students can soar in classrooms designed to meet their needs, but flounder when they are inappropriately placed in regular classes.

GIFTED AND TALENTED STUDENTS ARE AT PARTICULAR RISK

Gifted and talented students fall within the special needs category, and for them, mainstreaming is a disaster. If the gifted are not challenged, they will be turned off from school, and the gifts of our most able students will be lost to society.

WHEN SPECIAL NEEDS STUDENTS ARE MAINSTREAMED, STUDENTS WITHOUT DISABILITIES SUFFER

As teachers in regular classes adjust learning activities to accommodate the special needs students, other students lose out. The extra time, special curriculum, and attention given to special needs students amount to time and resources taken from others in the class.

SOURCE: Many of these arguments are found in greater detail in Jack L. Nelson, Stuart B. Palonsky, and Kenneth Carlson, *Critical Issues in Education: Dialogue and Dialectics* (New York: McGraw-Hill, 2004), pp. 441–67.

www.mhhe.com/
sadker

YOU DECIDE . . .

What training would help you meet the special needs of students mainstreamed into your classroom? Can "separate" ever be "equal"? Whose needs are most worth, those of special needs students, or of "regular" students? Do their needs actually conflict? As a teacher, would you want special needs children mainstreamed or pulled out? Imagine yourself the parent of a special needs child. Would you want your child mainstreamed or pulled out?

Effective teaching of students with special needs can be a challenging—and rewarding—experience. Here are a few practical suggestions to create an engaged *and* equitable learning environment for special needs students. In fact, these strategies are likely to improve learning for *all* students!

- **Establish and frequently review classroom rules, procedures, and academic directions.**
  Some students with special needs can become frustrated when they want to do the right thing, but get confused or forget. Repeating the rules keeps them—and all students—on track.

- **Set fair, yet challenging expectations for all students, and ask higher as well as lower order questions.**
  It can be difficult to keep expectations realistic, yet not underestimate the skills and insights of special needs students in your class. With experience you will learn how to continually challenge and not frustrate special needs learners.

- **Relate new learning to previous instruction, and to the students' backgrounds and experiences.**
  Seeing connections is central for special needs learners, since words alone are not always adequate. Think of connections that tie class learning to students' lives and to previous work.

- **Create high student engagement by using a variety of instructional strategies, including visual and auditory methods, hands-on activities, and shorter time segments for activities.**
  The more learning channels you open, the more engaged behavior you will encourage, and the more likely that students will connect with your academic goals.

- **Model skills and strategies, and always emphasize key words.**
  Be mindful that what you say and what you do is not incidental, casual, or secondary. Be purposeful and clear, for your words and behaviors teach powerful lessons.

- **Closely monitor independent work, and provide precise and immediate feedback.**
  Unlearning a behavior is more difficult than learning it correctly the first time. Monitoring and offering clear feedback can eliminate the need to unlearn and relearn.

- **Work to include joy and success in learning.**
  Design activities that will give students a sense of accomplishment. Provide additional time if needed to complete assignments, and don't forget to put joy and smiles in your teaching and in your students' learning.

REFLECTION: What words come to mind that characterize and help you remember these teaching tips (e.g., model, pacing)?

motor problems can use voice-activated software or specialized touch screens to direct the computer's actions. ERICA (Eyegaze Response Interface Computer Aid) allows students to control a computer's keyboard and mouse through eye movement alone, allowing even the most immobile learners to interact with teachers and peers. Those with learning disabilities report that computers (especially handheld computers) are useful for taking notes in class and keeping their schedules organized. And students with learning disabilities especially benefit from such tools as Spellcheck. Students with disabilities may use a variety of innovations to help achieve successful inclusion in regular classrooms, and the list of adaptive technology devices promises to grow in the years ahead.[38]

What are the pitfalls of such efforts, and can such "assistance" become too much? Some critics suggest that the use of spelling and grammar tools for special education students (as well as others) can short-circuit learning, and that sending laptops home can lead to inappropriate use, from visiting pornography and hate group Web sites to unsupervised Internet shopping excursions. In fact, the entire effort to include students with special needs has its critics, and even with technology and other resources, inclusion will not succeed unless teachers genuinely support the philosophy behind this approach. They must be committed to exploding stereotypes and able to recognize the essential value of helping all children to learn together. Their talents and commitment may be put to the test in communities like San Francisco, where students unable to feed themselves, or speak, or even go to the bathroom, are mainstreamed.[39] These students are part of a first wave of severely impaired children placed in regular classrooms. Although a difficult situation for teachers, students, and parents, the belief is that they will do far better there than in a segregated and restricted environment. Inclusion is at its heart a moral issue, one that raises the timeless principles of equality, justice, and the need for all of us to learn to live and grow together—not apart.

SUMMARY

**www.mhhe.com/
sadker8e**

CHAPTER REVIEW

Go to the Online Learning Center to take a chapter self-quiz, practice with key terms, and review concepts from the chapter.

1. **How do cognitive, affective, and physiological factors impact learning?**

   Individuals exhibit diverse styles of learning that are affected by attitudes (such as motivation), reasoning (organization and retention of information), and physical needs (preferences ranging from food and sleep needs to comfort levels for room sound or lighting). Because students exhibit a wide range of individual differences, there is no single optimal educational climate.

2. **How can teachers respond to different learning styles?**

   Teachers may need to adjust room temperature, lighting, and noise level, and plan a variety of activities to accommodate individual student needs. Teachers can work to complement various learning styles, such as visual, kinesthetic, or auditory.

3. **Is gender a learning style?**

   The jury is still out on this question. For example, a number of boys seem to prefer competitive learning, while many girls opt for cooperative learning activities. Is this due to genetics or socialization or some combination of the two? Certainly, the continued emphasis by schools on gender differences, segregating students by sex in comments, daily activities, and even in separate classrooms and schools does little to help cross-gender understanding or harmony.

4. **What are the classroom implications of Howard Gardner's theory of multiple intelligences?**

   Just as some educators challenge the concept of a single appropriate learning style, others challenge the notion of a single type of intelligence. Gardner's theory of multiple intelligences suggests that teachers plan their lessons to incorporate and develop these different intelligences (e.g., ask students to re-enact historical events through dance).

5. **How does emotional intelligence influence teaching and learning?**

   Daniel Goleman advocates that teachers develop students' emotional (EQ) as well as intellectual (IQ) gifts by helping students understand their emotions, "read" the emotions of others, and learn how to manage relationships.

6. **How are the needs of special learners met in today's classrooms?**

   The Individuals with Disabilities Education Act (IDEA) guarantees students with disabilities access to public education, and requires that individualized education programs document school efforts and student progress. Despite this law, there are no easy answers to identifying or educating special needs children, and there is much debate around the wisdom of inclusion or mainstreaming. Included in the special education category are gifted and talented students, who are often neglected. School programs for these students usually focus on either enrichment or acceleration.

THE *TEACHERS, SCHOOLS, AND SOCIETY* READER WITH CLASSROOM OBSERVATION VIDEO CLIPS

Go to your *Teachers, Schools, and Society* Reader CD-ROM to:

READ CURRENT AND HISTORICAL ARTICLES

2.1 **Differing Sexualities in Singular Classrooms,** Kevin Graziano, *Multicultural Education,* Winter 2003.

2.2 **An Educator's Primer to the Gender War,** David Sadker, *Phi Delta Kappan,* November 2002.

2.3 **Succeeding Through the Arts,** Sally Smith, *Their World,* 1996/1997.

ANALYZE CASE STUDIES

2.1 **Carol Brown:** A teacher, after socially integrating a diverse class, sees her efforts threatened when a child's pencil case disappears and is thought to have been stolen.

2.2 **Joan Martin, Marilyn Coe, and Warren Groves:** A classroom teacher, a special education teacher, and a principal hold different views about mainstreaming a boy with poor reading skills. The dilemma comes to a head over the method of grading him at the end of the marking period.

OBSERVE TEACHERS, STUDENTS, AND CLASSROOMS IN ACTION

Classroom Observation: A Multiple Intelligences Lesson in Action

As discussed in this section, Gardner's multiple intelligences theory indicates that recognizing and appealing to their different types of intelligences can support students' learning. In this observation, you will observe an elementary teacher using Gardner's theory of multiple intelligences in her instruction through the creation of learning centers based on the different intelligences.

Classroom Observation: Including Students with Special Needs

As a classroom teacher, you will most likely have at least one student with special needs and more likely several. In this observation, you will observe an elementary teacher demonstrating how he makes accommodations for his students with special needs. Teaching techniques, classroom organization, professional assistance and multiple instructional styles enable this instructor to reach ADHD, hearing impaired, PDD, and other students with special needs.

Classroom Observation: Identifying Classroom Bias and Analyzing the Role Play

David Sadker (coauthor of *Teachers, Schools, and Society*) often works with school administrators and teachers to demonstrate, through a role-play, several issues of bias that can overwhelm a classroom. In these two observations, you will observe David Sadker give one of these classroom bias workshops.

KEY TERMS AND PEOPLE

accelerated programs, 52

advanced placement, 52

affective domain, 35

appropriate education, 36

assistive or adaptive technology, 59

cognitive domain, 35

emotional intelligence quotient (EQ), 46

enrichment, 52

exceptional learners, 49

heteronormativity, 43

Howard Gardner, 44

generalizations, 41

gifted learners, 50

Daniel Goleman, 46

inclusion, 56

individualized education program (IEP), 57

Individuals with Disabilities Education Act (IDEA), 57

learning disabilities, 57

learning styles, 34

least-restrictive environment, 56

locus of control, 35

mainstreaming (inclusion), 56

multiple intelligences, 44–45

nondiscriminatory education, 56

portfolio, 46

procedural due process, 56

Public Law 94-142, 56

regular education initiative, 59

Sally L. Smith, 55

special education, 54

stereotypes, 41

zero reject, 54

DISCUSSION QUESTIONS AND ACTIVITIES

www.mhhe.com/
sadker8e

WEB-*TIVITIES*
Go to the Online Learning Center to do the following activities:
1. Learning Style Inventory
2. Multiple Intelligences
3. Exceptional Learners

1. How would you characterize your own learning style? Interview other students in your class to determine how they characterize their learning styles. Based on these interviews, what recommendations could you offer your course instructor about how to meet the needs of different students in your class?

2. Interview people who graduated from single-sex schools and ask them about their experiences. Did they find single-sex schools to be an advantage or not? In what ways? Do males and females have different assessments? What was lost by not attending a coed school? What was gained?

3. What steps can teachers take to create a safe classroom climate for GBLT students? How might the curriculum or school norms be made more inclusive?

4. Can you develop additional intelligences beyond the ones Gardner identifies? (This is often best accomplished in groups.)

5. Investigate a special education program in a local school. Describe its strengths. What suggestions do you have for improving it?

REEL TO REAL TEACHING

BEND IT LIKE BECKHAM (2002)
Run Time: 112 minutes

Synopsis: Jess Bhamra is an 18-year-old growing up in West London, where her family has taken every effort to stay in touch with its Indian heritage. Her father and mother want their daughter to go to law school, learn to cook a traditional Indian dinner, and settle down with a nice Indian boy. Much to her family's chagrin, however, Jess's talents and interests push her to pursue her love for soccer.

Reflection:

1. In the film, gender, culture, sexual orientation, religion, and ethnicity clash. How is Jess's identity affected by each of these dimensions? How do Pinky, Jules, and Jules's and Jess's parents serve as advocates of roles in society? Which of these characters reflect views that you experienced as you grew and developed? How did you resolve these conflicting views of the world—or did you?

2. Although Jess's family held to tradition in food, dress, and celebrations, identify times when they embraced new ideas. How did the greater British society influence them? How did they affect that British society? Can an individual pursue his or her dreams and passions without giving up cultural values and traditions? What is the cost of giving up these traditional values? What is the cost of closely adhering to tradition? Can/should these differences be bridged?

3. In the United States in 2001, Ashley Martin became the first woman to score in a NCAA Division I football game. She kicked three extra points. Should women play football? Do you have limits for certain groups to participate in athletics, classrooms, and careers? What's "too far"?

Follow-up Activity: What barriers have you struggled through? Are you the only *male* or *female* in the stands, the only *nonmajor* in the hall, the only *straight* or *gay* person in the room? How does difference feel? What did you learn from such an experience? What can others learn? How might a difference in social class, religion, gender, ethnicity, or sexuality affect your life as a teacher or a student? Do you feel ready for the challenge and opportunity to teach students who are quite different from you? How can you prepare yourself for teaching in diverse classrooms?

BUT I'M A CHEERLEADER (1999)
Run Time: 85 minutes

Synopsis: The hilarious satire of a cheerleader, who is sent by her parents to an ex-gay camp. Instead of coming out straight, she realizes that she is a lesbian.

Reflection:

1. How does the assumption that everyone is or should be heterosexual make it difficult for GLBT people to be open and honest about who they are?

2. What are some difficulties GLBT youth encounter with their families?

3. Imagine one of your students comes out as gay, lesbian, bisexual, or transgender and other students begin teasing him or her. How might you handle this situation?

Follow-up Activity: Compose a list of GLBT resources for teachers. What materials (posters of famous GLBT people, Safe Zone signs) can teachers hang in their classrooms to create an atmosphere inclusive of GLBT people? What Web sites provide ideas and resources for teachers and GLBT students? Are there curricula and lesson plan ideas that include GLBT people and perspectives? Where can students go for information on starting a Gay-Straight Alliance? What books does your university's library have on GLBT issues and education? How can a GSA engage the rest of the school and educate for liberty and justice for all?

www.mhhe.com/
sadker8e

How do you rate these films? Go to *Reel to Real Teaching* to review these films.

FOR FURTHER READING

The Children Are Watching, by Carlos E. Cortés (2000). This book analyzes both entertainment and news media, grappling with issues such as how media frame diversity themes, transmit values concerning diversity, and influence thinking about topics such as race, ethnicity, gender, religion, and sexual orientation.

Higher Order Thinking the Multiple Intelligences Way, by David Lazear (2004). This creative guidebook demonstrates new research about multiple intelligences that help students learn. Lesson plans for elementary, middle, and high school classes provide specific techniques for effectively teaching diverse subject matters and utilizing all of a student's abilities.

Pedagogies of Resistance: Women Educator Activists, 1880–1960, by Margaret Smith Crocco, Petra Munro, and Kathleen Weiler (1999). Chronicles the lives of women who resisted conventional gender roles to make education and society more equitable.

The Power of the Arts: Creative Strategies for Teaching Exceptional Learners, by Sally Smith (2001). Illustrates how to use the arts to teach academic subjects to children with learning disabilities. Includes step-by-step instructions for arts-based projects that teach science, math, and vocabulary.

Sexual Orientation and School Policy: A Practical Guide for Teachers, Administrators, and Community Activists, by Ian K. Macgillivray (2004). A case study of one school district's attempt to add sexual orientation to its nondiscrimination policy and the controversy that followed. Provides a successful approach for educators who want to make their schools safe for GLBT students.

Culturally Responsive Teaching

CHAPTER 3

FOCUS QUESTIONS

1. In what ways are American schools failing culturally diverse students?
2. How do deficit, expectation, and cultural difference theories explain different academic performance among various racial, ethnic, and cultural groups?
3. How do metaphors like "melting pot" and "tossed salad" both capture and mask American identity?
4. What are the political and instructional issues surrounding bilingual education?
5. What are the purposes and approaches of multicultural education?
6. Why is culturally responsive teaching important?
7. How can teachers use culturally responsive teaching strategies?

www.mhhe.com/ sadker8e

WHAT DO YOU THINK? Cultural diversity of students. Estimate the racial, ethnic, and social class backgrounds of today's students.

CHAPTER PREVIEW

America has just experienced the greatest immigration surge in its history. In the past few decades, newly minted Americans have arrived mainly from Latin America and Asia, but also from the Caribbean, the Middle East, Africa, and Eastern Europe. Today, about one in ten Americans is foreign born, and the native language of well over 30 million Americans is a language other than English. By 2030, half of all school children will be of color. These demographics create a remarkable and formidable challenge for the nation's schools.[1] Some advocate a multicultural approach to education that recognizes and incorporates this growing student diversity into teaching and the curriculum. Others fret that disassembling our Eurocentric curriculum and traditional approaches to education may harm our American culture. For many teachers, the struggle is to teach students with backgrounds different from their own. How to best do this is a tough question, and one that this chapter addresses directly not only with breath-taking information and some astute (we hope) insights, but with practical suggestions as well.

Student Diversity

Since the 1960s, more immigrants have come to this country than at the beginning of the twentieth century, a time often thought of as the great era of immigration and Americanization. Today, about one in three Americans are of color. **Demographic forecasting,** the study of people and their vital statistics, predicts that by 2020 almost half the school population will be from non-European ethnic groups. You will teach in a nation more diverse and less Eurocentric than the one you grew up in. (See Figure 3.1.) Here are some trends that underscore our growing diversity:

- By 2030, half of all school children will be children of color.
- By 2012, the west (the geographic area expected to witness the greatest changes) will become "minority majority," with no single racial or ethnic group having a majority.
- The nation has approximately 2.5 million Native Americans (also called Indians), a number that increases to about 4 million when including Americans claiming partial Indian heritage on the census.
- By 2000, the number of Asians, including Asian Indians, in the United States was over 10 million or 3.6 percent of the population.
- About 6 million Americans claimed multiracial heritage with two or more races indicated on Census 2000.
- By 2030, the number of U.S. residents who are nonwhite or Hispanic will be about 140 million or about 40 percent of the U.S. population.[2]

So let's begin to explore our changing student population by defining some basic terms that are critical, but often used incorrectly. **Race** refers to a group of individuals sharing common genetic attributes, physical appearance, and ancestry. **Ethnicity** refers to shared common cultural traits such as language, religion, and dress. A Latino or Hispanic, for example, belongs to an ethnic group, but might belong to the Negro, Caucasian, or Asian race. **Culture** is a set of learned beliefs, values, and behaviors, a way of life shared by members of a society. There is not only a

FIGURE 3.1

Percentage of public and elementary and secondary students by race/ethnicity.

SOURCE: U.S. Department of Education, National Center for Education Statistics, Common Core of Data (CCD), "State Nonfiscal Survey of Public Elementary/Secondary Education," 2003–2004.

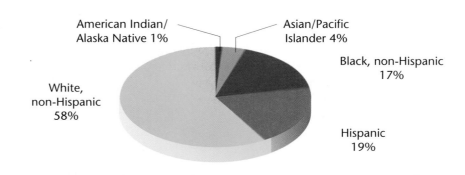

REFLECTION: Why should the lines between groups be blurred? In what ways does this graph represent, and misrepresent, America?

national culture, but microcultures or subcultures as well. There are cultures related to class, religion, or sexual orientation, to offer but a few examples. These sub-cultures carry values and behaviors that differ from others in the same nation or the same community. The willingness of people to understand and appreciate different cultures, races, and ethnicities is often at the heart of the diversity issue in America. The challenge for educators is to ensure that all our students will achieve.

Failing at Fairness

How are educators doing in meeting the needs of our diverse students? Here are some statistics that illustrate how far we have yet to go:[3]

- Hispanic, Native American, and African American students score consistently lower on standardized tests than do their Asian and white classmates.
- Almost half of the nation's historically under-resourced populations, Hispanic, African American, and Native American, are not graduating from high school.
- In Houston, Oakland, Cleveland, and New York, with large populations of poor and students of color, between 60 and 70 percent of the students do not graduate high school.
- Students from low-income families are six times more likely to drop out of school than are the children of the wealthy.

Are schools to blame for these dismal findings? Not according to most Americans.[4] In 1978, 80 percent of the public reported that schooling opportunities for all American children, regardless of race or ethnicity, were equal. In 2001, that figure was 79 percent, virtually unchanged. While most believe that educational opportunity is equal, they understand that student achievement is not. Nine out of ten agree that it is important to close the achievement gap between white students and students of color. An overwhelming 75 percent of those surveyed did not blame schools for the gap, but a majority (58 percent) felt it was up to the schools to fix the problem.[5]

This poll underscores the public understanding that issues outside of school affect what goes on in school. Even before children arrive at the schoolhouse door, poverty takes its toll. Lower birth weight, poor nutrition, and higher incidences of lead poisoning among the children from low-income families contribute to academic and cognitive problems.[6] Preschool children from low-income households know fewer words, speak less, and have fewer, if any, books. And "poverty" is not a synonym for color since most of the poor in the United States are white. Poverty affects students from all groups.

Race and ethnicity are of course well-publicized factors in academic performance. The test scores and graduation rates of African American and Hispanic American students lag behind those of white and Asian students, in part because of a

Being a good teacher in the years ahead will almost surely mean working with a culturally diverse population.

costly disconnect between school and home cultures. African American peers some-times mock school achievement as "acting white," suggesting academic success is racial or cultural treason. Hispanic families encounter not only cultural barriers, but language barriers as well. In truth, the failure of our society to bridge and honor differences among ethnic and racial groups contributes to the weaker test scores and lower graduation rates of many students. The home-school disconnect has other dimensions: Jewish and Moslem children encounter school obstacles to their religious practices, American Indian tribes have seen schools attack their cultures and beliefs, and even the cultural wars over sexual orientation affect student achievement. In this chapter, we will explore many of these diversity dimensions. As a teacher and as a citizen, working to eliminate social and economic injustice is as important to academic success as anything you do in the classroom.

This is not the first time that schools have been asked to solve society's prob-lems, and it will not be the last. Americans expect their schools to ensure that stu-dents from all groups are respected and honored, and able to achieve. Given the pervasive and persistent nature of bias, this task will require some creative responses. Here is one teacher's attempt to make invisible racism visible.

Putting a Price on Racism

"Welcome to class," says the professor as you take your seat. "I want you to respond to the following case study. This, of course, is fictional, but suspend belief, read the parable, and tell me what you think."

As a student in this class, you think this sounds kind of interesting (and a good grade in this course would be really nice). So you settle down and read the brief scenario:

> You are a white person and are visited by an official who explains that a mistake has been made. You were actually born to black parents who live far from where you grew up. The error has to be rectified. At midnight, you will become black, acquiring a darker skin, and body and facial features that reflect your African heritage. Your knowledge and ideas, your "inside," however, will remain the same.
>
> Now this is an unusual and rare problem, the official explains, but the error was not yours, and the organization that he represents is ready and able to offer you appro-priate recompense. His records indicate that you are likely to live another 50 years.
>
> How much financial recompense would you request?

You look around and see your classmates, each from their own unique perspec-tive of race and ethnicity, settle into the task. You wonder: How much money will your white classmates ask for? How will the students of color respond to this con-troversial, some would say offensive, class exercise? Now the BIG question: How much money would *you* ask for?

While the parable is not true, the scenario is. Professor Andrew Hacker at Cor-nell put this question to white students in his class, and asked them to come up with a settlement figure: How much money would they want to offset the "error"? If you are wondering what figure Hacker's students came up with, most felt that a reasonable payment for the "mistake" would be 50 million dollars, a million dol-lars for each coming black year.

The book that described this activity, *Two Nations: Black, White, Separate, Hostile, Unequal* (1992), received a great deal of media coverage in the 1990s. It raised some poignant questions, but we believe that it also left many unanswered.[7] What if Pro-fessor Hacker had continued the experiment with other groups? How much money

What do you see in this class? Hacker's anecdote unmasks the quiet racism that lurks in many adult minds as they view children's racial backgrounds as a predictor of future income and status.

would an Hispanic American, African American, and Asian American request if a mistake were made and they had to live the rest of their lives as a member of another race or culture? Would they request less compensation for the "administrative" blunder? The same 50 million dollars? Would they want more money?

Just posing the problem underscores the American tendency to look to the courts to fix any "mistake," no matter how bizarre. And of course, in this story, money is the all-American panacea, a salve for any social injury. But despite these confounding issues, the parable is fascinating, and the questions it raises are intriguing.

Why did Professor Hacker construct this strange story, and how did he interpret the payment? He believed that the story unmasks America's hidden racism. Professor Hacker considers white privilege to be so commonplace that most of us are no longer able to "see" it. He uses the parable because it makes visible the hidden advantage society gives to white Americans. In Hacker's estimation, the 50 million dollars that his students thought was "fair" compensation represents the value that white people place on the color of their own skin.

How do you interpret the story? Would you seek a legal settlement and monetary damages? (Here's an idea: perhaps you might feel privileged to experience more than one culture or one race in a single lifetime, and you should pay for this opportunity to see the world through another's eyes.) Or, like Hacker, do you believe that some races and cultures are more valued in America? And perhaps a more basic question: do you think that just going through this exercise is an appropriate classroom activity?

Theories of Why Some Groups Succeed and Others Do Not

A number of theories have emerged to explain why some groups soar in school, while others flounder. Some of the explanations are fatalistic, others more hopeful. Here are three—deficit theory, expectation theory, and cultural difference theory. The argument for **deficit theory** is that certain students do poorly in school because of their cultural, social, or linguistic background. The values, language patterns, and behaviors learned at home put these students at an academic disadvantage. Fewer books read, fewer vocabulary words used by parents, and little understanding of the relationship between education and careers contribute to the cultural deficit. A nefarious branch of this theory held that genetic and IQ deficiencies of certain groups, especially people of color, were the root cause of academic underachievement. Most deficit theory proponents today steer clear of such genetic claims.

Those who subscribe to **expectation theory** believe that some children do poorly because their teachers do not expect much of kids from certain racial and ethnic groups. As a result, they teach these students differently, and the students' academic performance suffers. This insight was first made popular by a classic study done by Rosenthal and Jacobson and is described in greater detail later in this text. In the study, students were randomly chosen and the teachers told that these students would experience an intellectual growth spurt during the year. Lo and behold, over the year, their grades improved. Teacher expectations of improved performance led to improved performance. Now imagine the opposite, teachers who expect less from certain students, and you see how harmful this "self-fulfilling prophesy" can be.

A third explanation for student achievement argues for better cross-cultural understanding. **Cultural difference theory** asserts that academic problems can be overcome if educators study and mediate the cultural gap separating school and home. Let's consider a case in point:

> Polynesian children in a Hawaiian village are performing poorly on the school reading tests. They seem unresponsive to the extra time and effort made by teachers to improve their reading performance. Why is this happening, and how can the situation be improved?

In this example, educators studied the Polynesian culture and discovered that older children, rather than adults, play a major role in educating the young. Accordingly, the school established a peer-learning center to provide the opportunity for older children to teach younger ones. By recognizing and adopting cultural traditions, the school was able to dramatically improve students' reading scores.[8]

What role do these theories play in the classroom? Deficit theory teaches us that groups bring different experiences and values to the classroom, and some of these differences do not mesh with mainstream school culture. Mainstream society terms this mismatch a deficit. The economic poverty of some groups contributes to such deficits, an issue that many believe should be addressed by the larger society. Expectation theory teaches us the power of teacher attitudes, that the attitudes you bring to the classroom influence your students, for better or worse. Cultural difference theory teaches us the rich nature of the human experience, and how much we can teach each other. This chapter is intended to do just that: help us appreciate each other.

The Melting Pot Has Melted

Start a discussion about cultural, racial or ethnic differences at a social gathering—or even more challenging, in a work environment—and just feel the tension grow as competing theories of group differences emerge. Introduce issues like affirmative action, immigration laws, classes being taught in Spanish or Laotian, or racial

Teaching Kids in Segregated Settings . . .

BY GENDER, CAN FOCUS ON ACADEMIC NEEDS

Same gender classes help students focus on academics, not on each other. Girls can get extra encouragement in math and science; boys can get special assistance in reading and language arts.

BY COMMUNITY, PROMOTES RACIAL AND ETHNIC PRIDE

Let's eliminate the alienation caused by busing students out of their neighborhood. Students feel accepted and take pride in local schools, where they can study with friends, and learn from a curriculum that reflects and honors their heritage.

BY RELIGION, ALLOWS APPROPRIATE AND SACRED OBSERVANCE

Secular American school norms and laws force all religious groups to make compromises. Some religious holidays are ignored, adult-led prayer in school is prohibited, school dress codes may conflict with religious requirements, and schools routinely ignore religious dietary law. By educating religious groups separately, different histories and beliefs can be honored and practiced. Students can pray as they like and pursue their religion without ridicule or taunting from peers, or interference from civil authorities.

BY NEED, OFFERS AN EDUCATIONAL HAVEN FOR GLBT STUDENTS

Special schools can help GLBT students cope with their unique personal and academic circumstances. Being with GLBT students protects them from comparisons and ridicule that might exist elsewhere.

Teaching Kids Together . . .

PROMOTES GENDER EQUALITY

Learning and succeeding together in the classroom prepares boys and girls to live and work together as adults. Equitable instruction and curriculum will teach students how to eliminate traditional gender barriers in society.

FOSTERS CULTURAL AND RACIAL UNDERSTANDING

We must not allow our nation to be fractured along racial, ethnic, and class lines. Integrating children of different backgrounds mirrors our ideal of a democratic society. Cross-cultural classrooms enrich the learning experience.

PROMOTES RESPECT AND UNDERSTANDING OF RELIGIOUS DIFFERENCES

Religious practices are the domain of religious institutions, and should not become the focal point of school life. Learning *about* different religions can help all of us to grow. Restricting each of us to one set of beliefs will eventually divide and separate Americans. By learning together, students gain valuable lessons as they prepare to live and work together as adults in a vibrant and diverse democracy. We see all too well in other countries how religion and government can create problems.

GIVES GLBT STUDENTS HOPE FOR THE FUTURE

Attending a regular school gives all students insight into more different lifestyles. Learning together as children can help us all live together as adults.

www.mhhe.com/
sadker8e

YOU DECIDE . . .

Do you believe equal educational opportunity is best achieved in separate or integrated classrooms? Is your position consistent or does it vary depending upon the identified group? Extend this *You Be the Judge* feature by developing the arguments for either integrating or separating two other groups discussed in this chapter (or identify new groups).

profiling, and some people become unglued. More than a few people will listen politely, carefully avoiding uttering a sound. Some might stay silent but wonder if the conversation is genuine or simply an attempt at "political correctness." Others, articulating beliefs they perceive as acceptable, may voice hopeful insights, but in their heart of hearts, they themselves do not believe them. A few may say things they will later regret, words that may spark an attack, or a charge of racism:

> "Why don't they learn to speak English? My grandparents had nothing, but they learned the language. Are they too lazy or do they simply not care?"

> "I am fine with racial equality. I like it as a concept. I just wonder why all my friends are my race."

> "I treat all people the same, but some groups have a chip on their shoulder."

Start a discussion about cultural, racial or ethnic differences at a social gathering, and you may wish you never did.

Many of us continue to live in silence about race and ethnicity. As a nation, we have yet to come to terms with our multicultural society. Many believe that America is a wondrous melting pot where the Statue of Liberty opens her arms to all the world's immigrants. This was the image painted by Israel Zangwill in a 1910 play that coined the term *melting pot.*

> America is God's Crucible, the Great Melting Pot where all races of Europe are melting and reforming . . . Germans and Frenchmen, Irishman and Englishmen, Jews and Russians—into the Crucible with you all! God is making the American . . . The real American has not yet arrived. He is only in the Crucible, I tell you—he will be the fusion of all races, the coming superman.[9]

For many, "melting in" became a reality. Groups incorporated into the mainstream culture are said to have gone through **assimilation** or **enculturation.** Countless immigrants today cling to this idea of being transformed into a new citizen, a new person, an American. But the melting pot image, while enticing, describes only a part of the American reality.

Many immigrants, even light-skinned Europeans, do not melt in. They settle in distinct communities, enclaves where traditional customs are maintained, not transformed, where, in some cases, native languages are preferred. From Germantown to Chinatown, and in countless less descriptive communities, Americans choose not to have their histories and traditions "melt" away. Others never had a choice. Indians, Mexican Americans, African Americans, and Asian Americans were excluded and isolated from mainstream American society. Although Zangwill called for the "fusion of all races" in his melting pot, it was painfully evident that the coming American "superman" would be white. History tells us that for many, a different metaphor is more apt: a "tossed salad." The tossed salad image underscores that either voluntarily or involuntarily, many Americans maintained their heritages and unique cultures. **Cultural pluralism** recognizes that some groups, voluntarily or involuntarily, have maintained their culture and their language, and that these group differences should be understood, appreciated, and even honored. In a tossed salad, ingredients keep their distinctive flavors.

These metaphors, aside from reminding you how close to meal time it may be, raise profound questions about the future of America. For teachers, the question that emerges is: how should we educate our increasingly diverse students?

Bilingual Education

What is going on in America? It is amazing, and disturbing, to ride on a road and see street signs that are printed not only in English but in other languages as well. What's more, even legal documents are now being written in foreign languages. How unnerving to walk down an American street and not understand what people are talking about. Maybe this isn't America. I feel like a stranger in my own land. Why don't they learn to speak English?

Sound like a stroll through today's Miami, or San Diego, or perhaps San Antonio? Good try, but you not only have the wrong city, you are also in the wrong century. Benjamin Franklin expressed this view in the 1750s.[10] He was disgruntled that Philadelphia had printed so many things, including street signs, in another language (German, in this case). Even the *Articles of Confederation* were published in German as well as English, and children were taught in Dutch, Italian, and Polish.

Bilingual education in America is hundreds of years old, hardly a "new" issue. In 1837, Pennsylvania law required that school instruction be given on an equal basis in German as well as English. In fact, that example provides us with a fairly concise definition of **bilingual education,** the use of two languages for instruction. But, almost a century later, as America was being pulled into World War I, foreign languages were seen as unpatriotic. Public pressure routed the German language from the curriculum, although nearly one in four high school students was studying the language at the time. Individual states went even further. Committed to a rapid assimilation of new immigrants, and suspicious of much that was foreign, these states prohibited the teaching of *any* foreign language during the first eight years of schooling. (The Supreme Court found this policy not only xenophobic but unconstitutional as well, in *Meyer* v. *State of Nebraska, 1923.)*[11]

In some bilingual education programs, English is learned as a second language while the student takes other academic work in his or her native language.

Despite the long history of bilingual education in this country, many school districts never really bought into the concept. In districts without bilingual education, students with a poor command of English had to sink or swim (or perhaps, more accurately, "speak or sink"). Students either learned to speak English as they sat in class—or they failed school, an approach sometimes referred to as **language submersion.** If submersion was not to their liking, they could choose to leave school. Many did.

Bilingual education had a rebirth in the 1960s, as the Civil Rights movement brought new attention to the struggles of many disenfranchised Americans, including non-English speakers trying to learn in a language they did not understand. And, unlike the 1800s, by the 1960s and 1970s education had become less an option and more a necessity, the threshold to economic success. To respond to this need, Congress passed the Bilingual Education Act in 1968. This act provided federal financial incentives, using what some people call "a carrot approach," to encourage schools to initiate bilingual education programs. Not all districts chased the carrot.

Why am I not allowed to speak Spanish at school? Why do Mexican students seem ashamed of speaking Spanish? Am I stupid for not learning English quickly so that I can do the assignments? Why are there no teachers who look like me and who share my culture and language? And why did my parents leave the warmth and comfort of Central America for the indifference and coldness of the United States?[1]

It was 1955. Carlos Julio Ovando had emigrated from Nicaragua and was anxious to show his teachers what he knew. But educationally disenfranchised by his linguistic and cultural background, he could not.

The promise of religious freedom and economic stability had motivated the Ovando family's move to Corpus Christi, Texas. In Nicaragua, the Somoza dictatorship opposed the vigorous attempts of Ovando's father, a former priest turned Protestant minister, to convert Catholics. The family was exiled. Yet, their Latin American heritage remained strong. Even after emigrating, Nicaraguan cultural traditions continued in the Ovando home and discussions of spiritual values were central to the family's daily life.

While home was a cultural touchstone for Ovando, school was foreign territory. Unable to understand the lessons in English, he felt abandoned. At age 14, Carlos was placed in the sixth grade and wondered, "Why do teachers show little interest in who I am?" In Nicaragua, the family was entrusted with home life and the school took care of the academic lessons. But school was clearly not working for Carlos.

> I do not recall my parents ever asking to see my report cards or expressing interest in visiting my school to talk to my teachers about my progress. As in the case with many other newly arrived immigrants, it may be that while tacitly interested in my academic well-being, my parents did not know how or were afraid to approach the unfamiliar American schools.[2]

Disconnected from school and doubtful of his own abilities, Ovando was experiencing education that was not so much immersion as submersion, the classic "sink or swim" approach, and Ovando was sinking, looking at America from the bottom of the pool. Ironically, a different kind of pool, a pool hall, provided to be the turning point in his life.

> The turning point in my academic career began when somebody in the church congregation saw me coming out of a pool hall and told my father. Soon after that, in the hope of saving me from sin, my father sent me to a Mennonite high school in northern Indiana.[3]

At the new school, a teacher saw Ovando in an entirely different way. Not so much English challenged, as Spanish blessed. He affirmed Ovando's Latin American roots and championed his native linguistic talent. Spurred by his teacher's encouragement, Ovando rediscovered confidence in his academic abilities. Rather than being punished for speaking Spanish, his language talents were acclaimed. He won honors, including college scholarships. Ovando now reveled in the world of ideas. He taught Spanish in a Midwest high school before going on to college teaching and writing.

His work shows how language is much more than a set of words and grammar rules: It can be a cultural link for students, one that promotes academic achievement. While critics see bilingual education as a threat to national identity, Ovando envisions a society built on the strengths of its diverse population. He challenges teachers to unlock each student's cultural touchstones: "Pedagogy that activates the student voice and embraces the local community provides a much richer environment for student understanding than pedagogy that treats students as if they were empty vessels into which knowledge is to be poured."[4]

[1] Adapted from Carlos J. Ovando and Virginia P. Collier, *Bilingual and ESL Classrooms: Teaching in Multicultural Contexts*, 2nd ed. (Boston: McGraw-Hill, 1998), p. 2. [2] Ibid, p. 2. [3] Ibid, p. 3. [4] Ibid, p. 24.

REFLECTION: How is the history of bilingual education in America reflected in Ovando's story? What is the downside of promoting a monolingual society? How do you explain the popularity of the effort to make English the "official language" in the United States? Why has the maintenance approach encountered so much difficulty? If you were to teach a student like Ovando, how could you tackle these linguistic and cultural challenges?

www.mhhe.com/ sadker8e

To learn more about Carlos Julio Ovando, click on *Profiles in Education.*

1700–1800S: THE PERMISSIVE PERIOD

Linguistic and cultural tolerance maintained the peace in the new nation. Many schools offered content-related classes in languages other than English.

1900–1960S: THE RESTRICTIVE PERIOD

The anti-German hostility during World War I linked foreign languages with alien ideologies. Most states required that all schools teach all content courses in English, and promoted the Americanization of all immigrants.

1950S TO 1980S: THE OPPORTUNIST PERIOD

The Cold War demonstrated that the lack of linguistic ability was a strategic vulnerability, and federal laws were passed to encourage foreign language instruction. The Bilingual Education Act and the *Lau* Supreme Court decisions affirmed the civil rights of language-minority speakers. Schools explored numerous approaches to bilingual education.

1980S TO THE PRESENT: THE DISMISSIVE PERIOD

With the arrival of Presidents Reagan and the two Bush administrations, an era of antibilingual education re-emerged. Federal support turned into federal hostility, and political movements such as "U.S. English," "English First," and "English Only" sprung up. State actions such as Proposition 227 in California required that English replace any other instructional language used in schools.

SOURCE: Carlos Ovando, "Bilingual Education in the United States: Historical Development and Current Issues." Paper presented at the American Educational Research Association annual convention, Montreal, Canada, April 19–23, 1999.

REFLECTION: Why has teaching in English become a political issue, rather than an educational one? How does political support for English-only courses conflict with economic goals to enhance the nation's performance in the global economy? Do you believe that bilingual education is a threat to national cohesion and stability?

During the early 1970s, disillusioned parents initiated lawsuits. In 1974, the Supreme Court heard the case of **Lau v. Nichols.** This class action lawsuit centered around Kinney Lau and 1,800 other Chinese students from the San Francisco area who were failing their courses because they could not understand English. The Court unanimously affirmed that federally funded schools must "rectify the language deficiency" of students. Teaching students in a language they did not understand was not an appropriate education. The Court's decision in *Lau* v. *Nichols* prompted the U.S. Department of Education Office of Civil Rights to issue the "*Lau* Remedies," guidelines for school districts which specify that "language minority students should be taught academics in their primary language until they could effectively benefit from English language instruction."[12] Under this provision, school districts must take positive steps to eliminate language barriers to learning.

Bilingual Education Models

More than 5 million **English language learners (ELL)** are enrolled in public elementary and secondary schools (nearly 10 percent of school enrollment), and the number is steadily increasing (see Figure 3.2). About half of these non-English-speaking youngsters are from families that have recently come to the United States. Surprisingly, many ELL students were born in this country but have not yet learned

FIGURE 3.2

The growing numbers of English language learners.

SOURCE: National Clearinghouse for English Language Acquisition, Washington, DC, December 2005.

REFLECTION: What are the implications of this demographic on your life in the classroom? How can your teacher preparation help you prepare to teach ELL students?

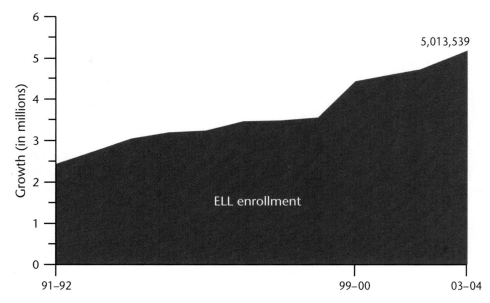

English at home or in their community. About one in five school-aged children speak a language other than English at home, and of these children, approximately one-third speak English with difficulty.[13] As these non-English-speaking students enter schools, most will need to make sense of a new language, a new culture, and possibly new ways of interacting with teachers and classmates. Teachers can greatly assist this transition by creating a stable classroom environment.

English language learners typically work to master English and academic content. Several models of bilingual education help students reach these goals. These models vary in ease of implementation and effectiveness, and often reflect the underlying philosophy of a local community or state. These philosophies fall along the continuum of cultural assimilation (immersion and ESL models) to cultural pluralism (maintenance methods).

Typically in bilingual education programs, English language learners acquire English as a second language while taking other academic subjects in their native language. The **transitional approach** uses the native language as a bridge to English language instruction. Academic subjects are first taught using the native language, but progressively students transition to English, to their new language. Cultural assimilation is often stressed. The goal is to prepare for English-only classrooms, typically within two to three years. The **maintenance** or **developmental approach** is designed to help children develop academic skills in both their native language and English. Instruction occurs in both languages to create a truly bilingual student. An ideal maintenance program provides dual-language instruction from kindergarten through twelfth grade, although few exist at the secondary level. Students develop cognitively in both languages, learning about the culture and history of their ethnic group as well as that of the dominant culture. Two-way bilingual education adapts the maintenance approach to develop the language abilities of ELLs *and* their English-speaking peers. For example, children who speak Spanish are placed in the same class with children who speak English, and students learn each other's languages and work academically in both languages.

In the **immersion** approach, instruction is exclusively in English. Immersion cannot truly be considered bilingual, but is used with ELLs nonetheless. Teachers using an immersion model often understand the students' native language but deliver lessons in a "sheltered" or simplified English vocabulary that attempts to familiarize students with English while learning academic content. **English as a Second Language (ESL)** supplements immersion programs by providing special pull-out classes for additional instruction in reading and writing English. The goal is to assimilate learners into the English language as quickly as possible. While research suggests that English-only instruction is not as cognitively effective as sound bilingual programs, ESL instruction may work well for students highly motivated to be part of a mainstreamed English-only classroom.[14]

Language submersion is an extreme example of immersion. Submersion places students in classes where only English is spoken, and instruction is not modified at all. It is fundamentally a "sink or swim" approach.

The Bilingual Controversy

As schools struggle to meet the needs of ELL students, bilingual education continues to spark political controversy. Millions of students speak hundreds of languages and dialects, including not only Spanish but Hmong, Urdu, Russian, Chinese, Polish, Korean, Tagalog, and Swahili (see Figure 3.3). Misunderstandings are multiplied when language barriers are accompanied by racial and ethnic differences, leading to even greater isolation and segregation for many ELL students. And, while some struggle to make bilingual education work, others believe that it never will.

Civil rights and cultural issues supporting bilingual education are challenged by concerns that many non-English speakers never master English and never fully participate in American life. Critics of bilingual education advocate an immersion model, claiming that many bilingual programs simply do not work, placing ELLs into lower academic tracks from which they may never emerge. Opponents point to studies showing that first- and second-generation Hispanic students who attended bilingual programs from the 1970s to the 1990s earned considerably less

FIGURE 3.3

Educational terms in other languages.

English	Spanish	Farsi	Korean	Urdu
Individualized educational program	Programa Educacional Individualizado	برنامه آموزش فردی	개별 교육 프로그램	انفرادی تعلیمی پروگرام
No Child Left Behind	Ley sobre No Dejar Atras a Ningún Niño	قانون هیچ کودکی عقب نماند	어느 아동도 뒤처져 있어서는 안된다는 법률	قانون بعنوان کسی بچے کو پیچھے نہیں چھوڑا جائے گا۔
Achievement gap	Brecha en el aprovechamiento	اختلاف میزان پیشرفت	성취의 갭	تعلیمی پیشرفت میں تفاوت
Paradigm	Paradigma	نمونه	범례	مثالی رویہ
Benchmark	Parámetro	معیار های ارزیابی	기준	معیار کا نشان

SOURCE: *The Washington Post*, January 24, 2006, p. B3.

REFLECTION: Educators find themselves translating key educational terms into many languages. Where could you go to find help in translating information into other languages?

money than Hispanics who attended "English-only" classes. Moreover, Hispanic students who dropped out of bilingual programs were less likely to return and complete high school than were Hispanics who attended English-only programs.[15] Today, the dropout rate for Hispanic students, the largest group of ELLs, remains high, hovering around 50 percent.[16]

Many parents of students in bilingual programs now oppose these programs, an ironic turnabout, since it was parent protests in the 1960s and 1970s that forced reluctant schools and the federal government to initiate bilingual education. In 1998, more than 60 percent of the voters in California, including a sizable minority of Hispanic voters, supported an initiative to replace most bilingual maintenance programs with a fast-track transition to English. Proposition 227 required that ELL students be provided a year of special pull-out English immersion instruction and then be shifted into mainstream English classrooms, unless their parents obtain a waiver. Several other states, including Arizona and Massachusetts, followed suit. Despite strong voter support for Proposition 227, recent studies reveal that English-only instruction has not improved student achievement in California schools.[17]

Many people worry that bilingual education threatens the status of English as the nation's primary vehicle of communication. As a result, an **English-only movement** has emerged (see Figure 3.4). Those who support this movement feel that English is a unifying national bond that preserves our common culture. They believe that English should be the only language used or spoken in public and that the purpose of bilingual education should be to quickly teach English to ELL students. It is not surprising that the Bilingual Education Act of 1968 expired in

FIGURE 3.4
States with official English language.

SOURCE: U.S. English, Inc. (2005), Washington, DC.

REFLECTION: Do you see any pattern in which states have passed this law? Does this influence your decision as to where you might want to teach? Do you believe such English-only laws have any practical impact?

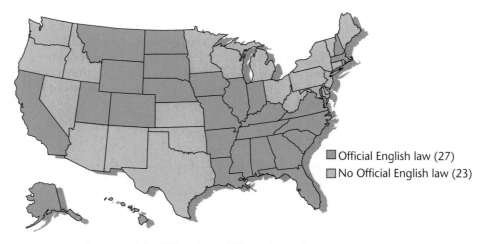

Official English law (27)
No Official English law (23)

States with Official English Rule and Year Enacted

Alabama (1990)	Indiana (1984)	New Hampshire (1995)
Alaska (1998)	Iowa (2002)	North Carolina (1987)
Arkansas (1987)	Kentucky (1984)	North Dakota (1987)
California (1986)	Louisiana (1811)	South Carolina (1987)
Colorado (1988)	Massachusetts (1975)	South Dakota (1995)
Florida (1988)	Mississippi (1987)	Tennessee (1984)
Georgia (1986 & 1996)	Missouri (1998)	Utah (2000)
Hawaii* (1978)	Montana (1995)	Virginia (1981 & 1996)
Illinois (1969)	Nebraska (1920)	Wyoming (1996)

*Hawaii recognizes English and Hawaiian languages.

2002 and was not renewed. Today, *No Child Left Behind* funds language programs that emphasize transition into English.

Bilingual education advocates argue that America is a mosaic of diverse cultures and that diversity should be honored and nurtured. One problem, they point out, is that we simply do not have enough competent bilingual teachers who can respond to the large numbers of ELL children now in our schools. They also point out that it is unfair to blame bilingual education for the slow progress some students are making. Achieving proficiency in any second language can take years.[18] Bilingual advocates oppose the English-only movement, and they feel that it promotes intolerance, will turn back the clock, and may very well be unconstitutional. Education writer James Crawford points out, "It is certainly more respectable to discriminate by language than by race. . . . Most people are not sensitive to language discrimination in this nation, so it is easy to argue that you're doing someone a favor by making them speak English."[19]

Research on Bilingual Education

What does the research say about the effectiveness of bilingual education? Unfortunately, the research is not clear. Educators are just now beginning to analyze long-term data, and they are uncovering some useful findings. In one case, the researchers found that when language-minority students spend more time learning in their native language, they are more likely to achieve at comparable and even higher levels in English.[20] Another study found that the earlier a student starts learning a new language, the more effective that language becomes in an academic setting.[21] Yet another study showed that no single approach holds a monopoly on success, and different approaches to bilingual education can each be effective, suggesting that local school systems should carefully select the programs and teachers most appropriate for their communities.[22]

One major bilingual study, directed by Virginia Collier and Wayne Thomas, evaluated the experiences by 42,000 students over a thirteen-year period. Early findings suggested that the students enrolled in well-implemented bilingual programs actually *outperform* the students in monolingual programs. One successful approach assumed bilingual education to be a two-way street, one in which English speakers and LEP students would learn from each other. In this model, during the Spanish part of the day, the Spanish-speaking students explained the lessons to native-English peers, while, during English instruction, the reverse took place. Collier and Thomas report that, by fourth grade, the students in these two-way classes had actually outperformed the native English speakers who attended English-only classes.[23]

More than two centuries ago, Ben Franklin expressed his fears about the multiple languages heard on America's streets. His concerns have echoed through the centuries, despite a world in which national borders seem to be blurring or even disappearing. In today's global community, Russians and Americans are working together in space, such international organizations as the United Nations and NATO are expanding their membership, and corporations are crossing national boundaries to create global mergers in an international marketplace. Moreover, technological breakthroughs, such as the Internet, have made international communications not just possible but commonplace. However, for most Americans, these international conversations are viable only if the other side speaks English. In this new international era, Americans find themselves locked in a monolingual society. How strange that, instead of viewing those who speak other languages as welcome assets to our nation, some seem eager to erase linguistic diversity.

Some teachers wonder how they can effectively teach English language learners. Here are several strategies for turning frustration into success for your ELL students.

- **Get to know your students, and when possible, use their backgrounds to make connections to the material being learned.**
  Creating a comfortable and safe classroom climate for your students despite the language and culture differences is an important first step. By connecting to their backgrounds, you will help ELL feel that their new classroom culture is less alien and distant.

- **Give explicit directions, emphasize key words, and offer concrete examples to enhance the understanding of ELL students.**
  Simple strategies such as emphasizing key words, offering examples of your main points, and using visuals such as the chalkboard, flash cards, games, graphics and puzzles can increase the understanding of ELL students.

- **Plan for and expect the active involvement of ELL students.**
  It is a good idea to call on all students to keep their attention and focus. ELL students are no exception. A preferred strategy is to ask a question before calling out a specific name so that all students have time to consider their answer. Feel free to use a variety of questioning strategies, but avoid rhetorical questions since ELL students may not understand them. Waiting a bit longer for students to respond will give ELL students more time to process the question in their new language.

- **Do not depend simply on verbal, teacher-centered learning, but incorporate a variety of instructional strategies.**
  Hands-on activities, cooperative learning groups, and other strategies will help ELL students develop their language skills and learn new information through avenues other than teacher talk.

- **Always provide time to check for understanding and be sure to provide precise and immediate feedback.**
  Unlearning the wrong word or behavior is more difficult than learning it correctly the first time. Monitoring and offering clear feedback can eliminate the need to unlearn and relearn.

REFLECTION: How would incorporating these skills for ELL students enhance your teaching effectiveness for all students?

Multicultural Education

Students in many urban and suburban schools speak scores of languages. In some urban communities, students of color comprise 70 to more than 90 percent of school enrollment. A successful teacher in these communities will need to bridge these possible racial, cultural, and language differences. In fact, even in very stable, overwhelmingly white school districts where all students share apparently similar backgrounds and are native speakers, cross-cultural knowledge is important. Many of these students will graduate, leave these communities, and work and live in more diverse areas. The success of their transition may depend on what they learned— or did not learn—in school. Moreover, communities that appear uniform and static may have differences in religion, social class, gender, sexuality. The controversial question facing the nation: how best to teach our multicultural students?

The Multiculturalism Debate

You enter teaching in a time of harsh and divisive "culture wars," as people argue about how diversity should be recognized in schools.[24] Some worry that overemphasizing diversity may pull us apart, and fear that multiculturalism will lead to a Dis-United States. Adversaries of multiculturalism point to Yugoslavia and Czechoslovakia, nations dissolved by the power of ethnic differences. They argue for a uniform national identity, and urge schools to promote one set of common beliefs

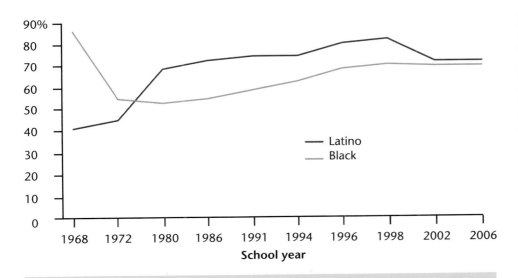

FIGURE 3.5
Students in *de facto* minority schools.

SOURCE: Gary Orfield and Chungmei Lee, "Racial Transformation and the Changing Nature of Segregation," Civil Rights Project, Harvard University, January 2006.

REFLECTION: Do you believe that desegregation of America's schools will ever be possible? Is desegregation important? Explain your position.

based on our English and European traditions. In their eyes, time spent teaching about different cultures poses a double threat: pulling apart the national fabric, while taking time from important academic subjects like math and reading. They would prefer students focus on academic achievement and adopt core values of America.

Others claim that multiculturalism is the nation's future. They believe that schools can no longer ignore or devalue cultural and ethnic differences either in this country, or throughout the world. National demographics are changing, and schools must recognize these changes. They argue that that current practices are failing in their mission to unite and educate all our students equitably, and point to statistics like these to underscore their point:[25]

- While schools were ordered to desegregate in the 1954 Brown decision, since the 1980s, schools have been resegregating. (See Figure 3.5.)
- Since the 1990s, the segregation of students of every racial group has increased.
- Nationally, Asians are more likely than students of other races to attend multi-racial schools.
- White students are the least likely to attend multiracial schools, and are the most isolated group.
- More than three-quarters of intensely segregated schools are also high-poverty schools.
- High school graduation rates are around 70 percent, and in many communities only 50 or 60 percent of Hispanic, African American, and Native American students are graduating from high school.

Is multicultural education part of the answer to these troubling statistics? Perhaps multiculturalism itself, specifically Eastern thought, can offer an answer. A sacred belief of the Hindu religion is "We are one," that all humans are connected.

During much of the twentieth century, African American students attended legally segregated schools. Today, while legal segregation has ended, segregation has not. Examine these two photos and suggest similarities and differences between segregation then
and now. During the past hundred years, what other ethnic or racial groups might be
photographed in much the same way?

A second Hindu truth is "Honor one another," emphasizing the importance of appreciating our differences. These Hindu beliefs are held simultaneously, and are not viewed as mutually exclusive. Perhaps the key to moving ahead and avoiding yet another culture war is for us to learn balance, to honor our national commonalities as we celebrate our group and individual differences.

Approaches to Multicultural Education

When multiculturalism began, the focus was on fighting racism. Over time, these programs expanded to confronting not only racism, but injustices based on gender, social class, disability, and sexual orientation. Today, there are many dimensions to **multicultural education** including (1) *expanding the curriculum* to reflect America's diversity; (2) *using teaching strategies* that are responsive to different learning styles; (3) *ensuring and supporting multicultural competence of teachers,* comfortable and knowledgeable working with students and families of different cultures; and (4) *a commitment to social justice,* efforts to work and teach toward local and global equity.

Multiculturalism has come to mean different things to different educators.[26] Some focus on *human relations,* activities that promote cultural and racial understanding among different groups. Others teach *single-group studies,* which you may know as Black Studies, Hispanic Studies, or Women Studies programs. Some educators believe multicultural education is all about creating close links between home and school so that minority children can succeed academically, an approach termed *teaching the culturally different.* Another tack, called simply *multicultural,* promotes different perspectives based on race, class, and culture; in a sense, developing new eyes through which students learn. And finally, the *multicultural reconstructionist* approach mobilizes students to examine and work to remediate social injustices. As you can see, multicultural education can mean different things to different people.

James Banks focuses specifically on developing a multicultural curriculum.[27] James Banks believes that one way to achieve greater understanding and more positive attitudes toward different groups is to integrate and broaden the curriculum to make it more inclusive and action oriented. He defines four approaches to a multicultural a curriculum which are related to several proposed by others[28] (Figure 3.6). As you read each description, consider if any of these approaches were used in your own schooling?

1. Multicultural education often begins with the *contributions approach,* in which the study of ethnic heroes (for example, Sacagawea, Rosa Parks, or Booker T. Washington) is included in the curriculum. At this superficial contributions level, one might also find "food and festivals" being featured or holidays such as *Cinco de Mayo* being described or celebrated.

2. In the *additive approach,* a unit or course is incorporated, often but not always during a "special" week or month. February has become the month to study African Americans, while March has been designated "Women's History Month." Although these dedicated weeks and months offer a respite from the typical curricular material, no substantial change is made to the curriculum as a whole.

3. In the *transformation approach,* the entire Eurocentric nature of the curriculum is changed. Students are taught to view events and issues from diverse ethnic and cultural perspectives. For instance, the westward expansion of Europeans can be seen as manifest destiny through the eyes of European descendants, or as an invasion from the east, through the eyes of Native Americans.

FIGURE 3.6

Banks' approach to multicultural education.

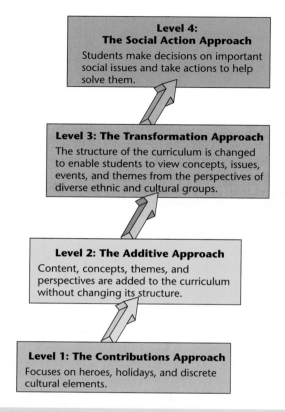

Level 4:
The Social Action Approach

Students make decisions on important social issues and take actions to help solve them.

Level 3: The Transformation Approach

The structure of the curriculum is changed to enable students to view concepts, issues, events, and themes from the perspectives of diverse ethnic and cultural groups.

Level 2: The Additive Approach

Content, concepts, themes, and perspectives are added to the curriculum without changing its structure.

Level 1: The Contributions Approach

Focuses on heroes, holidays, and discrete cultural elements.

REFLECTION: Think back to your own schooling. At which of Banks' levels would you place your own multicultural education? Provide supporting evidence. As a teacher, which of these levels do you want to reach and teach? Explain.

4. The fourth level, *social action,* goes beyond the transformation approach. Students not only learn to view issues from multiple perspectives but also become directly involved in solving related problems. At this level, a school would address social and economic needs here and abroad, advocate human rights and peace, and work to ensure that the school building and activities did not harm the environment. Rather than political passivity, the typical by-product of many curricular programs, this approach promotes decision making and social action to achieve multicultural goals and a more vibrant democracy.

Multicultural education also seeks to help all students develop more positive attitudes toward different racial, ethnic, cultural, and religious groups. According to a 1990s survey of more than 1,000 young people between the ages of 15 and 24 conducted by People for the American Way, most respondents felt their attitudes toward race relations were healthier than those of their parents. Yet about half described the state of race relations in the United States as generally bad. Fifty-five percent of African Americans and whites said they were "uneasy" rather than "comfortable" in dealing with members of the other racial group.[29] How to encourage students to become more "comfortable" with each other depends at least in part on the skills and insights the teacher brings to the classroom, what some term *culturally responsive teaching.*

As I look back over a lifetime of teaching, one special student stands out. Kou was the most memorable student I've ever taught. Short, bandy-legged, and incredibly strong for a 13-year-old, he had come from a rural mountain village deep within Laos to my special-education class in the Santa Barbara suburbs. Although he was no bigger than an American nine-year-old, the hormones of puberty had thrown a dark fuzz over his lip. His voice was deep, a shock coming from that small a body. Often, he wore a bemused expression, compounded of amazement and tolerance for the Americans who were so different from his countrymen in pastoral Laos.

On the playground, Kou was king. He could throw farther, higher, and harder than any other child in school. He was unsurpassed at *hack,* a Laotian game played with the head and feet that seemed like a cross between volleyball and soccer. And in soccer, he was the best. He also carved wonderful wooden tops, which served as trade goods for the American treasures the other boys had.

In the classroom, however, Kou had a problem. The letters, numbers, and words that he painfully memorized one week seemed to vanish during the next.

Although I tried every trick in my teaching bag, nothing seemed to work. With my help, Kou attempted all sorts of experiments designed to help him learn: writing in colored chalk, making clay letters, drawing on the playground. Throughout every effort, he remained cheerful and willing. His attitude seemed to be, "Well, this is how it is in America." But his skills did not improve.

Over time, I noticed that Kou often sang to himself as he worked. "Kou, tell me about your song," I said one day. In his halting English, he told me that the song was about a woman whose man had left her all alone.

"Write it down, Mrs. Nolan," demanded La, his friend. And so our song translation project began. As the class chimed in and squabbled over the meaning of different words, Kou sang, thought, then said the words in his fractured English. I wrote the song down on a sheet of paper. When I was finished, the children all read the song aloud, then sang it with Kou. The next day, my students brought tapes of their native music to school. Suddenly, we had a full-fledged language-experience project underway! As we listened, hummed, and made illustrated booklets about the songs and read them back, the legends and stories of Laos and the Hmong people began to tumble from Kou. For the first time, he had a reason to communicate.

Brief, primitive, and loaded with mistakes, Kou's stories became the foundation for his reading, writing, and language instruction. Never a fan of basal readers, I used this experience as an opportunity to leave the textbooks behind. Kou's quickly improving skills were a source of pride for both of us. When Kou was 15, he left us for junior high. By then he could read at a third-grade level and do survival math. He still had that sweet smile and he still sang softly as he worked. He still longed for the hills of Laos and his old job of herding ducks beside a lake, but he spoke and wrote much better English.

And me? How much I had learned from Kou. Not only did he open the door into a rich and mysterious realm where ghosts walked and crocodiles roamed, but he taught me something about how to be a teacher. From him I learned about the value of starting with a student's interests—and about how powerful a learning tool sharing a culture can be.

SOURCE: Virginia Nolan, "The Song in His Heart," *Instructor* 101, no. 8 (1992), p. 94.

REFLECTION: The section on Multicultural Education lists four levels devised by James Banks. On what level would you place Mrs. Nolan's cultural approach?

 ## Culturally Responsive Teaching

A key assumption of multicultural education is that students learn in different ways, and that effective teachers recognize and respond to these differences. **Culturally responsive teaching** focuses on the learning strengths of students, and mediates the frequent mismatch between home and school cultures. Gloria Ladson-Billings, a professor at The University of Wisconsin, offers a powerful example of culturally relevant teaching. She wanted to find out what behaviors make some teachers successful with African American children, while others are not. She asked parents and principals in four schools serving primarily African American students to nominate "excellent teachers," teachers they would rate as successful. As you might expect, principals chose teachers who had low numbers of discipline referrals, high attendance rates, and high standardized test scores. Parents, on the other hand, selected teachers who were enthusiastic, respectful, and understood that students need to operate in both the white world and their local community. Nine teachers, white and black, made both lists, and eight of them agreed to participate in her study. After several years of observations and interviews, she was baffled: their personalities, teaching strategies, and styles were entirely different; there seem to be no common patterns. She was close to throwing in the towel when she finally saw the subtle, but striking, commonalities.

First, all of these eight teachers had chosen to teach in these more challenging schools, and felt responsible for the academic success of each student. Second, they were sensitive to race discrimination in society; they actively fought bias and prejudice, and wanted their students to do the same. For example, some of these teachers had students rewrite out-of-date textbooks or work on projects to improve their community. And finally, the teachers viewed both the home and school as connected, and seized opportunities to learn from their neighborhoods. They honored the crafts and traditions in the community, inviting parents to share traditional cooking in the school. One teacher allowed students to use "home English" in class but required that students also master Standard English. Students were expected to learn both languages well. Teachers realized that they too were learners, and needed to be open to new information. **Gloria Ladson-Billings** developed three promising culturally responsive principles for teaching not only African American children, but others as well:[30]

1. **Students must experience academic success, which leads to a stronger self-esteem. Esteem is built on solid academic accomplishment.** We intuitively know that students who do not feel good about themselves have a tough time in (and beyond) school. But this is not enough. For school success, students' self-esteem needs to be built on solid academic accomplishment. Teachers must create lessons that are responsive to student learning styles, *and* allow student mastery of the basic knowledge and skills necessary for success in today's society. The bottom line: students feel good about themselves when there is real academic progress.

2. **Students should develop and maintain cultural competence, and the student's home culture is an opportunity for learning.** Too many teachers have been taught only about classroom teaching skills, and not about community outreach possibilities. Ladson-Billings' research teaches us that we must expand our concept of the classroom to include the community. When there is friction between school and home, academic progress suffers. Put more positively, when teachers move beyond their classroom and integrate learning with the local community, they can create a more positive, seamless, and mutually supportive academic environment. For example, a local African storyteller can visit the class and relate an African folktale. Students could use the experience as a springboard for their writing or drawing. Or a local politician could be invited to class to share his or her public service work, challenging students to develop their own vision of community service and social activism. Following the presentation, students might do just that: organize a class project to improve the quality of community life. Identifying community resources and connecting classroom activities to those resources are keystones to creating a fruitful academic climate for students.

3. **Students must develop critical consciousness and actively challenge social injustice.** A culturally relevant teacher needs to do more than connect with student needs and the local community; a culturally relevant teacher also works to improve the quality of life in the school and community. Do you remember the disconnect you may have felt between life in school, the world you read about in textbooks, and "the real world" you lived in? Schools too often live in a sanitized bubble, separate from the world's problems. Culturally relevant teachers break that bubble and, along with their students, work to improve the quality of life. For instance, if school textbooks are weak and dated, a teacher might encourage students to rewrite them. The result would be more realistic and current texts, as well as student practice in writing. Or perhaps there are serious health problems in the community. Students might volunteer to attract additional resources to the community health clinic and in the process learn how local government works. Confronting and eliminating real social problems is the third component of a culturally relevant classroom.

As you prepare to teach, it is helpful for you to consider what it means to be a culturally responsive teacher, to broaden your view of what it takes to be successful in the classroom. Let's take a moment to think about what this means for your own teacher preparation. To be competent in each of Ladson-Billings' three points, you will need to acquire certain *skills, attitudes,* and *knowledge.* What teaching *skills* will you need to be a culturally responsive teacher for all your students? You will want to diagnose different student needs and plan for different learning styles. You will want to develop critical thinking skills and include all your students in an equitable manner. You will even want to make certain that you can be silent and listen to the answers that are volunteered by all the students (a skill called "wait time"). Studies show that even teachers with the best of intentions too often fail to use these skills. (We describe equitable teaching skills later in this text in Chapter 11, Teacher Effectiveness.)

What *attitudes* will you need to be a culturally responsive teacher? How do you approach teaching students whose background may be quite different from your own? Since most of us have grown up in a segregated community, there is an excellent chance that most of your friends are similar to you in race, class, and ethnicity. You probably share a common set of values and opinions, seeing the world through a lens forged in your own socialization. As you prepare to teach, you may want to make an extra effort to move out of your familiar milieu and seek different views. The more voices you hear, the more likely you will be able to appreciate different life experiences and develop attitudes that are accepting of people who at first glance may seem very different from you.

Finally, as you prepare to teach, you will want to acquire *knowledge* about different group experiences in order to be a culturally responsive teacher. You already bring to the classroom some knowledge of other groups, but this knowledge is limited and some of it may be inaccurate. You will want to educate yourself about your future students, and the educational implications of their cultural backgrounds. This chapter helps you move down that path. For example, many African American communities often emphasize aural and participatory learning over writing. If you ignore this insight and use only writing activities in class, student performance may suffer.[31] As another example, research suggests that many girls and women personalize knowledge, and prefer learning through experience and first-hand observation.[32] Creating personal connections and examples may increase the success of your female students. In fact, responding to all types of student diversity is simply good teaching. A Head Start teacher in Michigan, in this case teaching poor, white, rural students, shares her view of culturally responsive teaching:

> I believe that it is my responsibility to learn as much as I can about the child's family and their culture and then implement that into my classroom, so that the child can see his/her culture is a part of our classroom and that I respect them and their family and their culture. It can be hard; I don't want to present any new stereotypes to these kids, so I ask the parents a lot of questions. Sometimes I get the answers and sometimes I don't, but at least they see I am trying.[33]

The challenge for teachers is to acquire useful and accurate cultural insights that help connect the classroom and the culture, while avoiding the trap of stereotypic thinking. What's the difference between a useful cultural insight and a damaging stereotype? That critical distinction is explored in the next section.

Stereotypes

In the last chapter, we outlined the differences between stereotypes and generalizations, and now we examine these concepts more closely. **Stereotypes** are absolute beliefs that all members of a group have a fixed set of characteristics. The word *stereotype* originated in the print shop. It is literally a type—a one-piece plate that repeats a pattern with no individuality. Today's cultural stereotypes also ignore individuality and are repeatedly applied to all members of a group. People who use stereotypes try to save time by short-circuiting the thinking process, just like the original stereotype saved time in the printing process. A set of characteristics is simply attributed to individuals based on their membership in a group with no qualifiers. Simplistic sentences are used with words like "all Hispanics are" and applied to every member of the group without distinction. Actually, stereotypes are examples of sloppy thinking that undermine the critical reflection that we want our students to develop. For example, a stereotype might naively proclaim that Hispanics are poor students, Asians are math geniuses, Jews are wealthy, and African Americans are great athletes. Stereotypes are impervious to contradictory information. Find a poor Jew, a Hispanic with a doctorate, an Asian dropping out of school, or an unathletic African American and each is thought to be an anomaly, the exception to the rule. The rule, the stereotype, endures. Stereotypes not only hurt people, they block learning. Stereotypic thinking obstructs a search for new information—not just "contradictory" information—but any information that might add to the complex, rich understanding of an individual or group. Stereotypes ignore nuances, qualifiers,

Consider these three students. What assumptions do you make about them based on this photo? Are these assumptions based on stereotypes?

and subtleties that might more accurately characterize the group. This willingness to engage in complex thinking is what students need and, unfortunately, stereotypes short-circuit thoughtful reflection.

Stereotype Threat

Let's look at an example of how damaging stereotypes can be. Opinion polls suggest that about half of white America endorses common stereotypes about blacks and Hispanics, such as the belief that they are not very intelligent. Such stereotypes influence expectations and behaviors not only of whites who hold them, but also of blacks and Hispanics who must live in a society marked by such beliefs. For example, an African American called on in class realizes that an incorrect answer may confirm the stereotype of inferior intelligence. For this student, simply speaking in class can be risky. As you might imagine, the risk intensifies on high-stakes tests. Consider the following studies: African American and white college students were asked to take a difficult standardized verbal examination. In the control group, the test was presented in a typical way, as a measure of intelligence. In the experimental group, the students were told that ability was not being assessed; rather the psychology of their verbal problem-solving was being researched. The two groups were matched so that student abilities, time to take the test, and the test itself were similar. In the nonthreatening experimental groups, black test takers solved about twice as many problems as the ones in the control group, while the white students solved the same number in both groups. In a similar study, researchers found that simply asking students to record their race before taking a test had a similar devastating impact on black performance.[34]

This dramatic outcome has been termed **stereotype threat,** a measure of how social context, such as self-image, trust in others, and a sense of belonging, can influence academic performance. When an individual is aware of a stereotype, he or she is more likely to behave like the stereotype than if it did not exist. Studies indicate that students who care the most about their academic performance are the most vulnerable to stereotype threat. Stereotype threat may explain in part why African Americans (and others) perform better in college than their SAT scores predict, and why standardized test scores can be so misleading. Nor are blacks alone. Latinos on English tests, females on math tests, and elderly people on short-term memory tests also fall victim to stereotype threat. In fact, even students with strong test scores can fall prey. White male engineering students with very high SAT scores were told that their performance on a test would help researchers understand the math superiority of Asians. Hearing about the comparison to strong Asian students, their scores fell. None of us is immune from stereotype threat.

Stereotypes limit students by teaching them that intellect is a fixed trait, that some groups are naturally brighter than others, and that their future was determined at birth. The belief that group differences are unchangeable is not a helpful construct for teachers. A person's intellect, like a person's brain, grows and changes. Human potential is amazing. If students see their brain and their intellect as muscles that can be taught to grow and become stronger, stereotype threat is diminished, and test scores rise.[35] Imagine the impact of stereotypes not only on intellectual performance, but on other characteristics as well. Teaching also deals with ethics, values, and character of students, and damaging stereotypes can inhibit this learning as well. Fortunately, stereotype threat can be overcome with proper instruction.[36]

You can diminish stereotype threat by ensuring that your curriculum represents diversity across race, ethnicity, gender, religious, and socioeconomic class. Or perhaps you prefer to confront the problem directly: explain stereotype threat in class and explore with your students strategies to neutralize it. The one thing you do not want to do is ignore the damage done by stereotype threat.

Generalizations

Generalizations recognize that there are trends over large numbers of people. Members of religious, racial, or ethnic groups share certain experiences and may share certain similarities. Generalizations offer insights, not hard and fast conclusions like stereotypes, and unlike a stereotype, a generalization does not assume that everyone in a group has a fixed set of characteristics. So the generalization that many Japanese value and seek higher education still holds if one encounters a Japanese dropout who dislikes school. The generalization is never intended to be applied to all; it is open to modification as new information is gathered, and there are always exceptions. Note that generalizations use words like "many," "often," or "tend to." Moreover, while stereotypes view people in one group or another, generalizations recognize that people belong to many groups simultaneously. Some Jews are Hispanic, some are Asian, and some are Arab, yet they are all Jews.

Generalizations offer us a hunch or clue about a group, and sometimes these clues are useful in planning for teaching. When you begin teaching you may know very little about your students, and a generalization offers a useful starting point. Think of it as an educated guess. As you learn more and more about each student, you will realize which generalizations are appropriate and which are not.

How can we use generalizations to develop culturally responsive teaching? Let's assume that a teacher has many Native American students in class, does some research and discovers that most Native American students prefer to learn in a cooperative group, valuing community and family over individual competition. Rather than teaching in the familiar teacher-centered manner, she modifies her plan and creates student groups to work on several academic topics. Using open-ended questions, she asks the groups to share their experiences, and patiently waits for each group response, realizing that Native American children may prefer to carefully consider their comments and compose their thoughts. When she can, the teacher uses natural phenomena in her explanations, since Native Americans often value both natural and supernatural forces. She may also integrate Indian words, symbols, or legends as appropriate. By building the learning on sharing rather than competition, and on valuing tribal experiences and beliefs, the teacher is increasing her chance of connecting with most of her students.[37] Since generalizations are flexible, the teacher is free to use a different approach with some or all of her students if she later discovers that they prefer a different learning style.

As you become a more experienced teacher, you will become more skilled at confronting all kinds of limiting stereotypes, developing useful teaching generalizations, and becoming a more culturally responsive teacher. In fact, let's start that process right now.

www.mhhe.com/ sadker8e

INTERACTIVE ACTIVITY
Multicultural Literacy.
Match multicultural terms
with their descriptions.

Teaching Your Diverse Students

Consider yourself a teacher working with the nation's diverse students. If you are teaching in a community that reflects the nation's population, your class of 40 students might include:[38]

17 white children

6 Hispanic children

6 children who do not speak English at home

5 poor children

5 African American children

1 Asian American child

The class might also include a Jewish, Native American, or Arab heritage child, not to mention multiracial or biracial students. Although we lack firm statistics concerning the number of gay, lesbian, bisexual, or transgendered children, estimates are that perhaps two or three of your students would fall into these categories. Planning for this class is quite a challenge!

The reality is that hyper-segregation of our schools makes it unlikely that you will be teaching students from all of these groups in the same class at the same time. Unlikely, but not impossible. And certainly, over time, you may teach many if not all of them. So let's meet your future students.

Meet Your Seventh-Grade Class

In this section, we profile eight students, students similar to ones you may some day teach. Each student is from a cultural, ethnic, racial, or other group, bringing to your class a rich history and different learning preferences. It is important to keep in mind that each student is an individual, and any generalizations you make initially may change over time. But for now, let's take step one of culturally responsive teaching and learn about our students. For each student, we ask you to identify a generalization that might influence your teaching and enhance learning. As you read each student's description, you will encounter hints about potential generalizations. You may want to draw on your own knowledge as well. When you teach, you will want to learn more about your students through reading and personal interactions. But for now, let's establish your baseline, what you know about groups as you begin your teacher education program, and what you will want to learn in the future.

This exercise is not simple. You may be pushed beyond your comfort zone, and formulating generalizations will be a demanding task. If you are baffled, venture your best guess. At the end of the section we shall provide you with sample generalizations that should help you think in new and constructive ways.

We will start you off by suggesting a few generalizations for the first student, Lindsey Maria Riley, who is Navajo. Then you are on your own. Try to identify at least one generalization for each of the other students. Later in the section you can compare your responses to our suggestions.[39] Now, meet (and begin thinking about) your students.

Lindsey Maria Riley (Navajo)

Lindsey grew up in a small, poor town in the Southwest. Although Lindsey did not live on a reservation, her family adhered to traditional Navajo ways. Lindsey followed tradition when not at school and spent time mostly with girls and women learning to cook, make pottery, and weave at an early age. Navajo boys would hunt, make tools, and live more physical lives, quite separate from the girls. Lindsey's family did not have a lot of money and received assistance for her school supplies from *Save the Children*, a nonprofit organization. Lindsey enjoyed the school she attended that was run by the Bureau of Indian Affairs. But this year, her family moved to your community and she is a new student in your class.

Most of the other students in your class have only seen Indians in movies, like *The Last of the Mohicans,* or on television. Some of Lindsey's classmates believe that Indians lived a long time ago on the frontier, and are surprised to learn they still exist. Some have heard their parents say that Indians make a fortune running casinos. But neither casinos nor movies explain Lindsey. And, Lindsey does not explain herself—she does not talk much. The students in your class like Lindsey, although they haven't really "figured" her out. To put it politely, Lindsey is a curiosity to them.

You recently asked the class to write a brief report on a president for Presidents Day. Lindsey never handed in her report. When you asked her about it, she said that all the presidents had done bad things to her people and that she would rather report on a different topic. Today, she told you that the school mascot, an Indian chief, bothers her.

Potentially Useful Generalization: _____

_____

_____.

Sample Response

[Note: Native Americans are not one group but hundreds of tribal nations with different languages and beliefs. Learning about tribal distinctions is a useful first step for teachers and students.] In this sample response, we will offer you a series of possible and well-accepted generalizations, but there are others as well. If we do not mention your generalization, you may want to research it to see if you are correct.

Potentially Useful Generalization: *Many tribes revere modesty. Group, rather than individual, recognition is typically preferred, as is cooperation over competition and patience rather than immediate gratification (qualities too often lost in contemporary classrooms). Additionally, visual and artistic learning, and "hands-on learning" are valued by many tribal cultures. Using American Indian cultural beliefs and insights during a lesson can help Native American students feel connected to the academic program. The supernatural, intuition, and spiritual beliefs are valued by many tribes and could also be incorporated in classroom instruction.*

[In terms of the casino-to-riches stereotype mentioned in the profile, less than 1 percent of Indians work in casinos, and the casino profits often go to schools and community improvement projects.]

Marcus Griffin (African American)

Marcus is in your class because of your school district's policy to voluntarily bus African American students from across the county line, a rare event these days. He lives with his mother, who works at the post office, about 10 miles from school. His older brother never attended this school; in fact, he never graduated from high school. You hear rumors that he is in and out of trouble. Marcus has only a few friends in class, a situation made worse by the bus schedule. After his last class, he hurries to catch his bus for the long ride home. Because of this schedule, he cannot participate in after-school activities, sports, and clubs. Marcus' neighborhood friends do not really talk much about school. They do not like the fact that Marcus chooses to bus to a white community instead of hanging out with them. Marcus feels that he is growing further and further away from his roots.

Marcus loves reading and writing, but feels like an alien in his new school. Virtually everything he sees or reads in school is about the history, accomplishments, and interests of whites. Only rarely are his people discussed, and then it is not in a very positive light. Marcus finds the teachers in your school pretty serious, and he decides not to rock the boat by suggesting different ideas in class. There is only one African American teacher in your school and only a few black students. Marcus would like to go to college, but his family's finances are limited. Some of the black kids talk about going to college on an athletic scholarship, but Marcus is not very athletic. You wish that you could connect with him, but when you try, he rarely looks at you. Like several other students in your school, he sometimes interrupts in class, a habit you find annoying. You hope for the best for Marcus, but you are not optimistic.

Potentially Useful Generalization: _____

_____

_____.

Ana Garcia (Mexican American)

Ana Garcia is one of the warmest and most involved students in your class. She is one of those students who actually hugs people, including you! She loves to ask questions, works closely with her peers, and seems eager to explore new topics. Her favorite topic is history. Ana loves doing class projects, yet she is quite modest about her work.

Although Ana was born in the United States, her parents, who work as laborers, emigrated from Mexico. Ana is the only one in her family who speaks any English, but most of the time she speaks Spanish with friends and family. Unfortunately, despite her motivation, Ana's English language skills lag behind those of her peers, and the gap seems to be widening. Since you do not speak Spanish, you suggest that she participate in some of the after-school activities where she might have more opportunities to work on her English. Ana listened to your advice, but explains that she goes right home after school to care for her younger siblings. Although Ana loves school, you get the sense that she is getting frustrated and is already focusing on her future family responsibilities and becoming a mother.

Potentially Useful Generalization: _____

_____

_____.

Myth 1—Culturally responsive teaching is a new approach intended to meet the needs of poor, urban students of color.   Teaching has always been culturally responsive, but primarily responsive to the values of white, Euro-American, middle-class students. That is why schools historically have emphasized individual success more than group success, strict adherence to time schedules, knowledge valued through analytical reasoning, self-sufficiency, and even dress codes. More inclusive culturally responsive teaching embraces the values and experiences of other cultures as well.

Myth 2—Only teachers of color can actually be culturally responsive to students of color.   Race is not an obstacle to culturally responsive teaching; ignorance is. Through teacher training, teachers of any cultural background can gain the knowledge, skills, and attitudes needed to teach children from diverse cultures. In turn, since most teachers are white, they can share important lessons about the dominant culture.

Myth 3—Culturally responsive teaching is little more than a collection of teaching ideas and practices to motivate students of color.   Culturally responsive teaching offers a new way of looking at the roles of teachers and students. Culturally relevant teachers are committed to valuing the experiences of their students and working toward a more just society, far more profound goals than simply a collection of teaching ideas.

Myth 4—Culturally relevant teachers must master all the critical details of many cultures.   It is unrealistic to expect teachers to master the intricacies of many cultures. But over time, thoughtful teachers will abandon simplistic, stereotypic thinking as they gain insights into cultural differences that influence behavior and learning.

Myth 5—Culturally relevant teaching categorizes children, which feeds stereotypic thinking.   Actually, culturally relevant teaching reduces stereotypic thinking by asking teachers to be reflective. They must consider student experiences and backgrounds, create teaching opportunities that respond to student learning styles, hold high expectations for all students, and help students experience academic success.

SOURCE: Adapted from Jacqueline Jordan and Beverley Jeanne Armento, *Culturally Responsive Teaching* (Boston: McGraw-Hill, 2001).

REFLECTION: Why do you think these myths are so prevalent? What additional myths about culturally relevant teaching can you add? How has your understanding of culturally relevant teaching expanded by reading this chapter?

Kasem Pravat (Asian American from Thailand)

Kasem is a very pleasant student who seems content in your class. He is always respectful and calm. Kasem works very hard. His papers are done with great care, and his test grades are strong. The one skill you would like him to develop is speaking up in class. Sometimes, he seems painfully shy.

You met Kasem's family briefly before school started, and they impressed you as agreeable, patient, and hard-working people. Kasem reflects those values. His family came from Thailand only recently, but since Kasem studied English in Thailand, his language adjustment here was relatively smooth. His favorite subject is math, and he is already talking about majoring in engineering in college. Kasem is one of the few students in your middle school class who is not only talking about college, but has already identified a major. Kasem is protective and caring of his younger sister, Keyo, who is in the neighboring elementary school.

Potentially Useful Generalization: _____

_____

_____.

Ariel Klein (Jewish American)

Ariel is an excellent student, in part because she is so hard working. Ariel's family is originally from an Orthodox Jewish neighborhood in New York City. Your community does not have an Orthodox synagogue for observant Jews who want to strictly follow their faith, so the Kleins now practice the more secular Conservative Judaism. Maintaining a *kosher* home has proven too difficult for the family since the nearest kosher food store is almost two hours away. Ariel and her family still observe Rosh Hashanah and Yom Kippur, which caused a major disruption in September when those holidays kept her from taking your academic skills assessment test. It was very difficult scheduling a re-test because the arranged make-up day was the following Saturday, her Sabbath. After several delays, she finally took the exam in the main office over two weekdays, but had to miss two more days of class, which troubled her.

Ariel is very outgoing. She can always be counted on to ask questions. Many questions. Her outspoken nature has turned some of the other students off, and to be honest, at times you too have found it irritating. Some call her "pushy." Lately, she seems to have more questions than you have answers. But she is a strong student who motivates others to work harder on school projects. She tells her friends that she would like to be a doctor some day, and if you were a betting sort, you would put your money on Ariel being just as hard working in medical school as she has been in middle school.

Potentially Useful Generalization: _____

_____

_____.

Mary Goode (rural white)

Mary grew up in a small town tucked away in the mountains of West Virginia. She attended a local elementary school with an enrollment of only 120 students in grades 1–8. Mary went through the first six years of elementary school with pretty much the same close group of 13 classmates. Her school only had nine classes and nine teachers. However, only a few teachers stayed during her entire time at the school. Since she helped out in the local food co-op, Mary knew virtually all of the families in town. The few she missed during the weekdays at the co-op she would see at church on Sunday. Her parents talked about her brother doing well in high school and then perhaps opening a business. For Mary, the conversation revolved around potential suitors and some day converting her parents into grandparents.

When Mary moved to your much larger community, she was overwhelmed. She says that she was never with so many students in one school or in one class in her life, and you suspect this might be why she is overwhelmed. You also think she might be reacting to the fact that the children in this town are all so different from those in her old town. Mary is now quite introverted and rarely speaks, in part because some students make fun of her accent. She is self-conscious about her background and all the things she does not seem to know that everyone else knows. Her clothes draw special attention by the other girls who explain how "yesterday" they are. When you finally meet her parents, they are very quiet and also a bit overwhelmed. They were reticent to come to school. Although Mary takes her school work seriously and is doing fine right now, you are concerned that she may get lost in this new crowd, perhaps turn off from school, or worse yet, drop out.

Potentially Useful Generalization: _____

_____

_____.

_____

Ibrahim Mouawad (Arab American)

Although Ibrahim has lived in your community his entire life, many see him as a foreigner. His family was one of the few who invited you over for dinner, and you still recall how warm they were toward you. The food was wonderful, although the names of some of those dishes fled your mind quickly.

When students ask Ibrahim where he is from, he says the Middle East, but avoids identifying a particular country. Since the September 11, 2001, attack and the war in Iraq, your community has been wary of the few Arab families living here. You can see that tension in the eyes and behaviors of some of your students. You find yourself paying a little more attention when Ibrahim and Ariel are in the same group or have extended interactions together. You too have been influenced by the Arab-Israeli conflict. Perhaps you are overreacting, but you wonder if Ibrahim's unnamed country is Palestine or Iraq.

Ibrahim enjoys school, and although quiet in class, he is extremely polite to you and his classmates. But it is clear that he does not always "fit in." During Ramadan, a Moslem religious time for fasting, for example, he avoided the cafeteria during lunch. No one talked much about it, but you wonder what it must be like to smell food and see everyone else eating while you are fasting. Lunchtime saw him sitting by himself for the whole month of Ramadan. Like Ariel, Ibrahim has real problems with cafeteria foods, which make no allowances for Jewish or Moslem dietary laws.

Potentially Useful Generalization: _____

_____

_____.

_____

Carlos Martinez (Gay)

Carlos always felt different from other boys. A year ago he realized that he was gay. His mom and dad had divorced when he was younger, and he is now estranged from his father, who is uncomfortable with Carlos' sexual orientation. His mother continues to accept him for who he is and relies on him to help care for his younger sister. Carlos is now in your class and he is doing well. Schoolwork has always been easy for him, but he and his friends are concerned about hateful comments, like "fag," they sometimes hear in the hallways. They decided to start a Gay-Straight Alliance (GSA) to educate their peers.

The GSA was approved by the principal and began planning a fundraiser to buy holiday gifts for underprivileged children in the community. When word reached a conservative community group, however, protests began pouring into the superintendent's office that the middle school has a "gay club that is promoting homosexuality."

The GSA was invited to speak at the school board meeting. Though a small group of parents complained about the GSA, the school board members were impressed with the maturity and compassion displayed by Carlos and the other students. The school board voted to affirm the right of the GSA, and other student clubs, like the Bible Club, to meet in the school. You are excited that next month, Carlos will be speaking at the state capitol to testify before the House Education Committee in support of antibullying legislation. But you worry, and hope that no *backlash* will follow him here.

Potentially Useful Generalization: _____

_____

_____.

So how did you do? Some of these scenarios may have been more challenging than others, and noting all the possible generalizations would be a Herculean task. Before we share our responses, look back at yours. Were some generalizations easier to identify than others? Or were all a challenge? What does that tell you about your own education, about what you have experienced and learned about other groups? Now you have an idea of what you need to learn to become more culturally knowledgeable. If you struggled with creating generalizations, you will want to learn more about different groups so that you can one day become a more effective culturally responsive teacher. Here are some generalizations for each student:

Marcus Griffin (African American)

Potentially Useful Generalizations: Research concerning African Americans indicates that many benefit from kinesthetic and activity-oriented learning; others have a strong oral language tradition—calling out in class may reflect interest and involvement, not rudeness; they tend to value imagination, imagery, and humor in learning; they also may value spirituality rather than a mechanistic approach to life. Also, not looking directly at an adult is often a sign of respect in this community.

Ana Garcia (Mexican American)

Potentially Useful Generalizations: One generalization is that many Mexican American students feel a loyalty and commitment to the family. Another, that many adhere to traditional gender roles in a patriarchal family. Mexican American students often prefer to work in peer groups rather than alone, and prefer structured learning environments; and the high school dropout rates of Latinos and Latinas are very high, with estimates ranging from 40 to 50 percent.

Kasem Pravat (Asian American from Thailand)

Potentially Useful Generalizations: [Note: Generalizations about Asian Americans are by nature a "broad brush" since Americans group Japanese, Indians, Chinese, Pakistanis, Indonesians, and Vietnamese—about half the world population—under the term "Asian." Learning about each unique culture and country is critical.] Thais typically honor their national independence, many are fatalistic, and they may be offended by someone touching their head, the most sacred part of their body. Many cast their eyes down as a sign of respect.

Thais often value self-discipline and academic success, seek cooperation and reconciliation, can be quite modest, might work hard to avoid confrontation, are often quiet, and typically revere teachers.

Ariel Klein (Jewish American)

Potentially Useful Generalizations: Jewish families in general are strong supporters of education and children are often academically diligent with high career expectations; Jewish holidays can conflict with school calendars, since schools are scheduled to conform to Christian holidays; observant Jews are unable to attend school functions on Friday nights and Saturdays, and may not be able to eat in the cafeteria; Jewish-Gentile conflict has existed for centuries and provides a disturbing undercurrent of anti-Semitism in some communities; and most Jews live in urban communities and on the east and west coasts.

Mary Goode (rural white)

Potentially Useful Generalizations: About one in five students attend rural schools; they are more likely to graduate from high school than urban or suburban students, but less likely to attend college; rural white students typically attend smaller schools and may struggle in a larger school community; Appalachian families are often traditional and patriarchal, with boys being favored.

Ibrahim Mouawad (Arab American)

Potentially Useful Generalizations: Arab homelands, rich heritage, and historical contributions are often discounted in the West and in the curriculum. Also, cultural, linguistic, religious, and national distinctions are typically ignored (the word *Arabs* refers to different nationalities, religions, and ethnic groups connected by a common language and culture). Close family relationships and respect for elders are common. Arabs are often generous and hospitable to friends and even strangers. Arabs often excel in math.

Carlos Martinez (Gay)

Potentially Useful Generalizations: GLBT students are often "overachievers" and show a high degree of creativity and energy. They are often committed to resolving social injustice. Some GLBT students, however, prefer to remain closeted.

And one last reminder that these generalizations offer you a starting point, a place where research suggests you are most likely to reach success. But once you get to know your students, each student becomes an individual and will not always "fit" the generalization. So after working with Ibrahim for several months, if you discover that despite the generalization about Arab proficiency in math, Ibrahim is struggling in that subject, then, of course, you would offer extra instruction in math. Individual needs always trump group tendencies.

Diversity Assets

Once you begin to formulate generalizations, you will realize that learning about students and their unique backgrounds can be a growth experience for the entire class, including the teacher. Even casual interactions can enhance learning for all, for each group brings rich and unique insights to school. These insights and experiences, these different ways of knowing and seeing the world, are *diversity assets*.

Let's visit those eight students in your class one more time. In each case, we will suggest a potential asset that the student's background may bring to your class, a way that this student's culture enriches learning.

Lindsey may be able to share her people's reverence for the earth and steward-ship of the environment, their spiritual insights, artistic talents, oral traditions, and preference for cooperative learning. Perhaps her tribe's warm interpersonal relationships will help build the class community.

Marcus may offer a "lens" to help others see invisible white privilege. Perhaps Marcus will share a history of oral traditions and be another voice for cooper-ative learning.

Ana can contribute a second language, helping monolingual students broaden their linguistic horizons. Mexican American warmth and loyalty may also help create a class community.

Kasem can share yet another language and culture, a culture that may also enhance class cohesion. He may also model academic persistence for others.

Ariel may support Kasem in promoting an academic focus and class dialogue. She may also offer insights into one of the world's oldest religions and cul-tures, and help others see how Christian beliefs and practices shape "secular" practices in America.

Mary can offer insights into life in rural America, and may be particularly resourceful since growing up in a rural community often fosters independence. Rural life also encourages a closer community, sometimes lost in today's fast-paced lifestyles.

Ibrahim brings another language to class, and may provide insights into the rich Arab culture and history, particularly crucial in today's world of ethnic and religious intolerance.

Carlos may be striving toward social justice and equality in the face of adver-sity. And in communities with little racial or ethnic diversity, Carlos may offer a diversity opportunity, a way to learn from the experiences and insights of others.

These students offer what a textbook or a curriculum cannot: a human con-nection to the world's diversity. Along with honoring their backgrounds and insights, their individual choices must be honored as well. Some teachers fall into the trap of inviting a Navajo, an African American, or a Mexican American student to be the voice of their people. How do black Americans feel about this, or what do Hispanics think about this? Crowning a black or Hispanic stu-dent as a spokesperson is unwise; one student can-not and should not speak for an entire group, and such a request can make a student feel uncomfort-able. But as students volunteer their stories and opin-ions, and communicate informally with each other, their diversity assets will enrich learning for all.

IMAGINE . . .

The Best Teachers for the Students with the Most Need

Imagine an immediate reassignment of the nation's best teachers to the schools serving the most needy students. Imagine that those same students were guaranteed places in state and regional colleges and universities. Imagine that within one generation we lift those students out of poverty.

SOURCE: Gloria Ladson-Billings, AERA Address, April 2006.

Diversity is a potential asset to every classroom.

Teaching Skills

Recognizing the experiences and histories of all your students is an important first step in creating a climate that honors and celebrates diversity. Your teaching behaviors should also reinforce your commitment to equity. All students benefit when they feel safe, their unique needs and interests are recognized, and they are part of classroom discourse. Teachers need to share their time and talent fairly, offering helpful feedback and encouragement to each student, and ensuring that the curriculum is meaningful. We will describe equitable teaching skills in Chapter 11, but here are some suggestions for effective and equitable teaching strategies. To help you remember them, we created the acronym *DIVERSE*.

Diverse Instructional Materials: Some say that an effective curriculum is both a window and a mirror. Are all your students able to see themselves in your curricular mirror? Are all parts of the world seen through your curricular window? Are diverse thoughts, views, and people woven into the curriculum? Do class and school displays reflect all the world's cultures and peoples?

Inclusive: Does your teaching provide opportunities for each student, especially those very quiet students, to participate in class discussions? Sometimes careful planning, thoughtful selection of particular students to respond, and patience can do wonders in encouraging even shy students to participate. Every student deserves a public voice and should be heard.

Variety: Using different teaching strategies—learning styles, sensory channels, and intelligences—can do wonders to involve all. Kinesthetic and artistic activities, cooperative learning, and other approaches honor different ways of learning and allow each student to experience success.

Exploration: Teachers should encourage students to explore new cultures and beliefs, and be open themselves to new ideas. Learning how different peoples view the world can unlock student (and teacher) minds.

Reaction: Often teacher feedback is given too quickly, with little thought, and is of little help. Each student deserves the teacher's specific, timely, honest, and precise comments. With effective feedback, patience, encouragement, and high expectation, all children can learn, and can learn well.

Safety: Without safety and security, little learning is possible. Offensive comments about religion, race, ethnicity, or sexuality and verbal or physical bullying should be quickly confronted and stopped by the teacher.

Evaluation: Teachers often forget that the achievement, aptitude tests, and high-stakes tests are often designed for white, middle-class culture. Teachers should consider a variety of evaluation strategies to assess the unique strengths of each student. Evaluation can assist in student diagnosis and planning effective instruction. It can serve a more constructive purpose than simply ranking and rating students.

These skills should help you to reach out to all your students. While they promote equity, they also promote good teaching. How fortunate we are that equitable teaching skills are also effective teaching skills.

We Are One

In this chapter, we recognize that group differences offer a way of broadening our perspective on what it means to be truly educated. While some have used our differences to demean, we as students and teachers can use these differences as an enormous opportunity to learn about ourselves, our communities, and the world. In this chapter, we see our differences as learning opportunities, assets for teachers and students. We have distinguished between stereotypes and generalizations, and the power of harnessing our diversity assets, the rich resources of experiences, values, and knowledge each group brings to the classroom. We should treat our wondrous diversity "as one of the most exciting parts of our education—an enormous opportunity to see the world in new ways and understand more about humanity. What is education about if not that."[40]

As Hindu tradition reminds us, as we honor one another's differences, we need also to honor what we hold in common. So let's close this chapter by recognizing that we are all part of the human family. In his 1963 commencement speech at American University, John F. Kennedy said: "For in the final analysis, our most basic common link is that we all inhabit this small planet, we all breathe the same air, we all cherish our children's futures, and we are all mortal." Those words still ring true today. According to genome research, human beings are 96 percent alike, no matter where we live, no matter what experiences we have, no matter our color, our language, or our God.[41] Yes, we can do both: honor our common humanity and the richness of our differences.

Not very long ago, an eighth-grade language arts teacher shared Langston Hughes' poem "I, Too, Sing America" with her students.[42] She asked them to create a similar poem based on their own experiences, and some remarkable insights emerged. Her students wrote poems that underscored the continuing racism and sexism in society, as well as profound universal desires to accept and be accepted by others. We use this same activity in our teacher education classes, and each year we learn from our students. Here are three poems written by our teacher education students. You can find more poems on the text Web site, and we invite you to write and submit your own to the Web site. As you read each of these, consider the unique group insights that emerge, as well as the universal connections. If we are to progress, we will need to honor both.

I, too, am an American
I am the trusting farm girl who grew up knowing no strangers
I ventured to the city, where they tell me I am too naïve
But I am not what my white, non-diverse, God-fearing, conservative roots suggest
I have experiences with the good and the bad this world has to offer
Yet, each day I choose to smile and look for the good

Maybe
I am the beginning of this cycle
One smile, one act of trust, one stranger turned friend at a time
I, too, am an American.

Lacey Rosenbaum

I, too, am an American
I am kind-hearted and mean-spirited
I expect everyone to tell me the truth
But I am not straight up with everyone I meet

To white folks, I am "a nice young man" and "a nigger"
To black folks, I am "a positive role model" and "a nigga"
To the rest of the folks, I am every image they see on television or on the streets

I am proud of the decisions I have made in this life
I am also proud of the decisions others have made for me
I am an American black male

John Burns

I, too, speak English
Yes, I am from Chicago
No, I don't have an Asian accent
Yes, I have a membership to a local gym
No, I don't do push-ups on my knuckles in the snow

Yes, I do well in my academics
No, I am not a computer genius
Yes, I am six feet, two inches tall
No, I am not under five feet eight inches tall

I am a human just like you
I eat, breathe, function, just like you
But I do eat with chop sticks
I, too, speak English

Jayson Chang

SUMMARY

www.mhhe.com/
sadker8e

CHAPTER REVIEW

Go to the Online Learning
Center to take a chapter
self-quiz, practice with key
terms, and review concepts
from the chapter.

1. In what ways are American schools failing culturally diverse students?

Today, about one in ten Americans is foreign born, and the native language of well over 30 million Americans is a language other than English. By 2030, half of all school children will be of color. Hispanic, Native American, and African American students score consistently lower on standardized tests than do their Asian and white classmates. Yet, almost half of the nation's historically under-resourced populations, Hispanic, African American, and Native American, are not graduating from high school. And students from low-income families are far more likely to drop out of school than are the children of the wealthy.

2. How do deficit, expectation, and cultural difference theories explain disparate academic performance among various racial, ethnic, and cultural groups?

Most white Americans believe that schools offer equitable educational opportunities to all children, and do not "see" the invisible privileges that many enjoy. Deficit, expectation, and cultural difference theories offer various explanations for the academic gaps that characterize different group performance in America's schools.

3. How do metaphors like "melting pot" and "tossed salad" both capture and mask American identity?

Traditionally, Americans viewed their identity as a simplistic *melting pot*, where the historical and cultural differences of immigrants are lost and a new American is forged. The *tossed salad* image views Americans as honoring their past cultures as well as their new nationality. Perhaps both are simplistic perceptions, but they influence people's mindset a great deal.

4. What are the political and instructional issues surrounding bilingual education?

In *Lau* v. *Nichols* (1974), the Supreme Court ruled that schools were deficient in their treatment of students with limited English proficiency. Many schools subsequently established a variety of bilingual programs. Some programs teach students in their native language until they learn English (the transitional approach), others teach in both languages (the maintenance approach), and some use English as a Second Language (ESL). Studies suggest that many bilingual programs often fall short of their goals, and some critics advocate fast-paced immersion (also termed "submersion"), an effort supported by those who want English to be declared the "official" American language. The future direction of bilingual education may be as much a political determination as an instructional one.

5. What are the purposes and approaches of multicultural education?

Multicultural education has multiple purposes, including *expanding the curriculum* to reflect the national diversity; *expanding teaching strategies* to respond to different learning styles; promoting the *multicultural competence of teachers;* and a *commitment to social justice,* to work and teach toward local and global equity. James Banks identifies four levels of a multicultural curriculum: contributions, additive, transformation, and social action. Those opposed to multicultural education fear it emphasizes differences at the expense of national unity, and takes time from critical academic subjects.

6. Why is culturally responsive teaching important?

As America's demographics become increasingly diverse, teachers will be expected to understand the needs and cultural learning styles of students with backgrounds very different from their own. Culturally responsive teaching focuses on mediating the frequent mismatch between the home and school cultures. Understanding and rejecting stereotypes, formulating generalizations about groups and their educational assets can offer a practical introduction for planning instruction.

7. How can teachers use culturally responsive teaching strategies?

In addition to recognizing cultural learning styles and bridging school and community cultures, a number of specific teaching strategies are also suggested. These range from an inclusive curriculum reflecting all groups, to inclusive classroom interactions where all students, even quiet ones, contribute to the learning community. Tomorrow's teachers will need to plan for diversity, which means using a variety of classroom strategies and techniques to respond to different learning styles.

THE *TEACHERS, SCHOOLS, AND SOCIETY* READER WITH CLASSROOM OBSERVATION VIDEO CLIPS

Go to your *Teachers, Schools, and Society* Reader CD-ROM to:

READ CURRENT AND HISTORICAL ARTICLES

3.1 **Profoundly Multicultural Questions,** Sonia Nieto, *Educational Leadership,* December 2002/January 2003.

3.2 **I, Too, Am an American: Preservice Teachers Reflect upon National Identity,** Nancy Gallavan, *Multicultural Teaching,* Spring 2002.

3.3 **The Threat of Stereotype,** Joshua Aronson, *Educational Leadership,* November 2004.

ANALYZE CASE STUDIES

3.1 **Helen Franklin:** A teacher who uses parents as volunteers to help with her unique classroom organization notices that a parent volunteer who has questioned the teachers' methods will work only with white students.

3.2 **Leigh Scott:** A teacher gives a higher-than-earned grade to a mainstreamed student on the basis of the boy's effort and attitude and is confronted by a black student with identical test scores who received a lower grade and who accuses her of racism.

OBSERVE TEACHERS, STUDENTS, AND CLASSROOMS IN ACTION

Classroom Observation: Immigrant Students

A growing number of students in today's schools are immigrants. In this observation, you will hear several high school students talk about their experiences in school as immigrants. You will also hear a teacher who works with them discuss her role in helping them to adapt to their new community and achieve academic and social success.

KEY TERMS AND PEOPLE

assimilation (enculturation), 74

James Banks, 85

bilingual education, 75

cultural difference theory, 72

cultural pluralism, 74

culturally responsive teaching, 87

culture, 68

deficit theory, 72

demographic forecasting, 68

English as a Second Language (ESL), 79

English language learners (ELL), 77

English-only movement, 80

ethnicity, 68

expectation theory, 72

generalizations, 92

immersion, 78

Gloria Ladson-Billings, 88

language submersion, 75

Lau v. *Nichols*, 77

maintenance (developmental) approach, 78

multicultural education, 85

Carlos Julio Ovando, 76

race, 68

stereotypes, 90

stereotype threat, 91

transitional approach, 78

DISCUSSION QUESTIONS AND ACTIVITIES

www.mhhe.com/ sadker8e

WEB-*TIVITIES*
Go to the Online Learning Center to do the following activities:

1. Today's Students: Patterns of Diversity
2. Native American Education Today
3. Black Americans and Desegregation
4. Multicultural Education
5. Bilingual Education

1. Observe a classroom, noting how many times teachers call on each student. Compare the amount of attention each student receives. Now determine group representation in the classroom. Does one group (boys or whites or native-English speakers) get more than its fair share of teacher attention? The online observation guide can be helpful in this activity.

2. How do you react to the various issues raised in this chapter? On a separate sheet of paper complete the following sentences as honestly as you can. If you wish, share your responses with your classmates.

    • To me, the phrase *invisible race privilege* means . . .

    • A great example of expectation theory is . . .

3. Given demographic trends, pick a region of the country and a particular community. Develop a scenario of a classroom in that community in the year 2030. Describe the students' characteristics and the teacher's role. Is that classroom likely to be affected by changing demographics? How are cultural learning styles manifested in the way the teacher organizes and instructs the class?

4. Choose a school curriculum and suggest how it can be changed to reflect one of the four approaches to multicultural education described by Banks. Why did you choose the approach you did?

5. Discuss the two main approaches to bilingual education in the United States: transitional and maintenance. Which do you favor, and why?

REEL TO REAL TEACHING

THE HEART OF THE GAME (2005)
Run Time: 105 minutes

Synopsis: What happens when you mix an eccentric tax law professor with Seattle's Roosevelt High's faltering girls' basketball team—a passionate story of athletics, the desire to win, and a reminder of the persistence of sexism in society. This movie includes the unforgettable tale of Darnellia Russell's legal battle to play the game that means everything to her.

Reflection:

1. Gender role stereotyping played a big part in this movie. In what ways were girls gender stereotyped? In what ways were boys gender stereotyped?

2. Do you think Darnellia Russell should have been allowed to play after she had her baby? Why do boys who father children rarely face penalties or public censure?

3. How did class and racial differences interfere with the team's performance? How did the coach handle the problem? If these very same differences emerged in your classroom, how would you respond?

4. Coach Resler created some fairly violent and fearsome animal images to motivate the girls. What was your reaction to such violent images being used as a motivational device? How does the culture of violence commonly associated with boys influence their development?

Follow-up Activity: As you think about this film, recall the description of culturally responsive teaching in this chapter. Now consider the concept of culturally responsive coaching. How did Coach Resler use the three components of culturally responsive teaching in his coaching style?

AKEELAH AND THE BEE (2006)
Run Time: 112 minutes

Synopsis: Akeelah Anderson, an African American girl from an impoverished South Los Angeles middle school, overcomes adversities at home and school on her path to the Scripps National Spelling Bee. Although she initially does what her peers do—hide her intelligence—encouragement from teachers and neighborhood residents, and eventually from her mother, enables Akeelah to realize not only her own potential but the potential in her community. An insightful piece of the film's "hidden curriculum" is how a competition like a National Spelling Bee can be transformed into encouragement of cooperation at home, at school, and across cultures.

Reflection:

1. Should competitions such as spelling or geography bees be an integral part of the curriculum? What were your reactions to competitions in your educational experience?

2. In what ways did Akeelah benefit from her participation in the spelling bee? How did her school, coach, and community benefit?

3. What examples of culturally relevant teaching do you see in this film?

4. Is this movie an example of the concept of "acting white" ("a set of social interactions in which minority adolescents who get good grades in school enjoy less social popularity than white students who do well academically")?

5. Would you describe the Asian father's presentation more a generalization of a stereotype? Were there other characterizations that stand out?

Follow-up Activity: Various cultural norms emphasize individual achievement. Extracurricular activities, including athletics, typically make winners and losers of us all, too often causing stress, anxiety, depression, and interpersonal stress. In small groups—or as an independent paper—analyze this issue, and see if you can develop appropriate and effective cooperative activities that promote learning and friendship. Can you create a sensitive and supportive learning competition? How will competition and cooperation be implemented in your own classroom? How can schools or teachers incorporate competitions into the curriculum in a culturally sensitive manner? How would you encourage community participation in your classroom?

How do you rate these films? Go to *Reel to Real Teaching* to review these films.

FOR FURTHER READING

Crossing Over to Canaan: The Journey of New Teachers in Diverse Classrooms, by Gloria Ladson-Billings (2001). Detailing the struggles and triumphs of eight novice teachers, this book shows how good teachers can use innovation and "teachable moments" to turn cultural differences into academic assets.

Culturally Responsive Teaching: Theory, Research, and Practice, by Geneva Gay (2000). The author discusses the role of teacher expectations and attitudes, formal and informal multicultural curricula, and diverse learning styles in the effort to improve the performance of underachieving students of color.

Ordinary Resurrections: Children in the Years of Hope, by Jonathan Kozol (2001). Kozol offers a hopeful vision of life in the South Bronx. Poverty and deprivation are viewed through the eyes of the children who live there, and an admiring portrait is painted of the teachers, priests, parents, and grandparents who strive against all odds to ensure that these children grow up with a strong sense of hope and pride.

There Are No Shortcuts, by Rafe Esquith (2003). What's a Los Angeles middle-school teacher to do with fifth and sixth graders, none of whom speak English at home and most of whom are eligible for free lunches? If you're Esquith, you have them read Twain, perform Shakespeare, play classical guitar, and study algebra. You take them camping and to concerts and the theater. And you teach them that "there are no shortcuts" to excellence.

Refusing Racism, by Cynthia Stokes Brown (2003). Why and how have whites joined people of color to fight against white supremacy in the United States? What have they risked and what have they gained? This book offers rich portraits of four contemporary white American activists who have dedicated their lives to the struggle for civil rights.

REFLECTIVE ACTIVITIES AND YOUR PORTFOLIO

Introduction

INTASC *Reflective Activities and Your Portfolio,* what we like to refer to as *RAPs*, give you a chance to explore your role as an educator by carefully considering what you have just read, and tying it to your own experiences. *RAPs* are intended to help you decide if teaching is right for you. And if it is right, these very same *RAPs* will give you direction as you prepare for a career in teaching.

RAPs follow and connect each of the four sections of the textbook. Each *RAP* includes a:

Purpose—explains why this activity is useful, and what it is intended to accomplish.

Activity—allows you to apply your readings through observations, interviews, teaching, and action research.

Artifact—challenges you to collect and manage the items you will find useful for developing your portfolio.

Reflection—helps you think deeply and realistically about education and your place in it.

Introduction to Portfolios

The term *portfolio* has traditionally been associated with artists and investors. Most artists maintain a showcase or portfolio of their best work to woo potential clients. Usually housed in a large portable attaché case, the portfolio is a pleasing way for clients to view an artist's best body of work. Similarly, investors keep track of their financial decisions with another type of portfolio. This portfolio tracks the gains and losses and helps determine short- and long-term investment strategies.

While rooted in the world of art and investing, educators have embraced portfolios. For the teacher-in-training, portfolios can also serve as a powerful forum in which to showcase their best work, as well as demonstrate their professional growth over time.

Multiple Purposes

Portfolios serve many purposes. They are used by states for licensure and licensure renewal, by school districts for merit pay increases, and by individual schools for hiring new staff. The National Board for Professional Teaching Standards (NBPTS) requires portfolios as part of the rigorous evaluation to reward and recognize high-achieving teachers with board certification. At the classroom level, teachers are using portfolios as an alternative evaluation method. Many teachers, students, and parents have found portfolios to be an authentic way to assess achievement.

Special thanks to Phyllis Lerner and Dan Otter for their help in creating and writing these *RAPs*.

Your Portfolio

As a teacher-in-training, your portfolio will be a valuable asset in your teacher education program and in your eventual search for a teaching position. Questions to keep in mind as you assemble this showcase include:

1. What do I want my portfolio to say about me as a teacher?
2. What do I want my portfolio to say about me as a student?
3. What do I want my portfolio to say about my relationship with students?
4. How can my portfolio demonstrate my growth as an educator and learner?
5. How can my portfolio demonstrate that I will be successful as a teacher?

Consider making your portfolio:[1]

- Purposeful—based on a sound foundation, such as the INTASC Standards for Licensing Beginning Teachers
- Selective—choosing only the appropriate materials for a specific purpose or circumstance, such as a job application
- Diverse—going beyond your transcript, student teaching critiques, and letters of recommendation to represent a broad array of teaching talent
- Ongoing—relaying your growth and development over time
- Reflective—both in process and product, demonstrating your thoughtfulness
- Collaborative—resulting from conversations and interactions with others (peers, students, parents, professors, teachers, and administrators)

Getting Started on Your Portfolio—Collect, Select, and Reflect

In four places in this book, we have placed INTASC *RAP*s to help you through the process of creating, collecting, researching, drafting, editing, and organizing your portfolio. The *RAP* activities in these sections are based on the INTASC standards and provide a springboard for your own creative portfolio artifacts. Read through the INTASC Standards for Licensing Beginning Teachers included in this section (p. 112) to understand the sections your portfolio will include. Of course, you are encouraged to include other material from other sources as well.

Building your portfolio is a three-step process—*collect, select, and reflect.*

1. *Collect* items for inclusion in your portfolio by completing *RAP*s and similar activities of your choosing.
2. *Select* items for inclusion in your portfolio from this pool of artifacts. You are encouraged to select at least one item from each of the ten INTASC Standards for Licensing Beginning Teachers.
3. *Reflect* on what was learned from each activity. This self-assessment should serve as a powerful learning tool, one you will be able to return to again and again.

Read through the INTASC standards for Licensing Beginning Teachers that follows to understand the sections. Your portfolio will include, of course, you are encouraged to include materials from other sources as well.

---

[1]Kenneth Wolf and Mary Dietz, "Teaching Portfolios: Purpose and Possibilities," *Teacher Education Quarterly,* Winter 1998, pp. 9–21.

Principle 1 Knowledge of Subject Matter
The teacher understands the central concepts, tools of inquiry, and structures of the discipline(s) he or she teaches and can create learning experiences that make these aspects of subject matter meaningful to students.

Principle 2 Human Development and Learning
The teacher understands how children learn and develop, and can provide learning opportunities that support their intellectual, social, and personal development.

Principle 3 Diversity in Learning
The teacher understands how students differ in their approaches to learning and creates instructional opportunities that are adapted to diverse learners.

Principle 4 Variety of Instructional Strategies
The teacher understands and uses a variety of instructional strategies to encourage students' development of critical thinking, problem solving, and performance skills.

Principle 5 Motivation and Management
The teacher uses understanding of individual and group motivation and behavior to create a learning environment that encourages positive and social interaction, active engagement in learning, and self-motivation.

Principle 6 Communication Skills
The teacher uses knowledge of effective verbal, nonverbal, and media communication techniques to foster active inquiry, collaboration, and supportive interaction in the classroom.

Principle 7 Instructional Planning Skills
The teacher plans instruction based upon knowledge of subject matter, students, the community, and curriculum goals.

Principle 8 Assessment
The teacher understands and uses formal and informal assessment strategies to evaluate and ensure continuous intellectual, social, and physical development of the learner.

Principle 9 Reflection and Responsibility
The teacher is a reflective practitioner who continually evaluates the effects of her or his choices and actions of others (students, parents, and other professionals in the learning community) and who actively seeks out opportunities to grow professionally.

Principle 10 Relationships and Partnerships
The teacher fosters relationships with school colleagues, parents, and agencies in the larger community to support students' learning and well-being.

SOURCE: Adopted from *Model Standards for Beginning Teacher Licensing and Development: A Resource for State Dialogue* developed by the Interstate New Teacher Assessment and Support Consortium (INTASC). Each principle includes knowledge, dispositions, and performance expectations for beginning teachers. INTASC updates can also be accessed online at www.ccsso.org/.

Housing Your Portfolio—from Traditional Methods to the Electronic Portfolio

The choices of where and how to store your portfolio can be as diverse as the contents of the portfolio itself. As mentioned earlier, artists often use a large portable attaché case to house their portfolios. Our best advice is to store your material as you see fit. Many teachers use portable plastic filing cases or crates. Others turn their portfolios into books for easy toting. Increasingly, teachers are employing a myriad of electronic tools to reach students. These can include video, the Internet, and computer activities such as PowerPoint presentations. How can teachers best include these artifacts in their portfolios? Through something called the *Electronic Portfolio or e-Portfolio*. Many software products exist to help in this process.

Final Thoughts

The first section of your portfolio should include an introduction to you and contact information, professional or present career objective, a brief résumé, transcripts, letters of support, and a mission or philosophy statement.

If you are new to portfolios, this all may seem a little overwhelming. Don't panic. We will guide you through much of the process in the chapters, discussion questions, and, of course, the INTASC *RAP* activities. Once you get the hang of portfolios—which won't take long—you should find them to be an extremely useful and meaningful professional tool. And like many of your colleagues, you may find yourself using portfolios to assess your own students.

INTASC

REFLECTIVE ACTIVITIES AND YOUR PORTFOLIO

Part I: Teachers and Students

INTASC PRINCIPLE 1
Knowledge of
Subject Matter

1:1 Teacher Interview in Your Subject Area

Purpose: Teachers are expected to have knowledge of both the subject(s) they teach and the students they are teaching. Deciding what to teach and how best to teach it are constant responsibilities. This activity gives you the opportunity to learn how teachers go through these tasks and to begin thinking how you might approach curricular decisions in your major subject area.

Activity: Interview a teacher in a subject area of special interest to you. Even if you plan to teach in an elementary program, select the curricular area that you savor. Focus on how the teacher decides what content to teach and how best to teach it. Here are some curricular questions to ask, but feel free to add your own to this list:

- What factors contributed to your decision to teach this subject and at this grade level?
- What do you enjoy most about teaching this curriculum? What do you enjoy least?
- How do you go about selecting what content and skills to teach?
- Do you try to offer different perspectives (multidisciplinary, multicultural) on these topics?
- Are there areas of this subject that are controversial? How do you handle these "hot" topics?
- How do you accommodate multiple intelligences in your classroom?
- How do you track and record grades? Does your school or district require a certain format? Do you use grading software?
- When do you do your planning? The week before, the night before, impromptu?
- Do you integrate other subject areas into your program?
- How do the school district's official curriculum and the textbook shape your decisions?
- Can you make your own decisions as to what topics to teach, or are you confined to the official school curriculum?
- Are selections made by you alone or with others in your department or grade-level team?
- Do professional associations influence your decisions?
- Do parents or students participate in deciding what is taught?

Artifact: "Teacher: Interview: Subject Specialty" For your portfolio, you will want to include the interview questions you ask, the teacher responses, and eventually, your reflection. Make certain that you include the place and date of the interview. You may want to re-read this artifact for some useful insights when you begin teaching. Or then again, you may want to read it in ten or twenty years, to see how much things have changed—or how much they haven't changed!

Reflection: What advice given by the teacher do you believe may influence your own decisions? How does the teacher's view of the content differ from your own? How will you decide what content to select when you become a teacher? What roles will professional associations play in your decision making? What role will parents and students play in your decision making? Why are you interested in this subject area, and how do you anticipate your interest will impact your students and teaching? What did you learn from this teacher that was surprising? Remember to attach your reflection to the artifact.

www.mhhe.com/
sadker8e

FORM:
Interview Questions for Teacher Interview in Your Major or Favorite Subject Area

1:2 Getting to Know Whom?

Purpose: Chapter 3, "Culturally Responsive Teaching," exposed some of life's heritage and happenings that influence who we are. Many of us have grown up in relatively homogeneous environments, knowing individuals of similar backgrounds and cultures. Meaningful conversations about how race, nationality, gender, religion, and socioeconomic status impact our own education are rare when diverse backgrounds are missing, yet such conversations could add essence and texture to your understanding of students.

INTASC PRINCIPLE 2
Human Development and Learning

Activity: Partner with a classmate, campus colleague, or friend who comes from a different background than you. Use the issues mentioned in the chapter to conduct an interview that will uncover information, stories, and perhaps feelings. Strive to interview more than one person. Concentrate on being a good and an active listener. Some opening thoughts might include:

- How do you identify your race or ethnicity?
- How would you describe your family heritage?
- How would you describe your family structure and patterns of daily life?
- Do you have memories of bias and discrimination?
- What are your recollections of your educational experience?
- What are some things you wished your teachers knew about you that perhaps they didn't?
- What are some things teachers could do to help all groups get along better?
- What other concerns have you experienced or witnessed that denied or impeded educational opportunity?
- How has diversity influenced you own education or your commitment to teach?

www.mhhe.com/
sadker8e

FORM:
Getting to Know You

Artifact: "Diversity Insights for My Classroom." From your interview, cull answers that relate directly to the classroom. In about a paragraph, sum up ways that you can apply what you learned during the interview to your teaching.

Reflection: How are you and your interviewee different? How are you similar? How might this anecdotal information add to your understanding of child and human development? What aspects of your partner's cognitive, social, and emotional growth paralleled your own schooling? All in all, what words might describe your conversation: *insightful, laborious, superficial, intimate?* What words do you think your partner might use as a description? Will this paragraph and the information learned during the interview be useful when you enter the classroom? Why or why not? Attach your reflection to your artifact and include in your portfolio.

1:3 Multiple Intelligence Bingo

INTASC PRINCIPLE 3
Diversity in Learning

Purpose: Educators are moving beyond the traditional IQ definition of intelligence. As the text discussed, Harvard professor Howard Gardner has identified at least eight intelligences—not all of which are commonly recognized in school settings—that he believes better define the unique nature of individual human capability. An effective teacher recognizes different types of intelligences and learning styles and adapts instruction accordingly. While some teachers still tend to focus on the logical and linguistic abilities, others enthusiastically incorporate Gardner's theory into their classrooms. You may even find "MI Schools" that demonstrate MI in action. In this activity, you will be challenged to identify intelligences and to see the theory applied in lessons.

Activity: Visit two classrooms. Try to include one that your professor recommends as an MI model. Observe in each room for at least 40 minutes. Use the following chart to record examples of multiple intelligences. Note both the instruction and the room displays or materials. Brainstorming with your peers before the observation will help you determine what might constitute evidence of a particular intelligence. See if your observation can fill every slot. Bingo!

www.mhhe.com/
sadker8e

FORM:
Multiple Intelligences Bingo

Artifact: Use accompanying "Multiple Intelligence Bingo Card" to record your observations, and file the chart in your portfolio. While this initial chart will help you to detect MI in action, in future years you may wish to use it for self-analysis, a way to make sure that you are including the multiple intelligences in your own teaching.

Classroom # _____ Bingo Card

Intelligence	Example During Instruction	Display or Material Example
Logical-mathematical		
Linguistic		
Bodily-kinesthetic		
Musical		
Spatial		
Interpersonal		
Intrapersonal		
Naturalist		
Others (your own)		

Reflection: Were any of your classrooms filled with examples of the multiple approaches to learning (any Bingo winners)? After your observations, were there any slots that remained empty? What could you do to fill those spaces? Were some classes totally geared to only one or two intelligence areas? Do you suspect that some intelligences are easy and some are always tough to use? How did particular students respond when given an opportunity to explore different intelligences? Were some confident with certain challenges and others withdrawn? How did the class respond, in general, when the lessons involved intelligences other than the logical and linguistic? What can you apply to your own classroom?

1:4 If the Walls Could Speak

INTASC PRINCIPLE 4
Variety of
Instructional
Strategies

Purpose: It is human nature to surround oneself with items that represent our unique heritage and experiences. Teachers cannot afford to fall into this pattern. Teachers can work to ensure that their classrooms reflect the rich diversity of both their students and their country. Teachers must work to ensure that their classrooms are nonsexist and nonracist. One way to achieve this goal is through classroom bulletin boards and other displays.

Activity: On a poster board or in your classroom, create a bulletin board representing diverse set of people and cultures. Use magazines, newspaper, the Internet, personal pictures, and so on. Strive to include "regular" people and events as well as famous people and events.

Artifact: "Seeing Diversity." Take a photo of your display, and if appropriate, save it for possible use in your classroom. Then stand back and be an objective judge by rating your bulletin board for diversity and equality using the following chart:

www.mhhe.com/
sadker8e
FORM:
Seeing Diversity

Seeing Diversity	Not at All				Very
	1	2	3	4	5
Clarity of Presentation					
Attractiveness					
Variety of Cultures Featured					
Equal Representation of Men and Women					
Mixture of Regular and Famous People					
Inclusion of Other Diversity Issues (Disability, Age, etc.)					
Overall Quality					
Overall Usefulness					

Reflection: What did you learn from this experience? Was it a challenge to create such a display? What part of this activity was easy? Did you learn how to improve this activity on your next try? Include both your photograph of your "Seeing Diversity" chart and the reflection in your portfolio.

1:5 Write a Letter to Yourself Detailing Why You Want to Become a Teacher

INTASC PRINCIPLE 5
Motivation and
Management

Purpose: People may have already asked you why you are considering teaching. Sometimes they ask with reverent tones, other times with disbelief. (In either case, they are probably sharing something about their own perspective regarding a teaching career.) Analyze your reasons to teach, so that you can provide a good answer to the question and uncover a bit about your own thinking.

Activity: Write a letter to yourself detailing why you want to become a teacher. Draw on your experience as a student. Perhaps you want to reflect on some of the teachers you have been fortunate to have, and some of the teachers you have been unfortunate to have. Include your hopes and dreams for your students. What do you want them to gain from being in your classroom? This letter will help you better understand why you want to become a teacher, and can be a useful addition to your portfolio.

Artifact/Reflection: This "Why I Am Teaching" letter will serve as both an artifact and a reflection. Over the years, your reasons for becoming a teacher may change, or weaken, or become even stronger. You may well want to repeat this process in five or ten years, and monitor your own development. The letter will provide you with an insight and a marker of your thinking as you first considered a teaching career.

1:6 Creating a Career Information Document

INTASC PRINCIPLE 6
Communication
Skills

Purpose: Applying for the right teaching position requires homework. You want to know where to apply, not only where the job openings are, but where you will find the "right" school for you. Visiting schools and meeting with administrators will help you learn about the school culture and offer insights into the kinds of questions you should be asking as you investigate teaching. An informational interview with a school administrator is a useful rehearsal for you and could provide timely information on the job market and hiring procedures, and a great way to begin your "Career Information" document.

Activity: Arrange an interview with a local school administrator (principal, personnel director). Consider going with a small group of peers (visitation team), so that your school leader is not inundated with too many requests. Review information in this text and in your community about teacher supply and demand. Develop questions as a visitation team. The following list of suggestions can also provide a framework for your conversation. Don't overstay your welcome—20 to 30 minutes should be adequate.

**www.mhhe.com/
sadker**8e

FORM:
Career Information
Document

- In terms of teacher openings, what grade levels, subject areas or specialties will likely be needed this year? What do you anticipate will be needed in the next few years?
- Are new schools being built? Are some being closed?
- Do teachers move in and out of the system (family leave, special grant projects)?
- What is the diversity breakdown of teachers in the district? How does this compare with the students in this school and districtwide? How do these factors affect screening and hiring?
- What is the application process for this district? Who else is involved in the hiring process? Are there individual or panel interviews? Do you require or recommend applicant portfolios?
- If you could describe a perfect candidate, what traits would that teacher possess?
- What other questions should we ask concerning the educational job market and hiring process?
- What advice would you offer beginning teachers?
- Do you have specific suggestions for the interview process?

Artifact: Building a "Career Information" document can help you keep and build on this information, and not let it slip through the cracks. One section might be your geographic preferences including city, suburbs, or rural areas. Another might be the kind of school you prefer, such as the school's educational philosophy, types of students, colleagues and administration, testing practices, diversity of staff, diversity of student body, salary/benefit package, community support, and so on.

This might be a good place to include job-seeking strategies, such as interviewing techniques. It is your document, so you decide what works for you. The purpose is to begin a process (that will be ongoing) that places you in the school that works best for you.

Reflection: Meet with other visitation teams and compare your interviews. Are certain trends evident in your locale? How do these realities influence your own decision making? What questions remain unanswered? Is more library or Internet research needed? Is a follow-up meeting or a phone call appropriate? Consider a similar interview during a trip home or while visiting another region of the country. How does all this information affect your teaching plans? Attach your reflections to your artifact.

1:7 Planning for Diversity: A Lesson Plan

Purpose: This activity will give you the opportunity to plan for (and even try) some of the diversity teaching skills discussed in this section.

INTASC PRINCIPLE 7
Instructional
Planning Skills

Activity: Develop a lesson plan related to a diversity topic. You are free to choose from a wide range of subjects (e.g., history of a group, cross-cultural understanding, a nontraditional hero, a religion that may not be familiar to many in your class, a social movement to create a more just society—you get the idea). Once you have selected a topic, begin to sketch out a lesson plan. Are you new to lesson planning? Here is a brief description from the noted educator, Dr. Madeline Hunter. She found that no matter what the teacher's style, grade level, subject matter, or economic background of the students, a properly taught lesson contained the following elements:

Dr. Madeline Hunter's Seven-Step Lesson Plan

1. **Anticipatory Set** (focus)—Focus learners' attention on the instruction that is about to begin. This could be a teacher demonstration, video, story, puzzle, or a handout prior to the actual lesson. This is also known as a "grabber," and it's a way to get your students' attention and interest.

2. **Purpose** (objective)—A clear explanation of what learners will understand and be able to do as a result of the lesson. This section should answer the question: "Why is this important to learn?"

3. **Instructional Strategy**—What content and skills need to be taught to accomplish this task? What are the best teaching strategies needed for this instructional task (lecture, activity, video, group work, etc.)?

4. **Modeling** (show)—Provide learners with examples or demonstrations of competencies associated with the lesson.

5. **Guided Practice**—Monitor learners as they apply new information.

6. **Check for Understanding**—Evaluate whether learners have the information needed to master the objective.

7. **Independent Practice**—Assign learners to work independently, without direct teacher assistance.

For more information on Dr. Hunter visit www.foothill.net/~moorek/lessondesign.html.

Since you are planning for diversity, you will want to include some of the effective teaching strategies described in Chapter 3. For example, did the topic you chose allow students to see themselves in your curriculum? Did you present a new insight about our world? Is a diverse view or person woven into the curriculum? Do your teaching strategies provide for different learning styles? Did you consider a variety of evaluation strategies to assess the unique strengths of each student?

If you decide to actually teach this lesson, other factors that you might consider include: Were all students participating in the lesson? Did you give thoughtful feedback to each student?

Artifact: The artifact is your lesson plan following Hunter's seven-step format.

Reflection: If this is your first lesson plan, you may want to save it for future reference. When you look back at your first attempt, you will be able to mark your professional growth and progress. For now, what were your reactions in planning for instruction? What questions came up? What did this process teach you? What do you want to learn more about?

If you have had previous practice in writing a lesson plan, reflect on what you liked and did not like with the Hunter format. Compare this approach to your previous experience and share your assessment of different lesson planning strategies. What elements do you value in a good lesson plan?

1:8 A Novel Read

Purpose: Great teachers have an incredible ability to care, really deeply, about children. Such teachers learn about their students, hold high expectations for them, and fully appreciate their diverse cultural perspectives and learning styles. One marvelous way to understand youngsters is to read literature about the challenges they face. The right books will not only inspire you, but also will expand your awareness of diverse learners.

Activity: Maybe this is a *RAP* activity you will save for summer vacation or a beach-based holiday. Or let this be a change of pace from your textbooks and research papers. Your education faculty will probably have additions to this book list. Pick a book and dig into it:

Teacher, Sylvia Ashton-Warner

Warriors Don't Cry: A Searing Memoir of the Battle to Integrate Little Rock's Central High, Melba Patillo Beals

Mentors, Masters and Mrs. MacGregor: Stories of Teachers Making a Difference, Jane Bluestein (Editor)

Bury My Heart at Wounded Knee, Dee Brown

America Is in the Heart, Carlos Bulosan

Family Values: A Lesbian Mother's Fight for Her Son, Phyllis Burke

Black Ice, Lorene Cary

House on Mango Street, Sandra Cisneros

The Water Is Wide, Patrick Conroy

Reflections of a Rock Lobster: A Story About Growing Up Gay Aaron Fricke

One Child, Torey Hayden

Up the Down Staircase, Bel Kaufman

Among Schoolchildren, Tracy Kidder

Coming of Age in Mississippi, Ann Moody

The Bluest Eye, Toni Morrison

900 Shows a Year, Stuart Palonsky

The Education of a WASP, Lois Stalvey

Native Son, Richard Wright

Artifact: "Lessons from Literature." After reading one of the selections from this list, or a book of your choice with a school/education theme, write a book review that focuses on lessons and themes from the book that can be applied to the classroom. The goal of your review is not only to assess the book's strengths and weaknesses, but also to extract lessons about effective and culturally responsive teaching practices.

Reflection: What did you learn from reading this book? Did you "unlearn" or abandon any misconceptions after your reading? Can you identify implications for your classroom? Would you assign this book to your students or suggest it for a faculty book club? How will you assess student learning? Your own understandings? Include your book report and reflection in your portfolio.

1:9 Nontraditional Hero

Purpose: We know that students need inspiring figures—individuals who serve as role models and motivate students. Although heroes come from all backgrounds, curricular materials do not always reflect diversity. The result is a disconnect between the growing diversity of America's students and the curriculum they study. You can enhance your curriculum by adding to the list of nontraditional champions in your texts. (Consider ethnicity, race, gender, age, class, lifestyle, disability, and circumstances as you select your hero.) You may also want to define different kinds of heroism as you tackle this project. Identifying such heroes has the additional advantage of broadening your own scholarship.

INTASC PRINCIPLE 9
Reflection and
Responsibility

Activity: Select a unique individual or hero who has made a difference. Strive to select someone from a subject area that you will be teaching. Develop a lesson about this person. Make the language, content, and style relevant to the grade level you plan to teach. Develop visuals to enhance your presentation, perhaps a billboard or poster of this person.

Artifact: "Nontraditional Hero Lesson." Save your lesson plan and supporting material for your portfolio, and for use when you begin teaching.

Bonus Artifact: As a way to blend technology with this activity, develop the lesson using PowerPoint software. Include ten or fewer slides in your presentation, and strive to limit text on each slide. Create a powerful presentation. Present the PowerPoint lesson to your college class. Afterward, tweak the presentation so that it is ready to be presented in your first classroom.

Reflection: What has this activity taught you about augmenting the curriculum? Was it a challenge to find a nontraditional hero—or a challenge to choose just one? Is it a teacher's professional responsibility to change instructional materials to better meet the needs of students? What are some of the arguments for and against modifying the curriculum? Will you consider modifying the curriculum in your own teaching? If you do make changes, what criteria should a teacher use when altering the curriculum? Did you try to do the bonus artifact? Will you consider using the PowerPoint in your own teaching? Be sure to include the artifact and the reflection in your portfolio.

1:10 Special Education Services

INTASC PRINCIPLE 10
Relationships and Partnerships

Purpose: For many preservice teachers, the laws and services for students with special needs can be complex and confusing. Gaining a professional understanding of these concerns will help anyone with career plans in education. It might even motivate you to teach children with disabilities. Begin by reviewing the information in Chapter 2 that covers special education.

Activity: Contact a local school district and identify the director of services for special education. Request a parent information packet that outlines the rights and responsibilities of the district regarding testing, resources, policy, practices, and all other information that would help you understand the Individuals with Disabilities Education Act (IDEA).

Highlight the key points in the literature, and take notes of what a teacher needs to do to meet the needs of special needs students.

Artifact: Create a document that will make this information more easily accessible to you when you begin teaching. Perhaps the title might be "Special Needs Reminders" or something similar. This should be an easy to read piece, perhaps even a checklist, to help you fulfill your responsibilities and create the best possible educational climate for special needs learners.

Reflection: What more did you learn about IDEA? How does it feel to look at this information from a parent's perspective? How does it feel to look at this information from a student's perspective? How does it feel to look at this information from a teacher's perspective?

PART

II

Schools and Curriculum

CLASS ACT

As an elementary school teacher, I was particularly eager to find good multicultural books. One day, I planned to read one of the many Juan Bobo stories. Juan Bobo (Simple John) depicts a "noodlehead" who does nothing right. This character is Puerto Rico's favorite fool and simpleton and has been the mainstay for generations.

Supposedly, Juan Bobo embodies the essence of Puerto Rico—the *jibaro*—a product of three cultures: Taino Indian, African, and Spaniard. The character stands for the honest and uncorrupted life of the country folks against the pomposity and falsehood of those in the city (i.e., the aristocratic Spaniards and those imitating them). But too often Juan Bobo is instead a mockery of the *jibaros*—equated with the poor and uneducated country folks. Additionally, Juan Bobo is frequently portrayed as either a person of apparent Black and/or Indian heritage. Among Puerto Ricans, it is highly insulting to be called either *jibaro* or Juan Bobo.

As I prepared to read to them, I looked into the face of one of my students—a Latino boy of African heritage. I was transported back to my childhood and saw myself—a little girl of African heritage, also waiting for the teacher to read a story to the class. I recalled painful memories.

Growing up biracial in Puerto Rico made me aware at a very young age of the deep racism in Latino culture. Although family and friends called me *triguena* (wheat colored), I recall classmates' and even teachers' crueler taunts.

I glanced at the cover of the book I was about to read. It clearly pictured Juan Bobo as a poor country boy of African heritage. I looked back at the faces of my students—innocent faces reflecting their African and Indian heritage. What was I doing? Persons of African and Indian ancestry are the majority in most Latino countries. Yet the folklore and literature, adults' and children's alike, predominantly present characters of Spanish ancestry. Country folks and Latinos of color disappear or are presented as ignorant and superstitious, as criminals, servants, and buffoons. Those in power are White Latinos.

Over the years, I have come to an important understanding. Just because a book is "multicultural" doesn't mean it is free of bias. Juan Bobo and other culturally authentic stories have been translated into English and other languages—they can now take their biases across cultures.

I placed the book down on my lap and told the class: "Today, we are going to do something really special. Books are stories that have been written by authors so others can read and hear them. Today, I am going to tell you a story from my childhood and then, we will tell each other our stories. We are going to write our stories down and publish them so others can read them later." I proceeded: "Once I climbed a tall mountain and thought I had reached the top of the world where the Taino Indian god Yukiyu lives . . . "

Marta I. Cruz-Jansen, Ph.D.
Professor
Multicultural Education
College of Education
Florida Atlantic University

SOURCE: M. I. Cruz-Jansen, (1998, Fall). "Culturally Authentic Bias." *Rethinking Schools,* 13, no 1 (Fall 1998), p. 5.

www.mhhe.com/ sadker8e

Read more *Class Acts* on the Online Learning Center.

CHAPTER 4

Schools: Choices and Challenges

FOCUS QUESTIONS

1. What expectations do Americans hold for their schools?
2. Should schools transmit the American culture or change it?
3. What school purposes are emphasized by educational reform?
4. How are magnet, charter and virtual schools, open enrollment, and vouchers reshaping our concept of the neighborhood public school?
5. Do the laws of the marketplace belong in public education?
6. Why are so many families choosing home schooling?
7. What are the characteristics of effective schools?

www.mhhe.com/
sadker8e

WHAT DO YOU THINK? What do you think schools and students are like today? Check off what you think and see how others respond.

CHAPTER PREVIEW

Although most of us take school for granted, the proper role of this institution continues to evoke heated debate. Are schools to prepare students for college, for a vocation, or to achieve high scores on standardized tests? Should schools help students develop good interpersonal relationships, patriotism, simply adjust to society or more ambitiously change and improve society?

In this chapter, you will have the opportunity to examine the major purposes assigned to schools and some of the major criticisms that have been leveled at them. The recent emphasis on standards and tests once again raises the crucial question: What's a school for? Some believe that poor test scores mean that America's schools are failing, and reform efforts have led to the creation of new schools, quite different from the old neighborhood school that you may have attended. The creation of virtual schools that teach via the Internet has made even a physical school building unnecessary. Competition among schools is being fueled by the business community, which views schools as potential profit centers. And more concerned parents than ever before are giving up on schools entirely, choosing to educate their children at home. Defining the place and purpose of schools has never been more challenging. And sorting out what makes one school effective while another is ineffective broadens the question from what is a school for to what does it take to make a school work well? As we close this chapter, we will look at the factors associated with effective schools.

A Meeting Here Tonight

Sam Newman has been principal of Monroe High School for just under five years. Becoming principal seemed a natural step to take after teaching and coaching for eight years.

Sam's plans to improve school morale and community relations, as well as to increase faculty involvement in key decisions, pleased the school board enough to give him the principalship over two, more senior candidates. He got off to a good start. He organized rallies, proclaiming, "Monroe is tops!"; he met with parents and teachers in endless meetings; and he created teacher management teams. But all that seems long ago.

Sam now spends his time rushing from one emergency to another. The latest emergency is the just-released statewide test scores. Monroe is a year behind the norm in both reading and math, and the angry calls from parents (and some pretty nasty stories in the local paper) have led to tonight's "emergency" meeting.

On his way to the meeting, Sam detours to the bathroom. As he stares into the mirror to comb his thin, graying hair, he notes sadly the almost complete disappearance of his belt beneath his belly. He once prided himself on staying in shape. Now his shape is mostly round.

But being a principal is not the same as being a coach, and a school is very different from a team. Each passing year has taught him how precious little he knows about schools. He schedules. He budgets. He writes plans. He calms parents. He disciplines students. But, all the while, he realizes that he has little time to shape and direct the school. He is not really leading the school—he is not even sure where to lead it; he is simply trying very hard to keep it afloat. Although he knows more about flowcharts than about philosophy, a line from his college philosophy course sticks in his mind. The line is Santayana's: Fanaticism consists of redoubling one's efforts after having forgotten one's aim.

A quick glance at his watch brings an abrupt end to philosophical speculation. He is already late. He hurries down the hallway to the meeting.

• • •

George Elbright unconsciously tugs at his tie as he mounts the long stairway to Monroe High School. He glances up at the motto, chiseled in stone. "Knowledge Is Power." He thinks back to the first time he read those words, as a 15-year-old freshman. Thirty years later, the memory still makes him perspire and pull at his tie. Funny how schools do that to you.

For George Elbright, Monroe High conjures up memories of hard work, graded homework assignments, and midterms so tough that kids sometimes broke down and cried, unable to go on. And finals! The whole year's work riding on one exam. Tests were rough then, but kids learned. Not like today. Not at all.

And that is why George is back at Monroe High. For years, he watched schools disintegrate, and complained bitterly about the lack of discipline; the growing permissiveness; courses in sex education, drug education, and environmental education; and the new teaching methods that sound as if the teachers do not have to teach at all. Finally things were changing. And no wonder. The test scores were in. George Jr. failed the standardized state test. So did many of the students at Monroe. No wonder George Elbright Sr. is about to attend his first parent-teacher meeting in six years.

George reaches into his pocket and pulls out his wrinkled, handwritten list. He has to be clear and forceful. He slowly rehearses his list:

1. Teachers must reassume their responsibility. Skills development, homework, and tests should be the main activities of the classroom. Free-for-all discussion, with the teacher acting as a television talk show host instead of a teacher, has to end. Children have to learn that learning is serious.

2. Students must learn the importance of discipline and respect. Students should speak to adults with respect. We should consider a new dress code or even school uniforms. Sloppy dress and poor manners lead to lazy attitudes and poor work.

3. Kids who do not pass tests should be left back until they do pass them. Too many high school graduates can't read or write well.

4. I am tired of trying to decipher "progress reports" about my child's "social adjustment" and "satisfactory efforts." I want to see report cards with grades and without educational jargon.

5. A school is supposed to teach fundamental skills, and not sex education, human relations, or other frills and electives. It is time that schools get back to the basics.

6. And it is high time that teachers taught kids morality and ethics.

Perhaps it will work; perhaps he can get the school back on the right track. The newspapers are filled with reports that seem to support his point of view. Why, he even read a report that said schools are so weak they jeopardize America's future. At any rate, he has to try for George Jr.'s sake. All the family's hopes are pinned on him. George Jr. would be the first Elbright to make it to college. This is no time for the school to let him down.

• • •

Shirley Weiss sits alone in her classroom, sipping lukewarm coffee from a commuter cup. She finished grading 15 minutes ago but is determined to wait until the last minute before going down to the auditorium for the meeting. She is amazed at public reaction to the poor scores on the state's standardized test. Given the teacher cuts and the large size of today's classes, it really isn't all that surprising. Everyone seems to be missing the point entirely. Teenagers today simply aren't contemporary versions of the kids who attended Monroe High 10 or 20 years ago. Violence, alienation, racism, sexism, drugs, terrorism—the world is so much more complex. Kids should find out who they are and where they are going. President Jackson's 1830s fight over the National Bank does not exactly speak to them.

That is why Shirley Weiss has restructured her American history course into a contemporary social problems course. Students have to *want* to learn and grow, and that's what her course is all about. And the students do well in her course. They are genuinely interested. They study and they learn. As a matter of fact, if those test makers ever were to leave their air-conditioned, swanky offices and rejoin the real world, they would revise their tests to parallel her authentic assessments, and her kids would soar! The problem is not really with the school or the kids at all! It is with the test makers and the parents who are stuck in the past!

Ever wonder how schools get their names—and which names are the most popular? The National Education Resource Center researched the most popular proper names for U.S. high schools: Washington, Lincoln, Kennedy, Jefferson, Roosevelt (both Franklin and Teddy), and Wilson. (Presidents do well.) Lee, Edison, and Madison round out the top ten names. But proper names are not the most common high school names. Directions dominate: Northeastern, South, and Central High School are right up there. While creativity obviously is not a criterion, politics is. Citizens fight over whether schools should be named after George Washington or Thomas Jefferson—who, after all, were slave holders—and over why so few African Americans, Hispanics, and people of non-European ancestry are honored by having a school named after them. And, considering how many women are educators, it is amazing that so few schools are named to honor women—Eleanor Roosevelt, Amelia Earhart, Christa McAuliffe, and Jacqueline Kennedy are exceptions. Some schools have honored writers (Bret Harte, Walt Whitman, and Mark Twain) or reflect local leaders and culture. (In Las Vegas, you will find schools named Durango, Silverado, and Bonanza, which some complain sound more like casinos than western culture.)

> **REFLECTION:** What choices do you think educators might make if they were responsible for school names? If students were in charge, would schools be named after sports figures or music and media stars? How do our school names reflect the power and culture in a society? What's in a name?

Shirley is good and angry as she pushes back her chair and makes her way down to the auditorium.

• • •

Phil Lambert begins to fidget as he waits for the meeting to begin. His physique and the 25-year-old wooden seat are less than perfect fits.

Phil, owner of Lambert's Department Store, is also president of the chamber of commerce. Every week, he is involved with enticing professionals, even high-tech firms, and developers to relocate in Monroe. Sooner or later, the talks always turn to the quality of the school system. In a sense, the success of the schools is a barometer of the town's future growth and development. And now the barometer is falling; stormy days are ahead. Declining test scores could cost the town plenty.

But Phil is particularly upset because he has warned people about this problem for years. High school kids are getting into more and more trouble. He has recently been to court three times to deal with teenage shoplifters. And, when kids today apply for work, it is so sad it is almost funny! Wearing baggy jeans and fouling up the application form, they just come off as irresponsible and stupid. For years, Phil has been asking rhetorically, "Didn't you learn *anything* in school?" Now his question is no longer rhetorical.

The schools simply have to get down to business, literally, and begin preparing kids for the real world. Our whole nation is in economic trouble because of weak schools. More courses should be offered, stressing not only the basics but also how to get a job and the importance of the work ethic. Students have to understand that school is not a place where they can come late, dress sloppily, and goof off. Once they understand how serious the real world is, how important getting a job is, they will get serious about their schoolwork.

Phil checks his cell phone for messages and makes a mental note that the meeting is starting sixteen minutes late. If he were to run the store the way they run the schools, he'd have been bankrupt years ago.

• • •

The late start of the meeting gives Mary Jackson a chance to unwind. She has rushed from her job to make the meeting and is beginning to feel the consequences of her long day.

As she gauges the audience, she sees that once again the "haves" outnumber the "have-nots." The middle-class, white, well-dressed parents don't look half as tired as Mary Jackson feels. But they sure do seem worried. For the first time, they are getting a small taste of the problem Mary has been fighting for years. Lower achievement scores are shaking them up. But they could never know the problem as well as Mary does. Even with the drop in scores for white kids, they are still scoring almost two years ahead of the African American students.

Mary has two daughters enrolled in Monroe High. Both are working hard, yet they cannot seem to catch up to the top students. Her kids have never had a non-white teacher. And her kids have never gotten into the honors track. Somehow it seems that only white students end up there.

She has tried to make the school aware of the special problems faced by students of color and females by organizing the Parents' Multicultural Task Force. Everyone at Monroe seems sympathetic, from Mr. Newman on down. But nothing has changed, and that makes her feel tired and discouraged—but not tired and discouraged enough to give up.

Mary looks around at the almost completely filled auditorium, spotting precious few black faces in the audience. But Mary would speak for those who could not come, and for those who have given up all hope of changing things. Monroe High should be their stepping-stone up, not an obstacle. Mary would tell them. The past few frustrating years have worn her patience thin.

• • •

This was the first time Karen Miller ever visited Monroe High, but it all seemed so familiar: unhappy parents gathering to complain about an underperforming school to a very tired-looking principal. This was the kind of scenario that was made-to-order for Unlimited Educational Opportunities, Inc. and their "Horizon" Schools. Karen glanced down to make certain that she had her carton filled with hundreds of multicolored brochures. She knew the plan well. She would let the parents complain, the principal would try to assuage their anxiety, and then she would announce the opening of her company's new charter school. A Horizon Charter School would promise a more focused educational program and guaranteed test score improvements by bringing business efficiency to education. No empty promise: There was a track record. She would explain that over 60 Horizon for-profit schools in other states were already compiling impressive reading and math scores. Horizon uses a Back to Basics curriculum and character education combined with extra time, extra teachers, and laptop computers to achieve its goals. But Karen would have to warn them as well: Although Horizon schools were open to all, it was likely that there would be more applicants than spaces. Karen would alert everyone to the obvious: A lottery system would have to be used to select which students will be admitted.

Karen felt good about the evening meeting, the ability of Horizon to enhance the test scores, and her own decision to leave Wall Street and use her Harvard M.B.A. to promote Unlimited Educational Opportunities. It was looking like another growth year.

● ● ●

Sam Newman twists the microphone stand to within a few inches of his mouth and prepares to open the meeting. He looks out at the packed auditorium and begins to assess the crowd:

> There is Pat Viola, the art teacher. What is she doing here? Art is never assessed on those tests.

> Oh, there's Mrs. Jackson, the chair of the Multicultural Task Force. She's not going to pull any punches about those test scores. The black students are two years behind the white students on achievement tests.

> And Dr. Sweig, the humanities' professor from the university, is here. He's probably going to make his pitch about requiring all students to study the classics. He must have given that "cultural literacy for all" speech a dozen times.

> Mrs. Benoit, president of the school board, looks distressed. As long as I can find a solution that pleases everyone and doesn't increase the budget, she'll be satisfied. She needs a magician, not a principal, to run this meeting.

> Phil Lambert is here and Shirley Weiss. Isn't that the Elbright kid's father? Wonder what's on their minds.

Sam Newman begins to perspire. He leans forward and announces, "Okay, let's begin."

The Purposes of School

Sam Newman has a dilemma on his hands. Parents and teachers are pulling him—and trying to pull Monroe High—in different directions. If it is any comfort to Sam—and it probably is not—he is confronting an old question: What is the purpose of a school?

Having spent much of your life as a student, you may find this question too basic, even obvious. Answers come quickly to mind. We go to school to learn things, to earn good grades, to qualify for better jobs, to become a better person—or to please our parents (or even ourselves). But these divergent reasons represent the view only from a student's side of the desk. There are other perspectives, broader views, and more fundamental definitions of the purposes of schools. Although brainstorming all the possible reasons for schools could lead to some creative insights, it may be more practical at this point to focus on two fundamental, yet somewhat antithetical, purposes of schools.

IMAGINE . . .

Japanese View of World War II

The Japanese are quite serious about transmitting a positive image of their culture and history, but World War II is a problem. However, it is not a problem for school children. The Hiroshima memorial explains that "the situation in Pearl Harbor hurtled Japan into the Pacific war." There is no mention of Japan's surprise attack, and no explanation why Japan invaded China four years before Pearl Harbor. China and South Korea have objected to what Japan teaches the young, and have threatened trade sanctions if these inaccuracies are not corrected. They demand a meaningful account of Japan's invasion and occupation of their nations. While many Japanese teachers support such revisions, Japan's Ministry of Education continually rejects any changes.

SOURCE: Jamie Miyazaki, "Textbook Row Stirs Japanese Concern," BBC online at http://news.bbc.co.uk, April 13, 2005.

Purpose 1: To Transmit Society's Knowledge and Values (Passing the Cultural Baton)

Society has a vital interest in what schools do and how they do it. Schools reflect and promote society's values. There is a world of knowledge out there, more than any school can possibly hope to teach, so one of the first tasks confronting the school is to *select* what to teach. This selection creates a cultural message. Each country chooses the curriculum to match and advance its own view of history, its own values, its self-interests, and its own culture. In the United States, we learn about U.S. history, often in elementary, middle, and high school, but we learn little about the history, geography, and culture of other countries—or of America's own cultural diversity, for that matter. Even individual states and communities require schools to teach their own state or local history, to advance the dominant "culture" of Illinois or of New York City. By selecting what to teach—and what to omit—schools are making clear decisions as to what is valued, what is worth preserving and passing on.

Literature is a good example of this selection process. American children read works mainly by U.S. and British writers, and only occasionally works by Asian, Latin American, and African authors. This is not because literary genius is confined to the British and U.S. populations; it is because of a selection process, a decision by the keepers of the culture and creators of the curriculum that certain authors are to be taught, talked about, and emulated and others omitted. Similar decisions are made concerning which music should be played, which art viewed, which dances performed, and which historical figures and world events studied. As each nation makes these cultural value decisions, it is the role of the school to transmit these decisions to the next generation.

As society transmits its culture, it also transmits a view of the world. Being American means valuing certain things and judging countries and cultures from that set of values. Democratic countries that practice religious tolerance and respect individual rights are generally viewed more positively by Americans than are societies characterized by opposing norms, standards, and actions—that is, characteristics that do not fit our "American values." Afghani women denied access to schools, hospitals, and jobs by the Taliban conflicted with our cultural and political standards and was repulsive to most Americans. Repression of religious, racial, and ethnic groups usually engenders similar negative feelings. By transmitting culture, schools breathe the breath of cultural eternity into a new generation and mold its view of the world.

But this process is limiting as well. In transmitting culture, schools are teaching students to view the world from the wrong end of a telescope, yielding a constricted view that does not allow much deviation or perspective. Cultural transmission may contribute to feelings of cultural superiority, a belief that "we are the best, number one!" Such nationalistic views may decrease tolerance and respect for other cultures and peoples.

Purpose 2: Reconstructing Society (Schools as Tools for Change)

If society were perfect, transmitting the culture from one generation to the next would be all that is required of schools. But our world, our nation, and our communities are far from ideal. Poverty, hunger, injustice, pollution, overpopulation, racism, sexism, and ethical challenges—and, of course, the dark clouds of terrorism, nuclear, chemical, and biological weapons—are societal problems on a depressingly long list. To **reconstructionists,** society is broken, it needs to be fixed, and the school is a perfect tool for making the needed repairs. Reconstructionists see successful students as citizens ready to make change by transforming injustices.

To prepare students for such engagement, *social democratic reconstructionists* believe that civic learning—educating students for democracy—needs to be on par with other academic subjects. Yet to achieve this goal, reconstructionists hold a wide spectrum of beliefs and strategies. At one end are those who believe that students should be made aware of the ills of society; study these critical, if controversial, areas; and equip themselves to confront these issues as they become adults.[1] Other reconstructionists are more action-oriented and believe that schools and students shouldn't wait until students reach adulthood. They call for a **social action curriculum,** in which students actively involve themselves in eliminating social ills. For example, to gain public and government support for increased school construction and repairs, high school students in Baltimore, Maryland, organized a photo exhibit of their decaying school buildings. State legislators received a guided tour of the photos, which showed broken heaters, moldy walls, library shelves with no books, cockroaches, a stairwell filled with garbage, and broken windows.[2] As another example, students of all ages can learn about poverty and hunger in their communities and then organize a food drive or work in a soup kitchen.

This idea of students contributing to society is not unique. The Carnegie Foundation for the Advancement of Teaching recommends that every student be required to earn a **service credit,** which might include volunteer work with the poor, elderly, or homeless. The idea behind a service credit is not only to reduce social ills but also to provide students with a connection to the larger community, to develop a sense of personal responsibility for improving the social condition.[3] In 1992, Maryland became the first state requiring students to perform community service before they would be granted their high school diploma, and service learning became more popular nationwide throughout the 1990s.[4] More than half of students in grades 6 through 12 participate in service learning, although who participates and what they do to gain service credits is somewhat erratic. Girls are more likely to participate than are boys, and whites outnumber students of color. Participation increases when schools take an active role in setting up the service opportunities, and when they require it for graduation. And student participation increases with the educational level of their parents.[5]

While social democratic reconstructionists are reform-minded, *economic reconstructionists* hold a darker view of society's ills and advocate more drastic, even revolutionary, action. They believe that schools generally teach the poorer classes to accept their lowly stations in life, to be subservient to authority, to unquestioningly follow rules while laboring for the economic benefit of the rich. To economic reconstructionists, schools are currently tools of oppression, not institutions of learning. They believe that students must be introduced to curricula that analyze and reform economic realities. For example, one such curriculum project targets a popular and highly visible athletic company, one that produces incredibly expensive sport shoes. This company manufactures its products in developing nations, maintaining horrid working conditions. Children in these poor countries are sold into labor bondage by their impoverished families. As young as 6, they work 12 or more hours a day, enduring cruelty and even beatings as they earn only pennies an hour. While the companies defend themselves by saying that they cannot change local conditions, economic reconstructionists believe that companies intentionally select locations because of their cheap labor costs. Economic reconstructionists point out that

Is the purpose of schools just academic learning, or might the goals include fostering an awareness of the benefits of community service, such as volunteering to tutor others?

American children play with products made through the agonizing toil of other children. All the while, the companies profit. Educators who focus on economic reform have developed materials, Web sites, and social action projects that not only teach children about such exploitation but also provide them with strategies to pressure companies into creating more humane and equitable working conditions.[6]

Perhaps the most noted contemporary economic reconstructionist was **Paulo Freire,** author of ***The Pedagogy of the Oppressed,*** a book about his efforts to educate and liberate poor, illiterate peasants in Brazil.[7] In his book, Freire describes how he taught these workers to read in order to identify problems that were keeping them poor and powerless. From this new awareness, they began to analyze their problems—such as how the lack of sanitation causes illness—and what they could do to solve specific problems and liberate themselves from their oppressive conditions. Freire highlighted the distinction between schools and education. Schools often miseducate and oppress. But true education liberates. Through education, the dispossessed learned to read, to act collectively, to improve their living conditions, and to reconstruct their lives. (See *The Education Hall of Fame* in Chapter 7 for more about Freire.)

Public Demands for Schools

While preserving the status quo and promoting social change represent two fundamental directions available to schools, they are not the only possible expectations. When you think about it, the public holds our schools to a bewildering assortment of tasks and expectations.

John Goodlad, in his massive study ***A Place Called School,*** examined a wide range of documents that tried to define the purposes of schooling over 300 years of history. He and his colleague found four broad goals:

1. *Academic,* including a broad array of knowledge and intellectual skills.
2. *Vocational,* aimed at readiness for the world of work and economic responsibilities.

FIGURE 4.1
Goals of schools.

REFLECTION: Under each goal, list specific efforts a school could make to reach the goal. How would you prioritize these goals? Explain.

3. *Social and civic,* including skills and behavior for participating in a complex democratic society.

4. *Personal,* including the development of individual talent and self-expression.[8]

Goodlad included these four goal areas in questionnaires distributed to parents, and he asked them to rate their importance. (See Figure 4.1.) Parents gave "very important" ratings to all four. When Goodlad asked students and teachers to rate the four goal areas, they rated all of them as "very important." When pushed to select one of these four as having top priority, approximately half the teachers and parents selected the intellectual area, while students spread their preferences fairly evenly among all four categories, with high school students giving a slight edge to vocational goals. When it comes to selecting the purpose of schools, both those who are their clients and those who provide their services resist interpreting the purpose of schools narrowly.

What do Americans want from their schools? Evidently, they want it all! As early as 1953, Arthur Bestor wrote, "The idea that the school must undertake to meet every need that some other agency is failing to meet, regardless of the suitability of the schoolroom to the task, is a preposterous delusion that in the end can wreck the educational system."[9]

Then, in the 1980s, Ernest Boyer conducted a major study of secondary education and concluded,

> Since the English classical school was founded over 150 years ago, high schools have accumulated purposes like barnacles on a weathered ship. As school population expanded from a tiny urban minority to almost all youth, a coherent purpose was hard to find. The nation piled social policy upon educational policy and all of them on top of the delusion that a single institution can do it all.[10]

 # Where Do You Stand?

Identifying school goals seems to be everyone's business—parents, teachers, all levels of government, and various professional groups. Over the years, dozens of lists have been published in different reform reports, each enumerating goals for schools. The problem arises when schools cannot fulfill all of these goals, either because there are too many goals or because the purposes actually conflict with one another. It is these smaller pieces that often dominate discussion. Should schools focus on preparing students for college? Should they try to inhibit drug use, or lessen the threat of AIDS? Perhaps schools ought to focus on the economy and train students to become members of a more efficient workforce, one that can successfully compete in the world marketplace.

Look at the following list of school goals. Drawn from a variety of sources, these goals have been advocated singly and in combination by different groups at different times and have been adopted by different schools. In each case, register your own judgment on the values and worth of each goal. When you have completed your responses, we shall discuss the significance of these goals, and you can see how your responses fit into the bigger picture.

Circle the number that best reflects how important you think each school goal is.

1   Very unimportant

2   Unimportant

3   Moderately important

4   Important

5   Very important

www.mhhe.com/ sadker8e

INTERACTIVE ACTIVITY

How Important Are These School Goals? Do this exercise online. See how others responded to each statement.

	Very Unimportant				Very Important
1. To transmit the nation's cultural heritage, preserving past accomplishments and insights	1	2	3	4	5
2. To encourage students to question current practices and institutions; to promote social change	1	2	3	4	5
3. To prepare competent workers to compete successfully in a technological world economy	1	2	3	4	5
4. To develop healthy citizens aware of nutrition, exercise, and good health habits	1	2	3	4	5
5. To lead the world in creating a peaceful global society, stressing an understanding of other cultures and languages	1	2	3	4	5
6. To provide a challenging education for America's brightest students	1	2	3	4	5
7. To develop strong self-concept and self-esteem in students	1	2	3	4	5
8. To nurture creative students in developing art, music, and writing	1	2	3	4	5
9. To prevent unwanted pregnancy, AIDS, drugs, addiction, alcoholism	1	2	3	4	5
10. To unite citizens from diverse backgrounds (national origin, race, ethnicity) as a single nation with a unified culture	1	2	3	4	5
11. To provide support to families through after-school child care, nutritional supplements, medical treatment, and so on	1	2	3	4	5
12. To encourage loyal students committed to the United States; to instill patriotism	1	2	3	4	5
13. To teach students our nation's work ethic: punctuality, responsibility, cooperation, self-control, neatness, and so on	1	2	3	4	5

	Very Unimportant				Very Important
14. To demonstrate academic proficiency through high standardized test scores	1	2	3	4	5
15. To provide a dynamic vehicle for social and economic mobility, a way for the poor to reach their full potential	1	2	3	4	5
16. To prepare educated citizens who can undertake actions that spark change	1	2	3	4	5
17. To ensure the cultural richness and diversity of the United States	1	2	3	4	5
18. To eliminate racism, sexism, homophobia, anti-Semitism, and all forms of discrimination from society	1	2	3	4	5
19. To prepare as many students as possible for college and/or well-paid careers	1	2	3	4	5
20. To provide child care for the nation's children and to free parents to work and/or pursue their interests and activities	1	2	3	4	5

Now, think about your three most valued goals for school and write those goals below:

Three valued goals:

_____ , _____ , _____

Do your responses to these items and your three priority goal selections cast you as transmitter of culture or as change agent for restructuring society? To help you determine where your beliefs take you, record your scores on the following selected items:

Purpose of Schools

Transmitting Culture		Reconstructing Society	
Focused Item		Focused Item	
1	_____	2	_____
3	_____	5	_____
10	_____	9	_____
12	_____	15	_____
13	_____	16	_____
19	_____	18	_____
Total	_____	Total	_____

REFLECTION: Do your responses reflect the school experiences you had, or the ones you had hoped for? Which camp are you in: transmitting culture or reconstructing society?

Let's investigate how your choices reflect your values. The current emphasis on standards, tests, and academic performance is reflected in items 1, 13, and especially 14. Are you in agreement with this contemporary educational priority? If you scored high on items 1 and 10, then you value the role schools serve in preparing Americans to adhere to a common set of principles and values. This has been a recurrent theme in schools as each new group of immigrants arrives. Some people called this the melting pot, more formally termed **acculturation,** or **Americanization** (replacing the old culture with the new American one). Others view diversity more as a tossed salad, an analogy that suggests that cultural traditions, practices and identity would be retained in America, and a high score on item 17 reflects a sensitivity to our nation's cultural diversity. Items 2, 17 and 18 suggest a commitment to civil rights and student empowerment, hallmarks of the 1960s and 1970s, and since history often runs in cycles, perhaps these goals will resurface in the not too distant future. Do you like the Horatio Alger folklore: hard work and a little elbow grease, and the poor become wealthy? Agree with this folklore and you probably rated items 15 and 19 pretty high. Take a little time and see where you stand on the other items. And while you look them over, consider item 20, which may seem a bit odd. After all, few people see schools as babysitters, but, without this "service," most parents would be overwhelmed. And consider the impact that millions of adolescents would have on the job market. Unemployment would skyrocket and wages would tumble. By minding the children, schools provide parents with time and keep our workforce down to a manageable size.

What did your ratings teach you about your values and your view of schools? Were your goals popular during particular periods of our past, or are you more future-oriented? You may want to compare your goals for education here with your philosophical preferences as identified in Chapter 8.

 ## Education Reform

> Our Nation is at risk. Our once unchallenged prominence in commerce, industry, science, and technological innovation is being overtaken by competitors throughout the world. . . . If an unfriendly foreign power had attempted to impose on America the mediocre educational performance that exists today, we might well have viewed it as an act of war. As it stands, we have allowed this to happen to ourselves. We have even squandered the gains in student achievement made in the wake of the *Sputnik* challenge. Moreover, we have dismantled essential support systems which helped make those gains possible. We have, in effect, been committing an act of unthinking, unilateral educational disarmament.[11]

So began the report of the National Commission on Excellence in Education, **A Nation at Risk: The Imperative for Educational Reform,** released in 1983. The report cited declining test scores, the weak performance of U.S. students in comparison with those of other industrialized nations, and the number of functionally illiterate adults. *A Nation at Risk* condemned the "cafeteria-style curriculum." The report called for a more thorough grounding in the "five new basics" of English, mathematics, science, social science, and computer science. It called for greater academic rigor, higher expectations for students, and better-qualified and better-paid teachers.

This report galvanized Americans, moving education to center stage. Remember, in 1983, we were in two wars: the Cold War with the Soviet Union and an economic war with Japan. Our national security was at stake, and poor school performance was putting the nation at risk. With the battle cry sounded, governors, state legislators, and foundations issued a wave of reports (see Online Appendix D for a summary of the salient reform reports). Within the next two years,

- Hundreds of local and state panels were formed.
- More than 40 states increased course requirements for graduation.
- Thirty-three states instituted testing for student promotion or graduation.
- Almost half the states passed legislation to increase qualification standards and pay for teachers.
- Most states increased the length of the school day and/or school year.
- Most states passed laws that required teachers and students to demonstrate computer literacy.[12]

Although state legislatures passed laws, many critics remained skeptical that such changes would truly improve education. They pointed out that these were top-down approaches, dictated from above and far removed from the real world of the classroom.[13] Teachers felt dumped on (*teacher bashing* was the phrase used to protest this), controlled, and regulated by new rules and requirements. Other critics worried that these new regulations might do more harm than good. Increasing student graduation requirements without providing for special programs could hurt racial and ethnic minorities, non-English speakers, females, special education students, and other groups not testing well. Different groups struggled to claim their place on the new list of educational priorities. To be left out of the goals for education reform could be costly, indeed.[14]

The reform reports—and there were many—came in three waves (see the *Frame of Reference* on p. 140). These **three waves of reform** continue to influence American education today. The first wave of reports came immediately after *A Nation at Risk* and, as previously described, viewed school reform in terms of national defense and economic competition. Corporations complained about the need to teach employees basic reading and math skills, and the military struggled to recruit technically skilled personnel for increasingly sophisticated equipment. Education critics pointed to low scores by American students on international tests, especially in math and science, as they made their case that schools were not meeting the nation's economic and technical needs. By the turn of the century, this first reform wave had trumped many educational issues and topics: It seemed as though everyone was talking about standards; the rapid growth of state tests; and the effort to identify weak performing students, teachers, and schools. While other, smaller waves followed, this first wave never ended. Politicians decried the inadequate performance of public schools; private for-profit companies sprung into existence, saying that their new schools could do a better job; and corporations lamented the fact that their new employees lacked fundamental skills.

Other critics point out that American industry has itself to blame for some of its problems, including many inefficient production practices. Educator Clinton Boutwell, author of *Shell Game: Corporate America's Agenda for Schools,* asserts that, contrary to popular belief, technical and scientific education in America's schools is stronger than ever. Boutwell believes that sinister motives might be at play. Many business leaders complaining about the lack of scientists and engineers are the same executives who fire tens of thousands of scientists and engineers as they downsize the workforce in an effort to increase profits.[15] In fact, the vast majority of new jobs are service-oriented and do not require large numbers of highly educated employees at all.

Wave 1—The goal of the first wave was to raise educational quality by requiring more courses and more testing of student and teacher performance. States were to assume the leadership in improving existing practices and this wave continues to be the strongest.

Wave 2—Again it was state governors who promoted improvement and accountability. Teachers were to be empowered, given more control over their schools. Some of the educational problems confronting children of color and some other students facing educational barriers were also addressed.

Wave 3—In this, the most ambitious wave, reformers called for reformulating our nation of schools. Schools should be seen as more than educational facilities. They should also provide health care, social services, and transportation. In short, the whole array of services needed to bring the child into successful adulthood should be offered at the school: one-stop shopping for educational, social, medical, and other services.

Wave I (began 1982 to present)	Wave II (began 1986)	Wave III (began 1988)
"Raise the Standards"	"Restructure the School"	"Comprehensive Services"

SOURCE: Adapted from Joseph Murphy, "The Educational Movement of the 1980s: A Comprehensive Analysis," in Joseph Murphy (ed.), *The Educational Reform Movement of the 1980s* (Berkeley: McCutchan, 1990).

REFLECTION: Which of these reform waves do you feel would be most effective? Why does the first persist? As familiar as these efforts have become, they are far from universally accepted. As Educator Larry Cuban has pointed out, "As economic productivity has gone up and down over the last twenty years, the argument has remained the same. But during the last eight years of unparalleled prosperity, nobody has given the public schools an Oscar for outstanding performance. And the reason is that there is no relationship." Researcher Gerald Bracey adds: "If you think about it, the kids who were in high school when *A Nation at Risk* was released became all the dot.com millionaires."[16]

The second wave of reform, which began in the mid- and late-1980s, was led by educators such as Theodore Sizer, John Goodlad, and Ernest Boyer, rather than by politicians and business leaders. Based on research and school observations, these educators stressed the need for basic reform of school practices. Theodore Sizer and others see the superficial nature of the curriculum as a central weakness, recommending that students cover fewer topics but study them in greater depth. The second wave of reformers were alarmed at the loss of teacher autonomy in oppressive school climates, bland teaching, and poor academic performance. They emphasize thoughtful changes: reducing bureaucracy; creating a more professionally trained, empowered, and well-salaried corps of teachers; implementing local decision making; strengthening the role of the school principal; and studying subjects in greater depth.

The third wave of reform recognizes that struggling families are unlikely to possess the time and resources required to ensure high-quality education. Underway since the late 1980s and early 1990s, the third wave advocates **full service**

A byproduct of recent calls for educational reform has been an explosion of student (and teacher) testing to ensure that revised school goals are being met.

schools, providing a network of social services, nutrition, health care, transportation, counseling, and parent education. School boards would be replaced by children's boards, made up of professionals and community members who work on the comprehensive needs of children. School policy, focused only on education, would be replaced by children's policy, responding to the multiple needs of children. In the late 1990s, full service schools in Florida, New York, and California were operating long hours and providing an array of community services.

> At Intermediate School 218, in the Washington Heights section of New York City, school is open by 7 a.m. for breakfast, sports activities, dance or Latin band practice, all before school "officially" opens. At the school's Family Resource Center, parents receive social services, including immigration, housing, and employment consultations. Social workers, mental health counselors, a health and dental clinic are all on site. After classes end, the building remains open until 10 p.m. for sports, computer lab, music, art, mentoring, English classes, parenting skills, and cultural classes. Intermediate School 218 is a full service school.[17]

 ## Beyond the Neighborhood Public School

At the beginning of the chapter, you listened in on the meeting held at Monroe High School. You had the opportunity to hear parents, educators, and businesspeople express their concern, frustration, and disappointment with the test scores at Monroe High. While that meeting was fictional, it offers an insight into the strong feelings and opinions found in communities around the nation, communities disappointed with their public schools. The future of the neighborhood school, for centuries the cornerstone of public education, is now in doubt. Many parents and political leaders, discouraged by the slow pace of educational change, have been experimenting with public schools beyond their neighborhoods, with open enrollments, vouchers, and charter schools, and even with business-sponsored schools designed to make money.[18] Some parents now send their children to these schools created to both educate and turn a profit. Other parents are refocusing their

FIGURE 4.2
Public attitudes: Reform-
ing or replacing public
schools.

SOURCE: *The 2006 Phi Delta
Kappa/Gallup Poll of the
Public's Attitudes Toward the
Public Schools.*

REFLECTION: Why
do you believe that
most people prefer
to reform the current
system rather than
find an alternative?

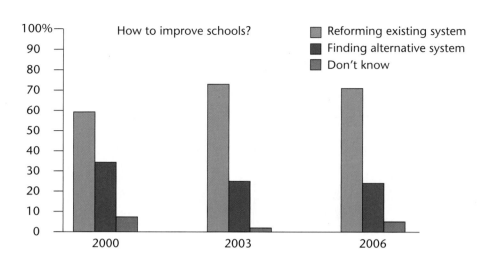

energies on getting their children into private schools. Other parents have given up on all schools, and have joined the growing number of Americans educating their children at home. Many parents are leaving what they consider to be a failing public school monopoly. Let's look at some of these dramatic changes, changes that may well influence where you teach. (See Figure 4.2.)

The Choice Concept

In the 1950s, economist **Milton Friedman** suggested that public schools would be more effective if they functioned as a free market, much as private schools do. Friedman believed that public schools were not working well, even back then, because there was no competition, no incentive for them to do their best. Parents were forced to send their children to the neighborhood school, and the neighborhood school had no incentive to compete with other schools or improve. It had a "trapped" clientele. But not everyone was trapped. Because they could afford private school tuition, wealthy parents were able to bail out if the public school was performing poorly. Friedman believed that everyone needed the same freedom to choose what the wealthy enjoyed.

In a 1981 study, James Coleman found that private schools were doing a better job of educating students than were the neighborhood public schools. Not only were the students attending independent, often religiously affiliated, private schools better behaved, but they also scored higher on tests. Coleman noted that the private schools enforced more rigorous academic standards and gave teachers and administrators more autonomy. In 1993, another study found that Catholic schools not only were providing particularly effective education for inner-city students of color but also were providing this education at a lower per-student cost and in less segregated classrooms than were neighboring public schools.[19] The call for **school choice** was getting louder.

Magnet Schools

Over a quarter century ago, a number of public schools actually began a choice program, although few called it that. In the 1970s, as schools struggled to desegregate, "forced" busing became quite unpopular. But, with neighborhoods so racially segregated, desegregating schools required that students and teachers attend schools outside their local communities. **Magnet schools** were created to draw, much like a magnet, diverse students to schools outside their neighborhoods. The magnet school "draw" is to offer high-quality education programs designed around a special theme or method of instruction, unique programs unavailable in local schools and well worth the bus ride.

Today, more than two million students attend several thousand magnet schools. Magnet schools offer unique educational programs in such areas as science and technology, communication skills, career specialties, mathematics and computer science, theater, music, and art. How effective have magnet schools been? After a quarter of a century, the results are mixed. About half of these schools have helped desegregation efforts, but, in hypersegregated cities and other areas, they have had little or no impact on desegregation. In terms of educational quality, some studies suggest that students in magnet schools outperform students in other public schools and in Catholic schools. Research also indicates that those attending career magnet schools that prepare students for the world of work are less likely to be involved in fighting and drinking, and they earn more college credits and demonstrate greater involvement in social justice issues than their contemporaries in public schools. Although magnet schools cost more than neighborhood public schools, these studies suggest that they may also be more effective.[20]

Open Enrollment

In 1988, Minnesota instituted **open enrollment,** which eliminated the requirement that students must attend the closest public school. Like the magnet schools, open enrollment encouraged parents to choose a school, but it greatly increased the number of schools to choose from. Any public school with available space became eligible. Arkansas, Iowa, Nebraska, and other states soon followed Minnesota's lead and introduced open enrollment legislation. Today, more than 40 states allow open enrollment within school districts. However, even more radical proposals are available that may redefine, if not eliminate, the neighborhood school.

Vouchers

The approach that Milton Friedman favored was neither open enrollment nor magnet schools: Friedman proposed that **educational vouchers** be given to parents. The vouchers would function like admission tickets. Parents would "shop" for a school, make their choice, and give the voucher to the school. The school would turn over the voucher to the local or state government, and the government would pay the school a fixed sum for each voucher. Good schools would collect many vouchers and thrive, while poor schools would not attract "customers" and would go out of business. Some voucher plans would give parents the choice of selecting either a public or a private school, while other plans would limit the choice to public schools.

In 1990, Milwaukee became the site of the first publicly financed voucher program. Wisconsin lawmakers approved a plan for Milwaukee students to receive about $3,000 each to attend nonsectarian private schools, then, in 1995, amended the law to allow students to attend religious schools as well. And it is the inclusion of religious schools first in the Milwaukee voucher plan, then in a similar plan in Cleveland, that sparked a heated controversy and a round of lawsuits. The reason that religious schools are so closely involved in the voucher dispute is that they are the prime beneficiaries, receiving upwards of 90 percent of the students using such vouchers. Why is this? Two reasons: First, most private schools are religious schools, and second, most religious schools charge less than other private schools. Most voucher plans offer modest financial support, too little for elite private schools but enough to cover the cost of many parochial schools. Many voucher students attend parochial schools like St. Agatha–St. Aloysius, housed in a crumbling brick hulk of a building on Cleveland's East Side. The neighborhood has changed much over the past decades, from mostly Irish American to mostly black, but the school has not. Boys wear white shirts and ties, shelves in the basement library are stocked with trophies won by teams a half-century ago, discipline is strict and daily homework is a given.[21] Yet, the First Amendment of the Constitution ensures the separation of church and state, and paying for a religious education with taxpayer funds violates the Constitution—or has all that changed?

In fact, the legal picture is in flux. In 1971 in **Lemon v. Kurtzman** and in 1973 in the *Nyquist* case, the Supreme Court constructed clear walls limiting the use of public funds to support religious education. What became known as the *Lemon* test provided three criteria to determine the legality of government funds used in religious schools. According to *Lemon,* the funds (1) must have a secular purpose, (2) must not primarily advance or prohibit religion, and (3) must not result in excessive government entanglement with religion. In **Zelman v. Simmons-Harris** (2002), a narrow 5–4 Supreme Court majority ruled that publicly funded vouchers could be used to send children to Cleveland's private religious schools. Chief Justice William Rehnquist wrote that such vouchers permit a "genuine parental, nongovernmental choice among options public and private, secular and religious." The ruling also asserted that the improvement of our nation's schools is "inherently a secular endeavor." Justice John Paul Stevens dissented, writing, "Whenever we remove a brick from the wall that was designed to separate religion and government, we increase the risk of religious strife and weaken the foundation of our democracy."[22] Even with these legal changes, in 2005 tuition vouchers were used in just five states and the District of Columbia. While Congress and the U.S. Supreme Court have given their approval to tuition vouchers, state courts and state lawmakers remain wary. Most state constitutions have so-called Blaine Amendments—named for a late-nineteenth century Republican legislator from Maine—that restrict aid to private and religious institutions.[23]

The public is also divided. Supporters extol vouchers for expanding educational choice. Yet a majority of Americans continue to oppose vouchers, concerned that tax monies are redirected from public to private education, particularly toward spreading religious doctrine. Both groups may be correct.[24] (See Figure 4.3.)

Charter Schools

In 1991, Minnesota was the first state to enact charter school legislation. Today more than 3,500 charter schools in 40 states plus the District of Columbia and Puerto Rico are educating over one million students. Arizona, California, Texas, and Florida have the greatest number of charter schools. So many were created so quickly that some states decided to slow the process down and take a closer look at these schools. Some charters had questionable educational impact, others were

Do you favor or oppose allowing students and parents to choose private schools at public expense?

FIGURE 4.3
How Americans view vouchers.

SOURCE: *The 2006 Phi Delta Kappa/Gallup Poll of the Public's Attitudes Toward the Public Schools.*

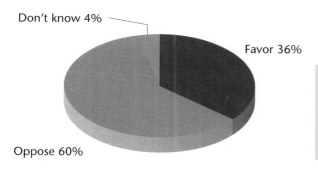

Don't know 4%

Favor 36%

Oppose 60%

REFLECTION: The public's view on vouchers, as depicted here, is far from firm or clear. Try your own skill at polling, and ask friends and family their responses to this question. How do their responses compare to national trends? How might you explain these similarities or differences?

drawing few students, and others raised even more serious legal and financial questions. Most charters, however, continued to enjoy public support.[25]

What are these **charter schools**? The concept is simple. The charter (or contract) represents legal permission from a local or state school board to operate the school, usually for a fixed period of time, perhaps five years, with the right to renew the charter if the school is successful. While charter schools must follow some of the same rules established for other publicly funded schools (for example, health and safety regulations, agreement not to discriminate), charter schools are exempt from many state and local laws and regulations. Charter schools, in effect, "swap" rules and regulations for greater freedom and the promise that they will achieve better results. A charter school typically

- Allows for the creation of a new or the conversion of an existing public school
- Prohibits admission tests
- Is nonsectarian
- Requires a demonstrable improvement in performance
- Can be closed if it does not meet expectations
- Does not need to conform to most state rules and regulations
- Receives funding based on the number of students enrolled

A charter school represents a break with the past, a new way to educate with tax dollars. A charter school might be established to improve academic performance or attendance, to explore a new organizational approach or teaching strategy, or to extend the hours of the school day or the length of the school year. Some charter schools are associated with national programs, such as the International Baccalaureate Degree, while others are independent, meeting local needs. In St. Paul, Minnesota, for example, the City Academy is a year-round charter school serving 40 at-risk students. Metro Deaf serves deaf students, while the Teamsters Union and the Minnesota Business Partnership sponsor a vocational and technical school, called Skills for Tomorrow, that uses internship placements to educate students interested in becoming skilled workers. The City on a Hill charter in Boston

A Harvard graduate and Rhodes scholar, Jonathan Kozol had no idea "what it was like to be a poor kid in America." He quickly learned. In 1964 the Klu Klux Klan in Mississippi murdered three young civil rights workers. The injustice ignited a need to act.

I'd never been involved with racial issues. I was not particularly political. In fact, I wasn't political at all. But this event had an extraordinary effect. I volunteered to spend the summer teaching at a black church which had set up a freedom school. When September came, I walked into the Boston school department and said, "I'm going to be a teacher."[1]

He was assigned to the fourth grade of an urban school in Boston, a school so impoverished he didn't have a classroom. Kozol and his disenfranchised students camped out in an auditorium. In an effort to resuscitate their interest in learning, he shared his favorite poetry. Students recited lines, asked questions, even cried as they identified with the words of Langston Hughes. While the words of the black poet may have inspired students, the author was not on the school's approved reading list. Kozol was fired. He chronicled his first year teaching in *Death at an Early Age* (1967), which alerted the nation to the wrenching injustices found in impoverished schools and the resiliency of their students.

For almost four decades, Kozol's compassionate spirit has given voice to the poor. In his best-selling book,

Savage Inequalities (1991), he describes life in destitute schools from East St. Louis to the Bronx. Kozol writes of schools so overcrowded that students only get desks when other students are absent. Of students who go for part, most, or all of the year without textbooks. While decrying this tragedy, Kozol does not find an answer in voucher programs.

[T]he idea behind choice (within the district), basically, is that if you let people choose, everybody will get the school they want. [But] people very seldom have equal choices, and even when they theoretically have equal choices, they rarely have equal access.

People can't choose things they've never heard of, for example. And lots of the poorest folks in our inner cities are functionally illiterate. In many of our inner cities, as many as 30 percent of our adults cannot read well enough to understand the booklets put out by school systems delineating their choices.

Even if they can understand and even if the school system is sophisticated enough to print these things in five different languages for all the different ethnic groups in cities like New York or Chicago, there's a larger point that those who hear about new schools, good schools, first are almost always the well connected.

And so, what often happens is that while everybody theoretically has the right to choose any school, the affluent, the savvy, the children of the academics, the children of the lawyers, the children of the doctors, the children of the school superintendent tend to end up in the same three little boutique elementary schools. And I call them boutique schools because they're always charming, and the press loves them, and they always have enough racial integration so it looks okay for the newspaper or the TV camera. But, in fact, they are separated by both race and class, and more and more by class.

What happens is that the poorest of the poor often do not get into these schools or very small numbers get in. Large numbers of the kids who nobody

wants end up concentrated in the schools that no one chooses except by default . . .

Now the dark, terrifying prospect of vouchers or a choice agenda, of a so-called market basis for our public schools, is that rather than encourage a sense of common loyalties among people, choice will particularize loyalties. It will fragmentize ambition, so that the individual parent will be forced to claw and scramble for the good of her kid and her kid only, at whatever cost to everybody else. There's a wonderful quote from John Dewey. He said "What the best and wisest parent wants for his own child, that must the community want for all its children. Any other ideal for our schools is narrow and unlovely. Acted upon, it destroys our democracy."

. . . The best known voucher advocate, John Chubb, of the Brookings Institute, in Washington, says something—I'm paraphrasing him—like this: "Democratic governance of schools is what's wrong with schools. We need a voucher plan in order to break the bonds of democratic education, because it hasn't worked." That's what he says.

When I hear that, I think to myself, "Wait a minute. We've never tried democratic education." We haven't yet given equal, wonderful, innovative, humane schools—at the level of our finest schools—to all our children. . . . I think we should try it first, see how it might work.[2]

[1] Mardell Raney. Interview with Jonathan Kozol. *Technos*, 7 no. 3 (Fall 1998), pp. 4–10.
[2] Reprinted with permission of *Educational Leadership* 50, no. 3 (November 1992), pp. 90–92.

REFLECTION: In your opinion, what American values are reflected—or undermined—in school choice?

www.mhhe.com/ sadker8e

To learn more about Jonathan Kozol, click on *Profiles in Education*.

was created by two veteran teachers committed to providing a more effective education for poor inner-city children.[26] Although charter schools operate differently in different states, the increase in the number of charter schools across the country has been spectacular. Why?

One reason is that charter schools are less controversial than voucher plans. They do not involve religious schools or competition between public and private schools. They appeal to people who support public schools but who have concerns about their quality. The enthusiasm generated by these supporters is contagious, and often translates into a robust educational effort, and a great deal of positive publicity. But is enthusiasm enough for the long haul? Are charters doing as well as some say?

While it is too early to reach a final assessment of charters, some problems are coming to light. Charters were created to experiment, promote innovation, and to trailblaze new educational approaches. This is not happening. Most charters, in fact, are mirroring the most traditional educational practices available. And they are teaching a very select student population. Critics point out that by doing this, they are actually segregating students, creating schools where all the children are similar and share similar goals, a far cry from the inclusive and democratic ideal of public education. Initially advocates proclaimed that the charters would cut the cost of education by eliminating a "bloated administration," but this has not been the case. Their low student enrollments and the need to duplicate resources like libraries and computers has translated into just the opposite, higher administrative costs than public schools. Added to these financial woes is the fact that many charters are located in inadequate buildings, either converted facilities or schools built with cheap materials, so we can include safety concerns to our list.[27] In Arizona, the state with the most charter schools, one out of every three charters is "underperforming," a rate twice as high as the state's noncharter public schools.[28] This does not appear to be only an Arizona problem. In 2003, a national study revealed that charter schools were plagued by problems. Nearly half of the teachers were unlicensed, poor and disabled students underfunded, black students isolated, and overcrowding common. Yet, in other instances, charters were performing far better than other public schools, fueling a movement that has seen amazing growth.[29] Whether charter schools will revolutionize public education or remain just a boutique innovation remains an unanswered question.

Who are the people who create such schools? Tom Watkins, director of the Detroit Center for Charter Schools, describes three types of charter advocates: reformers, zealots, and entrepreneurs. *Reformers* are those who want to expand public school options and create more teacher- and student-centered institutions. These are the most mainstream advocates, the ones who often engender positive reports in the press. Watkins also describes *zealots*, those who prefer private to public schools, who view teacher unions as the obstacle to change and many of whom are themselves politically quite conservative. The final group consists of *entrepreneurs*, those who view schools as untapped profit centers and charter schools as vehicles for combining business and education. In the next section, we will take a closer look at these educational entrepreneurs.[30]

Schools.com

One of the most unusual schools we shall look at (well perhaps not exactly "look at" because you cannot really see it) is a school that has no building, no parking lot, and no one actually goes there (some might call it a "dream school"). But before

How would you feel about teaching in a virtual school? What are the advantages, and disadvantages?

you get carried away, **virtual schools** provide a wealth of learning, usually via technology. Actually, a virtual school is a form of **distance learning,** or learning provided over long distances via television, the Internet, and other technologies. The first virtual high school (VHS) began in Massachusetts in 1997. Today K–12 online learning programs exist in about half of the states. Recognizing the importance of online literacy, in 2006 Michigan became the first state to require high school students to complete one online course in order to graduate.[31]

As with other schools, most virtual schools still have a central office, administrators, teachers, professional development, curriculum, daily attendance, grades, report cards, parent conferences, special-education and health services, field trips, rules, discipline infractions, state reporting, school board meetings, and even disgruntled parents. But they no longer have to be housed in big brick-and-mortar buildings. Rather than taking cars and buses to school, teachers and students ride the Internet.

One reason for the popularity of online learning is that it offers specialized courses not typically found in traditional high schools. The VHS in Massachusetts, for example, offers Bioethics Symposium, Earth 2525, A Model United Nations Simulation, and Folklore and Literature of Myth, Magic, and Ritual. Virtual classes are asynchronous (that is, people can join classroom activities at any time of the day or night), so students from around the nation or around the world can take the same course at a time that works for them. Students in a small town in Colorado can enroll online in an advanced anthropology course with classmates from New York, Los Angeles, and even Amman, Jordan. (For more information, visit "Welcome to the Virtual High School" at www.govhs.org.)

While many virtual high schools were formed to augment high school programs, some have been organized as full-time charter high schools, offering an entire high school curriculum online. Whether students attend full or part time, virtual high schools provide expanded opportunities, especially to students in under-resourced

www.mhhe.com/
sadker8e

INTERACTIVE ACTIVITY
Virtual High School Click on the Virtual High School Web site to observe an online classroom.

rural or urban schools. Homebound children with special needs; students who prefer to learn online; or students whose creativity, talent, and curiosity exceed the resources of their local school all benefit from online learning.

Critics of virtual schools argue that they isolate students and deprive them of important social interactions (one reason why there are so few virtual schools at the elementary level). But students learning online report that they find virtual courses more personal, interactive, and individualized than typical high school classes. Other supporters point out that virtual schools may hold the answer to a growing teacher shortage.[32] Clearly, virtual schools have become part of our educational landscape.

EMOs (Educational Maintenance Organizations): Schools for Profit

Wall Street calls them **EMOs,** paralleling the HMOs in the health maintenance industry. HMOs are big business, and many on Wall Street are predicting that EMOs will be too. During the past few years, for-profit businesses have contracted with local school districts to provide a wide range of services in an attempt to win a segment of the lucrative education market, a market that exceeds $300 billion a year. Not that the entrance of private companies onto the public educational scene is completely new. For years, school districts have contracted with private businesses to provide school lunches and bus transportation. But, to manage education itself, to be responsible for academic performance, *is* new.

The largest for-profit venture in public schools, the **Edison Schools,** took off after a chance encounter. In 1990, Benno Schmidt, the president of Yale University, was attending a party in the Hamptons, a posh section of Long Island. At that party, Schmidt met Chris Whittle, an entrepreneur who was involved with various education-related projects. Apparently, they hit it off. Whittle offered Schmidt a high salary, reported to be about $1 million a year, to leave Yale and assume leadership of the Edison Schools. Chris Whittle's vision called for creating a model school, one based on proven educational programs, and then franchising the model nationally.

Edison Schools lengthen the school day by one or two hours, while increasing the school year from 180 days to 210 days. In effect, these changes add about two more years of study before graduation. Curricular changes include devoting more school time to math and science, foreign language instruction starting from the early grades, and using proven programs, such as the University of Chicago's "Everyday Mathematics" approach to math and "Success for All," a reading program developed at Johns Hopkins University. Learning contracts are used to increase student accountability. Edison's plan calls for linking each student to the school by a company-provided home computer. The computer offers students a virtual library and gives both parents and students a dedicated communication link to teachers.

The project's start-up costs were enormous, and the franchise idea was not easy to implement. Whittle saw that opening charter schools would be an easier way to disseminate his plan.[33] The charter school movement was a wonderful opportunity for education companies like Edison. The company could work with an entire school district or deal directly with parents and neighborhood groups, selling its Edison concept as a charter school. Today Edison manages about 100 public schools throughout the country. Yet a critical question remains unanswered: Are these schools effective? A Columbia University study of Edison found that there was high teacher morale, enthusiasm for the curriculum, and satisfied parents. However, some Edison employees reported that the company was hiding its problems from the public and that the needs of special education students, among others, were not being met. Studies by the American Federation of Teachers, National Education Association, and RAND Corporation found Edison students doing no better than regular public school students, and sometimes worse.[34] Dogged by financial troubles and persistent questions, Chris Whittle turned his public venture into a private company. The future of Edison Schools remains rocky.

Yet private-sector education companies are undaunted and continue to multiply. Ten percent of charter schools are managed by for-profit companies. Advantage Schools, a Boston-based company, focuses on urban school districts, hires nonunion teachers, and promotes direct instruction, a program that relies on intense and frequent teacher-student interactions, and like other private companies, does not have a stellar record with special education students. Sylvan Learning Systems provides after-school instruction for students who are performing below expectations. In fact, Sylvan is piloting their centers at Wal-Mart, so students can be tutored while parents cruise the aisles. Advocates of the private management of schools, called **privatization,** argue that corporations can more effectively and less expensively provide specific services for and even run innovative schools, especially those serving underperforming children. Critics worry that schools fueled by a profit motive will shortchange students' academic and social needs in order to make money.[35] The business community is certainly not timid about investing in public education.

Brand Name Education: Should Schools Be "Open" for Business?

Is school choice a good idea? Is even asking the question somehow undemocratic? Choice supporters are quick to point out that vouchers and charters give poor families the kind of school choice that wealthy families already enjoy. Even a brief visit to an impoverished urban neighborhood public school underscores this sad reality: Many of these schools are doing a woefully inadequate job. Little wonder that many urban parents support choice plans, and would view a new charter school as an oasis in an educational desert.[36] But we need to look more carefully, for the charter oasis may turn out to be little more than an educational mirage.

It is convenient to group all choice options together. That is a big mistake. Choice options and charter schools vary greatly. One of the fundamental differences is whether a school is a nonprofit, public institution, or there to make a profit.[37] Along with a number of other writers and educators, the authors of this text have deep reservations about what happens to children when schools are turned into profit centers. Opening minds should be the goal of public education, not turning a profit. To ensure that we provide you with the other side of the issue, this chapter's *You Be the Judge* includes a business perspective. However, to be true to our beliefs, in this section, we will share some of our concerns.

Do the laws of the marketplace belong in public education? Should we give private companies access to public institutions? Business supporters answer in the affirmative and believe competition is the key to creating more efficient and effective schools. Not everyone agrees. Alex Molnar, for example, studied the economics of for-profit charter schools and discovered that they simply replace a public bureaucracy with a private one, are less efficient, less equitable, and less accountable than

Are a Good Idea Because . . .

COMPETITION LEADS TO BETTER SCHOOLS

For-profit schools will break down the public school monopoly by creating competition and choice. As schools compete, parents (particularly poor parents) will finally have a choice, and not be forced to place their children in the neighborhood school. Just like in business, the weak schools will lose students and declare "bankruptcy." The stronger schools will survive and prosper.

SCHOOLS WILL BE ABLE TO REWARD GOOD TEACHERS, AND REMOVE WEAK ONES

The current public school bureaucracy protects too many incompetent teachers through the tenure system, and does not recognize teaching excellence. Using sound business practices, for-profit schools will reward superior teachers through profit-sharing incentives, retain competent teachers, and terminate ineffective teachers.

BUSINESS EFFICIENCY WILL IMPROVE SCHOOL PERFORMANCE

Education needs the skills and know-how of the business community. For-profit schools will implement the most effective educational strategies in a business culture. The top-heavy management of today's schools will be replaced by only a handful of administrators, and teachers will be driven to greater productivity through the profit incentives.

FOCUSED PROGRAMS AND INVESTOR OVERSIGHT LEAD TO ACADEMIC SUCCESS

For-profit schools will do a better educational job because they provide a focused and proven instructional plan. These schools avoid the public school pitfall of trying to offer "something-for-everyone." And if they falter and profits disappear, investor pressure will put them back on track.

Are a Bad Idea Because . . .

COMPETITION LEADS TO WEAKER SCHOOLS

Transplanting businesslike competition into the education arena would be a disaster. Competition is not all that business brings: false advertising, "special" promotions, a "feel-good" education—all the hucksterism of the marketplace to mislead students and their parents. Worse yet, the local public school, which holds a community together, will be lost.

TEACHERS WILL LOSE THEIR INFLUENCE AND ACADEMIC FREEDOM

Teachers who speak out against the company, or teach a controversial or politically sensitive topic, will have a brief career. The business community is quite vocal about teachers sharing in the profits, but strangely silent about what will happen during economic hard times.

PROFITS AND EDUCATION DO NOT MIX

For-profit schools are exactly that, "for profit," and when the interests of children and investors clash, investor interests will prevail. If investors demand better returns, if the stock market drops, if the economy enters hard times, the corporate executives will sacrifice educational resources. After all, while students enjoy little leverage, stockholders can fire business executives.

FOCUSED PROGRAMS MEANS KEEPING SOME STUDENTS OUT

Their one-size-fits-all approach practiced by these schools might be good for efficiency, but it is bad for students. The more challenging students, those with special needs, non-native speakers of English, or those who need special counseling, will be left to the underfunded public schools to educate.

www.mhhe.com/
sadker

YOU DECIDE . . .

Do you believe that business and schools are a good or a bad match? Explain. Do you believe that profits can be made in schooling the nation's children? As a teacher, would you want to work for a for-profit school? Now here is your chance to be the author! What additional advantages and disadvantages of for-profit schools can you add to the above lists?

public schools.[38] Studies reveal that for-profit schools too often reject special needs students who may be more challenging and more costly to educate.[39] Molnar finds the HMO-EMO analogy troubling:

> The only reason that the health care industry can make a profit is that it has nothing to do with [social] equity. We've got 40 million Americans who on any given day don't have health insurance. Now that's a social catastrophe. The same thing would happen in education. If you cut the schools loose from any concern about equity, you could carve out schools that you could run for a profit. However, it would be at an enormous social cost.[40]

The competitive business model is all about mining a market segment, finding the consumers likely to buy the product, and shunning others. School choice programs are not the only schools drawn into this marketplace strategy. The traditional neighborhood public school increasingly turns to the business community for funds. The push for private money stems from several different pressures. New government requirements and rising operating costs are not being met by most state budgets.

If clever ads can convince Americans to pay $150 for athletic shoes or $100 for designer jeans, imagine the power of advertisements in hyping something really important, like education. School districts have begun a blitz of new efforts to attract private money. Many have hired development officers to seek out their community's big donors, and consider everything from corporate sponsorship of the high school prom to selling advertising space on school roofs. In states where it is legal, districts now sell advertisements on school buses. Critics complain that educational resources are being spent on questionable advertising rather than on improving educational programs. Will brand name schools be the designer clothes of the next decade? How far away are we from having our children attend Nike Elementary School or Dunkin' Donuts High? Perhaps closer than many imagine.

The school-business connection has been galvanized by the federal *No Child Left Behind* law, which factors attendance into its evaluations. Across the country, schools are offering cars, iPods, and even a month's rent to students just for showing up. Most of the prizes are paid for by local businesses or donors. For example, in Hartford, Connecticut, a 9-year won a raffle for students with perfect attendance and was given the choice of a new Saturn Ion or $10,000. (His parents chose the money.) At Oldham County High School in Buckner, Kentucky, a high school senior was awarded a canary yellow Ford Mustang. Krispy Kreme doughnuts awards students in Palm Beach County, Florida, a free doughnut for every report card A. And in Temecula, California, the school district prizes can include iPods, DVD players, and a trip to Disneyland. Describing his quest for additional school funds, one high school principal noted, "My approach is Leave No Dollar Behind."[41]

Brand naming is growing as schools enter "exclusive agreements" with companies to ensure that no competitive

What lesson is being taught in this school environment?

products are sold on school grounds. Coca-Cola promised Oakland, California, half a million dollars to support a community youth program in return for a 10-year agreement banning the sale of competing soft drinks on city property. These exclusive "pouring rights" contracts may turn out to be a very bad business deal as school officials find themselves targeted by lawsuits blaming them, along with fast-food and soft drink companies, for contributing to America's obesity epidemic.[42] Schools are also borrowing business practices of professional sports, selling naming rights to school property. When Brooklawn, New Jersey, needed funds for a new school gymnasium, the school board sold the name to the local supermarket, ShopRite. For this nonstop advertisement, ShopRite agreed to pay $100,000, prorated to $5,000 a year, a figure that only covered maintenance and operation costs. Naming rights was a smart business move since ShopRite did not have to pay even a single penny of actual construction cost.

Branding schools does not stop with athletic facilities. School districts now sell the naming rights of school buildings, offer companies the opportunity to put their corporate logos on textbooks and other curricular material, and hang advertising banners from school buildings. Sometimes the corporation simply pays a bounty to the school for getting students and parents to buy their products. General Mills donates funds to schools based on the number of box-tops turned in or other coupons showing proof of purchase. Television commercials now air during school time to a captive audience of future consumers. Channel One, for example, broadcasts commercials in school and students admit they are more likely to remember the ads than the educational programs.

Business interests have moved beyond commercials to prime time, working to inculcate business values into the curriculum. The paper company Weyerhauser pays teachers during the summer to join their "company science center," and the industry group Pacific Logging Congress provides photos and brochures explaining why clear-cutting forests is environmentally sound. Should cell phones be part of the curriculum? They already are as students learn proper cell phone use behind the wheel, courtesy of Verizon. "Nutrition curriculums" are being offered by fast food and snack companies. McDonald's Corporation sends its Ronald McDonald mascot into schools as the company's "ambassador for an active, balanced lifestyle." PepsiCo has also embraced the youth fitness cause. The company, a manufacturer of snack foods as well as soft drinks, has sent fitness education materials to elementary and middle schools. Since excess consumption of snack foods, soft drinks, and fast food has been implicated in the alarming rise in childhood obesity, companies that promote and profit from these sales are likely using "fitness" as a public relation fig leaf. As one critic noted, if you teach business values early enough, children accept it as truth.[43]

Profits and corporate values are well represented in everyday school practices. As Linda Darling-Hammond notes:

> The short segmented tasks stressing speed and neatness that predominate in most schools, the emphasis on rules from the important to the trivial, and the obsession with bells, schedules, and time clocks are all dug deep into the ethos of late nineteenth-century America, when students were being prepared to work in factories on predetermined tasks that would not require them to figure out what to do.[44]

Add to this analogy the impact of the current standards and testing movement, and we can more clearly see that we are in the midst of a major business incursion into public schools. The National Association of Manufacturers insists on more testing as well as "a national system of skills standards designed by industry." Today's testing industry is a two-prong profit center, funneling literally billions of dollars into corporate coffers. Profit Center #1: The sales and scoring of newly required standardized tests. Profit Center #2: Public schools that score poorly become prime targets to be replaced by for-profit companies. We discuss the current standards and testing movement in greater detail later in this text, and the business influence will once again become evident.

Whatever your personal belief about the importance of business in America, the growing influence of business in schools raises serious ethical and educational concerns. Is public education a venue for corporate profits? What happens if and when the private money dries up? And each time private money fills the gaps left by public financing, are legislators and taxpayers allowed to shrug off responsibility for supporting education? Are competition, advertising, and a commitment to materialism good for our children? We believe that schools should promote creative thinking, reflection, care for others and a commitment to improve the quality of life on this planet. These goals are not only more important than profits and crass materialism, they are in conflict with them.

Home Schools, Home Teachers

Thirteen-year old Taylor is working at the kitchen table, sorting out mathematical exponents. At 10, Travis is absorbed in *The Story of Jackie Robinson,* while his brother Henry is practicing Beethoven's Minuet in G on his acoustical guitar. The week before, the brothers had attended a local performance of a musical comedy, attended a seminar on marine life and participated in a lively debate about news reports concerning corporal punishment in Singapore. These boys are part of a growing number of students being educated at home. What makes their story somewhat unusual is that their father is unable to participate in their education as much as he might like, because he must spend time at his own work: teaching English at a local public high school.[45]

Home schooling, the practice of parents (even teachers) choosing to educate their children at home rather than have them attend school, is a growing trend. (See Figure 4.4.) Only a few decades ago, a mere 12,500 students were home schooled, yet today between one and two million children are taught at home.[46] Why the huge increase?

While concerns about the school environment, such as safety, drugs and peer pressure, are the primary motivations for home schooling, they are not the only reasons.[47] Many parents opt for home schooling to ensure specific religious and moral instruction. Other parents, disenchanted with school bureaucracies, choose to create home schools that nurture their children and individualize learning. But not all home schools are launched with such noble motivations. Sometimes racism, anti-Semitism, or another hateful reason can inspire a parent to home school. Researcher Van Galen describes parents who home school as either ideologues or pedagogues. **Ideologues** focus on imparting certain values. They create a home school where they choose the curriculum, create the rules, enforce a schedule, and promote their beliefs. **Pedagogues** are motivated by educational goals; they are interested in the process of learning, intrinsic motivation, and experiential activities.[48]

Technology has been a real boost to the movement. Some Internet service providers now offer a home-schooling forum, complete with lesson plans, tutoring, legislative updates, and group networking, while virtual schools bring education directly into the home.[49]

FIGURE 4.4

Who are home schoolers?

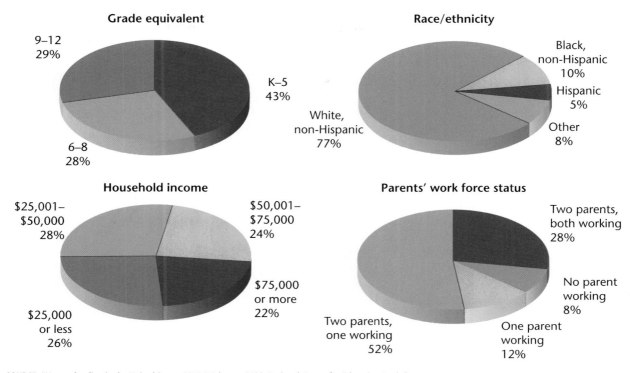

SOURCE: "Homeschooling in the United States: 2003," February 2006, National Center for Education Statistics.

REFLECTION: These percentages are based on a million home schoolers. Some believe that the true number may be at least twice that. Why do you believe so many home schoolers are not counted? How might these statistics change if those left out were included?

Does it work? Home-schooled children score between 15 and 30 percentile points higher than their peers on standardized tests.[50] In fact, home schoolers like Grant Colfax, have achieved some notoriety. Grant attended neither elementary nor secondary school, yet won admission to Harvard, graduated *magna cum laude,* became a Fulbright scholar, and eventually graduated from Harvard Medical School. His home-schooled brothers enjoyed similar success—all endorsements of home schooling.

But home schooling has its critics as well. Do children educated in isolation from their peers suffer any negative consequences? What is lost by not working and learning with other children of diverse beliefs and backgrounds? Since Americans were originally motivated to build schools in order to promote Americanization, to meld a single nation, to learn how to live and work together, it is logical to wonder if home schooling will adversely affect our national cohesion.[51]

This chapter has explored a deceptively simple question: What's a school for? The many approaches to schooling offer us a variety of insights into the purposes of schools, but there is one critical question that we have left unasked (until now): What makes a school effective? So let's close this chapter with a look at what we know (and don't know) about effective schools.

What does a school's name, mascot, message board, and presentation say about what's happening inside the classroom? What do these school signs tell you? Are there ways to identify a good school by its sign? How would your high school sign fit in the photo gallery?

 What Makes a School Effective?

Consider the following situation: Two schools are located in the same neighborhood and are considered "sister schools." They are approximately the same size, serve the same community, and the student populations are identical. However, in one school, state test scores are low and half the students drop out. In the other school, student test scores exceed the state average and almost all students graduate. Why the difference?

Puzzled by such situations, researchers attempted to determine what factors create successful schools. Several studies have revealed a common set of characteristics, a **five-factor theory of effective schools**.[52] Researchers say that effective schools are able, through these five factors, to promote student achievement. Let's take a look at these classic five factors, and then move on to some more recent studies.

Factor 1: Strong Leadership

In her book *The Good High School*, Sara Lawrence Lightfoot drew portraits of six effective schools.[53] Two, George Washington Carver High School in Atlanta and John F. Kennedy High School in the Bronx, were inner-city schools. Highland Park High School near Chicago and Brookline High School in Brookline, Massachusetts,

**www.mhhe.com/
sadker8e**

INTERACTIVE ACTIVITY

**What Makes Schools
Effective?** Rate What you
think makes schools
effective. Compare your
responses to those of
your colleagues.

were upper middle-class and suburban. St. Paul's High School in Concord, New Hampshire, and Milton Academy near Boston were elite preparatory schools. Despite the tremendous difference in the styles and textures of these six schools, ranging from the pastoral setting of St. Paul's to inner-city Atlanta, they all were characterized by strong, inspired leaders, such as Robert Mastruzzi, principal of John F. Kennedy High School.

When Robert Mastruzzi started working at Kennedy, the building was not yet completed. Walls were being built around him as he sat in his unfinished office and contemplated the challenge of not only his first principalship but also the opening of a new school. During his years as principal of John F. Kennedy, his leadership style has been collaborative, actively seeking faculty participation. Not only does he want his staff to participate in decision making, but he gives them the opportunity to try new things—and even the right to fail. For example, one teacher made an error about the precautions necessary for holding a rock concert (800 adolescents had shown up, many high or inebriated). Mastruzzi realized that the teacher had learned a great deal from the experience, and he let her try again. The second concert was a great success. "He sees failure as an opportunity for change," the teacher said. Still other teachers describe him with superlatives, such as "he is the lifeblood of this organism" and "the greatest human being I have ever known."[54]

Mastruzzi seems to embody the characteristics of effective leaders in good schools. Researchers say that students make significant achievement gains in schools in which principals

- Articulate a clear school mission
- Are a visible presence in classrooms and hallways
- Hold high expectations for teachers and students
- Spend a major portion of the day working with teachers to improve instruction
- Are actively involved in diagnosing instructional problems
- Create a positive school climate[55]

Factor 2: A Clear School Mission

A day in the life of a principal can be spent trying to keep small incidents from becoming major crises. But the research is clear: In effective schools, good principals somehow find time to develop a vision of what that school should be and to share that vision with all members of the educational community. Successful principals can articulate a specific school mission, and they stress innovation and improvement. In contrast, less effective principals are vague about their goals and focus on maintaining the status quo. They make such comments as, "We have a good school and a good faculty, and I want to keep it that way."[56]

It is essential that the principal share his or her vision, so that teachers understand the school's goals and all work together for achievement. Unfortunately, when teachers are polled, more than 75 percent say that they have either no contact or infrequent contact with one another during the school day. In less effective schools, teachers lack a common understanding of the school's mission, and they function as individuals charting their own separate courses.

The need for the principal to share his or her vision extends not only to teachers but to parents as well. When teachers work cooperatively and parents are connected with the school's mission, the children are more likely to achieve academic success.

A positive, energizing school atmosphere characterized by accepting relationships between students and faculty often begins and ends with the principal.

Factor 3: A Safe and Orderly Climate

Certainly before students can learn or teachers can teach, schools must be safe. An unsafe school is, by definition, ineffective. Despite the attention-grabbing headlines and the disturbing incidents of student shootings, schools today are safer than they have been in years.[57] (See Figure 4.5.) Nearly all public school teachers (98 percent) and most students (93 percent) report feeling safe in schools.[58] Yet the image of unsafe schools persists, and for more than two decades, opinion polls have shown that the public considers lack of discipline to be among the most serious problems facing schools (though LGBT students are three times more likely to feel unsafe at school).[59]

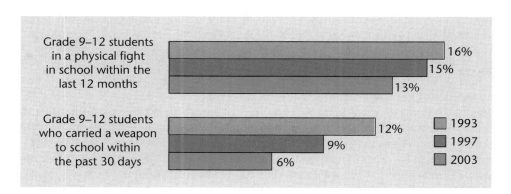

FIGURE 4.5

School-related violence: On the decrease

SOURCE: National Center for Education Statistics, Indicators of School Crime and Safety, 2005.

Grade 9–12 students in a physical fight in school within the last 12 months: 16%, 15%, 13%

Grade 9–12 students who carried a weapon to school within the past 30 days: 12%, 9%, 6%

- 1993
- 1997
- 2003

REFLECTION: How do you explain the popular perception of a more violent society contrasted with these statistics reflecting a decrease in school violence?

Good schools have safe
environments.

The vast majority of schools provide safe learning environments. This is accomplished by more than metal detectors and school guards. Safe schools focus on academic achievement, the school mission, involving families and communities in school activities, and creating an environment where teachers, students, and staff are treated with respect. Student problems are identified early, before they deteriorate into violence. School psychologists, special education programs, family social workers, and schoolwide programs increase communication and reduce school tension.

In some of America's most distressed neighborhoods, safe schools provide a much needed neighborhood refuge. Sara Lawrence Lightfoot tells of the long distances that urban students travel to reach John F. Kennedy High School in the Bronx. One girl, who did not have money to buy a winter coat or glasses to see the chalkboard, rode the subway 1 hour and 40 minutes each way to get to school. She never missed a day, because for her school was a refuge—a place of hope where she could learn in safety.[60]

Factor 4: Monitoring Student Progress

As the researcher walked through the halls of a school we will call Clearview Elementary School, she noted attractive displays of student work mounted on bulletin boards and walls. Also posted were profiles clearly documenting class and school progress toward meeting academic goals. Students had a clear sense of how they were doing in their studies; they kept progress charts in their notebooks. During teacher interviews, the faculty talked about the individual strengths and weaknesses of their students. Teachers referred to student folders that contained thorough records of student scores on standardized tests, as well as samples of classwork, homework, and performance on weekly tests.

A visit to Foggy Bottom Elementary, another fictitious school with a revealing name, disclosed striking differences. Bulletin boards and walls were attractive, but few student papers were posted, and there was no charting of progress toward academic goals. Interviews with students showed that they had only a vague idea of how they were doing and of ways to improve their academic performance. Teachers also seemed unclear about individual student progress. When pressed for more information, one teacher sent the researcher to the guidance office, saying, "I think they keep some records like the California Achievement Tests. Maybe they can give you what you're looking for."

Following the visit, the researcher wrote her report: "A very likely reason that Clearview students achieve more than Foggy Bottom students is that one school carefully monitors student progress and communicates this information to students and parents. The other school does not."

Effective schools carefully monitor and assess student progress in a variety of ways:

- **Norm-referenced tests** compare individual students with others in a nationwide norm group (e.g., the Stanford9).
- **Objective-referenced tests** measure whether a student has mastered a designated body of knowledge (e.g., state assessment tests used to determine who has "mastered" the material).

Other measures may be less formal. Teacher-made tests are an important (and often overlooked) measure of student progress. Some teachers ask students to track their own progress in reaching course objectives as a way of helping them assume more responsibility for their own learning.[61] Homework is another strategy to monitor students. Researcher Herbert Walberg and colleagues found that homework increases student achievement scores from the 50th to the 60th percentile. When homework is graded and commented on, achievement is increased from the 50th to nearly the 80th percentile. Although these findings suggest that graded homework is an important ingredient in student achievement,[62] how much homework to assign, and what kinds of homework tasks are most effective, continue to be points of contention.

Factor 5: High Expectations

The teachers were excited. A group of their students had received extraordinary scores on a test that predicted intellectual achievement during the coming year. Just as the teachers had expected, these children attained outstanding academic gains that year.

Now for the rest of the story: The teachers had been duped. The students identified as gifted had been selected at random. However, eight months later, these randomly selected children did show significantly greater gains in total IQ than did another group of children, the control group.

In their highly influential 1969 publication, ***Pygmalion in the Classroom,*** researchers Robert Rosenthal and Lenore Jacobson discussed this experiment and the power of teacher expectations in shaping student achievement. They popularized the term **self-fulfilling prophecy** and revealed that students may learn as much—or as little—as teachers expect.[63] Although methodological criticisms of the original Rosenthal and Jacobson study abound, those who report on effective schools say that there is now extensive evidence showing that high teacher expectations do, in fact, produce high student achievement, and low expectations produce low achievement.[64]

Too often, teacher expectations have a negative impact. An inaccurate judgment about a student can be made because of error, unconscious prejudice, or stereotype. For example, good-looking, well-dressed students are frequently thought to be smarter than their less attractive peers. Often, male students are thought to be

1800–1900	Memorization is the mark of an educated person, and homework consumes many hours
1900–1940	Homework is considered a form of child labor, and a health risk; memorization and homework are de-emphasized
1940–1957	Creative, individualized assignments usher in a more humane return to homework
1957–1967	The lunch of *Sputnik* sparks increased homework, especially in math and science
1968–1982	Social concerns and civil rights take precedence over academics and homework
1982–present	A *Nation at Risk* reports that homework is an effective counter to falling test scores, and homework increases dramatically, despite the concern of many parents

SOURCE: Laurel Graeber, "More Work, Less Play," in Education Life, *The New York Times*, January 3, 1999.

REFLECTION: Where do you predict the homework pendulum will be during your time in the classroom? Do you have a preference?

brighter in math, science, and technology, while girls are given the edge in language skills. Students of color are sometimes perceived as less capable or intelligent. A poor performance on a single standardized test (perhaps due to illness or an "off" day) can cause teachers to hold an inaccurate assessment of a student's ability for months and even years. Even a casual comment in the teachers' lounge can shape the expectations of other teachers.

When teachers hold low expectations for certain students, their treatment of these students often differs in unconscious and subtle ways. Typically, they offer such students

- Fewer opportunities to respond
- Less praise
- Less challenging work
- Fewer nonverbal signs (eye contact, smiles, positive regard)

In effective schools, teachers hold high expectations that students can learn, and they translate these expectations into teaching behaviors. They set objectives, work toward mastery of those objectives, spend more time on instruction, and actively monitor student progress. They are convinced that students can succeed.

Do high expectations work if students do not believe they exist? Probably not, and that is too often the case. While a majority of secondary school principals believe that their schools hold such expectations for their students, only 39 percent of teachers believe this to be true and, even more discouraging, only one in four students believe their school holds high expectations for them.[65] We need to do a better job of communicating these expectations to students, and making certain that these expectations truly challenge students.

And it is not only students who benefit from high expectations. In *The Good High School,* Sara Lawrence Lightfoot reported that when teachers hold high expectations for their own performance, the entire school benefits. At Brookline High School, "star" teachers were viewed as models to be emulated. Always striving for excellence, these teachers felt that no matter how well a class was taught, next time it could be taught better.

A Note of Caution on Effective Schools Research

Although the research on what makes schools effective has had a direct impact on national reform movements, it has limitations.[66] First, there is disagreement over the definition of an effective school. Researchers use varying descriptions, ranging from "schools with high academic achievement" to schools that foster "personal growth, creativity, and positive self-concept." Although the five factors we have described are helpful, they do not really provide a prescription for developing successful schools.

Another problem is that much of the research has been conducted in elementary schools. Although some researchers suggest applicability to secondary and even higher education, caution must be used in carrying the effective-schools findings to higher levels of education. The generalizability of the research is also limited, since several of the studies were conducted in inner-city schools and tied closely to the achievement of lower-order skills in math and science. If one wanted to develop a school that nurtures creativity rather than basic skills, another set of characteristics might be more appropriate.

Beyond the Five Factors

New effective-schools findings offer us insights beyond these original five factors of effective schooling:

- *Early start.* The concept that there is a particular age for children to begin school needs to be rethought. The earlier schools start working with children, the better children do. High-quality programs during the first three years of life include parent training, special screening services, and appropriate learning opportunities for children. While such programs are rare, those that are in operation have significantly raised IQ points and have enhanced language skills. It is estimated that $1 spent in an early intervention program saves school districts $7 in special programs and services later in life.

- *Focus on reading and math.* Children not reading at grade level by the end of the first grade face a one-in-eight chance of ever catching up. In math, students who do not master basic concepts find themselves playing catch-up throughout their school years. Effective schools identify and correct such deficiencies early, before student performance deteriorates.

- *Smaller schools.* Students in small schools learn more, are more likely to pass their courses, are less prone to resort to violence, and are more likely to attend college than those attending large schools. Disadvantaged students in small schools outperform their peers in larger schools, as achievement differences for the rich and poor are less extreme. Many large schools have responded to

In *Deschooling Society,* Ivan Illich compared schools to a medieval church, performing more a political than an educational role. The diplomas and degrees issued by schools provide society's "stamp of approval," announcing who shall succeed, who shall be awarded status, and who shall remain in poverty. By compelling students to attend, by judging and labeling them, by confining them, and by discriminating among them, Illich believed that schools harm children. He would replace schools with learning "networks," lifelong and compulsory. To Illich, the notion of waking up to a world without schools would be a dream fulfilled. Education reformer John Holt agreed, and coined the term "un-schooling" to describe an education where kids, not parents or teachers, decide what they will learn. Holt believed that children do not need to be coerced into learning; they will do so naturally if given the freedom to follow their own interests and a rich assortment of resources. For unschooled kids, there are no mandatory books, no curriculum, no tests, and no grades. Children are given complete freedom to learn and explore whatever they choose—from Chinese to aesthetic mathematics to tuba lessons to the Burmese struggle for civil rights.

SOURCE: Ivan Illich, *Deschooling Society* (New York: Harper & Row, 1973); John Holt, *Instead of Education* (New York: Dutton, 1976).

REFLECTION: How are schools more a political than an educational institution? What would your community be like if it were de-schooled?

these findings by reorganizing themselves into smaller units, into schools within schools. Research suggests that small schools are more effective at every educational level, but they may be most important for older students.

- *Smaller classes.* Although the research on class size is less powerful than the research on school size, studies indicate that smaller classes are associated with increased student learning, especially in the earlier grades. Children in classes of 15 outperform students in classes of 25, even when the larger classes have a teacher's aide present.

- *Increased learning time.* While not an amazing insight, research tells us what we already suspect: more study results in more learning. Longer school days, longer school years, more efficient use of school time, and more graded homework are all proven methods of enhancing academic learning time and student performance.

- *Teacher training.* Researcher Linda Darling-Hammond reports that the best way to improve school effectiveness is by investing in teacher training. Stronger teacher skills and qualifications lead to greater student learning. Conversely, students pay an academic price when they are taught by unqualified and uncertified teachers.

- *Trust.* Trusting relationships among parents, students, principals and teachers is a necessary ingredient to govern, improve, and reform schools. As trust levels increase, so does academic performance.

- *Parental Involvement.* Learning is a cooperative venture, and a strong school–home partnership creates a more positive attitude toward learning, and improves academic achievement and social well-being. Not surprisingly, teachers' expectations for student success also rise as parents become more engaged in school life.[67]

Research and experience will continue to offer answers to that pressing question, "What makes a school effective?" Are there factors that you believe might someday be added to this list? Perhaps we could expand the notion of "effective school" to venture beyond academics. Some schools are already doing this, adopting a broader view of an educated American. Such schools create a climate of kindness, teaching students to serve their community and to treat the earth and all its inhabitants with compassion. Perhaps one day more schools will be able to broaden their definition of "effective."

SUMMARY

1. What expectations do Americans hold for their schools?

Since their inception, public schools have been the focus of conflict as they work to meet society's academic, vocational, social, civic, and personal goals.

2. Should schools transmit the American culture or change it?

Two fundamental, often opposing, purposes of schools, are (1) to transmit society's knowledge and values, passing on the cultural baton, and (2) to reconstruct society, empowering students to promote social reform.

3. What school purposes are emphasized by educational reform?

In 1983, *A Nation at Risk* triggered increased testing and a back-to-basics school curriculum, an emphasis that is felt in today's schools. Other reform efforts, focusing on strengthening the teaching profession, restructuring education, and providing social and medical services for children, have had less impact.

4. How are magnet, charter and virtual schools, open enrollment, and vouchers reshaping our concept of the neighborhood public school?

These different schools offer parents choices, and free-market economists like Milton Friedman believe that such choices lead to more competitive and successful schools. As an examples, the charter school movement, which started in 1991, encourages groups to contract with school boards and open their own public school, and virtual schools allow students to take classes via the Internet.

5. Do the laws of the marketplace belong in public education?

For-profit education companies argue that they are more effective and efficient than public schools. But many parents and educators are concerned that profiteering and commercialism are compromising public education.

6. Why are so many families choosing home schooling?

The growth of home schooling is due not only to religious reasons, but also because many parents believe home schooling offers a more effective education that either private or public schooling.

7. What are the characteristics of effective schools?

The "five-factor theory" of effective schools includes: (1) strong administrative leadership, (2) clear school goals shared by faculty and administration, (3) a safe and orderly school climate, (4) frequent monitoring and assessment of student progress, and (5) high expectations for student performance. Newer research connects effective schools with early intervention programs, an emphasis on reading and math, smaller schools, smaller classes, increased learning time, assessment of student progress, expanded teacher training, and parental involvement.

www.mhhe.com/
sadker8e

CHAPTER REVIEW

Go to the Online Learning Center to take a chapter self-quiz, practice with key terms, and review concepts from the chapter.

THE *TEACHERS, SCHOOLS, AND SOCIETY* READER WITH CLASSROOM OBSERVATION VIDEO CLIPS

Go to your *Teachers, Schools, and Society* Reader CD-ROM to:

READ CURRENT AND HISTORICAL ARTICLES

4.1 **Questionable Assumptions about Schooling,** Elliot Eisner, *Phi Delta Kappan,* 2003.

4.2 **Teaching against Idiocy,** Walter Parker, *Phi Delta Kappan,* January 2005.

4.3 **Schools Our Teachers Deserve,** Rosetta Marantz Cohen, *Phi Delta Kappan,* March 2002.

ANALYZE CASE STUDIES

4.1 **Amy Rothman:** A high-school resource room teacher is confronted by a parent during a staffing meeting about a gifted, autistic student in her resource room for whom the parent wants a service not provided by the school district.

4.2 **Chris Kettering:** A teacher finds to his dismay that his white, middle-class students are not interested in social activism and that he is unable to promote awareness and openmindedness in them.

OBSERVE TEACHERS, STUDENTS, AND CLASSROOMS IN ACTION

Classroom Observation: Tour of a Charter School

You may one day want to explore teaching in a charter school. In this observation, you will observe the faculty and administrators of the Match charter school who provide insights into daily life and teaching in a charter school. A number of comparisons with typical public schools are made.

KEY TERMS AND PEOPLE

DISCUSSION QUESTIONS AND ACTIVITIES

1. Discuss your list of school goals that you recorded with your classmates. Which goals seem to be most important to your peers? to your instructor? Which do you consider most important? Give reasons for your priorities.

2. Congratulations! You have been put in charge of designing the next charter school in your district. Describe the charter school that you would design. Be sure to include the research on effective schools in your description. Going beyond the current research, what unique factor(s) would you make part of your school because you believe they would contribute to an effective school?

3. Imagine you are a school board member and your district is debating whether to move to an open enrollment or to a voucher system. Defend your opinion in a brief memo.

4. What do you think of private businesses contracting to run schools? What factors would cause you to seek or avoid teaching for a corporation? Would you feel secure in your job, even without tenure?

5. Does your local public school district have an official (or unofficial) policy concerning home schooling? Do home-schooled students participate in any school activities or receive any school resources? How do you feel about these (un)official policies?

WEB-*TIVITIES*

Go to the Online Learning Center to do the following activities:

1. The Purposes of Schools
2. Paulo Freire and Reconstructionism
3. Educational Vouchers and School Choice
4. Educational Maintenance Organizations (EMOs)
5. Home Schools, Home Teachers
6. Preventing School Violence
7. Monitoring Student Progress
8. The Virtual High School

REEL TO REAL TEACHING

SCHOOL TIES (1992)
Run Time: 110 minutes

Synopsis: A working-class Jewish quarterback is offered a senior year scholarship to a prestigious New England academy. It's his ticket to an Ivy League education, but there is one condition: The school's administration asks him to hide his religious identity.

Reflection:

1. What is the purpose of education at St. Matthew's Academy, according to the school administration? Teachers? Students? Parents? Alumni? Describe the similarities and differences you discover.

2. Would the school's mission have been different if David Greene were allowed to express his religious identity? How?

3. What characteristics, other than religion, do students formally or informally hide in schools?

4. School choice programs, similar to a private school like St. Matthew's, may be selective about who is admitted to a school. How is a school's purpose reflected in selective inclusion policies?

5. Who should have the final authority to determine a school's purpose? Who had the ultimate authority in *School Ties*?

Follow-up Activity: Using words and pictures, create a school logo that reflects St. Matthew's school mission in *School Ties*. Revisit the *Where Do You Stand* section in the chapter (pages 135–138). What school goals did you mark as very important? Design a logo that reflects these goals.

www.mhhe.com/
sadker8e

How do you rate this film? Go to *Reel to Real Teaching* to review this film.

FOR FURTHER READING

Common Sense School Reform, by Frederick Hess (2004). Based on real school stories, this book challenges traditional reform strategies like class size reduction, small schools, and enhanced professional development, and offers radical reforms based on accountability, teacher flexibility, competition, and strong leadership. The author argues that the problem with U.S. public schools has nothing to do with education, but with poor management.

Educating the "Right" Way: Markets, Standards, God, and Inequality, by Michael Apple (2001). Why have the needs of private business become top priorities in the public classroom? How did school vouchers move from the conservative fringe to the political mainstream? Why are scores on standardized tests falling, even as teachers are forced to cram more "facts" into their curricula? Apple offers concrete, common-sense solutions that show what critical educators and parents can do to interrupt these trends and develop a more democratic educational system, suited to the needs of all American children.

Inside Charter Schools: The Paradox of Radical Decentralization, by Bruce Fuller (2001). This book takes readers into six strikingly different schools, from an evangelical home schooling charter in California to a back-to-basics charter in a black neighborhood in Lansing, Michigan.

Powerful Reforms with Shallow Roots, by Larry Cuban and Michael Usdan (2003). Featuring close-up case studies of six urban districts (Philadelphia, Baltimore, Chicago, Boston, San Diego, and Seattle), this book explores the reasons why these cities chose to alter their traditional school governance structures and analyzes what happened when the reforms were implemented.

School-Family Partnerships for Children's Success, by Evanthia Patrikakou, Roger Weissberg, Sam Redding, and Herbert Walberg (eds). (2005). While research has shown that parental involvement plays a key role in academic achievement, most schools lack strong parental support. This book provides tools and strategies for teachers and administrators to create positive relationships and productive school-family partnerships by addressing the social and cultural realities of diverse families.

Tinkering towards Utopia: A Century of Public School Reform, by David Tyack and Larry Cuban (1996). Explores some basic questions about the nature of educational reform. Why has it been so difficult to change the basic institutional patterns of schooling? What actually happened when reformers tried to "reinvent" schooling? The authors also suggest that teachers must be at the heart of any effort to renew our schools.

Student Life in School and at Home

CHAPTER 5

FOCUS QUESTIONS

1. What rituals and routines shape classroom life?
2. How is class time related to student achievement?
3. How does the teacher's gatekeeping function influence classroom roles?
4. What is tracking, and what are its advantages and disadvantages?
5. Why has "detracking" become a popular movement?
6. How do peer groups impact elementary school life?
7. In what ways does the adolescent culture shape teenage perceptions and behaviors?
8. What impact do changing family patterns and economic issues have on children and schools?
9. How can educators respond to social issues that place children at risk?
10. What steps can educators take to create a more supportive school environment?

www.mhhe.com/
sadker8e

WHAT DO YOU THINK? What was your school experience like? See how it compares to that of your colleagues.

CHAPTER PREVIEW

School is a culture. Like most cultures, it is filled with its own unique rituals and traditions, and its own set of norms and mores. In school, even the familiar, like time, is made new. Time is told by subjects ("Let's talk before math") or periods ("I'm going home after seventh period"). Students are pinched into passive roles, following schedules created by others, sitting still rather than being active, and responding to teacher questions, but seldom asking any of their own. Such a system challenges and confines both teachers and students. Peer groups create friendships and popularity, a strong subculture that make winners and losers of us all—at least for a brief time. Adults pick up where children leave off, assigning students to what amounts to an academic caste system through *de facto* tracking or ability grouping. While adults focus on academics, many adolescents and preadolescents are focused on relationships and sexuality.

Economic and social factors are also powerful forces in today's classrooms, and have reshaped the family unit. New family patterns abound, challenging the traditional view of the mother, father, and two children (did we forget the dog?) as the "typical" American family. With these changes, economic and social problems threaten our children and challenge teachers. We will describe these challenges so that educators can work to create schools that are safe havens and institutions of hope.

Rules, Rituals, and Routines

Schools create their own cultures, replete with norms, rituals, and routines. Even simple tasks, like distributing textbooks, are clothed with cultural cues, but they are cues that differ for students and teachers.

"Come Right Up and Get Your New Books": A Teacher's Perspective

Dick Thompson looked at the pile of poetry anthologies stacked on his desk and sighed. Getting texts distributed and starting a new unit always seemed like such a chaotic ordeal, particularly with seventh-graders. But worrying over possible mishaps wouldn't get this poetry unit launched. Besides, his students were getting restless, so he had better get things started.

"Okay, class, quiet down. As you can see, the poetry books we've been waiting for have finally arrived. All right, you can cut out the groans. Give the books a fair trial before you sentence them. I'd like the first person in each row to come up, count out enough books for his or her row, and hand them out."

Six students charged to the front and made a mad grab for the books. In the ensuing melee, one stack of books went crashing to the floor.

"Hey, kids, take it easy and stop the squabbling. There are plenty of books to go around. Since this procedure obviously isn't working, we'll just have to slow down and do things one row at a time. Bob, you hand out the books for row 1 first; then Sally will come up and get the books for row 2. It will take a little longer this way, but I think things will go more smoothly. When you get your texts, write your name and room number in the stamped box inside the cover."

Since the dispensing of books now seemed to be progressing in an orderly fashion, Mr. Thompson turned his attention to the several hands waving in the air.

"Yes, Jessica?"

"I can't fill in my name because my pencil just broke. Can I sharpen it?"

"Go ahead. Jamie?"

"My pencil's broken too. Can I sharpen mine?"

"Yes, but wait until Jessica sits down. Let me remind you that you're supposed to come to class prepared. Now there will be no more at the pencil sharpener today. Scott?"

"Can I use the hall pass?"

"Is this absolutely necessary? All right then [responding to Scott's urgent nod]. Now I think we've had enough distraction for one morning. The period's half over and we still haven't gotten into today's lesson. After you get your book and fill in the appropriate information, turn to the poem on page 3. It's called 'Stopping by Woods on a Snowy Evening,' and it's by Robert Frost, one of America's most famous poets. Yes, Rosa?"

"I didn't get a book."

"Tomás, didn't you hand out books to your row? Oh, I see. We're one short. Okay, Rosa, go down to the office and tell Mrs. Goldberg that we need one more of the new poetry anthologies. Now, as I was about to say, I'd like you to think about the questions that I've written on the board: How does the speaker in this poem feel as he looks at the snow filling up the deserted woods? Why does he wish to stop, and what makes him realize that he must go on? The speaker says, 'I have miles to go before I sleep.' He may be talking about more than going to bed for the night. What else may 'sleep' mean in this poem? Yes, Timothy, do you have a comment on the poem already?"

"My glasses are being fixed and I can't read the board."

"All right. Take the seat by my desk. You'll see the board from there. April! Maxine! This is not a time for your private chat room. This is a silent reading activity—and I do mean silent. Okay, class, I think most of you have had enough time to read the poem. Who has an answer for the first question? Jordan?"

"Well, I think the guy in this poem really likes nature. He's all alone, and it's private, with no people around to interrupt him, and he thinks the woods and the snow are really beautiful. It's sort of spellbinding."

"Jordan, that's an excellent response. You've captured the mood of this poem. Now for the second question. Maxine?"

"I think he wants to stop because . . ."

Maxine's answer was cut short by the abrasive ring of the fourth-period bell.

"Class, sit down. I know the bell has rung, but it isn't signaling a fire. You'll have time to make your next class. Since we didn't get as far into our discussion as I had hoped, I want to give you an assignment. For homework, I'd like you to answer the remaining questions. Alice?"

"Is this to hand in?"

"Yes. Any other questions? Okay, you'd better get to your next-period class."

As the last student left, Dick Thompson slumped over his desk and wearily ran his fingers through his hair. As he looked down, he spotted the missing poetry anthology under his desk, a victim of the charge of the book brigade. The whole lesson was a victim of the book brigade. He had been so busy getting the books dispensed and fielding all the interruptions that he had forgotten to give his brief explanation on the differences between prose and poetry. He had even forgotten to give his motivating speech on how interesting the new poetry unit was going to be. Well, no time for a postmortem now. Stampedelike noises outside the door meant the fourth-period class was about to burst in.

"Come Right Up and Get Your New Books": A Student's Perspective

From her vantage point in the fourth seat, fifth row, Maxine eyed the stack of new books on the teacher's desk. She knew they were poetry books because she had flipped through one as she meandered into the room. She didn't care that it wasn't "in" to like poetry; she liked it anyway. At least it was better than the grammar unit they'd just been through. All those sentences to diagram—picking out nouns and pronouns—what a drag that was.

Maxine settled into her seat and began the long wait for her book. Her thoughts wandered: "Mr. Thompson seems like he's in some kind of daze, just staring at the new books like he's zoned out. Wonder what's bugging him. Good enough, the first kids in each row are heading up to get the books. Oh, right, they're getting into a brawl over handing out the stupid books. What a bunch of jerks; they must think they're funny or something. Now it'll be one row at a time and will take forever. I suppose I can start my math homework or write some letters."

Maxine got several of her math problems solved by the time her poetry anthology arrived, along with instructions to read the poem on page 3. She skimmed through the poem and decided she liked it. She understood how Robert Frost felt, watching the snowy woods and wanting to get away from all the hassles. It sure would be nice to read this poem quietly somewhere without listening to kids going on about pencil sharpeners and hall passes and seat changes. All these interruptions made it hard to concentrate.

As she turned around to share her observation about hassles with April Marston, Mr. Thompson's sharp reprimand interrupted her. She fumed to herself, "Private chat room. What's with him? Half the class is talking, and old Eagle Eyes Thompson has to pick on me. And they're all talking about the football game Saturday. At least I was talking about the poem. Oh well, I'd better answer one of those questions on the board and show him that I really am paying attention."

Maxine waved her hand wildly, but Jordan got called for question 1. Maxine shot her hand in the air again for a chance at question 2. When Mr. Thompson called on her, she drew a deep breath and began her response. Once again, she was interrupted in midsentence, this time by the fourth-period bell. Disgruntled, she stuffed her poetry book under her arm and fell into step beside April Marston.

"I really knew the answer to that question," she muttered under her breath. "Now we have to write all the answers out. Boring. Well, next period is science and we're supposed to be giving lab reports. Maybe we'll have a chance to finish the English homework there."

 ## Delay and Social Distraction

You have just read two capsular replays of a seventh-grade English lesson, one from the vantage point of the teacher, the other from the vantage point of a student. Mr. Thompson and Maxine play different roles, which cause them to have very different experiences in this class. In what ways is the same class experienced differently by teacher and student?

One difference you may have detected is that while Mr. Thompson was continually leapfrogging from one minor crisis to the next, Maxine was sitting and waiting. In his perceptive book **Life in Classrooms, Philip W. Jackson** describes how time is spent in elementary school.[1] He suggests that, whereas teachers are typically very busy, students are often caught in patterns of delay that force them to do nothing. Jackson notes that a great deal of teachers' time is spent in noninstructional busywork, such as keeping time and dispensing supplies. In the slice of classroom life you just read, Mr. Thompson spent a substantial part of the class time distributing new texts. Indeed, most teachers spend a good deal of time giving out things: paper, pencils, art materials, science equipment, floppy disks, exam booklets, erasers, happy faces, special privileges—the list goes on and on. The classroom scene described also shows Mr. Thompson greatly involved in timekeeping activities. Within the limits set by school buzzers and bells, he determines when the texts will be distributed, when and for how long the reading activity will take place, and when the class discussion will begin.

What do students do while teachers are busy organizing, structuring, talking, questioning, handing out, collecting, timekeeping, and crisis hopping? According to Jackson's analysis, they do little more than sit and wait.[2] They wait for the materials to be handed out, for the assignment to be given, for the questions to be asked, for the teacher to call on them, for the teacher to react to their response, and for the slower class members to catch up so that the activity can change. They wait in lines to get drinks of water, to get pencils sharpened, to get their turn at the

What are the pluses and pitfalls of posting a schedule like this? Do you recall your own feelings as a student about the routine and regimentation of school life?

computer, to go to the playground, to get to the bathroom, and to be dismissed from class. If students are to succeed in school, they must be able to cope with continual delay as a standard operating procedure.

One plea that is rarely granted is that of talking to classmates beyond controlled learning activities. Like the character from Greek mythology, Tantalus, who was continually tempted with food and water but was not allowed to eat or drink, students are surrounded by peers and friends but are restrained from communicating with them. In other words, students in the classroom are in the very frustrating position of having to ignore social temptation, of acting as though they are isolated despite the crowd surrounding them. Furthermore, while trying to concentrate on work and to ignore social temptations, students are beset by frequent interruptions— the public address system blaring a message in the middle of an exam, the end-of-class bell interrupting a lively discussion, a teacher's reprimand or a student's question derailing a train of thought during silent reading.

Consider how Maxine in Mr. Thompson's English class had to cope with delay, denial of desire, social distraction, and interruptions. She waited for the delivery of her new text. She waited to be called on by the teacher. Her attempt to concentrate on reading the poem was disturbed by frequent interruptions. Her brief communication with a classmate was interrupted by a reprimand. Her head was filled with ideas and questions. In short, there was a lot she would like to have said, but there was almost no opportunity to say it.

 ## Watching the Clock

Educators concerned about school improvement have called attention to the inefficient use of time in school, claiming that we lose between one-quarter and one-half of the time available for learning through attendance problems, non-instructional activities (such as class changes and assemblies), administrative and organizational activities, and disruptions caused by student misbehavior.[3]

FIGURE 5.1

School time.

SOURCE: From John Goodlad, *A Place Called School* (New York: McGraw-Hill, 1984).

REFLECTION: About three-fourths of class time is spent in instruction. Does that seem high, low, or about right? The instruction category is quite broad. How might you break it down into more meaningful subcategories?

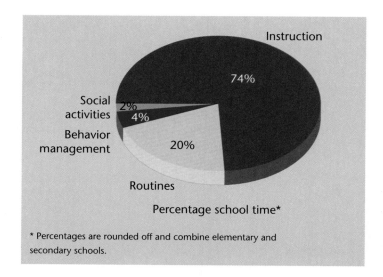

Percentage school time*

* Percentages are rounded off and combine elementary and secondary schools.

In a classic study of schools, **John Goodlad** found a fair degree of consistency in how time is spent in different activities as children go through the grades. As Figure 5.1 illustrates, about 2 percent of time is spent to social activities, 2 to 5 percent to behavior management, 20 percent to routines, and 74 percent to instruction.

In Goodlad's study, although there was a general consistency in how time was spent at different levels of schooling, one of the most astonishing findings was the enormous variation in the *efficiency* with which different schools used time. When examining the hours per week allocated to subject-matter learning, time ranged from a low of 18.5 hours in one school to a high of 27.5 hours in another. Goodlad was also surprised at the limited amount of time spent on the academic staples, such as reading and writing. He found that only 6 percent of time in elementary school was spent on reading. This dropped to a minuscule 2 percent at the high school level. In contrast, the amount of time students spent listening to teacher lectures and explanations increased from approximately 18 percent in elementary school to more than 25 percent in high school.[4] Many schools have responded by adopting alternative or block scheduling and special focus activities, such as sustained silent reading, to make better use of time in school.

While the business world may suggest "time is money," for educators, time is learning. As one teacher points out,

> Time is the currency of teaching. We barter with time. Every day we make small concessions, small trade-offs, but, in the end, we know it's going to defeat us. After all, how many times are we actually able to cover World War I in our history courses before the year is out? We always laugh a little about that, but the truth is the sense of the clock ticking is one of the most oppressive features of teaching.[5]

There is a limited amount of time set aside for the school day. Research shows that, when more time is allocated to subject-matter learning, student achievement increases.[6] When this valuable resource is spent handing out supplies or reprimanding misbehavior, it is lost for learning. Looked at from this perspective, Mr. Thompson's class was not only frustrating, but it also deprived students of a precious and limited resource—the time to learn.

The Teacher as Gatekeeper

Philip Jackson reports that teachers are typically involved in more than one thousand verbal exchanges with their students every day.[7] Count the number of verbal exchanges Mr. Thompson had with his students during our abbreviated classroom scene and you will get some idea of how much and how often teachers talk. One of the functions that keeps teachers busiest is what Philip Jackson terms **gatekeeping.** As gatekeepers, teachers must determine who will talk, when, and for how long, as well as the basic direction of the communication.

Consider what effect patterns of classroom interaction have on both teachers and students:

- Roughly two-thirds of classroom time is taken up by talk; two-thirds of that talk is by the teacher.[8]

- In the typical "pedagogical cycle," teachers structure (lecture and direct), question, and react to student comments. Teachers initiate about 85 percent of these verbal cycles.[9]

- While questioning signals curiosity, it is the teachers, not the learners, who do the questioning, asking as many as 348 questions a day.[10] The typical student rarely asks an academic question.[11]

- Most classroom questions require that students use only rote memory.[12]

- Students are not given much time to ask, or even answer, questions. Teachers usually wait less than a second for student comments and answers.[13]

- Teachers interact less and less with students as they go through the grades.[14]

Ironically, while a major goal of education is to increase students' curiosity and quest for knowledge, it is the teachers, not the students, who dominate and manage

Part of the hidden curriculum of schools is the "culture of waiting" that accompanies the many transition periods throughout the day. And often, waiting seems to be a gender-segregated activity.

After observing in more than one thousand classrooms, John Goodlad and his team of researchers found that the following patterns characterize most classrooms:

- Much of what happens in class is geared toward maintaining order among twenty to thirty students restrained in a relatively small space.
- Although the classroom is a group setting, each student typically works alone.
- The teacher is the key figure in setting the tone and determining the activities.
- Most of the time, the teacher is in front of the classroom, teaching a whole group of students.
- There is little praise or corrective feedback; classes are emotionally neutral or flat places.
- Students are involved in a limited range of activities—listening to lectures, writing answers to questions, and taking exams.

- A significant number of students are confused by teacher explanations and feel that they do not get enough guidance on how to improve.
- There is a decline in the attractiveness of the learning environment and the quality of instruction as students progress through the grades.

Goodlad concluded that "the emotional tone of the classroom is neither harsh and punitive nor warm and joyful; it might be described most accurately as flat."

SOURCE: John Goodlad, *A Place Called School* (New York: McGraw-Hill, 1984).

REFLECTION: Goodlad's classic study is now two decades old. How many of these findings continue to characterize classroom life?

classroom interaction. Classroom interaction patterns do not train students to be active, inquiring, self-reliant learners. Rather, students are expected to be quiet and passive, to think quickly (and perhaps superficially), to rely on memory, and to be dependent on the teacher. Silent, passive students have less positive attitudes and lower achievement. Perhaps the challenge new teachers should keep before them is finding a way to turn their gatekeeping role into a benefit for students, instead of a hindrance.

The Other Side of the Tracks

We have seen that teachers function as gatekeepers, controlling the amount and flow of student talk in the classroom. Let's step back a moment, and consider an even more basic question: Which students sit (for sit they mainly do) in which classrooms? That very crucial, political decision falls on teachers, counselors, and administrators. Many believe that it is easier for students with similar skills and intellectual abilities to learn together, in **homogeneous** classes. Educators following this belief, screen, sort, and direct students based on their abilities, and as a result, send them down different school paths, profoundly shaping their futures. Students of different abilities (low, middle, and high) are assigned to different "tracks" of courses and programs (vocational, general, college-bound, honors, and AP). **Tracking** is the term given to this process, and while some teachers believe that tracking makes instruction more manageable, others believe that it is a terribly flawed system.

In the 1960s, sociologist Talcott Parsons analyzed school as a social system and concluded that the college selection process begins in elementary school and is virtually sealed by the time students finish junior high.[15] Parsons's analysis has significant implications, for he is suggesting that future roles in adult life are determined by student achievement in elementary school. The labeling system, beginning at an early age, determines who will wear a stethoscope, who will carry a laptop computer, and who will become a low-wage laborer.

Several researchers consider students' social class a critical factor in this selection system. Back in 1929, Robert and Helen Lynd, in their extensive study of Middletown (a small midwestern city), concluded that schools are essentially middle-class institutions that discriminate against lower-class students.[16] Approximately 15 years later, W. Lloyd Warner and his associates at the University of Chicago conducted a series of studies in New England, the deep South, and the Midwest and came to a similar conclusion.

> One group [the lower class] is almost immediately brushed off into a bin labeled "nonreaders, first grade repeaters," or "opportunity class," where they stay for eight or ten years and are then released through a chute to the outside world to become hewers of wood and drawers of water.[17]

In his classic analysis of class and school achievement, August Hollingshead discovered that approximately two-thirds of the students from the two upper social classes but fewer than 15 percent of those from the lower classes were in the college preparatory program.[18] In midwestern communities, Robert Havinghurst and associates reported that nearly 90 percent of school dropouts were from lower-class families.[19] The unfortunate tracking by class is one of the oldest of school traditions.

Parents and peers may influence academic choices even more than guidance counselors do.[20] When family and friends encourage children with similar backgrounds to stay together, students of the same race and class typically find themselves on the same school tracks. When school norms and children's culture clash, the result can also lead to racially segregated tracks. For example, some students of color devote time and attention to "stage setting." Stage setting may include checking pencils, rearranging sitting positions, and watching others—all part of a pattern of readiness before work can begin. To a teacher unfamiliar with this learning style, such behavior may be interpreted as inappropriate or as avoidance of work. Some racial and ethnic groups value cooperation and teamwork, yet school norms frequently stress individual, competitive modes of learning. Such cultural clashes work to the detriment of certain groups, relegating them to lower-ability classes and tracks.[21]

Several studies document differences in how students in high-ability and low-ability tracks are treated. In a classic study done in the 1970s, Ray Rist observed a kindergarten class in an all-black urban school. By the eighth day of class, the kindergarten teacher, apparently using such criteria as physical appearance, socioeconomic status, and language usage, had separated her students into groups of "fast learners" and "slow learners." She spent more time with the "fast learners" and gave them more instruction and encouragement. The "slow learners" got more than their fair share of control and ridicule. The children soon began to mirror the teacher's behavior. As the "fast learners" belittled the "slow learners," the low-status children began to exhibit attitudes of self-degradation and hostility toward one another. This teacher's expectations,

The classroom language game, in which teachers talk and students listen, may encourage passivity and boredom.

Here are some disturbing facts about how tracking impacts students:

- Minority students are 3 times as likely as white students to be enrolled in low-track math classes and whites are more than 1.5 times more likely to be in high-track classes.
- Schools with predominately poor and minority populations offer fewer advanced and more remedial courses in academic subjects.
- When parents intervene, counselors place middle- and upper-class students with comparably low grades and test scores into higher groups.
- African American and Hispanic students are underrepresented in programs for the gifted.
- Asian students are more likely than Hispanic students to be recommended for advanced classes, even with equivalent test scores.
- Teachers with the least experience and the lowest levels of qualifications are assigned to students in the lowest tracks.
- Students are more likely to "choose" their friends from their ability groups and tracked classes in elementary through high school. The social network and peer status sorting system is linked to the academic sorting system.
- 73 percent of students completing an academic program are white, 10 percent are black, and 7 percent are Hispanic.
- 63 percent of Advanced Placement exam takers are white, 6 percent are black, 13 percent are Hispanic, 10 percent are Asian, and 1 percent are Native American.

SOURCE: "Race/Ethnicity of Students Taking Advanced Placement Exams, 2006," *The 2006 National Summary Report on Advanced Placement Program* (New York: College Board, 2006); Jeannie Oakes, *Keeping Track* (New Haven, CT: Yale University Press, 2005); Joseph Renzuli and Sunghee Park, *Giftedness and High School Dropouts: Personal, Family, and School-Related Factors* (Storrs, CT: National Research on the Gifted and Talented, 2002).

REFLECTION: Can a tracking or ability grouping program avoid segregating children by race and ethnicity? How would you create such a program?

formed during eight days at the beginning of school, shaped the academic and social treatment of children in her classroom for the entire year and perhaps for years to come. Records of the grouping that had taken place during the first week in kindergarten were passed on to teachers in the upper grades, providing the basis for further differential treatment.[22]

Jeannie Oakes's *Keeping Track* (1985/2005) was a scathing indictment of tracking, adding momentum to the effort to **detrack,** or eliminate tracking practices from the nation's schools. Oakes found that race more than ability determined which students were placed in which tracks, and that the lower-tracked students had fewer learning opportunities.[23] Other studies confirmed that low demands were placed on students in low-ability groups, and teachers expected little from them and offered fewer constructive comments to students in low ability groups. Low tracks suffered from more classroom management problems, and focused more on social rather than academic matters. Over the course of a year, a child in the highest group moved ahead as much as five times more quickly than a child in the lowest group. By the fourth grade, an achievement spread of a full four grades separated children at the top and the bottom of the class, a difference that increased with time.[24] (See *Frame of Reference:* Tracking and Race.)

"True," tracking advocates argue, "it would appear more democratic to put everyone in the same class, but such idealism is destined to fail." They contend that it is unrealistic to think everyone can or should master the same material or learn it at the same pace. Without tracking we have **heterogeneous,** or mixed ability classes. Tracking advocates are quick to point out that mixed ability classes have their own set of problems: In heterogeneous classes, bright students get bored, while slower students have trouble keeping up, and we lose our most talented and our most needy students. Teachers find themselves grading the brighter students on the quality of their work, and the weaker ones on their "effort," which is a big problem (especially with parents!). Teachers get frustrated trying to meet each student's needs, and hardly ever hitting the mark. Putting everyone in the same class simply doesn't work.[25]

Detracking advocates, as you might imagine, offer a different take on the issue. "No sorting system is consistent with equality of opportunity. Worse yet, the tracking system is not based on individual ability. It is badly biased in favor of white middle-class America. We must face the reality that poor children, often children of color, come to school far from being ready to learn. And the school, whose job it is to educate all our children, does little to help. The built-in bias in instruction, counseling, curricular materials, and testing must be overcome. Students get shoveled into second-rate courses that prepare them for fourth-rate jobs. Their track becomes 'a great training robbery,' and the students who are robbed may be ones with great abilities."

While the social pitfalls of tracking have been well documented, its efficacy has not. With little hard evidence supporting tracking, and a growing concern about its negative fallout, it is little wonder that the term "tracking" has fallen out of favor. By the 1990s, only 15 percent of schools had official tracking policies, down from 93 percent in 1965, a quiet but persistent change that has been termed the **unremarked revolution.**[26]

Most schools today work hard to avoid using the term "tracking." Middle and high schools are taking their cue from elementary schools, where "ability grouping" has been in favor. **Ability grouping** sorts students based on capability, but the groupings may well vary by subject. While tracks suggest permanence, ability grouping is more transitory. One year, a student might find herself in a high-ability math group and a low-ability English group. The following year, that same student might be reassigned to a new set of groups. Today, many middle and high schools talk about "ability grouping," but sometimes it is only the label that has been changed. (You may want to think of school tracking as a take-off on the federal "witness protection program": a reality functioning under an assumed identity.) By seventh grade, two-thirds of all schools have ability grouping in some classes, and about 20 percent have tracking or grouping in every subject.[27] Many educators charge that the United States relies more on tracking than any other nation in the world.[28]

Critics argue that we really can eliminate *de facto* tracking, whatever name it is given. They believe that detracking can work, if it is implemented correctly. Teachers, parents, and students should realize that although students arrive at school from very different backgrounds, learning from each other and together has great advantages. Instruction is best offered through individualized and cooperative learning, rather than the traditional approach of trying to teach all students simultaneously. Alternative assessments work far better than testing everyone with the same test (compare this view to the current emphasis on standardized tests). In fact, detracked schools can be authentic places of learning, academically challenging to all while teaching a living lesson in democracy. What is needed is time, careful planning, and adequate training for teachers so that they can succeed and all students can learn.[29]

As these arguments suggest, tracking is likely to remain an area of controversy in the years ahead, especially for educators who find it "the most professionally divisive issue" in the field.[30] One of the ironies of tracking is that it simply builds on an already divided school culture. What educators do not do to divide students, students often do to themselves.

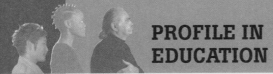

PROFILE IN EDUCATION Jeannie Oakes

Jeannie Oakes never dreamed of being a schoolteacher. "It was just too ordinary. I wanted adventure, unconventionality." So she embraced her passion for reading, earned a degree in American Literature, married, and had children. "It turned out that I was a lot more conventional than I thought I was!" While raising her children at home in the 1960s, Oakes decided that, she would become a teacher for the "same old-fashioned reasons for which women have always taught—I wanted to be with my children when they came home from school every day."[1] But the unconventional spirit in Jeannie Oakes hadn't disappeared. She championed the Civil Rights movement and anti-Vietnam war activities. And she realized that teaching was a vehicle for social justice, that teaching could be far from ordinary.

Her first day in the classroom made a lasting impression. She didn't announce to students they were taking basic English, but recalls how within five minutes they knew and announced, "Oh, we're in the dumb class!" During the seven years Oakes taught middle and high school English in suburban Los Angeles, she struggled to be as good a teacher to low track classes as to the high ones, and was astonished how her own instruction and expectations changed for students placed in honors, average, and basic classes. She also witnessed how tracking dictated disparate lives in schools. "In a

very public way, adults make judgments about students' current and future abilities that take on a hierarchical nature: We talk about top groups and bottom groups. And in the culture of schools, the top group becomes the top kids and the bottom group the bottom kids in a very value-laden and defining way."[2]

Creating innovative classrooms that unlocked successful learning for diverse students became her challenge. Each new school year, Oakes developed new curriculum and instructional strategies, hoping to invigorate enthusiasm for learning in students and fellow teachers. Her calls for change met with administrative resistance and her voice was increasingly silenced.

Her voice was heard as a doctoral student at UCLA, as Oakes researched with John Goodlad the varied aspects of life in schools. Oakes specifically explored how tracking and ability grouping limit the school experiences of low-income students and students of color. Her landmark book *Keeping Track: How Schools Structure Inequality* (1985/2005) brings the inequities of tracking into the national spotlight, casting a riveting portrayal of how tracking creates segregation within schools and shortchanges quality learning and resources. Yet despite the attention, tracking remains one of the most entrenched school practices, relegating students to separate classrooms based less on ability and more on race and socioeconomic status.

Oakes believes the persistence is rooted in a cultural notion that intelligence is immutable and that there is virtually nothing schools can do to alter a student's fundamental capability. She doesn't buy such a limited view.

Kindergartners show an enormous interest in learning, and this cuts across socioeconomic, racial, and ethnic lines. But as kids go through school, if they don't have successful experiences, they learn their efforts do not pay off. So by high school, we see disinterest unjustly interpreted by teachers as low ability.[3]

For Oakes, then, the fundamental goal of equalizing opportunity is not simply to detrack but to increase the quality of curriculum and instruction for everybody in schools, so that success is not limited to those in the high track. This requires a powerful shift in conventional norms, one that defines intellectual capacity as not fixed, but learned through interaction, problem solving, and critical thinking.

Oakes recognizes that the process of detracking schools is not easy. School reform efforts are often met with resistance by those who benefit from the current system. This political dimension of inequality cannot be underestimated. Parents of high-achieving students exert considerable pressure to ensure that their children have access to honors and AP classes. Moreover, teachers of high-track students often resist efforts to detrack, enjoying the intellectual challenge and prestige that come from teaching these students. School administrators and teachers who have undertaken detracking efforts often tell her it is their most difficult undertaking—and most rewarding. Oakes understands why: "It's about fairness and creating better schools. And getting there is half the fun."[4]

A conventional career, perhaps. But Jeannie Oakes is an unconventional advocate for equity and change.

[1] Carlos Alberto Torres, *Education, Power, and Personal Biography: Dialogues with Critical Educators* (New York: Routledge, 1998), pp. 224–25.
[2] John O'Neill, "On Tracking and Individual Differences: A Conversation with Jeannie Oakes," *Educational Leadership*, 50, no. 2 (October 1992), p. 18. [3] Ibid, p. 20. [4] Torres, *Education, Power, and Personal Biography*, p. 230.

REFLECTION: How has Jeannie Oakes made teaching an act of social justice? Why does tracking persist? How have you experienced or witnessed the impact of tracking?

www.mhhe.com/
sadker8e

To learn more about Jeannie Oakes, click on *Profiles in Education.*

The Power of Elementary Peer Groups

Educational researcher Raphaela Best wanted to capture a portrait of life in school as a group of elementary school children experienced it. During a multiyear study, she played the role of participant observer, working with children during class time, playing with them at recess, eating lunch with them in the cafeteria, talking with them, observing them, and taking notes. She found that the children "organized their own intense, seething little world with its own frontiers, its own struggles, its own winners and losers. It was a world invisible to outsiders, not apparent to the casual observer,"[31] where the peer group became increasingly important in the children's lives—eventually competing with and even eclipsing parental influence.

In the first grade, when so much about school seems gigantic and fearful, children look to adults for safety: What am I supposed to do in the classroom? Where do I get lunch? How do I find the bus to ride home from school? Both girls and boys look to the teachers and to the principal for answers, and for emotional support. In her study, Best found that the children ran to their first-grade teacher not only for this practical information but also for hugs, praise, and general warmth and affection. They climbed onto the teacher's lap and rested, secure, and comforted.

By the second grade, the boys had begun to break away from teacher dependence and to place more importance on their peer group. Though loosely structured, this group was largely sex-segregated, with its own leadership hierarchy. In the first grade, the boys and girls had sat side-by-side in the lunchroom, but, by the second grade, the boys had claimed one end of a lunchroom table for themselves. To ensure privacy from the female world, the group's meeting place became the boys' bathroom, where the boys talked about kids at school and decided what to play at recess.

By the third grade, the boys were openly challenging teacher authority. They banded together to organize an all-male club, complete with pecking order, assignments, secrets, and anti-establishment pranks, such as stuffing the locks with paper so the teachers could not get into the building in the morning. Also, by the third grade, the boys' territorial rights had increased, and they had staked out an entirely male lunchroom table for themselves. The playground also became increasingly sex-segregated, as blacktop and grassy areas were reserved for active boys' ball games, and the girls were relegated to the fringe areas, where they stood talking, played hopscotch, and jumped rope. The girls used their time to chat, giggle, and re-create game rules to discourage cut-throat competition. Occasionally, an athletic girl breached the cultural divide and played with the boys, yet her status as tomboy was always a limiting and non-inclusive role. A powerful male culture had evolved, with the entitlement and rights of the privileged.

Excluded from this all-male society were not only the girls but also some boys who were considered sissies. For these rejected boys, the consequences of being left out of the dominant male peer group were painful and severe. As they progressed through their elementary school years, these excluded male students exhibited an increasing number of social, emotional, and academic problems. Afraid of being teased by the male club, they avoided playing with the girls, even though they might have been very happy doing so. Belonging nowhere, they banded together loosely, not out of liking but out of need.

The girls spent the first few years of school helping the teacher, not switching their allegiance to the peer group until the fourth grade. Throughout their school years, this allegiance was rewarded, in part with good report card grades. Then, instead of joining a club, they formed best-friend relationships, in which pairs of girls pledged devotion to one another. Sometimes fights broke out, when two girls argued over having a third as best friend. In the upper elementary grades, the girls also began to fantasize about the "cute" boys in their class and about what being married and having a family would be like. Being a good student and having a pleasing personality were seen as important, but, by the upper elementary grades, appearance had become the key to social status.

The **gender wall** blocking boys and girls from interacting is stronger than barriers to racial integration; there is more cross-race than cross-sex communication during the elementary school years. When Best asked students why there was not more friendship between boys and girls, they reacted with embarrassment. "Everyone would make fun of you," said one girl. Another commented,

> If you say you like someone, other kids spread it all over the school and that's embarrassing. . . . If you even sit beside a boy in class, other kids say you like him. And they come to you in the bathroom and tease you about liking the boy. Once some of the girls put J. S. and B. B. on the bathroom walls. That was embarrassing.[32]

Every day, teachers must work to create humane and caring classrooms. When students respond to questions designed to measure their friendship patterns, 10 percent of them emerge as not being anybody's friend (isolates). About half of these are just ignored. The other half become the victims of active peer group rejection and hostility. In fact, elementary school sociometric measures predict social adjustment better than most other personality and educational tests do.[33] These social preferences can be graphically presented in **sociograms** (see Figure 5.2).

Most friendless children are aware of their problem and report feeling lonely and unsuccessful in relating to others. Rejection by the child's peer group is a strong indicator of future problems. Some public schools have simply given up trying to teach girls and boys in a caring coeducation climate, and established single-sex schools and classes. Rather than solve the relationship challenge, these schools have chosen to avoid it. This may not be the best long-term strategy for teaching girls and boys how to learn, work, and live together.

GUEST COLUMN: Haunted by Racist Attitudes

As graduation time approaches, I am supposed to get nostalgic about my community and my school. I should be thankful for how they have enriched my life, and I should expect to reminisce later on the "great things" about living here. Frankly, in my case, that will not be possible; I'll be trying to forget the bigotry here. Elementary school fostered my negative first impressions. One kid tried to insult me in the halls by calling me "African." My classmates told me to "go back where you came from." (Obviously they had no idea what country this was, but cultural education is another essay.) Often, I was used as an object in a "cooties" game. I was the contaminated one who had to touch all the other pure white-skinned kids. One day after school I was tied to a tree by some boys. The girls just stood around to laugh. They were the friendly ones because at least they did not inflict bodily pain. Wasn't I the naive buffoon to underestimate the burn of psychological humiliation?

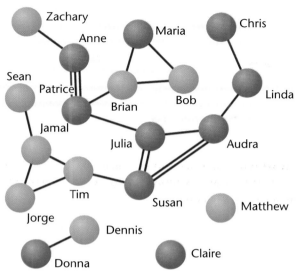

FIGURE 5.2
Sociogram: A teacher's tool.

Sociograms provide insights into the social life of a class. In this sociogram, circles represent students, and colors indicate gender. Lines are drawn connecting circles when students interact with one another. Each line reflects a verbal communication: the more lines, the greater number of interactions. In this sociogram it appears that Anne and Patrice are friends; Julia, Susan, and Audra may form a clique; while Matthew and Claire appear to be isolates. Charting several sociograms of these children over time would confirm or refute these initial perceptions.

REFLECTION: Construct your own sociogram, drawing a circle for each person in your class or in a class that you are observing, or even in a lunchroom or during recess. During a specific period of time, draw a line every time there is an interaction. Can you detect friends, cliques, and isolates? How does class seating impact relationships? What might you do as a teacher to influence these patterns?

Summer meant parks and recreation day camp, and that was hellish. Each day, I was depantsed by some fifth-grade boys in front of the amused campers. I was too embarrassed to tell my parents, and the counselors paid no attention to the foolish games all little boys play. Adult ignorance was by far the most agonizing injustice. In middle school, I sat in front of a boy who constantly whispered, "You f — nigger, black, disgusting" in my ear. Racism was intolerable. The teacher, I guess, disagreed. At least kids are honest. Isn't it amusing how they are little reflections of a community's attitudes? Today, the same people who tormented me as a child walk down the halls faceless. Once a racist reaches a certain age, he realizes that prejudice is not an outright verbal contract. It is subtle and "understood."

Just yesterday my five-year-old sister came home from her preschool and complained, "A girl said she didn't wanna play with me because I'm black." I said, "That's terrible! Did you tell the teacher?" My sister responded, "My teacher said, 'Just ignore her.'"

Yes, I'll have no trouble trying to forget this place.

—Student letter to the school paper[34]

The elementary school culture is driven by blatant and subtle peer group dynamics. An insightful teacher can structure a classroom to minimize negative and hurtful interaction and maximize the positive power of peer group relations. For instance, eliminating social cliques and race- and gender-based segregation is a precursor to successful cooperative groups. An "intentional" teacher often assigns students to seats or to group work to counter pupil favoritism and bias. A teacher's perceptiveness and skill in influencing the social side of school can mean a world of difference in the student's environment.

 ## The Adolescent Society

Was your transition from elementary to middle school smooth, filled with the excitement of new friends and independence? Or did the move spark angst as you navigated new buildings, teachers, and friendships? Not surprisingly, both experiences are common and have spurred debate on the educational effectiveness of middle schools.

Since the 1960s, many policymakers have advocated that middle school—generally grades 6, 7, and 8—should be a time when children have a chance to adjust to puberty. Attention to the emotional and physical developmental growth of adolescents is seen as the primary purpose of middle school life. However, some critics see middle schools as having gone "soft," overemphasizing self-esteem building at the expense of academic rigor. Describing the middle school years as the "Bermuda Triangle of American education," such critics call for a return to K–8 schooling and a more discipline-focused curriculum.[35] Since some adolescents can struggle with change, they argue that K–8 schools provide stability in neighborhood, building, peers, and staff for parents and students alike. Yet, advocates for middle schools argue that simply changing the grade configuration is no magic bullet. What happens in the classroom is what matters most. Noted one principal, "The challenge for us as middle-school educators in the age of high-stakes testing is to encourage teaching for understanding while addressing the myriad of social and emotional issues."[36] While the future of middle schools is in doubt, one adolescent struggle remains omnipresent: the need to develop an identity, including what it means to be male or female.

Middle School: A Gendered World

"I feel pressure from my parents and teachers to do well in school. But when I do, boys won't ask me to the school dance and even my girlfriends call me a 'nerd.' So now I talk less in class and don't study as much. The teasing hurts, so it's easier to hide being smart."

"Boys joke around too much so teachers pay more attention by disciplining rather than helping them to learn."

"Boys can't take music class without being called a fag. So I hide my musical talents, like playing Mozart on the keyboard."

"Girls do everything for men in marriage."

Do these words sound like sexist artifacts of the 1950s or 1960s, or perhaps the 1970s? In fact, these are the voices of today's middle-school students. Their words reveal how gender and peer relations play significant roles in their lives, expanding some options, but more often limiting academic and social development. When we asked more than 400 middle schoolers to identify the "best and worst thing about being a boy or girl," their stories lifted the veil on the pervasive sexism in today's schools and society.[37] Students unequivocally had more positive things to say about being a boy than being a girl. Male advantages focused on physical and athletic prowess, underscoring the central role physicality plays for boys. Students also described how boys "naturally" excel at sports: "Boys have more sports available and can play them better. It's fair to say that we are better athletes than girls."

Students also easily described male entitlements: they are listened to more, are naturally smarter, allowed to do more, have the dominant role in marriage, and receive greater respect. More than one in ten students wrote that one of the best things about being a boy was not being a girl, citing the perils of periods, childbirth, pressures to be thin, and limited high-paying career options. Yet middle school boys face challenges, too. When asked to describe the worst thing about being a boy, behavioral aggression and discipline topped the list followed by poor grades and homophobia. Despite the problems, male privilege remained evident as many students identified the worst thing about being a male as "nothing."

What are the joys for adolescent girls? Appearance was mentioned most often as the best reason for being a girl. Appearance comments included buying clothes, playing with hair styles, and taking beauty treatments, underscoring the need for females to seek approval outside of themselves. One seventh-grade girl vividly captured this salience of appearance: "Clothes make it fun to be a girl. THE perfect outfit can make you feel pretty and worth something." Academic advantage was another "best" reason for being a girl and included two opposing sets of comments, one that spoke to undue favoritism given girls—the "teacher's pet" idea—while the other described the extra effort given by girls and the intellectual satisfaction derived from their higher grades.

Nearly one in five students wrote "nothing" to describe the best thing about being a girl, and students had little difficulty identifying negative aspects of being female. Relational aggression ranked highest with students describing a peer culture of gossip, rumors, and distrust among friends. Girls also noted their deliberate efforts to take easier courses, perform poorly on tests and assignments, and "act dumb" to gain popularity or have a boyfriend. Girls further expressed frustration at being the "second class gender," describing limited career options, responsibility for domestic chores, and the fear of sexual harassment/rape.

Importantly, these experiences of middle schoolers are similar for students in urban, suburban, and rural America; in wealthy and poor communities; in schools that are diverse as well as those that are homogeneous. Relational aggression and discipline, appearance, entitlement, and homophobia can create pressures that detract from both the academic emphasis and social well-being of a school community. Schools that do not attend to these issues are placing a number of school goals at risk.

High School: Lessons in Social Status

Rock singer Frank Zappa said, "High school isn't a time and a place. It's a state of mind." Sociologist James Coleman said that high school is "the closest thing to a real social system that exists in our society, the closest thing to a **closed social system.**" Sociologist Edgar Friedenberg points out that most high schools are so

Many schools, public and private, have opted for official uniforms. Even when dress remains a student choice, peer pressure may create "unofficial" uniforms. Based on the appearance of these students, what assumptions might you make about their schools?

www.mhhe.com/
sadker8e

INTERACTIVE ACTIVITY
How Cool Are You? Test
how much of today's
slang you understand.

insular that they have their own mechanism for telling time—not by the clock but by periods, as in "I'll meet you for lunch after fourth period." In his inaugural speech before Congress, President Gerald Ford confided, "I'm here to confess that in my first campaign for president—at my senior class at South High School— I headed the Progressive party ticket and I lost. Maybe that's why I became a Republican." More than 40 years later, Gerald Ford still remembered high school. No matter where we go or who we become, we can never entirely run away from high school. It is an experience indelibly imprinted on our mind.[38]

More than thirteen million students arrive at twenty thousand public high schools every day. These schools run the gamut from decaying buildings plagued by vandalism and drugs to orderly, congenial places with modern technology and attractive facilities. They vary in size from fifty to five thousand students, who spend days divided into either six or seven 50-minute periods or perhaps fewer, longer blocks of time.

In his book *Is There Life After High School?* Ralph Keyes stirs up the pot of high school memories and draws a very lively picture of what life was like during that time and in that place and state of mind. In researching his book, he asked many people, both the famous and the obscure, about their high-school experiences. He was amazed at the vividness and detail with which their memories came pouring out—particularly about the status system, that pattern of social reward and recognition that can be so intensely painful or exhilarating. High school was remembered as a caste system of "innies" and "outies," a minutely detailed social register in which one's popularity or lack of it was continually analyzed and contemplated. In *The Adolescent Society,* James Coleman notes that a high school "has little material reward to dispense, so that its system of reward is reflected almost directly in the distribution of status. Those who are popular hold the highest status."[39]

In a major study conducted almost a quarter of a century after Coleman wrote *The Adolescent Society,* John Goodlad reached a similar conclusion; the junior and senior high school students he researched were preoccupied not with academics but, rather, with athletics, popularity, and physical appearance. Only 14 percent of the junior high and 7 percent of the senior high students said that "smart students were the most popular." Thirty-seven percent of the junior high students said that the "good-looking" students and 23 percent said the athletes were the most popular. In senior high, 74 percent of the students said that the most popular kids were "good-looking" and "athletes."[40]

When junior and senior high school students were asked to identify the one best thing about their school, they usually said, "My friends." Sports activities ranked second. "Nothing" ranked higher than "classes I'm taking" and "teachers." In some secondary schools, peer group interests bubbled so close to the surface that they actually pushed attention to academic subjects aside and almost took over the classroom. When asked to describe her school, one high school junior said,

> The classes are okay, I guess. Most of the time I find them pretty boring, but then I suppose that's the way school classes are supposed to be. What I like most about the place is the chance to be with my friends. It's nice to be a part of a group. I don't mean one of the clubs or groups the school runs. They're for the grinds. But an informal group of your own friends is great.[41]

Most informal groups are rigidly homogeneous, as becomes apparent in the seating arrangements of the secondary school cafeteria. A student in one high school described the cafeteria's social geography like this: "Behind you are the jocks; over on the side of the room are the greasers, and in front of you are the preppies—white preppies, black preppies, Chinese preppies, preppies of all kinds. The preppies are the "in" group this year; jocks of course are always in and greasers are always out."[42]

Perhaps high school students flock to others most like themselves because making their way in the adolescent society is so difficult. David Owen is an author who returned to high school undercover to study peer culture. Posing as a student who had just moved into the area, he enrolled in what he calls a typical American high school, approximately two hours out of New York City. He was struck by the power of the peer group and how socially ill at ease most adolescents are. He likened adolescents to adults visiting a foreign country and a different culture. Experimenting with new behavior, they are terrified of being noticed doing something stupid:

> Being an adolescent is a full-time job, an all-out war against the appearance of awkwardness. No one is more attentive to nuance than a seventeen-year-old . . . When a kid in my class came to school one day in a funny-looking pair of shoes that one of his friends eventually laughed at, I could see by his face that he was thinking, "well, that does it, there goes the rest of my life."[43]

The memory of high school rejection is powerful, even for generations of the rich and famous. Actress Mia Farrow recalls a high school dance at which every girl was on the dance floor except her. Cartoonist Charles Schulz never forgot the day the yearbook staff rejected his cartoon. No matter where we were in the high school system, few of us have egos so strong or skins so tough that we fail to get a psychological lift when we learn that beautiful actress Ali McGraw never had a date during high school, that actor Gregory Peck was regarded as least likely to succeed, that singer John Denver was called "four-eyes," or that no one wanted to eat lunch with former Secretary of State Henry Kissinger.[44]

For those who remember jockeying unsuccessfully for a place within the inner circle of the high school social register, it may be comforting to learn that the tables do turn. No study shows any correlation between high status in high school and later achievement as an adult. Those who are voted king and queen of the prom or most likely to succeed do not appear to do any better or any worse in adult life than those whose yearbook description is less illustrious. What works in that very insular adolescent environment is not necessarily what works in the outside world. One researcher speculates that it is those on the "second tier," those in the group just below the top, who are most likely to succeed after high school. He says, "I think the rest of our lives are spent making up for what we did or did not do in high school."[45]

Most students know the feeling of being judged and found wanting by high school peers, and some spend the rest of their lives trying to compensate or get even. Comedian Mel Brooks sums it up well:

> Thank God for the athletes and their rejection. Without them there would have been no emotional need and . . . I'd be a crackerjack salesman in the garment district.[46]

For some students, the impact of rejection does not lead to such positive outcomes. These students struggle to break through clique walls that are invisible but

---

IMAGINE . . .

Honors Bathroom

At Northgate High School near Pittsburgh, integrity and honesty pay off in unusual ways. Students who pledge not to smoke or damage the fixtures will be issued magnetized cards that admit them to an *honors bathroom.* Smoke-free lavatories are predicted to be the in thing, according to senior Rob S. *Most kids will want to be there,* he says. *I don't think the honors bathroom kids will be nerds.*

SOURCE: *Newsweek,* October 19, 1998.

---

www.mhhe.com/
sadker8e

INTERACTIVE ACTIVITY
The Popular Crowd?
Match celebrities with
their high school profiles.

Peer groups appear to be homogeneous and, more than anything else, tend to define the quality of students' school life.

impervious. As one student stated: "I've never really been part of any group. I suppose I don't have anything to offer."[47]

Being part of a group continues to be a challenge for today's adolescents. While historically, entire communities participated in child care, and extended families guided and monitored children, today this social fabric of adult supervision has disappeared. With increased mobility, the generations have been separated, and traditional child care is gone. Two-parent wage earners provide less supervision, and the absence of widespread quality day care has added to the stress of growing up in America.

In *A Tribe Apart: A Journey Into the Heart of American Adolescence* (1999), Patricia Hersch shares the story of three years she spent with seventh through twelfth graders in suburban Reston, Virginia.[48] What Hersch discovered was troubling: the development of a more isolated, intense, and perilous adolescent culture, where drugs, alienation, and violence represent ongoing threats. It is a teenage society unknown to many parents. Today's teenagers are less likely to form the tight teenage cliques that adults remember from their own childhood. Contemporary adolescent friendships appear to be more fluid: teenagers may have one group of friends in a drama club, another from math class, and a third set from sports activities. Today cross-gender friendships are also more common as boys and girls do a better job of developing relationships without the need for a romantic attachment.

But even as the number of friendships grows, the quality of adolescent relationships remains a problem. Today's teenagers, both girls and boys, report that although they have many friends, they lack intimate, close friends. Teenagers say that there is no one that they can really confide in, no one with whom to share their deepest thoughts. In the midst of a crowd, they feel alone. It is a disturbing admission, and some educators believe that schools can and should do something about it.

Our Children, Your Students

Have you ever felt the cold slap of rejection because of your social class? Have you ever denied a family history that includes divorce or unplanned pregnancy? Has your life been touched by depression, substance abuse, or bullying? Children across all racial, ethnic, and socioeconomic backgrounds may be plagued by such difficulties, affecting their academic and emotional well-being. Your students will likely carry these struggles and concerns with them as they walk through your classroom door. While schools and teachers cannot completely solve these social issues (as much as we may try), education can bring purpose, hope, and empowerment to our most troubled youth.

Family Patterns

Not too many years ago, the Andersons of *Father Knows Best* lived through weekly, if minor, crises on television; Dick and Jane lived trouble-free lives with their parents and pets in America's textbooks; and most real families contained a father, mother, and perhaps three children confronting life's trials and tribulations as a family unit. But today's family bears little resemblance to these images. In fact, just over half of American "families" have no children under 18 at home, and one-fourth of all households are people living alone.[49]

Leave It to Beaver may live in rerun land forever, but Beaver Cleaver resolves the bumps and bruises of childhood in a way that by today's standards appears half a step from a fairy tale. Only 50 years ago, a single-parent meant one thing: a premature death. Out-of-wedlock children and pregnant, unmarried teenagers were hidden from the public's attention. Divorce was rare. Mothers stayed at home and fathers went to work.

Stay-at-home moms, working dads, and two children populate television reruns like *Leave It to Beaver,* but they no longer reflect most of today's families.

Beaver Cleaver's family structure represents few families. Only two-thirds of children today live in two-parent families, with children of color far less likely than their white peers to live with both parents (Figure 5.3). Nearly one in four children live only with their mothers, 5 percent live only with their fathers, and 4 percent live with neither parent.[50] Research shows that children from single-parent families are less likely to achieve and more likely to be expelled or suspended.[51] Generally, our families are getting smaller, older, and more diverse. While Americans still prefer marriage, the past twenty-five years have seen the number of unmarried opposite and same sex partners living together more than double.

Wage Earners and Parenting

In 1960, fewer than half of married women with children between the ages of 6 and 17 worked outside the home; today, eight in ten do. The rise in salaried employment for married women with children under 6 has been even more striking, jumping from one in five in 1960 to three in five today.[52] Yet social changes lag

FIGURE 5.3
The changing American family.

SOURCE: Federal Interagency Forum on Child and Family Statistics, *America's Children: Key National Indicators of Well-Being*, 2005.

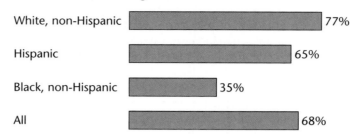

Children Living in Two-Parent Families

White, non-Hispanic — 77%
Hispanic — 65%
Black, non-Hispanic — 35%
All — 68%

REFLECTION: What factors might account for these family differences across racial groups?

behind. In one major study, following the birth of their first child, women placed a hold on their career (describing it as a job), while the majority of men waited until their career was successfully in place before scaling back work commitments.[53] And since about two-thirds of America's families do have both or only parent(s) working outside the home, a significant need also exists for quality child care. Parents who work are often in a bind, trying to balance the needs of child rearing and family life with work demands. Neither Mom nor Dad is likely to be readily available to attend daily to children's emotional, social, and intellectual development.

Latchkey Kids

Jennifer unlocked her door quickly, raced inside, and shut it loudly behind her. She fastened the lock, threw the bolt, dropped her books on the floor, and made her way to the kitchen for her usual snack. Within a few minutes, Jennifer was ensconced on the sofa, the television on and her stuffed animals clutched firmly in her hand. She decided to do her homework later. Her parents would be home then, and she tried not to spend too much time thinking about being lonely. She turned her attention to the television, to spend the next few hours watching talk shows.

Jennifer is a latchkey kid—left to care for herself after school. The estimates are that one in five children is latchkey. The term **latchkey** (sometimes called self-care) was coined to describe children who carry a key on a cord or chain around their necks to unlock their home door. These children are often from single-parent homes or families with two working parents, few extended family members, and no affordable, high-quality child care facilities nearby. Latchkey kids are found in all racial and socioeconomic groups, but the more educated the parents, the more likely they are to have a latchkey child. Although the average latchkey child is left alone two and a half hours per day, a significant number are alone much longer, more than 36 hours per week. Over 25 of those hours are spent watching television with the leftover time parceled into studies or play.[54]

Divorce

Although divorce is common, with half of new marriages end in divorce, it is hardly routine. The underlying stress can increase a child's anguish. Along with the emotional trauma of changing family dynamics, divorce can also create financial worries.

The divorced mom often struggles with a severe loss of income. Children living only with their mothers are five times more likely to live in poverty than children living in a married household.[55] Children who have experienced divorce may exhibit a variety of problem behaviors. Symptoms from depression to aggression diminish school performance. Children often go through a classic mourning process similar to that experienced after a death in the family. However, most children are resilient and can rebound from the trauma of divorce, with 80 to 90 percent recovering in about a year. Teachers should give children the chance to express their feelings about divorce and let them know they are not alone in their experience.[56]

America's New Families

By the turn of the 21st century, more Americans were living in stepfamilies than nuclear families, including about half of our children. Stepfamilies consist of biological and legal relationships with stepparents, stepsiblings, multiple sets of grandparents, and what often becomes a confusing array of relatives from old and new relationships.[57]

Other families are combined, not by remarriage, but through cross-cultural and racial unions. It was only in 1967 that the Supreme Court overruled antimiscegenation laws, which had banned interracial marriage. Interracial unions are a small yet rapidly growing portion of today's households.[58] The children of interracial marriages do not fit neatly into today's labels. Is the child of an African American and an Asian American to be categorized as African American, Asian American, "blended," or "other"?

Alternative families include family lifestyles other than a married male and female living with their children. Alternative families can consist of single moms or dads with children; biological parents who are not married; relatives or friends acting as child guardians; same-sex couples sharing parenting roles; nonmarried couples living as families; or serial relationships with continually changing partners. Yet, the conventional family stereotype still permeates the school curriculum, and children in nontraditional families may feel discomfort about their "abnormal" lifestyle. Clearly, many schools have a way to go before they successfully integrate all family structures into school life.

Poverty

Today, children are the poorest group in our society, and current programs and policies are woefully inadequate to meet their growing needs. Stanford's Michael Kirst sums it up this way:

> Johnny can't read because he needs glasses and breakfast and encouragement from his absent father. Maria doesn't pay attention in class because she doesn't understand English very well and she's worried about her father's drinking and she's tired from trying to sleep in her car. Dick is flunking because he's frequently absent. His mother doesn't get him to school because she's depressed because she lost her job. She missed too much work because she was sick and could not afford medical care.[59]

The one in five American children living in poor families are among the poorest in all developed nations (see Figure 5.4). Most parents of poor children work, but they don't earn enough to provide their families with basic necessities—adequate food, shelter, child care, and health care. When children are poor, they are more likely to drop out of school and be involved in violent crime, early sexual activity,

FIGURE 5.4
Children under 18 living in poverty.

SOURCE: U.S. Bureau of the Census, *Income, Poverty, and Health Insurance Coverage in the United States.* Current Population Reports (2005). Available at www.census.gov/prod/2005pubs/p60-229.pdf.

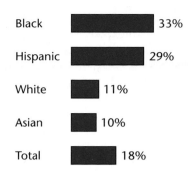

REFLECTION: What do you believe is the role(s) of schools to help poor children? The role of teachers? What steps will you take to better understand the needs of your students living in poverty?

and drugs. Children, with little voice and no votes, are among the first to lose services. Nearly 9 million children under age 18 have no medical coverage.[60] In short, poverty puts children at risk.

How can teachers understand the unique needs of children in poverty? According to educator Ruby Payne, we can find clues in the hidden rules governing different socioeconomic classes. (See the *Frame of Reference:* Hidden Class Rules.) Since schools tend to reflect middle-class values, children from poverty backgrounds often feel out of place, unaware of the unspoken rules guiding academic and social success. Payne describes, for example, how achievement and career are often driving forces for the middle class, while survival, entertainment, and relationships are more salient for individuals in poverty. These class differences can make both teaching and learning challenging. Too often, teachers don't understand why a student from poverty is chronically acting out or not grasping a concept, even after repeated explanations. Are poor children less capable or intelligent? Of course not. They simply have limited experience in the strategies, or hidden rules, needed for success in our schools.

Many of the culturally relevant teaching strategies described in Chapter 3 that help teachers create meaningful learning for children of diverse racial and ethnic backgrounds are also tools teachers can use to connect with students who are poor. To help lower-class children navigate school norms and value academic learning, Payne suggests cultivating meaningful relationships between teachers and peers and providing resources for cognitive, emotional, and physical well-being. Developing language skills is a particularly important resource since individuals in poverty typically have a limited vocabulary of 300–500 words. An expanded vocabulary offers students a broader perspective of the world as well as improved ability to communicate.[61] Along with resources, Payne proposes that academic learning should be connected with relationships. Consider the following example of how learning was framed in terms of a student's need for belonging and competence:

> A 17-year-old poor student in an alternative school refused to complete his daily math homework on positive and negative numbers. His teacher suggested that since he lacked understanding of positive and negative numbers, his friends could easily cheat him in cards, or exclude him from the game entirely. Furious and insulted, the student engaged his teacher in a card game to prove his ability. From that time on, the student faithfully completed his math homework and earned an A.[62]

From her extensive study of the impact of social class on education and career, Ruby Payne offers social class norms. These norms should be seen as helpful generaliza-tions, remembering that individuals within each group may have different experiences and values.

Poverty	Middle Class	Wealth
Decision making is based on survival, relationships, and entertainment.	*Decision making* is based on school and career achievement.	*Decision making* is based on social, financial, and political connections.
Possessions are people. A relationship is valued over achievement. Too much education is feared because a person might leave home and family.	*Possessions* are things. If material security is threatened by someone, often the relationship is broken.	*Possessions* are legacies, pedigrees, and one-of-a-kind objects.
The world is defined in local terms.	*The world* is defined in national terms, such as national news and travel.	*The world* is defined in international terms.
Fighting is physical and respect is given to those who resolve conflict with physical force.	*Fighting* is done verbally. Physical fighting is looked down upon.	*Fighting* occurs through social exclusion and through lawyers.
Food is valued for quantity.	*Food* is valued for quality.	*Food* is valued for presentation.

SOURCE: Ruby Payne, *Framework for Understanding Poverty* (Highlands, TX: Aha Process Inc., 2001).

REFLECTION: Which of these hidden rules surprises you? What rules do you value? Why? What values might be lost as one moves out of poverty? What additional unspoken social class rules can you add? How will you make learning culturally relevant for students from diverse economic backgrounds?

Hidden America: Homeless Families

In Washington, D.C., a 3-year-old girl and her 5-year-old brother spend their nights with their mother, assigned to a cubicle in a school gym. The mother lost her job because of unreliable child care. Unable to meet her rent payments, she lost her apartment. Now the family is awakened at 5:30 a.m. in order to catch the 7:00 a.m. bus to a welfare hotel where breakfast is served. After breakfast, it is another bus ride to drop the 5-year-old off at a Head Start program, then back to the welfare hotel for lunch. Another bus takes them to pick up the boy from day care and then transports them to dinner back at the hotel. The final bus ride takes them to their cubicle in the gym. The 3-year-old misses her afternoon nap on a daily basis. The mother does not have the time or means to look for a job.

The cycle continues.[63]

America's estimated one million homeless children are urban and rural, of every racial and ethnic background, and face significant school challenges. While most now attend school, there is constant turmoil and frequent transfers. Many arrive at school hungry and tired, lacking even rudimentary study facilities. Add to this equation the drugs, crimes, violence, and prostitution sometimes found in shelters, and it is clear that these children struggle against overwhelming odds.

WHAT TEACHERS NEED TO KNOW ABOUT THE EDUCATION OF HOMELESS CHILDREN

- No one needs a permanent address to enroll a child in school.
- The child may remain at the same school he or she attended before becoming homeless or may enroll at the school serving the attendance area where he or she is receiving temporary shelter.
- The homeless child cannot be denied school enrollment just because school records or other enrollment documentation are not immediately available.
- The child has the right to participate in all extracurricular activities and all federal, state, or local programs for which the child is eligible, including food programs; before- and after-school care; vocational education; Title I; and other programs for gifted, talented, and disadvantaged learners.
- The child cannot be isolated or separated from the mainstream school environment solely due to homelessness.

SOURCE: Adapted from the National Law Center on Homelessness & Poverty, "Educating Homeless Children and Youth: The 2005 Guide to Their Rights" (2005).

REFLECTION: Recall your earliest encounters with homelessness. How have those images changed and how have they remained the same? What would you do or say if you ran into the parent of one of your homeless students?

In 1987, Congress passed the **McKinney-Vento Homeless Assistance Act,** providing the homeless with emergency food services, adult literacy programs, access to schooling, job training, and other assistance. The act has been amended to facilitate the public education of homeless children. For example, families living "doubled up" in apartments are now considered homeless and entitled to certain educational rights. In the past, school districts had required proof of residency, birth certificates, proof of immunization—simple tasks for most families, but enough to keep many homeless children out of school. The amended act reduced or eliminated many such barriers, and required that each school have a liaison to ensure that homeless children are not segregated and receive a competent education.[64] Despite this progress and the potential of schools to be a stabilizing force, the educational needs of the nation's homeless children often go unmet.

Children: At Promise or at Risk?

It was not too long ago that family life was captured by simplistic TV images, with problems easily solved in fewer than 30, almost commercial-free, minutes. In the mid-1900s, teachers were concerned about students talking out of turn, chewing gum, making noise, running in the halls, cutting in line, and violating dress codes. Half a century later, teachers' top student concerns reflect the devastating changes in the lives of their pupils: drug and alcohol abuse, pregnancy, suicide, rape, robbery, and assault.

Dropping Out

Lamar was finishing junior high school with resignation and despair. He had just managed to squeak through Beaton Junior High with poor grades and no understanding of how this frustrating experience would help him. He wasn't good at schoolwork and felt that the classes he had to sit through were a waste of time. He wanted to end these long, boring days, get a job, and get a car. He'd had enough of school.

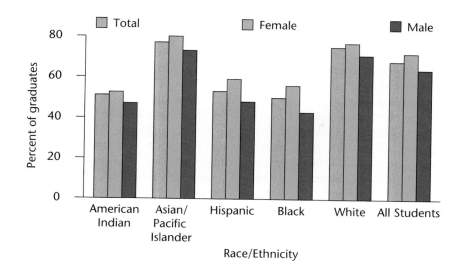

FIGURE 5.5
National graduation rates.

SOURCE: Gary Orfield, *Losing Our Future: How Minority Youths Are Being Left Behind by the Graduation Rate Crisis* (2004). Available at www.urban.org.

REFLECTION: What strategies would you suggest to improve graduation rates?

Lamar is a good candidate to join the nation's dropouts. In fact, poor students are six times more likely to drop out than wealthy ones, and students whose parents do not value schooling are also on the "most-likely-to-drop-out" list. Typically, dropping out is a long-term process with academic warning signs. In a Baltimore study, more than half of the students who eventually dropped out did poorly even in the first grade. Seventy-one percent of students who repeated a grade once, and 80 percent of students who repeated a grade twice, eventually dropped out. On the other hand, students who reported being "engaged" in school did not drop out.[65]

Are you surprised to learn that nationwide only two-thirds of students graduate from high school? Racial, ethnic, and gender patterns offer an even more disturbing picture of educational attainment (see Figure 5.5).[66] Most students don't drop out because they can't do the work. In fact, nearly 90 percent have passing grades when they leave school. The major reason for opting out? Classes are too boring, and students feel academically disengaged. Others are more worried about pregnancy, family issues, or financial concerns. Indeed, the immediate monetary rewards of the workplace lure some students. Yet, dropouts earn an average of almost $10,000 less a year than high school graduates, and are far more likely to need government assistance or end up in jail.[67] Many educators believe that the dropout rate can be reduced through early intervention, early literacy programs, one-on-one instruction, mentoring and tutoring, more relevant curricular materials, service learning, and family involvement.[68]

Sexuality and Teenage Pregnancy

Who can blame today's adolescents for being confused about sexuality? On the one hand, they see a "green light," as they are bombarded with suggestive advertising, graphic movies, bawdy television shows and sexualized cable channels. Contraceptives, including the morning-after pill, offer pregnancy safeguards that did not exist just a few years ago. Then students see a bright "red light" of morality standards preaching abstinence and the looming threat of sexually transmitted diseases (STDs). So how do schools respond to this conflict? The short answer is not well.

About a third of the school systems preach an "abstinence only until marriage" policy, which discourages sex outside of heterosexual marriage. Little if any other information is given. Other schools embrace comprehensive sex education, which stresses abstinence but also includes contraceptive information. What students are taught differs state to state, district to district, and school to school. The federal government, however, has weighed in on the side of abstinence-only programs, committing nearly 200 million dollars to these programs annually. Comprehensive sex education programs currently receive no federal support.[69]

One thing is certain: the current fractured approach is not working. Rates of pregnancy and STDs in this nation are the highest in the industrialized world, and many attribute the problem to the lack of a coherent sex education curriculum. A study of nine abstinence-focused programs found that the information being taught was inaccurate, outdated, and biased against reproductive choice options. Teens' sexual behavior, pregnancy rates, and rates of contracting STDs usually remain steady or increase following completion of abstinence-only courses. Some students have objected to abstinence-only programs, and demanded more complete information. A few states, including California, Oregon, Missouri, and Alabama, have passed laws requiring schools to teach up-to-date, judgment-free information about contraception, but these laws are difficult to enforce, and the majority of states simply look the other way, leaving sex education to local school systems.[70]

Substance Abuse

"I know personally kids who drink whole bottles of liquor on the weekends by themselves."

"You won't see the drug culture here unless you know what to look for. You'll get a lot of parent and school denial, but the reputation of this school is 'cocaine heaven.'"

"On an average week, I gross over $2,000 dealing drugs at this school."

These statements from high school students add a personal dimension to official reports indicating that the United States has the highest rate of teenage drug use of any industrialized nation in the world. Substance abuse ranges from alcohol and chewing tobacco to inhalants, cocaine, and LSD, to food abuse, from dieting to obesity. Sixty percent of high school students and 30 percent of middle schoolers say drugs are used, kept, and sold in their schools and are easily available.[71]

While alcohol, cigarette smoking, and marijuana use among teenagers are at historic lows, they remain serious problems for our youth. Alcohol represents, by far, the most widespread form of substance abuse. More than two-thirds of high school seniors admit to drinking regularly and one-third admit to binge drinking. The pattern of abuse starts early: more than one in five eighth-graders report drinking within the last year. Cigarette smoking is down for the population as a whole, yet more than a million young people start smoking each year. One-quarter of high school seniors and one in six eighth-graders light up at least once a month. Although teens understand that smoking is bad for their health, nearly one-fourth admit they cannot quit because they are addicted. Use of marijuana, the most widely used illicit drug, remains common. One-third of high school seniors and one in ten eighth-graders used the drug at least once in the past year. Asked whether they had used other illicit drugs such as cocaine and heroin, 20 percent of seniors and nearly one in ten eighth-graders said yes.[72]

An even darker "coming of age" picture emerges as researchers uncover a cultural shift in drug use. Today's youth grow up in a world where it is routine to reach for a prescription bottle to enhance performance, to focus better in school, and to stay awake or calm down. Not surprisingly, use of inhalants, diet pills, sedatives, and prescription drugs is rising. For example, by the eighth grade, one in five students has tried an inhalant—such as glue, paint, felt-tip markers, and air freshener—to get high. Equally troubling, prescription painkillers like Vicodin and Oxycontin are abused by one in ten high schoolers.[73]

What leads youth to substance abuse? Some blame the mixed messages children receive. Although parents and teachers may talk about the physical, emotional, and academic dangers, the media and pop culture often glorify alcohol and other drugs as methods for coping with stress and loneliness or to improve performance. Other contributing factors include family instability and the materialistic, success-driven nature of our culture that creates tremendous pressure on youth (and adults). And the problems of substance abuse are all too real for many students. When asked to describe their greatest concern, teens frequently cite the pressure to use drugs ahead of social and academic pressures.[74] We know all too well that substance abuse paves a risky, downward path:

- Grades go down as alcohol consumption and drug use go up. The average student who has one drink a day earns C or lower grades. Greater usage is associated with failing grades. Marijuana users are twice as likely as nonusers to average Ds and Fs.

- The more teenagers drink, the more likely they are to be involved in violent crime, such as murder, rape, or robbery, either as victim or perpetrator.

- Alcohol and drug abuse is associated with more unplanned pregnancies, more sexually transmitted diseases, and more HIV infections than any other single factor.

- Approximately 50 percent of all youth deaths from drowning, fires, suicide, and homicide are alcohol related.[75]

Schools may adopt programs such as Drug Abuse Resistance Education (D.A.R.E.) to help youth understand the facts about drugs and cope with peer pressures. Funded and run by local police departments, D.A.R.E. costs school districts very little and is popular in schools nationwide. Yet research reveals that D.A.R.E. and its "Just Say No" message are ineffective in curtailing drug use. Similar criticism has been leveled on the U.S. Department of Education's Safe and Drug-Free Schools program, a part of *No Child Left Behind*. The program provides more than half a billion dollars annually to local school districts. But there is no record of success, and the government requires no accountability of how funds are spent. In fact, a review of the program found that taxpayer money pays for a variety of questionable practices, such as spending $1.5 million for a human torso model, $18,500 for recordings of the song "Hokey Pokey" to be played at school parties, and millions on magicians and puppet shows.[76] Given the poor track record of these national programs, many local schools choose to develop their own substance abuse curricula and policies.

Youth Suicide

A closely knit New Jersey community across the Hudson River from Manhattan was viewed as a model town. The high school frequently won the state football championship, the police department won awards for its youth-assistance programs, and the town was known for the beauty of its parks and safety of its streets. On an early Wednesday morning in March, the citizens of Bergenfield woke up to discover that four of their teenagers had locked themselves in a garage, turned on a car engine, and left a note requesting that they be buried together. The group suicide brought the total of teen suicides in Bergenfield to eight that year.

In the past 25 years, while the general incidence of suicide has decreased, the rate for those between the ages of 15 and 24 has tripled. Suicide is the third most common cause of death among adolescents, and many health specialists suspect it is seriously underreported. Every day 14 adolescents (mostly males) will take their own lives. Particularly at risk are substance abusers, teens questioning their sexuality, victims of bullying, academic overachievers, and girls who have been physically or sexually abused.[77]

What should teachers look for? Depression often precedes suicide attempts. Manifestations include persistent sadness, boredom or low energy, loss of interest in favorite pastimes, irritability, physical complaints and illness, serious changes in sleeping and eating, and school avoidance or poor performance.[78] Impulsivity, which accounts for about one-fourth of all adolescent suicides, is particularly difficult for adults to deal with, since it may cause students to commit suicide in response to their first bout with depression. To date, teachers and parents have not done well in preventing youth depression and suicide.

Bullying

> Jared hides behind the school building for an hour, hoping Tom has forgotten about him and walked home already. Maybe this will be the first night he will make it home without being pushed or taunted. Jared slowly leaves his hiding spot, gripping his backpack as tight as he can. As he gets farther away from school, his stomach begins to unknot. He is relieved that he will make it home tonight without incident. Just then, Tom appears around the corner with a smirk on his face, ready to fight.[79]

While metal detectors and extra security measures have sharply reduced school violence, bullies still stalk. Playgrounds, hallways, cafeterias, and school buses—places where students interact informally with little adult supervision—are prime areas for bullying. One-third to a half of America's children report being bullied at least once a month and 10 percent feel continually targeted. In a typical classroom of 20 students, 2 or 3 come to school every day fearing being bullied, harassed, or worse. The most likely targets are gay students, or students perceived as gay. While most youth describe bullying as harmful, a gap exists between this belief and students' behaviors. More than 40 percent of students admit to bullying a classmate at least once; more than half have witnessed bullying and not stopped or reported it.[80]

Bullies seek control over others by taking advantage of imbalances in perceived power, such as greater size, physical strength, or social status. Bullies can use physical force or threats, but sticks and stones aren't the only tools. Social weapons, such as taunts and teases, name-calling, gossip-mongering, and exclusion, can cut children much deeper. The ways youngsters are tormented and ostracized by one another, often in the guise of being cool or hip, are the stuff of teenage nightmares: being made the butt of a clique's disdain, not being invited to the party everyone is talking about, and, increasingly, being eviscerated in nasty instant messages over the Internet. Cyber bullying is a relatively new phenomenon. Through e-mail, instant messaging, Internet chat rooms, and electronic gadgets

Social exclusion or relational aggression occurs in mixed sex or same sex peer groups. In either setting, rejection and isolation can be painful.

like camera cell phones, cyber bullies forward and spread hurtful images and/or messages. Bullies use this technology to harass victims at all hours, in wide circles, and at warp speed.

Bullying has been an accepted school tradition for decades, if not centuries, often because so many teachers accept the myths surrounding bullying: only a small number of children are affected, students are just "tattling, it's a natural behavior," and "boys will be boys." But these myths are dangerous. Boys *and* girls engage in bullying, though often with different behaviors. Boys are more likely to engage in physical bullying, while girls often revert to relational bullying, such as gossip and exclusion. Bullying is linked to academic difficulties, withdrawal from activities, depression, suicide, and eating disorders. And children who bully are more likely to get into fights, vandalize property, and drop out of school. The cost of bullying is high, and schools are finally "getting it." The rise of lawsuits, and the creation of antibullying programs have helped to keep the bully in his (or her) place. Effective antibullying practices ask teachers to be involved and interested in students, set firm limits on unacceptable behavior, apply consistent nonpunitive, nonphysical sanctions, and act as authorities and positive role models. Creating a safe classroom climate is the first step in effective teaching. Schools are also implementing peer mediation programs to help reduce bullying and school violence. Students are trained to help classmates peacefully solve problems, becoming empowered advocates against bullying.[81]

The Affective Side of School Reform

The message to children in this period of standards, testing, and competition is that the school is a place of academics, and that the nonacademic needs of students receive low priority. Students get this message. Students report that when they are feeling sad or depressed, overwhelmingly they turn for help to friends (77 percent) or family (63 percent); far less frequently do they seek out educators (33 percent).[82] Yet many teachers despair over the unmet **affective student**

needs of today's children. As a kindergarten teacher from an urban school system points out,

> The difficult part of teaching is not the academics. The difficult part is dealing with the great numbers of kids who come from emotionally, physically, socially, and financially stressed homes. Nearly all of my kindergarten kids come from single-parent families. Most of the moms really care for their kids but are young, uneducated, and financially strained. Children who have had no breakfast, or who are fearful of what their mom's boyfriend will do to them—or their moms—are not very good listeners or cooperative partners with their teachers or their peers. We are raising a generation of emotionally stunted and troubled youth who will in turn raise a generation of the same. What is the future of this country when we have so many needy youngsters?[83]

Those who teach in urban settings warn us that the future of poor and minority children is at risk. But all is not well in suburbia, either. Consider this comment from a teacher in suburban New Jersey: "In the large, efficient suburb where I teach, the pressure is on kids from kindergarten to high school to get good grades, bring up the test scores, and be the best on the test."[84] Another teacher says that there is such pressure to get high test scores that students are rushed from one workbook to another. There is no time for anything not directly related to cognitive achievement. "We feel guilty," she says, "doing an art lesson or having a wonderful discussion."[85]

In another study, Frances Ianni describes the affluent lifestyle in the suburb of Sheffield (name fictitious), a place where families keep well-manicured lawns and push their children to succeed. Students are groomed to be good at everything—athletics, social skills, academic achievement. "People in Sheffield will tell you," Ianni says, "that the two things you never ask at a cocktail party are a family's income and the Scholastic Assessment Test scores of their children."[86]

Pushed beyond their abilities and alienated from family, friends, and community, some teenagers develop a "delusion of uniqueness," a sense that "no one knows how I feel, no one else faces these problems, no one cares about me." When children feel cut off from what Urie Bronfenbrenner calls "the four worlds of childhood"—family, friends, school, and work—the situation can become serious and even life-threatening.[87] Sara Lawrence Lightfoot describes the following incident that took place in an elite school in a wealthy suburb in the Midwest:

> A student with a history of depression . . . had been seeing a local psychiatrist for several years. For the last few months, however, she had discontinued her psychotherapy and seemed to be showing steady improvement. Since September, her life had been invigorated by her work on *Godspell*—a student production that consumed her energies and provided her with an instant group of friends. After *Godspell*, her spirits and enthusiasm declined noticeably. In her distress, she reached out to a teacher who had given her special tutorial support in the past, and the school machinery was set in motion. A meeting was scheduled for the following day to review her case. That night, after a visit to her psychiatrist, she killed herself.
>
> The day after, the school buzzed with rumors as students passed on the gruesome news—their faces showing fear and intrigue. . . . But I heard only one teacher speak of it openly and explicitly in class—the drama teacher who had produced *Godspell*. Her words brought tears and looks of terror in the eyes of her students.
>
> "We've lost a student today who was with us yesterday. We've got to decide where our priorities are. How important are your gold chains, your pretty clothes, your cars? . . . Where were we when she needed us? Foolish old woman that I am, I ask you this because I respect you. . . . While you still feel, damn it, feel . . . reach out to each other."[88]

This "reaching out" is what Ianni recommends in her **youth charter** network. "Communities," she says, "can create youth charters that encourage youngsters to move from dependence to independence, from the ethnocentrism of early adolescence to the social competence of young adulthood." She urges the community to move from benign neglect or outrage at the young to an organized system of positive involvement and guidance. Many other child advocates are calling for a coordinated system of school-based social services to replace the existing maze of bureaucratic agencies.[89]

Alfie Kohn is one educator who claims that the social and affective sides of school must become an explicit part of the formal curriculum: "It is possible to integrate prosocial lessons into the regular curriculum. . . . Indeed to study literature or history by grappling with moral or social dilemmas is to invite a deeper engagement with these subjects." According to Kohn, such schools as the California-based Child Development Project, a long-term effort in prosocial education, teach children to take responsibility and care for one another.[90]

While most reform reports emphasize increased academic achievement, only a few recognize the social and emotional needs of children. The Carnegie Council on Adolescent Development report, *Turning Points: Educating Adolescents in the 21st Century,* warned that one in four adolescents are in serious jeopardy. Their basic human needs—caring relationships with adults, guidance in facing sometimes overwhelming biological and psychological changes, the security of belonging to constructive peer groups, and the perception of future opportunity—are unmet at this critical stage of life. Millions of these young adolescents will never reach their full potential.[91] Pointing to a society dangerous to adolescent health—one of drug abuse, poor school performance, alienation, and sexual promiscuity—the report called for comprehensive middle school reform to help protect these youngsters.

> Middle-grade schools—junior high, intermediate or middle schools—are potentially society's most powerful force to recapture millions of youth adrift. Yet all too often they exacerbate the problems youth face. A volatile mismatch exists between the organization and curriculum of middle-grade schools and the intellectual, emotional, and interpersonal needs of young adolescents.[92]

Describing the trauma students face when they shift from a neighborhood elementary school, where they spent most of the school day with one or two teachers who knew them well, to a larger, colder secondary institution, where they move through six or seven different classes daily, the Carnegie report made the following recommendations:

- Divide large schools into smaller "communities" for learning.
- Create a core curriculum.
- Eliminate tracking.
- Emphasize cooperative learning.
- Develop stronger partnerships between schools and communities.
- Assign teams of teachers and students, with an adult adviser for each student.
- Emphasize the link between education and good health.
- Strengthen teacher preparation for dealing with the adolescent age group.

Imagine life in a school that implements these recommendations. You would see a smaller middle school or high school, one emphasizing community activities and

A Major Part of a Student's Life Because . . .

THERE IS TOO MUCH MATERIAL TO BE MASTERED ONLY DURING SCHOOL TIME

Given demands on students to learn more and to increase their test scores, much study and learning needs to take place at home. After all, students are in school for just five hours of a 24-hour day.

IT BRINGS PARENTS INTO THE LEARNING PROCESS

School cannot accomplish its goals alone. Students achieve much more when academics are reinforced at home. By providing guidance and monitoring homework, parents demonstrate their support of learning, becoming true partners with teachers. Closing the school-home gap fosters competent and attentive students.

MANY STUDENTS DO NOT USE THEIR TIME WISELY

The average student comes home from school, talks on the phone with friends, "hangs out" at the mall, watches television for hours, and then plays a computer game or two before going to bed. Homework at least gives students something meaningful to do with their time.

Limited and Brief Because . . .

TOO MUCH STRESS IS PLACED ON STUDENTS AS IT IS

Schools have been taken over by this growing obsession with tests. The last thing we need to do is extend this angst to home life. Besides, homework is mostly busywork, unrelated to real learning.

IT FAVORS SOME STUDENTS AND PENALIZES OTHERS

Some children have highly educated parents, home computers, and the resources needed to produce quality homework. Other students have poor and uneducated parents, who may not even speak English, and who may be working two or more jobs. All too often homework is simply a measure of family resources.

MANY STUDENTS DO NOT HAVE THE LUXURY OF EXTRA TIME

Many students go directly from school to their part-time job. Their families may need the money. Other students must care for younger siblings at home while parents are at work. Increasing homework would place an enormous burden on these families.

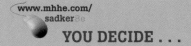

**www.mhhe.com/
sadker**

YOU DECIDE . . .

Will you be assigning homework? If so, how much do you think is appropriate, and how will homework factor into your assessment of student work? Do you have a plan to handle differences in family resources?

moving away from an atmosphere that produces "large-school alienation." Health issues would become more central, linking diet and exercise more directly to education, enhancing the longevity and quality of students' lives well into adulthood. But, to create such a caring and healthful school, teacher education itself would need to be changed. As you examine your own teacher education program, can you identify ways that these recommendations are being promoted? How does your teacher education program prepare you to develop school-community partnerships, promote cooperative learning, and respond more effectively to the needs of adolescents? Significant changes in many teacher education programs across the nation will need to be made if the recommendations of the Carnegie report are to be implemented.

SUMMARY

1. **What rituals and routines shape classroom life?**

   Students spend much of their time sitting still and waiting, denying their needs, and becoming distracted.

2. **How is class time related to student achievement?**

   John Goodlad and others have documented that while some teachers use instructional time efficiently, others are sidetracked by behavioral problems and administrative routine.

3. **How does the teacher's gatekeeping function influence classroom roles?**

   Phil Jackson and others have shown that while a major goal of education is to increase students' curiosity, teachers are the gatekeepers who determine what will be learned and who will be actively involved.

4. **What is tracking, and what are its advantages and disadvantages?**

   The practice of placing students into a specific class based on ability is called tracking, but Jeannie Oakes has found that a disproportionate number of poor children and students of color are tracked as slow learners and receive weaker teachers and fewer opportunities.

5. **Why has "detracking" become a popular movement?**

   Supporters of detracking call for more individualization of instruction, more authentic learning, and less reliance on a "one size fits all" view of teaching and learning.

6. **How do peer groups impact elementary school life?**

   Peer pressure wields great power in and out of school, and a gender wall rigidly segregates young children.

7. **In what ways does the adolescent culture shape teenage perceptions and behaviors?**

   Middle school years capture identity issues, including gender roles. Sociologist James Coleman described high school as an intense, almost "closed" social system, where peer status dominates, while author Patricia Hersch is troubled by the lack of community or parental values on the young.

8. **What steps can educators take to create a more supportive school environment?**

   Reformers have called for more humane, caring, and smaller schools; a greater student involvement in social services; elimination of tracking; and an increased attention to the affective development of adolescents.

9. **What impact do changing family patterns and economic issues have on children and schools?**

   Nearly one in six U.S. children lives in poverty, a condition that frequently short-circuits educational promise. Divorce, remarriage, and nontraditional family patterns have restructured the family and the home-school connection.

10. **How can educators respond to social issues that place children at risk?**

    Sexuality, AIDS, substance abuse, and bullying are just a few of the social and health issues faced by today's youth. Teachers are challenged to create classrooms where bias, hatred, and misinformation are replaced by a sense of security, trust, and truthful information concerning health, relationships, and sex education.

www.mhhe.com/ sadker8e

CHAPTER REVIEW

Go to the Online Learning Center to take a quiz, practice with key terms, and review concepts from the chapter.

Go to your *Teachers, Schools, and Society* Reader CD-ROM to:

READ CURRENT AND HISTORICAL ARTICLES

5.1 **Bullying Among Children,** Janis Bullock, *Childhood Education,* Spring 2002.

5.2 **Meeting the Challenge of the Urban High School,** Joyce Baldwin, *Carnegie Reporter,* Spring 2001.

5.3 **Profiles in Caring: Teachers Who Create Learning Communities in Their Classrooms,** David Strahan et al., *Middle School Journal,* September 2001.

ANALYZE CASE STUDIES

5.1 **Marsha Warren:** A teacher is overwhelmed by the problems created by her students, including eight children who have unique home problems and personal situations that are affecting their schooling.

5.2 **Anne Holt:** This case follows an experienced teacher through her morning routine with a diverse group of first-grade children. The case presents a detailed look at her organization and the climate she creates in the classroom.

OBSERVE TEACHERS, STUDENTS, AND CLASSROOMS IN ACTION

Classroom Observation: Adolescent Self-Concept at Age 16

Understanding your students and the issues they face is an important part of being an effective teacher. Adolescents particularly struggle with self-esteem. In this observation you will observe two adolescent girls as they discuss how their self-esteem fluctuates and is more influenced by the opinions of friends than family.

Classroom Observation: Talking about Drugs at Age 15

Understanding your students and the issues they face is an important part of being an effective teacher. Too many of today's adolescents will have some contact, direct or indirect, with illegal substances before they graduate from high school. In this observation you will observe three teenage girls discussing drug use at their school and that fact that they believe that most of the kids in their school have at least experimented with marijuana.

Classroom Observation: Characteristics of Children Who Bully

Being aware of the characteristics of bullying is an important first step in creating a safe classroom. In this observation you will observe an interview with Dr. Espelage, an educational psychologist, in which bullying behavior and its characteristics are defined and the sex differences in bullying behavior are described.

KEY TERMS AND PEOPLE

ability grouping, 179
The Adolescent Society, 188
affective student needs, 201
alternative families, 193
closed social system, 185
detrack, 178
gatekeeping, 175

gender wall, 182
John Goodlad, 174
heterogeneous, 178
homogeneous, 176
Philip W. Jackson, 172
latchkey, 192
Life in Classrooms, 172

McKinney Vento Homeless Assistance Act, 196
Jeannie Oakes, 178, 181
sociograms, 182
tracking, 176
unremarked revolution, 179
youth charter, 203

DISCUSSION QUESTIONS AND ACTIVITIES

1. Observe in a local elementary school. What are the rules and regulations that students must follow? Do they seem reasonable or arbitrary? Do students seem to spend a large amount of time waiting? Observe one student over a 40-minute period and determine what portion of those 40 minutes she or he spends just waiting.

2. Do you think that tracking is a valid method for enhancing student performance? Or do you think it is a mechanism for perpetuating inequality of opportunity based on social class, race, or sex? Debate someone in your class who holds an opposing point of view.

3. We have noted the vividness and detail with which many people recall their high school years. Try to answer the following:

   • Who was voted most likely to succeed in your high school class? (Do you know what he or she is doing today?)

   • What was your happiest moment in high school? your worst?

   • Name five people who were part of the "in crowd" in your class. What were the "innies" in your high school like?

   • Is there any academic experience in high school that you remember vividly? If so, what was it?

4. Research the issue of adolescent alienation. Make some recommendations on how secondary schools could get students to become more involved in academic and extracurricular activities.

WEB-*TIVITIES*
Go to the Online Learning Center to do the following activities:
1. Gender Equity: The Work of Myra Sadker
2. Hidden America: Homeless Families
3. Children: At Promise or at Risk?

5. What can schools do to address each of the following issues?

- Poverty
- High divorce rates
- Single-parent families
- Alternative families
- Parental income
- Substance abuse
- Dropping out

REEL TO REAL TEACHING

ELECTION (1999)
Run Time: 103 minutes

Synopsis: This satirical comedy takes an uncommon look at ambition, ethics, the power of peer groups, and the hidden curriculum of student elections. Jim McAllister is a popular teacher and student government adviser, but he will risk his reputation and career to stop the school's consummate overachiever from winning the school's election. As campaign fever sets in, both teachers and students blur the lines of right and wrong.

Reflection:

1. What purpose(s) did the election have for Tracy Flick? Paul Metzler? Tammy Metzler? Mr. McAllister?

2. Do you agree with Tammy Metzler that student government should be abolished? Can student government ever help create effective schools?

3. Some believe that school elections actually hurt democratic principles, teaching students to vote on popularity rather than substance, and to not expect any real change after the elections. Do student elections actually do more harm than good?

4. Recall your own experiences with high school student elections. Did you run for an office? Why or why not? In your high school, what was the social status of students serving in student government?

5. How were race, gender, and socioeconomic status represented in *Election*? In your own high school elections?

6. What personal boundaries will you establish with your students? Are teacher-student friendships appropriate? Teacher-student sexual relationships? How might the grade level of students influence your answers?

Follow-up Activity: You are Mr. McAllister's successor as student council adviser at George Washington Carver High. After this major election foul-up, it is up to you to spark participation, confidence, and enthusiasm for student government. You must propose election guidelines: Who is eligible to run for office? What power (if any) will each elected position wield? What are acceptable campaign platforms? Are candidates allowed to spend money? Where and when are candidates permitted to campaign? How will ballots be collected and counted?

www.mhhe.com/sadker8e

How do you rate this film? Go to *Reel to Real Teaching* to review this film.

FOR FURTHER READING

Bullying Prevention: Creating a Positive School Climate and Developing Social Competence, by Pamela Orpinas and Arthur M. Horne (2005). An overview of research that describes the causes of bullying, dispels myths, and suggests practical strategies to minimize risk factors and build safe and productive school environments.

Fires in the Bathroom: Advice for Teachers from High School Students, by Kathleen Cushman (2003). This collection of interviews conveys a uniform message: students do want to learn. They also have ideas for teachers on how to best make learning happen: from getting to know students, to earning their trust, to judging their behavior, to what to do when things go wrong.

A Framework for Understanding Poverty, by Ruby Payne (2001). Explains how children from generational poverty possess values and behaviors different from those usually emphasized in schools, and offers concrete strategies for working with some of our most misunderstood students.

Girlfighting: Betrayal and Rejection among Girls, by Lyn Mikel Brown (2003). Through interviews with over 400 girls of diverse racial, economic, and geographic backgrounds, Brown chronicles the journey girls take from direct and outspoken children who like and trust other girls, to distrusting and competitive young women. She argues that this familiar pathway can and should be interrupted and provides ways to move beyond girlfighting to build healthy relationships.

Keeping Track: How Schools Structure Inequality (2nd ed.), by Jeanne Oakes (2005). This provocative, carefully documented work shows how tracking—the system of grouping students for instruction on the basis of ability—reflects the class and racial inequalities of American society and helps to perpetuate them.

Visionary Middle Schools: Signature Practices and the Power of Local Invention, by Catherine Cobb Morocco, Nancy Brigham, and Cynthia Mata Aguilar (2006). An in-depth look at three schools, each organized around a "signature practice" that reflects the school's particular beliefs about learning. Despite obstacles such as poverty, low English-language proficiency, and new immigrant status, each of these schools is the strongest performing in their respective districts and presents approaches and lessons of relevance to urban schools across the country.

CHAPTER 6

Curriculum, Standards, and Testing

FOCUS QUESTIONS

1. What is the formal curriculum taught in schools?
2. How does the invisible curriculum influence learning?
3. What is the place of the extracurriculum in school life?
4. What forces shape the school curriculum?
5. How has technology affected the curriculum?
6. How do textbook publishers and state adoption committees "drive" the curriculum?
7. What is standards-based education?
8. What are the provisions and criticisms of *No Child Left Behind*?
9. What problems are created by high-stakes testing, and what are the testing alternatives?
10. How are cultural and political conflicts reflected in the school curriculum?
11. How can we rethink tomorrow's curriculum?

www.mhhe.com/ sadker8e

WHAT DO YOU THINK? **What books did you read in high school English?** Compare what you read to what others read for a larger view of the high school canon.

CHAPTER PREVIEW

"We shape our buildings and afterwards our buildings shape us," said Winston Churchill. Had the noted statesman been a noted educator, he might have rephrased this epigram, substituting curriculum for buildings, for what children learn in school today will affect the kind of adults they will become and the kind of society they will eventually create. In fact, it is the power of curriculum to shape students and, ultimately society, that takes curriculum development out of the realms of philosophy and education and into the political arena. Children learn through the formal curriculum, made up of objectives and textbook assignments, and through the more subtle lessons of the hidden, null, and extra curriculum. This chapter will provide a brief overview of what has been taught, and how curricular decisions are reached.

Several trends are pushing schools toward a similar curriculum: the indomitable textbook, the Internet, and the recent emphasis on state standards and testing. Protests (perhaps better titled "antitests") have been growing against the increasing influence of standardized tests in general, and *No Child Left Behind* in particular. The benefits of standards and the many problems with high-stakes tests are explored in this chapter, as are more positive and creative ways of looking at curriculum and testing.

The Faculty Room

A casual conversation in the faculty room opens this chapter door on the teacher's role in curricular decisions:

JO: Were you at yesterday's faculty meeting? The sales reps from the publishing company showed their new textbook series.

MAYA: No, I had an emergency dentist appointment—a root canal. That was painful enough! What's the new series like?

JO: Fabulous. It must be worth big money—superslick covers, beautiful photos, and graphics. And talk about supplementary materials. They have everything! It's got a Web site, which they promise to update regularly, that includes practical student projects. They went online for us yesterday, and it looks great. The objectives are totally spelled out, and there's a step-by-step teacher's guide saying exactly how to cover each objective. There are discussion questions after reading assignments and a student workbook with activities for the kids to do after we've finished the reading. They even have huge banks of test questions for weekly tests and unit exams on CD-ROM.

MAYA: What's got you so excited?

JO: Excited? The prep time alone is endless. Anything that saves me hours, I'm for. And these books look like a time-saving resource.

MAYA: Jo, we've been through so many TGIF afternoons—you know I need more "quality and quantity" time in my life. But some of these new comprehensive textbook systems make me nervous.

JO: What do you mean?

MAYA: I'm not so sure the people in slick offices (who do the slick covers) know what's best for our kids. What makes them so smart that they can determine what we should tell our students? I know my kids! What kind of expertise do they have to tell us how to teach? When was the last time those textbook writers were in a classroom, anyway? I'm a professional, and I am not ready to relinquish my control over what and how I teach.

JO: Sounds like you. But they can save you a lot of grief. You don't want to step on anyone's toes, or get the "Parents for an American Curriculum" breathing down your neck. Those textbooks sidestep a lot of those controversies for you.

MAYA: The other day I was talking with Jena, the new teacher who works across the hall from me. She just graduated from college a few years ago, and she has some terrific ideas. She's using an individualized reading program, and she's really got the kids into it. Instead of the basal reading selections, she's got the class reading everything from Judy Blume to Tolkien. And the kids are loving it. It's a tremendous success. But, instead of being psyched, she's in panic mode—afraid she's harming her students' reading development, because she's not following the official basal reader or the new state standards. The upcoming state reading assessment worries her. If her kids don't do well on that state exam, she's toast.

JO: You're kidding!

MAYA: I wish I were.

The Visible Curriculum

As you listen to the faculty room conversation, you sense how teachers struggle with the **curriculum.** If you asked these teachers for a copy of their curriculum, you will likely be handed a curriculum guide, a description of courses offered, or perhaps some syllabi describing what the students are supposed to be learning at each grade level and in each subject. Ask for more detailed information, and a teacher might share some specific lesson plans, classroom activities that will enable students to meet these objectives. Educator Hilda Taba emphasized the importance of a school curriculum: "Learning in school differs from learning in life in that it is formally organized. It is the special function of the school to arrange the experiences of children and youth so that desirable learning takes place."[1] This is a pretty good description of the **formal** or **explicit curriculum,** arranging experiences so that intended outcomes are reached. And if you could go back in time (and in this text, you can!), you soon realize that the formal curriculum is not a fixed course of study but changes to reflect the values of the time. Here is a quick tour of the changing formal curriculum.

The Two Rs in the Seventeenth Century

If you were a student in colonial America, your formal curriculum would focus on religion and reading, the "two *Rs.*" You might find yourself shaking with apprehension as you listened to a fear-inspiring dose of Puritan morality, and if you were among the few to graduate from secondary school, you would have memorized quite a bit of Latin and Greek. But if you were female, African American, Native American, or poor, you would find yourself standing outside a locked schoolhouse door.

Eighteenth Century: Focus on Building a New Nation

The new nation's emphasis on the secular began to free the formal curriculum from the tight bonds of religion. Studies still included reading, religion, and morality, but writing and arithmetic received more attention. At the secondary level, in addition to the classical Latin route, you could learn vocational skills, such as surveying, bookkeeping, accounting, and navigating. While the color barrier remained, more women were attending school.

A Secularized Curriculum for Students in the Nineteenth Century

As the nation developed, so did the curriculum. Elementary schools stressed writing, arithmetic, spelling, geography, and good behavior. As a secondary student, you would probably enroll in the academy, and select either the classic Latin curriculum or the newer English curriculum, which included grammar, public speaking, geography, history, and sometimes even science, geometry, algebra, and a modern language.

Progressive Education in the First Half of the Twentieth Century

Americanization of many new immigrants along with the new ideas from progressive education dominated the curriculum. Creativity and the arts were curricular touchstones, and traditional courses, like history, geography, civics, reading, writing, and spelling, were now combined into the social studies and language arts. The high school curriculum grew beyond college preparation to include vocational courses, such as typing, stenography, bookkeeping, domestic science, and industrial arts.

Sputnik in Space and a More Demanding Curriculum, 1950s–1960s

The launching of the Soviet *Sputnik,* the first artificial satellite, marked a low point for the West in the Cold War. America's schools were made the scapegoat for the U.S. failure to beat the Soviets into space. Prestigious university academics were recruited to develop a more rigorous curriculum, especially in science, math, and foreign languages. Courses were reorganized so that students would focus not on memorization, but on learning to think like mathematicians or scientists. Problems and issues pushed students to develop higher-order thinking skills.

Today's recycling efforts have their roots in the environmental education programs that emerged in the 1970s.

Social Concern and Relevance, 1960s–1970s

The Civil Rights movement and the protest against the war in Vietnam impacted the school curriculum. Reformers criticized the Cold War curriculum that emphasized academics at the expense of social reality. As a student in elementary school, you might decide for yourself what you wanted to learn in a new child-centered curriculum called an "open classroom." By high school, you would explore an exciting array of electives: Black Studies, Multicultural Education, Peace Studies, Ecology, Women's Studies, or perhaps Sexuality, Consumer Rights, or Film Making.

Back to Basics, Standards and Testing, 1980s–Today

The proliferation of electives in the 1960s and 1970s led to superficial course options and a less rigorous curriculum. Coupled with poor test scores and the publication of critical reports and books (*A Nation at Risk, A Place Called School,* and *Horace's Compromise*), America's schools began eliminating electives and increasing the number of basic courses required for graduation, sometimes referred to as a **core curriculum.** Support for clear academic standards and frequent test-ing increased. In many schools today, the curriculum is defined by the states, and school effectiveness is determined by standardized tests.

(Want to learn more about current trends in specific subject areas? Read Appen-dix A on the Online Learning Center.)

 # The Invisible Curriculum

Let's face it, some of the most powerful curricular lessons taught in school are not to be found in the formal curriculum at all. This "invisible curriculum" has two parts, and by describing each we hope to make it more visible for you. Let's start with what educators sometimes call the **implicit** or **hidden curriculum,** learn-ings that are not always intended but emerge as students are shaped by the school culture, including the attitudes and behaviors of teachers. Here is an example offered by Jules Henry, an anthropologist who has analyzed the hidden curriculum of the elementary school. Henry described a fourth-grade spelling bee. Team mem-bers were chosen by two team captains. When a student spelled a word correctly on the board, a "hit" was scored. When three spelling errors were made, the team was "out." Students cheered or groaned, depending on the outcome for their team. Did you see the hidden curriculum?

According to Henry, these students were learning powerful lessons: the impor-tance of winning, the pain of losing, how competition can turn a friend into an adversary, the joy of being chosen early for a team, and the embarrassment and rejection when you are not. Some of the more thoughtful students may have seen the absurdity of a spelling lesson being taught as a baseball game.[2] Schools teach many powerful but hidden lessons, from the importance of punctuality to follow-ing the rules, from social conformity to respecting authority. While some hidden lessons are useful; others can be destructive. The first step in evaluating the appro-priateness of the hidden curriculum is to actually see it.

Let's remove the veil from another part of the invisible curriculum, all the mate-rial that you do not learn in school. When some one or some group decides that a topic is unimportant or too controversial, inappropriate or not worth the time, that topic is never taught and becomes part of the **null curriculum.** If your American History class never went beyond World War II, then your null curriculum included the Korean and Vietnam Wars; the fall of communism, the Civil Rights and Women's Rights movements; an assassination and an impeachment, the disaster in Somalia; widespread corporate corruption, the technology revolution, the September 11, 2001, attack; and the abuses at Abu Ghraib prison in Iraq. When a school board decides not to teach about the theory of evolution or sex education, they have made a deci-sion that these topics will become part of the null curriculum. The null curriculum is rich, but invisible. (It would be fascinating to witness what students would learn if some enterprising educators created a school to focus on the null curriculum.)

 # The Extracurriculum

Now let's look at one last curriculum, a vibrant ingredient of school life but often not thought of as a curriculum at all. The **extracurriculum** teaches the lessons students learn in school activities such as sports, clubs, governance, and the stu-dent newspaper, places where a great deal of learning occurs, without tests or

Sports and varsity athletics comprise an important and influential part of school life.

grades. The Duke of Wellington was one of the first to highlight the importance of extracurricular activities when he remarked that "The Battle of Waterloo was won on the playing fields of Eton." A majority of students participate in at least one extracurricular activity, with students from smaller schools and with stronger academic records the most likely to be involved.[3] In high school, varsity sports attract about half of the boys and more than a third of the girls, reducing behavior problems and increasing positive attitudes toward school while teaching lessons in leadership, teamwork, persistence, diligence, and fair play.[4] While it may surprise some, the fastest growing high school sport for both girls and boys is bowling, defying the perception that it is a sport of a bygone era.[5] About one student in four participates in music and drama, while about the same percentage joins academic clubs in science, languages, computers, debate, and the like, clubs that enhance not only academic learning but social skills as well. Nationwide programs such as Odyssey of the Mind and Future Bowl promote cross-curricular interests and creative problem-solving skills. Advocates see these activities as so important that they refer to them not as the extracurriculum but as the *cocurriculum,* and believe that their value goes far beyond the high school years. Participation in the extracurricular activities has been connected with:

- Higher student self-esteem, school completion, and civic participation
- Improved race relations
- Higher SAT scores and grades
- Better health for females and less conformity to gender stereotypes
- Higher career aspirations, especially for boys from poor backgrounds[6]

But the extracurriculum is not without problems. The underrepresentation of low-socioeconomic students is evident in many programs, as are gender differences in participation in performing arts, athletics, school government, and literary activities.[7] Skeptics suggest that the best we can say "is that the effects of extracurricular participation on secondary school students' personal development and academic achievement

Across the nation, music programs range from grandiose spectacles to the sounds of silence. How does a school's music program amplify its culture?

are probably positive, but very modest, and are definitely different among students with different social or intellectual backgrounds."[8] And given the current emphasis on test scores and academic standards, the extracurriculum is sometimes viewed as little more than a distraction.[9] In Texas and other states, "no pass, no play" rules deny students in poor academic standing the right to participate in varsity sports. In other communities, budget tightening has led to "pay to play" rules, in which a fee is required for sports participation, posing a serious problem for low-income families and students. Such policies raise puzzling questions and issues. Should academic performance and financial constraints be factors in deciding who participates in extracurricular activities? Since the top academic students, more likely to be wealthy and white, already dominate the extracurriculum, will "pay to play" and "pass to play" regulations make this curriculum even more exclusive, driving deeper divisions between the haves and have-nots and further segregating racial and ethnic groups?

 ## Who and What Shape the Curriculum?

Although all three curriculums are powerful forces, the public and the press typically focus on the most visible—the formal or official curriculum—when evaluating schools. Given the current emphasis on standards and testing, and the recurrent controversies over the teaching of evolution or the place of religion in the curriculum, the formal curriculum is constantly in the news. As a future teacher, it makes a lot of sense for you to begin thinking about who decides what you should teach. In fact, what you teach is decided by competing interest groups, and the product sometimes feels as though it was created in a pressure cooker (see Figure 6.1). Anyone, from the president of the United States to a single parent, can impact what is taught in your classroom. Let's take a brief tour of some of the chefs at work on the curricular pressure cooker.

Teachers

Teachers develop curriculum both formally and informally. They may serve on textbook selection committees that determine what texts the school will purchase, or they may actually work on writing a district's curriculum. In a less formal but no

FIGURE 6.1
A pressure cooker of groups shapes the curriculum.

REFLECTION: What groups today exert the most influence on the curriculum? Do you see all these groups as a mark of democratic participation, or an inappropriate intrusion in curricular decision making?

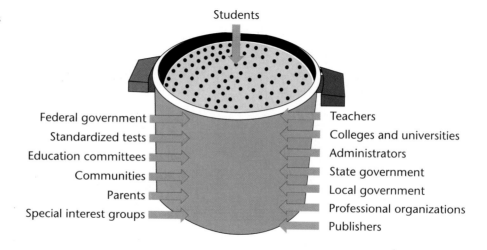

Students

Federal government
Standardized tests
Education committees
Communities
Parents
Special interest groups

Teachers
Colleges and universities
Administrators
State government
Local government
Professional organizations
Publishers

less powerful way, classroom teachers interpret and adapt whatever official text or curriculum guide has been assigned, stressing certain points in a text while giving scant attention to others; supplementing with teacher-made materials or directing students to the Internet.

Parental and Community Groups

Parents can be quite forceful in impacting the curriculum. They might advocate for more rigorous academic courses, concerned about poor student performance on standardized tests, or they may desire more practical vocational training, such as an increase in computer science courses. Banning certain books or videos from the curriculum is also not unusual. In conservative communities, religious fundamentalists have objected to the absence of Christian values, while liberal communities have objected to books that use racial, ethnic, or gender slurs and stereotypes.

Students

During the 1960s and 1970s, students demanded curricular relevance. Although students have not seemed particularly interested in influencing curriculum policy recently, they have been active in protests against standardized testing. Typically, students are given some freedom to select topics for independent projects, research papers, book reviews, and even authentic learning.

Administrators

Principals, in their role as instructional leaders, can wield substantial influence in shaping the curriculum. For example, a principal announces at a faculty meeting that the school's scores on the state standardized test in mathematics were disappointing, and this year's priority is to raise those scores. The result might well be a math curriculum that "teaches to the test." Sometimes central-office personnel, such as a language arts coordinator or a social studies supervisor, might create a new or revised school or district curriculum.

State Government

States are now assuming a larger role in education, and their interest in curriculum matters has sharpened through the creation of state standards, curriculum guides, and frameworks for all state schools to follow. In some states, the role of religion and the treatment of evolution versus intelligent design are hot-button issues. In other states, instructional materials are expected to include cultural diversity.

Local Government

Local school boards make a variety of curriculum decisions, requiring courses from AIDS education to technology. Supporters feel that local school boards should have a strong voice in the curriculum, because they are closest to the needs of the local community and the interests of the students. Others feel that school board members lack training to make curricular decisions.

Colleges and Universities

Institutions of higher learning influence curricula through their entrance requirements, which spell out courses high school students must take to gain admittance. As A. Bartlett Giamatti noted when he was president of Yale University,

> The high schools in this country are always at the mercy of the colleges. The colleges change their requirements and their admissions criteria and the high schools . . . are constantly trying to catch up with what the colleges are thinking. When the colleges don't seem to know what they think over a period of time, it's no wonder that this oscillation takes place all the way through the system.[10]

Standardized Tests

The results of state and national tests, from the state subject matter tests needed for graduation to the SATs, influence what is taught in the school. If students perform poorly in one or more areas of these standardized tests, the government or public pressure pushes school officials to strengthen the curriculum in these weak spots.

Schools of education are not immune from the current focus on test performance. Because an increasing number of states are requiring new teachers to take qualifying tests, such as the National Teacher Exam (NTE, Praxis series), these tests influence what is covered in teacher education programs. For example, if Benjamin Bloom's Taxonomy of Educational Objectives is emphasized on such tests, teacher education colleges will teach more about Bloom in their own programs.

Education Commissions and Committees

From time to time in the history of U.S. education, various committees, usually on a national level, have been called upon to study an aspect of education. Their reports often draw national attention and influence elementary and secondary curricula. The 1983 report, *A Nation at Risk,* and the National Education Summit in 1989 led to a more uniform core of courses, and a program for testing student progress.

Professional Organizations

Many professional organizations such as the National Education Association (NEA), the American Federation of Teachers (AFT), the National Association for the Education of Young Children (NAEYC), and numerous subject area associations (teacher groups in English, math, science, and the like) publish journals and hold conferences that emphasize curriculum needs and developments. Their programs and materials may focus on teaching with technology, multicultural education, or authentic learning. Teachers, inspired by these presentations, might choose to modify their curriculum and implement new approaches and ideas.

Special Interest Groups

Today's students are tomorrow's customers, so it is not surprising that businesses and interest groups offer teachers free (and attractive) curricular materials promoting their view of the world. A student-friendly magazine on protecting the environment looks wonderful at first glance, but how do you handle Company X's self-promoting distortion of its own environmental policies that may be part of the narrative? A month's supply of free newspapers for all students is appealing, but does acceptance mean that you are endorsing the editorial opinions of the paper? Teachers need to examine materials and products carefully in order to present a fair and accurate view.

Publishers

The major goal of textbook publishers is—not surprisingly—to sell books. That is why textbooks are attractively packaged and chock full of terms and names deemed important at the time (including this text!). Unfortunately, most elementary and secondary texts rarely provide in-depth coverage of topics and avoid unpopular points of view (unlike this text). Teachers need to remember that textbooks are published to meet market demands, and not necessarily objective or complex viewpoints.

Federal Government

The federal government influences the curriculum through judicial decisions, financial incentives, and legislation. In 2001, *No Child Left Behind* was a major piece of legislation that significantly altered the curricular landscape. (We will look closer at this law a little later in this chapter.)

Many times these groups have different agendas as they compete to shape the curriculum, but on one recent issue, technology, there is widespread agreement that computers should be part of the school curriculum. Prestigious commissions have issued reports about the importance of technology for the economy, parent groups pressure schools to buy computers for their children, and businesses arrange special prices and package deals to make such large-scale school purchases attractive. The federal government offers funds to help schools hop onto the Internet, and publishers sell new educational software. Clearly, the school curriculum is shaped by the computer age.

 ## Technology and the Curriculum

In the twentieth century, education was forever changed. Human beings serving as teachers, the core of schooling for centuries if not millennia, were made technologically obsolete. The new invention was used at home and then in the more affluent schools. Eventually, all schools were connected. Slowly but surely, the classroom teacher was replaced. These new machines took students where they had never been before, did things no human could do, and shared an unlimited reservoir of information. Clearly, this technological breakthrough had potential to teach more effectively at a far lower cost than human teachers. Predictions varied from the replacement of all teachers to the replacement of most teachers. Some even predicted the replacement of schools themselves.

Sound familiar? While today's computer revolution has sparked these sorts of predictions, the developments described above had nothing to do with computers or the Internet, or even the twenty-first century. These predictions were made in the 1950s about television. The popular perception back then was that educational television would reshape the classroom and revolutionize schools, and perhaps put a few million teachers out of work. That never happened. While television has reshaped much of the cultural landscape (and not all for the good), predictions about its impact on schools were greatly exaggerated. Americans are quick to see a brave new world with each new invention. Consider the following soothsayers:

> "The motion picture is destined to revolutionize our educational system, and . . . in a few years it will supplant largely, if not entirely, the use of textbooks."
>
> *Thomas Edison*

> "The time may come when a portable radio receiver will be as common in the classroom as is a blackboard."
>
> *William Levenson, director of Cleveland Public School's radio station*[11]

Technology brings students instant information, but educators wonder about its ultimate impact on learning.

So it should not be surprising that the monumental investments in computer technology have not been matched by monumental gains in student achievement. In fact, researchers are divided on the academic benefits brought by computers. Evidence suggests that drills and tutorials in science, social science, and math may be effective, but more advanced simulations, like virtual dissections, are not. Perhaps with more sophisticated uses of technology in the future, more effective learning will occur—or perhaps not.[12] Some educators believe that technology can also hamper learning. Students who become too dependent on calculators can see their mathematics test scores tumble.[13] Word processing has produced longer, higher-quality writing by students, but teachers complain about the spelling and grammatical shortcuts that characterize students' e-mail.[14] Technology has created some ethical dilemmas as well. Nearly 40 percent of college students use the cut-and-paste function on their computers to lift text from the Internet. Text-messaging on cell phones has been used to share information during exams. High-tech cheating is rarely reported by students.[15]

Ways Computers Are Used in the Classroom

Although computers have a mixed track record, most adults believe that computers offer essential workplace skills. The public sees computers in the classroom as a sign of educational progress, and increasingly, teachers view technology as a central part of classroom life. What technology? When asked to rank their needs, teachers listed a computer station with access to e-mail at the top of the list, followed by the Internet, a telephone (yes, a telephone!), encyclopedia and other reference materials on CD, and at least one computer for every four students. PowerPoint and multimedia authoring programs were also mentioned.[16] In the curriculum, teachers use technology in some exciting ways:

- *Simulations* recreate events, such as elections, cross-cultural meetings, and historical events, with amazing realism that pulls students into another time or place.

- *Virtual field trips* transport students to the ocean depths, to outer space on NASA's Shuttle site, and to the National Zoo where zookeepers share their knowledge of the animals and students can pose questions via a "chat interface."

- *Distance learning* provides courses online that instantly cross national borders. Distance learning is today's "e-quivalent" of correspondence courses, providing educational options to home-schooling families, those working unusual or unpredictable hours, commuters who would rather travel the Internet than the interstate, and individuals who simply like learning on their own time and in their own place. In fact, the Internet offers the potential of a world curriculum, as evidenced by some fascinating programs:

  - The First People's Project provides a site, in Spanish and English, for students from indigenous cultures. The goal is for students to learn about different cultures and perhaps become involved in humanitarian efforts (see www.iearn.org.au/fp/efphome.htm).

  - Over six thousand schools from Mexico, the United States, and Canada participate in wildlife migration studies in the western hemisphere by recording sightings in their areas. "Journey North: A Global Study of Wildlife Migration" teaches students to care for wildlife by creating or protecting habitats (see www.learner.org/jnorth).

  - At the Holocaust/Genocide Project, students produce a magazine called *An End to Intolerance* (see www.iearn.org/hgp/student-magazine.html).

  - World Wise Schools is a Peace Corps project where classrooms can partner with Peace Corps volunteers and follow them as they do their work during the course of a year (see www.peacecorps.gov/wws).

  - Podcasting lectures and discussions is a way of teaching students even when they are not in class. While teachers now podcast information to students, schools also are encouraging students to produce their own podcasts in various subjects.[17]

But Stanford University professor Larry Cuban, looking beyond even these positive signs, sees problems on the horizon. When academic advances do not follow technological advances, we often blame teachers for not adequately embracing new technology. If teachers are not to blame, we place our criticism on the doorstep of an unresponsive school bureaucracy unable to manage change. If that does not work, then we explain failure in terms of insufficient resources, a public unwilling to fund costly technology. Rarely do Americans question the technology itself. Cuban points out that we know little about using technology to enhance instruction, that the problem may not be teachers, administrators, or funding; it may be America's unbridled faith in technology.[18]

The Digital Divide

While technology offers hope to many, it does not always offer opportunity to everyone. The gap between technology haves and have-nots has been termed a **digital divide.** For years, African American, Hispanic, and female students had fewer computers and less access to or interest in the Internet, a technology gap with educational implications.[19] But in recent years, this gap has been closing due to the falling price of laptops, new cell phone technology, and the increasing number of school computers.[20] (Although at the college level, whites, Asians, and males continue to constitute the majority of computer science majors and professionals.[21])

But the digital divide has not disappeared. For instance, classrooms and homes in wealthier communities are more likely to have up-to-date technology and rapid Internet connections than poorer communities.[22] Geography matters since running fiber optic cables to rural schools is often an expense that telecommunications companies avoid. The connections that are made are often slow, posing difficulties for students participating in online classes, a digital divide that has its own title: the **last mile problem.**[23] Perhaps Internet connections via satellite or more advanced future technologies will resolve this geographic challenge, but for now, rural America is on the wrong side of the digital divide.[24]

Finally, let's focus on a more subtle digital divide: *how* technology is used.[25] You probably have some friends who struggle with technology, and others who are wizards. There is more to technology than simply access. Some schools use technology to promote drill and practice, while other schools use technology to challenge students. Professor Henry Jay Becker warns, "Efforts to ensure equal access to computer-related learning opportunities at school must move beyond a concern with the numbers of computers in different schools toward an emphasis on how well those computers are being used to help children develop intellectual competencies and technical skills"[26] (see Figure 6.2). While technology can awe us, in the end it is how well we use the technology that matters.

FIGURE 6.2

Playing or learning? In the summer between kindergarten and 1st grade, 80 percent of children from high-income families used their home computers on a weekly basis, compared with 60 percent of children from low-income families. There were also disparities in how those children used their home computers.

SOURCE: "Young Children's Access to Computers in the Home and at School in 1999 and 2000," U.S. Department of Education, National Center for Education Statistics, March 2003.

REFLECTION: Do you believe that teachers should work with poorer families to enhance the productive use of computers and the Internet at home? If so, how might this be done?

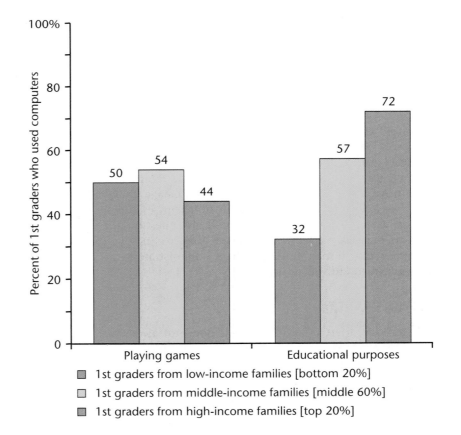

1st graders from low-income families [bottom 20%]
1st graders from middle-income families [middle 60%]
1st graders from high-income families [top 20%]

It is helpful for teachers to maintain perspective when it comes to technology. While it is unlikely that education will be redefined completely in the near future, it is also clear that technology's influence is growing. Consider technology mastery as part of your professional development. Attend relevant courses and workshops and observe colleagues applying technology, but do not lose your skepticism. Be wary of "magic bullets," simple solutions to complex educational problems.

The Reign of the Textbook

Although technology garners headlines, textbooks reign as the perennial shaper of the curriculum. So influential is the textbook that some consider it a *de facto* national curriculum. Students around the nation study from the same books, do the same exercises, and are expected to master the same material. Studies reveal that students spend as much as 95 percent of classroom time using textbooks. Teachers base more than 70 percent of their instructional decisions and as much as 90 percent of homework assignments on the text.[27] No wonder some are convinced that textbooks rule.

Before 1850, textbooks were made up of whatever educational materials children had in their homes. Students took these textbooks to school, and instruction was based on them. Picture yourself trying to teach a class with the wide array of random materials children have in their homes. Although today we might use these personal resources to supplement instruction, back then it was difficult to teach with such disparate materials. In fact, despairing teachers appealed for common texts, so that all students could use the same materials. Local legislators responded by requiring schools to select appropriate books, and then parents were required to buy them. When families moved, they often had to buy new books. Concerned about the costly burden this lack of consistency placed on families, legislators mandated commonly used textbooks across larger geographic areas.

Today, the process of textbook development and adoption has come under intense criticism. One of its chief critics, Harriet Tyson Bernstein, says,

> Imagine a public policy system that is perfectly designed to produce textbooks that confuse, mislead, and profoundly bore students, while at the same time making all the adults in the process look good, not only in their own eyes, but in the eyes of others. Although there are some good textbooks on the market, publishers and editors are virtually compelled by public policies and practices to create textbooks that confuse students with non sequitors, that mislead them with misinformation, and that profoundly bore them with pointedly arid writing.
>
> None of the adults in this very complex system intends this outcome. To the contrary, each of them wants to produce good effects, and each public policy regulation or conventional practice was intended to make some improvement or prevent some abuse. But the cumulative effects of well-intentioned and seemingly reasonable state and local regulations are textbooks that squander the intellectual capital of our youth.[28]

Here's how the system works and why Bernstein and other opponents are so angry. In 1900, when our current textbook system was designed, 22 states enacted laws that put in place a centralized adoption system. Today, about the same number

FIGURE 6.3

Textbook adoption states. While some school districts are free to choose any text, others are limited to state-approved textbooks.

SOURCE: American Association of Publishers, Washington, DC, 2006.

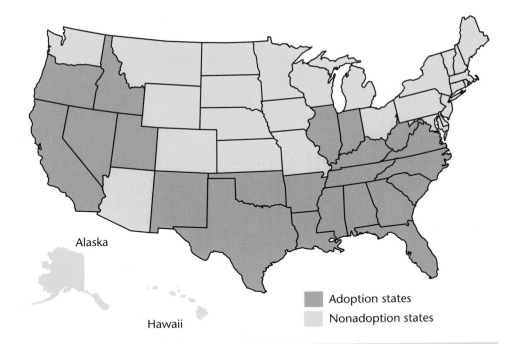

Alaska

Hawaii

Adoption states
Nonadoption states

REFLECTION: What patterns do you notice in the states that require texts be selected from an approved list? Would such state adoption procedures be a factor in deciding where you might teach? Visit the site for updates at www.publishers.org.

of states, located mainly in the South and the West, are **textbook adoption states.** (These states are indicated in Figure 6.3.)

Under a state adoption system, local school districts typically select their texts from an official, state-approved list. Those in favor of statewide adoption claim that this process results in the selection of higher-quality texts. This system creates a common, statewide curriculum, which unites educators and makes school life easier for students who move to different schools within the state. State adoptions also save time and work for educators at the local level, and, because of the large numbers of books purchased, the per-book cost is kept low.

Criticism of statewide adoptions focuses on what has been called the **Texas and California effect,** which might more accurately be termed the "Four States Effect" (including Florida and North Carolina). Together these four states exert an enormous influence on what is included—or omitted—from the texts. These states draw up plans for what they would like to see in a textbook, and the publishers design books to meet the states' "wish list." These four populous states account for a billion dollars of annual textbook sales.[29]

In a typical year, American schools spend upwards of four billion dollars on textbooks. The lure of such profits has created a corporate feeding frenzy, and in recent years, four publishing giants have gobbled up all competitors. Powerful adoption states, like Texas and California, have reduced the choices further by dictating to these companies what content to include, and sometimes what topics, words, or names to exclude. The remaining publishers cannot afford to lose the sales of these major adoption states, and so they comply. As a result, there is little competition about what should be included in the textbook, and all textbooks have become quite similar (and less than exciting). Since content does not vary much, to sell their books publishers must focus on sales techniques like give-away programs and colorful book design. Teachers and administrators asked to select a textbook, whether from a state-approved list or not, have very few options available to them, and can be influenced by superficial qualities like the cover, the graphics, and the design. While visual attractiveness can enhance learning, it is no substitute for well-written and accurate content.[30]

Since some states will buy texts only if they have a specified reading level, publishers are under pressure to develop books that meet this criterion. Often, authors avoid difficult words and long sentences, so that, for example, esophagus becomes food tube and protoplasm becomes stuff. The result, according to former secretary of education Terrell Bell and other critics, is the **dumbing down** of the textbook. Ironically, readability formulas may make books harder, not easier, to read. When authors simplify vocabulary, they replace precise and clear terminology with simple, vague, even ambiguous words. When authors shorten sentences, they often leave out the connective issue—and, but, therefore—words that clarify the relationships between events and ideas. Shortening sentences to make reading simple can make understanding challenging ideas even more difficult.

As textbooks skim over content, simply to cover it, the student loses information necessary for comprehension. Critics are frustrated by this **mentioning phenomenon,** and charge that texts typically include too many subjects and gloss over them to such a degree that students do not really understand what is going on.[31]

One reason for the mentioning phenomenon is the knowledge explosion. But another cause can be traced to the adoption process. In their quest for higher scores on standardized tests, many states have called for aligning the curriculum in textbooks with what is on standardized tests. Adoption committees have delineated in minute detail all the names, dates, and places they want included, and what skills they want students to attain. Frequently, in-depth analysis and clarifying examples are lost in favor of mentioning lots of names, places, and dates. Researchers have also found that basal readers and other texts, in attempting to be inoffensive to potential purchasers, include only a limited range of story types, often devoid of interpersonal and internal conflict.[32]

Textbooks offer an inviting target, but before we banish them from schools, let's consider some of their strengths, and some ways that teachers can use them effectively. With a clear narrative, informative graphics, and exercises that develop skills, students can learn a great deal from a textbook. And if a teacher is fortunate to be working with a well-crafted text, research suggests that the text can actually motivate the teacher to try new ideas in the classroom.[33] At its best, a good text is a catalyst for change. And even when a text is less well crafted and floods the reader with too much information, the teacher can make critical choices on how best to use it. One simple idea is to be selective: choose certain chapters while skipping others, assign a few of the better exercises in the book rather than require all be done. Here's one final idea: even a weak text can be used effectively. For example, while blatant stereotypes of the past are rarely found in today's texts, subtle bias persists. Rather than ignore this bias, teach your students how to see the inequity, offer examples of how bias appears in texts, then ask your students to evaluate their own books. This approach empowers students to become critical readers. (For more on this, see the Frame of Reference "Seven Forms of Bias.")

www.mhhe.com/ sadker8e

INTERACTIVE ACTIVITY

What Is the Bias? Match scenarios with the bias being displayed.

While yesterday's stark racist and sexist texts are thankfully gone, subtle bias persists. Here are descriptions of seven forms of bias that emerge in today's texts. These categories can identify bias toward racial and ethnic groups, the elderly, English language learners, females, gays and lesbians (and others). By teaching your students about the forms of bias, you can help them to become critical readers, an important skill they can take into adulthood.

Invisibility: Prior to the 1960s, African Americans, Latinos, Asian Americans, women, and Native Americans were largely invisible; that is, not even included in texts. Today, those with disabilities or gays and lesbians are often invisible.

Stereotyping: When rigid roles or traits are assigned to all members of a group, a stereotype is born. Examples include portraying all African Americans as athletes, Mexican Americans as laborers, and women only in terms of their family roles.

Imbalance and Selectivity: Texts can perpetuate bias by presenting only one side of an issue, such as describing how women were "given" the vote. In fact, women endured physical abuse and other sacrifices in their struggle to gain their civil rights.

Unreality: Curricular materials often paint a Pollyanna picture of the nation (and this goes for any nation!). Our history texts often ignore class differences, the lack of basic health care for tens of millions, as well as ongoing racism, classism, and sexism.

Fragmentation and Isolation: Have you ever seen a chapter or section focusing on one group, perhaps entitled "Ten Famous Asian Americans." When texts isolate groups in this way, they are subtly suggesting that they are not part of society's mainstream.

Linguistic Bias: Using words like "roaming" and "wandering" to describe Native Americans suggests nondirected behavior and relationships, language that implicitly justifies the seizure of native lands by white Americans who "settled" the lands. Or word choices that place men in primary roles, and women in family roles: "men and their wives."

Cosmetic Bias: Cosmetic bias offers the "illusion of equity" to lure educators into purchasing books that appear current, diverse, and balanced. A science textbook brandishes a female scientist on the cover, but alas, there is almost no content on female scientists in the text content.

SOURCE: The forms of bias were developed by Myra Sadker and David Sadker for Title IX equity workshops.

REFLECTION: These forms of bias emerge in more than just textbooks. Choose a television program or news show, and see how many of these biases you can identify.

 ## The Standards Movement

For as long as anyone can remember, schools have been the focal point of criticism. In recent times, the poor performance of American students on international test scores has led to headlines announcing: "America's Students Fall Further Behind." It was this growing pressure to "fix" the nation's schools that led to standards-based education. **Standards-based education** specifies precisely what students should learn, focuses the curriculum and instruction (and perhaps much more) on meeting these standards, and provides continual testing to see if the standards are achieved.

The first President Bush initiated the standards movement when he convened a "National Educational Summit" of governors in Charlottesville, Virginia, in 1989.[34] The summit produced "Education 2000" (modified as "Goals 2000" under the Clinton administration), a list of worthy, if unrealistically optimistic goals. The first goal was "All children will start school ready to learn," but only half of the nation's youth were enrolled in preschool by 2000, and many of those programs were of poor quality. "We will be first in the world in math and science by the year 2000," also missed the mark. In retrospect, the Education Summit was a transition between *A Nation at Risk* (1983) and today's emphasis on state standards and testing.

While the goals were never attained, they did put the nation on a course of self-examination, and developing standards of learning dominated much of the education literature of the 1990s. Professional education associations, business leaders, and citizen groups got into the content standards business. **Content standards** detailed precisely what students should know and be able to do in each subject at each grade level. As former Secretary of Education Richard Riley said: "Without knowing where you're going, you certainly cannot get there."[35] States echoed the call for better schools by adopting and adapting many of these national standards, and in some cases, developing their own. This step was crucial, for in the end the states have the major responsibility for creating the school curriculum. (See Frame of Reference: Selected State Content Standards.)

But the federal government, which supported standards, was not always happy with the standards developed by scholars. When the content standards in history were presented, dissatisfied political leaders rejected them. Some argued that the standards developed by history scholars slighted white men and maligned business leaders. The critics were led by Lynne Cheney, a former official in the first Bush administration, who characterized the new standards as "a warped view of American history."[36] No such outburst had accompanied the publication of the national standards for mathematics five years earlier. Forty-one states quickly adopted the mathematics standards, and math textbooks were modified accordingly. For mathematics, a national curriculum began to take shape.[37] Why was the process of adopting standards relatively easy for math but difficult for history? The basic reason is that mathematics raises fewer values questions, while other disciplines, such as history, live and breathe values. Here are just some of the questions raised by history standards:

- Should traditional heroes, sometimes called "DWM" (dead white males)—such as Washington, Jefferson, and other revered Americans—be the sole focus of the curriculum, or should the experiences and contributions of other groups, women and people of color, be researched and included?

- Should history continue to emphasize European roots, or should Afrocentric issues be included? What about the views of other groups? For instance, should schools teach a penetrating view of European settlement of the Americas as seen through the eyes of Native Americans and Mexicans?

- Should U.S. history tell only a story of wars and politics, or should it also relate varied views of social, cultural, and economic issues?

The new history standards did not please traditionalists. Familiar names like Daniel Webster, Paul Revere, and the Wright brothers were missing while unfamiliar names of women and people of color were now included. The Civil War received a different perspective as well, going beyond a chronology of battles to include an account of Northern riots by poor laborers who were being drafted for the deadliest war in American history, while rich men simply paid $300 and avoided the draft. It is clear that American history was in the eye of the beholder, and those funding the standards held a very different view of what children should be taught.[38] Political pressure rejected the scholars' proposals and traditional history standards were reinstated. Some suggest that over time, such pressure will create remarkably similar standards in all states.[39]

LANGUAGE ARTS

Grades K–4: Students communicate using standard English grammar including usage, sentence structure, punctuation, capitalization, spelling, and handwriting in final drafts of writing assignments. (Louisiana)

Grades 3–4: Write informational reports that include facts, details, and examples that illustrate an important idea. (Ohio)

Grade 8: Read, interpret, and critically analyze literature. Identify the defining features and structure of literary texts, such as conflict, representation of character, and point of view. Analyze the effect of characters, plot, setting, language, topic, style, purpose, and point of view on the overall impact of literature. (Wisconsin)

Grades 9–12: The student constructs meaning from a wide range of texts through a variety of reference materials, including indexes, magazines, newspapers, and journals; and tools, including card catalogs and computer catalogs, to gather information for research topics. (Florida)

MATHEMATICS

Grade 1: Identify and classify two- and three-dimensional shapes. Classify two- and three-dimensional figures according to characteristics (e.g., square, rectangle, circle, cube, prism, sphere, cone, and cylinder). (Mississippi)

Grade 5: Select and use appropriate statistical methods to analyze data. Compare two related sets of data using measures of center—mean, median, and mode—and range. (Oregon)

Grade 7: The student will solve consumer application problems involving tips, discounts, sales tax, and simple interest, using whole numbers, fractions, decimals, and percents. (Virginia)

Grades 8–12: Students apply basic factoring techniques to second-degree and simple third-degree polynomials. These techniques include finding a common factor for all terms in a polynomial, recognizing the difference of two squares, and recognizing perfect squares of binomials. (California)

SOCIAL STUDIES

Grade 2: Rules and Law: Students know why society needs rules, laws, and governments. Students know and are able to participate in class decision making. (Nevada)

Grade 3: Identify contributions of individuals to U.S. history, such as George Washington, Thomas Jefferson, Abraham Lincoln, Theodore Roosevelt, Franklin D. Roosevelt, Abigail Adams, Sacajawea, Frederick Douglass, Clara Barton, Jackie Robinson, Rosa Parks, Archbishop Patrick Flores, Jaime Escalante, Sally Ride, Tiger Woods, Cal Ripken, Jr., Sammy Sosa. (Pennsylvania)

Grades 5–8: The student uses maps, globes, graphs, charts, models, and databases to answer geographic questions. The student is expected to create thematic maps, graphs, charts, models, and databases depicting various aspects of world regions and countries such as population, disease, and economic activities. (Texas)

Grades 9–12: Discusses the limitations of the Articles of Confederation and the reasons for the calling of the Constitutional Convention. (Georgia)

SCIENCE

Grades 1–3: Describe the basic earth materials (rocks, soils, water, and gases) and their physical properties. (Arizona)

Grades 5–8: Students will understand that cells are the basic units of life. The functions performed by organelles (specialized structures found in cells) within individual cells are also carried out by the organ system in multicellular organisms. This standard requires that students be conversant with magnifying devices, cell structure and function, body systems, and disease causes and the body's defense against them. (Maine)

Grades: 12: The student will apply skills, processes, and concepts of biology, chemistry, physics, and earth/space science to societal issues. (Maryland)

Grades 9–12: Students will use chemical formulas and equations to obtain and communicate information about chemical changes. (Connecticut)

SOURCE: Education World. Online at www.educationworld.com/standards.

REFLECTION: Do you think these standards represent what and who is worth knowing? Why or why not? What content standards would you promote in our nation's schools?

Yet by 2000, the standards movement yielded encouraging results. Teachers reported that standards promoted higher student expectations and created a more demanding curriculum.[40] The second Bush administration then decided to take the standards movement national by passing a new and wide-ranging piece of legislation: *No Child Left Behind.*

No Child Left Behind: Tests and Protests

George W. Bush sponsored **No Child Left Behind (NCLB)** in the first year of his presidency, a law supported by both Democrats and Republicans and described as "the most significant change in federal regulation of public schools in three decades."[41] In the years that followed, *NCLB* changed the lives of teachers and students, labeled thousands of schools "in need of improvement," created a high-stakes testing culture, and sparked countless protests. Democrats and some Republicans who originally supported the legislation were now opposing it. Before we examine the problems, let's take a look at the major provisions of *NCLB*:

- *Annual Testing.* Reading and math assessments from grades 3–8 are required, with each state deciding on which test to use and what a passing or "proficient" grade is. In 2007–08, science assessments began in elementary, middle and high school. Schools report not only individual test scores, but also scores by race, ethnicity, disability, social class, and limited English proficiency to ensure that no group is left behind. Underperforming schools must improve—or be closed.

- *Academic Improvement.* States must define academic proficiency for all students, and all students must be proficient in reading and mathematics by 2013–14. The progress of each state and each school are measured annually, and schools that fail to make **adequate yearly progress (AYP)** for two consecutive years are labeled "underperforming." Such schools are entitled to special assistance, but they must also give parents the option of sending their children to "successful" schools, and pay transportation costs. If the school does not achieve AYP for three years, additional supplemental services must be provided to children, including private tutoring, also paid for by the school. After four years of unsatisfactory test grades, the state institutes major staff and curricular changes. After five years, the school is closed and is either reconstituted by the state or reopened as a charter school.

- *Report Cards.* States and school districts must provide the public with "Report Cards" of district and school progress—or lack of progress. Underperforming schools must be made public.

- *Faculty Qualifications.* All teachers must be "highly qualified," licensed with an academic major in the field they are teaching. Paraprofessionals must have at least two years of college or pass a rigorous test. Parents must be informed if their child's teacher is not "highly qualified."

Although these aspects of *NCLB* are often in the news, the law covers less-publicized areas, such as reading, bilingual education, charter schools, and technology, which have caused considerable consternation. For example, *NCLB* requires that high schools report personal student information to military recruiters, which critics argue violates students' privacy rights. The law supports "scientifically based" educational programs, but critics argue that too often ideology supplants science. For example, under *NCLB,* federal dollars assist local schools teach reading, but only if the school uses the phonics approach. Phonics programs associate letters with their sounds, and at times provide scripted lessons for teachers. Many educators argue that the research on effective reading programs is not that clear, and that promoting just one approach, no matter what that approach might be, does not work for all students. Nevertheless, only phonics is funded under *NCLB.*[42] The legislation also requires that school buildings be opened to Boy Scout meetings. This became an issue because the Boy Scouts do not allow homosexuals to join, and some schools do not open their facilities to groups that practice discrimination. *NCLB* requires schools to ignore such local antidiscrimination regulations. The law also requires school officials to certify in writing that every student has the right to pray, and to submit this certification to the federal government every two years. Detractors charge that such politically motivated provisions do not improve the nation's schools.[43]

Another point of contention is the requirement that all students be taught by skilled and competent teachers. The law defines a "highly qualified teacher" as holding a bachelor's degree from a four-year college, a state teacher's license, and demonstrated competency in the subject being taught. The intent is a strong focus on content mastery. Although highly qualified teachers are required for all core subjects (English, history, science, and math), that goal remains elusive. Highly qualified teachers are drawn to the most attractive and wealthiest school districts, leaving those schools most in need with the least trained teachers. Small rural schools can't afford to enlarge their faculties to include specialists in each subject area, and urban areas struggle even to attract teachers not categorized as "highly qualified." Without increased funding to improve teacher salaries and working conditions, it is difficult to imagine how nearly two million "highly qualified" teachers will be drawn to teaching, or even more challenging, stay in teaching.[44]

NCLB includes not only standards of what is to be learned, called content standards, but also **performance standards,** assessing how well students learn the content standards. While content standards were quite popular, performance standards led to federally mandated testing. And schools that do not test well are punished. This has created inequities, a "do-or-die" testing culture, and a backlash against the law. Much of the criticism of *NCLB* has been leveled at the testing provisions.

Each state has different rules for a school's passing or failing grades on these tests, and teachers and principals are often surprised when their schools fail. If scores for one group of students in a school are inadequate and AYP is not achieved, the entire school is considered "underperforming," and administrators must inform all parents that the school "needs improvement." Parents can then transfer their children to a "successful" school. Each year a school does not make annual yearly progress means a ratcheting up of penalties, and after five years, the school is reconstituted. Under *NCLB*, a school with insufficient test scores can disappear.

Supporters believe this approach will eliminate weak schools. Others feel that the law is simply too rigid or impractical. Let's listen to the voices of some principals whose schools were found to "need improvement."[45]

> "There is nothing positive I can say about *No Child Left Behind.* We were one of the schools that did make AYP at the beginning, so we were a school kids could transfer to. But that was almost like a Catch-22. If you get that designation, they send you kids with low test scores, which helps bring you down to 'needs improvement.'"
>
> *Reginald Ballard, Cardozo HS, Washington, DC*

> "I think *NCLB* is basically a good law, because no school should leave a child behind. You want everybody to learn, you want everybody to make progress, you want to make good citizens because that's good for everybody. But I don't think *NCLB* is properly funded."
>
> *Rhonda Pitts, Bladensburg ES, Maryland*

"There's no question that NCLB has benefited schools in many areas. But why do some schools continually miss AYP while others continually make it? There is a big disparity between the haves and the have-nots of education."

Rodney Henderson, Kenmoor ES, Maryland

"*No Child Left Behind* is not a bad law . . . The law has lofty goals. It is a noble effort, but it does need to be modified . . . I get my satisfaction from the fact that we are growing and our teachers are working hard. There's frustration but there's also improvement on the part of our kids. The states say that if you don't meet the standards, we can come in and take you over. But you just can't take over that many schools. We're doing the best we can, but if someone can do it better, let them show us how. Because we are all ears."

Sue Dziedzic, Oxon Hill ES, Maryland

Critics argue that deciding if a school is successful or not based on a single test score is fundamentally unsound, especially when there are huge resource differences in wealthy and poor schools. Worse yet, the way this legislation is written, even schools that improve on most measures are likely to find themselves labeled "underperforming." This is possible because schools are rated not only on school-wide test scores, but on the performance of particular groups. For example, if African Americans do poorly one year and improve the second year, but another group, let's say students with disabilities, do poorly the second year, that amounts to two years of poor scores, and the entire school is labeled "underperforming." In a small school or in a school with small numbers of these special groups, a change in scores of only a few students can make the difference, and some schools have been accused of under-reporting minority group scores.[46] Even those who crafted the legislation believe that the majority of the nation's schools will be cited as underperforming, although they predict this will motivate schools to become more effective. But that's not what happened in Michigan.[47]

When Michigan initially tested its schools, 1,513 were labeled underperforming by the state, and "failing" by the media. Michigan took decisive action to reverse this problem: it lowered the passing grade from 75 percent to 42 percent, and *voilá*, only 216 schools were problematic. Michigan is not alone; other states have also lowered standards, some to the point where no schools are underperforming.[48] "The severe sanctions may hinder educational excellence," explained University of Colorado Professor Robert Linn, "because they implicitly encourage states to water down their content and performance standards in order to reduce the risk of sanctions." Creating national standards for everyone would solve the problem, but convincing the states to voluntarily abandon control of school standards is unrealistic.[49]

The cost of testing and the other provisions of *NCLB* became particularly problematic in 2005 when federal budget cuts were announced, meaning state and local governments would have to pick up an even larger share of the cost. Some states decided to sue the federal government rather than join the costly testing culture. It is estimated that to comply with the law, states will spend between $1.9 and $5.3 billion to produce 460 new tests.[50] This led comedian David Letterman to quip: "Due to budget crunches, (President) Bush has had to scale back some of the programs. He has a new program, 'Leave a Couple of Kids Behind.'"[51]

Despite the criticism, the Department of Education is committed to testing and to giving parents educational options. In fact, the law obliges school districts to transfer students from failing schools to better schools, and to offer supplementary services, but this is not as easy as it sounds.[52] For example, free tutoring under

Are Desirable Because . . .

SCHOOLS AND EDUCATORS ARE NOT BEING HELD ACCOUNTABLE FOR STUDENT FAILURE

"If they don't want to learn, we can't make them," has been the modus operandi of educators. As a result, we have high school graduates who cannot read or write, and college graduates who do little better. Standards and tests will finally hold educators accountable. We will be able to see what students know, and how well they know it. We can reward successful schools, help troubled schools, and finally close failing schools.

THEY MAKE US EDUCATIONALLY AND ECONOMICALLY COMPETITIVE

Many of today's high school graduates must be retrained in basic literacy skills by the corporations that hire them, because they are unable to do the work that is required. This is a sign that schools are failing. This sort of educational inefficiency leads to technically incompetent workers, and weakens our ability to compete in world markets. We must have standards and tests to educate a first-class labor force and maintain our standard of living.

TEACHERS WORK COLLABORATIVELY RATHER THAN IN ISOLATION

A common set of standards promotes cooperation. Teachers and principals will work together to identify problems, develop instructional solutions, and collaborate as a professional team working to ensure that all the standards are met.

THEY WILL BIND THE NATION

National standards offer a unifying experience, as children learn about our common heritage. Without such standards, we become dangerously pluralistic and suffer the risk of becoming not one nation but several. There are already examples of countries that have lost this common thread and whose cultures have disintegrated.

LOCAL PAROCHIALISM WILL BE ELIMINATED

National standards will bring new insights and diverse points of view to the nation's children. Rather than being held hostage to the desires and views of local school boards, students will be able to consider broader perspectives. National standards can end debilitating local parochialism and broaden students' horizons.

Are a Mistake Because . . .

HIGH-STAKES TESTS REPRESENT A TERRIBLE ACCOUNTABILITY

Taking time from studies to prepare for a high-stakes test is not an effective demonstration of educational progress or school accountability. In fact, schools simply replace real learning with test preparation programs. One test is a terribly unreliable way to assess a person's knowledge, and flies in the face of all that we have learned about multiple intelligences, individual differences, and authentic assessment.

NATIONAL STANDARDS AND TESTS ARE A STEP BACKWARD FOR MANY STUDENTS AND SCHOOLS

National standards represent a step down for the nation's strongest school districts. The nation's best schools are well beyond such standards, yet must invest time and resources preparing for the state tests. Our schools prepare very competent scientists and engineers, many of whom are the first to be "downsized" by the same business executives who complain about educational quality. In fact, given our service economy, we may be overeducating our workforce.

TEACHERS WORK IN ISOLATION RATHER THAN COLLABORATIVELY

The pressure of tests and standards will drive teachers away from cooperative planning on educational goals, and into the trap of drilling their students to ensure that their class does well. Teachers will become competitors in a survival of the fittest scenario.

NATIONAL STANDARDS WILL DIVIDE THE NATION

We simply cannot agree on a single set of standards, on which facts to remember (and which to forget). What is important to one group of Americans may be unimportant or offensive to another. The effort to create unifying standards and tests will divide our people.

CENTRAL CONTROL OF OUR LIVES WILL GROW

The authors of the Constitution had it right, local communities and individuals know their children best, and they hold the practical wisdom that made this nation great. All we need is faith in the common sense of Americans, because they do know what's best for their children.

Are Desirable Because . . .

NATIONAL TESTS WILL GIVE US CRITICAL INFORMATION AND DIRECTION

Standardized tests will enable us to compare student performance, and to understand what it takes to earn an "A" in one school, versus an "A" in another. We will discover who is really learning, and who is not. Finally, we will be able to make sense out of what is going on in almost 100,000 school buildings.

Are a Mistake Because . . .

NATIONAL TESTS WILL HURT EDUCATION

High-stakes tests hurt students who are bright, but simply don't test well. Such standardized tests encourage a school curriculum based on test preparation, drive away talented teachers, increase pressure to cheat, and create the kind of boring, predictable, "one-size-fits-all" curriculum that is a disservice to a true democracy.

www.mhhe.com/
sadker

YOU DECIDE . . .

Where do you stand on the standards and the testing issue? Can you separate standards from testing? How might you determine if standards are being met—without using a standardized test? Some educators assert that test development should precede standards development. Do you agree or disagree? Why?

NCLB is available, but few students use this service.[53] If that doesn't work, the federal government recommends sending students to other school districts, although adequate funds to pay for all these recommendations are not provided. Some critics believe that *NCLB* is a Trojan horse: when public schools, teachers, and students fail, vouchers and private educational companies will be presented as the solution.[54] Whether this cynical view is accurate or not, a curious corner was turned when *NCLB* created the current testing culture. Equating test scores with education raises some troubling issues.

Test Problems: Seven Reasons Why Standardized Tests Are Not Working

In a New York City middle school, the principal asked teachers to spend fifteen minutes a day with students practicing how to answer multiple-choice math questions in preparation for the state-mandated test. One teacher protested, explaining she taught Italian and English, not math. But the principal insisted, and she followed his directive. As you might suspect, the plan failed, and in the end, fewer than one in four New York City middle schoolers passed the exam. While the importance of the test dominated the formal curriculum, the lessons learned through the hidden curriculum were no less powerful. Students learned that test scores mattered more than English or Italian, and that teachers did not make the key instructional decisions. In fact, once the test was over, one-third of the students in her class stopped attending school, skipping the last five weeks of the school year.[55]

Inner-city schools aren't the only ones experiencing testing woes; rural communities and wealthy suburbs have their own complaints. In Scarsdale, New York, an upscale, college-oriented community, parents organized a boycott of the eighth-grade standardized tests. Of 290 eighth-graders, only 95 showed up for the exam.[56] In Miami, protests erupted when over 12,000 Florida seniors were denied their high school diploma. Teachers in California and Chicago refused to give tests and faced disciplinary action.[57] Why are teachers, students, and parents protesting? What's wrong with

As national, state, and district decision makers require more testing, many teachers have protested or boycotted these exams.

measuring academic progress through standardized tests? Here are some reasons why high-stake tests are problematic:

1. *At-Risk Students Placed at Greater Risk.* Using the same tests for all students, those in well-funded posh schools along with students trying to learn in underfunded, ill-equipped schools is grossly unfair, and the outcome is quite predictable. Since students do not receive equal educations, holding identical expectations for all students places the poorer ones at a disadvantage. State data confirm that African Americans and Hispanics, females, poor students and those with disabilities are disproportionately failing "high-stakes" standardized tests. In Louisiana, parents requested that the Office for Civil Rights investigate why nearly half the students in school districts with the greatest numbers of poor and minority children had failed Louisiana's test, even after taking it for a second time. In Georgia, two out of every three low-income students failed the math, English, and reading sections of the state's competency tests. No students from well-to-do counties failed any of the tests and more than half exceeded standards. Even moderate income differences could result in major test score differences. In Ohio, almost half of the students from families with incomes below $20,000 failed the state exams, while almost 80 percent of students from families earning more than $30,000 passed those same exams.

Along with performance and content standards, a third kind of standard called an opportunity-to-learn standard, was supposed to remedy these social and economic challenges. **Opportunity-to-learn standards** were to ensure a level playing field by providing all students with appropriate educational resources, competent teachers and modern technology. Differences in student learning styles were to be accommodated and additional time provided for students to relearn material if they failed the test. Teachers were to be given quality in-service training. Yet half the states did not earmark money to remedy dramatic educational differences between school districts, and real barriers to achievement—racism, poverty, sexism, low teacher salaries, language differences, inadequate facilities—were lost in the sea of testing. Although the rhetoric of the standards movement is that a rising tide raises all ships, in fact, without the adequate resources, some ships do not rise. In the current standards and testing movement, opportunity-to-learn is the forgotten standard.[58]

2. *Lower Graduation Rates.* Grade-by-grade testing and graduation tests actually increase school dropouts. A Harvard University study found that students in the bottom 10 percent of achievement were 33 percent more likely to drop out of school in states with graduation tests. The National Research Council found that low-performing elementary and secondary school students who are held back do less well academically, are much worse off socially, and are far likelier to drop out than equally weak students who are promoted. Retention in grade is the single strongest predictor of which students will drop out—stronger even than parental income or mother's education level.

Former Education Secretary Paige was given credit for dramatic improvement of test scores in Houston, where he was superintendent. Houston was the centerpiece of the "Texas Miracle" and the foundation for *No Child Left Behind*. But by 2003, it became clear that under-reported dropouts contributed to test score gains. Houston reported a dropout rate of just over 1 percent a year, but that statistic was put in doubt by later studies that found the dropout rate was closer to 40 percent. When poor students, Latinos, African Americans, and Native Americans fail to meet graduation testing requirements, they are retained in grade and then likely to drop out. When their low scores disappear, the school's average test score improves, giving a picture of success when the real picture is failure.[59]

3. *Higher Test Scores Do Not Mean More Learning.* Evidence is mounting that for a growing number of schools, teaching is being redefined as test preparation. Seventy-nine percent of teachers surveyed by *Education Week* said they spent "a great deal" or "somewhat" of their time instructing students in test-taking skills, and 53 percent said they used state practice tests a great deal or somewhat. In Texas, James V. Hoffman and his colleagues asked reading teachers and supervisors to rate how often they engaged in test preparation. The study used a scale of 1 to 4, in which 1 stood for never, 2 for sometimes, 3 for often, and 4 for always. Most of those surveyed said that teachers engaged in the following activities "often" or "always":

- Teaching test-taking skills—3.5
- Having students practice with tests from prior years—3.4
- Using commercial test preparation materials—3.4
- Giving general tips on how to take tests—3.4
- Demonstrating how to mark an answer sheet correctly—3.2

In one school, for example, students were taught to cheer "Three in a row? No, No, No!" The cheer was a reminder that if students answered "c" three times in a row, probably at least one of those answers is wrong since the test maker is unlikely to construct three questions in a row with the same answer letter.[60]

Although this kind of test preparation may boost scores, it does not necessarily produce real gains in understanding that show up on other tests or performance measures or that students can apply in a nontesting situation. Consider these findings:

- A study of eighteen states with high-stakes testing compared trends in state test scores with long-term trends on other standardized tests. When state tests were given, performance went down on the ACT, SAT, and the math test of the National Assessment of Educational Progress (NAEP). The study concluded that higher state test scores were most likely due to direct test preparation rather than increased student learning, and to differences in how many students were excluded from testing based on disabilities or limited English proficiency.
- Three-quarters of fourth-grade teachers surveyed by RAND in Washington State, and the majority of principals, believed that better test preparation (rather than increased learning) was responsible for most of the score gains.
- In Kentucky's state assessment, scores went up on test items that were reused, then dropped when new items were introduced. This discrepancy between new and reused items was larger in schools that had greater overall test score gains, a relationship that suggests students were being coached on reused items.[61]

4. *Standardized Testing Shrinks the Curriculum.* Educator Alfie Kohn advises parents to ask an unusual question when a school's test scores increase: "What did

One day in 1967, fifth-grader Alfie Kohn received a class assignment. As expected, he wrote his name and the date at the top of the paper. The title he chose, though, was unanticipated: "Busywork." He doesn't remember the announced purpose of the assignment. He does remember that it was busywork. Over three decades later, Alfie Kohn still discriminates between genuine learning and mindless school routine. As a teacher, researcher, and journalist, his work carries a common theme: Educational excellence comes from personalized learning, from recognizing the uniqueness of each student, not from a lockstep curriculum. As a teacher, he remembers:

> I lovingly polished lectures, reading lists, and tests. I treated the students as interchangeable receptacles—rows of wide-open bird beaks waiting for worms.
>
> Finally I realized I was denying students the joy of exploring topics and uncovering truths on their own.[1]

In his own education, Kohn adopted this personalized approach to learning. As an undergraduate at Brown University, he created an interdisciplinary major, and dubbed it normativism. He again took an unbeaten path at the University of Chicago, writing his graduate thesis on humor. "Learning was meaningful because I started with the question and then drew from whatever fields were useful in exploring it, rather than being confined to the methods and topics of a particular discipline."[2] When he visits classrooms today, Kohn is often disheartened. Rarely does he witness such engaged learning. Instead, he sees students usually learning just to pass a test.

Kohn challenges today's popular clamor for higher standards and increased testing. "Standardized testing has swelled and mutated, like a creature in one of those old horror movies, to the point that it now threatens to swallow our schools whole."[3] He passionately warns educators, policymakers, and parents that raising standardized test scores is completely different from helping students to learn. And the pressurized culture of testing exacts a high cost. Every hour spent on such exam preparation is an hour not spent helping students to think creatively, to tackle controversial issues, and to love learning.

Common standards often begin with "all students will be able to . . ." and Kohn sees a harmful message in such wording: Individual differences don't exist or are unimportant. Often justified in the name of accountability or rigor, standards turn schools into fact factories. Students may recite Civil War battles, distinguish between phloem and xylem, and memorize prime numbers in hopes of meeting predetermined standards of excellence. Will they? Kohn doesn't think so.

With a focus on standards of outcome rather than standards of opportunity, real barriers to achievement—racism, poverty, low teacher salaries, language differences, inadequate facilities—are lost in the sea of testing. "[A]ll students deserve a quality education. But declaring that everyone must reach the same level is naïve at best, cynical at worst, in light of wildly unequal resources."[4] Equally troublesome is testing's unbalanced reward system. As a bonus for good scores, more money is often given to successful schools and less to those already deprived. Callous is how he describes such a retreat from fairness and the implication that teachers and students need only be bribed or threatened in order to achieve.

Alfie Kohn also knows that change in schools can be slow. Standardized curriculum and testing are fueled by concerns of competition in our global economy and reinforced by a tradition of teacher-centered instruction. "I am not a utopian. I am as aware as anyone of the difficulties of creating schools that are genuinely concerned about learning and about meeting children's needs, but that causes me to redouble my efforts rather than throw up my hands."[5]

[1] Jay Matthews, "Education's Different Drummer," *The Washington Post* (January 9, 2001), p. A10. [2] Ibid. [3] Alfie Kohn, "Standardized Testing and Its Victims," *Education Week* (September 27, 2000). [4] Alfie Kohn, "One-Size-Fits-All Education Doesn't Work," *Boston Globe* (June 10, 2001), p. C8. [5] Jay Matthews, "Education's Different Drummer."

REFLECTION: Do you agree with Kohn that standardized testing undermines learning? In the next decade, do you think schools in the United States will become more or less reliant on standardized tests? Justify your answer.

www.mhhe.com/ sadker8e

To learn more about Alfie Kohn, click on *Profiles in Education.*

FIGURE 6.4

Teaching to the test.

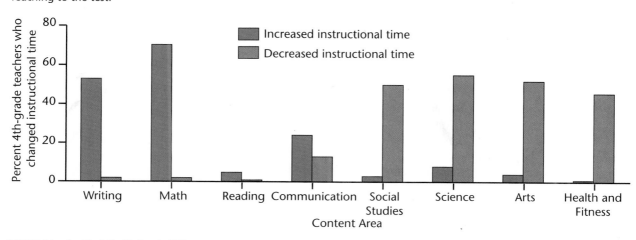

SOURCE: *Education Week*, Quality Counts, 2001.

REFLECTION: What would the curriculum be like if you planned the instructional schedule?

you have to sacrifice about my child's education to raise those scores?"[62] Most schools have reduced instructional time in art, music, foreign language, social studies, or science to give more time to reading and math and test preparation.[63] One teacher reports: "At our school, third- and fourth-grade teachers are told not to teach social studies and science until March."[64] As "real learning" takes a backseat to "test learning," challenging curriculum is replaced by multiple choice materials, individualized student learning projects disappear, and in-depth exploration of subjects along with extracurricular activities are squeezed out of the curriculum.[65] (See Figure 6.4.)

5. *When Tests Fail.* Tests themselves are often flawed, and high-stakes errors become high-stakes disasters. When Martin Swaden's daughter failed the state math test by a single answer, Swaden requested to see the exam so that he could help his daughter correct her errors and pass the test next time around. It took a threatened lawsuit before he was able to meet with a state official to examine the answers. Together they made an amazing discovery: six of the sixty-eight answers were keyed incorrectly, not only for his daughter, but for all the students in Minnesota. Jobs had been lost, summers ruined, the joy of graduation turned to humiliation for those students who were misidentified as having failed. Suits followed and $7 million in damages were eventually paid, but the testing company argued that it was not liable for "emotional damages."

Unfortunately, such stories continue to mount as the crush of millions of new tests overwhelms the handful of testing companies. In Massachusetts, a senior spotted an alternative answer to a math question, and the scores of 449 students were suddenly propelled over the passing mark. A Massachusetts teacher spotted a question with two correct answers, and when the scores were adjusted, 666 more students passed. A flawed answer key incorrectly lowered multiple-choice scores for 12,000 Arizona students, erred in adding up scores of essay tests for students in Michigan and forced the re-scoring of

204,000 essay tests in Washington. Another error resulted in nearly 9,000 students in New York City being mistakenly assigned to summer school, and $2 million in achievement awards being denied to deserving students in Kentucky.[66] The National Board on Educational Testing and Public Policy reported that fifty high-profile testing mistakes had occurred in twenty states from 1999 through 2002, and in 2006, rain fell on some SAT answer sheets, and 4,000 college hopefuls had their test scores affected, most in a negative direction.[67] Many question the wisdom of rewarding and punishing students, teachers, and schools based on the flawed history of the testing industry.[68]

6. *Teacher Stress.* While teachers support high standards, they object to learning being measured by a single test.[69] Not surprisingly, in a national study, nearly seven in ten teachers reported feeling test-stress, and two out of three believed that preparing for the test took time from teaching important but nontested topics.[70] Fourth-grade veteran teachers were requesting transfers, saying that they could not stand the pressure of administering the high-stakes elementary exams, and teachers recognized for excellence were leaving public schools, feeling their talents were better utilized in private schools where test preparation did not rule the curriculum.[71] When eighty Arizona teachers and teacher educators were asked to visually depict the impact of standardized tests, their drawings indicated test-driven classrooms where boredom, fear, and isolation dominate. Teachers feel that they are shortchanging schoolchildren from a love for learning. Figure 6.5 presents one of those drawings. (For others, visit Mr. Tirupalavanam Ganesh's Web site at http://ganesh.ed.asu.edu/aims.)

7. *What's Worth Knowing?* The fact that history, drama, the arts and a host of subjects are given less attention in the current testing movement raises

FIGURE 6.5

A teacher's impression of the testing movement.

SOURCE: A female teacher with a literature specialty teaching in a suburban elementary school. http:// ganesh.ed.asu.edu/aims/ view_image.php?image_id= 72& grade_range_id=3

REFLECTION: Try your own hand at drawing an image of how you feel when you are about to take a high-stakes test.

intriguing curricular questions: What is really important to teach? What is worth knowing? While it may sound pretty obvious, thinking beyond the obvious is often a good idea. Much of what is taught in schools is tradition and conventional wisdom, curricular inertia rather than careful thought. To see how society's notion of what is important can change, try your hand at the following test questions that were used to make certain that eighth-graders in Kansas knew "important information." We have shortened the exam, but all these questions are from the original. (Hint: Brush up on your orthography.) See if you would qualify to graduate from elementary school in 1895.[72]

8th Grade Examination Graduation Questions
Saline County, Kansas
April 13, 1895

Reading and Penmanship—The Examination will be oral and the Penmanship of Applicants will be graded from the manuscripts.

Grammar

1. Give nine rules for the use of Capital Letters.
2. Define Verse, Stanza, and Paragraph.
3. What are the Principal Parts of a verb? Give Principal Parts of do, lie, lay, and run.

Arithmetic

1. District No. 33 has a valuation of $35,000. What is the necessary levy to carry on a school seven months at $50 per month, and have $104 for incidentals?
2. What is the cost of a square farm at $15 per acre, the distance around which is 640 rods?
3. Write a Bank Check, a Promissory Note, and a Receipt.

U.S. History

1. Give the epochs into which U.S. History is divided.
2. Tell what you can of the history of Kansas.
3. Describe three of the most prominent battles of the Rebellion.

Orthography

1. What are the following, and give examples of each: Trigraph, subvocals, diphthong, cognate letters, linguals?
2. Give four substitutes for caret "u."
3. Mark diacritically and divide into syllables the following, and name the sign that indicates the sound: card, ball, mercy, sir, odd, cell, rise, blood, fare, last.

Geography

1. Name and describe the following: Monrovia, Odessa, Denver, Manitoba, Heela, Yukon, St. Helena, Juan Fernandez, Aspinwall, and Orinoco.
2. Name all the republics of Europe and give capital of each.
3. Describe the movements of the earth. Give inclination of the earth.

Physiology

1. How does nutrition reach the circulation?
2. What is the function of the liver? Of the kidneys?
3. Give some general directions that you think would be beneficial to preserve the human body in a state of health.

How did you do? Well, if you bombed it, don't feel too badly; few of today's PhDs would pass. So what does this teach us? Are today's schools far weaker than earlier ones? If we failed are we not truly educated? Or perhaps what we consider "important knowledge" is less enduring than we believe. How much of today's "critical" information will be a curious and unimportant footnote in the years ahead?

 ## Alternatives to High-Stakes Testing

The testing guidelines issued by the American Psychological Association specifically prohibit basing any consequential decisions about individuals on a single test score.[73] Most educational organizations and measurement experts agree that a better gauge of student performance is multiple assessments: tests, portfolios, formal exhibitions, independent student projects, and teacher evaluations. Standardized tests are popular because they are relatively inexpensive compared to other assessments, offer clear results, and can be rapidly implemented. Many educators are working to create tests that more fully and precisely assess learning. **Authentic assessment** (also called alternative or performance-based assessment) captures actual student performance, encourages students to reflect on their own work, and is integrated into the student's whole learning process. Such tests usually require students to synthesize knowledge from different areas and actively use that knowledge. The student might demonstrate what has been learned through a portfolio (like the ones we encourage you to develop in the *RAP*s found in this text), or a journal, or by undergoing an interview, conducting an experiment, or giving a presentation. Authentic assessment offers a focused and intense insight into what the student has learned, and requires evidence quite different from what is required by responding to questions on a typical high-stakes test.[74] Comparisons are often made with sports, in which participants are expected to demonstrate in a game what they have learned in practice. A tennis player works on her backhand, so that she can demonstrate mastery in a game; similarly, when students know that they will be called on to demonstrate and use their knowledge, they are more motivated to practice their academic skills. Many states are exploring authentic methods of assessment, especially the writing sample.[75]

Authentic assessment is used in the Coalition of Essential Schools, led by prominent educator Theodore Sizer. The coalition encourages schools to define their own model for successful reform, guided by nine basic principles that emphasize the personalization of learning. These principles include the requirement that students complete "exhibitions," tasks that call on them to exhibit their knowledge concretely. The high school curriculum is structured around these demanding, creative tasks, which may include:

- Completing a federal Internal Revenue Service Form 1040 for a family whose records you receive, working with other students in a group to ensure that everyone's IRS forms are correct, and auditing a return filed by a student in a different group

- Designing a nutritious and attractive lunch menu for the cafeteria within a specified budget and defending your definitions of nutritious and attractive

- Designing and building a wind instrument from metal pipes, then composing and performing a piece of music for that instrument

- Defining one human emotion in an essay, through examples from literature and history, and in at least three other ways (through drawing, painting, or sculpture; through film, photographs, or video; through music; through pantomime or dance; or through a story or play that you create)[76]

An increase in authentic assessment may contribute to a greater classroom focus on critical thinking and personal development. Authentic assessments may help us go beyond the current dependence on high-stakes standardized tests in determining the competence of students and the success of schools.

IMAGINE . . .

A Test of Goodwill

Colman McCarthy teaches high school Peace Studies, but has never given a test. In his own words, he prefers giving "tons of homework." His assignments include: Tell someone you love her or him. Do a favor for someone who will not know you did it. Thank the people who drive the school bus, cook the food, and clean the toilets. If students don't do the homework, McCarthy explains, they will fail. Worse than failing a standardized test, they will fail their better selves; they will fail to make the world a better place.

SOURCE: *The Washington Post*, March 18, 2006.

 Tension Points

You can read a curriculum the way you read the day's newspaper, for in it you can see the fractures in our society. Often, the curriculum becomes a battleground for competing political and cultural ideas. Here are some examples.

Intelligent Design versus Evolution

In colonial New England, the Bible was the major text, and religious instruction was the center of the curriculum. But the new nation's constitution changed all that. Or did it? From prayer in school to sex education, courts continually debate the role of religion in school. Here are two examples of too much religious influence.

The following questions were assigned to students in a public school in Virginia:

1. List six proofs that the Bible is God's word.
2. God is supreme ruler and has given man free choice. This shows that God is: A. Omniscient B. Good C. Sovereign D. Merciful[77]

A California public school system was using textbooks that taught that God helped Columbus discover America, that Native American accomplishments were "worthless" since they had no knowledge of the "true" God, described non-Christian religions as "cults," and asked students to punctuate a sentence that read: "The Hebrew people often grumbled and complained."[78]

These examples were clearly religious instruction and illegal. According to the Supreme Court, also illegal is the teaching of **creationism,** the position that God created the universe in six, 24-hour periods as described in the Bible. But does that mean that the theory of evolution should be taught as the only explanation of life's origin? **Evolution,** as put forth by Charles Darwin, is a keystone of modern biological theory and postulates that animals and plants have their origin in other pre-existing types and that there are modifications in successive generations. Christian fundamentalists (also referred to as religious fundamentalists or the religious right) do not believe that this explains the origin of human life, and they are not alone. They support the teaching of **intelligent design,** which credits an unnamed intelligence or designer for aspects of nature's complexity still unexplained by science, and that evolution is simply a theory, not a fact. While civil rights attorneys and many scientists argue that intelligent design is religious and unscientific, polls indicate that a large segment of the public is comfortable with this notion that students

A warning sticker placed in science textbooks in Cobb County, Georgia, saying evolution is "a theory, not a fact" was removed by court order.

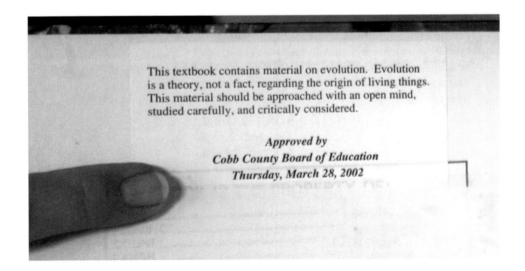

This textbook contains material on evolution. Evolution is a theory, not a fact, regarding the origin of living things. This material should be approached with an open mind, studied carefully, and critically considered.

Approved by
Cobb County Board of Education
Thursday, March 28, 2002

deserve to hear "competing theories."[79] More than a dozen states (a number likely to grow) are either considering or have already passed legislation requiring that when evolution is taught, that criticism be included, or that alternative explanations of the origins of humans, including the supernatural, be taught as well. Some states and school districts have actually removed the word evolution from the curriculum.

The subtlety of language is partially responsible for this tension point since "theory" has two separate meanings. In common language, "theory" means an idea or a hunch. In science, a theory is a thoroughly tested belief unlikely to change, such as the theory of gravitation or cell theory or evolutionary theory.[80] Scientific theories are the results of decades or centuries of insights drawn on many interconnected observations and ideas. The theory of evolution is more than a hunch, and needs to be understood as a well-founded scientific explanation. But that does not mean that evolution exists in a vacuum: perhaps intelligent design works through evolution. The bottom line is that we still have much to learn. It is unfortunate that such debates harden positions, instead of open minds.

These controversies frighten some teachers. The result is many shy away from teaching about religion or evolution.[81] This is unfortunate. Teaching should be about opening minds, not indoctrination. Teaching the theory of evolution is important; teaching *about* different religions is important. Promoting or disparaging religious or scientific beliefs is inappropriate. Unfortunately, many teachers, fearful of the consequences, avoid teaching about religion or evolution.[82] Teaching spirituality is even more rare. Spirituality, a personal and pluralistic view of life's meaning, is broader than any particular religion. **Spirituality** encompasses many ideas common to all religions; activities that renew, lift up, comfort, heal, and inspire both ourselves and others. Religion, science, and spirituality need not be in conflict. Religious intolerance, scientific hostility, and spiritual ignorance do not move the world forward; instead, they limit learning.[83]

Censorship and the Curriculum

Ruth Sherman lived just outside New York City, in a Long Island neighborhood known for its Italian community and easy commute to the city. Although she traveled only a short distance to P.S. 75, where she taught third grade, she might as well have been teaching in another country. P.S. 75 was in the Bushwick section of Brooklyn, a graffiti-filled neighborhood populated by poor black and Hispanic families living in the midst of a rampant drug culture. "Why there?" her friends asked her. "Because I want 'to turn things around,'" she responded. She was that kind of teacher. But, in just three months, it was Ruth Sherman, and not her students, who was turned around.

Her problems started in September, although she did not learn about it until later, when she assigned a book called *Nappy Hair*, by African American author Carolivia Herron. Her students loved the book, about a little black girl with "the nappiest, fuzziest, the most screwed up, squeezed up, knotted hair," and clamored for copies to take with them. By Thanksgiving, the parents in Ruth Sherman's class had also discovered the book, which they considered racially insulting. At a parents' meeting, she was confronted by 50 parents (most of them parents of children not in her class), who shouted racial epithets and eventually threatened her. The superintendent sent Ruth home, for her own protection. A review of the book followed. The review brought only praise for a book that promoted positive images for children and presented stories that appealed to them. Within a few days, the superintendent wrote her a letter, commending her performance, inviting her back to the school, and promising security escorts to protect her. But, by then, it was too late. Ruth Sherman, the teacher who wanted to make a difference, did not want to work in a climate that required "escorts" to ensure her safety. She transferred to another school.[84]

This incident occurred in 1998 in New York, but it could occur anywhere at anytime. Nearly everyone—teachers, parents, the general public, and various special interest groups—wants some say as to what is and is not in the school curriculum. No matter what content is found in a particular textbook or course of study, someone is likely to consider it too conservative or too liberal, too traditional or too avant-garde, racist, sexist, anti-Semitic, violent, un-Christian, or pornographic.[85] When this happens, pressure to censor the offending materials soon follows.

There is no such thing as a totally safe, acceptable, uncontroversial book or curriculum. Each of the following has been subjected to censorship at one time or another:

- Mary Rodgers's *Freaky Friday:* "Makes fun of parents and parental responsibility"
- Plato's *Republic:* "This book is un-Christian"
- Jules Verne's *Around the World in Eighty Days:* "Very unfavorable to Mormons"
- William Shakespeare's *Macbeth:* "Too violent for children"
- Fyodor Dostoyevsky's *Crime and Punishment:* "Serves as a poor model for young people"
- Herman Melville's *Moby Dick:* "Contains homosexuality"
- Anne Frank's *Diary of a Young Girl:* "Obscene and blasphemous"
- E. B. White's *Charlotte's Web:* "Morbid picture of death"
- J. R. R. Tolkien's *The Hobbit:* "Subversive elements"
- Roald Dahl's *Charlie and the Chocolate Factory:* "Racist"
- Mark Twain's *The Adventures of Huckleberry Finn:* "Racism, insensitivity, and offensive language"
- *Webster's Dictionary:* "Contains sexually explicit definitions"[86]

According to the American Library Association, more than 500 books are challenged each year.[87] But the incidences of **self-censorship,** which some term **stealth censorship,** is considered much higher.[88] Stealth censorship occurs when educators or parents quietly remove a book from a library shelf or a course of study in response to an informal complaint—or in order to avoid controversy. Teachers practice the same sort of self-censorship when they choose not to teach a topic or not to discuss a difficult issue. Numbers on the frequency of self-censorship are impossible to obtain. Tallying up the number of books that were officially removed or placed on restricted-access shelves in libraries is far easier.[89] Frequently challenged authors include J. K. Rowling, John Steinbeck, Judy Blume, Robert Cormier, Mark Twain, Phyllis Reynolds Naylor, Stephen King, Lois Duncan, S. E. Hinton, Maya Angelou, Roald Dahl, and Toni Morrison. Here are a few of today's most challenged books, and the reasons adults do not want children to read them:

- *It's Perfectly Normal* by Robie H. Harris for homosexuality, nudity, sex education, religious viewpoint, abortion, and being unsuited to age group.
- *Forever* by Judy Blume for sexual content and offensive language.
- *The Catcher in the Rye* by J. D. Salinger for sexual content, offensive language, and being unsuited to age group.
- *The Chocolate War* by Robert Cormier for sexual content and offensive language.
- *Whale Talk* by Chris Crutcher for racism and offensive language.
- *Detour for Emmy* by Marilyn Reynolds for sexual content.
- *What My Mother Doesn't Know* by Sonya Sones for sexual content and being unsuited to age group.
- *It's So Amazing! A Book about Eggs, Sperm, Birth, Babies, and Families* by Robie H. Harris for sex education and sexual content.[90]

At the heart of the case against censorship is the First Amendment, which guarantees freedom of speech and of the press. Those who oppose censorship say that our purpose as educators is not to indoctrinate children but to expose them to a variety of views and perspectives. The case for censorship (or, perhaps in a more politically correct phrase, *mature judgment and selection*) is that adults have the right and obligation to protect children from harmful influences. But "harmful influences" are in the eye of the beholder. For instance, challenges to books that include homosexuality have become commonplace. Critics say that these books promote homosexuality, and that is not acceptable in school. Others believe that such books teach tolerance of sexual differences, and serve a positive purpose for both heterosexual and homosexual students. Moreover, they argue, reading about different sexual orientations is a far cry from promoting any particular sexual outlook.[91] The censorship controversy is symbolic of how politicized the curriculum debate has become.

Cultural Literacy or Cultural Imperialism?

Both George Orwell and Aldous Huxley were pessimists about the future. "What Orwell feared were those who would ban books," writes author Neil Postman. "What Huxley feared was that there would be no one who wanted to read one."[92] Perhaps neither of them imagined that the great debate would revolve around neither fear nor apathy but, rather, deciding which books are most worth reading.

Proponents of **core knowledge,** also called **cultural literacy,** argue for a common course of study for all students, one that ensures that an educated person knows the basics of our society. Novelist and teacher John Barth laments what ensues without core knowledge:

> In the same way you can't take for granted that a high school senior or a freshman in college really understands that the Vietnam War came after World War II, you can't take for granted that any one book is common knowledge even among a group of liberal arts or writing majors at a pretty good university.[93]

Allan Bloom's *The Closing of the American Mind* (1987) was one of several books that sounded the call for a curricular canon. A canon is a term with religious roots, referring to a list of books officially accepted by the church or a religious hierarchy. A curricular **canon** applies this notion to schools by defining the most useful and valued books in our culture. Those who support a curricular canon believe that all students should share a common knowledge of our history and the central figures of our culture, an appreciation of the great works of art and music and, particularly, the great works of literature. A shared understanding of our civilization is a way to bind our diverse people.

Allan Bloom, professor of social thought at the University of Chicago, took aim at the university curriculum as a series of often unrelated courses lacking a vision of what an educated individual should know, a canonless curriculum. He claimed that his university students were ignorant of music and literature, and charged that too many students graduate with a degree but without an education.[94] One of the criticisms of Bloom's vision was that his canon consisted almost exclusively of white, male, European culture.

E. D. Hirsch, Jr., in his book *Cultural Literacy,* was more successful than Bloom in including the contributions of various ethnic and racial groups, as well as women. This is a rarity among core curriculum proponents. In fact, Hirsch believes that it is the poorer children and children of color who will most benefit from a cultural literacy curriculum. He points out that children from impoverished homes are less likely to become culturally literate. A core curriculum will teach them the names, dates, places, events, and quotes that every literate American needs to know in order to succeed. In 1991, Hirsch published the first volume of the core knowledge series, *What Your First Grader Needs to Know.* Other grades followed in these mass-marketed books directed not only at educators but at parents as well.[95]

Not everyone is enamored with the core curriculum idea. A number of educators wonder who gets included in this core, and, just as interesting, who gets to choose? Are Hirsch, Bloom, and others to be members of a very select committee, perhaps a blue-ribbon committee of "Very Smart People"? Why are so many of these curricular canons so white, so male, so Eurocentric, and so exclusionary?

Many call for a more inclusive telling of the American story, one that weaves the contributions of many groups and of women as well as of white males into the textbook tapestry of the American experience. Those who support **multicultural education** say that students of color and females will achieve more, will like learning better, and will have higher self-esteem if they are reflected in the pages of their textbooks. And let's not forget white male students. When they read about people other than themselves in the curriculum, they are more likely to honor and

www.mhhe.com/ sadker8e

INTERACTIVE ACTIVITY

Do You Know the "Basics"? See how you do on this hypothetical quiz created to test your cultural literacy. Get a first-hand feel for the testing issue.

appreciate their diverse peers. Educator and author James Banks calls for increased cultural pluralism:

> People of color, women, and other marginalized groups are demanding that their voices, visions, and perspectives be included in the curriculum. They ask that the debt Western civilization owes to Africa, Asia, and indigenous America be acknowledged. . . . However, these groups must acknowledge that they do not want to eliminate Aristotle and Shakespeare, or Western civilization, from the school curriculum. To reject the West would be to reject important aspects of their own cultural heritages, experiences, and identities.[96]

The Saber-Tooth Curriculum

Unless we carefully consider and resolve these tension points, we might end up with a "saber-tooth curriculum." What's that? It is a classic satire on Paleolithic curriculum written by Abner Peddiwell, known in real life as Harold Benjamin, and a great way to think about tomorrow's possibilities.

New-Fist was a brilliant educator and thinker of prehistoric times. He watched the children of his tribe playing with bones, sticks, and brightly colored pebbles, and he speculated on what these youngsters might learn that would help the tribe derive more food, shelter, clothing, security, and, in short, a better life. Eventually, he determined that in order to obtain food and shelter, the people of his tribe must learn to fish with their bare hands and to club and skin little woolly horses; and in order to live in safety, they must learn to drive away the saber-tooth tigers with fire. So New-Fist developed the first curriculum. It consisted of three basic subjects: (1) "Fish-Grabbing-with-the-Bare-Hands," (2) "Woolly-Horse-Clubbing," and (3) "Saber-Tooth-Tiger-Scaring-with-Fire."

New-Fist taught the children these subjects, and they enjoyed these purposeful activities more than playing with colored pebbles. The years went by, and by the time New-Fist was called by the Great Mystery to the Land of the Setting Sun, all the tribe's children had been systematically schooled in these three skills. The tribe was prosperous and secure.

All would have been well and the story might have ended here had it not been for an unforeseen change—the beginning of the New Ice Age, which sent a great glacier sliding down upon the tribe. The glacier so muddied the waters of the creeks that it was impossible for people to catch fish with their bare hands. Also, the melted water of the glacier made the ground marshy, and the little woolly horses left for higher and drier land. They were replaced by shy and speedy antelopes with such a scent for danger that no one could get close enough to club them. And finally, as if these disruptions were not enough, the increasing dampness of the air caused the saber-tooth tigers to contract pneumonia and die. The tigers, however, were replaced by an even greater danger: ferocious glacial bears, who showed no fear of fire. Prosperity and security became distant memories for the suffering tribe.

Fortunately, a new breed of brilliant educators emerged. One tribesman, his stomach rumbling with hunger, grew frustrated with fruitless fish-grabbing in cloudy waters. He fashioned a crude net and in one hour caught more fish than the whole tribe could have caught had they fish-grabbed for an entire day. Another tribesman fashioned a snare with which he could trap the swift antelope, and a third dug a pit that captured and secured the ferocious bears.

As a result of these new inventions, the tribe again became happy and prosperous.

Some radicals even began to criticize the school's curriculum and urged that net-making, snare-setting, and pit-digging were indispensable to modern life and should be taught in the schools. But the wise old men who controlled the schools objected:

With all the intricate details of fish-grabbing, horse-clubbing, and tiger-scaring—the standard cultural subjects—the school curriculum is too crowded now. We can't add these fads and frills of net-making, antelope-snaring, and—of all things—bear-killing. Why, at the very thought, the body of the great New-Fist, founder of our Paleolithic educational system, would turn over in its burial cairn. What we need to do is to give our young people a more thorough grounding in the fundamentals. . . . The essence of true education is timelessness. It is something that endures through changing conditions like a solid rock standing squarely and firmly in the middle of a raging torrent. You must know that there are some eternal verities, and the saber-tooth curriculum is one of them.[97]

The Saber-Tooth Curriculum was written in 1939, but it still resonates. How do educators avoid a curriculum programmed for obsolescence? What in today's curriculum is "Saber-Tooth-Tiger-Scaring-with-Fire," and what skills are we not teaching that we should be?

 ## New Directions for the Curriculum

What will tomorrow's curriculum look like? Predictions are only predictions, but here are a few ideas for you to consider.

The tremendous knowledge explosion has produced more information than schools can teach, and many believe that schools need to emphasize less content and more of the thinking skills needed in the new information society.

What are these more relevant thinking skills? Here are some examples:

Critical thinking skills—One of the pioneering works, *Teaching for Thinking: Theory and Application,* identified "thinking operations," that should be taught directly: comparing, interpreting, observing, summarizing, classifying, decision making, creating, and criticizing. *Teaching for Thinking* incorporates these critical thinking skills into such subjects as mathematics and history, in which teachers ask higher-order questions that prompt students to analyze and evaluate data. Research indicates that not only do students learn critical thinking skills in such programs, but their knowledge of the content also increases when they apply these skills in the classroom.[98]

Metacognition—Another approach, developed by Robert Marzano and his colleagues, stresses the importance of teaching students how to think about their own thinking, called metacognition. Metacognition includes active control over the thought processes in learning and teaches students how to plan to approach a given learning task, to monitor their own understanding, and to evaluate their own learning.

Critical pedagogy—This approach merges teaching and learning with social improvement. The purpose of critical pedagogy is to teach students how to identify and then remediate social challenges, such as eliminating pollution in a local lake or promoting consumer education in a poor community. Critical pedagogy connects schooling with actions to enhance the quality of life.[99]

Enduring Lessons: A Modest Proposal

While these are some of the ideas and approaches of leading educators, let's take a moment and do some critical thinking of our own. Imagine that you are in charge of taking the schools down an educational path. What path would you trailblaze? Standards and testing? Greater emphasis on reading and math? Higher-order thinking skills? Critical literacy?

We believe that today's society is in need of a strategic educational realignment. Our world is marked by hatred and misunderstanding, cultural and religious warfare, massive poverty, physical deprivation, and interpersonal conflicts. All these issues scream for the attention of not only political leaders, but educators and students as well. How can schools focus on more meaningful values, values that will always be timely. Perhaps we can call this curriculum one of "enduring lessons." Here is a sample of what we would teach.

Enduring Lesson Number 1: Understand Our Roots There is a fundamental, even driving need to more deeply understand ourselves both as individuals and as part of the wider community. We often learn only a few salient aspects of our backgrounds, such as personal and family history, cultural and religious beliefs, gender differences and challenges, and a single view of our national heritage. But these are incomplete lessons. We lack a healthy appreciation of how these key forces have shaped lives and limited our worldview. Only through greater self-insight can we begin to understand our perceptions and motivations, our strengths and weaknesses, and the way we behave and think. In so doing, we develop a realistic and healthy self-esteem, and learn the first enduring lesson: "know yourself."

Enduring Lesson Number 2: Celebrate Others Once we are understand ourselves, we can seek insights from other peoples and cultures. While some have called this *teaching tolerance,* we do not believe that diversity should be *tolerated.* Today, we tolerate things from sleazy politics to shoddy home repairs. Tolerance of diversity falls woefully short, and we believe that diversity should be celebrated. Cultural, racial and ethnic, and religious differences offer us wondrous insights into the human experience. We can learn so much from each other. Our challenge is to learn from our differences, not fear them.

Enduring Lesson Number 3: Encourage Individual Talents and Contributions

High test scores predict high test scores, but not much else: not problem-solving skills, not good work habits, not honesty, not dependability, not loyalty, nor any cherished virtue.

Schools should prepare students to live purposeful and satisfying lives. To do this, students need to learn and develop their own unique interests and abilities, skills, and talents. By measuring all students against the same yardsticks of literacy and numeracy, individual creativity and differences are lost or denigrated. Contrary to the current testing wave, we support less standardization and more individualization.

Enduring Lesson Number 4: Promote Purposeful Lives

At the Antioch College commencement in 1859, Horace Mann advised the graduates, "Be ashamed to die until you have won some victory for humanity." The real measure of an education is not what a student receives as a test grade or even does while in school; the real measure is what people do after graduation. Are students living higher lessons and working for noble purposes, or have they succumbed to baser temptations? Are adults honest and caring with one another, treating their children, families, colleagues, and even strangers with love, compassion, and forgiveness? The way we choose to live our lives as adults, and not our test scores, will be the true measure of our schooling.

SUMMARY

1. **What is the formal curriculum taught in schools?**

   The formal or visible curriculum is the school's official curriculum, but it is far from static. In colonial America, reading and religion were central. During the early part of the twentieth century, progressive ideas led to a curriculum that emphasized creative expression, social skills, and an integrated study of subject areas. By the 1980s and 1990s, spurred by poor standardized test scores, a back-to-basics curriculum with high-stakes testing dominated.

2. **How does the invisible curriculum influence learning?**

   Schools teach an invisible curriculum that has two components. The hidden or implicit curriculum offers lessons that are not always intended, but emerge as students are shaped by the school culture, including the attitudes and behaviors of teachers. Topics considered unimportant or too controversial, inappropriate or not worth the time, and therefore not taught comprise the null curriculum.

3. **What is the place of the extracurriculum in school life?**

   Most students participate in the extracurriculum, a voluntary curriculum that includes sports, clubs, student government, and school publications. While some see these activities as part of a rich cocurriculum, others discount their value.

www.mhhe.com/ sadker8e

CHAPTER REVIEW

Go to the Online Learning Center to take a chapter self-quiz, practice with key terms, and review concepts from the chapter.

4. What forces shape the school curriculum?

Many groups influence the content of the curriculum. In recent years, the federal government and specially appointed education commissions have been two groups promoting a standards-based, high-stakes testing curriculum.

5. How has technology affected the curriculum?

Exciting virtual field trips that take students around the world or the online activities that create fascinating learning communities illustrate technology's promise of rich learning activities. But American fascination with technology in the past has been overly optimistic, and that may also be true today. The jury is still out on technology's impact on learning. The presence of the digital divide reminds us that technology's potential benefits are not shared by all, that wealth and geography play a role.

6. How do textbook publishers and state adoption committees "drive" the curriculum?

More than 20 states, mainly located in the South and West, are textbook adoption states. Local school districts in these states must select their texts from an official, state-approved list. The most populous of these states exert considerable influence in the development of textbooks.

7. What is standards-based education?

The pressure to improve test scores led to standards-based education, a process of focusing the curriculum on specified topics and skills, followed by continuous testing to see if these standards have been learned.

8. What are the provisions and criticisms of *No Child Left Behind*?

One of the most far-reaching federal education plans, *No Child Left Behind,* includes annual testing, identification of underperforming schools, employing only "highly qualified" teachers, and providing additional learning options to students attending underperforming schools. Lack of funding and reliance on a single test to measure learning are just two of the criticisms leveled at the law.

9. What problems are created by high-stakes testing, and what are the testing alternatives?

High-stakes tests are believed to contribute to increases in the number of dropouts and the increase in teacher and student stress. High scores on such tests do not necessarily reflect greater learning, and teachers who teach to the test eliminate other important topics from the curriculum. One testing alternative, authentic assessment, evaluates students by asking them to synthesize what they have learned in a final product or "exhibit."

10. How are cultural and political conflicts reflected in the school curriculum?

Opposing the theory of evolution, some support intelligent design, an alternative explanation for the origin of humans. Cultural and political differences over what should be taught have led to book banning and censorship. Proponents of a core curriculum and cultural literacy argue with multiculturalists who advocate the greater inclusion of the roles, experiences, and contributions of women and people of color.

11. How can we rethink tomorrow's curriculum?

Because of the knowledge explosion, some educators believe that we should focus less on content and more on process, including critical thinking skills, metacognition, and critical pedagogy. The reader is invited to consider a new approach to the current curriculum, and the authors suggest a four-tier curriculum that promotes self-understanding, human relations, and greater individualization. *The Saber-Tooth Curriculum* teaches us that a curriculum should preserve the past, but not be limited by it.

Go to your *Teachers, Schools, and Society* **Reader CD-ROM to:**

READ CURRENT AND HISTORICAL ARTICLES

6.1 **Heightening Awareness about the Importance of Using Multicultural Literature,** Susan Colby and Anna Lyon, *Multicultural Education,* Spring 2004.

6.2 **Where Did We Come From?** Lottie Joiner, *American School Board Journal,* 2003.

6.3 **The Authentic Standards Movement and Its Evil Twin,** Scott Thompson, *Phi Delta Kappan,* January 2001.

ANALYZE CASE STUDIES

6.1 **Elaine Adams:** A student teacher near the end of her assignment observes her co-operating teacher give the students help while administering the district-mandated standardized tests. She finds herself unsure how to deal with the situation.

6.2 **Melinda Grant:** A teacher who has developed an innovative curriculum is concerned because another teacher continually warns her that she will be held responsible for her students' end-of-year standardized test scores.

OBSERVE TEACHERS, STUDENTS, AND CLASSROOMS IN ACTION

Classroom Observation: Explaining Standardized Test Scores

As a teacher, part of your job will be to be able to explain your students' assessment to their parents. In this observation you will observe a teacher discuss a student's test scores, and the meaning behind the norm-referenced scores, to his mother.

KEY TERMS AND PEOPLE

DISCUSSION QUESTIONS AND ACTIVITIES

www.mhhe.com/
sadker8e

WEB-*TIVITIES*
Go to the Online Learning Center to do the following activities:
1. The Formal or Explicit Curriculum
2. The Curriculum Time Machine
3. New Directions for the Curriculum
4. Censorship and the Curriculum
5. The Textbook Shapes the Curriculum
6. Is the United States Going Test Crazy?
7. The Teacher As the Curriculum Developer?
8. Computers in the Classroom, Virtual Field Trips, and Global Education

1. For some students, the hidden curriculum and the extracurriculum are most central to their school experience. Define the roles of these unofficial curricular experiences in your own education. If you were placed in charge of a school today, how would you change these hidden and extracurricular experiences? How might your changes be evident in elementary, middle, and high schools? Why?

2. What subject areas spark the greatest debate and controversy over creating a single, national curriculum? Are there strategies to help reach a consensus on these issues? How might a national history curriculum written today differ from one written a century from now? A century ago? Why?

3. Collect textbooks from your local elementary and secondary schools and analyze them according to the following criteria:

   - Do they include instructional objectives? Do these require students to use both recall of factual information and analytical and creative thinking skills?

   - Were readability formulas used in the preparation of the textbooks? If so, did this appear to have a negative or positive impact on the quality of the writing?

   - Are under-represented group members included in the textbooks' narrative and illustrations? Are individuals with disabilities included?

   - When various individuals are included, are they portrayed in a balanced or a stereotyped manner?

4. If you were given the job of developing a standards-based curriculum with assessment tools, where would you go to identify standards? What kinds of tests would you use? What kinds of tests would you avoid? What subjects and skills do you consider crucial? Why?

5. Do you believe that children's educational materials should be censored? Are there any benefits to censorship? Any dangers? What kinds of materials would you refuse to let elementary school students read? Middle or high school students? Postsecondary students?

REEL TO REAL TEACHING

MR. HOLLAND'S OPUS (1995)
Run Time: 142 minutes

Synopsis: Glenn Holland is an aspiring composer who takes a teaching job to support his family. As the years unfold, the joy of sharing his passion for music with his students becomes his new definition of success.

MUSIC OF THE HEART (1999)
Run Time: 124 minutes

Synopsis: This is a true story of Roberta Guaspari and her fight against the board of education. Her effort to teach music to underprivileged students in East Harlem involved an innovative violin program.

Reflection:

1. *Mr. Holland's Opus* chronicles a 30-year teaching career. What changes in the music curriculum did you observe? In Mr. Holland's instructional style? What personal and institutional factors influenced these changes?

2. How did gender, race, and socioeconomic status influence the curriculum, teaching, and efforts to save music education in *Music of the Heart?* In *Mr. Holland's Opus?*

3. How did the arts influence the education and life experiences of Gertrude and Sadler in *Mr. Holland's Opus?* Guadalupe and Naeem Adisa in *Music of the Heart?* What role did the fine arts play in your elementary and secondary education? In your life? Do your experiences parallel those of the films' characters?

4. Consider Mr. Holland's comment: "The day they cut the football budget in this state, that will be the end of Western Civilization as we know it!" Why do you think extracurricular athletics are often given priority in school budgets over music, art, and even physical education?

Follow-up Activity: It's time to take a stand! You are a colleague of Mr. Holland at John F. Kennedy High or Ms. Guaspari in East Harlem (or choose any school where the fine arts are targeted for elimination).* The local school board is holding finance hearings and you decide to share your opinion. In 500 words or less, create talking points. Use scenes from the films, information from the chapter, and your own life experiences as supporting evidence.

*If you feel strongly for or against another course potentially threatened by budget cuts (sign language, computer animation, child care) use this example for the position paper.

How do you rate these films? Go to *Reel to Real Teaching* to review these films.

**www.mhhe.com/
sadker8e**

FOR FURTHER READING

Connecting Girls and Science: Constructivism, Feminism, and Science Education Reform, by Elaine V. Howes (2002). Describes the powerful results that can occur in secondary science classrooms when students' interest and curiosity about science are brought firmly to the center of the curriculum.

The Case Against Standardized Testing: Raising Scores, Ruining Schools, by Alfie Kohn (2000). Argues that standardized tests undermine quality learning and reflect the interests of politicians and business leaders rather than students and educators.

Caught in the Middle: Nonstandard Kids and a Killing Curriculum, by Susan Ohanian (2001). Describes how curriculum standards impart a singular definition of success that fails many students. The lives of eight students who "think outside the box" are detailed.

Political Agendas for Education: From the Religious Right to the Green Party, by Joel Spring (2002). The political and religious background to the many controversies over American education today are explained. Topics include the Republican agenda for the twenty-first century, the meaning of "compassionate conservative," creationism, and commercialization of schools.

Protecting the Right to Learn: Power, Politics, and Public Schools, by James Daly, Patricia Schall, and Rosemary Skeele (2001). Investigates how censorship stifles the ability of schools and teachers to educate students in meaningful ways through a case study of one school district embroiled in a legal battle over control of the curriculum.

REFLECTIVE ACTIVITIES AND YOUR PORTFOLIO

Part II: Schools and Curriculum

INTASC PRINCIPLE 1
Knowledge of
Subject Matter

2:1 State and National Curricular Standards

Purpose: Many of today's schools are immersed in standards and testing, and being familiar with these policies can be enormously helpful. A knowledge of standards and testing can guide you during the hiring process, in deciding where to teach, and also in crafting and presenting effective lessons.

Activity: Perform an Internet search of "curriculum standards" at both the national and state level. For state curriculum standards, choose a particular state that interests you. As you get closer to the hiring process, you may want to investigate curriculum standards for specific school districts. Standards are typically broken into curricular areas, so choose at least one subject area for your focus. A useful resource for this activity is: www.educationworld.com/standards.

Artifact: "Venn Diagram: Curricular Standards" After reading through the curriculum standards at both the national and state level, complete the following Venn Diagram. Venn Diagrams are useful for examining similarities and differences. They help us to compare the elements of one or more items. Compare and contrast at least three standards.

Venn Diagram

Subject and Standard (*example* Math—numbers and operations grades 3–5):

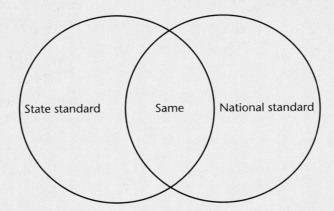

State standard   Same   National standard

Reflection: What did you learn from this activity? Any surprises? In your opinion, are these standards realistic? Useful? Support your opinion. What kind of similarities and differences do you find between the national curriculum standards and the state level curriculum standards? How do you envision using curriculum standards in planning lessons? Attach your reflections to your Venn Diagram and include in your portfolio.

2:2 Scoping School Culture

Purpose: Have you ever wanted to "stop the world" and, rather than get off, take the time to really observe people's behavior? Here's your chance with the added bonus that this experience will help you better understand your future teaching environment. Your inherent curiosity, coupled with some directed observations, can offer a rich opportunity to study the growth and development of students.

INTASC PRINCIPLE 2
Human Development and Learning

Activity: Visit an elementary, middle, or high school campus, preferably at the level you envision teaching one day. Set yourself up to the side of the major thoroughfares with notepad, laptop, or sketchbook and make "notes." Consider three public and informal spaces: cafeteria, hallways, open space quad, blacktop/field, or recess areas.

Artifact: Create a "School Observation Diary" by taking notes on what you observe. Below are some questions to guide you. Feel free to add your own thoughts, questions, and observations.

www.mhhe.com/sadker8e

FORM:
School Observation Diary

School Observation Diary

- What does the "scene" look like? How are individuals and groups dressed? What else do you see?
- Focus on students and their body language. Who's talking, touching, or teasing? Describe the behavior. Are groups divided along racial, gender, and/or economic lines?
- Focus on staff or faculty in the area. What are their roles? Are they detached, integrated, or "in charge"? Describe their actions. What is the ratio of male teachers to female teachers?
- What noise is evident—music, varied languages, general chatter, or the "sounds of silence"?
- Compare and contrast school geography to see if cliques dominate certain areas or activities?
- What other behaviors, in general, do you observe?

Reflection: Did the students' behavior appear to vary by such factors as gender, race, physical size, language fluency, and clothing? What insights did you have about this student body and individual pupils? How did their use of time and space in the halls, cafeteria, and open areas interest and inform you? What insights about student and teacher behavior might you draw from your observations? How might these observations help you understand human development? Has this observation experience influenced your opinion about a career in teaching? Attach your reflection to the "School Observation Diary" and include both in your portfolio.

2:3 Curriculum Bias Detectors

Purpose: The way curricular materials portray different groups can promote either knowledge or stereotypes. In this activity, you will refine your skills for detecting bias. As a teacher, once you recognize this problem, you can select or adapt materials to counter such biases.

INTASC PRINCIPLE 3
Diversity in Learning

Activity: Review the seven forms of bias discussed in Chapter 6. Borrow a K–12 textbook (appropriate for your subject major or grade level) from your college's curriculum resource center, a local school, or a teaching friend. Look for an example of each form of bias.

Bias Busters		
Book Title/Author/Reference Information:		
Brief description of text:		
Type of Bias	**Page #**	**Example**
1. Invisibility		
2. Stereotyping		
3. Imbalance and selectivity		
4. Unreality		
5. Fragmentation and isolation		
6. Linguistic bias		
7. Cosmetic bias		

Reflection: What did you learn from this experience? Was there more or less evidence of bias than you thought? What surprised you about this activity? Will this experience influence how you use materials in your classroom? Why or why not? How will you teach your students to become "Bias Detectors"? Attach your "Forms of Bias" notes to your reflection and include in your portfolio.

2:4 Visit a "Choice" School

Purpose: As Chapter 4 illustrates, public education is moving beyond the neighborhood school. An abundance of school choices now exist: magnet schools, charter schools, for-profit schools, voucher programs, and home schooling to name a few. If you choose to become a teacher you may find yourself working in a very different setting than the one you attended. For this reason it is important that you become familiar with the changing face of America's public schools, and how instructional strategies may differ in different schools.

Activity: Arrange to visit at least one "choice" school. Spend time in the classrooms and observe the school culture. If possible, speak with administrators, teachers, students, and (if possible) parents. What is the educational environment like? What instructional strategies are used? Are any of these strategies new to you? How are the instructional strategies different from or similar to public schools in your area?

Artifact: Create a "Choice School Instruction Diary" that includes your notes and observations about these teaching strategies and practices. Include your assessments of these strategies. Create a Venn Diagram comparing this school's instructional practices to those in a nonchoice school. You can compare it to the school you attended as a student or to the "Scoping School Culture" activity in 2.2.

Venn Diagram

Type of Choice School (*example* charter):

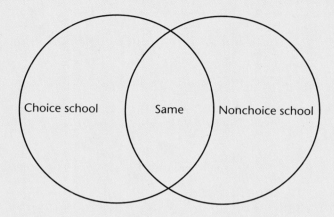

Reflection: What did you learn from observing these instructional strategies? Would you want to adopt or adapt some of these strategies? Why or why not? Attach your notes and Venn Diagram to your reflection and include in your portfolio.

2:5 Effective Schools

Purpose: Chapter 4, "Schools: Choices and Challenges," detailed five factors of effective schools: strong leadership, a clear school mission, a safe and orderly climate, the monitoring of student progress, and high expectations.

Activity: Visit one or more elementary, middle, or high schools in an effort to find evidence of these factors. Walk the halls of these schools and spend time in classrooms. Look for examples of how each of these five factors affects the motivation of students or contributes to a more effectively managed school. Keep in mind that it may be difficult to get a complete picture of a school from a few short visits, but look for specific examples of how each of these factors affects student motivation and management. Use the chart below to record your observations.

Artifact:

Effective Schools Observation	
	Management and Motivation Examples
Strong Leadership	
Clear School Mission	
Safe and Orderly Climate	
Monitoring of Student Progress	
High Expectations	

Reflection: Were some of the five factors easier to spot than others? Were you able to see examples of motivation and management associated with each of these five factors? What did you learn from your school observations? What do you recall of the management practices and that motivated (or did not motivate) you when you were a student? Attach your reflection to your artifact and store in your portfolio.

2:6 A Public Service Announcement: The Purpose of School

INTASC PRINCIPLE 6
Communication
Skills

Purpose: Chapter 4 details two diverse purposes of education: to transmit society's knowledge and values (passing the cultural baton), and to reconstruct society (schools as tools for change). Your ability to formulate and express your vision for education can guide your formal application for a teaching position. Communicating your goals clearly and concisely will let you practice verbal language skills, a foundation of effective instruction.

Activity: Develop a public service announcement (PSA) supporting one of these purposes of education. Think of it as a radio spot (thirty to forty-five seconds long) that tells the listening public just what *they* need to know.

Artifact: "Public Service Announcement for Schools." Write, edit, and practice your script with a stopwatch. Rewrite, edit again, and rehearse until it's right. You may not always be able to practice and tighten your lessons this thoroughly, but the strategies you use to develop and refine your PSA are a necessary part of your communication repertoire. Deliver your PSAs in small groups during a class session, maybe as a series of "commercial breaks." Perhaps you can record and broadcast your PSA. Challenge: Develop a second PSA supporting the other purpose of education.

Reflection: What did you learn from this activity? How were your peers' messages similar or different? Which PSAs appealed to you the most? Did you find yourself supporting the other purpose of education? Is it really possible to support only one of these purposes of education? Attach your PSA artifact to your reflection and include in your portfolio.

2:7 A Real Inservice Program

INTASC PRINCIPLE 7
Instructional
Planning Skills

Purpose: Several districts and states, along with independent schools, are instituting a service obligation as a high school graduation requirement. The intent is to instill a contributory ethic in students. While an ongoing service requirement may be one way to meet this principled goal, you as a teacher can help by integrating this "service ethic" in your lessons.

Activity: Recall a lesson or unit you have seen. Brainstorm (alone or with others) how you might add a service component. Use the following chart as a guide.

Artifact: "A Service Component." Briefly outline a lesson or unit that you will be teaching, and then describe in (about 150 words) how you would integrate a service project or activity into your lesson. The following sample chart can offer some suggestions.

Lesson	Sample Service Component
Language arts	Read with special population students, children, or seniors
Science	Assist with student health appraisal
Math	Be a homework helper, one on one, with a student
Social studies	Work on a student or teacher rights campaign
Technology	Teach computer skills at a local shelter
Physical education	Referee or supervise a children's sport event or recess
Health	Bring the Great American Smoke Out to a local school
Vocational and career	Review career materials for bias
Foreign language	Assist bilingual parents with school visits and conferences
Arts	Volunteer with children in theater, art, dance, or music

Reflection: This reflection might better be called a projection. Project yourself into the future, actually teaching your lesson. Describe your service component. What goals do you hope to accomplish? Your service component teaches "higher lessons" about honoring each other and developing a caring community. How can you integrate these lessons of caring and compassion with your official curriculum? Attach your reflection to the artifact and include in your portfolio.

2:8 Memoirs of a Time-Tested Student

Purpose: National, state, and district tests are a huge part of school culture, yet few teachers analyze their own role in the current testing climate. The following activity will help you define that role.

INTASC PRINCIPLE 8
Assessment

Activity: Think about the quizzes and tests you took as a student. Looking back, would you rate your teachers as helpful, or not so helpful? Either through your own journal entry or a conversation with a partner (live, taped, or online), consider the following questions below as you consider your testing experiences.

- What's an early memory of a "big deal" test? (Sharpening your number 2 pencil? unsealing special pamphlets in elementary school? being tucked in a cardboard "cubby" for privacy? proctors milling through rows, looking for cheating?) Consider thoughts from your classmates and see if more recollections are sparked.
- What did the teacher do that encouraged and supported you during the test?
- Do you remember any words or behaviors that distracted or annoyed you during the test?

Artifact: Review the *You Be the Judge* format that you find in this text, and create two columns that would be useful for your teacher-testing role. Prepare a *You Be the Judge* feature on testing by brainstorming what teachers can do to ensure a positive climate for student testing in one column, and list actions teachers should definitely avoid in the other.

FORM:
You Be the Judge: "Testing
Do's and Don'ts"

You Be the Judge: "Testing Do's and Don'ts"	
What Teachers SHOULD Do . . .	**What Teacher Should NOT Do . . .**
1. Describe the purpose of the test*	1. Leave the room*
2.	2.
3.	3.
etc.	etc.

*Sample items.

Reflection: What have you learned from this activity? Based on your analysis, what are some of the most critical factors in a testing climate? How can you remember to implement effective testing practices? Attach the *You Be the Judge* sheet to your reflection and store in your portfolio.

2:9 Reflections of a High School Yearbook

INTASC PRINCIPLE 9
Reflection and
Responsibility

Purpose: Part 2 of this text looked at all aspects of the school scene, from the student role to a teacher's reality. While you may have shifted perspective as you walked away from your high school graduation ceremony, the purpose of this activity is to look back and assess some of your choices and actions. Your high school yearbook symbolizes a snapshot of your school and a view of yourself in the social system. What does it show you about your school, yourself, and others?

Activity: Dig out your high school yearbook or see if it is posted on the Internet. Many schools now have their own Web pages. Read through the questions below before starting the artifact.

- Find yourself. Are you included? What is the caption under your senior photo? Did you get caught in candid shots? Are you with clubs, in activities, and on teams? Are you surrounded by your friends or often on your own? Which images recall emotions: pride, embarrassment, sadness? Did your school have an FTA (Future Teachers of America) organization? Were you pictured with them? How does being a future teacher or a member of that club look today? Were your curricular strengths evident by achievements, awards, and participation? (You were an officer for the Model UN and you're now a social studies major; you belonged to the Storyteller Society and you want to be an elementary teacher; you lettered in many sports and plan to teach physical education.) In what ways are you the same or different today?

- Find your friends. In what ways were you similar or different from them? When and where do they appear?

- Find lesser-known faces. Stop and really stare at students you may have walked by for years. What of their stories do you suspect or know? What groups were they in? What labels described their lives?

- Who is invisible or missing? Are there students who appear only in their "mug shot" and never as part of the campus culture? Do female or male students, from varied racial and ethnic groups, dominate particular activities or campus locales?

Artifact: Write a paragraph entitled "My High School Days" or "The Story Behind the Story" describing what really was going on with you socially, physically, and psychologically during this year in high school. Include both positive and negative experiences and feelings. (You can even compose a song or poem to share your high school years.)

Reflection: What do you notice about your school and yourself? How does it compare with the student cultures described in this text? Would you want to teach there or at a very different site? What stories from your yearbook pages would be valuable to share with classmates? Attach your reflection to your artifact and store in your portfolio.

2:10 Support Staff Interview

Purpose: When you have a teaching job, you become part of a learning community. Knowing about the roles and responsibilities of support personnel will enhance your understanding of the way schools work. Nonteaching employees contribute significantly to a well-functioning school. Bus drivers, clerical personnel, media and custodial staff, instructional aides, playground and lunch supervisors, resource specialists, medical and psychological professionals, and security and safety personnel all do their part. They befriend alienated kids, clean up after trashy nutrition breaks, reset chairs in an auditorium as many as eight times a day, frisk students with clothes baggy enough to cover goods and evils, know most students' names when they step up to the office counter, make lunchrooms smell like fresh cookies (maybe not quite often enough), find media materials with the leanest of hints from teachers and students, toss balls in one direction and *bench* students in another, and provide one-on-one practice for the most unique of tasks and talents. And these support personnel have their own special view of students, schools, and teachers. Fostering relationships with these colleagues is a way to create a valuable extension of your classroom community.

INTASC PRINCIPLE 10
Relationships and Partnerships

Activity: Try to schedule a 20-minute interview with one of the nonteaching employees at a local school. Here are some questions to ask, but feel free to add your own to the list.

- Describe your job duties.
- What do you like best about your job?
- What is the most challenging aspect of your job?
- How do students, teachers, and administrators affect your job?
- What is one thing about your job that you would like students to know about?
- What is one thing about your job that you would like teachers to know about?
- What is one thing about your job that you would like administrators to know about?
- Recount your best day on the job.

Artifact: Write a brief description entitled "A Day in the Life of _____." How do teachers support the support personnel, and more specifically, what can you do to create a positive relationship with school support personnel?

www.mhhe.com/ sadker8e

FORM:
Support Staff Interview

Reflection: What did you learn from this experience? How might this interview affect your rapport and behavior with support staff? Attach your reflection to your artifact and store in your portfolio.

PART III

Foundations

CLASS ACT

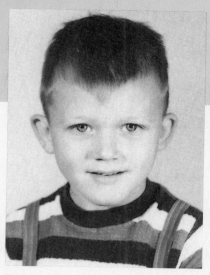

A chilly morning in early September 1952. My parents walked me down the dirt road to the state highway, where the No. 3 school bus passed by our farm. I boarded the faded yellow bus with no idea where I was going. Half an hour later, I was deposited in front of an old brick building: Dardanelle Elementary School.

I walked into a school that had been constructed in 1869, and had once housed both elementary and secondary students. Now grades one through six filled the school. Greeting me at the schoolhouse door, the principal escorted me to my first grade class. Stepping inside the classroom, it seemed as if I had entered the nineteenth century. The two-seat student desks were bolted to the floor, facing the teacher's desk that rested upon a wooden platform. A cracked chalkboard stood behind the teacher's desk. My assigned seat was next to a "town girl" on the first row.

After printing her name on the chalkboard, Mrs. "T" began the year-long process of teaching academic skills to students who had had no preparation for the first grade. We had no preschool, no kindergarten, and no educational television in those days. It was Mrs. T's job to fill our minds with basic academic knowledge. For seven hours each day, she lectured, recited, dictated, directed, questioned, and criticized. If we broke any of her many rules, we could expect a tongue-lashing or a public spanking, for physical punishment was not unusual back then.

Though she was a harsh taskmaster, Mrs. T proved an effective teacher. Using textbooks from the 1930s, she taught us how to read, write, and cipher. Our favorite class was spelling, because the textbooks were new, and it was also our last class of the day. At three o'clock every afternoon, the dismissal bell freed us. Mrs. T, who had been a member of the Woman's Army Corps during World War II, was a warrior on the educational front lines in 1952. This massive wave of children, which we now call the "baby boom," would strain the resources of America's educational system. It was left to the well-educated but ill-paid American teachers to cope with this flood of students. Mrs. T created a nineteenth-century style classroom climate to allow her to cope with thirty illiterate, rambunctious children, who came from the county seat, outlying hamlets, and scattered rural farms. She narrowed the curriculum to four essential subjects—reading, writing, spelling, and mathematics. Teaching the essential subjects in time-honored fashion, she tolerated no "misbehavior" and ruled her classroom with an iron hand.

In retrospect, I admire Mrs. T's accomplishments during the 1952–1953 school year. In one year, she taught us the basic academic skills we needed for success in the upper grades. Most of her students not only completed high school, but they also finished college. Several even managed to earn post-graduate degrees. However, her harsh classroom climate left its mark. Today, when I walk into a classroom, I feel the old fear that I experienced in her class fifty years ago. Mrs. T taught me about the lifelong influence that a powerful first grade teacher can have. And she taught me something about myself as well: my personal commitment to create a classroom without fear.

John Solomon Otto
American University

www.mhhe.com/ sadker8e

Read more *Class Acts* on the Online Learning Center.

CHAPTER 7

The History of American Education

FOCUS QUESTIONS

1. What was the nature and purpose of colonial education?
2. How did the Common School Movement promote universal education?
3. What developments mark the educational history of Native Americans?
4. How did teaching become a "gendered" career?
5. How did secondary schools evolve?
6. How have twentieth-century reform efforts influenced schools?
7. What were the main tenets of the Progressive Education movement?
8. What role has the federal government played in American education?
9. How did history shape the educational experiences of African Americans, Hispanics, Asian Americans/Pacific Islanders, and Arab Americans?
10. What educational barriers and breakthroughs have girls and women experienced?
11. Who are some of the influential educators who have helped fashion today's schools?

www.mhhe.com/
sadker8e

WHAT DO YOU THINK? How much do you already know about the history of education? Before reading the chapter, take a quiz that includes some "basics" and fun facts.

CHAPTER PREVIEW

Understanding the history of America's schools offers you perspective—a sense of your place in your new profession. Your classroom is a living tribute to past achievements and sacrifices.

In this chapter, we will trace American education from colonial times to the present. Education during the colonial period was intended to further religious goals and was offered primarily to white males—typically, wealthy white males. Over time, educational exclusivity diminished, but even today, wealth, race, and gender continue to impact educational quality. To a great extent, the story of American education is a battle to open the schoolhouse door to more of our citizens. In this chapter, we share the story of America's struggle to honor its commitment to equality.

The complex network of expectations surrounding today's schools is the product of a society that has been evolving for over three centuries. Individuals, groups, and the government all have contributed to making public schools more accessible. Benjamin Franklin, Horace Mann, Emma Hart Willard, and Mary McLeod Bethune, for example, fought to free America from historical biases. New federal laws were designed to create more equitable and effective educational opportunities. Today, the federal focus is to increase school competition, identify failing schools, and either "fix" them or replace them. But the notion of competition and standards is only the most recent chapter in the story of our nation's schools. In the colonial era, the goals were simpler: to teach the Scriptures and to develop a religious community. We will begin by looking into the classroom of Christopher Lamb, a New England teacher in one of the earliest American schools, over three centuries ago.

Christopher Lamb's Colonial Classroom

The frigid wintry wind knifed through Christopher Lamb's coat, chilling him to the bone as he walked in the predawn darkness. The single bucket of firewood that he lugged, intended to keep his seventeenth-century New England school-room warm all day, would clearly not do the job. Once the fire was started, Christopher focused on his other teaching tasks: carrying in a bucket of water for the class, sweeping the floor, and mending the ever so fragile pen points for the students. More than an hour after Christopher's predawn activities had begun, Margaret, the first student, arrived. Although Margaret, like most girls, would stay in school for only a year or two, Christopher believed that she should learn to read the Bible, so that she could be a better wife and mother. With any luck, she might even learn to write her name before she left school. But that was really not all that important for girls. As other students trickled in, they were directed to either the boys' bench or the girls' bench, where, in turn, they read their Testament aloud.

Those who read the Scriptures without error took their place at the table and wrote on their slates. Christopher was amazed at how poorly some students read, tripping over every other word, whereas others read quite fluently. The last student to finish, Benjamin, slowly rose from the bench, cringing. Christopher called out, "Lazy pupil," and a chorus of children's voices chimed in: "Lazy pupil. Lazy pupil. Lazy pupil." Benjamin, if not totally inured to the taunts, was no longer crushed by them, either. He slowly made his way to the end of the student line.

After the recitation and writing lessons, all the children were lined up and examined, to make certain they had washed and combed. A psalm was sung, and Mr. Lamb exhorted the students to walk in God's footsteps. For ten minutes, the class and teacher knelt in prayer. Each student then recited the day's biblical lesson. Those who had memorized their lessons received an *O*, written on their hand, a mark of excellence. Those who failed to recite their lessons correctly after three attempts once again were called "lazy pupil" by the entire class, and this time their names were written down. If by the end of the day they had finally learned the lesson, their names were erased from the list, and all the children called out "Diligent!" to those students.

Christopher Lamb had been an apprentice teacher for five years before accepting this position. He rejected the rod approach used so frequently by his master teacher. Using the children to provide rewards and punishments was far more effective than welts and bruises, marks left by a teacher's rod. Yes, Christopher was somewhat unorthodox, perhaps even a bit revolutionary, but the challenges of contemporary seventeenth-century society demanded forward-thinking educators, such as Christopher Lamb.

Colonial New England Education: God's Classrooms

One of the striking differences between Christopher Lamb's colonial classroom and today's typical public school is the role of religion in education. The religious fervor that drove the Puritans to America also drove them to provide religious education for their young, making New England the cradle of American education. In

Christopher Lamb's time, school was meant to save souls. Education provided a path to heaven, and reading, writing, and moral development all revolved around the Bible.

Early colonial education, both in New England and in other colonies, often began in the home. (Today's home schooling movement is not a *new* approach.) The family was the major educational resource for youngsters, and the first lessons typically focused on reading. Values, manners, social graces, and even vocational skills were taught by parents and grandparents. Home instruction eventually became more specialized, and some women began to devote their time to teaching, converting their homes into schools. These "dames" taught reading, writing, and computation, and their homes became known as **dame schools.** A "dame," or well-respected woman with an interest in education, became (for a fee) the community's teacher.

An **apprenticeship** program rounded out a child's colonial education. While boys, sometimes as young as 7 years of age, were sent to live with masters who taught them a trade, girls typically learned homemaking skills from their mothers. Apprenticeship programs for boys involved not only learning skilled crafts but also managing farms and shops. Many colonies required that masters teach reading and writing as well as vocational skills. The masters served *in loco parentis*—that is, in place of the child's parent. The competencies of the masters guiding apprentices varied greatly, as did the talents of family members, dames, ministers, and others fulfilling the teaching role. Not surprisingly, this educational hodgepodge did not always lead to a well-educated citizenry; a more formal structure was needed.

Twenty-two years after arriving in the New World, the Puritans living in the Commonwealth of Massachusetts passed a law requiring that parents and masters of apprentices be checked periodically to ensure that children were being taught properly. Five years later, in 1647, Massachusetts took even more rigorous measures to ensure the education of its children. The Massachusetts Law of 1647, more commonly known as the **Old Deluder Satan Law**—the Puritans' attempt to thwart Satan's trickery with Scripture-reading citizens—required that

Recitation lesson in a colonial classroom.

- Every town of 50 households must appoint and pay a teacher of reading and writing.
- Every town of 100 households must provide a (Latin) grammar school to prepare youths for the university, under a penalty of £5 for failure to do so.[1]

By 1680, such laws had spread throughout most of New England. The settlement patterns of the Puritans, who lived in towns and communities rather than scattered throughout the countryside, made establishing schools relatively uncomplicated. After learning to read and write, most girls returned home to practice the art of housekeeping. Boys who could afford to pay for their education went on to a **Latin grammar school.** In 1635, only fifteen years after arriving in America's wilderness, the Puritans established their first Latin grammar school in Boston. The Boston Latin Grammar School was not unlike a "prep" school for boys and was similar to the classical schools of Europe. The Boston Latin Grammar School was a rather exclusive school for boys of wealth, charging tuition to teach boys between the ages of 7 and 14.

Many consider the Boston Latin Grammar School to be the first step on the road to creating the American high school, although the school's curriculum reflected European roots. Students were expected to read and recite (in Latin, of course) the works of Cicero, Ovid, and Erasmus. In Greek, they read the works of Socrates and Homer. (Back to basics in colonial times meant back to the glory of Rome and Greece.) By the eighteenth century, the grammar school had incorporated mathematics, science, and modern languages. Classes started at 7 A.M., recessed at 11 A.M., and picked up from 1 P.M. until 5 P.M. Graduates were expected to go on to college and become colonial leaders, especially ministers.

Within a year of the founding of the Boston Latin Grammar School, Harvard College was established specifically to prepare ministers. Founded in 1636, Harvard was the first college in America, the jewel in the Puritans' religious and educational crown.[2]

For attendance at exclusive schools, such as Boston Latin Grammar, or at college, wealth was critical. The least desirable educational and apprenticeship opportunities were left to the poor. Some civic-minded communities made basic education in reading and writing more available to the poor, but only to families who would publicly admit their poverty by signing a "Pauper's Oath." Broadcasting one's poverty was no less offensive in colonial times than today, and many chose to have their children remain illiterate rather than sign such a public admission. The result was that most poor children remained outside the educational system.

Blacks, in America since 1619, and Native Americans were typically denied educational opportunities. In rare cases, religious groups, such as the Quakers, created special schools for children of color.[3] But these were the exceptions. Girls did not fare much better. After they had learned the rudiments of reading and writing, girls were taught the tasks related to their future roles as mother and wife. Later in this chapter, we will describe in more detail the barriers separating many Americans from a quality education.

Location greatly influenced educational opportunities. The northern colonies were settled by Puritans who lived in towns and communities relatively close to one another. Their religious fervor and proximity made the creation of community schools dedicated to teaching the Bible a predictable development.

In the middle colonies, the range of European religious and ethnic groups (Puritans, Catholics, Mennonites, the Dutch, and Swedes) created, if not a melting pot, a limited tolerance for diversity.[4] Various religious groups established schools, and apprenticeships groomed youngsters for a variety of careers, including teaching. In the middle colonies, the development of commerce and mercantile demands promoted the formation of private schools devoted to job training. By the 1700s, private teachers and night schools were functioning in Philadelphia and New York, teaching accounting, navigation, French, and Spanish.

The first city in North America was St. Augustine, Florida, where there is evidence that the Spanish settlers established schools. In terms of education, the southern English colonies trailed behind. The rural, sparsely populated southern colonies developed an educational system that was responsive to plantation society. Wealthy plantation owners took tutors into their homes to teach their children not only basic academic skills but also the social graces appropriate to their station in life. Plantation owners' children learned the proper way to entertain guests and "manage" slaves, using such texts as *The Complete Gentleman*. Wealthy young men seeking higher education were sent to Europe. Girls made do with just an introduction to academics and a greater focus on their social responsibilities. Poor white children might have had rudimentary home instruction in reading, writing, and computation. Black children made do with little if any instruction and, as time went by, encountered laws that actually prohibited their education entirely.[5]

Education has come a long way from colonial days and from Christopher Lamb's class—or has it? Consider the following:

1. The colonial experience established many of today's educational norms:
   - Local control of schools
   - Compulsory education
   - Tax-supported schools
   - State standards for teaching and schools

2. The colonial experience highlighted many of the persistent tension points challenging schools today:
   - What is the role of religion in the classroom?
   - How can we equalize the quality of education in various communities?
   - How can the barriers of racism, sexism, religious intolerance, and classism be eliminated, so that all children receive equal educational opportunity?
   - How can we prepare the most competent teachers?

 ## A New Nation Shapes Education

The ideas that led to the American Revolution revolutionized our schools. European beliefs and practices, which had pervaded America's schools, were gradually abandoned as the new national character was formed. None of these beliefs had been more firmly adhered to than the integration of the state and religion.

In sixteenth- and seventeenth-century England, the Puritans' desire to reform the Church of England was viewed as treason. The Puritans encountered both religious and political opposition, and they looked to the New World as an escape from persecution. However, they came to America *not* to establish religious freedom, as our history books sometimes suggest, but to establish their own church as supreme, both religiously and politically. The Puritans were neither tolerant of other religions nor interested in separating religion and politics. Nonconformers, such as the Quakers, were vigorously persecuted. The purpose of the Massachusetts colony was to establish the "true" religion of the Puritans, to create a "new Israel" in America. Schools were simply an extension of the religious state, designed to teach the young to read and understand the Bible and to do honorable battle with Satan.

During the 1700s, American education was reconstructed to meet broader, nonsectarian goals. Such leaders as **Thomas Jefferson** wanted to go beyond educating a small elite class or providing only religious instruction. Jefferson maintained that education should be more widely available to white children from all economic and social classes. Public citizens began to question the usefulness of rudimentary skills taught in a school year of just three or four months. They questioned the value of mastering Greek and Latin classics in the Latin grammar schools, when practical skills were in short supply in the New World.

In 1749, **Benjamin Franklin** penned *Proposals Relating to the Youth of Pennsylvania,* suggesting a new kind of secondary school to replace the Latin grammar school—the **academy.** Two years later, the **Franklin Academy** was established, free of religious influence and offering a variety of practical subjects, including mathematics, astronomy, athletics, navigation, dramatics, and bookkeeping. Students were able to choose some of their courses, thus setting the precedent for elective courses and programs at the secondary level. In the late 1700s, it was the Franklin Academy and not the Boston Latin Grammar School that was considered the most important secondary school in America.[6]

The Franklin Academy accepted both girls and boys who could afford the tuition, and the practical curriculum became an attractive innovation. Franklin's Academy sparked the establishment of 6,000 academies in the century that followed, including Phillips Academy at Andover, Massachusetts (1778), and Phillips Exeter Academy in Exeter, New Hampshire (1783). The original Franklin Academy eventually became the University of Pennsylvania.

Jefferson's commitment to educating all white Americans, rich and poor, at government expense, and Franklin's commitment to a practical program of nonsectarian study offering elective courses severed American educational thought from its European roots. Many years passed before these ideas became widely established practices, but the pattern for innovation and a truly American approach to education was taking shape.

The Common School Movement

During the early decades of the nineteenth century, education was often viewed as a luxury. However, even parents who could afford such a luxury had limited choices. The town schools still existed in Massachusetts, and some charity schools served the poor and orphans. Dame schools varied in quality. In some areas, religious schools of one denomination prevailed, while, in rural areas and the South, few schools existed at all. The United States was a patchwork quilt of schools, tied together by the reality that money was needed to attain a decent education.

During the early decades of the nineteenth century, the democratic ideal became popular as many "common people"—immigrants, small farmers, and urban laborers—demanded greater participation in the democracy. With the election of Andrew Jackson in 1828, the voices of many poor white people were heard, particularly their demands for educational access. Many more decades would pass before additional voices—particularly those of people of color—would also be heard.

Horace Mann became the nation's leading advocate for the establishment of a **common school** open to all. Today we know this common school as the public **elementary school.** Historians consider Horace Mann to be the outstanding proponent of education for the common person (the common school movement), and he is often referred to as "the father of the public school." (More about Mann appears in "The Education Hall of Fame," later in this chapter.) Mann helped create the Massachusetts State Board of Education and in 1837 became its secretary, a position similar to today's state superintendent of schools. In this role, Mann began an effort to reform education, believing that public education should serve both practical and idealistic goals. In practical terms, both business and industry would benefit from

FRAME OF REFERENCE   Early Textbooks

A rich variety of textbooks, media, library books, and computer software provide today's teachers with curricular resources unimaginable just a few years ago. As a teacher, you will come across references to some of the limited but influential curriculum materials of the past. Here is a brief profile of the best-known instructional materials from yesterday's schools.

HORNBOOK

The most common teaching device in colonial schools, the **hornbook** consisted of an alphabet sheet covered by a thin, transparent sheet made from a cow's horn. The alphabet and the horn covering were tacked to a paddle-shaped piece of wood and often hung by a leather strap around the student's neck. Originating in medieval Europe, the hornbook provided colonial children with their introduction to the alphabet and reading.

NEW ENGLAND PRIMER

The first real textbook, the **New England Primer** was a tiny 21/2- by 41/2-inch book containing 50 to 100 pages of alphabet, words, and small verses accompanied by wood-cut illustrations. First published in 1690, it was virtually the only reading text used in colonial schools until about 1800. The *Primer* reflected the religious orientation of colonial schools. A typical verse was

> In Adam's Fall
> We sinned all.
> Thy Life to mend,
> This Book attend
> The idle fool
> Is whipt at School.

AMERICAN SPELLING BOOK

The task undertaken by Noah Webster was to define and nourish the new American culture. His **American Spelling Book** replaced the New England Primer as the most common elementary textbook. The book contained the alphabet, syllables, consonants, rules for speaking, readings, short stories, and moral advice. The bulk of the book was taken up by lists of words. Royalty income from the sale of millions of copies of this book supported Webster in his other efforts to standardize the American language, including his best-known work, which is still used today, the *American Dictionary*.

MCGUFFEY READERS

William Holmes McGuffey was a minister, professor, and college president who believed that clean living, hard work, and literacy were the virtues to instill in children. He wrote a series of readers that emphasized the work ethic, patriotism, heroism, and morality. It is estimated that more than 100 million copies of *McGuffey Readers* educated several generations of Americans between 1836 and 1920. **McGuffey Readers** are noteworthy because they were geared for different grade levels and paved the way for graded elementary schools.

REFLECTION: Can you detect the morals and traditional values being promoted in today's texts? Can you cite any examples?

educated workers, resulting in a more productive economy. In idealistic terms, public schools should help us identify and nurture the talents in poor as well as wealthy children, and schools should ameliorate social disharmony.[7] Mann decried the rifts between rich and poor, Calvinists and religious reformers, new Irish immigrants and native workers. A common school instilling common and humane moral values could reduce such social disharmony (a popular belief today as well). Mann attempted to promote such values, but he encountered strong opposition when the values he selected revealed a distinct religious bias, one that offended Calvinists, atheists, Jews, Catholics, and others. His moral program to create a common set of beliefs had the opposite impact, igniting a dispute over the role of religion in school.

The idea of public education is so commonplace today that it seems difficult to imagine another system. But Horace Mann, along with such allies as Henry Barnard of Connecticut, fought a long and difficult battle to win the acceptance of public elementary schools. The opposition was powerful. Business interests predicted disaster if their labor pool of children were taken away. Concerned taxpayers protested the additional tax monies needed to support public education. There was also the competition. Private schools and religious groups sponsoring their own schools protested the establishment of free schools. Americans wondered what would become of a nation in which everyone received an elementary education. Would this not produce overeducated citizens, questioning authority and promoting self-interest? The opposition to public elementary schools was often fierce, but Horace Mann and his allies prevailed.

As he fought for public schools for all, Mann also waged a battle for high-quality schools. He continually attempted to build new and better schools, which was a problem, since so many Massachusetts schools were in deplorable condition. By publicly disseminating information about which communities had well-built or poorly built schools, he applied public pressure on districts to improve their school buildings. He worked for effective teacher training programs as well and promoted more stringent teacher licensing procedures. As a result of his efforts, several **normal schools** were founded in Massachusetts, schools devoted to preparing teachers in pedagogy, the best ways to teach children. He also championed newer teaching methods designed to improve and modernize classroom instruction. He opposed the routine practice of corporal punishment and sought ways to positively motivate students to learn. Mann emphasized practical subjects useful to children and to adult society, rather than the mastery of Greek and Latin. Mann saw education as a great investment, for individuals and for the country, and he worked for many years to make free public education a reality. He worked for the abolition of slavery, promoted women's educational and economic rights, and even fought alongside the temperance movement to limit the negative impact of alcohol. He was not only a committed educator but a committed reformer as well.

By the time of the Civil War, this radical notion of the public elementary school had become widespread and widely accepted. Educational historian Lawrence Cremin summarized the advance of the common school movement in his book *The Transformation of the School:*

> A majority of the states had established public school systems, and a good half of the nation's children were already getting some formal education. Elementary schools were becoming widely available; in some states, like Massachusetts, New York, and Pennsylvania, the notion of free public education was slowly expanding to include secondary schools; and in a few, like Michigan and Wisconsin, the public school system was already capped by a state university. There were, of course, significant variations from state to state and from region to region. New England, long a pioneer in public education, also had an established tradition of private education, and private schools continued to flourish there. The Midwest, on the other hand, sent a far greater proportion of its school children to public institutions. The southern states, with the exception of North Carolina, tended to lag behind, and did not generally establish popular schooling until after the Civil War.[8]

 ## Native American Tribes: The History of Miseducation

While the notion of universal education, especially at the elementary level, spread slowly among Americans of European ancestry, many who lived here were not European. In fact, Europeans were the late arrivals. It has been estimated that 50 to 100 million Native Americans occupied both North and South America before Columbus arrived.[9] Within a relatively brief time, over 90 percent of them would be dead from disease, starvation, and conquest. The survivors in the United States

YOU BE THE JUDGE
SCHOOL MASCOTS

Should Change with the Times Because . . .

MASCOT NAMES CAN BE HURTFUL

A pep rally featuring chanting "Indians" shaking rubber tomahawks trivializes meaningful rituals and cultural differences. Names such as the "Lady Bucks" or "Tigerettes" perpetuate an image of female inferiority and the second-class status of their sports.

MASCOT NAMES PROMOTE VIOLENCE

Stands filled with "Pirates" wielding sabers and chanting insults bring us all closer to potential violence and injury. Mascots should build a positive climate, not a destructive one.

WE SHOULD SET AN EXAMPLE FOR STUDENTS

We must teach by example, and changing offensive mascot names gives us that opportunity. By adopting names like "Freedom" or "Liberty," we teach our children how names can model our historical best, not our historical bigotries, and how adults can learn from past mistakes.

Should Not Change over Time Because . . .

IT'S JUST A NAME

There are more important issues to address than changing names of athletic teams. Exaggerated complaints about mascot names consume hours of school board meetings, and only show how political correctness is driving the times.

MASCOT NAMES BUILD SCHOOL SPIRIT

Proud mascot names like the "Patriots" highlight courage and bravery. Mascot names instill school spirit, a trait sorely needed by today's young people.

TRADITION MATTERS

Some things really do need to stay the same. Building a positive and stable school community is hard enough with people constantly moving and families splitting. School mascot names provide stability, and do not mindlessly mirror every passing fad.

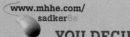

www.mhhe.com/
sadker

YOU DECIDE . . .

You and your classmates may want to share your own experiences on this hot-button issue. Should any mascot names be changed? Which names and why (or why not)? Brainstorm positive team names and mascots. This may be more challenging than you think. To understand more about mascots and American Indians, visit www.racismagainstindians.org.

would soon experience what many describe as an attempt to kill their culture through education.[10] Church missionaries educated native peoples to abandon their history and language in order to become "civilized Christians." Native beliefs, customs and languages were systematically ridiculed and repressed.[11]

Despite adverse conditions, Native Americans achieved some extraordinary educational accomplishments. For example, when their oral traditions and beliefs were discredited, Sequoyah invented a Cherokee syllabary in 1822. This permitted the Cherokee language to be written. Books were published in Cherokee; Cherokee schools became bilingual; and the Cherokee nation wrote, edited, and published the *Cherokee Phoenix,* a bilingual weekly newspaper. However, as federal interventions became more systematic, the tribes' control over their own education diminished.

After the Civil War, the federal government, through the Bureau of Indian Affairs (BIA), continued to use education as a tool of cultural conquest. Indian reservations saw more white superintendents, farm agents, teachers, inspectors, and missionaries. The largest of the tribes, the Navajos, despite their years of resistance,

Indian boarding schools attempted to supplant Indian culture with European values.

were assigned to a reservation. The treaty with the Navajos promised that schools would be built to educate their children. In 1892, almost 20 years after the treaty was signed, Indian boarding schools were established to assimilate young Native Americans into the dominant European-American values: veneration of property, individual competition, European-style domesticity, toil, and European standards of dress.

Many Native Americans refused to send their children to reservation schools. Arrest and kidnapping were common practices in forcing Native American children to attend. Rations were often withheld from parents as a means of compelling them to send their children to school.

After 1920, there was an increase in political and legal activity as Native Americans fought for tribal and educational rights. Native Americans challenged the federal government for violating treaties, including failure to provide adequate education. The federal courts were not responsive. Greater gains at the state level were made, and in several court cases Native Americans won the right to attend public schools.[12]

Today, over half of the Native Americans in this country do not live on reservations, and their youngsters have become invisible children of color in urban centers. As the students have been desegregated across neighborhoods, they have lost their "critical mass," which is often associated with higher achievement.[13]

The recent decades have witnessed continued activity by Native Americans to win control of the reservations, including the schools. The tribes feel strongly that such control will maintain cultural identity, as well as increase the academic achievement of their children. The vast majority of Indian children are educated in public schools. Most other Native youth are clustered in programs under the advisory of the Bureau of Indian Affairs or private schools.

The following Ancient Digger Indian proverb captures the last two centuries of Indian tribal education:

> In the beginning, God gave to every people a cup of clay, and from this cup they drank their life. They all dipped in the water, but their cups were different. Our cup is broken now. It has passed away.

Spinsters, Bachelors, and Gender Barriers in Teaching

Textbooks typically explore history's "big picture," focusing on how schools developed or how national reform movements grew. But too often this approach misses the personal, often moving, stories in history. One poignant thread of stories in our nation's history concerns how gender and sexuality have been used to short-circuit the contributions of both women and men in education. While some teachers have courageously fought such confining social conventions, many others have been victimized. Their stories are worth remembering.

Although today's popular perception is that teaching is predominantly a female career, in fact, men dominated teaching well into the mid-nineteenth century. Teaching was a **gendered career,** and it was gendered "male." Although a few women taught at home in *dame schools*, the first women to become teachers in regular school settings, earning a public salary, were viewed as gender trespassers, "unsexed" by their ambition, and considered masculine. Concerned by this negative characterization, early feminists such as Catherine Beecher implored female teachers to accentuate their feminine traits, highlight their domestic skills, and continue their preparation for marriage.[14] Despite the national reluctance to allow women into the workforce, and despite the perception that teachers should be male, the demand for more and inexpensive teachers created by common schools made the hiring of women teachers inevitable.

By the early part of the twentieth century, women constituted upwards of 90 percent of teachers. But not all women were equally welcome. School districts preferred "spinsters," women unmarried and unlikely to marry. Such women would not suffer the dual loyalties inherent in "serving" both husband and employer. Unmarried women were hired so frequently in the late nineteenth and early twentieth century that teaching and spinsterhood became synonymous. Cartoonists, authors, and reporters made the spinster school teacher a cultural icon. Boarding and rooming houses, and eventually small apartments, sometimes called *teacherages*, were built to provide accommodations for this new class of workers. Teaching was gendered again, but now it was gendered "female."

As women came to dominate teaching, the gender tables were turned, and a new concern arose: the fear that female teachers were "feminizing" boys. There were demands to bring men back to teaching, and to halt the "feminization" of young schoolboys. President Theodore Roosevelt added a touch of racism to the debate, arguing that since so many white women were choosing teaching over motherhood, they were committing "race suicide," and the continuance of the white race was in jeopardy.[15] School districts responded by actively recruiting male teachers, and male educators carved out their own niches in school systems. Administration, coaching, vocational education, and certain high school departments, specifically science and math, became male bastions.

For women, teaching meant economic and financial liberation. But not without cost. The dedicated teaching *spinsters* of the nineteenth century became the object of ridicule in the twentieth century. Women choosing teaching over motherhood were considered unnatural by a mostly male cadre of psychologists, physicians, and authors. Articles and books began to appear early in the twentieth century arguing that being unmarried caused women to be spiteful, hateful, and disgusting. The eminent psychologist G. Stanley Hall wrote an article entitled "Certain Degenerative

Tendencies among Teachers," explaining why unmarried women were frustrated, bitter, and otherwise unpleasant. Political opinions parading as research soon appeared claiming that as many as half of all single teachers were lesbians. Stage shows and movies picked up the theme, portraying lesbian relationships in and beyond school settings. The National Education Association reacted by campaigning for school districts to drop their ban against hiring married women. But when the depression hit in the 1930s, the idea of hiring wives and creating two-income families was anathema: the scarce jobs were to be funneled to women living alone or to men, the family "breadwinners." It was not until the end of World War II that most school districts even employed married women.

Men who remained in teaching also paid a price. Conventional wisdom early in the twentieth century held that effeminate men were gay men, and that gay men were naturally drawn to teaching. Worse yet, gay men were considered to be a teaching time bomb, since they would be poor role models for children. All male teachers became suspect, and few were drawn to teaching. School districts avoided hiring men who did not possess a clearly masculine demeanor. (Married men with children were preferred.) The Cold War and the accompanying McCarthy anti-Communist scare of the 1950s declared war on liberal ideas and unconventional choices: Homosexuality was seen as a threat to America. "There was a list of about 21 things that you could be fired for. The first was to be a card-carrying Communist, and the second was to be a homosexual."[16] Single teachers declared their "healthy" heterosexuality, and gay teachers stayed hidden. During this time, the number of married teachers doubled.

While recent years have witnessed a loosening of gender straightjackets, sex stereotypes, myths, and bigotry against gays continue to restrict and confine both women and men. Men drawn to teaching young children and women seeking leadership roles confront both barriers and social sanctions. Gay and lesbian teachers (and students) frequently endure hurtful comments and discriminatory treatment. As long as these gender and sexual barriers persist, we are all the poorer.

 ## The Secondary School Movement

With Mann's success in promoting public elementary schools, more and more citizens were given a basic education. In 1880, almost 10 million Americans were enrolled in elementary schools, and, at the upper levels of schooling, both private and public universities were established. But the gap between the elementary schools and the universities remained wide.

Massachusetts, the site of the first tax-supported elementary schools and the first college in America, was the site of the first free secondary school. Established in Boston in 1821, the **English Classical School** enrolled 176 students (all boys); shortly thereafter, 76 students dropped out. The notion of a public high school was slow to take root. It was not until 1852 that Boston was able to maintain a similar school for girls. The name of the boys' school was changed to The English High School and, even more simply, Boys' High School, to emphasize the more practical nature of the curriculum.

As secondary schools spread, they generally took the form of private, tuition-charging academies. Citizens did not view the secondary schools as we do today, as a free and natural extension of elementary education.[17] On the eve of the Civil War, over a quarter of a million secondary students were enrolled in six thousand tuition-charging private academies. The curricula of these academies varied widely, some focusing on college preparation and others providing a general curriculum for students who would not continue their studies. For those wanting to attend college, these academies were a critical link. In academies founded for females or in coeducational academies, "normal" courses were often popular. The normal course prepared academy graduates for teaching careers in the common schools. A few academies provided military programs of study.

A major stumbling block to the creation of free high schools was public resistance to paying additional school taxes (sound familiar?). But, in a series of court cases, especially the **Kalamazoo, Michigan, case** in 1874, the courts ruled that taxes could be used to support secondary schools. In Michigan, citizens already had access to free elementary schools and a state-supported university. The courts saw a lack of rationality in not providing a bridge between the two. The idea of public high school slowly took hold.

During the last half of the nineteenth century, the nation moved from agrarian to industrial, from mostly rural to urban, and people viewed the elementary school as inadequate to meet the needs of a more sophisticated and industrialized society. More parents viewed the high school as an important stepping-stone to better jobs. With the gradual decrease in demand for teenage workers, high school attendance grew. Half a century earlier, the public elementary school had reflected the growing dreams and aspirations of Americans and their changing economy. Now the public high school was the benchmark of these changes.

In the United States, although the high school served the dual purposes of vocational and college preparation, the rigid European tracking system was less pronounced, and early decisions did not predetermine a child's destiny. The high school became a continuation of elementary education, a path to public higher education, and an affirmation of democracy.

While the high school grew in popularity, it did not meet the needs of all its students. The junior high school, first established in 1909 in Columbus, Ohio, included grades 7, 8, and 9, and was designed to meet the unique needs of preadolescents. More individualized instruction, a strong emphasis on guidance and counseling, and a core curriculum were designed to respond to the academic, physiological, social, and psychological characteristics of preadolescents. The junior high school concept was further refined in the middle school, which included grades 5–8. Created in 1950, the middle school was built on the experiences of the junior high school, while stressing team teaching, interdisciplinary learning, de-emphasizing the senior high school's heavy emphasis on both subject matter mastery and competitive sports. During the last decades of the twentieth century, middle schools were rapidly replacing junior high schools, but the academic effectiveness of both schools was being questioned.[18]

 ## School Reform Efforts

In 1890, the United States was a vibrant nation undergoing a profound transformation. Vast new industries were taking shape; giant corporations were formed; labor was restive; massive numbers of immigrants were arriving; population was on the upsurge; and traditional patterns of life were changing. In fact, these descriptions parallel changes much later, at the close of the twentieth century. How would education generally, and the new high schools specifically, respond to these changes?

In 1892, the National Education Association (NEA), one of the oldest teacher organizations, established the **Committee of Ten** to develop a national policy for high schools.[19] Chaired by Charles Eliot, president of Harvard University, the committee was composed, for the most part, of college presidents and professors who wanted to bring consistency and order to the high school curriculum. This committee of college professors viewed high schools in terms of preparing intellectually gifted students (typically, white males) for college. The Committee of Ten did not envision today's high school, one that serves all our youth. Nonetheless, many of the committee's recommendations have been influential in the development of secondary education. In 1893, the committee recommended the following:

- A series of traditional and classical courses should be taught sequentially.
- High schools should offer fewer electives.
- Each course lasting for one year and meeting four or five times weekly should be awarded a **Carnegie unit.** Carnegie units would be used in evaluating student progress.
- Students performing exceptionally well could begin college early.

A generation later, in 1918, the NEA once again convened a group to evaluate the high school. Unlike the Committee of Ten, this committee consisted of representatives from the newly emerging profession of education. Education professors, high school principals, the U.S. commissioner of education, and other educators focused concern not on the elite moving on to college but on the majority of students for whom high school would be the final level of education. This committee asked the question, What can high school do to improve the daily lives of citizens in an industrial democracy? This committee's report, *Cardinal Principles of Secondary Education,* identified seven goals for high school: (1) health, (2) worthy home membership, (3) command of fundamental academic skills, (4) vocation, (5) citizenship, (6) worthy use of leisure time, and (7) ethical character. The high school was seen as a socializing agency to improve all aspects of a citizen's life.

Since the publication of the *Cardinal Principles* in 1918, not a decade has passed without a committee or commission reporting on reforms needed to improve U.S. schools. During the 1930s, the Progressive Education Association (PEA) provided suggestions to promote social adjustment as well as individual growth. Similar findings reported in the 1940s and 1950s noticeably influenced the evolution of our high schools. More electives were added to the high school curriculum. Guidance counselors were added to the staff. Vocational programs were expanded. The result was the formation of a new, comprehensive institution.

In time, the United States has come full circle, echoing the original call for intellectual rigor first voiced by the Committee of Ten in 1893. In 1983, the federal government's National Commission on Educational Excellence issued *A Nation at Risk: The Imperative for Educational Reform,* maintaining that mediocrity, not excellence, characterized U.S. schools. The commission declared that the inadequate rigor of U.S. education had put the nation at risk, losing ground to other nations in commerce, industry, science, and technology. The commission called for fewer electives and a greater emphasis on academic subjects.

Reports on the status of education and recommendations for school reform have become a U.S. tradition. These reports have underscored a built-in dichotomy in public education, a conflict between intellectual excellence and basic education for the masses, between college preparation and vocational training, between

The Development of American Schools

ELEMENTARY SCHOOLS

Dame Schools (1600s) These private schools taught by women in their homes offered child care for working parents willing to pay a fee. The dames who taught here received meager wages, and the quality of instruction varied greatly.

Local Schools (1600s–1800s) First started in towns and later expanded to include larger districts, these schools were open to those who could afford to pay. Found generally in New England, these schools taught basic skills and religion.

Itinerant Schools (1700s) and Tutors (1600s–1900s) Rural America could not support schools and full-time teachers. As a result, in sparsely populated New England, itinerant teachers carried schooling from village to village; they lived in people's homes and provided instruction. In the South, private tutors taught the rich. Traveling teachers and tutors, usually working for a fee and room and board, took varying levels of education to small towns and wealthy populations.

Private Schools (1700s–1800s) Private schools, often located in the middle colonies, offered a variety of special studies. These schools constituted a true free market, as parents paid for the kind of private school they desired. As you might imagine, both the curricula and the quality of these schools varied greatly.

Common Schools (1830–present) The common school was a radical departure from earlier ones in several ways. First, it was free. Parents did not have to pay tuition or fees. Second, it was open to all social classes. Previously, schools usually taught either middle-class or upper-class children. Horace Mann's common school was intended to bring democracy to the classroom. By the mid-nineteenth century, kindergarten was added. In the past few decades, many common schools, now called *elementary schools,* have added Head Start and other prekindergarten programs.

SECONDARY SCHOOLS

Latin Grammar Schools (1600s–1700s) These schools prepared wealthy men for college and emphasized a classical curriculum, including Latin and some Greek. From European roots, the curriculum in these schools reflected the belief that the pinnacle of civilization was reached in the Roman Empire.

English Grammar Schools (1700s) These private schools moved away from the classical Latin tradition to more practical studies. These schools were viewed not as preparation for college but as preparation for business careers and as a means of instilling social graces. Some of these schools set a precedent by admitting white girls, thus paving the way for the widespread acceptance of females in other schools.

Academies (1700s–1800s) The academies were a combination of the Latin and English grammar schools. These schools taught English, not Latin. Practical courses were taught, but history and the classics were also included. Some academies emphasized college preparation, while others prepared students to enter business and vocations.

High Schools (1800s–present) These secondary schools differed from their predecessors in that they were free; they were governed not by private boards but by the public. The high school can be viewed as an extension of the common school movement to the secondary level. High schools were open to all social classes and provided both precollege and career education.

Junior High Schools (1909–present) and Middle Schools (1950s–present) Junior high schools (grades 7–9) and middle schools (grades 5–8) were designed to meet the unique needs of preadolescents and to prepare them for the high school experience.

> **REFLECTION:** If you were responsible for creating a new school based on contemporary needs, what kind of school would you create?

student-centered education and subject specialization. Some of the reports have called for more focus on the student, on programs to enhance the student's entrance into society and the workplace. Others have cited the need for more emphasis on academic and intellectual concerns, as well as for programs to enhance the student's preparation for college. This dichotomy has been and continues to be an integral feature of American education. Regardless of the particular reforms advocated, all the reports, from the 1890s to the present, have had a common theme: a faith in education. The reports have differed on solutions but have concurred on the central role of the school in maintaining a vibrant democracy.

John Dewey and Progressive Education

John Dewey was possibly the most influential educator of the twentieth century—and probably the most controversial one. Some saw him as a savior of U.S. schools; others accused him of nearly destroying them. Rather than become engrossed in the heated controversy surrounding Dewey, however, let us look at *progressivism,* the movement with which he is closely associated, and later in this text, explore the philosophy behind progressivism.

As early as 1875, Francis Parker, superintendent of schools in Quincy, Massachusetts, introduced the concepts of progressivism in his schools and by 1896, John Dewey had established his famous laboratory school at the University of Chicago. But it was not until the 1920s and 1930s that the progressive education movement became more widely known. During the 1920s and 1930s, the Dalton and Walden schools in New York, the Beaver Country Day School in Massachusetts, the Oak Lane Country Day School in Pennsylvania, and laboratory schools at Columbia and Ohio State universities began to challenge traditional practices. The progressive education approach soon spread to suburban and city public school systems across the country. Various school systems adapted or modified progressive education, but certain basic features remained constant, and elements of progressive education can still be found in many schools.

Progressive education included several components. First, it broadened the school program to include health concerns, family and community life issues, and a concern for vocational education. Second, progressivism applied new research in psychology and the social sciences to classroom practices. Third, progressivism emphasized a more democratic educational approach, accepting the interests and needs of an increasingly diverse student body.

This model of education assumed that students learn best when their learning follows their interests. Passively listening to the teacher, according to the progressive movement, is not the most effective learning strategy. The role of the teacher is to identify student needs and interests and provide an educational environment that builds on them. In fact, progressive education shares some characteristics with problem-based and authentic learning, popular innovations in some of today's schools.

Although not involved in all the progressive education programs, John Dewey, in many minds, is the personification of progressive education, as well as its most notable advocate. (See "The Education Hall of Fame" later in this chapter for a description of Dewey and his achievements.) In no small part, this is due to the tens of thousands of pages that Dewey wrote during his long life. (Dewey was born on the eve of the Civil War in 1859 and died during the Korean War in the early 1950s.) Toward the end of Dewey's life, both he and progressive education came under strong attack.

The criticism of Dewey and progressive education originated with far-right political groups, for it was the era of Senator Joseph McCarthy and his extremist campaign against communism. While McCarthy's hunt for communists was primarily directed at the government and the military, educators were not immune. Some viewed progressive education as an atheistic, un-American force that had all but destroyed the nation's schools. Because students were allowed to explore and question, many critics were able to cite examples of how traditional values were not being taught. Although these critics were generally ignorant of Dewey's ideas and progressive practices, a second group was more responsible in its critique.

This second wave of criticism came from individuals who felt that the school curriculum was not academically sound. Hyman Rickover, a famous admiral and

For over one hundred years, many classrooms have looked strikingly similar. What does each of these rooms say about the roles of teachers and students? How would you describe the aesthetic of these spaces? How will you design your classroom?

developer of the nuclear submarine, and Arthur Bestor, a liberal arts professor, were among the foremost critics decrying the ills of progressive education. They called for an end to "student-centered" and "life-adjustment" subjects and a return to a more rigorous study of traditional courses. While the arguments raged, the launching of *Sputnik* by the Soviet Union in 1957 put at least a temporary closure on the debate. The United States was involved in a space race with the Soviets, a race to educate scientists and engineers, a race toward the first moon landing. Those arguing for a more rigorous, science- and math-focused curriculum won the day. Although many still argued vociferously over the benefits and shortcomings of progressive education, traditionalists were setting the direction for the nation's curriculum.

Before leaving progressive education, however, it will be beneficial to examine one of the most famous studies of the progressive movement. The Progressive Education Association, formed in 1919, initiated a study during the 1930s that compared almost three thousand graduates of progressive and of traditional schools as they made their way through college. The study, called the Eight-Year Study, was intended to determine which educational approach was more effective. The results indicated that graduates of progressive schools:

1. Earned a slightly higher grade point average
2. Earned higher grades in all fields except foreign languages

3. Tended to specialize in the same fields as more traditional students

4. Received slightly more academic honors

5. Were judged to be more objective and more precise thinkers

6. Were judged to possess higher intellectual curiosity and greater drive

 ## The Federal Government

As World War II drew to a close, the United States found itself the most powerful nation on earth. For the remainder of the twentieth century, the United States reconstructed a war-ravaged global economy while confronting world communism. In fact, the United States viewed education as an important tool in accomplishing these strategic goals. When the Soviets launched *Sputnik,* for example, the government enlisted the nation's schools in meeting this new challenge. Consequently, Congress passed the **National Defense Education Act (NDEA)** in 1958 to enhance "the security of the nation" and to develop "the mental resources and technical skills of its young men and women." The NDEA supported the improvement of instruction and curriculum development, funded teacher training programs, and provided loans and scholarships for college students that allowed them to major in subjects deemed important to the national defense (such as teaching). However, looking back in history, it is not at all clear how the federal government was legally able to do this. After all, the framers of the Constitution made their intentions clear: Education was to be a state responsibility, and the federal government was not to be involved. How did the NDEA and other federal acts come to pass?

Many people are unaware that the responsibility for educating Americans is not even mentioned in the Constitution. Under the **Tenth Amendment,** any area not specifically stated in the Constitution as a federal responsibility is automatically assigned to the states. Why was education a nontopic? Some historians believe that, since the individual colonies had already established disparate educational systems, the framers of the Constitution did not want to create dissension by forcing the states to accept a single educational system. Other analysts believe that education was deliberately omitted from the Constitution because Americans feared control of the schools by a central government, any central government, as had been the case in Europe. They saw central control as a possible threat to their freedom. Still others suggest that the framers of the Constitution, in their haste, bartering, and bickering, simply forgot about education (what a depressing thought!). Whatever the reason, distinct colonial practices continued, as each state created its own educational structure—its own approach for preparing teachers and funding schools.

Over time, however, the federal government discovered ways to influence education. As early as the revolutionary period, the new nation passed the **Land Ordinance Act** of 1785 and the **Northwest Ordinance** of 1787. These acts required townships in the newly settled territories bounded by the Ohio and Mississippi Rivers and the Great Lakes to reserve a section of land for educational purposes. The ordinances contained a much-quoted sentence underscoring the new nation's faith in education: "Religion, morality, and knowledge being necessary to good government and the happiness of mankind, schools and the means of education shall forever be encouraged."

The federal government also exerted its influence through targeted funding, or categorical grants. By using federal dollars for specific programs, the government was able to create new colleges and universities, to promote agricultural and

The following is a partial list of legislation indicating the long history of federal involvement in education.

1. *Land Ordinance Act* and *Northwest Ordinance* (1785 and 1787). These two ordinances provided for the establishment of public education in the territory between the Appalachian Mountains and the Mississippi River. In these new territories, 1 square mile out of every 36 was reserved for support of public education, and new states formed from these territories were encouraged to establish "schools and the means for education."

2. *Morrill Land Grant College Acts* (1862 and 1890). These acts established sixty-nine institutions of higher education in the various states, some of which are among today's great state universities. These acts were also called simply the *Land-Grant College Acts,* since public land was donated to establish these colleges.

3. *Smith-Hughes Act* (1917). This act provided funds for teacher training and program development in vocational education at the high school level.

4. *Servicemen's Readjustment Act* (G.I. Bill of Rights, 1944). This act paid veterans' tuition and living expenses for a specific number of months, depending on the length of their military service.

5. *National Defense Education Act* (1958). In response to the Soviet launching of *Sputnik,* the NDEA provided substantial funds for a variety of educational activities, including student loans, the education of school counselors, and the strengthening of instructional programs in science, mathematics, and foreign languages.

6. *Elementary and Secondary Education Act* (1965). This law provided financial assistance to school districts with low-income families, to improve libraries and instructional materials, and to promote educational innovations and research. In the 1970s, this legislation was expanded to include funding for bilingual and Native American education, drug education, and school lunch and breakfast programs.

7. *Project Head Start* (1964–1965). This act provides medical, social, nutritional, and educational services for low income children 3 to 6 years of age.

8. *Bilingual Education Act* (1968–2001). In response to the needs of the significant number of non-English-speaking students, Congress authorized funds to provide relevant instruction to these students. The primary focus was to assist non-English speakers, particularly Spanish-speaking students, almost 70 percent of whom were failing to graduate from high school. Although many other languages besides Spanish are included in this act, a relatively limited percentage of non-English-speaking students participate in these programs, due to funding shortfalls.

9. *Title IX of the Education Amendments* (1972). This regulation prohibits discrimination on the basis of sex. The regulation is comprehensive and protects the rights of both males and females from preschool through graduate school, in sports, financial aid, employment, counseling, school regulations and policies, admissions, and other areas. Title IX enforcement has been lax and many schools violate one or more parts of the regulation.

10. *Individuals with Disabilities Education Act* (1975, 1991, 1997, 2004). This act provides financial assistance to local school districts to provide free and appropriate education for the nation's 8 million children with disabilities who are between 3 and 21 years of age.

11. *No Child Left Behind Act* (2001). This act revises the Elementary and Secondary Education Act (ESEA, 1965) and calls for state standards and annual testing of math, reading and eventually science in grades 3–8. Schools that test poorly may receive additional funds for improvement, but also face the possibility of being closed. Parents are given greater freedom to select schools, with increased federal support for charter schools. The act also attempts to improve teacher quality, assist students with limited English skills, and encourage tutoring and supplemental educational services, even when carried out by private and religious organizations.

REFLECTION: Current federal initiatives promote standards and testing. How is this a departure from the general history of federal legislation?

industrial research efforts, and to provide schools for Native Americans and other groups. During the Great Depression of the 1930s, the federal government became even more directly involved with education, constructing schools, providing free lunches for poor children, instituting part-time work programs for high school and college students, and offering educational programs to older Americans. With unemployment, hunger, and desperation rampant in the 1930s, states welcomed these federal efforts. More and more Americans were coming to realize that some educational challenges were beyond the resources of the states. But federal involvement in education was sometimes resisted by states and local communities. In the case of African American education, it took nearly a century for the federal government to move forcefully to end racial segregation. And then, a few decades later, most students found themselves once again racially segregated.

Black Americans: The Struggle for a Chance to Learn

Much of the history of African American education in the United States has been one of denial. The first law prohibiting education of slaves was passed in South Carolina in 1740. During the next hundred years, many states passed similar and even stronger compulsory-ignorance laws. For example, an 1823 Mississippi law prohibited six or more Negroes from gathering for educational purposes. In Louisiana, an 1830 law imposed a prison sentence on anyone caught teaching a slave to read or write. However, because education has always been integral to African Americans' struggle for equal opportunity, they risked the penalties of these laws and even the dangers of violence for a chance to learn. They formed clandestine schools throughout most large cities and towns of the South. Suzie King Taylor described what it was like to attend one of those secret schools in Savannah, Georgia:

> We went every day about nine o'clock with our books wrapped in paper to prevent the police or white persons from seeing them. We went in, one at a time, through the gate, into the yard to the L Kitchen which was the schoolroom.[20]

The Civil War brought an end to policies of compulsory ignorance and an affirmation of black people's belief in the power of education. Most of the schooling of African Americans immediately following the Civil War was carried out by philanthropic societies. These associations worked with the Freedmen's Bureau, a federal agency established to provide various services, including the establishment of schools. School staffs were usually a mixture of instructors from the North, blacks of Caribbean island heritage, and formerly enslaved literate blacks.

Many white Southerners responded to the education of blacks with fear and anger. Sometimes there was terrorism against black schools. State after state passed laws that explicitly provided for segregated schools. With the 1896 *Plessy* **v.** *Ferguson* Supreme Court decision, segregation became a legally sanctioned part of the American way of life. In this landmark case, the Court developed the doctrine of **separate but equal.** Separate but equal initially legalized separate railway passenger cars for black and white Americans, and was also used to justify a legally segregated school system, which in many states lasted for more than half a century.

"Separate but equal" was not equal. In 1907, Mississippi spent $5.02 for the education of each white child but only $1.10 for each black child. In 1924, the state paid more than $1 million to transport whites long distances to schools. No money was spent for blacks, and for them a daily walk of more than twelve miles was not out of the question. Attending schools without enough books, seats, space, equipment, or facilities taught African American children the harsh reality of "separate but unequal." In the South, a dual school system based on race was in existence. This was **de jure segregation**—that is, segregation by law or by official action.

In the North, school assignments were based on both race and residence. **De facto** (unofficial) **segregation** occurred as the result of segregated residential patterns, patterns that were often prompted by discriminatory real estate practices. As housing

Scenes like this one became commonplace all across America in the years following the landmark *Brown* v. *Board of Education of Topeka* decision in 1954 and the passage of the Civil Rights Act in 1964.

patterns changed, attendance zones were often redrawn to ensure the separation of white and black children in schools. Even in schools that were not entirely segregated, black children were routinely placed in special classes or separate academic tracks, counseled into low-status careers, and barred from extracurricular activities. Whatever the obstacle, however, African Americans continued their struggle for access to quality education. As W. E. B. DuBois noted: "Probably never in the world have so many oppressed people tried in every possible way to educate themselves."[21]

Political momentum for civil rights reform grew with the participation of African Americans in World War II and the 1954 Supreme Court decision that schools must desegregate "with all deliberate speed." In ***Brown v. Board of Education of Topeka*** (Kansas), the court ruled unanimously that "in the field of public education the doctrine of 'separate but equal' has no place. Separate educational facilities are inherently unequal." Yet a decade after *Brown,* almost 91 percent of all African American children in the South still attended all-black schools.

In 1964, President Johnson and Congress moved boldly to eradicate racial segregation. The Civil Rights Act gave the federal government power to help local school districts desegregate (Title IV), and when necessary, to initiate law suits or withhold federal school funds to force desegregation (Title VI). The Civil Rights Act produced more desegregation in the next four years than the Supreme Court's *Brown* decision had in the preceding decade. All branches of the federal government now moved in concert to desegregate the nation's schools.

During the late 1960s and early 1970s, the Supreme Court also attacked de facto segregation stemming from racially imbalanced neighborhoods. Courts supported busing, racial quotas and school pairing to eradicate school segregation in both the North and the South. But opposition to these measures grew, and school districts began to experiment with magnet schools, choice plans, and voluntary metropolitan desegregation, remedies more acceptable to many school families.

Even as some schools became more racially balanced, a new barrier to equality appeared. In the same school building, black and white students found themselves separated by tracking, treated differently by teachers and administrators, and even gravitating to different areas of the school.[22] This within school

---

IMAGINE . . .

KKK Wizard Honored

School board member Roberta W. is trying to change the name of Nathan Bedford Forrest middle school in Gadsden, Alabama. Named for the Confederate general who went on to become the first grand wizard of the Ku Klux Klan, Ms. Roberta W. feels the time to change the name is long overdue. Her request to explore a new name was defeated when no one seconded her motion.

SOURCE: *The American School Board Journal,* April 1998.

Many students avoid academic excellence because they fear their peers will label them nerds. According to B. Bradford Brown and Laurence Steinberg, who sampled eight thousand high school students in California and Wisconsin, this fear is warranted. Unlike athletes, who are offered adulation, high academic achievers often get resentment instead of respect.[1] To avoid the "nerd" label and the social rejection that comes with it, students learn that they should do well, but not too well. This brain-nerd connection causes students to put the brakes on academic achievement, cut corners, and do only what is necessary to get by. The anti-achievement climate is even stronger for African American students. Signithia Fordham and John Ogbu reported the results of a fascinating ethnographic study in a Washington, DC, high school, where the student population was 99 percent black.[2] They found that the students actively discouraged each other from working to achieve because attaining academic success was seen as "acting white." "Acting white" was understood to include speaking standard English, listening to white music and radio stations, being on time, studying in the library, working hard, and getting good grades. students who did well in school were called "brainiacs," a term synonymous with jerk. The students who managed to achieve academic success and still avoid the "brainiac" label developed ingenious coping strategies. Some students camouflaged high achievement by "acting crazy," as class clowns or comedians. Others chose friends who would protect them in exchange for help with homework. Female achievers were more likely to hide out, keeping a low profile, so their peers would not know they were smart.

[1] B. Bradford Brown and Laurence Steinberg. "Academic Achievement and Social Acceptance," *The Education Digest* 55 (March 1990), pp. 57–60. Condensed from *National Center on Effective Secondary Schools Newsletter* 4 (fall 1989), pp. 2–4.
[2] Signithia Fordham, *Blacked Out: The Dilemmas of Race. Identity, and Success at Capital High* (Chicago: University of Chicago Press, 1996); Signithia Fordham and John Ogbu, "Black Students' School Success: Coping with the Burden of 'Acting White,'" *Urban Review* 18, no. 3 (1986), pp. 176–205.

REFLECTION: What can teachers do to break the brainiac-jerk association? How can the power of peer pressure be unleashed for success instead of mediocrity or failure? What do you think?

segregation was termed **second-generation segregation.** In the 1960s, the Kerner Commission warned: "Our nation is moving toward two societies, one black, and one white—separate and unequal." The commission charged that white society must assume responsibility for the black ghetto. "White institutions created it, white institutions maintain it, and white society condones it."[23]

But the Kerner Commission's warning was not heeded. As the century drew to a close, affirmative efforts such as busing were abandoned, and in the *Hopwood* (1996) and the *University of Michigan* decisions (2003), firm racial set-asides for college and law school admissions were eliminated. Although the courts said that race could be a factor in promoting student diversity, it could not be a major factor. The consequences of these actions are now evident in the nation's schools.[24]

Professor Gary Orfield at the Harvard Civil Rights Project reports that segregation is once again common. Today's students are more segregated than they were three decades ago, with white students experiencing the most segregated educational environment. The relatively few students attending diverse schools are more comfortable with other racial and ethnic groups and more understanding of diverse points of view. The Harvard Project points out that most students will not see these benefits. Orfield puts most of the responsibility for allowing schools to resegregate on the courts:[25]

Past and present policies which made it extremely difficult for black Americans to achieve at the level of their ability are like dropping the baton. And black America is not another team in competition with white America. Black Americans are part of America's team. If America keeps running without the baton, no matter how fast or how far, we're going to lose.[26]

The Supreme Court decision in *Brown* v. *Board of Education of Topeka,* followed by the 1964 Civil Rights Act, made it possible for students of all races, cultures, and disabling conditions to receive a desegregated education.

Hispanics: Growing School Impact

Over 40 million Hispanics live in the United States, including Puerto Rico, up more than 75 percent since 1980. Most Hispanics living in the United States are U.S. citizens and constitute 14 percent of the nation's population, the largest minority group in the nation.[27] Because many Latinos immigrated to the United States to escape economic and political repression, they did not all enter the country legally. Consequently, their numbers may be underestimated. Ongoing legal and illegal immigration, together with high birth rates for young families in their childbearing years, have made Hispanics the youngest and fastest-growing school-age population in the United States. By 2020, Hispanic children will represent one-fourth of the total school-age population.[28] Latino children confront numerous educational barriers. As early as kindergarten, Hispanic students are less able than their white peers to identify colors, recognize letters, count to fifty, or write their first name. Approximately half of Hispanics drop out of school.[29]

Hispanics consist of several subgroups, which share some characteristics, such as language, but differ in others, such as race, location, age, income, and educational attainment. The three largest Hispanic subgroups are Mexican Americans, Puerto Ricans, and Cuban Americans. There is also significant representation from other Latin American and Caribbean countries, such as the Dominican Republic, El Salvador, Nicaragua, and Honduras. (See Figure 7.1.) In contrast to these new immigrants, many from war-torn or poverty-stricken countries, there is also an "old" population of Mexican and Spanish descent living in the Southwest with a longer history on this continent than those who trace their ancestors to the New England colonies. Let's briefly look at some of the groups that comprise the Hispanic community.

FIGURE 7.1

U.S. Hispanic subgroups.

SOURCE: The Hispanic Population in the United States, U.S. Census Bureau, December 2005.

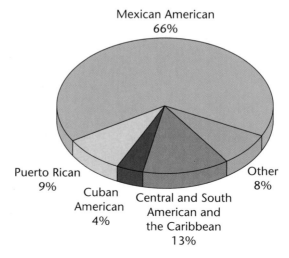

Mexican American
66%

Puerto Rican
9%

Cuban
American
4%

Central and South
American and
the Caribbean
13%

Other
8%

U.S. Hispanic subgroups

REFLECTION: While many refer to Hispanics as a homogeneous community, they are not. What distinctions can you make for each of these segments? What similarities have you observed or studied?

In the late 1960s, Cesar Chavez led the fight of migrant Mexican American laborers to organize themselves into a union and to demand a more responsive education that included culture-free IQ tests, instruction in Spanish, smaller classes, and greater cultural representation in the curriculum.

Mexican Americans

At the end of the United States' war with Mexico (1846–1848), the Mexicans who decided to stay in the new U.S. territories were guaranteed full citizenship. By 1900, approximately 200,000 Mexican Americans were living in the Southwest, having built the cities of Los Angeles, San Diego, Tucson, Albuquerque, Dallas, and San Antonio. The devices that were used to deny educational opportunity to Mexican Americans were similar to those imposed on African Americans. By 1920, a pattern of separate and unequal Mexican American schools had emerged throughout the Southwest.

A significant number of Mexican American families migrated once or twice a year, exploited as a source of cheap labor in rural, agricultural communities. With constant transitions, children's learning suffered. One superintendent in Texas, reflecting deeply engrained prejudice, argued that education was actually dangerous for Mexican Americans:

> Most of our Mexicans are of the lower class. They transplant onions, harvest them, etc. The less they know about everything else, the better contented they are . . . so you see it is up to the white population to keep the Mexican on his knees in an onion patch. . . . This does not mix well with education.[30]

Today, more than one in four public schools enroll migrant students, mostly Mexican Americans. The greatest numbers are in rural sections of California, Texas, and North Carolina.[31]

Puerto Ricans

During the nineteenth century, many of the Puerto Ricans in the United States were highly respected political exiles striving for the independence of their homeland. But all that changed in 1898, when Puerto Rico was acquired from Spain and became a territory of the United States. Citizenship, through the Jones Act in 1917, provided free movement between the continent and the island. Migration to the mainland peaked during the 1950s, with the majority of Puerto Ricans settling in New York City. By 1974, there were more than a quarter of a million Puerto Rican students in the New York City public schools. Currently, about half the Puerto Rican population lives within the fifty states, and the other half lives in Puerto Rico.[32] The frequent passage between the island and the United States, as families search for a better economic life, makes schooling all the more difficult for Puerto Rican children.

Cuban Americans

Following the Castro-led revolution in the 1950s, Cuban immigration to the United States increased significantly. During the 1960s, Cubans who settled in the United States were primarily well-educated, professional, and middle- and upper-class. By 1980, 800,000 Cubans—10 percent of the population of Cuba—were living in the United States. For the most part, Cubans settled in Miami and other locations in southern Florida, but there are also sizable populations in New York, Philadelphia, Chicago, Milwaukee, and Indianapolis. Cubans, considered one of the most highly educated people in American immigration history, tend to be more prosperous and more conservative than most of the other Latino groups.[33] In the second immigration wave, during the 1980s, there were many more black and poor Cubans, who have not been accepted as readily into communities in the United States.

 ## Asian Americans and Pacific Islanders: The Magnitude of Diversity

The term "Asian Americans and Pacific Islanders" embraces peoples from nations as diverse as India, Vietnam, China, Pakistan, Korea, Samoa, Japan, and Native Hawaii, about half the world's population. Over 14 million Americans have roots in Asia, although demographers predict that this figure will increase severalfold by the year 2050.[34] As a group, these Americans have attained a high degree of educational and economic success. This section will describe the differing experiences of four of the largest Asian immigrant groups—Chinese, Filipinos, Asian Indians, and Japanese—as well as problems faced by refugees from Southeast Asia.[35]

Many of these cultures hold education in high esteem, and well-mannered, respectful, and studious Asian American students have earned themselves the moniker of model minority. In kindergarten, Asian American children outscore their peers in both reading and math.[36] Over 40 percent of Asian American/Pacific Islanders graduate from college. One year after graduation, they have a higher starting salary than any racial or ethnic group.[37] However, diversity within the Asian community is often overlooked, and as with many stereotypes, misconceptions abound. Fewer than half of Vietnamese and Samoan Americans graduate from high school, and Asian New Wavers reflect the current countercultural pattern, with baggy pants, combat boots, and dyed hair, challenging the model minority stereotype.[38]

Chinese Americans

When the Chinese first began immigrating to the West Coast in the 1850s, they were mostly young, unmarried men who left China, a country ravaged by famine and political turmoil, to seek their fortune in the "Golden Mountains" across the Pacific and then take their wealth back to their homeland. By 1880, approximately 106,000 Chinese had immigrated to the United States, fueling a vicious reaction: "The Chinese must go." With the passage of the Immigration Act of 1882, along with a series of similar bills, further Chinese immigration was blocked. The Chinese already in this country responded to increasing physical violence by moving eastward and consolidating into ghettos called Chinatowns. Inhabited largely by male immigrants, these ghettos offered a grim and sometimes violent lifestyle, one with widespread prostitution and gambling. Chinatowns, vestiges of century-old ghettos, can still be found in many of America's cities.

In 1949, the institution of a Communist government in mainland China caused Congress to reverse more than a century of immigration quotas and naturalization and antimiscegenation laws and grant refugee status to five thousand highly educated Chinese in the United States. Despite facing active prejudice and discrimination, Chinese Americans today have achieved a higher median income and educational level than that of white Americans.

Filipino Americans

After the 1898 Spanish-American War, the United States acquired the Philippines. Filipinos, viewed as low-cost labor, were recruited to work in the fields of Hawaii and the U.S. mainland. Thousands left the poverty of their islands to seek economic security.

With a scarcity of women (in 1930, the male–female ratio was 143 to 1) and the mobility of their work on farms and as fieldhands, the Filipinos had difficulty establishing cohesive communities. Like other Asian immigrants, they came with the goal of taking their earnings back to their homeland; like other Asian immigrants, most found this an impossible dream.

Because of their unique legal status (the United States had annexed the Philippines in 1898), Filipinos were not excluded as aliens under the Immigration Act of 1924. However, the Tydings-McDuffie Act of 1934 was a victory for those who wanted the Filipinos excluded from the United States. Promising independence to the Philippines, this act limited immigration to the United States to fifty per year.

All that changed in 1965, when a new immigration act allowed a significant increase in Filipino immigration. Between 1970 and 1980, the Filipino population in the United States more than doubled. The earlier presence of the U.S. military in Manila generated an educated elite who spoke English, studied the American school curriculum, and moved to the United States with professional skills, seeking jobs commensurate with their training.[39] Concentrated in urban areas of the West Coast, Filipinos are the second-largest Asian American ethnic group in the United States.

Asian Indian Americans

Traders from India arrived in New England in the 1880s, bartering silks and spices. Intellectuals Henry David Thoreau, Ralph Waldo Emerson, and E. M. Forester (*Passage to India*) gravitated to the culture, religion, and philosophy of the Eastern purveyors. On the West Coast, Indians from Punjab migrated to escape British exploitation, which had forced farmers to raise commercial rather than food crops. With farming conditions in California similar to those in India, Punjabees became successful growers and landowners. They were destined to lose their lands, however, and even their leasing rights, under the California Alien Land Law, which recalled the ownership of land held by Indians and Japanese.

In addition to legal restrictions, Indian laborers were attacked by racist mobs in Bellingham, Washington, in 1907, triggering other riots and expulsions throughout the Pacific region. U.S. government support for British colonial rule in India became the rationale to further restrict Indian immigration. It was not until 1946 that a law allowing Indian naturalization and immigration was passed.

During the 1980s and 1990s, tens of thousands of Indians arrived in America. Most Indians are extremely well educated, and many are professionals. More than 85 percent have graduated from high school, over 65 percent have college degrees, and 43 percent have graduate or professional degrees. Their educational and income levels are the highest of any group in the United States, including other Asians.[40]

Japanese Americans

Only when the Japanese government legalized emigration in 1886 did the Japanese come to the United States in significant numbers. For example, in 1870, records show only 50 Japanese in the United States, but, by 1920, the number had increased to more than 110,000.

With the immigration of the Chinese halted by various exclusion acts, Japanese immigrants filled the need for cheap labor. Like the Chinese, the early Japanese immigrants were males who hoped to return to their homeland, an unfulfilled dream. Praised for their willingness to work when they first arrived in California, the Japanese began to make other farmers nervous with their great success in agriculture and truck farming. Anti-Japanese feelings became prevalent along the West Coast. Such slogans as "Japs must go" and warnings of a new "yellow peril" were frequent. In 1924, Congress passed an immigration bill that halted Japanese immigration to the United States.

After Japan's attack on Pearl Harbor on December 7, 1941, fear and prejudice about the "threat" from Japanese Americans were rampant. On February 19, 1942, President Franklin Roosevelt issued Executive Order No. 9006, which declared the West Coast a "military area" and established federal "relocation" camps. Approximately 110,000 Japanese, more than two-thirds of whom were U.S. citizens, were removed from their homes in the "military area" and were forced into ten internment camps in California, Idaho, Utah, Arizona, Wyoming, Colorado, and Arkansas. Located in geographically barren areas, guarded by soldiers and barbed wire, these internment camps made it very difficult for the Japanese people to keep their traditions and cultural heritage alive. Almost half a century later, the U.S. government officially acknowledged this wrong and offered a symbolic payment ($20,000 in reparations) to each victim.

Despite severe discrimination in the past, many of today's Japanese Americans enjoy both a high median family income and educational attainment. Their success is at least partially due to traditional values, a heritage some fear may be weakened by increasing assimilation.

Southeast Asian Americans

Before 1975, the United States saw only small numbers of immigrants from Southeast Asia, including Vietnam, Laos, and Kampuchea/Cambodia. Their arrival in greater numbers was related directly to the end of the Vietnam War and resulting Communist rule.

The refugees came from all strata of society. Some were wealthy; others were poverty stricken. Some were widely traveled and sophisticated; others were farmers and fishing people who had never before left their small villages. Most came as part of a family, and almost half were under age 18 at the time of their arrival. Refugee camps were established to dispense food, clothing, medical assistance, and temporary housing, as well as to provide an introduction to U.S. culture and to the English language.

By December 1975, the last refugee camp had closed and the U.S. government had resettled large numbers of Southeast Asians across the nation without too high a concentration in any one location. This dispersal was well intentioned but often left the refugees feeling lonely and isolated. In fact, many moved from original areas of settlement to cities where large numbers of Asian Americans were already located.

A second wave of Southeast Asian refugees followed in the years after 1975. Cambodians and Laotians migrated to escape poverty, starvation, and political repression in their homelands. Many tried to escape in small fishing boats not meant for travel across rough ocean seas. Called *boat people* by the press, almost half of them, according to the estimates, died before they reached the shores of the United States.

Similar to war refugees from Latin America, these children brought memories of terrible tragedy to school. For example, a teacher in San Francisco was playing hangman during a language arts lesson. As the class was laughing and shouting out letters, she was shocked to see one child, a newcomer, in tears. The girl spoke so little English she could not explain the problem. Finally, another child translated. The game had triggered a traumatic memory. In Cambodia, the girl had watched the hanging of her father.[41] Since the fall of Saigon in 1975, more than 1.4 million Southeast Asians have resettled in the United States. Their struggle to find a place in this society remains conflicted as most Americans associate Vietnam with war.

Although often grouped together, Asian Americans and Pacific Islanders reflect great ethnic and cultural diversity.

Arab Americans: Moving Beyond the Stereotype

Misunderstanding and intolerance have been all-too-common facts of life for three million Americans of Arab descent. Arab Americans' quality of life is often influenced by events taking place in other parts of the world. The Iraq wars, assaults on the terrorist camps in Taliban-ruled Afghanistan, the September 11, 2001, attacks on the World Trade Center and the Pentagon, and the continuing conflict between Israelis and Palestinians create tension and anxiety for Americans of Arab descent. While these news events are troubling enough, media portrayals can exacerbate the problem. Books and movies depict a strange melange of offensive Arab caricatures: greedy billionaires, corrupt sheiks, immoral terrorists, suave oil cartel magnates, and even romantic, if ignorant, camel-riding Bedouins. Nor are children's books immune from such characterizations. Caroline Cooney's *The Terrorist* (1999), a popular book for children in grades 5 through 10, is the fictional tale of an American teenager who tries to find the Arab terrorist responsible for her younger brother's death. It is not surprising that polls taken as far back as the 1980s reveal that most Americans perceive Arabs as anti-American, warlike, anti-Christian, and cunning.[42] The challenge to educators could not be clearer. Students and teachers need to learn about Arab Americans, as well as the Arab world.

The first wave of Arab immigrants, mostly from Syria and Lebanon, came to America at the end of the nineteenth century, for the same reasons that have driven so many immigrants: political freedom and economic opportunity. Toledo, Ohio, and Detroit, Michigan, became important centers of Arab immigration, and business became the economic mainstay of this first wave. Other waves of immigration followed, one just after World War II, and the third as a result of the Palestinian–Israeli conflict. Arabs arrived from over a score of countries, typically settling in major urban centers. (See Figure 7.2.)

Many Americans confuse Arabs and Moslems, mistaking Islam, a religion, with Arabs, a cultural group. While Islam is the predominant religion of the Middle East, and most Arabs living there are Moslems, there are also millions of Christian Arabs

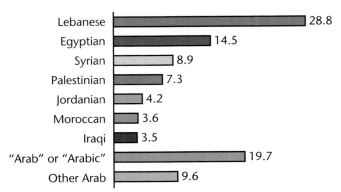

FIGURE 7.2
Arab Americans
by ancestry.

SOURCE: U.S. Census Bureau, Census 2000 special tabulation (www.census.gov/prod/cen2000/doc/sf4.pdf), issued March 2005.

Note: Other Arab (9.6 percent) includes Yemeni, Kurdish, Algerian, Saudi, Tunisian, Kuwaiti, Libyan, Berber, Emirati (United Arab Emirates), Omani, Bahraini, Alhuceman, Bedouin, Rio de Oro, and the general terms Middle Eastern and North African.

REFLECTION: As a teacher, what steps can you take to help your students appreciate the diversity obscured by broad labels such as "Arab American"?

(as well as those who are Jewish or Druse). In the United States, the vast majority of the three million Arab Americans are Christian. And, in contrast, the majority of America's eight million Moslems are not Arab. While Arabs practice different religions, they do share the same language and culture, a culture that is at times in conflict with Western values.[43]

Such differences can create friction, in and beyond school. For example, Arabs enjoy close social proximity, and members of the same sex often walk arm-in-arm or hold hands, behaviors at odds with American practice. Features of the Arabic language, including loudness and intonation, may be perceived in America as too loud, and even rude. While punctuality is considered a courtesy in the United States, being late is not considered a sign of disrespect in Arab culture. In addition to these cultural disconnects, more profound differences emerge, such as the disparity between the role of women in Arab society and the role of women in Western society. Many Arab nations cast women in an inferior position, denying them education, inheritance, and power. Saudi Arabia, for example, still forbids women to drive, prohibits coeducation, and requires that women wear veils in public. Arranged marriages and polygamy are practiced in several Arab nations. While the birth of a son is celebrated in conventional Arab families, the birth of a daughter may be met with silence.[44] Yet, change is also sweeping part of the Arab world. Several Arab states have opened schools and the workplace to women, with dramatic results.

Today, students of Arab heritage can be found in all 50 states, and as a group, do well in American schools. The proportion of Arab Americans who attend college is higher than the national average and Arab Americans earn postgraduate degrees at a rate nearly double the national average. Yet they still face challenges. They learn from textbooks that have little if anything to say about their history or experiences. American teachers lack basic information about Arab culture, which may present problems. For example, a traditional Arab student may be troubled or confused in an American school where women can be both teachers and principals. In a similar way, an American teacher who criticizes an Arab student in public may have unintentionally erected a wall of hard feelings. Arabs put a lot of emphasis on personal and family honor, and public ridicule is a serious matter.

If the Arab student happens to be of the Moslem faith, additional issues emerge. Moslems discover that while schools typically celebrate Christmas, they ignore Moslem holidays. For instance, during Ramadan, Moslems fast for a month during daylight hours, yet few schools recognize this observance, much less make provision for it. In terms of dietary restrictions, school cafeterias serve, but do not always label, pork products, a food Moslems are prohibited from eating. Clearly, Arab and Moslem American students are all but invisible in the official and hidden curriculum of most American schools. Teacher training, curricular revision, and a greater understanding of these cultural and religious issues are needed if equal educational opportunities are to become a reality for these Americans.

 # Women and Education: A History of Sexism

The peopling of America is a story of voluntary immigration and forced migration. The story of women's struggle for educational opportunity may be just as hard to uncover but equally important to reclaim.

For almost two centuries, girls were barred from America's schools.[45] Although a woman gave the first plot of ground for a free school in New England, female children were not allowed to attend the school. In 1687, the town council of Farmington,

Connecticut, voted money for a school "where all children shall learn to read and write English." However, the council quickly qualified this statement by explaining that "all children" meant "all males." In fact, the education of America's girls was so limited that fewer than a third of the women in colonial America could even sign their names. For centuries, women fought to open the schoolhouse door.

In colonial America, secondary schools, called female seminaries, appealed to families financially able to educate their daughters beyond elementary school. In New York, Emma Hart Willard struggled to establish the Troy Female Seminary, while, in Massachusetts, Mary Lyon created Mount Holyoke, a seminary that eventually became a noted women's college. Religious observance was an important part of seminary life in institutions such as Mount Holyoke. Self-denial and strict discipline were considered important elements of molding devout wives and Christian mothers. By the 1850s, with help from Quakers, such as Harriet Beecher Stowe, Myrtilla Miner established the Miner Normal School for Colored Girls in the nation's capital, providing new educational opportunities for African American women. While these seminaries sometimes offered superior educations, they were also trapped in a paradox they could never fully resolve: They were educating girls for a world not ready to accept educated women. Seminaries sometimes went to extraordinary lengths to reconcile this conflict. Emma Willard's Troy Female Seminary was devoted to "professionalizing motherhood" (and who could not support motherhood?). But, en route to reshaping motherhood, seminaries reshaped teaching.

For the teaching profession, seminaries became the source of new ideas and new recruits. Seminary leaders, such as Emma Hart Willard and Catherine Beecher, wrote textbooks on how to teach and on how to teach more humanely than was the practice at the time. They denounced corporal punishment and promoted more cooperative educational practices. Since school was seen as an extension of the home and another arena for raising children, seminary graduates were allowed to become teachers—at least until they decided to marry. Over 80 percent of the graduates of Troy Female Seminary and Mount Holyoke became teachers. Female teachers were particularly attractive to school districts—not just because of their teaching effectiveness but also because they were typically paid one-third to one-half of the salary paid to male teachers.

By the end of the Civil War, a number of colleges and universities, especially tax-supported ones, were desperate for dollars. Institutions of higher learning experienced a serious student shortage due to Civil War casualties, and women became the source of much-needed tuition dollars.

Female funding did not buy on-campus equality. Women often faced separate courses and hostility from male students and professors. At state universities, male students would stamp their feet in protest when a woman entered a classroom.

In *Sex in Education* (1873), Dr. Edward Clarke, a member of Harvard's medical faculty, argued that women attending high school and college were at risk because the

Low teacher salaries can be traced back to the late nineteenth century, when communities found that they could hire capable women teachers for approximately 60 percent of what men teachers were paid.

blood destined for the development and health of their ovaries would be redirected to their brains. The stress of study was no laughing matter. Too much education would leave women with "monstrous brains and puny bodies . . . flowing thought and constipated bowels." Clarke recommended that females be provided with a less demanding education, easier courses, no competition, and "rest" periods, so that their reproductive organs could develop. He maintained that allowing girls to attend such places as Harvard would pose a serious health threat to the women themselves, with sterility and hysteria potential outcomes.

M. Carey Thomas, future president of Bryn Mawr and one of the first women to earn a Ph.D. in the United States, wrote in her diary about the profound fears she experienced as she was studying: "I remember often praying about it, and begging God that if it were true that because I was a girl, I could not successfully master Greek and go to college, and understand things, to kill me for it."[46] In 1895, the faculty of the University of Virginia concluded that "women were often physically unsexed by the strains of study." Parents, fearing for the health of their daughters, often placed them in less demanding programs reserved for females, or kept them out of advanced education entirely. Even today, the echoes of Clarke's warning resonate, as some people still see well-educated women as less attractive, view advanced education as "too stressful" for females, or believe that education is more important for males than for females.

In the twentieth century, women won greater access to educational programs at all levels, although well into the 1970s gender-segregated programs were the rule. Even when females attended the same schools as males, they often received a less valuable education. Commercial courses prepared girls to become secretaries, while vocational programs channeled them into cosmetology and other low-paying occupations. After World War II, it was not unusual for a university to require a married woman to submit a letter from her husband, granting her permission to enroll in courses, before she would be admitted. By the 1970s, with the passage of Title IX of the Education Amendments of 1972, females saw significant progress toward gaining access to educational programs, but not equality. The opening section of Title IX states

> No person in the United States shall, on the basis of sex, be excluded from participation in, be denied the benefits of, or be subjected to discrimination under any education program or activity receiving federal financial assistance.

The law is straightforward, but misperceptions are common. For example, many equate Title IX only with athletics, yet the law prohibits gender discrimination in admissions, treatment of students, counseling, financial aid, employment, and health benefits, to name but a few. Nor is Title IX only about females; males are protected from gender discrimination as well. Ignorance of the law is widespread, one reason why it is so rarely enforced. In fact, in over three decades since Title IX became law, no school has ever been financially penalized by the federal government for violating Title IX.

Unfortunately, sexism still thrives in today's classrooms, affecting attitudes and careers.[47] Nursing, teaching, library science, and social work continue to be predominantly female while engineering, physics, and computer science are male domains. Even in medicine and law, where women have made progress, they find themselves channeled into the least prestigious, least profitable specialties. A "glass wall" still divides the sexes, and some call for the glass wall to become permanent, believing that males and females are so different that the nation should return to single-sex schools, an idea that popular in colonial America, bringing us full circle in this chapter.

SEVENTEENTH CENTURY

Informal family education, apprenticeships, dame schools, tutors

1635	Boston Latin Grammar School
1636	Harvard College
1647	Old Deluder Satan Law
1687–1890	*New England Primer* published

EIGHTEENTH CENTURY

Development of a national interest in education, state responsibility for education, growth in secondary education

1740	South Carolina denies education to blacks.
1751	Opening of the Franklin Academy in Philadelphia
1783	Noah Webster's *American Spelling Book*
1785, 1787	Land Ordinance Act, Northwest Ordinance

NINETEENTH CENTURY

Increasing role of public secondary schools, increased but segregated education for women and minorities, attention to the field of education and teacher preparation

1821	Emma Willard's Troy Female Seminary opens, first endowed secondary school for girls.
1821	First public high school opens in Boston.
1823	First (private) normal school opens in Vermont.
1827	Massachusetts requires public high schools.
1837	Horace Mann becomes secretary of board of education in Massachusetts.
1839	First public normal school in Lexington, Massachusetts
1855	First kindergarten (German language) in United States
1862	Morrill Land Grant College Act
1874	*Kalamazoo case* (legalizes taxes for high schools)
1896	*Plessy v. Ferguson* Supreme Court decision supporting racially separate but equal schools

TWENTIETH CENTURY

Increasing federal support for educational rights of under-achieving students; increased federal funding of specific (categorical) education programs

1909	First junior high school in Columbus, Ohio
1919	Progressive education programs
1932	New Deal education programs
1944	G.I. Bill of Rights
1950	First middle school in Bay City, Michigan
1954	*Brown v. Board of Education of Topeka* Supreme Court decision outlawing racial segregation in schools
1957	*Sputnik* leads to increased federal education funds.
1958	National Defense Education Act funds science, math, and foreign language programs.
1964–1965	Job Corps and Head Start are funded.
1972	Title IX prohibits sex discrimination in schools.
1975	Public Law 94-142, Education for All Handicapped Children Act (renamed Individuals with Disabilities Education Act, 1991), is passed.
1979	Cabinet-level Department of Education is established.
1990– present	Increased public school diversity and competition through charter schools, for-profit companies, open enrollment, and technological options. Promotion of educational goals, standards and testing.
2001	Passage of *No Child Left Behind* Act.

SOURCE: Compiled from Edward King, *Salient Dates in American Education, 1635–1964* (New York: Harper & Row, 1966); National Center for Education Statistics, U.S. Department of Education, *Digest of Education Statistics, 1994.*

REFLECTION: What milestones do you believe may occur in the years ahead?

At the beginning of the chapter, we peeked into Christopher Lamb's colonial classroom to watch our school traditions take root. Unfortunately, one such tradition was that education was reserved for some, and denied to others. We still struggle to create fair schools. In a sense, today's teachers stand on the shoulders of Christopher Lamb and other educators as each generation makes its own contribution to creating fairer, more effective schools. We have chosen to conclude this chapter with a Hall of Fame, a small tribute to those whose shoulders we stand on.

Hall of Fame: Profiles in Education

A "hall of fame" recognizes individuals for significant contributions to a field. Football, baseball, rock and roll, and country music all have halls of fame to recognize outstanding individuals. We think education is no less important and merits its own forum for recognition. In fact, Emporia State University in Kansas houses a Teachers' Hall of Fame. Following are the nominations we would offer to honor educators who we believe should be in a hall of fame.

Obviously, not all influential educators have been included in these brief profiles, but it is important to begin recognizing significant educational contributions. Indirectly or directly, these individuals have influenced your life as a student and will influence your career as a teacher.[48]

For his work in distinguishing schooling from education and for his concern with the stages of development—

Jean-Jacques Rousseau (1712–1778). French philosopher Rousseau viewed humans as fundamentally good in their free and natural state but corrupted as a result of societal institutions, such as schools. Like Comenius, he saw children as developing through stages and believed that the child's interests and needs should be the focus of a curriculum. In *Emile,* a novel he wrote in 1762, Rousseau described his educational philosophy by telling the story of young Emile's education, from infancy to adulthood. Emile's education took place on a country estate, under the guidance of a tutor and away from the corrupt influences of society. The early learnings came through Emile's senses and not through books or the words of the teacher. The senses, which Rousseau referred to as the *first teachers,* are more efficient and desirable than learning in the schoolroom. Nature and related sciences were acquired through careful observation of the environment. Only after Emile reached age 15 was he introduced to the corrupt influences of society to learn about government, economics, business, and the arts. Rousseau emphasized the senses over formalized teaching found in books and classrooms, nature over society, and the instincts of the learner over the adult-developed curriculum of school. Rousseau's visionary education for Emile can be contrasted with the sexist education he prescribed for Sophie, the book's female character. Sophie's education amounted to little more than obedience school, because Rousseau expected women to be totally subservient to men. (This terribly restricted view of the role of women is an indication that even members of the Education Hall of Fame have their limitations.)

Rousseau was a pioneer of the contemporary deschooling movement, as he separated the institution of the school from the process of learning. His work led to the child study movement and served as a catalyst for progressive education. Rousseau's romantic view of education influenced many later reformers, including Pestalozzi.

For establishing the kindergarten as an integral part of a child's education—

Friedrich Froebel (1782–1852). Froebel frequently reflected on his own childhood. Froebel's mother died when he was only nine months old. In his recollections, he developed a deep sense of the importance of early childhood and of the critical role played by teachers of the young. Although he worked as a forester, chemist's assistant, and museum curator, he eventually found his true vocation as an educator. He attended Pestalozzi's institute and extended Pestalozzi's ideas. He saw nature as a prime source of learning and believed that schools should provide a warm and supportive environment for children.

In 1837 Froebel founded the first **kindergarten** ("child's garden") to "cultivate" the child's development and socialization. Games provided cooperative activities for socialization and physical development, and such materials as sand and clay were used to stimulate the child's imagination. Like Pestalozzi, Froebel believed in the importance of establishing an emotionally secure environment for children. Going beyond Pestalozzi, Froebel saw the teacher as a moral and cultural model for children, a model worthy of emulation (how different from the earlier view of the teacher as disciplinarian).

In the nineteenth century, as German immigrants came to the United States, they brought with them the idea of kindergarten education. Margaretta Schurz established a German-language kindergarten in Wisconsin in 1855. The first English-language kindergarten and training school for kindergarten teachers were begun in Boston in 1860 by Elizabeth Peabody.

For his contributions to moral development in education and for his creation of a structured methodology of instruction—

Johann Herbart (1776–1841). German philosopher Herbart believed that the primary goal of education is moral education, the development of good people. He believed that through education, individuals can be taught such values as action based on personal conviction, concern for the social welfare of others, and the positive and negative consequences associated with one's behavior. Herbart believed that the development of cognitive powers and knowledge would lead naturally to moral and ethical behavior, the fundamental goal of education.

Herbart believed in the coordinated and logical development of all areas of the curriculum. He was concerned with relating history to geography and both of these to literature—in short, in clearly presenting to students the relationships among various subjects. Herbart's careful and organized approach to the curriculum led to the development of structured teaching. His methodology included preparing students for learning (readiness), helping students form connections by relating new material to previously learned information, using examples to increase understanding, and teaching students how to apply information.

Herbart's concern for moral education paved the way for contemporary educators to explore the relationship between values and knowledge, between a well-educated scientist or artist and a moral, ethical adult. His structured approach to curriculum encouraged careful lesson planning—that is, the development of a prearranged order of presenting information. Teachers who spend time classifying what they will be teaching and writing lesson plans are involved in the kinds of activities suggested by Herbart.

For opening the door of higher education to women and for promoting professional teacher preparation—

Emma Hart Willard (1787–1870). The sixteenth of seventeen children on a farm in Connecticut, Willard was fortunate enough to be born of well-educated and progressive parents who nurtured new ideas. At a time when it was believed that women could not learn complex subjects, Willard committed her life to opening higher education to women. In her own education, she pursued as rigorous an academic program as was permitted women at the time. She had mastered geometry on her own by the age of 12. At 17, she began her career in teaching. In 1814, she opened the Middlebury Female Seminary. In reality, the seminary offered a college-level program, but the term *college* was avoided and *seminary* was used so as not to offend the public. Although she herself was denied the right to attend classes at nearby Middlebury College, she learned college-level material on her own and incorporated this curriculum into the subjects she taught her female students at the seminary.

She put forth her views on opening higher education to women in a pamphlet entitled *An Address to the Public; Particularly to the Members of the Legislature of New York, Proposing a Plan for Improving Female Education* (1819). The pamphlet, written and funded by Willard, won favorable responses from Thomas Jefferson, John Adams, and James Monroe, but not the money she sought from the New York State Legislature to open an institution of higher learning for women. Eventually, with local support, she opened the Troy Female Seminary, establishing a rigorous course of study for women, more rigorous than the curriculum found in many men's colleges. Moreover, the seminary was devoted to preparing professional teachers, thus providing a teacher education program years before the first normal (teacher training) school was founded. To disseminate her ideas and curriculum, Willard wrote a number of textbooks, especially in geography, history, and astronomy. In 1837, she formed the Willard Association for the Mutual Improvement of Female Teachers, the first organization to focus public attention on the need for well-prepared and trained teachers.

Emma Hart Willard was a pioneer in the struggle for women's intellectual and legal rights. She wrote and lectured in support of the property rights of married women and other financial reforms, and she dedicated her life to promoting the intellectual and educational freedom of women. Her efforts promoted the recognition of teaching as a profession and the creation of teacher education programs. In the years that followed, colleges, graduate schools, and the professions opened their doors to women. It was Emma Hart Willard's commitment to providing educational opportunities for women that has shaped the past two centuries of progress, not only for women but for all Americans.

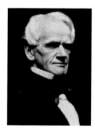

For establishing free public schools and expanding the opportunities of poor as well as wealthy Americans, and for his visions of the central role of education in improving the quality of American life—

Horace Mann (1796–1859). Perhaps the most critical factor in shaping the life of Horace Mann was not what he was given but what he was denied. Although he proved to be an able and gifted student, he was not afforded very much in the way of formal schooling. Forced to learn on his own, he acquired an education and was eventually admitted to Brown University. Before him was a career in law as well as a career in politics, but neither influenced his life as much as his struggle to gain an education. He worked to ensure that others would not be denied educational opportunities. That struggle directed his life and altered the history of U.S. education.

As an educator and a member of the Massachusetts House of Representatives, he worked to improve the quality of education. Corporal punishment, floggings, and unsafe and unsanitary school buildings were all denounced by Mann in speeches, letters, and his lobbying efforts before the state legislature and the U.S. Congress. Of the numerous challenges Mann confronted, he was probably most violently denounced for his efforts to remove religious instruction from schools. He also worked to lengthen the school term; to increase teacher salaries; and, by establishing the first public nor-mal school in 1839, to prepare better teachers. He organized school libraries and encouraged the writing of textbooks that included practical social problems. Mann's efforts resulted in the establishment of the Massachusetts Board of Education, and he became the board's first secretary of education, a position equivalent to a state super-intendent of schools.

Of the many achievements attributed to Mann, he is probably best remembered for his leadership in the common school movement, the movement to establish free, publicly supported schools for all Americans. He viewed ignorance as bondage and education as a passport to a promising future. Through education, the disadvantaged could lift themselves out of poverty, blacks could achieve freedom, and children with disabilities could learn to be productive members of society. Mann's credo was that social mobility and the improvement of society could be attained through a free edu-cation for all.

However, Mann's fervor was not confined to establishing quality public educa-tion. As a member of Congress, he denounced slavery, child labor, worker exploita-tion, workplace hazards, and the dangers of slum life. Later, as president of Anti-och College, he provoked further controversy by admitting women and minority members as students. In the 1850s, this was not only a radical move; for many, it suggested the imminent collapse of higher education. Mann did more than ver-balize the importance of freedom and education; his life and actions were a com-mitment to these principles. The fruits of Mann's efforts are found in our public school system; the education of minorities, the poor, and women; and efforts to provide well-trained teachers working in well-equipped classrooms.

For her integrity and bravery in bringing education to African American girls—

Prudence Crandall (1803–1889). Born of Quaker parents, Prudence Crandall re-ceived her education at a school in Providence, Rhode Island, founded by an active abolitionist, Moses Brown. Her upbringing within Quaker circles, in which discus-sions of abolition were common, may have inspired her interest in racial equality, an interest that led her to acts of personal courage as she strove to promote edu-cation among people of all colors.

After graduating from the Brown Seminary around 1830, Crandall taught briefly in Plainfield, Connecticut, before founding her own school for girls in the neigh-boring town of Canterbury. However, her decision to admit a black girl, Sarah Harris, daughter of a neighboring farmer, caused outrage. While African Americans in Connecticut were free, a large segment of the white population within Canterbury supported the efforts of the American Colonization Society to deport all freed blacks to Africa, believing them to be inherently inferior. Many were adamant that anything but the most basic education for African Americans would lead to dis-content and might encourage interracial marriage. The townspeople voiced fears that Crandall's school would lead to the devaluation of local property by attract-ing a large number of blacks to the area. Prudence Crandall was pressured by the local population to expel Sarah Harris. However, she was determined to defy their wishes. When the wife of a prominent local clergyman suggested that, if Harris remained, the school "could not be sustained," Crandall replied, "Then it might sink then, for I should not turn her out."

When other parents withdrew their children, Crandall advertised for pupils in *The Liberator,* the newspaper of abolitionist William Lloyd Garrison. A month later, the school reopened with a student body comprising 15 black girls. However, the townspeople made life difficult for Crandall and her students. Supplies were hard to obtain, and Crandall and her pupils faced verbal harassment, as well as being pelted with chicken heads, manure, and other objects. Nonetheless, they persisted.

In 1833, only one month after Crandall had opened her doors to African American girls, the Connecticut legislature passed the notorious "Black Law." This law forbade the founding of schools for the education of African Americans from other states without the permission of local authorities. Crandall was arrested and tried. At her trial, her counsel advised the jury, "You may find that she has violated an act of the State Legislature, but if you also find her protected by higher power, it will be your duty to acquit." Her conviction was later overturned on appeal, but vandalism and arson continued. When a gang stormed the school building with clubs and iron bars, smashing windows and rendering the downstairs area uninhabitable, the school finally was forced to close.

Prudence Crandall's interest in education, racial equality, and women's rights continued throughout her life. Several of her students continued her work, including her first African American student, Sarah Harris, who taught black pupils in Louisiana for many years.[49]

For her work in identifying the educational potential of young children and crafting an environment in which the young could learn—

Maria Montessori (1870–1952). Montessori was no follower of tradition, in her private life or in her professional activities. Shattering sex-role stereotypes, she attended a technical school and then a medical school, becoming the first female physician in Italy. Her work brought her in contact with children regarded as mentally handicapped and brain-damaged, but her educational activities with these children indicated that they were far more capable than many believed. By 1908, Montessori had established a children's school called the Casa dei Bambini, designed to provide an education for disadvantaged children from the slums of Rome.

Montessori's view of children differed from the views held by her contemporaries. Her observations led her to conclude that children have an inner need to work at tasks that interest them. Given the right materials and tasks, children need not be rewarded and punished by the teacher. In fact, she believed that children prefer work to play and are capable of sustained periods of concentration. Young children need a carefully prepared environment in order to learn.

Montessori's curriculum reflected this specially prepared environment. Children learned practical skills, including setting a table, washing dishes, buttoning clothing, and displaying basic manners. They learned formal skills, such as reading, writing, and arithmetic. Special materials included movable sandpaper letters to teach the alphabet and colored rods to teach counting. The children developed motor skills as well as intellectual skills in a carefully developed sequence. Montessori worked with each student individually, rather than with the class as a whole, to accomplish these goals.

The impact of Montessori's methods continues to this day. Throughout the United States, early childhood education programs use Montessori-like materials. A number of early childhood institutions are called **Montessori schools** and adhere to the approach she developed almost a century ago. Although originally intended for disadvantaged students, Montessori's concept of carefully preparing an environment and program to teach the very young is used today with children from all social classes.

For his work in developing progressive education, for incorporating democratic practices in the educational process—

John Dewey (1859–1952). John Dewey's long life began before the Civil War and ended during the Korean War. During his 93 years, he became quite possibly the most influential educator of the twentieth century. Dewey was a professor at both the University of Chicago and Columbia University, as well as a prolific writer whose ideas and approach to education created innovations and provoked controversies that continue to this day.

Dewey's educational philosophy has been referred to as *progressivism, pragmatism,* and *experimentalism.* Dewey believed that the purpose of education is to assist the growth of individuals, to help children understand and control their environment. Knowledge is not an inert body of facts to be committed to memory; rather, it consists of experiences that should be used to help solve present problems. Dewey believed that the school should be organized around the needs and interests of the child. The learner's interests serve as a springboard to understanding and mastering contemporary issues. For example, a school store might be used to teach mathematics. Students involved in the store operation would learn mathematics by working with money. Education consists of creating these experiences, and having students learn by doing—not just by listening. Dewey believed that an autocratic school where adults decided what would be taught is not wise. Creating a democratic school where students make decisions about their learning is the way to truly teach democracy and create good citizens. Today, Dewey's writings and ideas continue to motivate and intrigue educators, and there still exist educational monuments to Dewey, both in a variety of school practices and in professional organizations, such as the John Dewey Society. Dewey's philosophy helped open schools to innovation and integrated education with the outside world.

For her contributions in moving a people from intellectual slavery to education—

Mary McLeod Bethune (1875–1955). The first child of her family not born in slavery, Bethune rose from a field hand, picking cotton, to an unofficial presidential adviser. The last of 17 children born to South Carolina sharecroppers, she filled the breaks in her fieldwork with reading and studying. She was committed to meeting the critical need of providing education to the newly freed African Americans, and, when a Colorado seamstress offered to pay the cost of educating one black girl at Scotia Seminary in Concord, New Hampshire, she was selected. Bethune's plans to become an African missionary changed as she became more deeply involved in the need to educate newly liberated American blacks.

With $1.50, five students, and a rented cottage near the Daytona Beach city dump in Florida, Bethune founded a school that eventually became Bethune-Cookman College. As a national leader, she created a number of black civic and welfare organizations, serving as a member of the Hoover Commission on Child Welfare, and acting as an adviser to President Franklin D. Roosevelt.

Mary McLeod Bethune demonstrated commitment and effort in establishing a black college against overwhelming odds and by rising from poverty to become a national voice for African Americans.

For his creation of a theory of cognitive development—

Jean Piaget (1896–1980). As a student at the University of Paris, Swiss psychologist Piaget met and began working for Alfred Binet, who developed the first intelligence test (a version of which we know today as the Stanford-Binet IQ test). Binet was involved in standardizing children's answers to various questions on this new test, and he enlisted Jean Piaget to assist. Piaget not only followed Binet's instructions, but he went beyond them. He not only recorded children's answers but also probed students for the reasons behind their answers. From the children's responses, Piaget observed that children at different age levels see the world in different ways. From these initial observations, he conceptualized his theory of cognitive, or mental, development, which has influenced the way educators have viewed children ever since.

Piaget's theory outlines four stages of cognitive development. From infancy to 2 years of age, the child functions at the *sensorimotor stage*. At this initial level, infants explore and learn about their environment through their senses—using their eyes, hands, and even mouths. From 2 to 7 years of age, children enter the *preoperational stage* and begin to organize and understand their environment through language and concepts. At the third stage, *concrete operations*, occurring between the ages of 7 and 11, children learn to develop and use more sophisticated concepts and mental operations. Children at this stage can understand numbers and some processes and relationships. The final stage, *formal operations*, begins between 11 and 15 and continues through adulthood. This stage represents the highest level of mental development, the level of adult abstract thinking.

Piaget's theory suggests that teachers should recognize the abilities and limits at each stage and provide appropriate learning activities. Children should be encouraged to develop the skills and mental operations relevant to their mental stage and should be prepared to grow toward the next stage. Teachers, from early childhood through secondary school, need to develop appropriate educational environments and work with students individually according to their own levels of readiness.

Piaget revealed the interactive nature of the learning process and the importance of relating the learner's needs to educational activities. His work led to increased attention to early childhood education and the critical learning that occurs during these early years.

For his contributions in establishing a technology of teaching—

Burrhus Frederick (B. F.) Skinner (1904–1990). When poet Robert Frost received a copy of young B. F. Skinner's work, he encouraged the author to continue writing. But Skinner's years of serious writing in New York's Greenwich Village were unproductive. As Skinner explained, "I discovered the unhappy fact that I had nothing to say, and went to graduate study in psychology, hoping to remedy that short-coming."

Skinner received his doctorate from Harvard, where he eventually returned to teach. He found himself attracted to the work of John B. Watson, and Skinner's ideas became quite controversial. One critic described him as "the man you love to hate."

Skinner's notoriety stemmed from his belief that organisms, including humans, are entirely the products of their environment; engineer the environment, and you can engineer human behavior. Skinner's view of human behavior (called **behaviorism**) irked individuals who see it as a way of controlling people and enslaving the human spirit. Skinner's response was that he did not create these principles but simply discovered them and that a constructive environment can "push human achievement to its limits."

Skinner's early work included the training of animals. During World War II, in a secret project, Skinner trained, or conditioned, pigeons to pilot missiles and torpedoes. The pigeons were so highly trained that they were capable of guiding a missile right down the smokestack of an enemy ship.

Skinner believed that children could be conditioned to acquire desirable skills and behaviors. By breaking down learning into small, simple steps and rewarding children after the completion of each step, learning mastery is achieved. This approach laid the foundation for the later development of behavior modification and computer-assisted instruction.

Skinner's creative productivity resulted in both inventions and numerous publications. The "Skinner box" enabled researchers to observe, analyze, and condition pigeons and other animals to master tasks, while teaching machines translated these learning principles into human education. Skinner's books, including *Walden Two*, *The Technology of Teaching*, and *Beyond Freedom and Dignity*, spread his ideas on the importance of environment and behaviorism to educators, psychologists, and the general public. He provided guiding principles about the technology of learning, principles that can be used to unleash or to shackle human potential.

For her creative approaches placing children at the center of the curriculum—

Sylvia Ashton-Warner (1908–1984). Sylvia Ashton-Warner began her school career in her mother's New Zealand classroom, where rote memorization constituted the main avenue for learning. The teaching strategies that Ashton-Warner later devised, with their emphasis on child-centered learning and creativity in the classroom, stand in opposition to this early experience.

Ashton-Warner was a flamboyant and eccentric personality; throughout her life, she considered herself to be an artist rather than a teacher. She focused on painting, music, and writing. Her fascination with creativity was apparent in the remote New Zealand classrooms, where she encouraged self-expression among the native Maori children. As a teacher, she infuriated authorities with her absenteeism and unpredictability, and in official ratings she was never estimated as above average in her abilities. However, during the peak years of her teaching career, between 1950 and 1952, she developed innovative teaching techniques that influenced teachers around the world and especially in the United States.

Realizing that certain words were especially significant to individual pupils because of their life experiences, Ashton-Warner developed her "key vocabulary" system for teaching reading to young children. Words drawn from children's conversations were written on cards. Using these words, children learned to read. Ashton-Warner asserted that the key to making this approach effective lay in choosing words that had personal meaning to the individual child: "Pleasant words won't do. Respectable words won't do. They must be words organically tied up, organically born from the dynamic life itself. They must be words that are already part of the child's being."

Bringing meaning to children was at the center of Ashton-Warner's philosophy. This belief provided the foundation of several reading approaches and teaching strategies used throughout the United States. Her work brought meaning to reading for millions of children. In her best-selling book, *Teacher*, she provided many future teachers with important and useful insights. Her emphasis on key vocabulary, individualized reading, and meaningful learning is evident in classrooms today in America and abroad.

For his work in identifying the crippling effects of racism on all American children and in formulating community action to overcome the educational, psychological, and economic impacts of racism—

Kenneth Clark (1914–2005). Kenneth Clark attended schools in Harlem, where he witnessed an integrated community become all black and felt the growing impact of racism. He attended Howard University, was the first African American to receive a doctorate in psychology from Columbia University, and in 1960 became the first black to be tenured at City College of New York. His concern with the educational plight of African Americans generally, and the Harlem community in particular, was always central in his professional efforts.

Beginning in the 1930s, Clark and his wife, Mamie Phipps Clark, assessed black children's self-perceptions. They bought black dolls for 50 cents each at a store in Harlem, one of the few places where black dolls could be purchased. They showed black and white children two white dolls and two black dolls, and asked the children to pick out the "nice" doll, the "pretty" doll, and the "bad" doll. Both groups tended to pick the white dolls as nice and pretty, and the black doll as bad. He repeated the study in the 1950s in South Carolina, where white students received far more funds for education than black children. The results were similar. He concluded that the lesson of black inferiority was so deep in society that even young black children understood it and believed it. As Clark noted, "A racist system inevitably destroys and damages human beings; it brutalizes and dehumanizes blacks and whites alike." In *Brown* v. *the Topeka Board of Education* (1954), the Supreme Court cited Clark's "doll" study in deciding that "separate was inherently unequal."

For his global effort to mobilize education in the cause of social justice—

Paulo Reglus Neves Freire (1921–1997). Abandoning a career in the law, Brazilian-born Freire committed himself to the education of the poor and politically oppressed. His efforts moved literacy from an educational tool to a political instrument.

Freire denounced teacher-centered classrooms. He believed that instructor domination denied the legitimacy of student experiences and treated students as secondary objects in the learning process. Freire championed a *critical pedagogy*, one that places the student at the center of the learning process. In Freire's pedagogy, student dialogues, knowledge, and skills are shared cooperatively, legitimizing their experiences. Students are taught how to generate their own questions, focus on their own social problems, and develop strategies to live more fruitful and satisfying lives. Teachers are not passive bystanders or the only source of classroom wisdom. Freire believed that teachers should facilitate and inspire, that teachers should "live part of their dreams within their educational space." Rather than unhappy witnesses to social injustice, teachers should be advocates for the poor and agents for social change. Freire's best known work, **Pedagogy of the Oppressed**, illustrated how education could transform society.

Freire's approach obviously threatened the social order of many repressive governments, and he faced constant intimidation and threats. Following the military overthrow of the Brazilian government in 1964, Freire was jailed for "subversive" activities and later exiled. In the late 1960s, while studying in America, Freire witnessed racial unrest and the antiwar protests. These events convinced Freire that political oppression is present in "developed nations" as well as third world countries, that economic privilege does not guarantee political advantage, and that the pedagogy of the oppressed has worldwide significance.

www.mhhe.com/
sadker8e

INTERACTIVE ACTIVITY
Who Am I? Using hints, determine the identity of famous educational figures.

SUMMARY

1. **What was the nature and purpose of colonial education?**

   Much of colonial education took place in the home through dame schools, in the church, and through apprentice programs, with instruction dominated by religious teachings. In 1647, Massachusetts passed the "Old Deluder Satan Law," requiring every town to provide for education; although throughout the colonies, whites, males, and wealthier individuals were most likely to be schooled. Thomas Jefferson and Benjamin Franklin viewed the new nation's schools as a continuation of democratic principles and as a break from classist European traditions. By omitting any mention of education as a federal responsibility, the Constitution left schooling to the states, and so each state developed its own educational culture—although textbooks, from the rudimentary hornbook to the *McGuffey Reader*—created a minimal national curriculum. From colonial times to the present, continuing educational disputes include: the role of religion in schools, local control and state standards, and inequities in educational opportunities for women, people of color, and the poor.

2. **How did the Common School Movement promote universal education?**

   Nineteenth-century leader Horace Mann fought for the establishment of the common school, today's elementary school, and also for quality teacher education through normal schools. He believed that education should develop the talents of the poor as well as the wealthy.

3. **What developments mark the educational history of Native Americans?**

   In the early years, Native Americans (or Indians) were attacked by disease and warfare, and almost annihilated. During the nineteenth century, schools were used to "civilize" them into Western ways, degrading their culture, beliefs, and languages. While most Native Americans are currently in public schools, some are educated in private schools or through schools run by the Bureau of Indian Affairs (BIA).

4. **How did teaching become a "gendered" career?**

   Although teaching was initially "gendered" male, the advent of the common school created a demand for a large number of inexpensive teachers, and women were recruited. Since the late nineteenth century, teaching positions have been dominated by women, and teaching "re-gendered" female. Both female and male teachers continue to confront issues of sexuality and sexism. Gendered enclaves persist in today's schools, as women dominate elementary teaching, and men dominate certain academic specialties and leadership positions.

5. **How did secondary schools evolve?**

   The first publicly supported secondary school was the English Classical School in Boston. As America became more industrial and urban, public support for high schools grew, and the Kalamazoo case (1874) created the legal basis for high school funding. By the twentieth century, junior high schools and middle schools were established.

6. **How have twentieth century reform efforts influenced schools?**

   From the Committee of Ten in 1892 to the 1989 National Education Summit, waves of educational reform have become part of the American landscape. While the purpose of reform movements vary, one idea remains key: Schools should have a central role in maintaining a vibrant democracy.

www.mhhe.com/ sadker8e

CHAPTER REVIEW

Go to the Online Learning Center to take a quiz, practice with key terms, and review concepts from the chapter.

7. **What were the main tenets of the Progressive Education movement?**

Progressivism, led by John Dewey, emphasized learning by doing and shaping curricula around children's interests, but has frequently been attacked. Extremists of the 1950s saw progressivism as communistic, and after the 1957 Soviet *Sputnik* launching, progressivism was blamed for America's poor science and math performance.

8. **What role has the federal government played in American education?**

While the Constitution leaves the responsibility for schooling to the states, the federal government has played an increasing role in education over the past century, promoting teacher training, science and math instruction, and desegregation. More recently, the emphasis has been on school standards and testing.

9. **How did history shape the educational experiences of African Americans, Hispanics, Asian Americans/Pacific Islanders, and Arab Americans?**

Despite a national commitment to educate all citizens, bias and discrimination characterize the histories of many of ethnic and racial groups. The doctrine of "separate but equal" (*Plessey* v. *Ferguson*) was the law of the land until the 1954 *Brown* decision. Today, more than half a century after *Brown,* de facto resegregation has once again separated black and white. Hispanics (or Latinos) are now the largest minority group in the United States and face challenges in a culture that often fears people who speak another language. Asian is a broad label assigned to several billion people from a score of nations, and Asian Americans and Pacific Islanders are a rapidly growing population. Students from China, Japan and India are stereotyped as model minorities, a label that often masks the impact of prejudice on these children. Many Americans confuse Arabs and Moslems, mistaking Islam, a religion, with Arabs, a cultural group.

10. **What educational barriers and breakthroughs have girls and women experienced?**

For much of this nation's history, females were denied access to or segregated within schools. Although options have improved dramatically for girls and women, much of that progress due to Title IX, subtle bias continues to send boys and girls down different career paths.

11. **Who are some of the influential individuals who have helped fashion today's schools?**

Each of the chapters in this text highlights a significant educator through the *Profile in Education* feature. In this chapter, 14 noted educators from eighteenth-century Rousseau to twentieth-century Paulo Freire are profiled.

THE *TEACHERS, SCHOOLS, AND SOCIETY* READER WITH CLASSROOM OBSERVATION VIDEO CLIPS

Go to your *Teachers, Schools, and Society* Reader CD-ROM to:

READ CURRENT AND HISTORICAL ARTICLES

7.1 **Hamilton High:** From the 1950s through the 1980s, this case presents how a school has changed in reaction to societal and educational changes.

OBSERVE TEACHERS, STUDENTS, AND CLASSROOMS IN ACTION

Classroom Observation: Progressivism in Action

John Dewey believed in learning by doing, one of the keystones of progressive education. In this observation you will observe students in an American Civics class learning about the law by role playing different legal cases. In this instance, the students are arguing the pledge of allegiance case.

KEY TERMS AND PEOPLE

KEY TERMS

academy, 271, 280

American Spelling Book, 272

apprenticeship, 268

behaviorism, 306

Brown v. *Board of Education of Topeka,* 287

Cardinal Principles of Secondary Education, 279

Carnegie unit, 279

Committee of Ten, 279

common school, 271

dame schools, 268

de facto segregation, 286

de jure segregation, 286

elementary school, 271

English Classical School, 277

Franklin Academy, 271

gendered career, 276

hornbook, 272

in loco parentis, 268

Kalamazoo, Michigan, case, 278

kindergarten, 301

Land Ordinance Act, 284

Latin grammar school, 268

McGuffey Readers, 272

Montessori schools, 304

A Nation at Risk: The Imperative for Educational Reform, 279

National Defense Education Act (NDEA), 284

New England Primer, 272

normal schools, 273

Northwest Ordinance, 284

Old Deluder Satan Law, 268

Pedagogy of the Oppressed, 308

Plessy v. *Ferguson,* 286

progressive education, 281

second-generation segregation, 288

separate but equal, 286

Tenth Amendment, 284

KEY PEOPLE

Sylvia Ashton-Warner, 307

Mary McLeod Bethune, 305

Kenneth Clark, 308

Prudence Crandall, 303

John Dewey, 281, 305

Benjamin Franklin, 271

Paulo Reglus Neves Freire, 308

Friedrich Froebel, 300

Johann Herbart, 301

Thomas Jefferson, 270

Horace Mann, 302

Maria Montessori, 304

Jean Piaget, 306

Jean-Jacques Rousseau, 300

Burrhus Frederick (B. F.) Skinner, 306

Emma Hart Willard, 301

DISCUSSION QUESTIONS AND ACTIVITIES

www.mhhe.com/
sadker8e

WEB-*TIVITIES*
Go to the Online
Learning Center to do
the following activities:
1. Historical Events and
   Trends: Shaping
   American Education
2. American Schools of the
   Past: A Day in the Life
3. Early Textbooks
4. The Education Hall
   of Fame
5. American Schools:
   What's in a Name?

1. In the colonial period, a number of factors influenced the kind of education you might receive. Describe how the following factors influenced educational opportunities:
   - Geography
   - Wealth
   - Race/ethnicity
   - Gender

2. Progressive education has sparked adamant critics and fervent supporters. Offer several arguments supporting the tenets of progressivism, as well as arguments against this movement.

3. In what ways are terms like African American, Asian Americans, Hispanic Americans, or Arab Americans helpful? In what ways are these labels misleading?

4. Identify the contributions made by the following educators, whom some might consider candidates for the Hall of Fame: Septima Poinsette Clark, Madeline C. Hunter, Charlotte Hawkins Brown, Johnetta Cole, Joyce Ladner, Henri Mann.

5. Some teacher preparation programs do not consider or discuss the history of education, while other programs devote courses reviewing and analyzing educational history. Set up a debate (or use another *academic controversy* strategy) arguing the pros and cons of the following proposition. Resolved: Teacher preparation programs should focus on current issues and not consider the history of education.

REEL TO REAL TEACHING

You can find a wealth of classic movies with an education twist. Watch one of the four oldies but goodies described here, or visit the classics section of your local video store and check out a film "new" to you.

BLACKBOARD JUNGLE (1955)
Run Time: 101 minutes

Synopsis: The story of an idealistic teacher on his first job in a tough, urban, all male high school. A shocking film for its time, *Blackboard Jungle* was banned in some cities for its multiracial content and fear that it would spark violence.

THE MIRACLE WORKER (1962)
Run Time: 107 minutes

Synopsis: The true story of Anne Sullivan's devotion to teaching Helen Keller—a girl whose childhood illness caused her to become blind and deaf—how to communicate.

TO KILL A MOCKINGBIRD (1962)
Run Time: 129 minutes

Synopsis: Atticus Finch, a lawyer and single parent in a small Southern town during the Great Depression, defends an African American man wrongfully accused of raping a white woman. During the trial, his children and the community learn lessons of racial and disability tolerance.

TO SIR, WITH LOVE (1967)
Run Time: 105 minutes

Synopsis: Unable to find work as an engineer, an African American engineer accepts a teaching job in the slums of London. To motivate his rebellious students, he rejects traditional textbooks and lectures, and endeavors to earn their trust through unorthodox instruction.

Reflection:

1. Does the film you viewed remind you of a current issue? Which one(s)? Describe the similarities and differences.

2. What elements of effective teaching did you observe in the film? Is good teaching in the 1950s and 1960s still considered good teaching today?

3. Would you like to teach in the school depicted in the film? Why or why not?

Follow-up Activity: If there were an Education History Movie Hall of Fame, which classic film would you honor? Visit the *Reel to Real Teaching* on our Web site and post your nomination. Tell us why this film is a timeless winner!

How do you rate these films? Go to *Reel to Real Teaching* review these films.

www.mhhe.com/
sadker8e

FOR FURTHER READING

American Education, by Wayne Urban and Jennings Wagoner, Jr. (3rd ed., 2004). Chronicles the history of American education from precolonial times to the present, setting the discussion against the broader backdrop of national and world events.

The American School 1642–2004, by Joel Spring (2005). A critical analysis of the economic, political, and multicultural forces that have shaped education from colonial times to the present.

Cultural History and Education, by Thomas Popkewitz, Barry Franklin, and Miguel Pereyra (2001). Traces historical changes in the definitions of student, teacher, school, and community across Europe, Latin America, and North America.

Echoes of Brown, by Michelle Fine (2004). Integrating a book and DVD, *Echoes of Brown* features a performance by a diverse ensemble of youth from suburban and urban schools who speak of the victories and continuing struggles for justice and democracy in public schools.

Images of Schoolteachers in America, by Pamela Bolotin Joseph and Gail Burnaford (Editors) (2001). The question "What does it mean to be a teacher during the past 100 years?" is explored through a variety of media including film, television, portraits, photographs, fiction, comic strips, oral histories, and poetry.

A Place to be Navajo: Rough Rock and the Struggle for Self-Determination in Indigenous Schooling, by Teresa L. McCarty (2002). An ethnographic account of the Rough Rock Demonstration School in Arizona, home of the first American Indian community-controlled school. The author uses Indigenous oral testimony to describe this community's struggle for language, culture, and education rights. She also discusses the broader implications of the Rough Rock experience for self-determination by Indigenous communities elsewhere.

313

CHAPTER 8

Philosophy of Education

FOCUS QUESTIONS

1. What is a philosophy of education, and why should it be important to you?
2. How do teacher-centered philosophies of education differ from student-centered philosophies of education?
3. What are some major philosophies of education in the United States today?
4. How are these philosophies reflected in school practices?
5. What are some of the psychological and cultural factors influencing education?
6. What were the contributions of Socrates, Plato, and Aristotle to Western philosophy, and how is their legacy reflected in education today?
7. How do metaphysics, epistemology, ethics, political philosophy, aesthetics, and logic factor into a philosophy of education?

www.mhhe.com/
sadker8e

WHAT DO YOU THINK? What is your philosophy of education? Take an electronic version of the quiz on pages 317–318. Then, submit your responses to see how they compare to those of your colleagues.

CHAPTER PREVIEW

The root for the word **philosophy** is made up of two Greek words: *philo*, meaning "love," and *sophos*, meaning "wisdom." For thousands of years, philosophers have been wrestling with fundamental questions: What is most real—the physical world or the realm of mind and spirit? What is the basis of human knowledge? What is the nature of the just society? Educators must take stances on such questions before they can determine what and how students should be taught.

Since educators do not always agree on the answers to these questions, different philosophies of education have emerged. Although there are some similarities, there are also profound differences in the way leading educators define the purpose of education, the role of the teacher, the nature of the curriculum and assessment, and the method of instruction.

This chapter is intended to start you on a path of thoughtfully considering your values and beliefs. Five influential philosophies will be described, and you will see how each can shape classroom life. We invite you to consider how psychological and cultural beliefs can also affect schools. We then revisit the roots of Western philosophy with three ancient Greeks as our guides: Socrates, Plato, and Aristotle. Finally, we briefly examine the building blocks of philosophy, the divisions within philosophy that focus on questions pertinent to educators (what is of worth? how do we know what we know?). The ideas in this chapter will spark some very basic questions about your role in the classroom, and the school's role in society. Your answers to these questions will help you frame your philosophy of education.

Finding Your Philosophy of Education

What is a philosophy of education? Do you have one? Do you think it matters? If you are like most people, you probably have not given much thought to philosophy, in education or elsewhere. Being a practical person, you may be more concerned with other questions: Will I enjoy teaching? Will I be good at it? How will I handle discipline problems? Believe it or not, underlying the answers to these practical questions *is* your philosophy of education.

At this point, your philosophy may still be taking shape (not a bad thing). Your beliefs may reflect an amalgam of different philosophies. Unfortunately, they may also be filled with inconsistencies. In order to help you shape a coherent and useful educational philosophy, you must consider some basic—and very important—questions, such as:

What is the purpose of education?

What content and skills should schools teach?

How should schools teach this content?

What are the proper roles for teachers and students?

Still not sure what a philosophy of education is all about, or how it shapes classroom and school life? Let's listen to some teachers discussing the direction a new charter school should take. You'll see that each teacher has very clear ideas about what schools are for, what students should learn, and how teachers should teach.

Hear that noise coming from the faculty room down the hall? Your potential colleagues sometimes get a bit loud as they debate the possible directions for the new charter school. As you listen in, try to sort out which of these educational directions appeals to you.

JACK POLLACK: I am so excited! This new charter school can be just what we need, a chance to reestablish a positive reputation for the quality of public education! Let's face it, we are competing in a global economy, against nations whose students outscore ours on all the standardized tests that matter. It's embarrassing. If we can create a rigorous school (I'd prefer to call it an "Academy") with tough standards and a real commitment to learning, then look out! We'll make those "preppie" kids from Country Day School sorry they ever opted out of the public school system. I'd love to see a school with a strict code of conduct and core courses, like literature, history, math, and science, without those silly electives like "mass media." I would love to see our students wear uniforms and enroll in courses at the Advanced Placement level. What a great school not only for kids to learn, but for us to teach! It's all about rigorous standards.

MYRA MILLER: Jack, you and I both would like to teach in a more rigorous school, one with a tougher curriculum. But I am getting tired of standards and testing. I'll tell you a secret: I don't much care whether South Korean kids score better than Americans on some silly short answer test. I'm interested in a school committed to learning, not testing or competing. The new school should replace these boring textbooks with Great Books, books that intrigue, entice, and teach. Kids thirst for meaningful ideas. The school I envision would focus on classic works of literature and art. We would teach through intellectual questioning, a

"Socratic dialogue." What exciting discussions we could have about *The Old Man and the Sea,* Plato's *Republic,* and Homer's *Iliad.* Maybe we can re-invent the all-but-extinct American student: One who knows not only how to read, but a student who actually *wants* to read, *enjoys* reading, and best of all, knows how to *think.* Jack, I like the name you came up with—"Academy"—but I want our new charter school to create great minds, not just great test scores.

MARK WASHINGTON: I agree with Myra that we need to move beyond today's tyranny of testing, but Hemingway and Homer are not the answers. Problem is, we have more relevant issues and skills to deal with, issues never dreamed of in Plato's or Shakespeare's day. Our job as teachers is to make certain that our students can do well in the real world. We must be practical. Let me give you an example: When I was in eighth grade, my class took a three-week trip around the Midwestern states by train. Most of the semester was spent planning this trip. We worked together, researching different areas of the region and deciding where to go. We learned how to read train schedules and maps because we had to. We had to be organized and run meetings effectively. Math, history, geography, writing . . . talk about an integrated curriculum! We learned by doing. I still remember that trip and what went into it as a high point in my life. I want all students to have that kind of intense experience, to learn how to solve real world problems, not just answer test questions or discuss books.

TED GOODHEART: I want students to do more than simply fit into society; I want them to leave the world a better place than they found it. Behind our community's pretty façade are people in pain. We need to educate kids to care more about these people than we did. One out of six children is born into poverty here. One out of six! I want to teach kids to make a difference, and not let books and homework insulate them from real world concerns. The new charter school must equip children to tackle issues like poverty, violence, pollution, bigotry, and injustice. We need to prepare students with both a social conscience and the political skills needed to improve our society. I want to teach students whose actions will make me, and all of us, proud. Teaching in a socially responsible charter school would be my dream.

CARA CAMUS: Everyone in this room has been trying to design a charter school backwards, thinking mostly about what we teachers think. Here's a revolutionary idea: Let's build an education around the students. Why not have the students decide what they will learn? Students must assume primary responsibility for their own learning. I would like our charter school staffed by teachers who are skilled in facilitating and counseling children to reach their personal goals. Believe it or not, I trust students, and I would give every child (even the youngest or least able) an equal voice in decision making. It's not enough to slowly reform education; we need to rebuild it from the center, from where the students are.

As you might have suspected, these teachers are not only discussing different approaches to a proposed charter school, they are also shedding light on five major educational philosophies. Do any of these diverse views sound attractive to you? Do any sound particularly unappealing? If so, note which of these teachers you thought reflected your own beliefs, and which were really off the mark. If you found that you had strong opinions—pro or con—about one or more of these teachers' positions, then you are beginning to get in touch with your educational philosophy. Let's leave the faculty room conversation, and take a closer, more orderly look at your own philosophical leanings. The following inventory can help you sort out tenets of your educational philosophy.

 ## Inventory of Philosophies of Education

As you read through each of the following statements about schools and teaching, decide how strongly you agree or disagree. In a bit, we will help you interpret your results. Write your response to the left of each statement, using the following scale:

5   Agree strongly

4   Agree

3   Neither agree nor disagree

2   Disagree

1   Disagree strongly

_____ 1. A school curriculum should include a common body of information that all students should know.

_____ 2. The school curriculum should focus on the great ideas that have survived through time.

_____ 3. The gap between the real world and schools should be bridged through field trips, internships, and adult mentors.

_____ 4. Schools should prepare students for analyzing and solving the social problems they will face beyond the classroom.

_____ 5. Each student should determine his or her individual curriculum, and teachers should guide and help them.

_____ 6. Students should not be promoted from one grade to the next until they have read and mastered certain key material.

_____ 7. Schools, above all, should develop students' abilities to think deeply, analytically, and creatively, rather than focus on transient concerns like social skills and current trends.

_____ 8. Whether inside or outside the classroom, teachers must stress the relevance of what students are learning to real and current events.

_____ 9. Education should enable students to recognize injustices in society, and schools should promote projects to redress social inequities.

_____ 10. Students who do not want to study much should not be required to do so.

_____ 11. Teachers and schools should emphasize academic rigor, discipline, hard work, and respect for authority.

_____ 12. Education is not primarily about workers and the world economic competition; learning should be appreciated for its own sake, and students should enjoy reading, learning, and discussing intriguing ideas.

_____ 13. The school curriculum should be designed by teachers to respond to the experiences and needs of the students.

_____ 14. Schools should promote positive group relationships by teaching about different ethnic and racial groups.

_____ 15. The purpose of school is to help students understand themselves, appreciate their distinctive talents and insights, and find their own unique place in the world.

_____ 16. For the United States to be competitive economically in the world marketplace, schools must bolster their academic requirements in order to train more competent workers.

_____ 17. Teachers ought to teach from the classics, because important insights related to many of today's challenges and concerns are found in these Great Books.

_____ 18. Since students learn effectively through social interaction, schools should plan for substantial social interaction in their curricula.

_____ 19. Students should be taught how to be politically literate, and learn how to improve the quality of life for all people.

_____ 20. The central role of the school is to provide students with options and choices. The student must decide what and how to learn.

_____ 21. Schools must provide students with a firm grasp of basic facts regarding the books, people, and events that have shaped the nation's heritage.

_____ 22. The teacher's main goal is to help students unlock the insights learned over time, so they can gain wisdom from the great thinkers of the past.

_____ 23. Students should be active participants in the learning process, involved in democratic class decision making and reflective thinking.

_____ 24. Teaching should mean more than simply transmitting the Great Books, which are replete with biases and prejudices. Rather, schools need to identify a new list of Great Books more appropriate for today's world, and prepare students to create a better society than their ancestors did.

_____ 25. Effective teachers help students to discover and develop their personal values, even when those values conflict with traditional ones.

_____ 26. Teachers should help students constantly reexamine their beliefs. In history, for example, students should learn about those who have been historically omitted: the poor, the non-European, women, and people of color.

_____ 27. Frequent objective testing is the best way to determine what students know. Rewarding students when they learn, even when they learn small things, is the key to successful teaching.

_____ 28. Education should be a responsibility of the family and community, rather than delegated to formal and impersonal institutions, such as schools.

Interpreting Your Responses

Write your responses to statements 1 through 25 in the columns on the next page, tally up your score in each column. (We will return to items 26 to 28 in a bit.) Each column is labeled with a philosophy and the name of the teacher who represented that view in this chapter's opening scenario (the charter school discussion). The highest possible score in any one column is 25, and the lowest possible score is 5. Scores in the 20s indicate strong agreement, and scores below 10 indicate disagreement with the tenets of a particular philosophy.

A	B	C	D	E
Essentialism (Jack)	Perennialism (Myra)	Progressivism (Mark)	Social Reconstructionism (Ted)	Existentialism (Cara)
1. _____	2. _____	3. _____	4. _____	5. _____
6. _____	7. _____	8. _____	9. _____	10. _____
11. _____	12. _____	13. _____	14. _____	15. _____
16. _____	17. _____	18. _____	19. _____	20. _____
21. _____	22. _____	23. _____	24. _____	25. _____
Scores _____	_____	_____	_____	_____

Your scores in columns A through E, respectively, represent how much you agree or disagree with the beliefs of five major educational philosophies: essentialism, perennialism, progressivism, social reconstructionism, and existentialism. Check back to see if your scores reflect your initial reactions to these teachers' points of view. For example, if you agreed with Jack's proposal to create an "Academy," then you probably agreed with a number of the statements associated with essentialist education, and your score in this column may be fairly high.

Compare your five scores. What is your highest? What is your lowest? Which three statements best reflect your views on education? Are they congruent and mutually supporting? Looking at the statements that you least support, what do these statements tell you about your values? You may notice that your philosophical leanings, as identified by your responses to statements in the inventory, reflect your general outlook on life. For example, your responses may indicate whether you generally trust people to do the right thing, or if you believe that individuals need supervision. How have your culture, religion, upbringing, and political beliefs shaped your responses to the items in this inventory? How have your own education and life experiences influenced your philosophical beliefs?

Now that you have begun to examine varying beliefs about education, you may even want to lay claim to a philosophical label. But what do these philosophical labels mean? In the following pages we will introduce you to all five of these educational philosophies, and look at their impact in the classroom.

www.mhhe.com/
sadker8e

INTERACTIVE ACTIVITY

Where Do You Stand on the Philosophy Spectrum? Note where you think your philosophy of education falls, and compare where you stand to where your colleagues do.

Five Philosophies of Education

Essentialism, perennialism, progressivism, social reconstructionism, and existentialism. Taken together, these five schools of thought do not exhaust the list of possible educational philosophies you may consider, but they present strong frameworks for you to refine your own educational philosophy. We can place these five philosophies on a continuum, from teacher-centered (some would say "authoritarian"), to student-centered (some would characterize as "permissive").

Are you politically conservative or liberal? (Great, now we are bringing politics into this discussion.) Actually, your political stance is one predictor of your

IMAGINE . . .

Reflection

After a hectic school year, Kentucky High school graduate Juan C. avoided the beach graduation celebration and chose instead to spend the week in reflection at a Trappist monastery. The student explained: We spend a lot of time nourishing our bodies, but we spend little time nourishing our souls.   •

SOURCE: *American School Board Journal,* 1998.

FIGURE 8.1

Teacher- and student-centered philosophies of education.

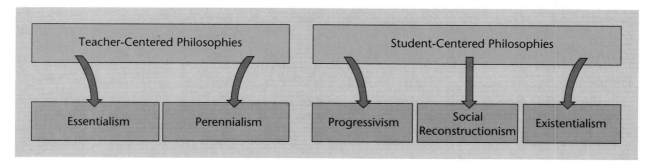

Teacher-Centered Philosophies		Student-Centered Philosophies		
Essentialism	Perennialism	Progressivism	Social Reconstructionism	Existentialism

REFLECTION: Check back with your scores on the Inventory of Philosophies in Education (p. 319). Now consider your scores in terms of teacher- or student-centered philosophies. What does this tell you about your own educational priorities?

educational philosophy. Traditionalists often champion teacher-centered philosophies and practices that emphasize the values and knowledge that have survived through time, while those committed to change find student-centered approaches more to their liking. (See Figure 8.1).

Let's begin our discussion with the teacher-centered philosophies, for they have exerted significant influence on American education during the past two decades.

 ## Teacher-Centered Philosophies

Traditionally, **teacher-centered philosophies** emphasize the importance of transferring knowledge, information, and skills from the older (presumably wiser) generation to the younger one. The teacher's role is to instill respect for authority, perseverance, duty, consideration, and practicality. When students demonstrate through tests and writings that they are competent in academic subjects and traditional skills, and through their actions that they have disciplined minds and adhere to traditional morals and behavior, then both the school and the teacher have been successful. (If you recall from Chapter 4, "Schools: Choices and Challenges," these philosophies view the primary purpose of schools as "passing the cultural baton.") The major teacher-centered philosophies of education are essentialism and perennialism.

Essentialism

Essentialism strives to teach students the accumulated knowledge of our civilization through core courses in the traditional academic disciplines. Essentialists aim to instill students with the "essentials" of academic knowledge, patriotism, and character development. This traditional or **back-to-basics** approach is meant to train the mind, promote reasoning, and ensure a common culture among all Americans.

American educator **William Bagley** popularized the term *essentialism* in the 1930s,[1] and essentialism has been a dominant influence in American education since World War II. Factors such as the launching of *Sputnik* in 1957, the 1983 report *A Nation at Risk,* intense global economic competition and increased immigration into the United States have all kept essentialism at center stage. Some educators refer to the present period as neoessentialism because of the increased core graduation requirements, stronger standards and more testing of both students and teachers.

Whether they call themselves essentialists or neoessentialists, educators in this camp are concerned that the influx of immigrants threatens American culture. In response, they call for rigorous schools teaching a single, unifying body of knowledge for all Americans. One of the leading essentialists, **E. D. Hirsch, Jr.,** authored *Cultural Literacy: What Every American Needs To Know,* and *The Schools We Need and Why We Don't Have Them.* Hirsch provides lists of people, events, literature, historical facts, scientific breakthroughs, and the like, lists that specify what students at every grade level should know to be "culturally literate."

Most of you reading this chapter have been educated in essentialist schools. You were probably required to take many courses in English, history, math, and science but were able to enroll in only a few electives. Such a program would be typical in an essentialist school.

The Essentialist Classroom Essentialists urge that traditional disciplines such as math, science, history, foreign language, and literature form the foundation of the curriculum, which is referred to as the **core curriculum.** Essentialists frown upon electives that "water-down" academic content. Elementary students receive instruction in skills such as writing, reading, measuring, and computing. Even when studying art and music, subjects most often associated with the development of creativity, students master a body of information and basic techniques, gradually moving to more complex skills and detailed knowledge. Only by mastering the required material are students promoted to the next higher level.

Essentialists maintain that classrooms should be oriented around the teacher, who should serve as an intellectual and moral role model for the students. The teachers or administrators decide what is most important for the students to learn and place little emphasis on student interests, particularly when such interests divert time and attention from the academic curriculum. Essentialist teachers rely on achievement test scores to evaluate progress. Essentialists expect that students will leave school possessing not only basic skills and an extensive body of knowledge, but also disciplined, practical minds, capable of applying schoolhouse lessons in the real world.

Essentialism in Action: Rancho Elementary School Rancho Elementary School in Marin County, California, proudly promotes its essentialist philosophy, and announces on its Web page that "students will participate in a highly enriched environment exposing them to rigorous academics, foreign language, citizenship/ leadership opportunities, and grade appropriate technology." Its mission is the acquisition of basic skills through direct instruction in the core academic areas, including reading through phonics. As a testament to its success, the school boasts high test scores. Beyond academics, the school also emphasizes "firm, consistent discipline" and close parent-teacher relationships.

If you do not live in Marin County, you may not have heard of Rancho, but you may have heard of a school belonging to The Coalition of Essential Schools, as 200 schools nationwide are members. But don't be misled by the name. Although these schools promote intellectual rigor, test students for mastery of information, and emphasize strong thinking skills across subjects, they are not pure examples of essentialism. The schools do not share a fixed core curriculum, they emphasize the study of single topics or issues in depth, and incorporate components of perennialism, which brings us to the other teacher-centered philosophy.

Perennialism

Perennialism is a cousin to essentialism. Both advocate teacher-centered classrooms. Both tolerate little flexibility in the curriculum. Both implement rigorous standards. Both aim to sharpen students' intellectual powers and enhance their moral qualities. So what are the differences?

Perennialists organize their schools around books, ideas, and concepts and criticize essentialists for the vast amount of factual information they require students to absorb in their push for "cultural literacy." Perennial means "everlasting"—a perennialist education focuses on enduring themes and questions that span the ages. Perennialists recommend that students learn directly from the **Great Books**—works by history's finest thinkers and writers, books as meaningful today as when they were first written.

Perennialists believe that the goal of education should be to develop rational thought and to discipline minds to think rigorously. Perennialists see education as a sorting mechanism, a way to identify and prepare the intellectually gifted for leadership, while providing vocational training for the rest of society. They lament the change in universities over the centuries, from institutions where a few gifted students (and teachers) rigorously pursued truth for its own sake, to a glorified training ground for future careers.

Those of you who received a religious education might recognize the perennialist philosophy. Many parochial schools reflect the perennialist tradition with a curriculum that focuses on analyzing great religious books (such as the *Bible, Talmud,* or *Koran*), discerning moral truths, and honoring these moral values. In the classroom description that follows, we will concentrate on secular perennialism as formulated in the twentieth-century United States by such individuals as Robert Hutchins and Mortimer Adler.

The Perennialist Classroom As in an essentialist classroom, students in a perennialist classroom spend considerable time and energy mastering the three "Rs," reading, 'riting, and 'rithmetic. Greatest importance is placed on reading, the key to unlocking the enduring ideas found in the Great Books. Special attention is given to teaching values and character training, often through discussion about the underlying values and moral principles in a story. (Former Secretary of Education Bill Bennett wrote a collection of such stories in 1993, entitled *Book of Virtues.*) High school marks an increase in academic rigor as more challenging books are explored, including works of Darwin, Homer, and Shakespeare. Few elective choices are allowed. In an extreme example, in his **Paideia Proposal,** published in 1982, **Mortimer Adler** proposed a single elementary and secondary curriculum for all students, with no curricular electives except in the choice of a second language.

Electives are not the only things perennialists go without. You find few if any textbooks in a perennialist class. **Robert Hutchins,** who as president of the University of Chicago introduced the Great Books program, once opined that textbooks "have probably done as much to degrade the American intelligence as any single force."[2] Because perennialist teachers see themselves as discussion seminar leaders and facilitators, lectures are rare. Current concerns like multiculturalism, gender stereotypes, or computer technology would find no place in a perennialist curriculum.

While both essentialism and perennialism promote a conservative, status quo approach to education and schools, these teacher-centered philosophies draw their curricula from different sources. The first column includes excerpts from a typical essentialist list (we included a few of the words and phrases under the letter "c"); the second column provides selections from the perennialists' *Great Books* curriculum. Remember, these are only a few suggestions from very long lists!

The List (Essentialism)

centigrade	Calvary
center of gravity	cast pearls before swine
cerebellum	Cascade Mountains
carry coals to Newcastle	cadre
capital expenditure	catharsis
Cèzanne	carbon dioxide
Canberra	carte blanche
Cain and Abel	Caruso, Enrico
Caesar Augustus	cathode ray tube
Candide	

Great Books (Perennialism)

Aristotle, *Sense and Sensible*

The Bible

Geoffrey Chaucer, *Canterbury Tales*

Charles Darwin, *On the Origin of Species*

Charles Dickens, *Oliver Twist*

F. Scott Fitzgerald, *The Great Gatsby*

Homer, *The Iliad*

Henry James, *In the Cage*

James Joyce, *Ulysses*

The Koran

Thomas Mann, *Death in Venice*

Karl Marx, *Das Kapital*

Herman Melville, *Moby Dick*

George Orwell, *Animal Farm*

Thomas Paine, *Common Sense*

Plato, *Charmides*

Jonathan Swift, *Gulliver's Travels*

Virginia Woolf, *Night and Day*

Leo Tolstoy, *War and Peace*

REFLECTION: How many of these names and terms can you identify? Does this list make you feel culturally literate—or illiterate? Do you believe that lists like this one should be important? Why or why not?

While critics chastise perennialists for the lack of women, people of color, and non-Western ideas in the Great Books they teach, many perennialists are unmoved by such criticism. To them, "training the mind" is ageless, beyond demographic concerns and transient trends. As Mortimer Adler wrote,

> The Great Books of ancient and medieval as well as modern times are a repository of knowledge and wisdom, a tradition of culture which must initiate each generation.[3]

Perennialism in Action: St. John's College The best-known example of perennialist education today takes place at a private institution unaffiliated with any religion: St. John's College, founded in 1784 in Annapolis, Maryland (www.sjcsf.edu). St. John's College adopted the Great Books as a core curriculum in 1937 and assigns readings in the fields of literature, philosophy and theology, history and the social sciences, mathematics and natural science, and music. Students write extensively and attend seminars twice weekly to discuss assigned readings. They also complete a number of laboratory experiences and tutorials in language, mathematics, and music, guided by the faculty, who are called *tutors*. Seniors take oral examinations at the beginning and end of their senior year and write a final essay that must be approved before they are allowed to graduate.

Although grades are given in order to facilitate admission to graduate programs, students receive their grades only upon request and are expected to learn only for learning's sake. Since the St. John's experience thrives best in a small-group atmosphere, the college established a second campus in 1964 in Santa Fe, New Mexico, to handle additional enrollment.

Student-Centered Philosophies

Student-centered philosophies are less authoritarian, less concerned with the past and "training the mind," and more focused on individual needs, contemporary relevance, and preparing students for a changing future. Progressivism, social reconstructionism, and existentialism place the learner at the center of the educational process: Students and teachers work together on determining what should be learned and how best to learn it. School is not seen as an institution that controls and directs youth, or works to preserve and transmit the core culture, but as an institution that works with youth to improve society or help students realize their individuality.

Progressivism

Progressivism organizes schools around the concerns, curiosity, and real-world experiences of students. The progressive teacher facilitates learning by helping students formulate meaningful questions and devise strategies to answer those questions. Answers are not drawn from lists or even Great Books; they are discovered through real world experience. Progressivism is the educational application of a philosophy called pragmatism. According to **pragmatism,** the way to determine if an idea has merit is simple: test it. If the idea works in the real world, then it has merit. Both pragmatism and progressivism originated in America, the home of a very practical and pragmatic people. John Dewey refined and applied pragmatism to education, establishing what became known as progressivism.

John Dewey was a reformer with a background in philosophy and psychology who taught that people learn best through social interaction in the real world. Dewey believed that because social learning had meaning, it endured. Book learning, on the other hand, was no substitute for actually doing things. Progressivists do not believe that the mind can be disciplined through reading Great Books, rather that the mind should be trained to analyze experience thoughtfully and draw conclusions objectively.

Dewey saw education as an opportunity to learn how to apply previous experiences in new ways. Dewey believed that students, facing an ever-changing world, should master the scientific method: (1) Become aware of a problem; (2) define it; (3) propose various hypotheses to solve it; (4) examine the consequences of each hypothesis in the light of previous experience; and (5) test the most likely solution. (For a biography of John Dewey, see the "Hall of Fame: Profiles in Education" in Chapter 7.)

Dewey regarded democracy and freedom as far superior to the political ideas of earlier times. Dewey saw traditional, autocratic, teacher-centered schools as the antithesis of democratic ideals. He viewed progressive schools as a working model of democracy. Dewey wrote:

> To imposition from above is opposed expression and cultivation of individuality; to external discipline is opposed free activity; to learning from texts and teachers, learning through experience; to acquisition of isolated skills and techniques by drill is opposed acquisition of them as means of attaining ends which make direct vital appeal; to preparation for a more or less remote future is opposed making the most of the opportunities of present life; to statistics and materials is opposed acquaintance with a changing world.[4]

The Progressive Classroom Walk into a progressivist classroom, and you will not find a teacher standing at the front of the room talking to rows of seated students. Rather, you will likely see children working in small groups, moving about and talking freely. Some children might be discussing a science experiment, while another group works on a model volcano, and a third prepares for a presentation. Interest centers would be located throughout the room, filled with books, materials, software, and projects designed to attract student interest on a wide array of topics. Finally you notice the teacher, walking around the room, bending over to talk with individual students and small groups, asking questions and making suggestions. You sense that the last thing on her mind is the standardized state test scheduled for next week.[5]

Progressivists build the curriculum around the experiences, interests, and abilities of students, and encourage students to work together cooperatively. Teachers feel no compulsion to focus their students' attention on one discrete discipline at a time, and students integrate several subjects in their studies. Thought-provoking activities augment reading, and a game like Monopoly might be used to illustrate the principles of capitalism versus socialism. Computer simulations, field trips, and interactive Web sites on the Internet offer realistic learning challenges for students, and build on students' multiple intelligences.

Progressivism in Action: The Laboratory School In 1896, while a professor at the University of Chicago, Dewey founded the Laboratory School as a testing ground for his educational ideas. Dewey's writings and his work with the **Laboratory School** set the stage for the progressive education movement. Based on the view that educators, like scientists, need a place to test their ideas, Dewey's Laboratory School eventually became the most famous experimental school in the history of U.S. education, a place where thousands observed Dewey's innovations in school design, methods, and curriculum. Although the school remained under Dewey's control for only eight years and never enrolled more than 140 students (ages 3 to 13) in a single year, its influence was enormous.

Dewey designed the Lab School with only one classroom but with several facilities for experiential learning: a science laboratory, an art room, a woodworking shop, and a kitchen. Children were likely to make their own weights and measures in the laboratory, illustrate their own stories in the art room, build a boat in the shop, and learn chemistry in the kitchen. They were unlikely to learn through isolated exercises or drills, which, according to Dewey, students consider irrelevant. Since Dewey believed that students learn from social interaction, the school used many group methods such as cooperative model-making, field trips, role-playing, and dramatizations. Dewey maintained that group techniques make the students better citizens, developing, for example, their willingness to share responsibilities.

Children in the Laboratory School were not promoted from one grade to another after mastering certain material. Rather, they were grouped according to their individual interests and abilities. For all its child-centered orientation, however, the Laboratory School remained hierarchical in the sense that the students were never given a role comparable to that of the staff in determining the school's educational practices.

Social Reconstructionism

Social reconstructionism encourages schools, teachers, and students to focus their studies and energies on alleviating pervasive social inequities, and as the name implies, reconstruct society into a new and more just social order. Although social reconstructionists agree with progressivists that schools should concentrate on the needs of students, they split from progressivism in the 1920s after growing impatient with the slow pace of change in schools and in society. **George Counts,** a student of Dewey, published his classic book, *Dare the Schools Build a New Social Order?*, in which he outlined a more ambitious, and clearly more radical, approach to education. Counts's book, written in 1932, was no doubt influenced by the human cost of the Great Depression. He proposed that schools focus on reforming society, an idea that caught the imagination and sparked the ideals of educators both in this country and abroad.

Social challenges and problems provide a natural (and moral) direction for curricular and instructional activities. Racism, sexism, environmental pollution, homelessness, poverty, substance abuse, homophobia, AIDS, and violence are rooted in misinformation and thrive in ignorance. Therefore, social reconstructionists believe that school is the ideal place to begin ameliorating social problems. The teacher's role is to explore social problems, suggest alternate perspectives, and facilitate student analysis of these problems. While convincing, cajoling, or moralizing about the importance of addressing human tragedy would be a natural teacher response, such adult-led decision-making flies in the face of reconstructionist philosophy. A social reconstructionist teacher must model democratic principles. Students and teachers are expected to live and learn in a democratic culture; the students themselves must select educational objectives and social priorities.

The Social Reconstructionist Classroom A social reconstructionist teacher creates lessons that both intellectually inform and emotionally stir students about the inequities that surround them. A class might read a book and visit a photojournalist's exhibit portraying violent acts of racism. If the book, exhibit, and the class discussion that follows move the students, the class might choose to pursue a long-term project to investigate the problem. One group of students might analyze news coverage of racial and ethnic groups in the community. Another student group might conduct a survey analyzing community perceptions of racial groups and race relations. Students might visit city hall and examine arrest and trial records in order to determine the role race plays in differential application of the law. Students might examine government records for information about housing patterns, income levels, graduation rates and other relevant statistics. The teacher's role would be as facilitator: assisting students in focusing their questions, developing a strategy, helping to organize visits, and ensuring that the data collected and analyzed meet standards of objectivity. Throughout, the teacher would be instructing students on research techniques, statistical evaluation, writing skills, and public communications.

In a social reconstructionist class, a research project is more than an academic exercise; the class is engaged in a genuine effort to improve society. In this case, the class might arrange to meet with political leaders, encouraging them to create programs or legislation to respond to issues the students uncovered. The students might seek a *pro bono* attorney to initiate legal action to remedy a social injustice they unmasked. Or perhaps the students might take their findings directly to the media by holding a press conference. They might also create a Web page to share their findings and research methods with students in other parts of the country, or other parts of the world. How would the teacher decide if the students have met the educational goals? In this example, an objective, well-prepared report would be one criterion, and reducing or eliminating a racist community practice would be a second measure of success.

Social Reconstructionism in Action: Paulo Freire **Paulo Freire** believed that schools were just another institution perpetuating social inequities while serving the interests of the dominant group. Like social reconstructionism itself, Freire's beliefs grew during the Great Depression of the 1930s, when he experienced hunger and poverty firsthand. Influenced by Marxist and neo-Marxist ideas, Freire accused schools of perpetuating the status quo views of the rich and powerful "for the purpose of keeping the masses submerged and content in a culture of silence."[6] Schools were endorsing **social Darwinism,** the idea that society is an ingenious "sorting" system, one in which the more talented rise to the top, while those less deserving find themselves at the bottom of the social and economic pecking order. The conclusion: Those with money deserve it, those without money deserve their lot in life, and poverty is a normal, preordained part of reality.

Freire rejected this conclusion. He did not believe that schools should be viewed as "banks," where the privileged deposit ideas like social Darwinism to be spoon fed into the limited minds of the dispossessed. He envisioned schools as a place where the poor can acquire the skills to regain control of their lives and influence the social and economic forces that locked them in poverty in the first place. Freire engaged the poor as equal partners in dialogues that explored their economic and social problems and possible solutions. Freire believed in **praxis,** the doctrine that when actions are based on sound theory and values, they can make a real difference in the world. (It is no accident that the term praxis is also the name given to the teacher competency tests required by many states.) Freire's ideas took hold not only in his native Brazil, but in poor areas around the globe. As poor farm workers became literate and aware, they organized for their self-improvement, and began to work for change. It is not surprising that the autocratic leaders of his country eventually forced him into exile, for he had turned schooling into a liberating force. (For a biography of Paulo Freire, see the "Hall of Fame: Profiles in Education" in Chapter 4.)

Existentialism

Existentialism, the final student-centered philosophy we shall discuss, places the highest priority on students directing their own learning. **Existentialism** asserts that the purpose of education is to help children find the meaning and direction in their lives, and it rejects the notion that adults should or could direct meaningful learning for children. Existentialists do not believe that "truth" is objective and applicable to all. Instead, each of us must look within ourselves to discover our own truth, our own purpose in life. Teaching students what adults believe they should learn is neither efficient nor effective; in fact, most of this "learning" will be forgotten. Instead, each student should decide what he or she needs to learn, and when to learn it. As the Buddhist proverb reminds us: When the student is ready, the teacher will appear.

There is little doubt that for many readers this is the most challenging of all the philosophies, and schools built on this premise will seem the most alien. We are a culture very connected to the outside world, and far less connected to our inner voice, or as an existentialist might say, our essence. We compete with each other for material goods, and we are distracted by hundreds of cable channels, iPods, and a constant array of external stimuli. Thinking about why we are here and finding our purpose in life is not what schools typically do, but existentialists believe it is precisely what they should do. Schools should help each of us answer the fundamental questions: Why am I here? What is my purpose?

The Existentialist Classroom   Existentialism in the classroom is a powerful rejection of traditional, and particularly essentialist, thinking. In the existentialist classroom, subject matter takes second place to helping the students understand and appreciate themselves as unique individuals. The teacher's role is to help students define their own essence by exposing them to various paths they may take in life and by creating an environment in which they can freely choose their way. Existentialism, more than

"Domephobia," the fear of things domestic, is Jane Roland Martin's word for gender bias in schools and in society. She coined the term when she compared the distinct educations Jean-Jacques Rousseau designed for his fictitious students Emile and Sophie. Martin was frustrated that while the boy, Emile, was said to revel in intellectual exploration, Sophie was to receive second-rate training—to be a wife and mother.

Martin deplores the disconnect between intellectual development and the development of abilities to love and care for a family. She recognizes that today's schools continue to craft different expectations for males and females. In fact, she knows this inequity firsthand. Teaching philosophy at the University of Massachusetts at Boston for over thirty years, Martin found herself fighting to have her intellectual voice heard in a traditional male discipline. Her experience of bias fueled her anger that equal opportunity education is still so far from reality.

Yet, Jane Roland Martin knows "women are barometers of change." Feminism today, like Sophie's education 300 years ago, gives men and women a special gift—a new perspective on gender roles. At the dawn of a new millennium, women's roles at work and in the family are indeed changing. Not only are women wives and mothers, they are corporate CEOs, medal-winning soccer players, and Supreme Court justices. Yet even as society may champion the greater earning power and talents of women, we are seeing a backlash against the more liberated roles of women. The trouble? The changes have cast as fiction the rosy Norman Rockwell portrait of the American family: More than half of all mothers work outside the home and single-parent homes number 1 in 5. These numbers stir concern that day care is bad, working mothers are neglectful and the well-being of the nation's children is threatened.

What society may see as problematic, Jane Roland Martin envisions as opportunity. Historically the physical, emotional, and social needs of children have been met by family, primarily mothers. Today, women are drawn by economic need and personal desire to enter the workforce. Martin sees these changes as a defining moment for schools, a chance to recreate within schools the nurturing tasks traditionally performed at home.

Martin's critics say no, schools should focus only on intellectual development. Not Martin. A social reconstructionist, she challenges schools to open their doors to what she calls the 3Cs—caring, concern, and connection. As more children are cared for outside the home, she fears the 3C curriculum is in danger of being lost. And American society has paid a heavy price for ignoring such domestic needs. Social inequalities continue and children are often the victims. Martin has an antidote: transform schoolhouses into "schoolhomes."

The schoolhome is far different from traditional "factory-model schooling which views children as raw material, teachers as workers who process their students before sending them on to the next station on the assembly line, [and] curriculum as the machinery that forges America's young into marketable products."[1] Instead, Martin's schoolhome focuses on students' individual emotional and cognitive needs. It embraces the experience of all learners and welcomes racial, cultural, and gender diversity. Martin's vision of schools reflects her vision of American society as everyone's home:

> Instead of focusing our gaze on abstract norms, standardized tests, generalized rates of success, and uniform outcomes, the ideas of the schoolhome direct action to actual educational practice. Of course a schoolhome will teach the 3Rs. But it will give equal emphasis to the 3Cs—not by designating formal courses in these but by being a domestic environment characterized by safety, security, nurturance, and love. In the schoolhome, mind and body, thought and action, reason and emotion are all educated.[2]

The schoolhome will incorporate the 3Cs into our very definition of what it means for males and females to be educated. Creating such nurturing and equitable schools will require "acts of both great and small, strategic and utterly outrageous. The cause demands no less, not one whit less."[3]

[1] Jane Roland Martin. *The Schoolhome: Rethinking Schools for Changing Families* (Cambridge, MA: Harvard University Press, 1992), p. 41. [2] Jane Roland Martin. "Women, School, and Cultural Wealth." In Connie Titone and Karen Maloney (eds.). *Thinking Through Our Mothers: Women's Philosophies of Education* (Upper Saddle River, NJ: Merrill, 1999), pp.161–62. [3] Jane Roland Martin. *Coming of Age in Academe: Rekindling Women's Hopes and Reforming the Academy* (New York: Routlege, 2000), p. 182.

REFLECTION: Do you agree with Jane Roland Martin that the 3Cs should be an integral part of the curriculum? Explain. Describe what a 3C curriculum might look like in schools today.

www.mhhe.com/ sadker8e

To learn more about Jane Roland Martin, click on *Profiles in Education.*

other educational philosophies, affords students great latitude in their choice of subject matter and activity.

The existentialist curriculum often emphasizes the humanities as a means of providing students with vicarious experiences that will help unleash their creativity and self-expression. For example, existentialists focus on the actions of historical individuals, each of whom provides a model for the students to explore. Math and the natural sciences may be de-emphasized because their subject matter is less fruitful for promoting self-awareness. Career education is regarded more as a means of teaching students about their potential than of teaching a livelihood. In art, existentialism encourages individual creativity and imagination more than it does the imitation of established models.

Existentialist learning is self-paced, self-directed, and includes a great deal of individual contact with the teacher. Honest interpersonal relationships are emphasized; roles and "official" status de-emphasized. According to philosopher Maxine Greene, teachers themselves must be deeply involved in their own learning and questioning: "Only a teacher in search of his freedom can inspire a student to search for his own." Greene asserts that education should move teachers and students to "wide awakeness," the ability to discover their own truths.[7]

Although elements of existentialism occasionally appear in public schools, this philosophy has not been widely disseminated. In an age of high-stakes tests and standards, only a few schools, mostly private, implement existentialist ideas. Even Summerhill, the well-known existentialist school founded in England by A. S. Neill in 1921, struggles to persevere with its unusual educational approach.

Existentialism in Action: The Sudbury Valley School   Visit Sudbury Valley School just outside of Boston, Massachusetts, look around, look closely, and you still may not see the school. The large building nestled next to a fishing pond on a 10-acre campus looks more like a mansion than a school. Walk inside, and you will find students and adults doing pretty much as they please. Not a "class" in sight. Some people are talking, some playing, some reading. A group is building a bookcase over there, a student is working on the computer in the corner, another is taking a nap on a chair. All ages mix freely, with no discernable grade level for any activity. In fact, it is even difficult to locate the teachers. If there is a curriculum, it is difficult to detect. Instead, the school offers a wide variety of educational options, including field trips to Boston, New York, and the nearby mountains and seacoast, and the use of facilities that include a laboratory, a woodworking shop, a computer room, a kitchen, a darkroom, an art room, and several music rooms.

Sudbury Valley provides a setting, an opportunity, but each student must decide what to do with that opportunity. Students are trusted to make their own decisions about learning. The school's purpose is to build on the students' natural curiosity, based on the belief that authentic learning takes place only when students initiate it. The school operates on the premise that all its students are creative, and each should be helped to discover and nurture his or her individual talents.

Sudbury Valley is fully accredited, and the majority of Sudbury Valley's graduates continue on to college. The school accepts anyone from 4-year-olds to adults and charges low tuition, so as not to exclude anyone. Evaluations or grades are given only on request. A high school diploma is awarded to those who complete relevant requirements, which mainly focus on the ability to be a responsible member of the community at large. More than 30 schools follow the Sudbury model, including schools in Canada, Europe, Israel and Japan.[8]

Teacher-Centered Approaches Are Best Because . . .

AFTER CENTURIES OF EXPERIENCE, WE KNOW WHAT TO TEACH

From Plato to Orwell, great writers and thinkers of the past light our way into the future. We must pass our cherished cultural legacy onto the next generation.

TEACHERS MUST SELECT WHAT IS WORTH KNOWING

The knowledge explosion showers us with mountains of new, complex information on a daily basis. Selecting what students should learn is a daunting challenge. Teachers, not students, are trained and best equipped to determine what is of value. To ask students to choose what they should learn would be the height of irresponsibility.

SCHOOLS MUST BE INSULATED FROM EXTERNAL DISTRACTIONS

Students can be easily distracted by the "excitement" of contemporary events. While academic and rigorous school-based learning may be less flashy and less appealing, in the long run, it is far more valuable. Once schoolwork has been mastered, students will be well prepared to leave the sanctuary of learning and confront the outside world.

WE ARE FALLING BEHIND OTHER NATIONS

U.S. student performance on international tests lags behind that of students from other nations. We have grown "educationally soft," lacking the challenging teacher-centered curriculums that other nations use. Only by creating a tough and demanding curriculum can we hope to compete with other nations.

COMPETITION AND REWARDS ARE IMPORTANT FOR MOTIVATING LEARNERS

Most people want and need to be recognized for their effort. Students are motivated to earn good report card grades and academic honors, to "ace" the SATs and be admitted to a prestigious college. Competition to earn high grades is the engine that drives successful school performance. Competition and rewards also drive the nation's productive workforce.

Student-Centered Approaches Are Best Because . . .

GENUINE LEARNING ORIGINATES WITH THE LEARNER

People learn best what they want to learn, what they feel they should or need to learn. Students find lessons imposed "from above" to be mostly irrelevant, and the lessons are quickly forgotten.

THEY BEST PREPARE STUDENTS FOR THE INFORMATION AGE

The knowledge explosion is actually a powerful argument for student-directed learning. Teachers can't possibly teach everything. We must equip students with research skills, then fan the flames of curiosity so they will want to learn for themselves. Then students can navigate the information age, finding and evaluating new information.

EDUCATION IS A VITAL AND ORGANIC PART OF SOCIETY

The most important lessons of life are found not on the pages of books or behind the walls of a school, but in the real world. Students need to work and learn directly in the community, from cleaning up the environment to reducing violence. Social action projects and service learning can offer a beacon of hope for the community, while building compassionate values within our students.

MULTIPLE CHOICE TESTS ARE NOT AN OLYMPIC EVENT

Education is not a competition, and academic tests are not a new Olympic event where youngsters have to get the highest score to please the cheering crowd. National success will come from living up to our beliefs, not "beating" the children of some other nation on a multiple-choice test.

MEANINGFUL REWARDS DO NOT COME FROM ACADEMIC COMPETITIONS

Grades, funny stickers, and social approval are poor sources of motivation. Authentic learning rests on a more solid foundation: intrinsic motivation. Real success comes from an inner drive, not from artificial rewards. Schools need to develop students' inner motivation and stress student cooperation, not competition.

continued

Teacher-Centered Approaches Are Best Because . . .

DISCIPLINED MINDS, RESPECTFUL CITIZENS

Students who listen thoughtfully and participate respectfully in classroom discussions learn several important lessons. For one, they learn the worth and wisdom of Western culture. They also learn to appreciate and to honor those who brought them this heritage, the guardians of their freedom and culture: their teachers.

Student-Centered Approaches Are Best Because . . .

HUMAN DIGNITY IS LEARNED IN DEMOCRATIC CLASSROOMS

Democracy is learned through experience, not books. Students flourish when they are respected; they are stifled when they are told what and how to think. As students manage their own learning, they master the most important lesson any school can teach: the importance of the individual's ideas.

www.mhhe.com/
sadker

YOU DECIDE . . .

Do you find yourself influenced more by the arguments supporting teacher-centered approaches, or those advocating student-centered approaches? Are there elements of each that you find appealing? How will your classroom practices reflect your philosophy?

Can Teachers Blend These Five Philosophies?

Some of you might be drawn to (and let's face it, sometimes repelled by) one or more of these philosophies. A social reconstructionist idea like students learning as they work to improve the world sounds perfect to some of us, while a more traditional approach focused on reading and discussing great books (preferably on a tropical island) is a dream come true to others. But for many, elements from both of these approaches are appealing. So you might be wondering if this is an either/or proposition; must we be purists and choose one philosophy, or can we mix and match, blending two or more philosophies?

As you probably have guessed, people differ on the answer, which means you get to think it through and come to your own conclusion. Some schools blend several philosophies. For example, the YES College Preparatory School in Houston and Wakefield High School in Maryland mix several different philosophies in their programs. There is both traditional academic emphasis on content mastery, with many AP tests being offered, as well as a more progressive approach as students create independent senior projects. And the faculty and students seem to appreciate the blending. But others are not so sure this is a good idea.

Advocates of a purist model argue that while blending sounds like a comfortable and reasonable compromise, much is lost. For example, if we want children to be independent problem solvers, then we must promote that approach. Blending independent problem solving with a traditional philosophy of teachers telling students what they are to learn does not work. Either students are taught how to think for themselves, or they are told what to think, and compromise is not an option. More traditional teachers have their reservations as well. They fear that much of progressive education, although replete with lofty goals, actually leads to little real learning. They claim that blending student centered philosophies with a demanding traditional curriculum actually dilutes learning.[9] As you consider where you want to teach geographically, you might also want to consider where you want to teach philosophically. Are you comfortable with the school's educational philosophy? If you have some freedom in structuring your classroom, which philosophy or philosophies will you follow? Are you a purist, or will you be blending several philosophies? (See Table 8.1.)

TABLE 8.1
Five philosophies of education.

	Focus of Curriculum	Sample Classroom Activity	Role of Teacher	Goals for Students	Educational Leaders
Student-Centered Philosophies					
Progressivism	Flexible; integrated study of academic subjects around the needs, and experiences of students	Learning by doing—for example, students plan a field trip to learn about history, geography, and natural science	Guide and integrate learning activities so that students can find meaning	To become intelligent problem solvers, socially aware citizens who are prepared to live comfortably in the world	John Dewey, Nel Noddings
Social Reconstructionism	Focus on social, political, and economic needs; integrated study of academic subjects around socially meaningful actions	Learning by reconstructing society—for example, students work to remove health hazards in a building housing the poor	Provide authentic learning activities that both instruct students and improve society	To become intelligent problem solvers, to enjoy learning, to live comfortably in the world while also helping reshape it	George S. Counts, Jane Roland Martin, Paulo Freire, bell hooks
Existentialism	Each student determines the pace and direction of his or her own learning	Students choose their preferred medium—such as poetry, prose, or painting—and evaluate their own performance	One who seeks to relate to each student honestly; skilled at creating a free, open, and stimulating environment	To accept personal responsibility; to understand deeply and be at peace with one's own unique individuality	A. S. Neill, Maxine Greene
Teacher-Centered Philosophies					
Essentialism	Core curriculum of traditional academic topics and traditional American virtues	Teacher focuses on "essential" information or the development of particular skills	Model of academic and moral virtue; center of classroom	To become culturally literate individuals, model citizens educated to compete in the world	William Bagley, E. D. Hirsch, Jr., William Bennett
Perennialism	Core curriculum analyzing enduring ideas found in Great Books	Socratic dialogue analyzing a philosophical issue or the meaning of a great work of literature	Scholarly role model; philosophically oriented, helps students seek the truth for themselves	To increase their intellectual powers and to appreciate learning for its own sake	Robert Hutchins, Mortimer Adler

REFLECTION: How many of these philosophies have you experienced in your own education? Describe the circumstances. Would you like to encounter others as a student? a teacher? Explain.

FRAME OF REFERENCE
Voices of the Five Philosophies

YESTERDAY'S VOICES

William Bagley (1874–1946) *Essentialism* Bagley believed that the major role of the school is to produce a literate, intelligent electorate; argued against electives while stressing thinking skills to help students apply their academic knowledge.

Robert M. Hutchins (1899–1979) *Perennialism* During the sixteen years he served as president of the University of Chicago, Hutchins abolished fraternities, football, and compulsory attendance, and introduced the Great Books program.

John Dewey (1859–1952) *Progressivism* A founder of progressivism, Dewey not only worked to democratize schools, he also fought for women's suffrage and the right of teachers to form unions.

George S. Counts (1907–1974) *Social Reconstructionism* Counts viewed education as an important tool to counter social injustices, and, if educators questioned their own power to make critical decisions, Counts's plea was to "Just do it!"

A. S. Neill (1883–1973) *Existentialism* Neill's attitude toward education stemmed from his own problems as a student, problems that fueled his creation of Summerhill, a school that encouraged youngsters to make their own decisions about what and when to learn.

TODAY'S VOICES

E. D. Hirsch, Jr. (1928–) *Essentialism* He established the Core Knowledge Foundation to develop a prescribed curriculum in subject areas, including technology. Visit your local bookstore and browse through his books delineating what educated people should know.

Mortimer Adler (1902–2001) *Perennialism* He renewed interest in perennialism with the publication of *The Paideia Proposal* (1982). Adler advocated that all students be educated in the classics and that education be a lifelong venture.

Nel Noddings (1929–) *Progressivism* She believes that an ethic of care can best be cultivated when the curriculum is centered around the interests of students. Schools are challenged to nourish the physical, spiritual, occupational, and intellectual development of each child.

bell hooks (1952–) *Social Reconstructionism* Her theory of education, *engaged pedagogy*, helps students and teachers develop a critical consciousness of race, gender, and class biases. A prolific writer, her books include *Ain't I a Woman: Black Women and Feminism* (1981) and *Teaching to Transgress: Education as the Practice of Freedom* (1994).

Maxine Greene (1917–) *Existentialism* She believes that it is crucial for students and teachers to create meaning in their lives. Greene sees the humanities and the arts as catalysts for moving people to critical awareness and conscious engagement with the world.

REFLECTION: The ideas of Dewey and Counts were particularly popular in the 1930s, 1960s, and 1970s, while the teacher-centered philosophies were popular in the other decades of the twentieth century. Existentialism drew a few influential supporters, but never many adherents. How did historical events during the twentieth century influence which of these voices were heard?

REFLECTION: How do these spokespersons reflect current political trends? Which voices are being heard in public policy circles today, and which are not? Why is this the case?

Each of these four photographs reflect four educational philosophies in action. Can you name them? Which is missing? What might that photo look like?

A

B

C

D

The missing philosophy is existentialism, which would portray students involved in a wide range of different activities, based on their desires.

Answers: (A) Social reconstructionism; (B) Progressivism; (C) Perennialism; (D) Essentialism.

Psychological Influences on Education

While essentialism, perennialism, progressivism, social reconstructionism, and existentialism are influential philosophies of education, they are far from the only forces shaping today's schools. Teachers who take their profession seriously pay attention to work in other fields, such as psychology, and may modify their teaching based on models proposed there. The following descriptions offer a glimpse into some of these forces guiding current school practices.

Constructivism

Constructivism, like existentialism, puts the learner at the center of the educational stage. **Constructivism** asserts that knowledge cannot be handed from one person to another (from a teacher to a learner), but must be *constructed* by each learner through interpreting and reinterpreting a constant flow of information. Constructivists believe that people continually try to make sense and bring order to the world.

Built on the work of Swiss and Russian psychologists, Jean Piaget and Lev Vygotsky, constructivism reflects the cognitive psychologists' view that the essence of learning is the constant effort to assimilate new information. Let's take a brief spin in your car to see how this works. You are driving happily along the highway and don't you know it—you hear an odd noise. No, it's not your passenger, it is coming from the engine. Just before panic sets in, you remember that your friend Karen mentioned that the air pressure looked low in your left front tire. You suspect that is causing the noise. You are doing just what a constructivist would expect you to do: looking for a pattern, a meaning to explain the noise. You step out of the car, look at the tires, but they all seem just fine. Now you need to figure out another explanation for the noise, another meaning. You open the hood, look around the engine, and find the fan belt waving wildly, hitting everything in sight. You back off, relieved that you have "learned" what is making the noise. You have reconstructed your thoughts based on new information. Next time you hear that noise, you might look first for that pesky fan belt. If that is not the problem, you will start the process again, and build more knowledge about what could go wrong in your car.

In a constructivist classroom, the teacher builds knowledge in much the same way, gauging a student's prior knowledge and understanding, then carefully orchestrating cues, penetrating questions, and instructional activities that challenge and extend a student's insight. Teachers can use **scaffolding,** that is, questions, clues, or suggestions that help a student link prior knowledge to the new information. The educational challenges facing students in a constructivist classroom could be creating a new way to handle a math problem, letting go of an unfounded bias about an ethnic group, or discovering why women's contributions seem all but absent in a history textbook. In a constructivist classroom, students and teachers constantly challenge their own assumptions. (If you check back to the philosophy inventory, see how you responded to item 26, which captured this aspect of constructivism.)

While constructivism runs counter to the current emphasis on uniform standards and testing, it is enjoying popularity, especially among school reformers. Perhaps part of the reason for its growing acceptance is that constructivism dovetails with authentic learning, critical thinking, individualized instruction, and project-based learning, ideas popular in reform circles.

Behaviorism

In stark contrast to both existentialism and constructivism, **behaviorism** is derived from the belief that free will is an illusion, and that human beings are shaped entirely by their environment. Alter a person's environment, and you will alter his or her thoughts, feelings, and behavior. People act in response to physical stimuli. We learn, for instance, to avoid overexposure to heat through the impulses of pain our nerves send to our brain. More complex learning, such as understanding the material in this chapter, is also determined by stimuli, such as the educational support you have received from your professor or parents and the comfort of the chair in which you sit when reading this chapter.

Harvard professor **B. F. Skinner** became the leading advocate of behaviorism, and he did much to popularize the use of positive reinforcement to promote desired learning. (For a biography of B. F. Skinner, see the "Hall of Fame: Profiles in Education" in Chapter 7.) Behaviorists urge teachers to use a system of reinforcement to encourage desired behaviors, to connect learning with pleasure and reward (a smile, special privilege, or good grades). In a program termed **behavior modification,** extrinsic rewards are gradually lessened as the student acquires and masters the targeted behavior. By association, the desired behavior now produces its own reward (self-satisfaction). This process may take minutes, weeks, or years, depending on the complexity of the learning desired and on the past environment of the learner. The teacher's goal is to move the learner from extrinsic to intrinsic rewards. (If you check the inventory at the chapter's opening, behaviorism was represented by statement 27. How did you respond?)

Behavior modification is perhaps most commonly used to manage student behavior. One well-known program is **assertive discipline,** developed by Lee and Marlene Canter. "The key to assertive discipline is catching students being good, recognizing and supporting them when they behave appropriately, and letting them know you like it, day in and day out."[10]

Critics of behaviorism decry behaviorists' disbelief in the autonomy of the individual. They ask, Are people little more than selfish "reward machines"? Can clever forces manipulate populations through clever social engineering? Are educators qualified to exert such total control of students? Those who defend behaviorism point to its striking successes. Behaviorism's influence is apparent in the joy on students' faces as they receive visual and auditory rewards via their computer monitor, or in the classroom down the hall where special needs learners make significant progress in a behaviorist-designed curriculum.

 ## Cultural Influences on Education

Most of the ideas and philosophies discussed in this chapter are drawn from Western culture. As a nation, we rarely identify or reflect on the ideas that derive from many parts of Asia, Africa, and Latin America. We are guilty of **ethnocentrism,** the tendency to view one's own culture as superior to others, and (perhaps worse) a failure to consider other cultures at all. Let's broaden our view, and examine education as practiced in other cultures.

In much of the West, society's needs dictate educational practices, with statewide standards, national goals, and high-stakes testing. In the rest of the world, that is to say, in most of the world, the child's education is primarily a concern of the family, not the society. A child's vocational interests, for example, might mirror the

---

**www.mhhe.com/
sadker8e**

INTERACTIVE ACTIVITY

What Philosophy or Approach Is This?
Read scenarios and match the philosophy or approach being exhibited.

IMAGINE . . .

Toward Enlightenment: Are Schools *Feng Shui*?

Dècor makes a difference, at least that's what some researchers say about the link between school architecture and student achievement. As classroom daylight increases, so does student performance in math and reading. In windowless classrooms (typical of the energy efficient 1970s and security conscious 1990s), students experience a kind of jet lag, which contributes to a lag in academic success.

SOURCE: *The New York Times*, August 5, 2001.

occupation of a parent or be built around the unique interest or talent of the child, rather than respond to the broader employment market or societal priorities. Family and community are foremost; the nation is a weaker influence.

In Western society, formal schools, formal certification and degrees are valued; in other societies, more credence is placed on actual knowledge and mastery rather than educational documentation. The notion of *teachers* and *nonteachers* is foreign in many cultures, since all adults and even older children participate in educating the young. Children learn adult roles through observation, conversation, assisting, and imitating, all the while absorbing moral, intellectual, and vocational lessons. This shared educational responsibility is called **informal education.**[11] (What does calling this practice "informal education" reveal about Western values and assumptions? Would someone in a culture practicing this integrated education call it "informal education"?) In the process, adults also learn a great deal about the children in the community. Strong bonds are forged between the generations. (As you probably already concluded, item 28 on our opening inventory describes informal education. You might want to check your answer to that statement.)

Oral traditions enjoy particular prominence in many parts of the world, even in literate societies where reading and writing are commonplace and valued. In the **oral tradition,** spoken language becomes a primary method for instruction: Word problems teach reasoning skills; proverbs instill wisdom; and stories, anecdotes, and rhymes teach lessons about nature, history, religion, and social customs. The oral tradition refines communication and analytical skills, and reinforces human connections and moral values. Not infrequently, religious and moral lessons were passed on initially through oral communication, only later to be written. In fact, the word Qur'an (Koran) is often translated as "the Recitation."

The practices and beliefs of peoples in other parts of the world offer useful insights for enhancing—or questioning—our own educational practices, but they are insights too rarely considered, much less implemented. Perhaps this will change in the years ahead as immigration continues to bring these ideas to our communities, while technological advances bring all world cultures closer together. For now, however, our education philosophies are rooted in the ideas and thoughts of Western thinkers. Let's visit some of these powerful thinkers and their influential, enduring contributions.

The Three Legendary Figures of Classical Western Philosophy

To understand Western philosophy, we must look back to the birthplace of Western philosophy—ancient Greece. Specifically, we must begin with a trio of philosopher-teachers: Socrates, Plato, and Aristotle. Together they laid the foundation for most of Western philosophy. It is likely that you are familiar with at least their names. Let's review their lasting contributions to the world of philosophy.

TEACHER: Today we will try to understand what we mean by the concepts of right and wrong. What are examples of conduct you consider wrong or immoral?

STUDENT: Lying is wrong.

TEACHER: But what if you were living in Germany around 1940 and you were harboring in your house a certain Jewish man named Nathan Cohen, who was wanted by the Nazis? If asked by a Nazi if you knew the whereabouts of that Mr. Cohen, wouldn't it be acceptable, even obligatory, to lie?

STUDENT: I suppose so.

TEACHER: So could you rephrase what you meant when you said that lying is wrong or immoral?

STUDENT: I think what I meant is that it is usually wrong to lie. But it is true that there are times when lying is acceptable, because the overall effects of the lie are good. Look at how much your Mr. Cohen was helped; the lie about where he was may have saved his life.

TEACHER: So you are saying that it is okay to lie, as long as the consequences of the lie are positive. But consider this hypothetical situation: I am a business tycoon who makes millions of dollars selling diamonds to investors. I sell only to very rich people who can afford to lose the money they invest in my diamonds. I tell my customers that my diamonds are worth $10,000 each, but they really are fakes, worth only $2,000 each. Rather than keeping the profits myself, I give all the money to the poor, helping them obtain the food and shelter they need to live. If you look at the obvious consequences of my business—the rich get slightly poorer and the needy are helped out immensely—you may conclude that my business has a generally positive effect on society. And, yet, because the business is based on fraud, I find it immoral. Do you agree?

STUDENT: Yes, I find it immoral. I suppose I was wrong in saying that whenever a lie has generally good results it is morally acceptable. In your diamond example, unlike the Nazi example, the lie was directed at innocent people and the harm done to them was significant. I want to change my earlier statement that a lie is acceptable whenever it has generally good results. What I want to say now is that you should never lie to innocent people if that would cause them significant harm.

As is typical of Socrates' dialogue, this one could go on indefinitely, because there is no simple, "correct" solution to the issues being discussed—the meaning of right and wrong and, more specifically, the contours of when a lie is morally acceptable. By asking questions, the teacher is trying to get the student to clarify and rethink his or her own ideas, to come eventually to a deep and clear understanding of philosophical concepts, such as right and wrong.

REFLECTION: Have you ever experienced the Socratic Dialogue as a student? What were your reactions? Would you like to develop this teaching technique? Why or why not?

The name of **Socrates** is practically synonymous with wisdom and the philosophical life. Socrates (469–399 B.C.E.) was a teacher without a school. He walked about Athens, engaging people in provocative dialogues about questions of ultimate significance. Socrates is hailed as an exemplar of human virtue whose goal was to help others find the truths that lie within their own minds. In that regard, he described himself as a "midwife"; today we call his approach the **Socratic method.** By repeatedly questioning, disproving, and testing the thoughts of his pupils on such questions as the nature of "love" or "the good," he helped his students reach deeper, clearer ideas.

Socrates's method did not just promote intellectual insights in his students; it also challenged the conventional ideas and traditions of his time. Socrates offended many powerful people and was eventually charged with corrupting the youth of Athens. Even in this, Socrates provides a lesson for today's teachers: challenges to popular convention may lead to community opposition and sanctions. (Luckily, sanctions today are less severe than those meted out to Socrates, who was condemned to death for his "impiety.")

We know about Socrates and his teachings through the writings of his disciples, one of whom was **Plato** (427–347 B.C.E.). Plato's writing is renowned for its depth, beauty, and clarity. His most famous works were dialogues, conversations

- **Socrates.** His philosophical lifestyle; the Socratic method, in which students are provocatively questioned so that they can rethink what they believe; his noble death
- **Plato.** Discussions of philosophy through eloquent dialogues; the theory of "forms," or "ideas," that exist in an eternal, transcendent realm; a vision of utopia, where an elite group of philosopher-kings rules over other members of society
- **Aristotle.** The breadth of his knowledge; the synthesis of Plato's belief in the eternal "forms" and a scientist's belief in the "real" world that we can see, touch, or smell; the theory of the Golden Mean (everything in moderation)

> **REFLECTION:** How might your current classroom instruction change if your education professor was Dr. Socrates, Plato, or Aristotle? Detail aspects of a "typical" lesson.

between two or more people, that present and critique various philosophical viewpoints. Plato's dialogues feature Socrates questioning and challenging others and presenting his own philosophy. After Socrates was put to death, Plato became disillusioned with Athenian democracy and left the city for many years. Later, he returned to Athens and founded **The Academy,** considered by some to be the world's first university.

Plato held that a realm of eternally existing "ideas" or "forms" underlies the physical world. In Plato's philosophy, the human soul has three parts: intellect, spirit, and appetite (basic animal desires). Plato believed that these faculties interact to determine human behavior. Plato urged that the intellect, the highest faculty, be trained to control the other two. For a look at Plato's famous "Parable of the Cave," from *The Republic*, setting out his political philosophy (he envisioned a class of philosopher-kings that would rule over the warriors and the common people), visit the Online Learning Center.

Just as Plato studied under Socrates, **Aristotle** (384–322 B.C.E.) studied under Plato. Aristotle entered Plato's Academy at age 18 and stayed for 20 years. In 342 B.C.E., Aristotle went to northern Greece and, for several years, tutored a young boy named Alexander, later known as Alexander the Great. After educating Alexander, Aristotle returned to Athens to set up his own school, the **Lyceum,** adjacent to Plato's Academy.

The depth and breadth of Aristotle's ideas were unsurpassed in ancient Western civilization. In addition to tackling philosophical questions, Aristotle wrote influential works on biology, physics, astronomy, mathematics, psychology, and literary criticism. Aristotle placed more importance on the physical world than did Plato. Aristotle's teachings can, in fact, be regarded as a synthesis of Plato's belief in the universal, spiritual forms, and a scientist's belief that each animal, vegetable, and mineral we observe is undeniably real.

Aristotle also won renown for his ethical and political theories. He wrote that the highest good for people is a virtuous life, fully governed by the faculty of reason, with which all other faculties are in harmony. Aristotle promoted the doctrine of the **Golden Mean,** or the notion that virtue lies in a middle ground between two extremes. Courage, for example, is bordered on the one side by cowardice and on the other side by foolhardiness.

Many of the ideas first formulated by Socrates, Plato, and Aristotle have long been integrated into Western culture and education.

Basic Philosophical Issues and Concepts

Philosophy has many subdivisions that are of particular significance to educators: metaphysics, epistemology, ethics, political philosophy, aesthetics, and logic. (See Figure 8.2.) These fields are where key educational questions are raised, including: How do we know what we know? What is of value? What is education's role in society? As you ponder these questions, you should find elements of your philosophy of education coming into sharper focus.

Metaphysics and Epistemology

Metaphysics deals with the origin and structure of reality. Metaphysicians ask: What really is the nature of the world in which we live? **Epistemology** examines the nature and origin of human knowledge. Epistemologists are interested in how we use our minds to distinguish valid from illusory paths to true knowledge. It may be easiest to remember the scope of these closely related disciplines by considering that epistemology and metaphysics address, respectively, *how* we know (epistemology) *what* we know (metaphysics) about reality.

Is Reality Composed Solely of Matter?   One of the most basic metaphysical issues is whether anything exists other than the material realm that we experience with our senses. Many philosophers assert the existence only of the physical, affirming fundamentally the existence of matter, a philosophy called **materialism.** By emphasizing in their curriculum the study of nature through scientific observation, modern public schools clearly deem that the material world is real and important. Other philosophers contend that the physical realm is but an illusion. They point out that matter is known only through the mind. This philosophy is called spiritualism or **idealism.** The physical world exists to teach us higher principles and meaningful lessons, but life is far more than a drive to acquire physical things. Spiritual leaders like Jesus and Gandhi have taught these lessons. Educators focused on idealism might teach students the importance of finding their place and purpose in the world, the importance of helping one another, and the need to protect the environment rather than abuse it. A third group of philosophers asserts that reality is composed of both materialism and idealism, body and mind, a belief associated with French philosopher René Descartes and called **Cartesian dualism.**

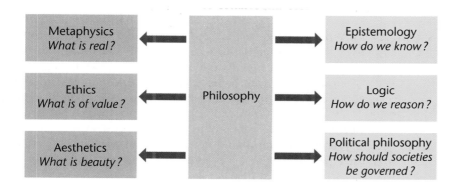

FIGURE 8.2
Branches of philosophy.

Is Reality Characterized by Change and Progress? Metaphysicians question whether nature is constantly improving through time. The belief that progress is inevitable is widely held in the United States. On the other hand, some philosophers hold that change is illusory and that a foundation of timeless, static content underlies all reality. Still others believe that change is cyclical, swinging widely from one side of center to the opposing side.

Teachers who believe in the inevitability of progress seek new approaches to teaching and new subjects to be taught, thereby "keeping up with the times." Other teachers, less enamored with change, pay little heed to current trends and technologies. They may prefer to teach everlasting, timeless truths discovered by great thinkers, such as Plato and Aristotle. Finally, some teachers suggest that, with change such a constant, it is pointless to try to keep pace. They choose to ignore these cycles and to simply select the teaching methods they find most comfortable.

What Is the Basis of Our Knowledge? **Empiricism** holds that sensory experience (seeing, hearing, touching, and so on) is the source of knowledge. Empiricists assert that we experience the external world by sensory perception; then, through reflection, we conceptualize ideas that help us interpret that world. For example, because we have seen the sun rise every day, we can formulate the belief that it will rise again tomorrow. The empiricist doctrine that knowledge is gained most reliably through scientific experimentation may be the most widely held belief in Western culture. People want to hear the latest research or be shown documentation that something is true. Teachers expect students to present evidence before drawing conclusions. Even children demand of one another, "Prove it."

Rationalism emphasizes the power of reason—in particular, logic—to derive true statements about the world, even when such realities are not detected by the senses. Rationalists point out that the field of mathematics has generated considerable knowledge that is not based on our senses. For example, we can reason that 7 cubed equals 343 without having to count 7 times 7 times 7 objects to verify our conclusion experientially. Whereas educational empiricists would support hands-on learning activities as the primary source for discovery and validation of information, rationalists would encourage schools to place a greater emphasis on teaching mathematics, as well as such nonempirical disciplines as philosophy and logic.

Ethics, Political Philosophy, and Aesthetics

Whereas metaphysics focuses on what "is," ethics, political philosophy, and aesthetics are concerned with what "ought to be." In these disciplines, philosophers grapple with the issue of what we should value. As you read on, consider the place of ethics, political philosophy, and aesthetics in the classroom.

Ethics is the study of what is "good" or "bad" in human behavior, thoughts, and feelings. It asks, What is the good life? and How should we treat each other? (What should schools teach children about what is "good" and what is "bad"?)

Political philosophy analyzes how past and present societies are arranged and governed and proposes ways to create better societies in the future. (How might schools engage in an objective evaluation of current governments, including our own?)

Aesthetics probes the nature of beauty. It asks, What is beauty? Is beauty solely in the eyes of the beholder? Or are some objects, people, and works (music, art, literature) objectively more beautiful than others? (How can teachers help students understand how their personal experiences, peer group values, and cultural and ethnic history shape their standards of what is beautiful?)

Logic

Logic is the branch of philosophy that deals with reasoning. Logic focuses on how to move from a set of assumptions to valid conclusions and examines the rules of inference that enable us to frame our propositions and arguments. While epistemology defines reasoning as one way to gain knowledge, logic defines the rules of reasoning.

Schools teach children to reason both deductively and inductively. When teaching **deductive reasoning,** teachers present their students with a general rule and then help them identify particular examples and applications of the rule. Inductive reasoning works in the opposite manner. When teaching **inductive reasoning,** teachers help their students draw tentative generalizations after having observed specific instances of a phenomenon.

A teacher who explains the commutative property of addition ($a + b = b + a$) and then has the student work out specific examples of this rule (such as $3 + 2 = 2 + 3$) is teaching deductive reasoning. Contrast this with a teacher who begins a lesson by stating a series of addition problems of the form $3 + 2 = 5$ and $2 + 3 = 5$, then asks, "What do you notice about these examples?" If students can draw a generalization about the commutative property of addition, they are reasoning inductively. While math is a natural field to isolate examples of deductive and inductive reasoning, logic equips students to think more precisely in virtually any field.

Your Turn

[I]n modern times there are opposing views about the practice of education. There is no general agreement about what the young should learn either in relation to virtue or in relation to the best life; nor is it clear whether their education ought to be directed more towards the intellect than towards the character of the soul. . . . [A]nd it is not certain whether training should be directed at things useful in life, or at those conducive to virtue, or at nonessentials. . . . And there is no agreement as to what in fact does tend towards virtue. Men [sic] do not all prize most highly the same virtue, so naturally they differ also about the proper training for it.[12]

Aristotle

More than 2,300 years later, we still find that reasonable people can come to entirely different points of view on all kinds of issues in education. (Remember the charter school discussion in the faculty room at the beginning of the chapter?) If everyone agreed on what should be taught, and how to teach it, there might be just one philosophy of education. But it is not so simple.

Rereading the inventory statements at the beginning of this chapter can help you determine if one of the five major philosophies speaks for you. You may be more eclectic in your outlook, picking and choosing elements from different philosophies. Your responsibility as an educator is to wrestle with tough questions, to bring your values to the surface and to forge a coherent philosophy of education.

You might say a clear philosophy of education is to a teacher what a blueprint is to a builder—a plan of action; reassurance that the parts will fit together in a constructive way. With a clear philosophy of education, you will not ricochet from one teaching method to another, and will not confuse students, parents, and administrators with conflicting messages about the role of students and teacher in the classroom. If you have a well-honed philosophy of education, you will be better able to assess whether you will find a comfortable fit in a school and a community. Simply put, a philosophy brings purpose and coherence to your work in the classroom.

SUMMARY

www.mhhe.com/
sadker8e

CHAPTER REVIEW

Go to the Online Learning
Center to take a quiz,
practice with key terms,
and review concepts from
the chapter.

1. **What is a philosophy of education, and why should it be important to you?**

   Behind every school and every teacher is a set of related beliefs—a philosophy of
   education—that influences what and how students are taught. A philosophy of
   education answers questions about the purpose of schooling, a teacher's role, and
   what should be taught and by what methods.

2. **How do teacher-centered philosophies of education differ from student-centered
   philosophies of education?**

   Teacher-centered philosophies, like essentialism and perennialisim, are more conservative,
   emphasizing the values and knowledge that have survived through time. Student-centered
   philosophies focus on individual needs, contemporary relevance, and a future orientation.
   Progressivism, social reconstructionism, and existentialism place the learner at the center
   of the educational process.

3. **What are some major philosophies of education in the United States today?**

   Essentialists urge that schools return to the basics through a strong core curriculum
   and high academic standards. Perennialists value the Great Books and the philosophical concepts that underlie human knowledge. The curriculum of a progressivist school
   is built around the personal experiences, interests, and needs of the students. Social
   reconstructionists more directly confront societal ills. Existentialism is derived from
   a powerful belief in human free will, and the need for individuals to shape their
   own futures.

4. **How are these philosophies reflected in school practices?**

   Essentialism and perennialism give teachers the power to choose the curriculum, organize the school day, and construct classroom activities. The curriculum reinforces a predominantly Western heritage. Progressivism, social reconstructionism, and existentialism
   focus on contemporary society and student interests and needs, while teachers serve as
   guides and facilitators.

5. **What are some of the psychological and cultural factors influencing education?**

   Constructivist teachers gauge a student's prior knowledge, then carefully orchestrate
   cues, classroom activities, and penetrating questions to push students to higher levels
   of understanding. According to Skinner, behavior can be modified through an extrinsic reward system that motivates students even if they do not fully understand the
   value of what they are learning. The practices and beliefs of peoples in other parts of
   the world, such as informal and oral education, offer useful insights for enhancing
   our own educational practices, but they are insights too rarely considered, much
   less implemented.

6. **What were the contributions of Socrates, Plato, and Aristotle to Western philosophy,
   and how are their legacies reflected in education today?**

   Socrates is hailed today as the personification of wisdom and the philosophical
   life. He used persistent questions to help students clarify their thoughts, a process
   now called the Socratic method. Plato, Socrates' pupil, crafted eloquent dialogues
   that present different philosophical positions on a number of profound questions.
   Aristotle, Plato's pupil, provided a synthesis of Plato's belief in the universal, spiritual
   forms and a scientist's belief in the physical world. He taught that the virtuous life
   consists of controlling desires by reason and by choosing the moderate path
   between extremes.

7. **How do metaphysics, epistemology, ethics, political philosophy, aesthetics, and logic factor into a philosophy of education?**

Metaphysics deals with the nature of reality, its origin and its structure, and poses curricular choices: Should we study the natural world, or focus on more meaningful lessons? Epistemology examines the nature and origin of human knowledge, and influences teaching methods. "How we know" is closely related to how we learn and therefore, how we should teach. Ethics is the study of what is "good" or "bad" in human behavior, thoughts, and feelings. Political philosophy proposes ways to create better societies in the future, and asks: How will a classroom be organized, and what will that say about who wields power? Aesthetics is concerned with the nature of beauty, and raises the issue: What works are deemed of value to be studied or emulated?

THE *TEACHERS, SCHOOLS, AND SOCIETY* READER WITH CLASSROOM OBSERVATION VIDEO CLIPS

Go to your *Teachers, Schools, and Society* Reader CD-ROM to:

READ CURRENT AND HISTORICAL ARTICLES

8.1 Text excerpts from **Experience and Education,** John Dewey.

8.2 **Pathways to Reform: Start with Values,** David Ferrero, Jr., *Educational Leadership,* February 2005.

8.3 **Teaching Themes of Care,** Nel Noddings, *Phi Delta Kappan* 76, no. 3 (1995).

ANALYZE CASE STUDIES

8.1 **Brenda Forester:** A preservice education student is concerned that one of her methods classes will not prepare her for teaching. Her philosophy of education is challenged when she observes a writing process classroom.

8.2 **Michael Watson:** A teacher finds that the assistant principal's evaluation of his class calls into question his teaching style as well as his philosophy of education. The evaluation suggests that his style and rapport with the students are getting in the way of his being more demanding.

OBSERVE TEACHERS, STUDENTS, AND CLASSROOMS IN ACTION

Classroom Observation: Essentialism in Action

It is hard to visualize how different philosophies might manifest themselves in the classroom. In this observation you will observe essentialism in action as an elementary teacher organizes an exciting class competition based on a television game. The involvement and excitement of the students is apparent.

x

345

KEY TERMS AND PEOPLE

KEY TERMS

The Academy, 340
aesthetics, 342
assertive discipline, 337
back-to-basics, 320
behavior modification, 337
behaviorism, 337
Cartesian dualism, 341
constructivism, 336
core curriculum, 321
deductive reasoning, 343
empiricism, 342
epistemology, 341
essentialism, 320
ethics, 342
ethnocentrism, 337
existentialism, 327
Golden Mean, 340
Great Books, 322
idealism, 341
inductive reasoning, 343

informal education, 338
Laboratory School, 325
logic, 343
Lyceum, 340
materialism, 341
metaphysics, 341
oral tradition, 338
Paideia Proposal, 322
perennialists, 322
philosophy, 314
political philosophy, 342
pragmatism, 324
praxis, 327
progressivism, 324
rationalism, 342
scaffolding, 336
social Darwinism, 327
social reconstructionism, 325
Socratic method, 339
student-centered
   philosophies, 324

teacher-centered
   philosophies, 320

KEY PEOPLE

Mortimer Adler, 322, 333
Aristotle, 340
William Bagley, 320, 333
George Counts, 325, 333
John Dewey, 324, 333
Paulo Freire, 326
Maxine Greene, 333
E. D. Hirsch, Jr., 321, 333
bell hooks, 333
Robert Hutchins, 322, 333
Jane Roland Martin, 328
A. S. Neill, 333
Nel Noddings, 333
Plato, 339
B. F. Skinner, 337
Socrates, 339

DISCUSSION QUESTIONS AND ACTIVITIES

**www.mhhe.com/
sadker8e**

WEB-*TIVITIES*
Go to the Online
Learning Center to
do the following
activities.
1. What Is Your Philosophy
   of Education?
2. Philosophies of
   Education
3. Progressivism and
   Dewey's Laboratory
   School
4. Existentialism
5. Behaviorism

1. Suppose that you are a student who must choose one of five schools to attend. Each reflects one of the five major philosophies. Which would you choose and why? Which school would you choose to work in as a teacher? Why?

2. Interview a teacher who has been teaching for several years. Find out what that teacher's philosophy was when he or she started teaching and what it is today. Is there a difference? If so, try to find out why.

3. Reread the five statements by the teachers in the faculty room at the beginning of the chapter. In what areas do you think these teachers could agree? In what areas are their philosophies distinct and different? What do you predict will be the result of their meeting? Which of the statements by the five teachers do you agree with most? Are there elements of each teacher's philosophy that could combine to form your own philosophy of education?

4. How would you describe your own philosophy of education? Imagine you are a teacher. Create a 3-minute speech that you would give to parents on back-to-school night that outlines your philosophy of education and identifies how it would be evident in the classroom.

5. The key terms and people in this chapter could be dramatically expanded by including Far Eastern and Middle Eastern philosophy. Consider the following additions: Buddhism, Confucius, Hinduism, Islam, Jainism, Judaism, Mohammed, Shinto, Taoism, Zen Buddhism. Research and briefly describe each of these. What has been (or might be) the impact of these religions, principles, and individuals on our present school philosophy?

REEL TO REAL TEACHING

QUIZ SHOW (1992)
Run Time: 130 minutes

Synopsis: By giving answers to the players they wanted to win, the producers of the popular 1950s game show *Twenty-One* had their trump card for capturing huge audience ratings. Charles Van Doren, college professor and scion of a great literary family, was the "perfect" game show contestant. The fact that the handsome and genteel Van Doren was prepared to participate in the cheating was an extra benefit. Based on a true story, the film probes the fault lines between knowledge, privilege, and scandal, and raises serious questions about what is most worth knowing.

Reflection:

1. What hooks you into a good game show or causes you to quickly flip channels? How is your educational philosophy reflected in your passion (or distaste) for game shows?

2. Which educational philosophy is best represented in *Quiz Show*? What elements of the classroom are seen on the game show stage?

3. How did factors such as race, religion, gender, and socioeconomic class determine who knew the answers on *Twenty-One*? Compare how these same factors shape how we define who is intelligent in schools.

4. After the scandal, Charles Van Doren noted that he believed the difference between good and evil was "not cut and dried." How is this statement revealed in the motives of the *Twenty-One* producers? Contestant Herb Stempel? Charles Van Doren? What power did each have? What power did each believe he had? How is this "winning at all costs" attitude reflected in schools and the testing culture?

5. What accounts for the popularity of quiz shows in the 1950s? Today? Consider the events, people, and values of each time period. How do game shows reflect American society and the value it places on knowledge?

Follow-up Activity: It's Game Night at your school. Choose a subject area and design your own "quiz show" based on one of the five philosophies discussed in the chapter. How will you define winning? How will the host, contestants, questions/answers, interactions, seating arrangements, and prizes reflect the key principles of the philosophy? Consider the many variables, such as the "facts"; the roles of gender, race, and class; and political motivations, among other things, that go into creating a "quiz show."

How do you rate this film? Go to *Reel to Real Teaching* to review this film.

www.mhhe.com/ sadker8e

FOR FURTHER READING

Approaches to Teaching, by Gary Fenstermacher and Jonas Soltis (3rd ed., 1998). Through an interactive, case studies approach, the authors explore the strengths and weaknesses of various philosophical perspectives. Readers are challenged to critically assess their own philosophical positions on education and to unpack the meaning of teaching.

Children as Philosophers, by Joanna Haynes and Tony Brown (2001). This book was written with the belief that philosophy can assist with children's thinking, speaking, and listening skills as well as provide a stimulus and structure for moral inquiry.

Happiness and Education, by Nel Noddings (2005). When parents are asked what they want for their children, they usually answer that they want their children to be happy. Why, then, is happiness rarely mentioned as a goal of education? Criticizing the current cultural emphasis on economic well-being and pleasure, the author explores what we might teach if we were to take happiness seriously as an aim of education.

Schools with Spirit: Nurturing the Inner Lives of Children and Teachers, by Linda Lantieri (ed), (2001). Fourteen respected educators describe how schools can nurture the inner life of students without violating the beliefs of families or the separation of church and state. *Schools with Spirit* inspires educators to develop "spiritual intelligence" in themselves and their students, from the first tentative steps of fostering emotional growth to the bold movement of welcoming the spiritual dimension in our schools.

Zen and the Art of Public School Teaching, by John Perricone (2005). This book is based on the assumption that "we teach who we are," and that our philosophy determines if we find joy and passion in teaching. With quick wit and poignant examples, the author invites readers to participate in an introspective journey designed to help them better know themselves and the professional path upon which they have embarked.

Financing and Governing America's Schools

CHAPTER 9

FOCUS QUESTIONS

1. Why do teachers need to know about finance and governance?
2. How is the property tax connected to unequal educational funding?
3. What is the distinction between educational equity and educational adequacy?
4. What are the sources of state revenues?
5. How does the federal government influence education?
6. What current trends are shaping educational finance?
7. How do school boards and superintendents manage schools?
8. What is the "hidden" government of schools?
9. How does the business community influence school culture?
10. How are schools being made more responsive to teachers and the community?

www.mhhe.com/
sadker8e

WHAT DO YOU THINK? What costs more? Try your hand at ranking the cost of several items on a state education budget.

CHAPTER PREVIEW

Do you know who pays for U.S. schools, and how? You might be surprised. In this chapter we introduce you to the decentralized, politically charged systems of school funding and school governance in the United States. You will become familiar with the sources of financial inequity in schooling, and, more important, learn how reformers are pursuing strategies to keep effective education within the reach of all, not just the very wealthy. Both the formal structure of power in school governance (school boards, school superintendents, and the like) and the informal, hidden government will impact your life in the classroom. By understanding the mechanics behind school finance and governance, you will be more empowered as a classroom teacher, and better able to influence decisions that shape the education of our nation's children.

Local and state governments have long grappled with the difficult proposition of raising enough public funds to adequately support education while dodging taxpayer ire over high taxes. Students in wealthy neighborhoods attend modern, well-equipped schools; poorer children make their way to decaying, ill-equipped school buildings in impoverished communities. Courts have forged solutions aimed at reducing these glaring disparities and bringing a measure of fairness to education. Many states are now focusing on guaranteeing that every student receives an adequate and appropriate education.

Day-to-day classroom life is influenced not only by economic issues but also by the ways in which schools are governed. In this chapter, you will learn how schools are managed, officially and unofficially. Your knowledge of educational decision making can be a powerful ally in shaping a successful teaching career.

Follow the Money: Financing America's Schools

Why Should Teachers Care Where the Money Comes From?

Why should a teacher be concerned about school finance? (Put another way, why should I want to read this chapter?) Doesn't a teacher's responsibility pretty much start and end at the classroom door?

Sounds reasonable, but here is where the authors jump in. We believe that it is unwise, and even dangerous, for teachers to invest their time and talent in a career where the key decisions are considered beyond their knowledge or influence. Educational finance may well determine not just the quality of life you experience as a teacher, but the very futures of the students you teach. Common sense tells us that the amount of money spent in a school is directly related to how well students learn, but not everyone agrees. What is the wisest way to invest educational dollars—and who should decide?

In the Watergate scandal that toppled Richard Nixon from the presidency, the *Washington Post* reporters who broke the story were given invaluable advice from a then anonymous source: "Deep Throat." Deep Throat advised the reporters to "Follow the money." He explained that in politics, the money trail reveals what is happening and who is benefiting. Money is the key to what is happening in schools as well.

We believe that teachers should be major participants in financial and governance policy decisions. The current trend toward testing teachers and developing school standards is an example of what happens when teachers are left out of policy circles. The emphasis on standards and testing too often casts the teacher in the role of a technician, implementing other people's goals with the resources other people decide they should have. And in the end, other people evaluate how well teachers (and students) perform. We believe that this system serves neither teachers nor students well. We see teachers as advocates for children, children who themselves are excluded from policy decisions. Teachers and students find themselves the victims of rising educational expectations but limited educational resources. Teachers should have a voice, and be a voice for children as well. Consider this chapter a step in that direction, and a primer on both the economics and governance of schools.

The Property Tax: The Road to Unequal Schools

> The method of financing public schools . . . can be fairly described as chaotic and unjust.
>
> *(Supreme Court Justice Potter Stewart)*

To someone from another country, the way the United States funds its schools must seem bizarre, and certainly unfair. Unlike many other nations, which use a centralized funding system, we have a very decentralized system. In fact, we have three levels of government—local, state, and federal—all raising and distributing funds. Currently, the local and state governments share the biggest burden of funding schools, with the federal government responsible for just 6 to 8 percent of the total. What a tangled web we weave when 50 states, 15,000 local governments,

Steadily increasing property taxes have led to taxpayer revolts in such states as California, Texas, and Massachusetts, where voters have passed propositions limiting such taxes.

and one enormous federal government become involved in funding and managing 90,000 schools.

How did this financial hodgepodge begin? In colonial America, schools were the concern of local communities. Then, at the birth of our nation, the Constitution did not designate a federal role in education, effectively leaving it the responsibility of the states. "Local control" of schools became a well-established tradition, one that still holds sway today.

In the agrarian society of colonial times, wealth was measured by the size of people's farms. So to raise money for schools, colonial towns and districts assessed a **property tax.** Although today only 2 percent of Americans still work the land, the property tax continues to be the major source of school revenue. Today's property taxes are levied on real estate (homes and businesses) and sometimes personal property (cars and boats). Whether a school district will find itself rich in resources, or scrambling to make ends meet, depends largely on the wealth of the community being taxed. Not surprisingly, a tax on a Beverly Hills mansion raises many more thousands of dollars than a tax on a house in South Central Los Angeles. Communities blessed with valuable real estate can easily raise funds for their schools. Impoverished communities are not so fortunate. Urban areas struggle the most, suffering not only from lower property values, but also the need to use those limited resources to fund more police officers, hospitals, subways, and other services than their suburban counterparts, a phenomenon known as **municipal overburden.**[1]

Reforming Education Finance

Unequal school funding results in stark differences, sometimes in close quarters. In 1968, 48-year-old sheetmetal worker Demetrio Rodriguez looked with despair at his children's school in a poor Latino section of San Antonio, Texas. Not only did Edgewood Elementary School lack adequate books and air conditioning, the

Growing up in South Carolina (vintage 1940s), Marian Wright Edelman learned to counter the summer heat with a swim. African American children were not allowed in the public pool, so Marian and her friends did their summer swimming, diving, and fishing in the creek, despite the fact that it was polluted with hospital sewage. One of her friends decided that the bridge spanning the creek would be a good diving platform, but that decision turned out to be fatal: He broke his neck on impact. His death was one of several tragedies that taught Edelman early lessons on the deadly impact of race segregation. In recalling these tragedies, Edelman says: "You never, ever forget."[1]

Marian Wright Edelman's family provided a refuge from this racial hatred. Her father was a Baptist minister, her mother a devout Sunday schoolteacher, and both instilled a sense of service. Sharing a bed, a meal, or a pair of shoes with foster children or neighbors in need was a common event for Edelman and her four siblings. While public playgrounds were closed to black children, her parents made Shiloh Baptist Church a community resource center for black sports teams, Boys Scouts, and Girl Scouts. Edelman learned that "[s]ervice is the rent we pay for living. It is the very purpose of life and not something you do in your spare time."[2]

During the 1960s, Edelman worked as a volunteer at the National Association for the Advancement of Colored People (NAACP), campaigning for passage of the Voting Rights Act as well as finding legal assistance for students jailed during sit-ins and demonstrations. As she sorted through requests for NAACP assistance from poor black citizens, Edelman realized that law could be a vehicle to social justice. She attended Yale University Law School and became the first black woman to pass the bar exam in Mississippi. Although she practiced civil rights law, Edelman's work with poor children helped her to see that they were the most vulnerable and voiceless group in our society. Children "had no one to speak out on their behalf—no one to make sure that there were laws and government policies in place to protect them."[3] During the next four decades, Marian Wright Edelman became their voice.

Edelman founded the Children's Defense Fund (CDF) in 1973, with the mission to "Leave No Child Behind." The CDF works to ensure that every child has a Healthy Start, a Head Start, a Fair Start, a Safe Start, and a Moral Start in life. The CDF strives to protect all children—and particularly children of low-income and minority families—through research, community organization, federal and state government lobbying, and public education. Among those who worked for the CDF was a young Wellesley graduate named Hillary Rodham, who continued to advocate for children's rights later when she became the First Lady and then U.S. Senator from New York.

CDF also sponsors Freedom Schools that recruit college students to serve as mentors to over 12,000 students both after school and during the summer. Edelman understands the lasting influence mentors give students, and she has a message for all teachers:

> Teaching is a mission, not just a task or a job. I don't care how fancy the school, how low the student-teacher ratio (which I believe should be lower), how high the pay (which I think should be higher): If children don't feel respected by adults who respect themselves, and don't feel valued, then they lose and all of us lose. Make it a reality that all children, especially poor children, are taught how to read, write, and compute so they can have happy and healthy options in their future. We need to understand and be confident that each of us can make a difference by caring and acting in small as well as big ways."[4]

[1] Marian Wright Edelman, *The Measure of Our Success: A Letter to My Children and Yours* (Boston: Beacon Press, 1992), p. 8; [2] Ibid, p. 6; [3] Marian Wright Edelman, *Lanterns: A Memoir of Mentors* (Boston: Beacon Press, 1999), p. 28; [4] Ibid, p. 22.

REFLECTION: Go to the Children's Defense Fund Web site at www.childrens defensefund.org and click on State Data. Compare the social problems and needs of children in your state with national averages. Which statistics surprised you? What responsibilities do you believe teachers have to ensure equal educational opportunity for children in poverty?

www.mhhe.com/ sadker8e

To learn more about Marian Wright Edelman, click on *Profiles in Education*.

top two floors were condemned and barely half the teachers were certified.[2] Ten minutes away, in affluent Alamo Heights, children were taught by certified teachers, in comfortable surroundings with ample materials. The educational cards were stacked against Rodriguez and his neighbors: even though Edgewood residents paid one of the highest tax rates on their property of any Texas community, the property itself was not worth much. Edgewood raised only $37 per student; Alamo Heights raised $412 per student. Rodriguez went to court, claiming that the system violated the U.S. Constitution's guarantee for equal protection under the law.

In a landmark decision, **San Antonio v. Rodriguez** (1973), the Supreme Court ruled against Rodriguez, deferring to the long history of local communities funding neighborhood schools. The Court declared that education was not a "fundamental right" under the U.S. Constitution, and that preserving local control was a legitimate reason to use the property tax system. While the Court recognized that educational funding through the property tax was a seriously flawed system, it was left up to the states to change it. It took sixteen more years before the Texas Supreme Court would act on the Rodriguez case. By the mid-1980s, Edgewood had neither typewriters nor a playground, but affluent Alamo Heights had computers and a swimming pool. Throughout Texas, per-pupil expenditures ranged from $2,112 in the poorest community to $19,333 in the wealthiest. In *Edgewood* v. *Kirby* (1989) the Texas Supreme Court issued a unanimous decision that such differences violated the Texas constitution, and ordered Texas to devise a fairer plan.

Reformers had more courtroom success under state constitutions' equal protection clauses. The California Supreme Court, in **Serrano v. Priest** (1971), struck down the state's financing system as unconstitutional. The court, faced with the glaring differences between Beverly Hills spending $1,232 per student, and nearby Baldwin Park spending only $577 a student, declared that education was a fundamental right under the California constitution and that the property tax system violated equal protection of that right. The court found that heavy reliance on the local property tax "makes the quality of a child's education a function of the wealth of his parents and neighbors. . . . Districts with small tax bases simply cannot levy taxes at a rate sufficient to produce the revenue that more affluent districts produce with a minimum effort." *The Serrano* v. *Priest* decision ushered in both a wave of litigation in other states and an increase in the state share of school funding.[3] (See Figures 9.1 and 9.2.) **Robin Hood reformers,** as they were called, won a victory as they took funds from wealthy districts and redistributed the monies to the poorer districts, much like the Robin Hood hero of Sherwood Forest fame. States have used different programs to try to equalize funding. In the foundation program, the state provides funds to ensure that each student receives a minimal or "foundation" level of educational services. Unfortunately, the established minimum is frequently far below actual expenditures. Another approach is the guaranteed tax base program, which adds state funds to poorer districts, helping to reduce economic inequities.

The Serrano victory in California was short-lived. Many voters feared tax increases, and wealthy voters revolted as their tax dollars were transported from their own children's schools to faraway poor schools. Proposition 13 was passed to limit the property tax. With decreased tax revenue, California saw its schools go into a rapid decline. California schools were finally becoming equal, but equally bad.

FIGURE 9.1

The public education dollar: Where the money comes from.

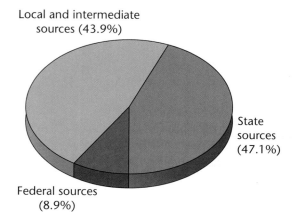

Local and intermediate
sources (43.9%)

State
sources
(47.1%)

Federal sources
(8.9%)

SOURCE: *Public Education Finances, 2004*, U.S. Census Bureau, March 2006.

REFLECTION: Is the proportion of revenue spent by local, state, and federal governments on education different from your initial perceptions? If you were able to suggest changes in this pie graph, what would they be? Why?

FIGURE 9.2

The public education dollar: Where the money goes.

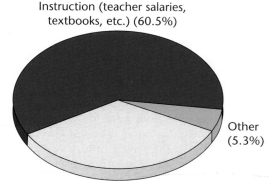

Instruction (teacher salaries,
textbooks, etc.) (60.5%)

Other
(5.3%)

Support services (school maintenance,
nurses, administration, library, etc.) (34.2%)

SOURCE: *Public Education Finances, 2004*, U.S. Census Bureau, March 2006.

REFLECTION: Does the distribution of educational funds surprise you? Are there changes that you would suggest?

Robin Hood's New Arrow: Adequacy

California provided an early example of the growing opposition to Robin Hood laws. In New Jersey, for example, the legislature was dominated by wealthy interests and middle-class communities who fought the Robin Hood idea. The state court shut down the schools to force the legislature to distribute more funds to poorer districts. In *Abbott* v. *Burke* (1990, 1998), the state court identified twenty-eight failing districts (known as "Abbott districts") where the rights of poor students were being denied. The court mandated that significantly greater funds be spent to transform their students into "productive members of society."[4] For school districts like Camden, with buildings in disrepair and students failing, Robin Hood funds were seen as the solution. But even after Camden received tens of millions of dollars in additional aid, academic statistics remained dismal. Critics of Robin Hood charged that increased funding could not turn failing school districts into successful ones. Redistributing tax dollars was not only politically unpopular, now it was considered ineffective.[5] (No wonder Robin Hood chose Sherwood Forest instead of New Jersey.)

The *Abbott* cases in New Jersey contributed to a new line of litigation focusing on *educational outcome* (student achievement) rather than *financial input* (per-pupil expenditures). State constitutions do not guarantee that every student is entitled to either an equal education or equal funding, but they do guarantee a basic education to all. States use different words to express this right. Some states require

We Should Seek Educational "Equity" Because . . .

MONEY TALKS

The gap between wealthy and poor communities makes a mockery of democracy and fairness. Poor students attend schools with leaking roofs and uncertified teachers; wealthy students learn in schools with computers, swimming pools, and well-paid and qualified teachers. No real democracy can ignore such glaring inequities.

EQUALIZING INPUT IS CRUCIAL

Isn't it strange that those who advocate business values like choice and competition ignore the most fundamental business value of all: money. Wealth creates good schools; poverty creates weak ones. Invest money wisely over a period of time, and watch those once-poor schools thrive.

EQUITY IS POWERFUL

Democracy and equity are powerful words representing powerful ideals. Adequacy is a feeble word subject to interpretation and compromise. What's adequate? Is it the ability to read at a high school level, or at an eighth grade level? Does an adequate education lead to a minimum wage job? Only "Equity" can serve as a rallying cry.

We Should Seek Educational "Adequacy" Because . . .

MONEY DIVIDES

Robin Hood is dead. Wealthy communities are not going to fund poor ones, happily sending their hard-earned dollars to fund someone else's school. The cornerstone of democracy is local control, and trying to redistribute wealth is fundamentally unfair, and smacks of the approach used by Communists (another failed system).

EQUALIZING INPUT IS INEFFECTIVE

We will never make schools more effective by throwing dollars at them. When California moved toward equitable input, the quality of its public schools deteriorated. Our goal is not to increase school budgets and per-pupil expenditures, but to increase student achievement.

ADEQUACY IS ATTAINABLE

Equity is a powerful dream, but adequacy is an attainable one. We are unlikely to achieve a completely equitable school system, but we can demand reasonable and reachable educational standards. Moreover, we are on firmer legal footing, since state constitutions guarantee not identical expenditures, but an adequate education for all.

www.mhhe.com/
sadker

YOU DECIDE . . .

Do you believe that adequacy or equity provides the best foundation for reforming schools? Explain. Can these approaches be blended, or are they mutually exclusive?

that every student receives an "efficient" education, others a "sound basic" education or a "thorough" education, or that all schools need to be "free and uniform."[6] Together, these constitutional clauses are referred to as **adequate education** guarantees, intended to ensure that all students have the basic skills they need to be effective citizens and compete in the labor market.[7] States differ dramatically in how they interpret adequate education. In Kentucky, the court ruled that the state's "entire system of common schools was infirm."[8] The court defined an "efficient" education as one that provides students with oral and written communications skills; knowledge of economics, history, and social systems; and sufficient preparation for academic and career success. To meet these goals, the state legislature enacted the Kentucky Education Reform Act in 1990, launching a new curriculum, statewide performance tests, preschool programs for at-risk students, multiple grades in the same class, and economic incentives for educational progress. New York took a minimalist approach, requiring all schools to provide students with desks and pencils, but not up-to-date science textbooks.[9] States from Wyoming to Ohio endured years of litigation as they struggled to define adequate education.

Perhaps the purest example of the adequacy approach is found in Maryland. Historically, states decided how much money they could afford to spend on education, and then decided how best to distribute those funds. Maryland turned that approach upside down. The state appointed a commission that defined adequate education, then computed how much money was needed to achieve it. Adequate education was defined as a school with at least 94 percent student attendance, less than a 4 percent dropout rate, and 70 percent or more of the students passing state achievement tests. Then the state commission studied successful schools that were meeting these goals, and found that they were spending about $6,000 per pupil. At the other end of the spectrum, low-performing schools had high numbers of poor children, non-English speakers, and children with special needs. Maryland determined that those schools would require an additional $4,500 per pupil to reach the goals of an adequate education. Final bill: Maryland would need an additional $1.1 billion. Although Maryland struggles to find these funds, the state tackled the problem voluntarily, and without litigation.[10]

Does Money Matter?

> To my knowledge, the U.S. is the only nation to fund elementary and secondary education based on local wealth. Other developed countries either equalize funding or provide extra funding for individuals or groups felt to need it.[11]

Why do Americans tolerate such dramatic inequities in school funding? Here are a few explanations:[12]

1. *Local Control.* In colonial times, it was left to individual communities in rural America to support their local schools. The Constitution codified this practice, and even after urbanization and suburbanization, Americans continue to believe that local taxes should be used to educate neighborhood children.

2. *Horatio Alger.* The rags to riches story of fictional Horatio Alger symbolizes the strongly held American belief that wealth and success are the fruits of individual effort, and that an individual's circumstances are merely obstacles to be overcome. It stands to reason, therefore, that if hard work and motivation alone are responsible for success, poverty comes from a lack of effort and a lack of talent. Individualism absolves communities from any collective responsibility for the poverty of others.

3. *Genetics.* For centuries, genetic differences have been used to explain why some succeed and others fail. The notion that certain groups are genetically deficient was promoted as recently as 1994 in Richard Hernstein and Charles Murray's book, *The Bell Curve.*

4. *Culture of Poverty.* Some believe that poor people live in and are shaped by the problems inherent in impoverished communities, problems that cannot be remedied through additional school funding.

5. *Flawed Studies.* Back in the 1960s, the classic Coleman study reported that school quality and funding had less of an effect on student achievement than family background or peer groups, and critics of equity efforts echo this notion that school funding is unrelated to student achievement. However, such studies have been cited for major methodological flaws.

6. *Previous Funding Increases Have Not Resulted in Achievement Gains.* Critics point out that although education spending has increased, test scores have not. However, most of these new funds were not for instructional improvement or test preparation, but to respond to targeted education needs, including special education, dropout prevention, expanded school lunch programs, and higher teacher salaries.

Does money matter? Of course it matters. Both common sense and a number of studies teach us that wealthier schools attract better-qualified teachers and have smaller class sizes. Both of these factors are associated with higher student achievement. Gaps in achievement between students from high- and low-socioeconomic-status homes are greater in poorly funded schools than in well-funded schools. The funding disparities are stunningly depressing. In Illinois, for example, one wealthy district spends about $20,000 more per student than a poor district. Schools with educational everything continue to exist in the same states with schools struggling to keep the building heated and the rats out. Law suits to close these gaps are commonplace.[13]

But if states went beyond just providing an "adequate" education and actually provided equitable funding for all schools, problems would persist. Money alone will not cure all the educational ills. Well-funded urban districts often post dismal results. Urban districts may have students with challenging needs which are costly to address, so equitable funding is still woefully inadequate. And in the real world, mismanagement, bureaucracy, poor decisions, and ineffective yet tenured teachers also sabotage even well-funded education programs.[14] While money alone is not the answer, it is part of the answer. Current financial inequities, both within a state and among the states, make providing even an "adequate" education difficult. Many believe that this problem can only be resolved by the federal government (an unlikely volunteer). For now, it is up to each state to "find the money."

States Finding the Money

Let's assume that you have been asked by your (choose one or more of the following): (a) education professor, (b) teacher association, (c) favorite political candidate, or (d) spouse, to "follow the money" and find out how states raise their educational funds. States have a dizzying number of budget items to fund. But for our purposes, the basic question is: Where do we find the money for our schools?

At the state level, a common revenue source is the **sales tax,** which is simply a charge added to all sales. Consumers pay a few extra pennies for small purchases or a few extra dollars for large purchases. The sales tax accounts for 30 percent of the typical state's income.[15] More than forty states use a sales tax, usually collecting between 2 percent and 8 percent of the item's value. A problem with the sales tax is that some people may choose to avoid paying the tax by taking their business to a neighboring state with a lower tax rate. And the tax is regressive: poor families must spend most of their income purchasing necessities, and end up feeling the impact of the tax much more than wealthy people.

Another popular option is the **personal income tax,** used in more than forty states. The personal income tax brings in more than 25 percent of state revenues.[16] Like the federal income tax, the personal income tax is collected through payroll deductions, even before a worker receives his or her paycheck. The tax is a percentage of income, typically above a particular threshold of income, so how each state determines these percentages in the end will resolve how equally, or unequally, the tax burden falls on the poor, the middle class, and the rich.

In a relatively new funding source, state lotteries, poorer people once again bear the greatest burden. **State lotteries** offer holders of winning tickets the chance to collect millions in prize money. But there are few winners and a disproportionate percentage of the poor purchase these long-shot lottery tickets. Roughly two-thirds of the states now have lotteries, and nearly half of those claim to dedicate at least a portion of the revenues to education. In reality, however, most states use lottery revenues to supplement, not fund, parts of an established education budget.[17]

Other common state sources of funding include: excise taxes (on tobacco, gasoline, and liquor, sometimes known as sin tax); severance tax (based on the state's mineral wealth); motor vehicle license fee; and estate or gift taxes.

Your brief course in "State Finance 101" is over. You can see some of the limits of state revenue sources. For extra credit, can you devise an entirely new scheme to raise state funds? As you can tell from Figure 9.3, states vary widely in how much money is invested in education.

FIGURE 9.3

Per-pupil expenditures for elementary and secondary schools: School year 2003–2004

Note: Current expenditures include salaries, employee benefits, purchased services, and supplies, but exclude capital outlay, debt service, facilities acquisition and construction, and equipment. Dollar amounts for states and the District of Columbia were grouped in $500 ranges (e.g., $8,501–$9,000).

SOURCE: U.S. Department of Education, National Center for Education Statistics, Common Core Data, "National Public Education Financial Survey" School year 2003–2004.

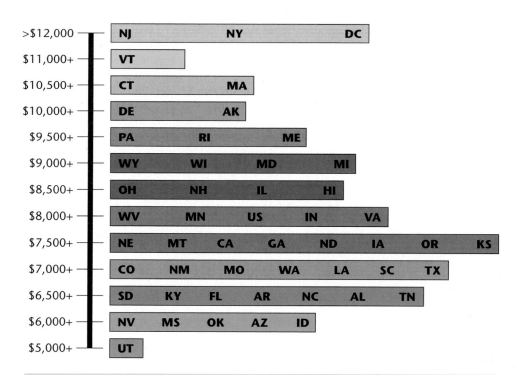

REFLECTION: Do your teaching plans include any of the states at the top or bottom of this list? Will this spending information influence your decision on where to teach? For more information on how different states respond to the needs of children, visit www.childrendefense.org.

The Federal Government's Role in Financing Education

At this point, some of you might be thinking: Even if every state provided every school district with adequate funding and a great education plan, the economic gaps among the states would still be enormous. If you thought about that, congratulations, you have put your finger on a systemic problem. For instance, in Connecticut, students throughout the state typically receive far more education dollars than students in Mississippi, regardless of what finance plans each of those states use. While we have been discussing *intrastate* equity, we have yet to explore *interstate* equity. Because of the Constitution, this is a problem the United States seems unable to correct.

If the Constitution had assigned education as a federal responsibility, we might expect to see the federal government close the economic gap between states. U.S. schools might be centrally financed and governed; or at the very least, the Supreme Court might rule funding inequities among states unconstitutional. But this is not the case. The Supreme Court has ruled that education is not a "fundamental right" under the U.S. Constitution, and has left education to the states. Accordingly, the federal government's role in the financing of education is relatively small. In fact, the federal government typically pays only 6 to 8 percent of the nation's educational costs.

However, the federal government still manages to influence schools. How does it do this? One way has been through **categorical grants**—funds directed at specific categories and targeted educational needs. Categorical grants have provided funding for preschool programs for poor children, library construction, acquisition of new technology, educational opportunities for veterans, the training of teachers and administrators, educational research, lunches for low-income youth, and loans to college students. By targeting funds into these categories, federal aid, although limited, has had a significant impact on schools.

More recently, there has been a shift away from categorical grants to "block grants." The obligations, rules, and even competition associated with seeking federal dollars were greatly reduced in the 1980s and 1990s. States were awarded **block grants,** lump sums of money, and were given great latitude in how to spend this money. As a result, there were educational winners and losers in the quest for federal dollars:

Winners. Under the block grant system, more funds went to purchase instructional materials, including computers. Many rural communities that lacked the resources even to apply—much less compete—for federal dollars, received federal support. The paperwork for all districts was reduced.

Losers. Desegregation efforts were cut by two-thirds under the block grant approach. Programs for disadvantaged and urban students, women's equity, and many other targeted programs were reduced or eliminated. Long-range programs lost support, and accountability for how the funds were spent was greatly weakened.[18]

In 1979, President Jimmy Carter established the **United States Department of Education,** raising federal involvement in education to cabinet status. The Department of Education influences schools by conducting research, publishing information, proposing legislation, and disbursing targeted, if limited,

IMAGINE . . .

Bonus Pay

Governor Jeb Bush of Florida decided to give teachers and schools millions of dollars in "bonus pay" as a reward for high scores on standardized tests. But when two middle schools offered the cash bonuses directly to high scoring students, as much as $150 per student, the governor objected. The chair of the school board argued that if adults get bonuses, so should children. Florida Congressman Jim Davis characterized the episode as "a new and inevitable low in testing run amok."

SOURCE: "Cash for Success," *The Washington Post,* August 21, 2001.

FIGURE 9.4

Federal budget. Within the federal budget, education expenditures remain quite small.

SOURCE: Federal Role in Education, U.S. Department of Education (2005). www.ed.gov/about/overview/fed/role.html

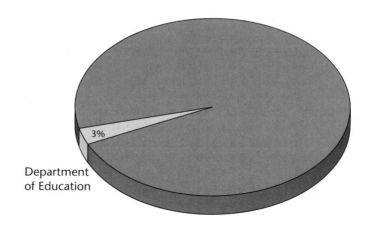

3%

Department
of Education

REFLECTION: Can you think of an area of the federal budget that receives fewer dollars than education?

federal funds. Expenditures for the Department of Education are dwarfed by other federal priorities. (See Figure 9.4.)

Although the federal government's financial role is limited, the federal government can exert tremendous influence on our schools through federal laws and court actions. For example, the 1954 *Brown* decision desegregated schools, and civil rights laws have increased educational opportunities for students of color, limited speakers of English, females, and others while *No Child Left Behind* (2001) brought high-stakes testing to center stage. (You will read about these laws and court cases, and more, in Chapter 10, "School Law and Ethics.")

 ## What the Future May Hold for School Finance

Today, we are in a period of shifting governmental responsibility for the financing of schools. Reformers are focusing less on financial inequity and more on educational inadequacy. What are some other trends in educational finance, and what issues are likely to surface in the years ahead?

Accountability

The public wants to see academic progress for their tax dollars—in short, **accountability.** Students will be tested, and so will educators. Graduation will be based less on time spent in school and more on proven performance. Teachers may find tenure more difficult to obtain. Schools will be required to identify specific goals, such as minimum achievement levels on standardized tests, and will be held responsible for reaching these goals, as in *No Child Left Behind.*

Choice Programs

The neighborhood school, long a mainstay of public education, may be radically reshaped (or even eliminated) in the years ahead. Many reformers are promoting a business culture and the value of competition as the keys to school improvement. Choice programs, charter schools, and vouchers are front burner issues in education (See Chapter 4, "Schools: Choices and Challenges").

The Economy's Impact on School Budgets

When our cyclical economy takes a downturn, state and local budgets are cut. This means fewer teachers are employed, class sizes increase, sports and extracurricular activities are eliminated, and courses like art and music are seen as "nonessential." School systems have even been known to end the school year early, or move to a four-day school week. Few governments maintain the public reserves necessary to avoid such cutbacks.[19]

Local Fundraising

Wealthier school districts are developing creative strategies to ensure that their schools are not endangered by funding redistribution plans. Through Parent Teacher Association donations, online fundraisers, cooperative agreements with local businesses, and tax-sheltered private educational foundations, additional dollars are collected for advanced science equipment, computers, special devices for disabled students, and college scholarships. Wealthy communities defend such practices as a way to prevent parents from fleeing "to private school if they don't perceive the public education to be excellent."[20]

Decaying Infrastructure

www.mhhe.com/sadker8e

INTERACTIVE ACTIVITY
Know Your School Finance Lingo! Match economic terms with educational definitions.

Here we are in the twenty-first century, using schools that were built in the nineteenth. When local governments need to replace these aging buildings, they usually resort to issuing bonds. A **bond** is a certificate of debt issued by a government guaranteeing payment of the original investment plus interest by a specified future date. Bonds give the local communities the money they need to build the schools and fifteen to 20 years to pay off the debt.

But for most schools, repair not replacement is the remedy for antiquated buildings. While keeping schools current means new wiring and electrical outlets for computer and Internet installation, teachers and principals give higher priority to "adequate" heating, lighting, acoustics, ventilation, and air conditioning. The Department of Education estimates that 25,000 schools need major repairs, at an estimated cost of over $112 billion.[21] One piece of good news: Polls indicate that the public recognizes the financial need of our schools suggesting that local bonds will be approved.

Governing America's Schools

School Governance Quiz

The following quiz should help you focus on how schools are governed. If you are puzzled at some of these questions, fear not; the remainder of the chapter is organized around a discussion of these questions and their answers.

Students and staff arrive to very different school buildings. What attitudes might develop as a result of learning in these dissimilar facilities? What physical improvements would you make to the dilapidated school building? List the physical characteristics of a school building that you believe are needed to ensure an "adequate education."

www.mhhe.com/
sadker8e

INTERACTIVE ACTIVITY

School Governance Quiz
Take an electronic version
of this quiz.

1. Most school board members are (choose only one)
   a. White, male, and middle or upper class.
   b. Middle-class women, about half of whom have been or are teachers.
   c. Middle of the road politically, about evenly divided between men and women, and representing all socioeconomic classes.
   d. So diverse politically, economically, and socially that it is impossible to make generalizations.

2. State school boards and chief state school officers are
   a. Elected by the people.
   b. Elected by the people's representatives.
   c. Appointed by the governor.
   d. Appointed by officials other than the governor.
   e. All of the above.
   f. None of the above.

3. During the past two decades, the influence of local school boards has
   a. Increased.
   b. Decreased.
   c. Remained unchanged.

4. Local school district superintendents are (you may choose more than one)
   a. Often mediating conflicts.
   b. Civil service–type administrators.
   c. Elected officials.
   d. Sometimes powerless figureheads.

5. Who might be considered part of the "hidden school government"? (you may choose more than one)
   a. The school principal.
   b. The state school superintendent.
   c. The U.S. secretary of education.
   d. The school secretary.
   e. Parents.
   f. The Teacher Arbitration and Labor Relations Board.

6. The influence of the business community in U.S. schools can best be characterized as
   a. Virtually nonexistent.
   b. Felt only in vocational and commercial programs.
   c. Extensive and growing.
   d. Usually illegal.

7. In most schools, teachers are expected to
   a. Design the policies guiding their schools.
   b. Collaborate with principals and district officials to create policies to suit their schools.
   c. Comply with policies made by principals and by district and state officials.
   d. Comply with policies that seem appropriate and change those that do not.

School Governance Answer Key

1. a   2. e   3. b   4. a, b, d   5. d, e   6. c   7. c

0 to 1 wrong: You receive the Horace Mann Award.

2 wrong: You may want to run for school board.

3 wrong: Read the rest of the chapter carefully.

4 or more wrong: Take detailed notes on this part of the chapter; become a frequent visitor to the text Web page; find a friend to quiz you; and whatever you do, stay away from TV quiz shows.

The Legal Control of Schools

The following sections review and discuss the quiz you have just taken, beginning with the first two questions:

1. Most school board members are . . . *white, male, and middle or upper class.*
2. School boards and chief state school officers are . . . *elected by the people, elected by the people's representatives, appointed by the governor, or appointed by officials other than the governor.*

School boards, whether at the state or local level, determine educational policy and their members tend to be male (over 60 percent), white (over 85 percent), and not young (most are 50 years of age or older). In short, school board members look like the leaders we find in corporate America or government.[22] As for the second question, in some states, school boards and chief state school officials are elected; in others, they are appointed. Even the name for the chief state school officer differs from place to place: superintendent, commissioner, or even secretary. Why the differences? The **Tenth Amendment** reminds us that: "The powers not delegated to the United States by the Constitution, nor prohibited by it to the States, are reserved to the states, respectively, or to the people." More than 200 years ago, the authors of the Constitution did not discuss education, so each state was free to create its own school system. While most nations have one national ministry of education to determine what and how all students will be taught, in our country, each of the 50 states, the District of Columbia, and several U.S. territories make those decisions.

The governor, legislature, state superintendent, or the state school board typically consider different ideas for improving education. One state might require that all schools have a certain number of computers, while another might decide that all high school students must pass four years of science. Let's say you apply for a position in a state that passed a new requirement: all candidates for a teaching license must pass a course in "Instructional Strategies for Improving Student Test Performance." The state superintendent and the state department of education would inform all teacher candidates (including you) of the new course requirement. If you wanted to teach in the state, someone in the state department of education would review your transcript to make certain that you had successfully completed the new course on improving test scores before issuing you a teacher's license. If you took the course, voila, you will be issued your license, you are qualified to be a teacher in that state. But (nothing personal) don't expect the state to hire you.

Although states issue teacher licenses, hiring and firing of teachers is done by the local school district, about 14,000 of them across the country. So you don't

FIGURE 9.5
Structure of a typical
state school system.

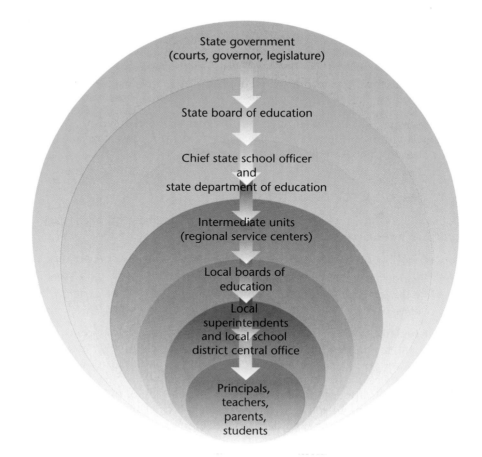

State government
(courts, governor, legislature)

State board of education

Chief state school officer
and
state department of education

Intermediate units
(regional service centers)

Local boards of
education

Local
superintendents
and local school
district central office

Principals,
teachers,
parents,
students

REFLECTION: What are some of the difficulties in these many levels of governance? Do you favor elected or appointed school boards? Why?

apply to the state for a teaching position, but to the local district. The district will check to make certain that you have your teacher's license, and then consider you for a position. Figure 9.5 describes these levels of school governance:

State Board of Education   The **state board of education** is responsible for formulating educational policy. The members are usually appointed by the governor, but sometimes they are chosen in a statewide election.

Chief State School Officer   Called *superintendent, commissioner, secretary of education,* or *director of instruction,* the **chief state school officer** is responsible for overseeing, regulating, and planning school activities, as well as implementing the policies of the board of education. The state superintendent is usually selected by the board of education but sometimes campaigns for the position in an election.

State Department of Education   The **state department of education** performs the administrative tasks needed to implement state policy. This includes

STATE GOVERNMENTS

- Levy taxes
- License teachers and other educators
- Set standards for school attendance, safety, etc.
- Outline minimum curricular and graduation standards (sometimes including specific textbooks to be used and competency tests for student graduation and teacher certification)
- Regulate the nature and size of local school districts

LOCAL SCHOOL DISTRICTS

- Implement state regulations and policies
- Create and implement local policies and practices for effective school administration
- Hire school personnel
- Provide needed funds and build appropriate facilities
- Fix salaries and working conditions
- Translate community needs into educational practice
- Initiate additional curriculum, licensing, or other requirements beyond state requirements
- Create current and long-range plans for the school district

REFLECTION: As a classroom teacher, offer some examples of the issues that would lead you to deal with state government. Which issues would send you down a path to the local government?

licensing teachers, testing student progress, providing information and training to teachers, distributing state and federal funds, seeing that local school systems comply with state laws, and conducting educational research and development. The state superintendent usually manages state department of education activities.

School Districts—Local School Boards and Superintendents All states except Hawaii have delegated much of the responsibility for local school operations to local school districts. (Hawaii treats the entire state as a single school district.) School districts vary in size from those serving only a few students to those with more than a million. Most local school districts mirror the state organization, with a local school board that is usually elected, a superintendent, and an office of education. Local school districts may be responsible for school construction, taxing, budgeting, the hiring of school personnel, curriculum decisions, and local school policy. Although school districts operate at the local level, their authority derives from the state, and they must operate within the rules and regulations specified by the state. (The *Frame of Reference:* Who Controls What? Levels of Educational Power summarizes the relationships between state and local control of schools.)

www.mhhe.com/
sadker8e

INTERACTIVE ACTIVITY
Who Is in Control? Test your knowledge of who controls different aspects of the school.

State Influence Grows as School Boards Come Under Fire

3. During the past two decades, the influence of local school boards has . . .
decreased.

Forged in the hamlets of colonial New England, school boards have symbolized small-town democracy. School board meetings evoke the essence of Americana—the kind painted by Norman Rockwell and made into a Frank Capra movie entitled "Mr. Deeds Elected to the School Board" (starring Jimmy Stewart as the beleaguered school board president). But Americana aside, many criticize school boards as unresponsive and entrenched bureaucracies.

Part of the problem is that there is little consensus on how school boards should operate.[23] Most school board members view themselves as *trustee representatives,* selected to serve because of their educational expertise and good judgment, and independent of ever-changing popular opinions. But others, including many voters, see school board members as *delegate representatives,* responsible for implementing the will of the public (or being voted out of office if they do not). The type of elections used to select school board members can shape the kind of school board that will emerge. When school boards are selected through "at-large" elections, in which the entire school district votes for all the members of the school board, the school board is expected to represent the interests of the entire community—in line with the notion of trustee representatives. But some school districts do not have at-large elections, instead choosing to have smaller geographic areas vote. In this type of election each of these smaller neighborhoods selects a board member to represent its interests (delegate representation).

While it might appear that at-large elections are less partisan, they do have serious drawbacks. Districtwide, at-large elections typically result in more elite, politically conservative and upper class individuals being elected to school boards. After all, it is the well-established individual who is likely to have the financial resources and educational and business background needed to win a big, districtwide election. Poorer citizens, people of color, and women are less likely to find themselves on school boards selected through at-large elections. Unfortunately, many citizens feel disenfranchised when it comes to school board elections.

Other criticisms of school boards run deeper. The Twentieth Century Fund and the Danforth Foundation conducted an intensive study of school boards, and recommended a total overhaul of the system, charging that

- School boards have become *immersed in administrative details,* at the expense of more important and appropriate policy issues. One study of West Virginia school boards showed that only 3 percent of all decisions made concerned policy.

- School boards are *not representing local communities,* but only special interest groups. Elections to the school board receive little public support. In a New York City school board election, for instance, only 7 percent of the voters participated.

- The *politics of local school board elections* have a negative impact on attracting and retaining superintendents and lead to conflict with state education agencies.

- The composition of the boards is *not representative,* with individuals of color, women, the poor, and the young unrepresented or underrepresented.

- School boards have been in the *backseat when it comes to educational change and reform.* As a matter of fact, many school boards do not support current educational reform proposals, and members have lagged behind public opinion on such issues as school choice and educational vouchers.

- The education of children goes beyond school issues to include health, social, and nutritional concerns. School boards are *too limited in scope* to respond to all the contemporary concerns of children.

- If schools continue to be *financed less from local funds and more from state funds,* local boards could become less influential.

- Many of the new reforms call for *new governance organizations,* site-based management, or choice programs that relegate the school board to a less important, perhaps even unnecessary, role.[24]

While these criticisms suggest a dismal future for school boards, preparing their obituary may be premature. School boards have endured a long time and may be around long after many of the reform recommendations are forgotten.

The School Superintendent and Principal

4. Local school district superintendents are . . . *often mediating conflicts, civil service–type administrators, sometimes elected and sometimes powerless figureheads.*

The first superintendents were hired to relieve school boards of their growing administrative obligations. The year was 1837, and these new superintendents worked in Buffalo and Louisville. As the nineteenth century progressed, more communities followed this example. Superintendents were expected to supervise and hire teachers, examine students, and buy supplies, which had become too burdensome for the school boards themselves. Superintendents also kept school records, developed examinations, chose textbooks, and trained teachers.

By the twentieth century, the superintendent's role had changed from the board's administrative employee to its most knowledgeable educational expert—from helper to chief executive officer. Today, the superintendent is the most powerful education officer in the school district, responsible for budgets; buildings; new programs; daily operations; long-term goals; short-term results; and recruiting, hiring, demoting, and firing personnel. When things are going well, the superintendent enjoys great popularity. But, when things are going poorly, or school board members are not pleased, or local community groups are angry, or teacher organizations turn militant, or . . . you get the picture. When there is a problem, it is usually the head of the system, the superintendent, who gets fired. The superintendent lives and works in a fishbowl, trying to please various groups while managing the school district. It is a very insecure existence of sidestepping controversies, pleasing school board members, responding to critics, juggling many different roles and goals, and living with conflict. Between 1990 and 2001, in thirty large urban school districts, superintendents served less than three years before they were fired, resigned, or retired.[25] Many believe that this high-visibility, high-stress position is also subject to subtle forms of racism and sexism. Over 80 percent of superintendents are male, and over 90 percent are white.[26]

One need not look hard for the reasons for this turnover. Successful superintendents must win and maintain public support and financing for their schools. This involves forming political coalitions to back their programs and to ward off attacks from those more concerned with rising taxes than with the school budget. In an era in which most citizens in many communities do not have children in schools, this becomes a real test of political acumen. Superintendents find themselves serving on a number of civic committees, speaking to community groups, and being the public relations spokesperson for the school district.

School superintendents who survive and thrive are the politically savvy administrators who can "read" their school board. In *The School Managers: Power and Conflict in American Public Education,* Donald McCarty and Charles Ramsey provide a useful classification system that matches school board types with different superintendent styles.[27]

School Boards in Communities That Are . . .	*Prefer Superintendent Style That Is . . .*
Dominated: School boards run by a few local elite who dominate community and school policies	*Functionary:* Follows wishes of the board
Factional: Divided community, competing factions	*Political:* Balances often opposing concerns, avoids appearance of favoritism
Pluralistic: Competition among interest groups	*Advisor:* Moves cautiously as advisor among shifting community coalitions
Inert: No visible power structure, little interest in schools	*Decision maker:* Board relies on superintendent for leadership and decision making

An effective superintendent must be an effective manager, and a number of new superintendents of large school districts have been selected for their management skills rather than their educational expertise. New York City, San Diego, Seattle, and Los Angeles have chosen generals, lawyers, and a former governor to lead their schools.[28] Because a large school district employs thousands of professionals and serves tens of thousands of students, these districts chose managers instead of educators. And good management is essential. Superintendents have been terminated when textbooks or teacher paychecks arrive late, or when the school days chosen for closing prove unpopular. And as if that were not enough, some school districts have adopted performance-based contracts that link superintendent compensation directly to student performance.[29]

While the superintendent is the focal point of district pressures, the principal bears the brunt of the school pressure. "Stress, testing, and social problems are all in the schools now. AIDS education, security, parenting classes, language programs. There are so many things that they are responsible for that they might not have control over, and it's led to concern about principal burnout."[30] Even at the elementary level, where many consider the stress most tolerable, a typical elementary principal supervises 30 teachers, 14 other staff members, 425 students, and works an average of nine or ten hours a day, 54 hours or more a week.[31] Amazingly, 20 percent of principals report spending five to ten hours a week in efforts aimed at a single purpose: avoiding lawsuits.[32] Principal recruiters struggle to overcome persistent racial and ethnic imbalances as well.[33] (Figure 9.6 provides insight into principal demographics and Figure 9.7 shows the average salaries of school administrators across the country.)

Covert Power in Schools

5. Who might be considered part of the "hidden school government" . . . *the school secretary and parents.*

So you think that the school principal is the only one responsible for school personnel decisions, including hiring and firing? Think again. Parents, vocal individuals, the school secretary, and community groups have **covert power** and can bring significant pressure to bear on which teachers stay in a school, and which leave. These unofficial but highly involved persons and groups constitute the **hidden government** of schools.[34]

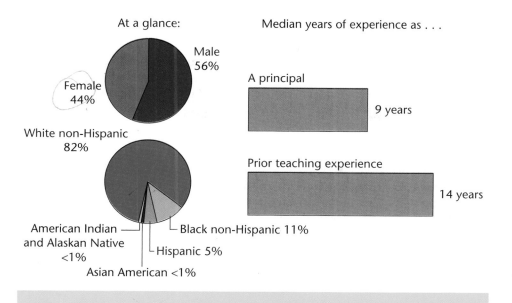

At a glance:

Male 56%

Female 44%

White non-Hispanic 82%

American Indian and Alaskan Native <1%

Asian American <1%

Hispanic 5%

Black non-Hispanic 11%

Median years of experience as . . .

A principal — 9 years

Prior teaching experience — 14 years

FIGURE 9.6

Elementary and secondary public school principals.

SOURCE: National Center for Educational Statistics, "Principals in Public and Private Elementary and Secondary Schools, by Selected Characteristics, 1999–2000," *Digest of Educational Statistics* (Washington, DC: U.S. Department of Education, 2005).

REFLECTION: What are the potential challenges for schools with white principals and a majority of students of color?

Rocky Mountains
Superintendent: $97,868
High school principal: $73,260

Mideast
Superintendent: $130,870
High school principal: $98,198

Plains
Superintendent: $90,591
High school principal: $70,627

Far West
Superintendent: $122,500
High school principal: $89,409

Great Lakes
Superintendent: $114,026
High school principal: $85,771

Southeast
Superintendent: $110,055
High school principal: $76,497

New England
Superintendent: $118,424
High school principal: $95,559

Southwest
Superintendent: $100,582
High school principal: $68,334

FIGURE 9.7

Regional public school administrator salaries.

SOURCE: Educational Research Service, "National Survey of Salaries and Wages in Public Schools, 2004–05."

REFLECTION: While administration pays more than teaching, there is also a trade-off. What is the trade-off? What are some valid reasons for pursuing administration? What are some less than appropriate reasons?

The concept of hidden government is not unique to schools. In fact, most of our institutions, including the White House, have developed their own unique forms of hidden government. There, decision making is often influenced more by old colleagues back home (the "kitchen cabinet") than by the president's official advisers and cabinet members.

How does hidden government operate in schools? Following are some examples.

Example 1   A first-year teacher in a New England junior high school spent long hours after school, preparing lessons and working with his students. Admirable as all this appeared, the school secretary, Ms. Hand, advised the teacher not to work with female students after school hours, because "You may get your fingers burned." The teacher smiled, ignored the secretary's advice, and continued providing students with after-school help.

Within a week, the principal called the teacher in for a conference and suggested that the teacher provide extra help to students only if both male and female students were present. The teacher objected to the advice and to the secretary's complaining to the principal. The principal responded, "You're new here, and I can understand your concern. But what you have to learn is that Ms. Hand is more than a secretary. She knows this school better than I do. Follow her advice and you'll do just fine."

Lesson: You can't always tell which people hold the real power by their official position.

Lesson: The school secretary is often the eyes and ears of the principal. In some cases, the secretary manages the day-to-day operations of the school.

Example 2   A young teacher in an elementary school in the Midwest was called into the principal's office for a conference. The principal evaluated her teaching as above average but suggested that she maintain greater discipline. Her classroom was

The school secretary holds a position that can exert significant covert power in his or her pivotal role as the principal's "eyes and ears."

simply too noisy, and the students' chairs were too often left in disarray. The conference was over in ten minutes.

The teacher was offended. She did not feel her classroom was too noisy, and the chairs were always arranged in a neat circle. Moreover, the principal had visited her class for only five minutes, and during that time the students had said hardly a word.

The next day, in the teacher's lounge, all became clear when she discussed the conference with another teacher. The teacher nodded, smiled, and explained:

"Mr. Richards."

"The custodian?"

"Yup. He slowly sweeps the halls and listens for noisy classrooms. Then he tells the principal. He also hates it when the chairs are in a circle, since it makes sweeping harder. Nice straight rows are much easier. Just make sure your classroom is quiet when he's in the halls and have your students put the chairs in neat, straight rows at the end of the day. That's the ticket for getting a good evaluation!"

Lesson: School custodians are often a source of information for principals and of supplies for teachers. They make very helpful allies and powerful adversaries.

Example 3   An elementary school teacher in a rural southern community was put in charge of the class play. Rehearsals were under way when the teacher received a note to stop by the principal's office at 3:00 p.m.

The principal had received a call from a parent who was quite disappointed at the small part her daughter had received in the play. The principal wanted the teacher to consider giving the child a larger part. "After all," he explained, "her mother is influential in the PTA, and her father is one of the town's most successful businessmen. It's silly for you to alienate them. Give her a bigger part. Life will be easier for both of us, and we may be able to get her parents' support for the next school bond issue. That would mean a raise for all of us."

Lesson: Parents can also be influential in school decisions by applying pressure on principals, school boards, and community groups. When you decide to make a stand in the face of parental pressure, choose a significant issue and be able to substantiate your facts.

Business and Schools

6. The influence of the business community in U.S. schools can best be characterized as . . . *extensive and growing.*

Business values have long influenced school practices, and decades ago educators adopted a business vocabulary. *Superintendent,* the title originally given to a factory supervisor, was assigned to the school district leader. Both a factory and a school have been called a *plant. Quality control, accountability, management design,* and *efficiency* were also expropriated. Little surprise that a growing number of superintendents come from the business sector. School values often mirror those of business: hard work, competition, dependability, punctuality, neatness, conformity, and loyalty.[35] Companies that formalize a relationship with a school, by dedicating personnel or products or signing exclusive rights contracts, are said to have formed an **educational partnership.** A number of educators express concerns about these developments, an issue we explored earlier in this text. But whether we are comfortable or uncomfortable with this trend, "The most far-reaching initiative in education to emerge in recent years is the growing corporate interest in public schools."[36]

Competition and other business-oriented values have become so familiar and pervasive in our schools that we have become inured to them.

Making Schools More Responsive

7. In most schools, teachers are expected to . . . *comply with policies made by principals and by district and state officials.*

While parents, community groups, and the business sector carve out their roles in schools, teachers traditionally have been omitted from meaningful involvement in school governance. To get a sense of what that might feel like, imagine that you are the senior faculty member at Someplace High School. Having taught there for thirty years, you know the school like the back of your hand. You are regarded as an excellent teacher, an expert at judging the needs of your students. Should you participate in making decisions affecting the management of your school?

To get a sense of how little say teachers have once they leave their own classrooms, let's join the first faculty meeting of the fall at Someplace High. The principal, Mr. Will E. Tell, is discussing the new teacher assessment forms with the faculty:

MR. TELL: If you all look in your folders, you'll see the criteria on which you will be assessed when I observe in your classrooms. Look these forms over carefully, and let me know if you have any questions. I'll be scheduling my school observation visits with you shortly. Another issue I wanted to raise with you concerns our need to develop better relations with the community. I've passed around a sign-up sheet for a committee to turn around the low attendance at parent conferences. What I have in mind is a car wash or a bake sale or another fund-raising activity to bring the community together. Ms. Johnson, you have a question?

MS. JOHNSON: Yes, Mr. Tell. I thought that we were going to talk about setting up a better school Web site, one that can pull parents into school conferences and activities, assist students with their homework, have links to resources, and address special interest topics for teachers and parents. We all indicated at last year's faculty meeting that this should be a top priority.

MR. TELL: You're absolutely right, Louise, and I'm glad you raised the topic. That was going to be our first order of business, but I'm happy to report that the district office called yesterday and has promised us Web site support by the second semester. I'll be getting out my first newsletter to the faculty in a few weeks, and I'll be sure to include that information. I'll also be announcing the in-service training sessions for the fall semester. I heard some interesting speakers at the national convention I attended, and I think I'm going to be able to get some of them to come to our district. Before we end the meeting, I want to introduce our new faculty member. I hired Ms. Wetherby over the summer, and she'll join the teachers in our English department. I know you'll all do everything you can to make sure that Ms. Wetherby feels welcome. Now, if there are no further topics for discussion, let's all get back to our classrooms. Tomorrow the kids arrive. It's time for a new year.

From listening in on this faculty meeting, you can tell that many of the most crucial decisions were made by others. Whether a teacher will be assigned to advanced placement literature classes or remedial English is a decision usually made by the principal. Teachers, as a rule, do not participate in hiring new teachers, in developing criteria by which their teaching will be evaluated, in setting graduation requirements, or in scheduling classes.

One reason for unresponsive schools is sheer size: over the past centuries, schools and school districts continue to grow. Larger districts are considered more cost-effective because they lower the per-pupil expenses, from preparing food to building maintenance, and bigger school districts are able to offer more courses, extracurricular activities, and sports programs.[37] Merging smaller schools and districts into larger ones is called **consolidation.** (See *Frame of Reference:* Consolidation in Action.) But larger schools and school districts also mean more red tape, greater

Teachers, who know more than most people in the educational chain about the needs and interests of individual students, have often been excluded from school management and policy-making.

The following numbers show the dramatic reduction in school districts. Still, 75 percent of the remaining districts are fairly small, servicing fewer than 2,500 students each.

SOURCE: *Digest of Education Statistics 2005,* U.S. Department of Education, National Center for Education Statistics.

School Year	Number of Public School Districts
1939–1940	117,108
1949–1950	83,718
1959–1960	40,520
1970–1971	17,995
1980–1981	15,912
1989–1990	15,367
1999–2000	14,928
2003–2004	14,383

REFLECTION: While district size is difficult for a student to gauge, school size is far easier. In your opinion, what is the "ideal" size for a high school? What was the size of your high school? How does your experience influence the notion of an "ideal" size?

student alienation, and reduced parent-teacher involvement; in other words, less responsive schools.[38] Many districts are now reversing the trend, creating smaller schools and smaller districts, a process called **decentralization.**[39]

In addition to size, top-down decision making by principals and superintendents also contributes to a sense of teacher powerlessness.[40] Efforts to empower teachers include site-based or school-based management and collaborative decision making. **Site-based** or **school-based management** shifts decision making from the central district office to individual schools, while **collaborative decision making** creates teacher committees to share power between the principal and the faculty. While you may find yourself teaching in a school using one or both of these approaches, keep in mind that the results have been mixed. While some teachers enjoy making curricular and budgetary decisions, others feel such participation simply becomes "just another meeting you've got to go to."[41] To complicate these efforts even further, federally mandated tests have preempted many local decisions.[42] One of the challenges facing you as a teacher or administrator will be to create more responsive and humane school climates, both for yourself and your students.

SUMMARY

www.mhhe.com/
sadker8e

CHAPTER REVIEW

Go to the Online Learning Center to take a quiz, practice with key terms, and review concepts from the chapter.

1. Why do teachers need to know about finance and governance?

For teachers to influence the direction of schools, they need to become more involved in finance and governance issues. Unfortunately, the insights of students and teachers are rarely heard in policy circles.

2. How is the property tax connected to unequal educational funding?

Local communities generally fund their schools through a property tax, which many people consider outdated and unfair. Since some areas are wealthier than others, some school districts generate more than enough money for schools, while others must struggle to keep schools open. Robin Hood laws, built on the California *Serrano* decision, attempted to equalize educational funding between wealthy and poor communities. Resistance to these attempts led to passage of laws such as Proposition 13, which limited property taxes. Although the Supreme Court recognized that school financing is a flawed system, it did not rule the process unconstitutional. State courts continue to address these financial inequities.

3. **What is the distinction between educational *equity* and educational *adequacy*?**

Opposition grew as state court decisions, for example *Abbott* v. *Burke* in New Jersey, directed funds be moved from wealthier districts to poorer communities. Because increased funding did not always lead to higher test scores, courts began to differentiate between financial input and educational outcome. Several state court decisions have cited state constitutional language guaranteeing adequate or efficient education, and focus on the educational skills of graduates, rather than per pupil expenditures. While critics of educational equity charge that money will not solve poor educational performance, well-funded schools draw more qualified teachers and have smaller classes, two factors associated with student achievement.

4. **What are the sources of state revenues?**

The most common state sources of school funding are property tax, sales tax, personal income tax, and state lotteries. Many of these revenue sources are regressive, putting most of the burden on the poorest citizens. Although states have experimented with different funding methods, such as foundation programs and a guaranteed tax base for all districts, none has proved very successful.

5. **How does the federal government influence education?**

According to the Tenth Amendment of the U.S. Constitution, education is the responsibility of the states. Still, the federal government exercises great influence through court actions, funding leverage, and specific programs sponsored by the U.S. Department of Education. Federal monies provide between 6 and 8 percent of K–12 educational costs, much of which is in block grants.

6. **What current trends are shaping educational finance?**

School financing in the future will be influenced by demands tying school performance to funding levels (accountability), the popularity of choice programs, the economy's impact on school budgets, the great need for repairing deteriorating school buildings (infrastructure), and the continuing effort of wealthy communities to retain their tax revenues in their own community, which perpetuates educational inequality.

7. **How do school boards and superintendents manage schools?**

At the state level, the legislature, state board of education, state superintendent, and state department of education administer schools, and delegate some of its power to local school boards and superintendents. Boards of education formulate education policy and can act as trustee representatives, serving the interests of the entire community, or as representative delegates, serving the interests of their neighborhoods. The chief state school officer, often called the superintendent, is responsible for implementing those policies of the state board of education, just as the local superintendent implements the policies of the local board of education. Several large school districts are turning to former lawyers, business executives, political leaders, and even military officers to lead their school districts.

8. **What is the "hidden" government of schools?**

Parents, school secretaries, and custodians influence school life, and are part of the hidden government of schools.

9. **How does the business community influence school culture?**

The business community significantly impacts schools through its ethos, vocabulary, and value system, which promote competitiveness, conformity, and punctuality. Many question the motivation, tactics, and commercialism involved in those efforts.

10. **How are schools being made more responsive to teachers and the community?**

Traditionally, teachers have not had a significant role in school governance. Recent trends of school-based management, also called site-based management, and collaborative decision making, may provide teachers with a more influential position in school governance. Consolidation has decreased the number of school districts while increasing the average size of schools. Supporters believe that this increases educational opportunities and efficiency by absorbing small school districts with limited educational resources and electives into larger districts. Critics claim that it increases alienation and red tape.

THE *TEACHERS, SCHOOLS, AND SOCIETY* READER WITH CLASSROOM OBSERVATION VIDEO CLIPS

Go to your *Teachers, Schools, and Society* Reader CD-ROM to:

READ CURRENT AND HISTORICAL ARTICLES

9.1 **The Invisible Role of the Central Office,** Kathleen Grove, *Educational Leadership* 59, no. 8, 2002.

9.2 **Putting Money Where It Matters,** Karen Hawley Miles, *Educational Leadership,* September 2001.

ANALYZE CASE STUDIES

9.1 **Kate Sullivan:** A principal faces the problems endemic to the students served by her school, which is located in a very low socioeconomic area. Issues of drugs, poverty, neglect, hunger, and homelessness are compounded by the underfunding for the school.

9.2 **Jane Vincent:** A teacher is asked by her principal to reconsider her grading of a student whose numerical average for the marking period is just below the department's cutoff score for that grade.

OBSERVE TEACHERS, STUDENTS, AND CLASSROOMS IN ACTION

Classroom Observation 9.1: School Board Meeting

As a teacher, you will be affected by decisions made by your local school board. In this observation you will observe an actual Montgomery County (MD) School Board meeting during which officials struggle with a proposal for the district's first charter school.

KEY TERMS AND PEOPLE

accountability, 360

adequate education, 355

block grants, 359

bond, 361

categorical grants, 359

chief state school officer, 366

collaborative decision making, 376

consolidation, 375

covert power, 370

decentralization, 376

Marian Wright Edelman, 352

educational partnerships, 373

hidden government, 370

municipal overburden, 351

personal income tax, 358

property tax, 351

Robin Hood reformers, 353

sales tax, 357

San Antonio v. *Rodriguez,* 353

school boards, 365

Serrano v. *Priest,* 353

site-based (school-based) management, 376

state board of education, 366

state department of education, 366

state lotteries, 358

Tenth Amendment, 365

United States Department of Education, 359

DISCUSSION QUESTIONS AND ACTIVITIES

1. Create a plan for (a) raising funds for education and (b) distributing funds equitably to all school districts within a state.

2. What is your opinion of the "adequacy" argument? Do you have any reservations about this approach? Do you believe that educational expenditures and educational quality are directly related? Support your position.

3. Research the average costs of educating a student in a local district. Discuss with classmates as you compare district programs, tax base, facilities, and student achievement.

4. Which of the four types of school boards would you prefer to serve on, or work for? Why? Which of the four types of school superintendents would you prefer to be, or to work for? Why?

5. Have you had any personal experience in an organization that had both a formal and a "hidden" government? Explain how these governments operated.

www.mhhe.com/ sadker8e

WEB-*TIVITIES*

Go to the Online Learning Center to do the following activities:

1. States to the Rescue
2. The Federal Government's Role in Financing Education
3. The Legal Control of Schools
4. Superintendents
5. School Boards Under Fire
6. The Business of America Is Business
7. Trends in School Governance: Educational Partnerships

REEL TO REAL TEACHING

OCTOBER SKY (1999)
Run Time: 108 minutes

Synopsis: The true story of Homer Hickam, a high school student seemingly destined to repeat his father's harsh life in the West Virginia coal mines, until the Soviet launch of *Sputnik* in 1957 sparks his own scientific aspirations. With the encouragement of a science teacher, Homer and his fellow "Rocket Boys" venture to launch their own homemade rockets.

Reflection:

1. This chapter emphasizes the financing and governing of schools. How did these two factors shape students' lives in Coalwood? Give examples from the film. How did your schooling reflect educational governance and financing?

2. Consider how inequitable funding is related to geography. How does school finance impact educational opportunities in rural, suburban, and urban schools?

3. *October Sky* is set in the late 1950s, prior to many of the landmark legal rulings on educational funding discussed in this chapter. How might these court decisions have altered educational opportunities at Coalwood High?

4. What student expectations are revealed in the principal's comment to Ms. Riley: "Our job is to give these kids an education, not false hopes. Once in a while a lucky one gets out on a football scholarship. The rest work in the mines."

5. What academic and social purposes do events such as science fairs, spelling bees, and music festivals play in schools and communities? How do these differ in wealthy and poor schools? Interview classmates who attended rural, suburban, and urban schools to learn about these differences.

Follow-up Activity: *October Sky* is a "coming of age" film. Homer Hickam wrestles with accepting life in the mines and pursuing his own dreams. It is a common theme not only in film, but also in life. Interview older friends or family members about whether they were ever expected to "follow in the footsteps" of others. How did they feel about it? Why did they choose to follow tradition or make a new path? Was their decision influenced by a pivotal schooling experience, a motivating teacher, or inspiring hero? What do they think now of the decisions they made then? Capture their stories by audiotaping, video recording, or taking notes on the interviews.

www.mhhe.com/sadker8e

How do you rate this film? Go to *Reel to Real Teaching* to review this film.

FOR FURTHER READING

Cultivating Leadership in Schools: Connecting People, Purpose, and Practice, by Gordon Donaldson, Jr. (2000). Enter the real-life world of decision making by administrators, teachers, parents, and school boards. "See" how interpersonal and intrapersonal skills are the keys to successful leadership.

Reframing the Path to School Leadership, by Lee Bolman and Terrence Deal (2002). A rare blend of storytelling and analysis between teachers and principals, the authors give an optimistic view of what can go right in schools today, and what possibilities lie ahead for classroom and school leadership.

School Finance: A Policy Perspective, by Allan Odden and Larry Picus (3rd ed., 2003). Provides a roadmap through recent research on equity and adequacy, case studies on state plans for resource allocation, and a simulation allowing readers to manipulate school finance data and see the effects on resources and achievement.

Shame of a Nation: The Restoration of Apartheid Schooling in America, by Jonathon Kozol (2005). Public school resegregation is a "national horror hidden in plain view," writes former educator turned public education activist Kozol. The author visited 60 schools in 11 states over a five-year period and finds, despite the promise of *Brown* v. *Board of Education*, many schools serving black and Hispanic children are spiraling backward to the pre-Brown era. These schools lack the basics: clean classrooms, hallways, and restrooms; up-to-date books in good condition; and appropriate laboratory supplies. Kozol presents sharp and poignant portraits of the indignities vulnerable individuals endure, yet tempers the injustice with some hopeful interactions between energetic teachers and receptive children.

Who Governs Our Schools? Changing Roles and Responsibilties, by David T. Conley (2003). Provides valuable insights on and implications for the current transfer of power from local and state school governments to the national level. Examines the new federal role, including the *No Child Left Behind* Act.

School Law and Ethics

FOCUS QUESTIONS

1. What are your legal rights and responsibilities as a teacher?
2. What legal rights do students enjoy (and do they have legal responsibilities)?
3. What are today's main approaches to moral education?

**www.mhhe.com/
sadker8e**

WHAT DO YOU THINK? What is your rights quotient? Take an electronic version of the quiz starting on page 383.

CHAPTER PREVIEW

- An honors student sues the school district after being randomly strip-searched.

- A teacher is reprimanded for allowing a first grader to read a Bible story to the class.

- A school puts the senior yearbook on its Web page and finds that it helps pedophiles identify potential targets.

- A student complains that peer grading of assignments is a violation of privacy.

- A homosexual student sues a school district for discrimination.

Today, lawyers and judges are increasingly a part of school life. In this chapter, you will have the opportunity to respond to actual legal situations that have con-fronted teachers and students. (Get ready to determine your RQ—Rights Quotient.) Also included are some pragmatic steps for your legal self-defense, steps that you can take to avoid potential problems. But, beyond the nitty-gritty of these legal case studies, we will ask more penetrating questions about right and wrong, questions that go beyond the law, such as: How should teachers deal with ethical issues that emerge in the classroom? Should teachers take positions on moral issues? Or should they play a more neutral role? To handle these important but difficult ethical dilemmas, we will offer some suggestions for ways teachers can organize their classrooms, and themselves.

Classroom Law

You have probably heard it before: the United States is a litigious society. "Take them to court," "I'll sue," and "Have your lawyer call my lawyer" are phrases that have worked their way into the American lexicon. And actions match words. People sue companies. Companies sue people. Governments sue companies. Companies and people sue governments. We tend to seek redress in the courts for all kinds of problems, from divorce to physical injury, from protecting our beliefs to complying (or not complying) with laws.

Today, parents sue teachers. Students sue teachers. Teachers sue schools. Despite the growing importance and influence of school-related law, many educators are still unaware of their basic legal rights and responsibilities.[1] This can be a costly professional blind spot.

What rights do you have in the classroom? Consider this exchange between a college professor and a former associate superintendent of public instruction for California:

SUPERINTENDENT: "Teaching is a privilege, not a right. If one wants this privilege, he or she has to give up some rights."

PROFESSOR: "Just what constitutional rights do people have to give up in order to enter teaching?"

SUPERINTENDENT: "Any right their community wants them to give up."[2]

Although such simplistic attitudes still exist, recent years have seen extraordinary changes in the legal rights of both teachers and students. Once the victims of arbitrary school rules and regulations, today's teachers and students can institute legal action if they believe that their constitutional rights are being threatened. In an increasing number of cases, the courts are finding school administrators guilty of violating the rights of both teachers and students.

As a classroom teacher, what can you legally say and do? Can you let your students log freely onto the Internet? What disciplinary methods are acceptable? How does your role as teacher limit your personal life? Knowing the answers to these questions *before* you step into a classroom can help you avoid costly mistakes.

While teachers would like to know definitively what is legal and what is not, courts often set forth standards with such terms as "reasonable care" or "appropriately under the circumstances." Courts try to balance legitimate concerns that can be raised on both sides of an issue and to keep their options open. Staying legally up-to-date is an ongoing professional task.

 # What Is Your Rights Quotient?

The following case studies focus on court cases or federal law.[3] The vignettes are divided into two parts: teachers' rights and students' rights. In each case, an issue is identified, a situation is described, and you are asked to select an appropriate (legal) response. After your selection, the correct response and relevant court decisions or laws are described. Keep track of your rights and wrongs; a scoring system at the conclusion will help you determine your RQ (rights quotient). Good luck!

I. Teachers' Rights and Responsibilities

Issue

Applying for a position

Situation 1

You did it! You finished student teaching (you were great!) and the school district you most want to teach in has called you for an interview. Mr. Thomas, from the personnel office, seems impressed with your credentials and the interview is going well. He explains that the school district is very committed to its teachers and invests a great deal of resources in training. He wants to make certain that this investment makes sense, so he asks you for your long-range plans with such questions as: "Do you see yourself teaching in this system for a long time?" and "Are you planning to get married or have children in the near future?"

_____ You answer the questions realizing that the district is entitled to know about your long-range plans.

_____ You avoid answering the questions. You think it's none of his business, but you are worried that you won't get the position.

Legal Decision   Not too long ago, school districts regularly considered marital and parenthood status in employment decisions. For women these were critical factors in being offered a job, and the "right" answer was: "No, I am not going to get married or have children." For male candidates, the question was less important and rarely asked. Now a variety of federal and state laws and court decisions make such inquiries illegal. Interview questions must be related to the job requirements. Questions about race, creed, marital status, sex, religion, age, national origin, and physical or other disabilities and even a request for photographs along with an application are generally illegal. **Title IX of the Education Amendments (1972)** and **Title VII of the Civil Rights Act (1964)** are two federal laws that prohibit many of these practices. In situation 1, the questions are inappropriate and illegal, and you need not answer them. You may wish to notify the school district or even the Office for Civil Rights in order to stop the school district from asking such discriminatory questions in the future. The challenge, of course, is how you could answer such questions without ruining your chances for being offered a position—that is, if you still want the job.[4]

Issue

Sexual harassment

Situation 2

After surviving the gender discriminatory interview, you are offered a teaching position and decide to take it. After all, you like the community and the children, and with any luck you will never run into Mr. Thomas (the interviewer) again. You are very excited as you prepare for your first day. You are up an hour early, rehearsing your opening remarks. You enter the school, feeling hopeful and optimistic. Then it's your worst nightmare. You meet the new principal, Mr. Thomas, recently transferred from the personnel office. You spend the next year dodging his lewd comments, his unwanted touches, and his incessant propositions. At

Federal, state, and local governments all have a voice in education, although they don't necessarily speak in unison. To help you navigate the legal landscape, here's a brief look at how the different branches and levels of government influence school law.

THE U.S. CONSTITUTION

While the Constitution does not mention education, it does guarantee to individuals basic rights, rights that are of concern in schools. Three Constitutional Amendments are of special interest to teachers and students.

- **First Amendment** protects freedom of religion and speech. An important part of this Amendment is the **establishment clause,** which prohibits government (including school) advancement of religion.
- Fourth Amendment protects basic privacy and security.
- Fourteenth Amendment protects right to due process and equal protection.

FEDERAL LAWS

Many federal laws influence education. The Civil Rights Act of 1964 bars discrimination on the basis of race, color, or national origin. Title IX prohibits discrimination on the basis of sex. The Individuals with Disabilities Education Act expands educational opportunities to persons with disabilities. By funding certain programs, and withholding funds from others, from elementary school through college, the federal government exerts a significant influence on education.

STATE AND LOCAL LAWS

State constitutions as well as state and local laws influence education, so there are significant local differences throughout the nation. State and local laws (also known as statutes) often deal with school financing, collective bargaining, teacher certification, and compulsory attendance.

THE COURTS

A dual judicial system of state and federal courts exists in the United States. State courts initially hear most legal issues in education. Only cases challenging the U.S. Constitution or federal laws are heard in federal courts, including the U.S. Supreme Court.

SOURCE: Michael LaMorte, *School Law: Cases and Concepts,* 8th ed. (Boston: Allyn & Bacon, 2004).

REFLECTION: What are the advantages and disadvantages of these different government jurisdictions determining school law? Offer at least two benefits and drawbacks of this system.

the end of the year, you find yourself in counseling and worried about your job. You decide that

_____ Your initial instincts were right. You should never have taken this job. Quit before things get worse.

_____ Enough is enough. You sue the district for damages.

Legal Decision Anita Hill's charges against Supreme Court nominee Clarence Thomas, as well as similar charges against former President Clinton, a stream of Senators, and other officials have awakened millions of Americans to the issue of sexual harassment. The principal's behavior, both verbal and physical, is clearly an example of this problem. The Supreme Court ruled that under Title IX, victims of sexual harassment are also victims of sex discrimination and can recover monetary damages. Keeping a record of the principal's behavior and having witnesses will strengthen your case. You certainly can sue, and, if you are successful, you may be awarded significant monetary damages. You can also file a grievance with the Office for Civil Rights, without even having a lawyer. This grievance will launch an investigation of the school's practices.[5]

Along with protecting teachers from sexual harassment and sex discrimination in employment, Title IX prohibits sex discrimination in many areas of education for employees and students, males and females. The law covers federally funded institutions—schools, colleges, vocational training centers, public libraries and museums—and ensures fairness in athletics, employment, counseling, financial aid, admissions, and treatment in classrooms.

Issue   ***Situation 3***

Personal   After your first few months, your reputation is estab-
lifestyle   lished: You are known as a creative and effective
                          teacher and are well liked by students and colleagues
                          (isn't that wonderful!). But your life outside the class-
                          room is not appreciated by school officials. You are
                          single and living with your "significant other." Several
                          school officials have strong feelings about this and
                          believe that you are a poor role model for the
                          students. The school system publicly announces that
                          your cohabitation is having a negative influence on
                          your elementary-age students and suspends you.

_____ You are the victim of an illegal action and should sue to be reinstated.

_____ The school board is within its rights in dismissing you and removing
a bad role model from the classroom.

Legal Decision   This case hinges on how much personal freedom an individual abandons as a teacher and role model for students. Although court decisions
have varied, the following general standard should be kept in mind: Does your
behavior significantly disrupt the educational process or erode your credibility
with students, colleagues, or the community? If the school district can demonstrate that you have disrupted education or have lost credibility, then you may
be fired.

In the case outlined here, the teacher sued the school district (*Thompson* v.
Southwest School District). The court indicated that, until the school district took
action to suspend the teacher on grounds of immorality, the public was generally
unaware of the teacher's cohabitation with her boyfriend. The court decided that
it was unfair of the board of education to make the issue public in order to gain
community support for its position. Furthermore, the court ruled that the teacher's
behavior had not interfered with her effectiveness in the classroom. With neither
a loss of credibility nor a significant disruption of the educational process, the board
lost its case and the teacher kept her job.

What if the teacher's "significant other" was of the same sex? Whether gay and
lesbian teachers need legal protection from dismissal based on sexual orientation
is a divisive and unsettled debate. Several states and more than 100 cities and counties prohibit sexual orientation discrimination in employment. Even in places without specific laws protecting gay and lesbian teachers, it is unlikely that they can be
dismissed without direct evidence showing that a homosexual lifestyle negatively
impacts their teaching.

Court decisions regarding the personal lifestyles of teachers have differed from
state to state. Driving while intoxicated or smoking marijuana was found to be
grounds for dismissal in one state but not in another, depending on whether the
behavior resulted in "substantial disruption" of the educational process. On the
other hand, an attempt to dismiss a teacher because she did not attend church was
not upheld by the court. In fact, the teacher in this case actually won financial
damages against the school district.

What about your personal appearance? What can a school district legally require
in terms of personal grooming and dress codes for teachers? Courts have not been
consistent in their decisions, although the courts may uphold the legality of dress

Do you believe that a teacher's sexuality is a legitimate consideration for employment?

codes for teachers if the dress requirements are reasonable and related to legitimate educational concerns.[6]

Issue	*Situation 4*
Teachers' academic freedom	As a social studies teacher, you are committed to teaching about the futility of hate and discrimination. You assign your middle school students the fictional mystery *The Terrorist*, a novel that evokes strong feelings on ethnic and religious issues. Class discussions and activities focus on challenging stereotypes and creating peaceful responses to violence. Your students find the novel engaging, and class discussions are lively and respectful. But in the post-9/11 climate, some parents are upset, and the school board asks you not to teach such a controversial lesson. Committed to your beliefs, you persist. At the end of the school year, you find that your teaching contract is not renewed.

_____ Since you think your academic freedom has been violated, you decide to sue to get your job back.

_____ You realize that the school board is well within its rights to determine curriculum, that you were warned, and that now you must pay the price for your indiscretion.

Legal Decision   The right to **academic freedom** (that is, to teach without coercion, censorship, or other restrictive interference) is not absolute. The courts will balance your right to academic freedom with the school system's interests in its students' learning appropriate subject matter in an environment conducive to

The courts are constantly asked to draw the line between a teacher's personal freedom and the community's right to establish teacher behavior standards. Historically, the scales have tilted toward the community, and teachers have been fired for wearing lipstick, joining a certain church, or getting married. Today's courts make more deliberate efforts to balance personal liberty and community standards. Although each case must be judged on its own merits, some trends do emerge. The courts have ruled that the community has the right to fire a teacher for

- Making public homosexual advances to nonstudents
- Incorporating sexual issues into lessons and ignoring the approved syllabus
- Inciting violent protest among students
- Engaging in sex with students
- Encouraging students to attend certain religious meetings
- Allowing students to drink alcohol
- Drinking excessively
- Using profanity and abusive language toward students
- Having a sex-change operation
- Stealing school property (even if it is returned later)
- Not living within his or her district if that is listed as a condition of employment

On the other hand, courts have ruled that teachers should not be fired for

- Smoking of marijuana
- Private homosexual behavior
- Obesity (unless it inhibits teaching performance)
- Adultery
- Use of vulgar language outside of school
- AIDS or disability

Why are teachers dismissed in some cases and not in others? Often, the standard the courts use is whether the behavior under question reduces teacher effectiveness. Public behavior, or behavior that becomes public, may compromise a teacher's effectiveness. In such cases, the courts find it reasonable and legal to terminate the teacher. If the behavior remains private, if the teacher shows discretion, the teacher's "right to privacy" often prevails.

SOURCE: These examples have been adapted from Louis Fischer, David Schimmel, and Leslie Stallman, *Teachers and the Law* (New York: Longman, 2006).

REFLECTION: Courts have disagreed on whether the following three situations constitute grounds for dismissal of a teacher. If you were the judge, how would you rule on the following issues?

- Unwed cohabitation
- Unwed parenthood
- Conviction for shoplifting

learning. Courts look at such factors as whether your learning activities and materials are inappropriate, irrelevant to the subjects to be covered under the syllabus, obscene, or substantially disruptive of school discipline. In this case, the lesson related to ethnic and religious differences appears to be appropriate, relevant, and neither obscene nor disruptive. If you were to sue on the grounds of academic freedom, you would probably get your job back.[7]

Issue	Situation 5
Legal liability (negligence)	You are assigned to cafeteria duty. Things are pretty quiet, and you take the opportunity to call a guest speaker and confirm a visit to your class. While you are gone from the cafeteria, a student slips on some spilled milk and breaks his arm. His parents hold you liable for their son's injury and sue you for damages.

_____ You will probably win, since you did not cause the fall and were on educational business when the accident occurred.

_____ The student's parents will win, since you left your assigned post.

www.mhhe.com/sadker8e

INTERACTIVE ACTIVITY
What Can a Teacher Be Fired For? Test your knowledge of teacher's rights.

Academic freedom protects a teacher's right to teach about sensitive issues, such as AIDS or other sex education topics, as long as the topic is relevant to the course, is not treated in an obscene manner, and is not disruptive of school discipline.

_____ The student who spilled the milk is solely responsible for the accident.

_____ No one will win, because the courts long ago ruled that there is no use crying over spilled milk. (You knew that was coming, right?)

Legal Decision In recent years, litigation against teachers has increased dramatically. The public concern over the quality of education, the bureaucratic and impersonal nature of many school systems, and the generally litigious nature of our society have all contributed to this rising tide of lawsuits. Negligence suits against teachers are common. In the cafeteria example, you would be in considerable jeopardy in a legal action. A teacher who is not present at his or her assigned duty might be charged with negligence, unless the absence is "reasonable." The courts are very strict about what is "reasonable" (leaving your post to put out a fire is reasonable, but going to the telephone to make a call is unlikely to be viewed as reasonable). It is a good practice to stay in your classroom or assigned area of responsibility unless there is an emergency.

Teacher liability is an area of considerable concern to many teachers. Courts generally use two standards in determining negligence: (1) whether a reasonable person with similar training would act in the same way and (2) whether or not the teacher could have foreseen the possibility of an injury. Following are some common terms and typical situations related to teacher liability:

- *Misfeasance.* Failure to conduct in an appropriate manner an act that might otherwise have been lawfully performed; for example, unintentionally using too much force in breaking up a fight is **misfeasance.**

- *Nonfeasance.* Failure to perform an act that one has a duty to perform; for example, the cafeteria situation is **nonfeasance,** since the teacher did not supervise an assigned area of responsibility.

- *Malfeasance.* An act that cannot be done lawfully regardless of how it is performed; for example, starting a fistfight or bringing marijuana to school is **malfeasance.**

- *Educational malpractice.* Although liability litigation usually involves physical injury to students because of what a teacher did or failed to do, a new line of litigation, called **educational malpractice,** is concerned with "academic damage." Some students and parents have sued school districts for failing to provide an adequate education. Many courts have rejected these cases, pointing out that many factors affect learning and that failure to learn cannot be blamed solely on the school system.

Issue	*Situation 6*
Teachers' freedom of speech	As a teacher in a small school district, you are quite upset with the way the school board and the superintendent are spending school funds. You are particularly troubled with all the money being spent on high school athletics, since these expenditures have cut into your proposed salary raise. To protest the expenditures, you write a lengthy letter to the local newspaper, criticizing the superintendent and the school board. After the letter is published, you find that the figures you cited in the letter were inaccurate.

The following week, you are called into the superintendent's office and fired for breaking several school rules. You have failed to communicate your complaints to your superiors and you have caused harm to the school system by spreading false and malicious statements. In addition, the superintendent points out that your acceptance of a teaching position obligated you to refrain from publicizing critical statements about the school. The superintendent says although no one can stop you from making public statements, the school system certainly does not "have to pay you for the privilege." You decide to

_____ Go to court to win back your position.

_____ Chalk it up to experience, look for a new position, and make certain that you do not publish false statements and break school rules in the future.

Legal Decision This situation is based on a suit instigated by a teacher named Marvin Pickering. After balancing the teacher's interests, as a citizen, in commenting on issues of public concern against the school's interests in efficiently providing public services, the Supreme Court ruled in favor of the teacher. It found that the disciplined operation of the school system was not seriously damaged by Pickering's letter and that the misstatements in the letter were not made knowingly or recklessly. Moreover, there was no special need for confidentiality on the issue of school budgets. Hence, concluded the Court, prohibiting Pickering from making his statements was an infringement of his First Amendment right to freedom of speech. You, too, would probably win in court if you were to issue public statements on matters of public concern, unless your statements were intentionally or recklessly inaccurate, disclosed confidential material, or hampered either school discipline or your performance of duties.[8]

Issue	*Situation 7*
Copying published material	You read a fascinating two-page article in a national magazine, and, since the article concerns an issue your class is discussing, you duplicate the article and distribute it to your students. This is the only article you have distributed in class, and you do not bother to ask either the author or the magazine for permission to reprint it. You have

_____ Violated the copyright law, and you are liable to legal action.

_____ Not violated any copyright law.

Legal Decision   Initially, as copiers became commonplace in staff rooms, teachers could reproduce articles, poems, book excerpts, or whatever they pleased with virtually no fear of legal repercussions. But, in January 1976, Congress passed the **Copyright Act** (PL 94-553) and teachers' rights to freely reproduce and distribute published works were greatly curtailed. Under this law, in order to use a published work in class, teachers must write to the publisher or author of the work and obtain written permission. This sometimes requires the payment of a permission fee, something that teachers on a limited budget are usually unwilling to do. Under certain circumstances, however, teachers may still reproduce published material without written permission or payment. This is called **fair use,** a legal principle that allows the limited use of copyrighted materials. Teachers must observe three criteria in selecting the material: brevity, spontaneity, and cumulative effect.

1. *Brevity.* A work can be reproduced if it is not overly long. It is always wise to contact publishers directly, but typical limits might include the following criteria. Poems or excerpts from poems must be no longer than 250 words. Articles, stories, and essays of less than 2,500 words may be reproduced in complete form. Excerpts of any prose work (such as a book or an article) may be reproduced only up to 1,000 words or 10 percent of the work, whichever is less. Only one illustration (photo, drawing, diagram) may be reproduced from the same book or journal. The brevity criterion limits the length of the material that a teacher can reproduce and distribute from a single work. If you were the teacher in this example and you reproduced only a two-page article, you probably would not have violated the criterion of brevity.

2. *Spontaneity.* If a teacher has an inspiration to use a published work and there is simply not enough time to write for and receive written permission, then the teacher may reproduce and distribute the work. The teacher in our vignette has met this criterion so is acting within the law. If the teacher wishes to distribute the same article during the next semester or the next year, written permission would be required, since ample time exists to request such permission.

3. *Cumulative effect.* The total number of works reproduced without permission for class distribution must not exceed nine instances per class per semester. Within this limit, only one complete piece or two excerpts from the same author may be reproduced, and only three pieces from the same book or magazine. Cumulative effect limits the number of articles, poems, excerpts, and so on that can be reproduced, even if the criteria of spontaneity and brevity are met. The teacher in our vignette has not reproduced other works and therefore has met this criterion also.

Under the fair use principle, single copies of printed material may be copied for your personal use. Thus, if you want a single copy for planning a lesson, that is not a problem. Whenever multiple copies are made for classroom use, each copy must include a notice of copyright.

What about videotapes, computer software, and mixed media? Without a license or permission, educational institutions may not keep copyrighted videotapes (for example, from a television show) for more than forty-five days. The tape should not be shown more than once to students during this period, and then it must be erased. The growing use of computers prompted the amendment of the Copyright Act in 1990 to prohibit the copying of software for commercial gain. In 1998, Congress further amended the Copyright Act and passed the Digital Millennium Copyright Act to protect the vast amount of material published on the World Wide Web. Text, graphics, multimedia materials, and even e-mail are copyright protected, and teachers must follow fair use guidelines when using information obtained from the Internet and gleaned from e-mail attachments. With so much information at our fingertips, both teachers and students need to be aware that all work posted on the Internet is copyright protected, whether or not a specific notice is included. It is always advisable to check with your local school district officials to determine school policy and procedures.[9]

What are the three criteria for fair use of copyrighted materials in your classroom—and can you answer this without peeking at the text?

Issue

Labor rights

Situation 8

Salary negotiations have been going badly in your school district, and at a mass meeting teachers finally vote to strike. You honor the strike and stay home, refusing to teach until an adequate salary increase is provided. During the first week of the strike, you receive a letter from the school board, stating that you will be suspended for 15 days without pay at the end of the school year, owing to your participation in the strike. You decide

_____ To fight this illegal, unjust, and costly suspension.

_____ To accept the suspension as a legal action of the school board.

Legal Decision   In a number of cases, courts have recognized the right of teachers to organize; to join professional organizations, such as the NEA (National Education Association) and the AFT (American Federation of Teachers); and to bargain collectively for improved working conditions. You cannot legally be penalized for these activities. On the other hand, courts have upheld teachers' right to strike in only about half the states. (In some states, the courts have determined that teachers provide a vital public service and cannot strike.) You need to understand your state laws to know if you are breaking the law by honoring the strike. The school board may be within its rights to suspend, fine, or even fire you for striking.

Although about half of the states have laws that prohibit strikes, many communities choose not to prosecute striking teachers. Conversely, even though

New teachers, without the protection of tenure, can be particularly vulnerable during a strike. If you find yourself in a school district where a strike has been called, you must decide if you believe the strike is justified and if you will join it or not. These are difficult decisions. Part of your decision process should consider whether the strike is legal or not. Sometimes the answer is "yes," but most times it is "no." To help you with the legal question, you should know that strikes are legal for K–12 educators in Alaska, California, Colorado, Hawaii, Illinois, Louisiana, Minnesota, Montana, North Dakota, Oregon, Pennsylvania, and, in very limited cases, Wisconsin.

SOURCE: National Education Association, *Collective Bargaining Laws for Public Sector Education Employees* (Washington, DC: NEA, October 2001).

REFLECTION: Can you offer any generalizations about the states that permit K–12 teachers to strike? What specific circumstance would cause you to strike?

membership in teacher organizations and the right to collective bargaining have been upheld by the courts, some communities and school boards are adamantly opposed to such organizations and refuse to hire or to renew contracts of teachers who are active in them. Such bias is clearly illegal; nevertheless, it is very difficult to prove in court and, consequently, it is very difficult to stop.

In summary, law and reality do not always coincide. Legally speaking, teachers may be prohibited from striking by state law but are rarely prosecuted or penalized. In some communities, however, active involvement in teacher organizations may result in discriminatory school board actions. If you choose to strike, do so with the realization that such activity makes you liable to legal sanctions.[10]

Issue

Sex-segregated classes

Situation 9

As a physical education teacher, you have grown to dislike coed classes, where students seem to abandon athletic skill development for social skill development. To avoid these coeducational problems, you try to separate the sexes so each can focus on athletic skills at their own level. You are pleased to learn that the local country club will now allow the school to use its golf course, but you worry that having female students swinging widely at the country club might lead to the end of the school's golf course privileges. You also note that in a coeducational class, more time is needed for teaching basic skills, but in the boys' class, more time is spent actually playing golf. It makes sense to have the boys register for the country club golf class while the girls register for the golf section that meets on the school field. You are amazed (and relieved) how the two classes fill up, but something still is troubling: are these all-boys and all-girls' classes legal?

_____ Yes. Title IX requires that males and females be given equitable opportunities to learn and explore their athletic interests. The two-course solution allows both sexes to play golf and makes good pedagogical sense.

_____ No. Girls and boys may be separated under certain circumstances, but golf is not one. This violates the law.

Although many states have laws prohibiting teachers from striking, most communities choose not to penalize striking teachers.

Legal Decision   No, this is not legal. Using skill levels to group students is legal, BUT using gender to group students usually is not. For example, if the teacher gave a skill test to each student to gauge golf skills, and then grouped students by ability as beginner, mid-level, and advanced, that would be legal. If all the boys were tested and found to be at the advanced level and all girls tested and found to be beginners, that would be legal as well. But it is ability level—not an assumption of one gender being better in a sport—that must determine assignments. Obviously, some girls may be more skilled than boys, and an objective assessment of all students will best determine this, not sexist assumptions.

Title IX prohibits sex segregation in physical education classes except for the following:

- Students may be separated by sex within coeducational classes when participating in wrestling, boxing, rugby, ice hockey, football, basketball, and other sports, the purpose or major activity of which involves bodily contact.

- Students may be grouped according to ability for instruction if the assessment is made using objective standards of individual performance.

- If students' religious beliefs prohibit them from participating in coeducational physical education, they may be excused from such classes or offered sex-segregated physical education.[11]

II. Students' Rights and Responsibilities

Issue

Student records

Situation 10

You are a high school teacher who has decided to stay after school and review your students' records. You believe that learning more about your students will make you a more effective teacher. As you finish reviewing some of the folders, Brenda, a 16-year-old student of

...UNTIL JUSTICE ROLLS DOWN LIKE WATERS AND RIGHTEOUSNESS LIKE A MIGHTY STREAM
MARTIN LUTHER KING JR.

"Flight delayed." For most, those two words evoke frustration and impatience. But for Morris Dees, a delayed flight was a life-changing event. At the airport bookstore, he bought a used copy of Clarence Darrow's *The Story of My Life.* While he had long admired Darrow for his defense of John Scopes in the famous "Monkey Trial," Dees had not known of Darrow's decision to leave the security and success of corporate litigation to practice civil rights law. Darrow's choice inspired Dees. "[A]ll the pulls and tugs of my conscience found a singular peace. It did not matter what my neighbors would think or the judges, the bankers, or even my friends. I had found an opportunity to return to my roots, to fight for racial equality."[1] He sold the profitable book company that he had started with a friend, and began to practice civil rights law full time.

Dees had earned a law degree from the University of Alabama and had become quite successful, both at his small law firm and at his book company, Fuller & Dees, which became one of the country's largest publishing houses. The company was based in Montgomery, Alabama. While Dees turned profits, Martin Luther King, Jr. was in the same city, focused on turning hearts. As Dees points out, back then, he didn't pay much attention to King.

"The Movement happened all around me, but I was oblivious, too caught up in the finesse of business . . . until [that] stormy night in 1967 at a Cincinnati airport."[2]

Not that Dees was new to the racial struggle of the South. Growing up in Alabama, Morris Dees worked with black laborers in the cotton fields his father owned, an unusual partnership in the deeply segregated South of the 1940s. As he worked alongside them, he learned about the scars of prejudice, both physical and emotional. The seeds of his career in civil rights advocacy were sown on those Alabama cotton fields, but needed time to take root.

In 1969, Dees sued the YMCA. Fifteen years after *Brown* v. *Board of Education,* the YMCA still refused to admit African American youth to its summer camp. Dees filed a class action suit to stop the YMCA's policy of racial discrimination. The suit was a long shot. Private organizations were considered beyond the scope of civil rights law—the business and social stalwarts untouchable. Morris Dees didn't flinch, and because of *Smith* v. *YMCA,* the Montgomery YMCA was forced to desegregate.

Lawyer Joe Levin, another Alabamian, followed *Smith* v. *YMCA* closely, impressed with the imagination and dogged determination of Dees. In 1971, the two joined forces to create a small civil rights firm, the Southern Poverty Law Center (SPLC). Today the SPLC is a national nonprofit organization known for its legal victories against white supremacist groups, tracking of hate groups, and sponsorship of the Civil Rights Memorial.

Dees' call for justice and understanding can be heard in the class-room as well. Dees has created Teaching Tolerance, a collaboration between the SPLC and teachers across the country. The project features a magazine, videos, and curriculum to help teachers and students collectively tackle issues of racial, religious, class, and gender bias.

After completing a study that showed an increase of hate Web sites, Dees realized that "[h]ate has a new home. The Internet. We need to recapture the wonder of the Internet and use it to spread fairness."[3] Dees and Teaching Tolerance created Tolerance.org, an interactive site of antibias lessons and classroom activities. After more than thirty years of litigation and education, Morris Dees has adopted this latest tool in his quest for social justice. "To everything there is a season. There will be a season of justice."[4]

[1] Morris Dees, *A Season for Justice: The Life and Times of Civil Rights Lawyer Morris Dees* (New York: Charles Scribner, 1991). [2] Ibid. [3] Morris Dees, "About Tolerance.org," www.tolerance.org (July 29, 2001). [4] Dees, *A Season for Justice.*

REFLECTION: Will you choose to confront discriminatory attitudes and behavior in your classroom? In yourself? (Yes, we all have biases.) How? Take a tour of http://tolerance.org. Submit an original antibias teaching idea to Tolerance.org.

www.mhhe.com/sadker8e

To learn more about Morris Dees, click on *Profiles in Education.*

yours, walks in and asks to see her folder. Since you
have several sensitive comments recorded in the folder,
you refuse. Within the hour, the student's parents call
and ask if they can see the folder. At this point, you

_____ Explain that the information is confidential and sensitive and cannot
be shared with nonprofessional personnel.

_____ Explain that the parents can see the folder and describe the procedure
for doing so.

Legal Decision The Family Rights and Privacy Act, commonly referred to as the
Buckley Amendment (1974), allows parents and guardians access to their children's educational records. The amendment also requires that school districts inform
parents of this right and establish a procedure for providing educational records on
request. Moreover, written parental permission is needed before these records can be
shared with anyone other than professionals connected with either the school the
student attends or another school in which the student seeks to enroll, health or
safety officials, or persons reviewing the student's financial aid applications. If the
student has reached 18 years of age, he or she must be allowed to see the folder and
is responsible for granting permission for others to review the folder. The Buckley
Amendment was recently tested by the common teacher practice of asking students
to exchange and grade others' papers. In *Owasso Independent School District* v. *Falvo*
(2002), the Supreme Court ruled that students can grade their peers' academic work
and even announce the results in class without violating the privacy act. The Court
determined that under the Buckley Amendment grades do not become private and
part of students' educational records until they are recorded in a teacher's grade book.

Under this law, you should have chosen the second option, for it is the parents'
right to see this information.[12]

Issue	*Situation 11*
Distribution of scholarships	As a secondary teacher, you are concerned with the manner in which scholarships and other financial awards (donated by the local booster club and neighborhood businesses) are distributed at graduation. You notice that nearly all the awards are going to boys. You mention this to the principal, who explains that this has been the case for as long as anyone can remember. The groups donating the scholarship funds use such categories as leadership skills and sports abilities in choosing the recipients. The principal says that, although this is not exactly equitable, it is realistic, because future financial burdens hit males more than females. You decide that

_____ It is an unfortunate but realistic policy.

_____ It is unfair, unreasonable, and unrealistic. You file a complaint with the
Office for Civil Rights.

Legal Decision Title IX prohibits using sex as a criterion by which to grant awards,
scholarships, or financial aid. Scholarships and aid must be awarded by objective
criteria fairly applied without regard to sex. If it turns out that the most qualified
students in a given year are predominantly or entirely of one sex, that is acceptable,

Corporal punishment, the physical discipline of students, is deplored by most educators, yet it remains legal in approximately half the states.

The Children's Defense Fund estimates that a public school student is physically punished every 13 seconds.

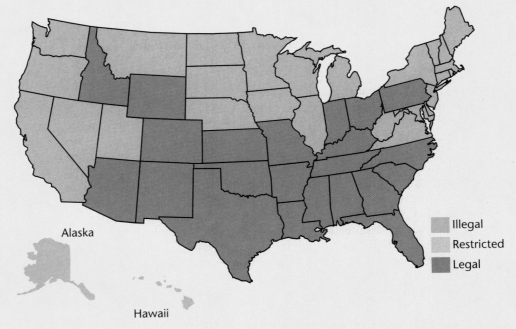

Alaska

Hawaii

Illegal

Restricted

Legal

SOURCE: Children's Defense Fund, "Moments in America for Children," *Children's Defense Fund Online,* November 2005; Louis Fischer, David Schimmel, and Leslie Stallman, *Teachers and the Law* (New York: Longman, 2006).

REFLECTION: Knowing whether corporal punishment is legal in your state and in your school is only part of the issue; sorting out your philosophy on this issue is more to the point. As a teacher, would you use physical punishment against a student? Explain your reasoning.

as long as the procedures and criteria have been fairly applied. But sex itself should not be a criterion; this example is a violation of Title IX and should be corrected.[13]

Issue	Situation 12
Suspension and discipline	You are teaching a difficult class, and one student is the primary source of trouble. After a string of disorderly episodes on this student's part, the iPods for the entire class mysteriously disappear. You have put up with more than enough, and you send the student to the principal's office to be suspended. The principal backs you up, and the student is told not to return to school for a week. This action is

_____ Legal and appropriate (and probably long overdue!).

_____ Illegal.

Legal Decision   Although troublesome and disorderly students can be disciplined, suspension from school represents a serious penalty, one that should not be taken lightly. In such cases, the Supreme Court has ruled (***Goss v. Lopez***) that teachers and administrators are required to follow certain procedures in order to guarantee the student's **due process** rights granted by the 14th Amendment. In this case, the student must be informed of the rule that has been broken and of the evidence. The student is also entitled to tell his or her side of the story in self-defense. For suspensions in excess of ten days, the school must initiate more formal procedures. School officials can be held personally liable for damages if they violate a student's clearly established constitutional rights (*Wood* v. *Strickland*).

If you look back at this vignette, you will notice that you do not know for sure that this student is responsible for the missing iPods, nor is the student given the opportunity for self-defense. If you selected "illegal," you chose the correct response.

Many schools have adopted zero-tolerance policies in an attempt to create safe schools. A **zero-tolerance policy** typically sets out predetermined consequences or punishment for specific offenses, regardless of the circumstances or disciplinary history of the student involved. Nine out of ten schools report zero-tolerance policies for firearms. Many schools have zero-tolerance policies covering possession of alcohol, drugs, and tobacco, as well as incidents of violence. Courts have generally ruled that students' constitutional right to due process is not violated by zero-tolerance policies.

Zero tolerance sends a powerful message to the school community that violent, aggressive behavior is not acceptable. However, opponents point out that zero-tolerance policies are inherently unfair and can backfire. For example, one six-year-old was expelled for bringing a weapon into school. His grandmother had placed a "weapon" in his lunch sack—a plastic knife for spreading peanut butter. The American Bar Association has denounced zero-tolerance policies that mandate expulsion or referral to juvenile court for minor offenses that do not compromise school safety.

While considering discipline, let us look at the legality of **corporal punishment**. In *Ingraham* v. *Wright* (1977), the Supreme Court ruled that physical punishment may be authorized by the states. The Court ruled that the corporal punishment should be "reasonable and not excessive," and such factors as the seriousness of the student offense, the age and physical condition of the student, and the force and attitude of the person administering the punishment should be considered. Although the courts have legalized corporal punishment, many states and school districts do not believe in it and have prohibited the physical punishment of students; other districts and states provide very specific guidelines for its practice. You should be familiar with the procedures and norms in your district before you even consider this disciplinary strategy.[14]

Issue	*Situation 13*
Freedom of speech	During your homeroom period, you notice that several of your more politically active students are wearing T-shirts with a red line drawn through "www." You call them to your desk and ask them about it. They explain that they are protesting censorship, the new school board policy that limits student access on the Internet. You tell them that you share their concern but that wearing the T-shirts is specifically forbidden by school rules. You explain that you will let it go this time, since

they are not disturbing the class routine, but that if they wear them again, they will be suspended.

Sure enough, the next day the same students arrive at school still wearing the T-shirts, and you send them to the principal's office. The students tell the principal that, although they understand the rule, they refuse to obey it. The principal, explaining that school rules are made to be followed, suspends them. The principal's action is

_____ Legally justified, since the students were given every opportunity to understand and obey the school rule.

_____ Illegal, since the students have the right to wear T-shirts if they so desire.

Legal Decision   In December 1965, three students in Des Moines, Iowa, demonstrated their opposition to the Vietnam War by wearing black arm bands to school. The principal informed them that they were breaking a school rule and asked that they remove the arm bands. They refused and were suspended.

The students' parents sued the school system, and the case finally reached the Supreme Court. In the landmark ***Tinker*** case, the Court ruled that the students were entitled to wear the arm bands, as long as the students did not substantially disrupt the operation of the school or deny other students the opportunity to learn. Since there was no disruption, the Court ruled that the school system could not prohibit students from wearing the arm bands or engaging in other forms of free speech. The school system in this vignette acted illegally; it could not prevent students from wearing the protest T-shirts. Hate speech is another matter. For example, a California high school prevented a student from wearing a T-shirt with the slogan "Homosexuals are shameful." The student argued that such a dress code

Courts have upheld students' freedom of speech in a number of cases, so long as the protests were not disruptive of other students' right to learn and were not obscene.

policy violated his First Amendment right to free speech. But a federal court ruled that "demeaning of young gay and lesbian students in a school environment is detrimental not only to their psychological health and well-being, but also to their educational development" and that students should feel safe from attacks based on sexual orientation, race, religion, and gender while at school.[15]

Does *Tinker* apply in cyberspace? Probably. Although the courts have not definitely resolved the issue, early "cyberTinker" decisions support First Amendment rights. One of the first lawsuits arose after a Missouri high school suspended a student for creating an Internet homepage that criticized his school administration. The student, Brandon Buessink, created the homepage outside of school on his home computer. The Web site caused no documented disturbance at this school and a federal district court reversed the suspension, citing the principal's simple dislike of the content as "unreasonable justification for limiting it."[16]

The issue of allegedly "obscene" speech has been considered by the Supreme Court. In a 1986 decision (*Bethel School District* v. *Fraser*), the Court evaluated the First Amendment rights of a high school senior, Matthew Fraser. Fraser presented a speech at a school assembly that contained numerous sexual innuendoes, though no explicit, profane language. After Fraser was suspended for his speech and told that he was no longer eligible to speak at his class's graduation, his father sued the school district. The Court upheld the suspension on the grounds that the language in the speech was indecent and offensive and that minors should not be exposed to such language. Obscene speech posted on the Internet from a student's home computer is also not constitutionally protected. A Pennsylvania district court upheld the suspension of a middle school student for posting inflammatory and perverse comments about his principal and algebra teacher.[17]

Issue	*Situation 14*
School prayer	A student on your team objects to the daily prayer recitation. You are sensitive to the student's feelings, and you make certain that the prayer is nondenominational. Moreover, you tell the student that he may stand or sit silently without reciting the prayer. If the student likes, he may even leave the gym while the prayer is being recited. As a teacher, you have

_____ Broken the law.

_____ Demonstrated sensitivity to individual needs and not violated the law.

Legal Decision   You were sensitive but not sensitive enough—you violated the law. As a result of leaving the gym, the student might be subjected to embarrassment, ostracism, or some other form of social stigma. The Supreme Court has ruled that educators must be completely neutral with regard to religion and may neither encourage nor discourage prayer. The Court has ruled that the separation of church and state prevents educators, but not necessarily students, from promoting religious activities. For example, students may engage in private prayer and religious discussion during school, and form religious clubs on school property if other, nonreligious clubs are also given school space. "Official"

IMAGINE . . .

Religious Freedom for All?

In Alabama, a family of Jewish children was repeatedly harassed after complaining about the promotion of Christian beliefs in their public schools. One of the students was forced to write an essay on "Why Jesus Loves Me." At a mandatory school assembly, a Christian minister condemned to hell all people who did not believe in Jesus Christ.

SOURCE: Anti-Defamation League, May 19, 2006, www.adl.org/issue_religious_freedom/separation_cs_primer _violations_schools.asp.

prayers given by school personnel are not permitted, even at graduation ceremonies (where they frequently are heard despite the law). State laws vary on whether a student can give a graduation speech when the speech becomes a platform for prayer. However, the Court has declared that student-led public prayers at athletic events constitute school sponsorship of religion, a violation of the establishment clause of the First Amendment. The Pledge of Allegiance also sparks controversy in public schools. Though many state and local school districts often champion the need for patriotism when requiring students to recite the pledge, students cannot be compelled to salute the flag. Finally, a moment of silence can be observed in schools as long as it does not encourage prayer over any other quiet, contemplative activity. Students can, however, voluntarily choose to pray during this time.

No Child Left Behind legislation gives special attention to school prayer, requiring states to certify that their school policies do not prevent constitutionally protected prayer. If states fail to comply, they can lose funding, connecting for the first time federal money to student prayer rights. Such mandates will undoubtedly continue debate on the role of religion in public schools.[18]

Issue	*Situation 15*
Search and seizure	The drug problem in your school is spreading, and it is clear that strong action is needed. School authorities order a search of all student lockers, which lasts for several hours. Trained police dogs are brought in, and each classroom is searched for drugs. The dogs sniff suspiciously at several students, who are taken to the locker rooms and strip-searched.

_____ School authorities are well within their rights to conduct these searches.

_____ Searching the lockers is legal, but strip-searching is inappropriate and illegal.

_____ No searches are called for, and all of these activities present illegal and unconstitutional violation of student rights.

Legal Decision Courts have ruled that school authorities have fewer restrictions than do the police in search-and-seizure activities. Courts have indicated that school property (such as lockers or cars parked in the school lot) are actually the responsibility of the school. Moreover, the school has a parentlike responsibility (termed **in loco parentis**) to protect children and to respond to reasonable concerns about their health and safety. Even random drug testing of students participating in extracurricular activities is permissible.

In situation 15, the search of lockers is legal. However, using police dogs to sniff students (rather than things) is allowable only if the dogs are reliable and the student is a reasonable suspect. The strip-search is illegal.

The second choice is the correct response. Although school personnel have great latitude in conducting school search and seizures, educators should be familiar with proper legal procedures and should think carefully about the related ethical issues.[19]

Issue	*Situation 16*
Freedom of the press	*The Argus* is the official student newspaper, written by students as part of a journalism course, but it has run afoul of school administrators. First the student newspaper ran a story critical of the school administration.

How might these students (and their teachers) feel as they begin the school day? How do search and seizure responsibilities in schools contrast with those for the general public?

In the next edition, the paper included a supplement on contraception and abortion. With their patience worn thin, school administrators closed the publication for the remainder of the school year.

_____ Closing the student newspaper is a legal action.

_____ Closing the student newspaper is an illegal action.

Legal Decision In 1988, a relatively conservative Supreme Court ruled in the *Hazelwood* case that student newspapers may be censored under certain circumstances. The Court held that student newspapers written as part of a school journalism course should be viewed as part of the official school curriculum. School administrators, according to the Court, can readily censor such a paper. In situation 16, since the publication is part of a journalism course, closing the school newspaper would be legal.

On the other hand, if the newspaper were financed by the students and not associated with an official school course, the students would enjoy a greater degree of freedom. Additional grounds for censoring a school newspaper include obscenity, psychological harm, and disruption of school activities.[20]

Issue	*Situation 17*
HIV-infected students	As you enter school one morning, you are met by a group of angry parents. They have found out that Randy, one of your students, is HIV positive, and hence can transmit the AIDS-related virus to others. There is no cure for AIDS, and there is no compromise in the voices of the parents confronting you. Either Randy goes, or they will keep their children at home. You listen sympathetically, but find your mind wandering to your own contact with Randy. You worry that you, too, may be at risk. In this case, you decide

_____ It's better to be safe than sorry, so you ask Randy to return home while you arrange a meeting with the principal to discuss Randy's case. There is no cure for AIDS and no reason to put every child's life in jeopardy.

_____ It's probably okay for Randy to attend school, so you check with your principal and try to calm the parents down.

Legal Decision   In a case very similar to this situation, Randy, a hemophiliac, and his brothers were denied access to De Soto County Schools in Florida when they tested positive for the HIV virus. The court determined that the boys' loss of their education was more harmful than the remote chance of other students' contracting AIDS. In fact, in this 1987 case, Randy's parents won an out-of-court settlement in excess of $1 million for the pain the school system inflicted on the family. In *Bragdon* v. *Abbott* (1998), the court determined that HIV-infected students are protected under PL 94-142, the Individuals with Disabilities Education Act. Clearly, medical guidelines direct the court. If some AIDS children present more of a public risk (for example, because of biting behavior, open sores, and fighting), more restrictive school environments may be required. To date, however, HIV-infected students and teachers are not viewed as a significant risk to the health of the rest of the population and cannot be denied their educational rights.[21]

Issue	*Situation 18*
Sexual harassment	One of your favorite students appears particularly upset. You are concerned, so you go over to Pat and put your arm around him. Pat stiffens his shoulder and pushes you away. He is obviously distressed about something. The next day, you offer to take Pat to a local fast-food restaurant after school, to cheer him up with a hot fudge sundae. He refuses to go but thanks you for the gesture. A few weeks later, the principal calls you into her office to explain that you have been charged with sexual harassment.

_____ You decide not to respond to the principal until you seek legal advice.

_____ You decide to apologize, realizing that you have overstepped the boundaries of propriety.

Legal Decision   In *Franklin* v. *Gwinnett* (1992), the Supreme Court extended the reach of Title IX, allowing students to sue a school district for monetary damages in cases of sexual harassment. The Gwinnett County case involved a Georgia high school student who was sexually harassed and abused by a teacher, a case much more serious than the pat on the back and offer of a hot fudge sundae described in the vignette above. In Georgia, the teacher's behavior was extreme and the school district's response inadequate. The school district was instructed to pay damages to the student—establishing a precedent.

However, just a few years later the Court made collecting personal damages from school districts more difficult. The Court ruled that the school district had to show "deliberate indifference" to complaints about teacher and peer sexual harassment before the district would be forced to pay damages [*Gebser* v. *Lago Independent School District* (1998) and *Davis* v. *Monroe County Board of Education* (1999)]. In fact, just notifying the principal when sexual harassment occurred was insufficient, according to the Court. More powerful officials would need to know and not act on this information before damages could be collected—clearly, an extremely difficult standard. The school district could suffer Title IX penalties (lose federal funds), and the individual accused of harassment could be forced to pay personal damages, but the school district, the place where large funds are available, could not be sued.[22]

Teachers have both a legal and ethical responsibility to prevent and respond to harassment. Sexual harassment is a pervasive, harrowing part of everyday school life for both males and females. (See Figure 10.1.) Four out of five students report being harassed at school. Harassment ranges from sexual comments and gestures, to inappropriate touching, to rape—and the consequences are troubling. Students fear attending school, withdraw from friends and activities, and suffer sleep and eating difficulties.

Title IX protections against sexual harassment also apply to gay and lesbian students. Hostility and ridicule toward homosexual students may be actionable in court if they are sufficiently severe and pervasive. For example, a gay student in

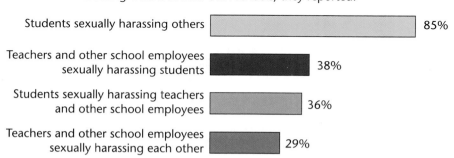

When students were asked for their perceptions of who is harassing whom in their own schools, they reported:

Students sexually harassing others — 85%

Teachers and other school employees sexually harassing students — 38%

Students sexually harassing teachers and other school employees — 36%

Teachers and other school employees sexually harassing each other — 29%

FIGURE 10.1

Who harasses whom?

SOURCE: Harris Interactive, *Bullying, Teasing and Sexual Harassment in School.* Commissioned by AAUW Educational Foundation (Washington, DC: American Association of University Women, 2001), p. 14.

REFLECTION: Girls' and boys' assessments of their school climate generally mirror their personal experiences, with one exception. Students perceive that teachers and other school adults harass students more than they personally have experienced. What reasons might you offer for this discrepancy? As a teacher, if you observed each of these four kinds of harassment, how would you respond?

The following summaries highlight the critical cases that have defined the boundaries of civil rights and liberties in American schools. You may not agree with all these Supreme Court decisions, but for now, they are the law of the land.

TEACHERS' RIGHTS
Freedom of Speech
Pickering v. Board of Education (1968)

A teacher's letter to the newspaper, a letter that criticized the school board, contained some false statements made because of incomplete research. The teacher was fired. The Court determined that the teacher's letter neither seriously damaged the disciplined operation of the school, disclosed confidential information, nor contained any misstatements that were made knowingly or recklessly. Under the First Amendment, a teacher has the same rights as all other citizens to comment on issues of legitimate public concern, such as a school board's decisions in allocating funds.

Separation of Church and State
Engel v. Vitale (1962)

A local school board instructed that a prayer composed by the New York Board of Regents be recited aloud every day by each class. The prayer was nondenominational and voluntary. Students who did not want to recite the prayer were permitted to remain silent or leave the classroom while the prayer was said. The Supreme Court held that the New York statute authorizing the prayer in school violated the First Amendment, particularly the establishment clause, and that official, organized prayer in school is not permitted.

Wallace v. Jaffree (1985)
Lee v. Weisman (1992)

Alabama enacted a law that authorized a 1-minute period of silence in all public schools for meditation or voluntary prayer. The Supreme Court held that the Alabama law violated the establishment clause. To determine whether the Alabama law was constitutional, the Court applied the three-part test established in *Lemon v. Kurtzman,* (1971): did the policy (1) have a secular purpose, (2) have a primarily secular effect, and (3) avoid excessive government entanglement with religion? In *Wallace,* the Alabama statute was found to have a religious rather than a secular purpose and was thus ruled unconstitutional. A moment of silence may be observed when its purpose is secular and does not require or encourage prayer over other contemplative activities. In *Weisman,* the court declared prayer led by school personnel at public school graduation to violate the establishment clause.

McCollum v. Board of Education (1948)
Board of Education of the Westside Community Schools v. Mergens (1990);
Good News Club v. Milford Central Schools (2001)

In *McCollum,* an Illinois school district allowed privately employed religious teachers to hold weekly religious classes on public premises. The students who chose not to attend these classes in religious instruction pursued their secular studies in other classrooms in the building. The Court ruled that a program allowing religious instruction inside public schools during the school day was unconstitutional, because it violated the establishment clause. However, in 1990, the Court modified this somewhat by allowing the use of school facilities by student organizations after school hours if other student clubs had similar access. In *Milford,* the Court allowed adult-led religious organizations the use of school facilities, further lowering the figurative wall of separation between church and state.

Stone v. Graham (1980)

A Kentucky statute required the posting of a copy of the Ten Commandments, purchased with private contributions, on the wall of each public classroom in the state. Despite the fact that the copies of the Ten Commandments were purchased with private funds and had a notation describing them as secular, the statute requiring that they be posted in every public school classroom was declared unconstitutional. Under the three-part *Lemon* test, the Court concluded that the statute requiring posting of the Ten Commandments failed under part 1 of the test in that it lacked a secular purpose. Merely stating that the Ten Commandments are secular does not make them so.

Academic Freedom and Teaching Evolution
Epperson v. Arkansas (1968)
Edwards v. Aquillard (1987)

In *Epperson,* the Court ruled that the teaching of evolution does not violate the First Amendment's call for separation of church and state. During the 1980s, religious fundamentalists won state "balanced" rulings that required science teachers to give equal instructional time to Biblical creationism and evolution. But the Supreme Court did not agree. In *Edwards,* the Court declared that policies *requiring* instruction in creationism violate the First Amendment's establishment clause.

Sexual Harassment
North Haven Board of Education v. Bell (1982)

The Court affirmed that Title IX protects teachers from discrimination based on sex. Title IX joined two other federal statutes, Title VII of the 1964 Civil Rights Act and the 1963 Equal Pay Act, to protect employees from sex discrimination.

STUDENTS' RIGHTS
Freedom of Speech (Symbolic)
Tinker v. Des Moines Independent Community School District (1969)

Unless there is substantial disruption in the school caused by student protest, the school board cannot deprive the students of their First Amendment right to freedom of speech. Students do not shed their constitutional rights at the school door. (See situation 13.)

West Virginia State Board of Education v. Barnette (1943)

A compulsory flag-salute statute in the public school regulations required all students and teachers to salute the U.S. flag every day. Two Jehovah's Witness students refused to salute the flag, because doing so would be contrary to their religious beliefs, and they were not permitted to attend the public schools. The Court determined that students cannot be compelled to pledge allegiance to the flag in public schools, a right protected by the First Amendment.

Freedom of Speech (Verbal)

Bethel School District v. Fraser (1986)

The Supreme Court, balancing the student's freedom to advocate controversial ideas with the school's interests in setting the boundaries of socially appropriate behavior, found that the First Amendment does not prevent school authorities from disciplining students for speech that is lewd and offensive.

Freedom of the Press

Hazelwood School District v. Kuhlmeir (1988)

Two articles about divorce and teenage pregnancy that were written in the student paper were deleted by the principal. The Supreme Court held that, since the student paper was school-sponsored and school-funded and was part of the school's journalism class, the school principal had the right to control its content. On the other hand, the courts have ruled that school authorities may not censor student newspapers produced at the students' own expense and those produced off school property, papers not part of any school's curriculum.

Freedom of Access to the Printed Word

Board of Education, Island Trees Union Free School District No. 26 v. Pico (1982)

A school board decided to remove nine books from the school library because the board members felt the books were objectionable and improper for students. The court ruled that school boards may not suppress ideas by removing books from a school library based on their feelings that the material contains controversial or unpopular viewpoints.

Right to Due Process

Goss v. Lopez (1975)

New Jersey v. T.L.O. (1985)

In Goss, several high school students were suspended from school for ten days. The Supreme Court held that before a principal can suspend a student, he or she must present the student with the charges and provide the student with a hearing or opportunity to defend against the charges. The 14th Amendment's due process procedures mandated as a result of this decision can be compared to the "Miranda rights" required in criminal cases. In T.L.O. the Court determined that school officials are not necessarily bound by the Fourth Amendment but by reasonable cause when engaged in a search.

Ingraham v. Wright (1977)

Florida statute allowed corporal punishment. Two students were punished by being hit with a flat wooden paddle and later sued the schools. The Supreme Court held that corporal punishment, such as the paddling, is not cruel and unusual punishment and does not necessarily deprive the student of his or her rights.

Separation of Church and State

Santa Fe Independent School District v. Doe (2000)

In a 6–3 ruling, the Supreme Court held that student-led prayer at football games violated the U.S. Constitution's prohibition against a government establishment of religion. The majority said the Texas school district's authorization of a student vote on whether to have an invocation before games and the election of a student speaker amounted to government sponsorship of prayer.

School Attendance and Choice

Pierce v. Society of Sisters of the Holy Names of Jesus & Mary (1925)

Plyer v. Doe (1982)

Zelman v. Simmons-Harris (2002)

Although most of us take school for granted, the right to an education and freedom to choose a school often spark legal debate. School choice appeared on the legal landscape with Pierce. The Court deemed unconstitutional an Oregon law requiring parents to send their children to public schools. Such a law denied parents the right to control their children's education. Plyer extended the reach of public education. The Court ruled that Texas could not withhold free public education from illegal immigrants because "education provides the basic tools by which individuals might lead economically productive lives to the benefit of us all." Zelman ushered in a new era of school choice as the Court affirmed that parents could use public vouchers to send their children to private religious schools.

Sexual Harassment

Franklin v. Gwinnett County Public Schools (1992)

The Franklin case involved a Georgia high school student who alleged that a teacher-coach engaged in behavior toward her ranging from unwelcome verbal advances to pressured sexual intercourse on school grounds. The Court ruled that "victims of sexual harassment and other forms of sex discrimination in schools may sue for monetary damages" under Title IX of the Education Amendments of 1972.

continued

Gebser v. *Lago Vista Independent School District* (1998)

The Court limited the circumstances under which a school district can be held liable for monetary damages for a teacher's sexual harassment of a student. The court ruled 5–4 that a district cannot be held liable under Title IX unless a district official with the authority to take corrective action had actual knowledge of teacher misconduct and was deliberately indifferent to it.

Davis v. *Monroe County Board of Education* (1999)

In a 5–4 ruling, the Court held that districts may be found liable under Title IX only when they are "deliberately indifferent" to information about peer harassment at school and when the harassment is so "severe, pervasive, and objectively offensive" that it bars the victim's access to an educational program or benefit.

> **REFLECTION:** Can you recall a time when you believe your rights as a student (or the rights of a classmate) were denied? Describe those events. What court cases and parts of the U.S. Constitution would apply to the situation?

Wisconsin was awarded a $900,000 judgment when his school district failed to end the violence he endured at the hands of classmates from grades 7 through 11. This landmark case established that school districts must take action to protect gay and lesbian students. Title IX does not apply, however, to heckling about a person's sexual orientation. For example, Title IX does not prohibit comments like "Gay students not welcome here" or "We fear queers," although such comments might well violate other civil rights or school conduct policies. For example, a lesbian student in California was barred from gym class after her teacher learned of her sexual orientation. A federal court determined that the school violated the young woman's constitutional right to equal protection and could be sued for monetary damages.[23]

Sexual harassment complaints against teachers have been increasing. Teachers need to realize that **sexual harassment** laws protect individuals not only from extreme actions, as in the Georgia case, but from offensive words and inappropriate touching. The mild scenario of comforting words, touching, and an offer of ice cream can indeed lead to problems. While the teacher's intention might have been pure and caring, the student's perception might have been quite different. The threat of the legal broadside that can result from this gap between teacher intentions and student perceptions has sent a chill through many school faculties. Teachers now openly express their fears about the dangers of reaching out to students, and some teachers are vowing never to touch a student or be alone in a room with a student, no matter how honorable the intention. Many teachers lament the current situation, recalling earlier times, when a teacher's kindness and closeness fostered a caring educational climate, rather than a legal case.[24] In the above situation, the first course of action would be the most prudent, to seek legal advice.

Scoring   What is your RQ (Rights Quotient)?

15 to 18 correct:	Legal eagle
13 or 14 correct:	Lawyer-in-training
11 or 12 correct:	Paralegal
9 or 10 correct:	Law student
8 or fewer correct:	Could benefit from an LSAT prep course

This brief review of the legal realities that surround today's classroom is not meant to be definitive. These situations are intended to highlight the rapid growth and changing nature of school law and the importance of this law to teachers. It will be your responsibility to become informed, and stay current, on legal decisions that influence your actions inside and outside your classroom. Ignorance of the law, to paraphrase a popular saying, is no defense. More positively, knowledge of fundamental legal principles allows you to practice "preventive law"—that is, to avoid or resolve potential legal conflicts so that you can attend to your major responsibility: teaching.

www.mhhe.com/
sadker8e

INTERACTIVE ACTIVITY
Practice with Court Cases. Match names of court cases with their description.

Teaching and Ethics

Some citizens believe that the most important issues facing U.S. schools are the ethical ones. Beyond simply following the law, they believe that students need to learn enduring moral lessons. Some moral lessons gain a quick consensus: students should not cheat. Yet cheating is clearly a lesson not yet learned. Nine out of ten high schoolers admit to some form of academic cheating (see Figure 10.2). Forget the traditional crib sheet tucked away under a sleeve; students today have discovered more high-tech forms of cheating. Cell phones and other palm-size gadgets are the new crib sheets at school, while the Internet has become a powerful temptation at home. The Internet has made it easy for students to cut-and-paste their way to a term paper, downloading a few sentences or even entire essays and then weaving them into their papers, without crediting the original sources. Such practice constitutes plagiarism, grounds for suspension from many schools. Yet more than half of high school students admit to this "cut-and-paste" method to complete assignments. One-fifth of students do not even cut and paste; they buy ready-made term papers from commercial Web sites. Students describe pressure to perform and the competitive college-admissions process, as well apathy toward many assignments, as reasons driving such spurious behavior.[25]

Just how easy is it to plagiarize online? Type *"Scarlet Letter* essay" into the popular Google Internet search engine, and dozens of Web sites pop up offering hundreds of essays on topics from symbolism to adultery. Fortunately, online

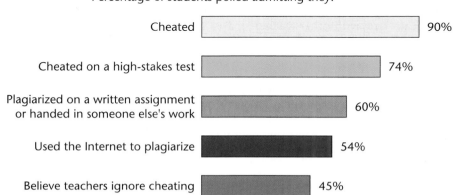

Percentage of students polled admitting they:

Cheated — 90%
Cheated on a high-stakes test — 74%
Plagiarized on a written assignment or handed in someone else's work — 60%
Used the Internet to plagiarize — 54%
Believe teachers ignore cheating — 45%

FIGURE 10.2
The dishonor role.

SOURCE: The Center for Academic Integrity (June 2005).

REFLECTION: This is from a recent study of 18,000 students in 61 high schools. Is cheating an acceptable norm in American schools? Why or why not? As a teacher, how might you approach the cheating dilemma?

companies, such as Turnitin.com, offer schools plagiarism detection programs. Students submit their completed work online, and the detection program then produces a report for teachers that highlights material copied from other sources. Teachers can also simply type a suspicious sentence or two from a student essay into a search engine such as Google to identify plagiarized material. And perhaps most important, teachers can be proactive and work with students to promote honesty over deceit. When teachers help students to explore values related to cheating, such as integrity and honesty, and when a consistent a no-cheating policy is applied, students get the message and cheating is less likely.[26]

Cheating is only one of a myriad of ethical issues teachers and students will confront in and beyond the classroom; a reminder that all is not well in our school culture. As a teacher, you will be called to follow your ethical compass to protect the physical and emotional well-being of your students and to guide students' own ethical development.

Protecting Your Students

Sam, the new student, seems so awkward in school, and he is often late. You have asked him more than once why he can't get to class on time, but he is barely audible as he mumbles, "I dunno." What's more, his behavior is strange. He seems to have an aversion to chairs, and, whenever possible, he prefers to stand in the back of the room alone. His clothes are not the neatest or cleanest, which is unusual in your class, where most of the children come from middle-class homes and dress fairly well. You have never seen Sam laugh or even smile. Every day, even on the hot ones, he wears a long-sleeve shirt. What is that all about? What a puzzle.

Then, one day, Sam arrives in class with some bruises on his face, and you begin to suspect that there is more to this story. You ask Sam, who shrugs it off and says that he fell and bruised his face. But you are not so sure. You begin to put the puzzle pieces together: quiet . . . standing rather than sitting . . . wearing long-sleeve shirts all the time . . . late . . . no smiles . . . no real friends . . . and now bruises. You arrive at a frightening thought: Could Sam be an abused child? How horrible! Now, what do you do?

In this case, you are confronting both an ethical dilemma and a legal challenge. Maybe you should speak to Sam's parents. Or should you press Sam for more information? Checking with other teachers makes sense, to see how they would handle the problem. Or perhaps it is time to go to the administration and let them find out what is going on.

Wait a second. What if you are wrong? Sam says he fell down and bruised himself. Maybe that is all it is. You should not go around accusing people without real evidence. Are you responsible for Sam's family situation? Is that a private concern rather than your business? Maybe the prudent course of action would be to monitor the situation for now and keep your suspicions to yourself. What would you do?

The ethical issue is pressing. If Sam is being injured, if his safety is in jeopardy, then waiting could be costly. Many would find that the most ethical course to follow would be to share your concerns with an appropriate person in your school, perhaps a school psychologist, counselor, or administrator, or to notify Child Protective Services, a report which can be confidential. The potential for injury is simply too great to remain silent. Sharing your concern is not the same as making an accusation of child abuse, which may be false. By bringing the situation to the school's attention, you start the wheels in motion to uncover facts.

Children who suffer physical abuse may

- Exhibit signs of frequent injury—burns, black eyes, welts, or bite marks
- Refuse to change into gym clothes; wear longsleeves even in very warm weather
- Not want to sit down
- Show unusually aggressive or unusually withdrawn behavior
- Not show emotion—no joy, pain, or anger
- Be unusually eager to please
- Show a significant change in school attitude, behavior, or achievement

Children who suffer sexual abuse may

- Demonstrate overcompliances or excessive aggression
- Exhibit unusual odors or signs of trauma in the genital area
- Wear bloody, torn, or stained undergarments
- Create stories or drawings of an unusually sexual nature
- Exhibit unusually sophisticated knowledge of sexual behavior
- Have difficulty sitting or walking
- Talk about sexual involvement with an adult
- Fear adults
- Show signs of an eating disorder

Children who suffer from emotional abuse or neglect may

- Show signs of depression
- Be apathetic toward school and friends
- Lack concentration
- Demonstrate hostility or distress
- Wear clothing unsuitable for the weather
- Be extremely hungry or have drastic changes in appetite
- Be frequently absent or tardy

SOURCE: Childhelp USA, *Signs and Symptoms of Child Abuse*, www.childhelpusa.org (2006).

REFLECTION: If one of your students showed warning signs of abuse, whom in your school would you approach first? How would you phrase your concern?

The American Humane Institute states that very few child abuse reports come from educators, yet it is the ethical responsibility of teachers to report the abusive treatment of children. Fortunately, as far as suspicion of child abuse is concerned, this ethical responsibility is reinforced by the law. Every state requires that teachers report "suspected" cases of abuse, and failure to report such cases can result in the loss of a teacher's license. Most of these laws also protect teachers from any legal liability for reporting such cases.

As a teacher, you may well encounter child abuse. In the last 20 years, reports of child maltreatment more than doubled, although as many as two-thirds of these reports are never investigated.[27]

Child abuse and neglect include a range of mistreatment, such as the following:

- Physical abuse, evidenced by cuts, welts, burns, and bruises
- Sexual molestation and exploitation
- Neglect: medical, educational, or physical
- Emotional abuse

Moral Education: Programs That Teach Right from Wrong

During the American colonial experience, schools transmitted a common set of values, an approach called **traditional inculcation.** Back then (and in many places today) it was the Protestant ethic: diligence, hard work, punctuality, neatness, conformity, and respect for authority. Those few individuals who received a college education during the eighteenth and nineteenth centuries received, above all, an experience in character development. The most important course in the college curriculum was moral philosophy, required of all students and often taught by the college president. Even those receiving a minimal education got a heavy dose of morality, perhaps illustrated best by McGuffey Readers, replete with tales and poems of moral elevation. The tremendous influx of immigrants in the early part of the twentieth century prompted a resurgence of this traditional approach in order to "meld" these new Americans by teaching core U.S. values.

During the social and political uncertainty of the 1960s and 1970s, a more analytical and individual approach to moral education became popular. This **individual analysis** method emphasized the decision-making process of students and avoided prescribing a fixed set of beliefs or values. Students were encouraged to consider the moral implications of past and present events and to formulate a set of values based on their analyses. Today's schools can choose from several different approaches to moral education, ranging from student decision-making to the more traditional paths. Four of the most widely known are (1) values clarification, (2) character education, (3) moral stages of development, and (4) comprehensive values education.

Values Clarification   The controversial **values clarification** program is designed to help students develop and eventually act on their values. Students might explore questions such as: What qualities do you value in a friend? When is lying acceptable? Would you be willing to donate your body to science when you die? How do you feel about competition? Would you welcome a person of a different race into your neighborhood? Throughout such values clarification exercises, students begin to bring their private values into a public light, where they can be analyzed, evaluated, and eventually put into action. This allows students to respond to each others' beliefs, to consider different points of view, and to analyze their own values. Many believe that values, like plants, need light and thoughtful nurturing to be healthy.

Critics charge that values clarification is itself valueless. In this approach, all values are treated equally, and there is no guarantee that good and constructive values will be promoted or that negative ones will be condemned. If, for example, a student decides that anti-Semitism or fascism is a preferred value, values clarification might do little to contradict this view. This "value neutral" stance is troubling to some and has led to the barring of values clarification in several school districts.

Character Education   **Character education** programs assume that there are core attributes of a moral individual that children should be directly taught in school. Forty states either are recipients of federal character education grants or require character education through legislation.[28] (To see if your state requires character education, visit www.character.org.) While still a form of moral inculcation, character education programs are less didactic and more analytic than some of the more traditional approaches.[29] What values are promoted? Core values include trustworthiness, respect, responsibility, fairness, caring, and good citizenship, and are encouraged through the school culture, conduct codes, curriculum, and community service. Younger students may be asked to find examples of these qualities in literature and history, while older students may consider these values through ethical reasoning exercises. Along with developing core values, character education programs can challenge students to act on these values. For example, students may debate how best to implement a school's honor code, organize a food drive, or plan a ceremony honoring local military veterans. Some character education programs include training in conflict resolution to develop problem-solving skills and respect. School districts using character education report a drop in discipline problems, enhanced student responsibility, and improved academic performance.[30]

Not everyone is enamored with character education. Opponents view this approach as superficial, artificially forcing a diverse student population into a simplistic and narrow set of unexamined values that does not really alter behaviors. Character education is often criticized for relying on testimonials to prove effectiveness. Although the federal government is committed to funding "scientifically based" programs, it has nevertheless distributed over $50 million to fund character education programs despite the lack of proven effectiveness.[31]

Other critics believe that character education is little more than the old-fashioned "fix-the-kids" approach, a return to a traditional or religious agenda that simply rewards students who do what adults desire. Who selects the values or the way the values are taught are issues at the heart of the concerns expressed by these critics. Although character education attempts to walk a middle ground, not all Americans find the values or the approach appropriate.[32]

> ## IMAGINE . . .
>
> ### Nice Not 2B 4-Gotten
>
> At Thomas Jefferson Middle School in Arlington, Virginia, yearbook signing has a new twist: Students are required to "write nice." Principal Sharon M. implemented the rule to ensure that these keepsakes would be filled with fond remembrances, not hurtful memories. So when Jotana C. was asked to sign a former friend's yearbook, there wasn't a hint of nastiness. She even wrote K.I.T. (keep in touch). Students who choose to pen yearbooks with profane or harassing words can be suspended, dismissed from award ceremonies, or required to buy replacement yearbooks.
>
> SOURCE: *The Washington Post,* June 17, 2001.

Moral Stages of Development   Based on the work of Jean Piaget, the psychologist who identified stages of intellectual development (see "The Hall of Fame" in Chapter 7), a schema proposed by **Lawrence Kohlberg** identifies **moral stages of development.** The earliest stages focus on simple rewards and punishments. Young children are taught "right" and "wrong" by learning to avoid physical punishment and to strive for rewards. Most adults function at a middle, or conventional, stage, in which they obey society's laws, even laws that may be unjust. At the highest level, individuals act on principles, such as civil rights or pacifism, that may violate conventional laws. Kohlberg believes that teachers can facilitate student growth to higher stages of morality. In Kohlberg's curriculum, students are encouraged to analyze moral dilemmas presented in brief scenarios. For example, one such scenario might tell the story of someone breaking into a store and stealing, and the question is posed: isn't stealing always wrong, or could it ever be justified? What if the person was stealing medicine needed to save a life; would that justify the theft? The teacher's role in this curriculum is to help students move to higher stages of moral development.

Detractors express concern that traditional (what Kohlberg calls "conventional") values are attacked. Kohlberg pushes toward higher levels of moral development, principled beliefs that may run counter to current law. Other critics point out that Kohlberg's theory was developed on an all-male population and that females may go through different stages of moral reasoning. Harvard professor **Carol Gilligan,** for example, found that women and men react differently when responding to moral dilemmas. While males seem to strongly value those who follow the rules and laws, females value relationships and caring. Kohlberg rated males as reaching a higher level of moral development than females, because the scales he developed were male-oriented. Finally, Kohlberg's stages are intellectually based. Some critics believe that behavior, not intellect, is the real measure of one's morality.

Comprehensive Values Education   Now that we have reviewed three approaches to teaching about values and ethics, it is worth noting that some teachers "mix and match," creating what might be considered a hybrid or fourth approach. Howard Kirschenbaum suggests that both values clarification and traditional inculcation have important lessons for children. In his approach, **comprehensive values education,** traditional values such as honesty, caring, and responsibility are taught and demonstrated directly. However, since other values are less straightforward, such as favoring or rejecting the death penalty, students are taught the analytical skills that will help them make wise decisions. There is an appropriate place in the school curriculum for each approach, Kirschenbaum insists, and many teachers instinctively apply multiple approaches.[33]

Classrooms That Explore Ethical Issues

For many educators and parents, concerns about values are daily events, too important to be left solely to a specific program or curriculum. How should teachers handle matters of ethics that appear on a daily basis? Consider that as a teacher, you might find

> A student complains that her Vietnamese culture is being demeaned by the Christian and Western classroom activities.
>
> A student with learning disabilities is ignored by classmates at lunchtime. Rather than sitting alone in the cafeteria, he hides in the bathroom.
>
> A gifted student with advanced verbal skills is frequently bullied by a classmate in the locker room before gym class. Other students remain bystanders and do not stop or report the bullying.
>
> Your best student, the one you just recommended for a special award, stored exam answers on her cell phone.

How are teachers to navigate this tricky moral minefield? Educators have offered several recommendations, summarized below:

The Setting

Climate. Create an environment that respects and encourages diverse points of view and that promotes the sharing of diverse opinions, by both the teachers and the students.

School and class rules. Requiring that students unquestioningly follow rules does not lead to democratic values. School and class rules need to be explained to students, and the reasons behind them understood. Many teachers go further and ask students to participate in formulating the rules they will live by.

Parents and community. Citizens and community leaders should participate with the school in developing mission statements and ethical codes of responsibility. One way to encourage such cooperation is to plan joint efforts that tie the family and civic organizations into school-sponsored programs. The key is to reinforce ethical lessons in the school, the home, and the community.

Are Best Taught by Instilling American Values Through Character Education Because . . .

OUR YOUTH ARE BEING CORRUPTED BY THE MEDIA

Television, music, and videos bombard children with commercialism, violence, and sex. Schools must be proactive in helping families instill the moral attitudes and values needed to counteract our lax social mores.

CHILDREN ARE UNABLE TO MAKE THEIR OWN MORAL CHOICES

Throughout history, educators have recognized that children have "impressionable" minds. Without moral training at a young age, as Theodore Roosevelt once noted, they can quickly become "a menace to society."

SHARED VALUES AFFIRM A NATIONAL IDENTITY

Americans believe in a common code of values to teach our children: respect, patriotism, tolerance, and responsibility. Our national fabric is built on such values, and our nation's future depends on them.

Should Help Students Develop Their Own Values Because . . .

SOCIETAL INDIFFERENCE IS CORRUPTING OUR YOUTH

Traditional character education adopts a "blame the media" approach while neglecting real social needs. By ignoring poverty, racism, and sexism, traditionalists inculcate their own rosy picture of America, overlooking genuine if unattractive social injustices.

CHILDREN MUST LEARN TO MAKE MEANINGFUL MORAL CHOICES

Through character indoctrination, students are manipulated to adopt a narrow set of values. Far better is for teachers to help students become reflective thinkers, active citizens ready to work for social justice.

INDIVIDUAL VALUES HONOR DIVERSITY

In a nation of people with diverse cultural backgrounds, indoctrinating one set of fixed values is undemocratic and unwise. Respect for different cultural values will help create a safe and fair society marked by tolerance.

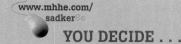

www.mhhe.com/
sadker8e

YOU DECIDE . . .

What role should character education play in public schools? Examine textbooks and curriculum used in a local school to determine the major values being taught to students. Are students expected to accept the values or to critically examine them? Which strategy do you support?

The Teacher

Model. You need to demonstrate the ethical lessons you teach. Teacher behavior should reflect such values as tolerance, compassion, forgiveness, and open-mindedness. (Values are often *caught not taught.*)

Interpersonal skills. You need effective communication skills to encourage students to share their concerns. A critical component of interpersonal skills is empathy—the ability to see problems from more than one point of view, including through the eyes of students.

Commitment. It takes determination and courage on your part to confront ethical dilemmas, rather than to take the easier path of indifference or even inattention.

Reflection skills. To unravel moral questions, you must know how to analyze a dilemma objectively and how to evaluate its essential components. Teachers with effective and deliberate reasoning skills are best suited for this challenge.

Personal opinions. You should not promote or indoctrinate students with your personal points of view, nor should you shy away from showing students that you have strong beliefs. The key is to create a classroom in which individuals can freely agree or disagree, as they see fit.[34]

While laws direct us to what we can and cannot do, moral guidelines direct us in what we should and should not do. Moral issues will continue to be a major concern in the years ahead, in many ways a measure of the quality of our culture. Indeed, even as our society grows in wealth and makes great scientific strides and technological breakthroughs, the final measure of our worth may not be our materialistic accomplishments but, rather, the way we treat each other.

SUMMARY

**www.mhhe.com/
sadker8e**

CHAPTER REVIEW

Go to the Online Learning Center to take a quiz, practice with key terms, and review concepts from the chapter.

1. **What are your legal rights and responsibilities as a teacher?**

   A teacher enjoys job security as long as the teacher's behavior and personal life do not disrupt or interfere with teaching effectiveness. Teachers may copy material for classroom use by adhering to three criteria: brevity, spontaneity, and cumulative effect.

2. **What legal rights do students enjoy (and do they have legal responsibilities)?**

   Parents and guardians have the right to see their child's educational record, and at 18 years of age, students become responsible for providing permission for others to see it. Title IX prohibits many forms of sexual harassment and sex discrimination, and students have constitutionally protected rights to due process before they can be disciplined or suspended from school. As long as students do not disrupt the operation of the school or deny other students the opportunity to learn, they have the right to freedom of speech within the schools. The school's *in loco parentis* responsibility allows it to search school lockers and cars in school parking lots and submit student athletes to random drug testing. Student publications can be censored if they are an integral part of the school curriculum, such as part of a course, or if they are obscene, psychologically damaging, or disruptive.

3. **What are today's main approaches to moral education?**

   Historically, traditional values were imparted in a didactic style. Another approach, called values clarification, promotes values through personal reflection and individual analysis. Character education is a popular approach that promotes a core set of values, including respect, responsibility, citizenship, caring, and fairness. What teachers do and say provides a model for students, serving as an "informal" curriculum on ethical behavior.

Go to your *Teachers, Schools, and Society* Reader CD-ROM to:

READ CURRENT AND HISTORICAL ARTICLES

10.1 **Teaching about Religion,** Susan Black, *American School Board Journal* 190, no. 4, 2003.

10.2 **Seven Worlds of Moral Education,** Pamela Bolotin Joseph and Sara Efron, *Phi Delta Kappan,* March 2005.

10.3 **Decisions That Have Shaped U.S. Education,** Perry Zirkel, *Educational Leadership,* December 2001/2002.

ANALYZE CASE STUDIES

10.1 **Amanda Jackson:** A teacher discovers that her principal has a drinking problem, which is well known but never discussed among the staff. She faces a dilemma when she realizes that the principal is planning to drive a student home during a snowstorm.

10.2 **Ellen Norton:** A teacher whose concern for a shy, underachieving student has led to the student becoming her "shadow," learns that another student may be the victim of child abuse at home. The teacher has to decide if she should become involved.

OBSERVE TEACHERS, STUDENTS, AND CLASSROOMS IN ACTION

Classroom Observation: Cheating: A Dramatization

As a teacher you will be faced with difficult decisions that will test your ethics. In this two-part observation you will observe a scenario in which students cheat during an exam. In part one, when the teacher is called out of class during an exam, some students take to cheating. When the teacher returns, some students tell him what happened, and he must decide how to deal with the cheating. In part two, the students and teacher discuss the incident during an interview.

KEY TERMS AND PEOPLE

DISCUSSION QUESTIONS AND ACTIVITIES

www.mhhe.com/
   sadker8e

WEB-TIVITIES
Go to the Online-
Learning Center to
do the following
activities.
1. Teachers' and Students'
   Rights and
   Responsibilities
2. Students' Rights: Title IX
   and Sexual Harassment
3. Values Clarification
4. Character Education
5. Classrooms That Explore
   Ethical Issues

1. If you were to suggest a law to improve education, what would that law be? Would you make it federal, state, or local? Why?

2. The role of religion and prayer in schools has always been controversial, and teachers are advised to neither *encourage* nor *discourage* religious observances. As a teacher, what religious celebrations or practices might you encounter in your class? How would you respond to these issues while maintaining your neutrality?

3. Construct an argument to support the principle that students and their property should not be searched without the students' consent.

4. Which of the paths to moral education (values clarification, moral development, character education, or comprehensive values education) appeals to you most? Why?

5. Describe some steps you might explore to promote ethical student behavior in your classroom.

REEL TO REAL TEACHING

FINDING FORRESTER (2000)
Run Time: 133 minutes

Synopsis: *Finding Forrester* is a telling portrayal of ethics and expectations as an African American teen writing prodigy and star athlete finds a mentor in a reclusive author.

Reflection:
1. What expectations did William Forrester, Dr. Crawford, and Clarie hold for Jamal? What social factors influenced these expectations? Did they change throughout the film. Why or why not?

2. How would you describe a successful student? An athlete? Did you picture this student as male or female? As a person of color or white? Now imagine that your successful student (and successful athlete) is the opposite sex or another race. Did your description change? What values are embedded in your answer?

3. As a teacher, how will you confront cheating and plagiarism in your classroom?

4. What lessons in character did Forrester and Jamal learn from each other?

Follow-up Activity: As part of a character education program, create an Honor Code to help students learn about academic integrity. You may want to consider the following questions: Is your Code a teacher's solo creation or a teacher-student partnership? What aspects of school life (such as bullying, lying, and punctuality) are included in the Code? Who will enforce the Code, and what are the rewards and punishments? What values will students learn from following (or breaking) the Honor Code?

How do you rate this film? Go to *Reel to Real Teaching* to review this film.

www.mhhe.com/sadker8e

FOR FURTHER READING

Building Character in Schools: Practical Ways to Bring Moral Instruction to Life, by Kevin Ryan and Karen Bohlin (2003). The authors provide a blueprint for educators who wish to translate a personal commitment to character education into a schoolwide vision and effort. Principles and strategies of effective character education are outlined for teaching students habits and dispositions that lead to responsible adulthood—from developing curriculum that reinforces good character development to strengthening links with parents.

Character Matters: How to Help Our Children Develop Good Judgment, Integrity, and Other Essential Virtues, by Thomas Lickona (2004). The author suggests how irresponsible and destructive behavior can be traced to the absence of good character and its 10 essential qualities—wisdom, justice, fortitude, self-control, love, a positive attitude, hard work, integrity, gratitude, and humility. He offers practical guidelines for building these core virtues through family, school, and community partnerships.

Protecting the Right to Teach and Learn, by James Daly, Patricia Schall, and Rosemary Skeele (2001). Explores the legal and pedagogical implications of academic freedom in the face of political and religious challenges to what is taught in schools.

The Respectful School: How Educators and Students Can Conquer Hate and Harassment, by Stephen Wessler (2003). Teachers may not always see it, but every day, students are being harassed and intimidated because of their race, religion, gender, or other personal characteristics. This book draws on definite research and experiences of young victims to explain fundamental changes that every school should make to protect students.

School Law and the Public Schools: A Practical Guide for Educational Leaders, 3rd ed., by Nathan Essex (2004). Summarizes educational laws and their impact on the organization of schools and daily classroom practices. Policy guidelines for issues such as school prayer, disability, sexual harassment, and freedom of speech are featured.

REFLECTIVE ACTIVITIES AND YOUR PORTFOLIO

Part III: Foundations

3:1 Self-Fulfilling Prophecy

INTASC PRINCIPLE 1
Knowledge of
Subject Matter

Purpose: Someday, at the end of your career in education, you will no doubt recall your early hopes and dreams. Will you have realized your goals? Project yourself into the future, and imagine you have accomplished all that you set out to do. An orientation toward the future can help you attain your goals.

Activity: Time flies: A new generation has decided to become teachers and they open *Teachers, Schools, and Society* (25th edition!), which they bought for only $1,284 and wondered if it was really worth it. They turn to the history chapter and begin reading the profiles in the "Hall of Fame." And you are there. Why? Let's find out.

Artifact: "My Hall of Fame Entry." Write yourself into *The Education Hall of Fame* by following the format in Chapter 7. Provide a graphic image, a statement of significant contribution, and about 250 words that detail your accomplishments in education. Be sure to include your unique skills and expertise to describe your achievement.

Reflection: The activity should help you define your professional values. What actions might help you reach your long-time goals? What steps should you consider now? Are there mentors and professional relationships that might help support your success? Keep this *Hall of Fame* entry in your portfolio. You could even seal and date it in an envelope to be opened when you teach your first class of students, receive your doctorate in education, are named U.S. Secretary of Education, or attend your retirement dinner. Attach your reflection to the artifact and include in your portfolio.

3:2 Money Matters

INTASC PRINCIPLE 2
Human
Development and
Learning

Purpose: Most state offices of education work to equalize per-pupil expenditures. Still, children live with very different financial realities at home and at school. A family's income influences a student's physical, social, emotional, moral, and cognitive growth.

Activity: To better understand and meet the needs of your learners, consider how economics has impacted you and your education.

Artifact: "Finances and Me." Under each developmental area, list ways your education was helped and/or hindered by money. While we all realize to one degree or another that money matters, we rarely take the time to consider specifically how it has shaped our own lives.

Physical (such as size, shape, fitness, health, medical resources):

Social (such as autonomy, civility, relationships):

Emotional (such as expressiveness, empathy, motivation):

Moral (such as ethics, honesty, good will):

Cognitive (such as intellectual resources, academic services, inherent abilities):

Reflection: Consider how your childhood financial security (or lack thereof) contributed to your educational reality. How was your growth and development distinguished by economic class? How might your life have been different if you were raised with a very different financial base? What is the correlation between financial resources and academic success? Attach your reflection to the artifact and include in your portfolio.

3:3 Philosophy on the Big Screen

Purpose: The philosophies of education are captured not just in this section of the book, but in classic and contemporary films about schools. Movies reflect diverse (and sometimes overdramatized versions) of teaching philosophies, and watching these movies critically can help you analyze and explore your own philosophical preferences.

Activity: Before you choose a movie to watch, refresh your memory of the major philosophies by scanning the philosophy discussion in Chapter 8 (essentialism, perennialism, progressivism, existentialism, social reconstructionism). Select a video by reviewing the *Reel to Real Teaching* feature after each chapter, or browse through your local video rental store and choose a film about schools and teaching.

Artifact: "Philosophy in Action." Use the simple chart below to record evidence of the major philosophies that appeared in the film. As you watch (with or without popcorn), attend to the various techniques the teachers use to meet the needs of the learners. Can you match the theories of philosophy to the cast of characters? Take notes and try to capture the indicators of educational philosophy that appear in the film.

www.mhhe.com/ sadker8e

FORM:
Developmental Areas and Socioeconomic Class

INTASC PRINCIPLE 3
Diversity in Learning

Philosophy on the Big Screen	
Movie _____	
Major Education Philosophy	**Cinematic Evidence**

Reflection: What philosophy was most prevalent? Why do you think the filmmaker chose to highlight this philosophy? What appealed or disappointed you about the film? What did you learn about teaching and educational philosophies from this film? What traits of the cinematic teacher might you adapt . . . avoid? Attach your reflection to the artifact and include in your portfolio.

3:4 The Great Lecture Theory of Learning

INTASC PRINCIPLE 4
Variety of
Instructional
Strategies

Purpose: Most of us have attended, even been moved by, a great lecture, yet, when we learn about strategies for classroom instruction, the lecture is often relegated to the least effective method or, simply, disparaged. Lecturing is not inherently evil. While it can be tiresome and boring, it can also be motivating, filled with information, clearly understood, and easily recalled. In some cases, the lecture format may be the best way to convey information. There are reasons that great lecturers are great, and the sooner you figure out some of those reasons, the sooner you will be able to give terrific lectures yourself.

Activity: Check around the campus with friends and acquaintances to find out which professors give great lectures. You may also want to inquire at a local elementary, middle, or high school. Choose one teacher to observe and ask permission to attend a class. (Or, if necessary, check into television courses, videotapes from a distance learning course, or satellite seminar series.)

Artifact: "Effective Lecture Ideas." Take notes, but not on the specific lecture information—rather on presentation strategy and style. Ask some of the following questions about lecture technique:

- What pulled you into the lecture? (a great story? a provocative question?)
- How did you know where the lecture was going? (Was the purpose or objective stated or implied?)
- How did the speaker use presentation or communication skills?
  Facial expressions?
  Gestures?
  Eye contact?
  Voice?
  Movement?
  Interaction with the audience?
  Other skills?
- What technical aids or materials (videotapes, PowerPoint presentation) enhanced your understanding and interest?

- Did the speaker use vivid examples, stories, metaphors, or role-play to enhance your comprehension?
- How might you assess the speaker's expertise in the lecture's content?

Reflection: All in all, was this lecturer worthy of his or her reputation? Why? How are you when it comes to public speaking? What's your comfort zone? Given what you know about yourself, which of the observed lecturer's strengths might be strengths of yours as well? Which might you want to add to your repertoire? Attach your reflection to the artifact and include in your portfolio.

3:5 What You See and What You Get

Purpose: The philosophy of a classroom can be seen, felt, and heard, yet future teachers sometimes have a difficult time "getting" it, even when examples of educational philosophy surround us. This activity will help you connect with specific clues that signal a teacher's philosophy.

Activity: Arrange to observe several classrooms of the age of student you would like to teach. If this is not possible, do this activity in your college classrooms. Record observations on the following chart. Gather at least three different observations.

Artifact:

> **INTASC PRINCIPLE 5**
> Motivation and Management

www.mhhe.com/ sadker8e

FORM:
Indicators of Education Philosophy

Philosophy-in-the-Classroom Observations

Indicators of Education Philosophy
Course: _____
Room arrangement:
Teacher-student interactions:
Student-initiated actions:
Instructional grouping and organization (full class, individuals/groups, centers/stations):
Instructional resources:
Other:

Reflection: What classroom indicators have you observed? What do these indicators suggest about the philosophy of your teachers, classes, program, or institution? What do your notes tell you about how faculty members manage instruction and motivate learning? Which elements do you want to include in your teaching? Which would you prefer to omit or avoid? Attach your reflection to the artifact and include in your portfolio.

3:6 Putting Your Philosophy into the Classroom

INTASC PRINCIPLE 6
Communication
Skills

Purpose: What is your educational philosophy? Is it teacher-centered or student-centered? Do you subscribe to essentialism, perennialism, progressivism, existentialism, or social reconstructionism? Or do you prefer a cafeteria approach—that is, picking and choosing from several approaches? A strong sense of your educational philosophy will guide and shape your development as an educator. Refining and declaring your beliefs will allow you to sharpen your professional communication skills.

Activity: Using the discussion on educational philosophies from Chapter 8 as a guide, formulate your educational philosophy. Begin by brainstorming thoughts and ideas about your own beliefs. Work to hone your beliefs into a concise one-page declaration. It may be useful to begin a number of your philosophy statements with the phrase, "I believe . . ."

Artifact: "My Philosophy of Education." Using this one-page declaration as a guide, create a poster describing your philosophy. Use pictures and words (or be more creative) to convey your philosophy. Can the poster convey a sense of your personal commitment? Challenge classmates to guess your philosophy by viewing your poster. How can you adopt this poster idea for your classroom, and share with your students your educational philosophy when you begin teaching?

Reflection: Was it difficult to formulate a philosophy? How did your beliefs evolve during the course of this assignment? What surprised you about this activity? What did you learn about yourself from this activity? Do you have—or are you moving toward—a consistent philosophy? Were classmates able to guess your philosophy? Attach your one-page declaration and reflection to the artifact and include in your portfolio.

3:7 Students' Bill of Rights and Responsibilities

INTASC PRINCIPLE 7
Instructional
Planning Skills

Purpose: When rights and responsibilities are handed down from higher authorities, or if a teacher simply reads out loud "class rules" at the beginning of the semester, democracy and the value and meaning of individual rights may well be lost. But when students actively participate and write these rules, they are creating a living social contract, and are more likely to understand, appreciate, and follow them. This RAP helps you to plan a student-centered lesson that will establish a classroom climate that promotes learning, an appreciation of individual rights, and ethical behavior among students.

Activity: This RAP asks you to plan a lesson that emphasizes student rights and responsibilities. Using the following outline developed by Madeline Hunter, describe how you would plan such a class.

Dr. Madeline Hunter's Seven-Step Lesson Plan

Anticipatory Set (focus)—Focus learners' attention on the instruction that is about to begin. This could be a teacher demonstration, video, story, puzzle, or a handout prior to the actual lesson. This is also known as a "grabber" and it's a way to get your students' attention and interest.

Purpose (objective) —A clear explanation of what learners will understand and be able to do as a result of the lesson. This section should answer the question: "Why is this important to learn?"

Instructional Strategy—What content and skills need to be taught to accomplish this task? And what are the best teaching strategies needed for this instructional task (lecture, activity, video, group work, etc.)?

Modeling (show) —Provide learners with examples or demonstrations of competencies associated with the lesson.

Guided Practice—Monitor learners as they apply new information.

Check for Understanding—Evaluate whether learners have the information needed to master the objective.

Independent Practice—Assign learners to work independently, without direct teacher assistance.

For more information on Dr. Hunter visit www.foothill.net/~moorek/lessondesign. html

Artifact: The artifact for this RAP is a lesson plan in the Hunter format. (You may want to include some material that reflects student rights established by courts. For example, the right to free speech that is not disruptive, due process rights of students, etc.) How will you ensure that all students understand these rights?

Reflection: How do you predict that students will respond to this activity? What are the differences between teacher-imposed rules and rules that students develop? How can you ensure that these rules will be followed and not forgotten? How might students view school differently when they are aware of the rights the courts have awarded them? How will you help students (and yourself) understand that these rights are only theoretical unless students and teachers know and honor them? What are the challenges in planning an instructional strategy that focuses on student decisions?

3:8 Assessing the Assessor

Purpose: With all the attention being given to the performance of American students on national and local tests, it makes sense for you to explore the promise and problems of districtwide evaluation.

INTASC PRINCIPLE 8
Assessment

Activity: Invite a school district administrator with assessment responsibilities to your class or study group for one hour. (Create a class chat room on your department's Web site or conduct an interview, if that works better.) Ask your guest to describe the district's history and current evaluation procedures.

Artifact: "Testing Practices." Use the following questions (or your own) to expand your guest's commentary. Record the answers.

www.mhhe.com/
sadker8e

FORM:
Testing Practices

- What are the purposes behind these tests?
- Give examples of when these policies and procedures work effectively—and when there are problems.
- What is the best thing about these tests, and what is the worst?

- What is the biggest problem you face?
- What role does the public (parents, media, chamber of commerce) play?
- How do special interest groups influence testing policies?
- How do teachers, students, and parents react to these tests?
- Can you suggest other approaches to gauge achievement?

Bonus Artifact: Assume you are writing for a newspaper and turn the administrator's presentation and interview into a story for your local newspaper.

Reflection: What have you learned? What information surprised you? What do you still have on your "need to know" list? Do you support the current testing culture? What are the pros and cons? Attach your reflection to the artifact and include in your portfolio.

3:9 Publication of the Month

INTASC PRINCIPLE 9
Reflection and
Responsibility

Purpose: While the Internet represents ready sources of information, not all of the information on the Internet is of high quality. Professional journals and magazines often include the best writing in our field. Journal articles are submitted and reviewed by educational experts, selected for their high standards of excellence. To be a reflective and responsible teacher, you will need to keep current by reading one or more professional journals.

Activity: Pick a journal or an educational magazine that is new to you. Try one at your professor's suggestion or use sources listed in the endnotes of this text. Spend at least one hour reading through the journal.

Artifact: "Journal Review." Harvest a sense of what this journal offers by analyzing its intended audience, format, content, style, policy, and readability. Write up your findings in a review format and present to the class or a small group of classmates. You may want to create a class scrapbook that describes these journals by sharing all the descriptions created by your classmates.

Refection: In describing this journal to your peers, what positive points would you stress? What are its weaknesses? If you could read only one journal a month, would it be this one, or perhaps another reviewed by a classmate? Why? Attach a sample article and your artifact to the reflection and include in your portfolio.

3:10 Get on Board

INTASC PRINCIPLE 10
Relationships and
Partnerships

Purpose: One seemingly distant group, the school board, influences every teaching day. As an elected agency of the community, school boards hold regular meetings, usually open to visitors. Because their norms and procedures vary, you have to see one to understand one. The purpose of this activity is to better understand how school boards function and how they might impact your life in the classroom.

Activity: Attend a school board meeting or watch one on television (many are broadcast by local cable networks). Imagine you are covering the meeting for your district's teacher association. Note what is going on. Try to grasp the formal curriculum (old and new business and procedures). Look also at the hidden curriculum, the cultural cues, and the nonverbal signals that tell you what else is going on.

Artifact: "A School Board Column." Write your notes into a news column for a teachers' newsletter that might be distributed in a local school system. Limit your article to a single page. Read your article in class and lead a class discussion.

Reflection: What were your personal and professional impressions of the meeting? What rituals and routines did you observe? How were your assumptions about school boards and meetings altered by your attendance? Were underlying politics evident? How were attendees treated? Did any of the school board's decisions directly impact district teachers? How? Based on your observation of the school board meeting, would you consider teaching in this district? Would you consider running for a school board position? Why or why not? Attach your reflection to your article and include in your portfolio.

CLASS ACT

At this time of year, graduates may feel a little lost. We have been students for SO long, and now suddenly things are changing. At such time of transition, we need a larger purpose to guide us—why have we chosen these careers as educators? It certainly wasn't for the money! I would like to share some words that I have turned to for a sense of purpose.

Over thirty years ago, W.E.B. DuBois, the great African American writer and activist, said from his death bed: "One thing alone I charge you: As you live, believe in life! Always human beings will live and progress to greater, broader, and fuller life. The only possible death is to lose belief in this truth . . . "

Despite all the injustice he experienced, DuBois died believing that the future will be ever brighter. In our line of work, it is not always easy to believe in progress. Apparently, DuBois never tried to get licensed at the New York City Board of Ed.! I have had many discussions with other students, wondering how to tackle problems such as glaring educational inequity based on race and class, negative or indifferent attitudes toward bilingual and special education, international disparities in the quality of education, and a general lack of respect in this country for the work that we do. What impact can I have as one individual educator? True, one person alone cannot change society. But each of us does have the power to change other people, and collectively we are an impressive force. For example, think of a teacher or family member who has passed on a legacy to you.

I am imagining two people up here with me: my mother's mother and my father's father. My grandmother, Mercy Oduro, was a West African woman who touched hundreds as a teacher and headmistress of an elementary school. It's a testament to her life's work that, although she died six years ago, I am still called "Teacher Mercy's granddaughter" when I go back to Ghana. To me, she has passed on a flair for celebration and an unshakeable belief in her students, and I will pass these on to my own students.

My American grandfather, William Steel, 83 years old, is a retired teacher, but STILL tutoring daily at his local school. His legacy is so strong that on his eightieth birthday he got letters from people he taught over fifty years ago, acknowledging his influence on them. To me, he has passed on a fantastic curiosity about the world and a playful sense of humor, and I will pass these on when I teach.

Imagine now that all the people we will reach ARE crowded in this room today—hundreds, thousands of them. In each of these people there is a piece of one of us, continuing the legacy of those who came before. Look around. Can you see the ocean of possibility flowing from us here today? Together, how can we NOT create DuBois' vision of greater, broader, and fuller life? Let me tell you, we are powerful: We are educators.

Melissa Steel
Teachers College Graduation Speech
Columbia University

www.mhhe.com/
sadker8e

Read more *Class Acts* on the Online Learning Center.

Teacher Effectiveness

FOCUS QUESTIONS

1. Are teachers born, or made?
2. How is class time organized and what is academic learning time?
3. What classroom management skills foster academic achievement?
4. What are the roles of teachers and students in the pedagogical cycle?
5. How can teachers set a stage for learning?
6. What questioning strategies increase student achievement?
7. How can teachers best tap into different student learning styles?
8. What are several salient models of instruction?
9. How can teachers use technology to support effective instruction?
10. What are the future directions of effective teaching research?

**www.mhhe.com/
sadker8e**

WHAT DO YOU THINK? **Qualities of a good teacher.** Rate the qualities of a good teacher, and see how other students rated these qualities.

CHAPTER PREVIEW

Albert Einstein believed that they awakened the "joy in creative expression and knowledge." Elbert Hubbard saw them as those who could make "two ideas grow where only one grew before." Gail Godwin surmised that they are "one-fourth preparation and three-fourths theater." Ralph Waldo Emerson believed that they could "make hard things easy." About whom are these talented geniuses talking? You guessed it: teachers. Although these intellectual leaders shared an insight into the importance of teaching, even these artists and scientists could not decide if teaching was an art or a science, a gift or a learned skill. Perhaps it is both.

Some individuals seem to take to teaching quite naturally. With little or no preparation, they come to school with a talent to teach and touch the lives of students. Others bring fewer natural talents to the classroom yet, with preparation and practice, become master teachers, models others try to emulate. Most of us fall in the middle, bringing some skills to teaching but also ready to benefit and grow from teacher preparation and practice teaching.

In this chapter, we present recent research findings on effective instruction, focusing on a core set of skills that comprise good teaching. We also detail the prevailing models of instruction, such as cooperative learning, problem-based learning, and computer-supported learning—classroom approaches that have become particularly popular in recent years. You may draw on these skills and models in your own classroom, selecting those that best fit your subject, students, and purpose.

Are Teachers Born or Made?

Think about the best teacher you ever had: Try to evoke a clear mental image of what this teacher was like. How do your memories compare with what some of today's teachers say about their favorite teachers from the past:

- The teacher I remember was charismatic. Going to his class was like attending a Broadway show. But it wasn't just entertainment. He made me understand things. We went step-by-step in such a clear way that I never seemed to get confused—even when we discussed the most difficult subject matter.

- I never watched the clock in my English teacher's class. I never counted how many times she said uh-huh or okay or paused—as I did in some other classes. She made literature come alive—I was always surprised—and sorry—when the bell rang.

- When I had a problem, I felt like I could talk about it with Mrs. Garcia. She was my fifth-grade teacher, and she never made me feel dumb or stupid—even when I had so much trouble with math. After I finished talking to her, I felt as if I could do anything.

- For most of my life, I hated history—endlessly memorizing those facts, figures, dates. I forgot them as soon as the test was over. One year I even threw my history book in the river. But Mr. Cohen taught history in such a way that I could understand the big picture. He asked such interesting, provocative questions—about our past and the lessons it gave for our future.

The debate has been raging for decades: Are teachers born, or made? What do you think?

If you think it is a combination of both, you are in agreement with most people who have seriously considered this question. Some individuals—a rare few—are naturally gifted teachers. Their classrooms are dazzlingly alive. Students are motivated and excited, and their enthusiasm translates into academic achievement. For these truly talented educators, teaching seems to be pure art or magic.

But, behind even the most brilliant teaching performance, there is usually well-practiced skill at work. Look again at those brief descriptions of favorite teachers: Each of them used proven skills—structure, motivation, clarity, high expectations, and effective questioning.

- "We went step-by-step in such a clear way that I never seemed to get confused—even when we discussed the most difficult subject matter." *(structure and clarity)*

- "She made literature come alive." *(motivation)*

- "After I finished talking to her, I felt as if I could do anything." *(high expectations)*

- "He asked such interesting, provocative questions—about our past and the lessons it gave for our future." *(questioning)*

Although there is ample room for natural talent, most teaching is based on "tried and true" practices. Research helps us distinguish between what we "think" will work and what really works. In this chapter, we describe what research tells us about teaching skills and models of instruction that raise student achievement. If you decide to teach, it will be your responsibility to keep up with the burgeoning and sometimes shifting teacher effectiveness research through conferences, course work, and education journals.[1] For now, let's explore together the current findings supporting teacher effectiveness.

Academic Learning Time

Research shows that students who spend more time pursuing academic content achieve more. That's the commonsense part, and it's hardly surprising. What is startling is how differently teachers use their classroom time. For example, the classic Beginning Teacher Evaluation Study[2] showed that one teacher in the Los Angeles school system spent 68 minutes a day on reading, whereas another spent 137 minutes; one elementary school teacher spent only 16 minutes per day on mathematics, whereas another spent more than three times that amount. Similarly, John Goodlad's comprehensive research study, *A Place Called School,* found that some schools devote approximately 65 percent of their time to instruction, whereas others devote almost 90 percent.[3] The variation is enormous.

Although allocating adequate time to academic content is obviously important, making time on the schedule is not enough. How this allocated time is used in the classroom is the real key to student achievement. To analyze the use of classroom time, researchers have developed the following terms: allocated time, engaged time, and academic learning time.

Allocated time is the time a teacher schedules for a subject—for example, thirty minutes a day for math. The more time allocated for a subject, the higher student achievement in that subject is likely to be.

Engaged time is that part of allocated time in which students are actively involved with academic subject matter (intently listening to a lecture, participating in a class discussion, writing an essay, solving math problems). When students daydream, doodle, write notes to each other, talk with their peers about nonacademic topics, or simply wait for instructions, they are not involved in engaged time. When there is more engaged time within allocated time, student achievement increases.[4] As with allocated time, the amount of time students are engaged with the subject matter varies enormously from teacher to teacher and school to school. In some classes, engaged time is 50 percent; in others, it is more than 90 percent.

Academic learning time is engaged time with a high success rate. Many researchers suggest that students should get 70 to 80 percent of the answers right when working with a teacher. When working independently, and without a teacher available to make corrections, the success rate should be even higher if students are to learn effectively. Some teachers are skeptical when they hear these percentages; they think that experiencing difficulty challenges students and helps them achieve. However, studies indicate that a high success rate is positively related to student achievement.[5]

In the following sections, you will learn about research-based teaching skills that you can use to increase academic learning time and student achievement. Since much time can be frittered away on organizational details and minor student disruptions (see Figure 11.1), we will look first at effective strategies for classroom management. Then we will consider the instructional skills that seem consistently to produce higher academic achievement in students.

Academic learning time is engaged learning time in which students have a high success rate. When working independently, as here, the success rate should be particularly high.

FIGURE 11.1

Estimated time available for academic learning.

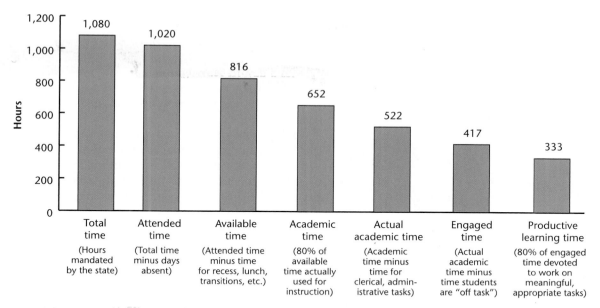

SOURCE: Carol Simon Weinstein and Andrew Migano, Jr., *Elementary Classroom Management: Lessons from Research and Practice,* 4th ed. New York: McGraw-Hill, 2006.

REFLECTION: Only half of school time is available for instruction, and only half of that is used effectively. Identify three classroom practices that you can implement to recapture productive learning time available to your students.

 ## Classroom Management

The observer walked to the back of the room and sat down. It seemed to him that the classroom was a beehive of activity. A reading group was in progress in the front of the room, while the other children were working with partners on math exam-ples. The classroom was filled with a hum of children working together, and in several languages—but the activity and the noise were organized and not chaotic.

The observer had been in enough schools over the past twenty years to know that this well-managed classroom did not result from magic but that carefully established and maintained procedures were at work. The observer scrutinized the classroom, searching for the procedures that allowed twenty-six students and one teacher to work together so industriously, har-moniously, and effectively.

First he examined the reading group, where the teacher was leading a discussion about the meaning of a story. "Why was Tony worried about the trip he was going to take?" the teacher asked (a few seconds' pause, all the children with eyes on the teacher, several hands raised). "Sean?"

IMAGINE . . .

How Bad Do You Have to Go?

Even though Daniel Thornton occasionally needed to go to the bathroom during his AP history course last year, he also needed a B on the midterm to maintain his grade. So he did what lots of students at Forest Park Senior High School in Woodbridge, Virginia, do in their Darwinian pursuit of academic success: Thornton endured a full bladder and hoarded two restroom passes, which, unused, were worth six points of extra credit. It was enough to bump the 18-year-old's midterm grade from a C+ to a B. Critics say it is unfair to give anyone an academic advantage based on something as unacademic as bathroom habits.

SOURCE: "How Bad Do You Have to Go?" *The Washington Post,* June 6, 2006, p. A1.

Modern classrooms are complex environments that require carefully planned rules and routines.

As Sean began his response, the observer's eyes wandered around the rest of the room, where most of the children were busy at work. Two girls, however, were passing notes surreptitiously in the corner of the room.

During a quick sweep of the room, the teacher spotted the misbehavior. The two girls watched the teacher frown and put her finger over her lips. They quickly returned to their work. The exchange had been so rapid and so quiet that the reading group was not interrupted for even a second.

Another student in the math group had his hand raised. The teacher motioned Omar to come to her side.

"Look for the paragraph in your story that tells how Tony felt after his visit to his grandmother," the teacher instructed the reading group. "When you have found it, raise your hands."

While the reading group looked for the appropriate passage, the teacher quietly assisted Omar. In less than a minute, Omar was back at his seat, and the teacher was once again discussing the story with her reading group.

At 10:15, the teacher sent the reading group back to their seats and quietly counted down from ten to one. As she approached one, the room became quiet and the students' attention was focused on her. "It is now time for social studies. Before you do anything, listen carefully to *all* my instructions. When I tap the bell on my desk, those working on math should put their papers in their cubbies for now. You may have a chance to finish them later. Then all students should take out their social studies books and turn to page 67. When you hear the sound of the bell, I want you to follow those instructions." After a second's pause, the teacher tapped the bell, and the class was once again a sea of motion, but it was motion that the teacher had organized while the students were now taking responsibility for their own learning.

The observer made some notes. There was nothing particularly flashy or dramatic about what he had seen. But he was satisfied, because he knew he had been witnessing a well-managed classroom.

• • •

Can you remember from your childhood those activity books in which you had to find the five things wrong in a picture? Let us reverse the game: Try rereading this classroom vignette and look for all the things that are *right* with the picture. Underline four or five examples of what the teacher did well.

The teacher in this vignette used several strategies to avoid interruptions and to keep instruction proceeding smoothly and keep students on task.[6] Did you notice that

1. The teacher used a questioning technique known as **group alerting** to keep the reading group involved. By asking questions first and then naming the student to respond, she kept all the students awake and on their toes. If she had said, "Sean, why did Tony feel concerned about his trip?" the other students in the group would have been less concerned about paying attention

and answering the question. Instead, she asked her question first and then called on a student to respond.

2. The teacher seemed to have "eyes in the back of her head." Termed **withitness** by researcher Jacob Kounin, this quality characterizes teachers who are aware of student behavior in all parts of the room at all times. While the teacher was conducting the reading group, she was aware of the students passing notes and the one who needed assistance.

3. The teacher was able to attend to interruptions or behavior problems while continuing the lesson. Kounin calls the ability to do several things at once **overlapping.** The teacher reprimanded the students passing notes and helped another child with a math problem without interrupting the flow of her reading lesson.

4. The teacher managed routine misbehavior using the principle of **least intervention.** Since research shows the time spent disciplining students is negatively related to achievement, teachers should use the simplest intervention that will work. In this case, the teacher did not make a mountain out of a molehill. She intervened quietly and quickly to stop students from passing notes. Her nonverbal cue was all that was necessary, and did not disrupt the students working on math and reading. The teacher might also have used some other effective strategies. She could have praised the students who were attending to their math ("I'm glad to see so many partners working well on their math assignments"). If it had been necessary to say more to the girls passing notes, she should have alerted them to what they *should* be doing, rather than emphasize their misbehavior ("Deanne and U-Mei, please attend to your own work," *not* "Deanne and U-Mei, stop passing notes").

5. The teacher managed the transition from one lesson to the next smoothly and effectively, avoiding a bumpy transition, which Kounin termed **fragmentation.** When students must move from one activity to another, a gap is created in the fabric of instruction. Chaos can result when transitions are not handled competently by the instructor. Did you notice that the teacher gave a

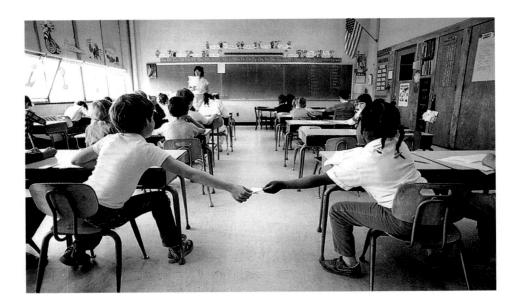

Good classroom management requires constant monitoring of student behavior.

Teachers must manage more than thirty major transitions every day, from one content area to another, through different instructional activities and through a myriad of routines, including having students line up, collecting papers, distributing texts, and the like. During these transitions, discipline problems occur twice as often as in regular classroom instruction. Classroom management expert **Jacob Kounin** identified five common patterns that can derail classroom management during **times of transition:**

- **Flip-flops.** In this negative pattern, the teacher terminates one activity, begins a new one, and then flops back to the original activity. For example, in making a transition from math to spelling, the teacher says, "Please open your spelling books to page 29. By the way, how many of you got all the math problems right?"

- **Overdwelling.** This bad habit includes preaching, nagging, and spending more time than necessary to correct an infraction of classroom rules. "Anna, I told you to stop talking. If I've told you once, I've told you 100 times. I told you yesterday and the day before that. The way things are going, I'll be telling it to you all year, and, believe me, I'm getting pretty tired of it. And another thing, young lady . . ."

- **Fragmentation.** In this bumpy transition, the teacher breaks directions into several choppy steps instead of accomplishing the instructions in one fluid unit—for example, "Put away your reading books. You shouldn't have any spelling books on your desk, either. All notes should be off your desk," instead of the simpler and more effective "Clear your desk of all books and papers."

- **Thrusts.** Classroom momentum is interrupted by *non sequitors* and random thoughts that just seem to pop into the teacher's head—for example, the class is busily engaged in independent reading, when their quiet concentration is broken by the teacher, who says, "Where's Roberto? Wasn't he here earlier this morning?"

- **Dangles.** Similar to the thrust, this move involves starting something, only to leave it hanging or dangling—for example, "Richard, would you please read the first paragraph on page 94. Oh, class, did I tell you about the guest speaker we're having today? How could I have forgotten about that?"

SOURCE: Jacob Kounin, *Discipline and Group Management in Classrooms* (New York: Holt, Rinehart & Winston, 1970).

REFLECTION: Since each of the above patterns represents a problem, can you reword the dialogue to produce a more effective transition?

clear transition signal, either the countdown or the bell; gave thorough instructions so her students would know exactly what to do next; and made the transition all at once for the entire class? These may seem simple, commonsense behaviors, but countless classes have come apart at the seams because transitions were not handled effectively.

Research also shows that effective classroom managers are good planners.[7] They are waiting at the door when the children arrive, rather than entering a room late, after noise and disruption have had a chance to build. Starting from the very first day of school, they teach standards or norms of appropriate student behavior, actively and directly. Often they model procedures for getting assistance, leaving the room, going to the pencil sharpener, and the like. The more important rules of classroom behavior are posted, as are the consequences of not following them.[8]

In traditional teacher-centered schools, rules usually mean obeying the teacher, being quiet, and not misbehaving. When schools move away from autocratic teaching styles, student responsibility and ownership of rules (or as one teacher calls them "Habits of Goodness") are embraced. Some teachers like to develop the list of rules together with their students; other teachers prefer to present a list of established practices and ask students to give specific examples or to provide reasons for having such rules. The bottom line: when rules are easily understood and convey a sense of moral fairness, most students will comply. We can create a productive

A time-out area, a visit to the principal, or an hour of detention are typical disciplinary practices in elementary, middle, and high school. What school-based discipline programs can you recall from your K–12 years? Are your recollections influenced by any first-hand experiences?

learning community when rules are (1) few in number, (2) fair and reasonable, and (3) appropriate for student maturation.

Good managers also carefully arrange their classrooms to minimize disturbances, provide students with a sense of confidence and security, and make sure that instruction can proceed efficiently. They set up their rooms according to the following principles:

- *Teaching eye to eye.* Teachers should be able to see all students at all times. Research shows that students who are seated far away from the teacher or the instructional activity are less likely to be involved in class discussions. As teachers intentionally move about the room, they can short-circuit off-task student behavior. Placing instructional materials (video monitor, overhead projector, demonstration activity, flip chart, lab station, and the like) in various parts of the room also gives each student "the best seat in the house" for at least part of the teaching day.

- *Teaching materials and supplies should be readily available.* Arranging a "self-help" area so that students have direct access to supplies encourages individual responsibility while freeing up the teacher to focus on instructional activities.

- *High-traffic areas should be free of congestion.* Place student desks away from supply cabinets, pencil sharpeners, and so on. Minor disturbances ripple out, distracting other students from their tasks.

- *Procedures and routines should be actively taught in the same way that academic content is taught.* Initial planning for classroom management is often rewarded with fewer discipline problems and smooth transitions to classroom routines and procedures.[9] For students who come from chaotic home environments, these routines offer a sense of stability. Once established, they allow teachers and all students more time for academic learning.

A child's misbehavior—from minor classroom disruptions to emotional outbursts to violence—is often rooted in trauma, feelings of powerlessness, or even "normal" daily events beyond a teacher's control. Yet, teachers must understand and manage student anger and aggression. Several classroom strategies can help:

- *Choice.* Constantly taking away privileges and threatening punishment can cause students to feel intimidated and victimized. Teachers can provide appropriate options to give a student a sense of some control and freedom. Encouraging a student to select a lunch mate or to choose a project topic offers a reasonable decision-making opportunity and can help avoid minor disruptions as well as aggressive acts.

- *Responsibility.* Rechanneling student energy and interest into constructive activities and responsibilities can reduce misbehavior. When instruction is meaningful and worthwhile, boredom and fooling around are less likely to occur.[10] When students are empowered, they are less likely to act out.

- *Voice.* Listening to young people is one of the most respectful skills a teacher can model. Students who feel they are not heard feel disrespected. Hearing and honoring students' words (and feelings) reduce the likelihood of misbehavior.[11]

Listening to students was exactly what Kathleen Cushman did when she wrote *Fires in the Bathroom.* Adolescents from around the nation were asked to tell teachers what they would like to see in their classrooms. Students advised teachers to: share your plans with me and tell me how I will be evaluated, be excited about what you teach, be firm when rules are broken, treat me fairly but remember I am an individual, give me feedback and encouragement, don't say "please" too much, and don't push yourself into my personal life.[12]

While we can't always detect the signs of danger, we can be on the lookout and can create management plans to handle small distractions as well as major incidents. As researcher David Berliner says, "In short, from the opening bell to the end of the day, the better classroom managers are thinking ahead. While maintaining a pleasant classroom atmosphere, these teachers keep planning how to organize, manage, and control activities to facilitate instruction."[13] Berliner makes an important connection between management and instruction. Effective teachers, in addition to being good classroom managers, must also be good organizers of academic content and instruction.

Picture a disruptive classroom, and you are likely to envision a few boys as troublemakers. Why boys? Male aggression is often connected with the more active male stereotype. Society teaches boys to project an outward appearance of strength, confidence, and security even when all are lacking. William Pollack calls this bravado the "boy code" or the "mask of masculinity"—a kind of swaggering posture that boys embrace to hide their fears, suppress dependency and vulnerability, and present a stoic, impervious front. When boys explore behaviors beyond the typical male role, they risk being called a "wuss," "fag," or "sissy" or identified as feminine.[1] This "boy code" contributes to school discipline problems.

Teachers are well aware of the "boy code," so it is hardly surprising that boys are targeted for swift and strict discipline. Girls, on the other hand, fit neatly into their stereotype and are afforded more gentle, if no less sexist, treatment. These gender disparities are readily detected by students who report that innocent boys are often targeted unfairly by teachers, and girls are able "to get away" with inappropriate and hurtful behavior.[2] When teachers appear to be unfair to students, classroom management suffers and a sense of security is lost for all students.

But all this does not mean that girls are problem-free. While overt male misbehavior captures teacher attention, girls' misbehavior is often more covert and subtle. Girls may create unhealthy relationship dynamics in an effort to gain social power or hurt a peer. These covert emotional bullying behaviors can be delivered in a whisper, more difficult to detect than the public male aggression, but no less painful. The term for this type of destructive behavior is **relational aggression,** and it includes:

- Purposefully ignoring someone (giving the "silent treatment").
- Calling each other "hos," "wimps," "sluts," "sissies," "loser."
- Making fun of someone's clothes, appearance, or weight.
- Telling others not to play with a certain classmate.
- Making mean jokes and then saying "just kidding."
- Spreading rumors and gossip.

When asked what sparks relational aggression, students identify three general motivations: *Belonging*—If I share the secret she told me with you, my information gets me "in"; *Fear*—I'm afraid of being rejected by my classmates, I'll go along with it; and *Drama*—I'm bored, and relationship aggression creates drama and excitement.[3]

Educators committed to creating fair and effective classrooms would be wise to listen to girls'—and boys'—voices to address and correct damaging classroom aggression, both physical and relational.

[1] William. S. Pollack, *Real Boys: Rescuing Our Sons from the Myths of Boyhood* (New York: Holt and Company, 1998). [2] Karen Zittleman, "Title IX and Gender: A Study of the Knowledge, Perceptions, and Experiences of Middle and Junior High School Teachers and Students," *Dissertation Abstracts International* 66, no.11 (2005) (UMI No. 3194815). [3] Lyn Mikel Brown, *Girlfighting: Betrayal and Rejection Among Girls* (New York: New York University Press, 2003).

REFLECTION: Why are gender stereotypes so persistent? How can teachers address relational aggression?

The Pedagogical Cycle

How does one organize classroom life? Researcher **Arno Bellack** analyzed verbal exchanges between teachers and students and offers a fascinating insight into classroom organization, likening these interactions to a pedagogical game.[14] The game is so cyclical and occurs so frequently that many teachers and students do not even know that they are playing. There are four moves:

1. *Structure.* The teacher provides information, provides direction, and introduces the topics.
2. *Question.* The teacher asks a question.
3. *Respond.* The student answers the question, or tries to.
4. *React.* The teacher reacts to the student's answer and provides feedback.

These four steps make up a **pedagogical cycle,** diagrammed in Figure 11.2. Teachers initiate about 85 percent of the cycles, which are used over and over again in

www.mhhe.com/
sadker8e

INTERACTIVE ACTIVITY
Pedagogical Cycle
Identify the moves in
a sample classroom
dialogue.

FIGURE 11.2
Pedagogical cycle and sample classroom dialogue.

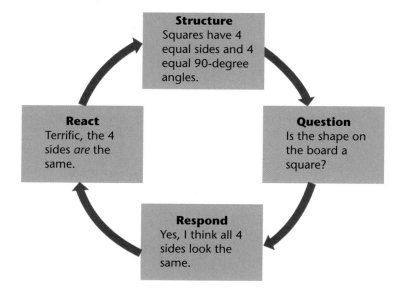

Structure
Squares have 4 equal sides and 4 equal 90-degree angles.

Question
Is the shape on the board a square?

Respond
Yes, I think all 4 sides look the same.

React
Terrific, the 4 sides *are* the same.

REFLECTION: Continue the classroom dialogue around the cycle again. What might the teacher and the student(s) say?

classroom interaction. When teachers learn to consciously enhance and refine each of the cycle's moves, student achievement is increased.[15]

Clarity and Academic Structure

Have you ever been to a class where the teacher is bombarded with questions? "What are we supposed to do?" "Can you explain it again?" "What do you mean?" When such questions are constant, it is a sure sign that the teacher is not setting the stage for instruction. Students need a clear understanding of what they are expected to learn, and they need motivation to learn it.[16] Effective **academic structure** sets the stage for learning and occurs mainly at the beginning of the lesson. Although the specific structure will vary depending on the students' backgrounds and the difficulty of the subject matter, an effective academic structure usually consists of

- **Objectives.** Let the students know the objectives (or purpose) of each lesson. Students, like the teacher, need a road map of where they are going and why.

- **Review.** Help students review prior learning before presenting new information. If there is confusion, reteach.

- **Motivation.** Create an "anticipatory set" that motivates students to attend to the lesson. Consider throwing out an intriguing question, an anecdote, a joke, or a challenging riddle.

- **Transition.** Provide connections to help students integrate old and new information.

- **Clarification.** Break down a large body of information. (This is sometimes called "chunking.") Do not inundate students with too much too fast. This is particularly true for young children, English language learners, and slower learners.

- **Scaffolding.** Step-by-step practice and well-crafted questions support and encourage student understanding.
- **Examples.** Give several examples and illustrations to explain main points and ideas.
- **Directions.** Give directions distinctly and slowly. If students are confused about what they are supposed to do, repeat or break information into small segments.
- **Enthusiasm.** Demonstrate personal enthusiasm for the academic content. Make it clear why the information is interesting and important.
- **Closure.** Close the lesson with a brief review or summary. If students are able to provide the summary, so much the better, for it shows that they have really understood the lesson.[17]

Through effective and clear structure, the stage is set for the remaining steps of the pedagogical cycle.

Questioning

Good questioning is at the very core of good teaching. As John Dewey said,

> To question well is to teach well. In the skillful use of the question more than anything else lies the fine art of teaching; for in it we have the guide to clear and vivid ideas, and the quick spur to imagination, the stimulus to thought, the incentive to action.[18]

Since questioning is key in guiding learning, all students should have equal access to classroom questions and academic interaction. Yet sitting in the same classroom taught by the same teacher, students experience significant differences in the number of questions they are asked. Research shows that male students are asked more questions than female students, and white students are asked more questions than nonwhite students. One of the reasons boys get to answer questions as well as to talk more is that they are assertive in grabbing teacher attention. Boys are more likely than girls to call out the answers to the questions. In addition, when boys call out the answers to questions, teachers are likely to accept their responses. When girls call out the answers, teachers often remind them to raise their hands. Teacher expectations also play a role and are frequently cited as one of the reasons white students (perceived as higher achievers) receive more questions and more active teacher attention than students who are members of other racial and ethnic groups.[19]

If you want all students, not just the quickest and most assertive, to answer questions, establish a protocol for participation. For example, make a rule that students must raise their hands and be called on before they may talk. Too many classes offer variations of the following scene:

TEACHER: How much is 60 + 4 + 12? *(Many students raise their hands—both girls and boys.)*

TONY: *(Shouts out)* 76!

TEACHER: Okay. How much is 50 + 9 + 8?

This scene, repeated again and again in classes across the country, is a typical example of the squeaky wheel—not necessarily the most needy or most deserving student—getting the educational oil. Once you make the rule that students should raise their hands before participating, *hold to that rule.*

Many teachers are well-intentioned about having students raise their hands, but, in the rapid pace of classroom interaction, they sometimes forget their own rule. If you hold to that "wait to be recognized" rule, you can make professional decisions about who should answer which questions and why. If you give away this key to classroom participation, you are abandoning an important part of your professional decision making in the classroom.

There is more to managing classroom questions than taking the role of a traffic cop. For instance, you might assign pairs of students to work together (sometimes called "Think-Pair-Share") to develop and record answers and then present them to the class as a whole. Or perhaps teams of four or five students can be established to tackle academic questions on a regular basis. When students are actively involved in either of these approaches, the teacher can move around the room as a facilitator, answering questions, motivating student groups, and assessing how the groups are doing. More important, the students take ownership of the questions, asking sincere questions reflecting their genuine interests.

While the distribution and ownership of questions are important, the type of question asked is also meaningful. This section provides more information about the different levels of classroom questions, as well as strategies for using them fairly and effectively.

Many educators differentiate between factual, lower-order questions and thought-provoking, higher-order questions. Perhaps the most widely used system for determining the intellectual level of questions is Benjamin **Bloom's taxonomy,** which proceeds from the lowest level of questions, knowledge, to the highest level, evaluation.[20]

A **lower-order question** can be answered through memory and recall. For example, "What is the name of the largest Native American nation?" is a lower-order question. Without consulting outside references, one could respond with the correct answer only by remembering previously learned information. (Cherokee for those who do not recall.) Students either know the answer or they don't. Research indicates that 70 to 95 percent of a teacher's questions are lower-order.

A **higher-order question** demands more thought and usually more time before students reach a response. These questions may ask for evaluations, comparisons, causal relationships, problem solving, or divergent, open-ended thinking. Following are examples of higher-order questions:

1. Do you think that William Clinton was an effective president? Why or why not?

2. What similarities in theme emerge in the three Coen movies: *Oh Brother, Where Art Thou, Raising Arizona,* and *Fargo?*

3. Considering changes that have taken place in the past decade, describe the impact of computer technology on campus life.

4. Create your own pledge of allegiance to a cause or organization.

5. What could happen if our shadows came to life?

Although higher-order questions have been shown to produce increased student achievement, most teachers ask very few of them.[21]

Many educators think that different questioning levels stimulate different levels of thought. If you ask a fifth-grade student to define an adjective, you are working on lower-level basic skills. If you ask a fifth-grade student to write a short story, making effective use of adjectives, you are working on a higher level of student

www.mhhe.com/
sadker8e

INTERACTIVE ACTIVITY
Questioning Levels
Match questions to the
different questioning
levels.

achievement. Both lower-order and higher-order questions are important and should be matched to appropriate instructional goals:

Ask Lower-Order Questions When Students Are

- Being introduced to new information
- Working on drill and practice
- Reviewing previously learned information

Ask Higher-Order Questions When Students Are

- Working on problem-solving skills
- Involved in a creative or affective discussion
- Asked to make judgments about quality, aesthetics, or ethics
- Challenged to manipulate already established information in more sophisticated ways

**www.mhhe.com/
sadker8e**

INTERACTIVE ACTIVITY
**The Question Master
Game** Test your
knowledge of Bloom's
Taxonomy

Student Response

If you were to spend a few minutes in a high school English class, you might hear a classroom discussion go something like this:

TEACHER: Who wrote the poem "Stopping by Woods on a Snowy Evening"? Tomàs?

TOMÀS: Robert Frost.

TEACHER: Good. What action takes place in the poem? Kenisha?

KENISHA: A man stops his sleigh to watch the woods get filled with snow.

TEACHER: Yes. Denise, what thoughts go through the man's mind?

DENISE: He thinks how beautiful the woods are. *(Pauses for a second)*

TEACHER: What else does he think about? Russell?

RUSSELL: He thinks how he would like to stay and watch. *(Pauses for a second)*

TEACHER: Yes—and what else? Rita? *(Waits half a second)* Come on, Rita, you can answer this. *(Waits half a second)* Well, why does he feel he can't stay there indefinitely and watch the woods and the snow?

RITA: He knows he's too busy. He's got too many things to do to stay there for so long.

TEACHER: Good. In the poem's last line, the man says that he has miles to go before he sleeps. What might sleep be a symbol for? Krista?

KRISTA: Well, I think it might be . . . *(Pauses for a second)*

TEACHER: Think, Krista. *(Waits for half a second)* All right then—Eugene? *(Waits again for half a second)* James? *(Waits half a second)* What's the matter with everyone today? Didn't you do the reading?[22]

The teacher is using several instructional skills effectively. His is a well-managed classroom. The students are on task and engaged in a discussion appropriate to the academic content. By asking a series of lower-order questions ("Who wrote the poem?" "What action takes place in the poem?"), the teacher works with the students to establish an information base. Then the teacher builds to higher-order questions about the poem's theme and meaning.

Bloom's Taxonomy Applied to Questioning Levels

LEVEL I: KNOWLEDGE

Requires student to recall or recognize information. Student must rely on memory or senses to provide the answer.

Sample Questions What does "quixotic" mean?

List the first ten presidents of the United States.

LEVEL II: COMPREHENSION

Requires student to go beyond simple recall and demonstrate the ability to mentally arrange and organize information. Student must use previously learned information by putting it in his or her own words and rephrasing it.

Sample Question In our story, the author discusses why the family left Oklahoma. Can you summarize why in your own words?

LEVEL III: APPLICATION

Requires student to apply previously learned information to answer a problem. At this level the student uses a rule, a definition, a classification system, or directions in solving a problem with specific correct answer.

Sample Questions Applying the law of supply and demand, solve the following problem. *(applying a rule)*

Identify the proper noun in the following sentences. *(applying a definition)*

Solve the quadratic equation. *(applying a rule)*

LEVEL IV: ANALYSIS

Requires student to use three kinds of cognitive processes: (1) To identify causes, reasons, or motives (when these have not been provided to the student previously), (2) To analyze information to reach a generalization or conclusion, (3) To find evidence to support a specific opinion, event, or situation.

Sample Questions Why do you think King Lear misjudged his daughter? *(identifying motives)*

What generalizations can you make about the climate of Egypt near the Nile River basin? *(analyze information to reach a conclusion)*

Many historians think that Abraham Lincoln was our finest president. What evidence can you find to support this statement? *(find evidence to support a specific opinion)*

LEVEL V: SYNTHESIS

Requires student to use original and creative thinking: (1) To develop original communications, (2) To make predictions, and (3) To solve problems for which there is no single right answer.

Sample Questions Write a short story about life on another planet. *(developing an original communication)*

What do you think life would be like if Germany had won World War II? *(making predictions)*

How can our class raise money for the dance festival? *(solving problems for which there is no single right solution)*

LEVEL VI: EVALUATION

Requires student to judge the merits of an aesthetic work, an idea, or the solution to a problem.

Sample Questions Which U.S. senator do you think is most effective? Support your selection.

Do you think that schools are too hard or not hard enough? Explain your answer.

REFLECTION: Starting with your own sample question at Level I (Knowledge) can you expand your questioning to Level VI (Evaluation)? Or, using Bloom's taxonomy as the content, create a question at each level about this classification system (e.g., Level I; List the six levels of Bloom's Taxonomy).

If you were to give this teacher suggestions on how to improve his questioning techniques, you might point out the difficulty students have in answering the more complex questions. You might also note the lightning pace at which this lesson proceeds. The teacher fires questions so rapidly that the students barely have time to think. This is not so troublesome when they are answering factual questions that require a brief memorized response. However, students begin to flounder when they are required to answer more complex questions with equal speed.

Although it is important to keep classroom discussion moving at a brisk pace, sometimes teachers push forward too rapidly. Slowing down at two key places during classroom discussion can usually improve the effectiveness and equity of classroom responses. In the research on classroom interaction, this slowing down is called **wait time.**[23]

Mary Budd Rowe's research on wait time shows that, after asking a question, teachers typically wait only one second or less for a student response (wait time 1). If the response is not forthcoming in that time, teachers rephrase the question, ask another student to answer it, or answer it themselves. If teachers can learn to increase their wait time from one second to three to five seconds, significant improvements in the quantity and quality of student response usually will take place.

There is another point in classroom discussion when wait time can be increased. After students complete an answer, teachers often begin their reaction or their next question before a second has passed (wait time 2). Once again, it is important for teachers to increase their wait time from one second to three to five seconds. Based on her research, Mary Budd Rowe has determined that increasing the pause after a student gives an answer is equally as important as increasing wait time 1, the pause after the teacher asks a question. When wait time 1 and wait time 2 are increased, classroom interaction is changed in several positive ways.

Changes in Student Behavior

- More students participate in discussion.
- Fewer discipline problems disrupt the class.
- The length of student response increases dramatically.
- Students are more likely to support their statements with evidence.
- Speculative thinking increases.
- There are more student questions and fewer failures to respond.
- Student achievement increases on written tests that measure more complex levels of thinking.

Changes in Teacher Behavior

- Teacher comments are less disjointed and more fluent. Classroom discussion becomes more logical, thoughtful, and coherent.
- Teachers ask more sophisticated, higher-order questions.
- Teachers begin to hold higher expectations for all students.

Research indicates that teachers give more wait time to students for whom they hold higher expectations. A high-achieving student is more likely to get time to think than is a low-achieving student. If we do not expect much from our students, we will not get much. High expectations and longer wait times are positively related to achievement. Researchers suggest that white male students, particularly high achievers, are more likely to be given adequate wait time than are females, English language learners, quiet students, and students of color. Students who are quiet and reserved or who think more slowly may obtain special benefit from increased wait time. In fact, a key benefit of extended wait time is an increase in the quality of student participation, even from students who were previously silent.

Usually when teachers learn that they are giving students less than a second to think, they are surprised and have every intention of waiting longer, but that is easier said than done! In the hectic arena of the classroom, it is all too easy to slip into split-second question-and-answer patterns.

Sometimes teachers fall into a pattern of quickly repeating every answer that students give. Occasionally this repetition can be helpful—if some students may not have heard it or if an answer merits repetition for emphasis. In most cases, however, this "teacher echo" is counterproductive. Students learn they do not need to listen to one another, because the teacher will repeat the answer anyway. The teacher echo also reduces valuable wait time and cuts down on the pause that allows students to think. Teachers who have worked on increasing wait time offer some useful tips.

Some teachers adopt self-monitoring cues to slow themselves down at the two key wait-time points. For example, one teacher says that he puts his hand behind his back and counts on his fingers for three seconds to slow himself down. Another teacher says that she covers her mouth with her hand (in a thoughtful pose) to keep herself from talking and thereby destroying "the pause that lets them think."

As mentioned previously, wait time is more important in some cases than in others. If you are asking students to repeat previously memorized math facts and you are interested in developing speed, a three- to five-second wait time may be counterproductive. However, if you have asked a higher-order question that calls for a complicated answer, be sure that wait times 1 and 2 are ample. Simply put, students, like the rest of us, need time to think, and some students may need more wait time than others. For example, when a student speaks English as a newly acquired language, additional wait time could help that student accurately translate and respond to the question. And many of us could profit by less impulsive, more thoughtful responses, the kind that can be engendered by a five-second wait time.

When teachers allow more wait time, the results can be surprising. Not only do more students answer questions, there is also an increase in student-initiated questions. While many educators believe that questioning is at the heart of learning, students ask remarkably few content-related questions. (Students in the upper grades ask fewer than 15 percent of classroom questions.)[24] Teachers can nourish genuine inquiry and tap student curiosity by encouraging student-initiated questions. As one teacher said, "I never thought Andrea had anything to say. She just used to sit there like a bump on a log. Then I tried calling on her and giving her time to answer. What a difference! Not only does she answer, she asks questions that no one else has thought of."

Reaction or Productive Feedback

"Today," the student teacher said, "we are going to hear the story of *The Three Billy Goats Gruff*." A murmur of anticipation rippled through the kindergarten children comfortably seated on the carpet around the flannel board. This student teacher was a favorite, and the children were particularly happy when she told them flannel-board stories.

"Before we begin the story, I want to make sure we know what all the words mean. Who can tell me what a troll is?"

A five-year-old nicknamed B.J. raised his hand. "A troll is someone who walks you home from school."

"Okay," the teacher responded, a slightly puzzled look flickering over her face. "Who else can tell me what a troll is?"

Another student chimed in, "A troll is someone with white hair sticking out of his head."

"Okay," the teacher said.

Another student volunteered, "It hides under bridges and waits for you and scares you."

"Uh-huh," said the teacher.

Warming to the topic, another student gleefully recounted, "I saw a green troll named Shrek who lives in the woods."

"Okay," the teacher said.

Wide-eyed, B.J. raised his hand again, "I'm sure glad we had this talk about trolls," he said. "I'm not going home with them from school anymore."

"Okay," the teacher said.

This is a classroom in which several good teaching strategies are in operation. The teacher uses effective academic structure, and the students are on task, interested, and involved in the learning activity. The teacher is asking lower-order questions appropriately, to make sure the students know key vocabulary words before the flannel-board story is told. The problem with this classroom lies in the fourth stage of the pedagogical cycle: This teacher does not provide specific reactions and adequate feedback. Did you notice that the teacher reacted with "uh-huh" or "OK," no matter what kind of answer the students gave? Because of this vague feedback and "OK" teaching style, B.J. was left confused about the difference between a troll and a patrol. This real-life incident may seem amusing, but there was nothing funny to B.J., who was genuinely afraid to leave school with the patrol.

Recently, attention has been directed not only at how teachers ask questions but also at how they respond to student answers. When Myra and David Sadker analyzed classroom interaction in more than 100 classrooms in five states, they found that teachers generally use four types of reactions:

1. **Praise.** Positive comments about student work, such as "Excellent, good job."

2. **Acceptance.** Comments such as "Uh-huh" and "OK," which acknowledge that student answers are acceptable. These are not as strong as praise.

3. **Remediation.** Comments that encourage a more accurate student response or encourage students to think more clearly, creatively, or logically. Sample remediation comments include "Try again," "Sharpen your answer," and "Check your addition."

4. **Criticism.** A clear statement that an answer is inaccurate or a behavior is inappropriate. This category includes harsh criticism ("This is a terrible paper"), as well as milder comments that simply indicate an answer is not correct ("Your answer to the third question is wrong").[25]

Which of these reactions do you think teachers use most frequently? Did you notice that the kindergarten teacher relied heavily on the acceptance, or "okay," reaction? So do most teachers from grade school through graduate school. The Sadkers' study found that acceptance was the most frequent response, accounting for more than half of all teacher reactions. The second most frequent teacher response was remediation, accounting for one-third of teacher reactions. Used infrequently, praise comprised only 11 percent of reactions. The rarest response was criticism. In two-thirds of the classrooms observed, teachers never told a student that an answer was incorrect. In the classrooms where criticism did occur, it accounted for only 5 percent of interaction. (See Figure 11.3.)

In *A Place Called School*, John Goodlad writes that "learning is enhanced when students understand what is expected of them, get recognition for their work, learn about their errors, and receive guidance in improving their performances."[26] But many students claim that they are not informed or corrected when they make mistakes.[27] Perhaps this is caused by overreliance on the acceptance response, which

FIGURE 11.3
Teacher reactions.

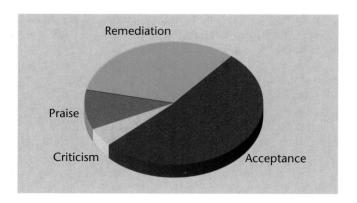

is the vaguest kind of feedback that teachers can offer. Since there is more accept-ance than praise, criticism, and remediation combined, some educators are begin-ning to wonder: "Is the 'OK' classroom OK?"

Although the acceptance response is legitimate and often appropriate, it is overused. Since achievement is likely to increase when students get clear, specific productive feedback about their answers, it is important for teachers to reduce the "OK" reaction and to be more varied and specific in the feedback they provide. Researcher Jere Brophy has done an analysis of praise and student achievement. He found that praise may be particularly important for low-achieving students and those from low socio-economic backgrounds. Additional studies show that praise is most effective when:

1. *Praise is contingent upon student performance.* Praise should closely follow stu-dent behavior the teacher wants to recognize.

2. *Praise is specific.* When teachers praise, they should clearly indicate what aspect of the student behavior is noteworthy (for instance, creative problem solving or good use of evidence to support an argument).

3. *Praise is sincere.* Praise should reflect the experiences, growth, and development of the individual student. Otherwise, it may be dismissed as being disingenuous.

4. *Praise lets students know about their competence and the importance of their accomplishments*—for instance, "The well-documented review of studies on your Web site and the connection you made between the two tobacco filters may eventually impact the industry."

5. *Praise attributes success to ability or effort*—for example, "Your analysis of the paintings of the Impressionists is excellent. I'll bet you spent a long time studying their work in the museum" *(attribution to effort).* Or "This story is fantastic. You've got a real flair for creative writing" *(attribution to ability).* When praise is attributed to abilities or effort, students know that successful performance is under their own control.

6. *Praise uses past performance as a context for describing present performance*—for example, "Last week you were really having trouble with your breast stroke kick. Now you've got it together—you've learned to push the water behind you and increase your speed."[28]

Just as students need to know when they are performing well, they need to know when their efforts are inadequate or incorrect. If students do not have information about their weak areas, they will find it difficult to improve. Here are some tips for effective feedback:

1. *Corrective feedback is specific and contingent on student performance.* The teacher's comments should closely follow the student behavior the teacher wants to improve.

2. *Critical comments focus on student performance and are not of a personal nature.* All of us find it easier to accept constructive criticism when it is detached from our worth as a person, when it is not personal, hostile, or sarcastic.

3. *Feedback provides a clear blueprint for improvement.* If you merely tell a student that an answer is wrong and nothing more, the student has clear feedback on level of performance but no strategies for improvement. Effective feedback suggests an approach for attaining success, such as "Check your addition," "Use the bold headings as a reading guide when you study for the exams," or "Let's conjugate this verb in both French and English, to see where the error is."

4. *An environment is established that lets the student know it is acceptable to make mistakes.* "We learn from our errors. Hardly any inventions are perfected on the first try."

5. *Corrective feedback relates eventual success to effort.* "Now you have demonstrated the correct sequence in class. Give yourself a solid half-hour tonight working on this, and I bet that you will get most of it correct. I'll check with you tomorrow."

6. *Corrective feedback recognizes when students have made improvements in their performance.* "Last week you were having trouble identifying which of Newton's Laws are applicable in each of these time motion studies. Now you've mastered the skill. You've done a good job."

An "okay classroom" allows student error and misunderstanding to go uncorrected; it lets B.J. think that the patrol will eat him up after school. In classrooms where there is appropriate use of remediation and constructive criticism, students know not only when they have made mistakes but also how to correct them. They also recognize that this process leads to growth and achievement.

Variety in Process and Content

Variety is the spice of life, the saying goes—the spice of lessons also, because variety can enhance both teaching effectiveness and student achievement.[29] Have you ever listened to a lecture for an hour and found your initial interest lapsing into daydreams? Have you ever watched a class begin a seatwork assignment with active concentration and found, after 30 minutes, that involvement had turned into passing notes and throwing paper airplanes? When the teacher fails to provide sufficient variety, lessons become monotonous and students get off task.

Effective teachers provide variety in both content and process. In elementary school, variety in content can involve moving from one subject area to another. In secondary instruction, the move might be in the same subject area, such as the switch from memorizing vocabulary to analyzing symbols in a short story.

As any savvy teacher knows, student interest can be maintained by moving from one activity to another during a single lesson. For example, a 60-minute lesson on the American Revolution might begin with a 10-minute overview providing the structure for the class, then move into a 15-minute question-and-answer session, then change to a 25-minute video, and conclude with a 10-minute discussion and closure. Another motivation to vary content and process in teaching is to accommodate different student learning styles. Some students might miss what is said in a lecture (not being auditory learners), but easily get it when the teacher shows pictures (because the visual

www.mhhe.com/
sadker8e

INTERACTIVE ACTIVITY
Create a Class Schedule
What do you think your
students' week should
consist of?

connection is clear). Gardner's growing inventory of intelligences (introduced in Chapter 2) offers another strong argument for instructional variety. Following is a sample of activities teachers can use to maintain student interest by varying the pattern of the lesson.

discussions	student presentations	music activities
lectures	tests	art activities
films, videos, DVDs, PowerPoint	visits to Web sites	tutoring
role plays	silent reading	spot quizzes
simulations	games	panel discussions
small-group activities	contests	brainstorming sessions
software for individuals and groups	creative writing	students tutoring one another
guest speakers	theater and drama	cooperative learning activities
independent seatwork	field trips	debates
guided practice	boardwork	
	learning centers	

Many of these activities can be described as "hands-on" or active learning and can be captivating for students, but more is needed. Variety alone will not produce achievement: Connections with content must be made, or variety will be reduced to mere activity. Teachers must consider individual students and tailor activities based on their interests, learning styles, and abilities. This is no easy task, as Figure 11.4 indicates. Consider an elementary student happily pasting animal

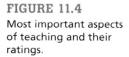

FIGURE 11.4

Most important aspects of teaching and their ratings.

SOURCE: *The MetLife Survey of the American Teacher 2001: Key Elements of Quality Schools* (New York: Harris Interactive, Inc., 2001).

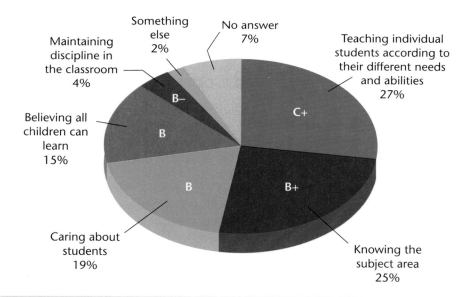

REFLECTION: The above pie chart reflects student responses to two questions: (1) Which of the following aspects of teaching do you think is most important? And (2) How would you grade your teacher on each of them? Why do you think that the most important area according to students is also the one with the lowest student rating? Can you identify two strategies that you can use to individualize your teaching?

pictures on charts, yet unable to explain what (if anything) he is learning about animal families. Students in a middle school may be dressing up for an evening on the Titanic, and from the lower to the upper decks, their clothing and accents reflect different social classes. Yet, if students have not connected their dress with social class and deck classifications, then they may miss learning about the relationship between social class and survival rate. Challenging students with engaging activities is admirable, but the effort must clearly connect the activity to both the content and the student.[30]

Models for Effective Instruction

Part of the challenge for teachers is knowing which model of instruction to choose for particular educational purposes. The following four models differ dramatically from one another, yet each may find a productive use in your classroom.

Direct Teaching

Also called *systematic, active,* or *explicit teaching,* the **direct teaching** model emphasizes the importance of a structured lesson in which presentation of new information is followed by student practice and teacher feedback. In this model, which has emerged from extensive research, the role of the teacher is that of a strong leader, one who structures the classroom and sequences subject matter to reflect a clear academic focus.

Researchers put forward six principles of effective direct teaching.

1. *Daily review.* At the beginning of the lesson, teachers review prior learning. Frequently, teachers focus on assigned homework, clarify points of confusion, and provide extra practice for facts and skills that need more attention.

2. *New material.* Teachers begin by letting students know the objectives to be attained. New information is broken down into smaller bits and is covered at a brisk pace. Teachers illustrate main points with concrete examples. Teachers ask questions frequently to check for student understanding and to make sure that students are ready for independent work using new skills and knowledge.

3. *Guided practice.* Students use new skills and knowledge under direct teacher supervision. During guided practice, teachers ask many content questions ("What is the definition of a paragraph?") and many process questions ("How do you locate the topic sentence in a paragraph?"). Teachers check student responses for understanding, offering prompts and providing corrective feedback. Guided practice continues until students answer with approximately 70 to 80 percent accuracy.

4. *Specific feedback.* Correct answers to questions are acknowledged clearly, so that students will understand

With direct teaching, teachers carefully explain what students must do to accomplish a task, then present a carefully structured lesson that is usually broken down into small, manageable steps.

when their work is accurate. When student answers are hesitant, the teacher provides process feedback ("Yes, Juanita, that's correct because . . ."). Teachers correct inaccurate responses immediately, before errors become habitual. Frequent errors are a sign that students are not ready for independent work, and guided practice should continue.

5. *Independent practice.* Similar to guided practice, except that students work by themselves at their seats or at home. Independent practice continues until responses are assured, quick, and at a level of approximately 95 percent accuracy. Cooperative learning (see the next section) and student tutoring of one another are effective strategies during independent practice.

6. *Weekly and monthly reviews.* Regular reviews offer students the opportunity for more practice, a strategy related to high achievement. Barak Rosenshine, a pioneering researcher in developing the principles of direct teaching, recommends a weekly review every Monday, with a monthly review every fourth Monday.[31]

Direct teaching works well when you are teaching skill subjects, such as grammar or mathematics, or helping students master factual material. The direct teaching model is particularly helpful during the first stages of learning new and complex information, but it is less helpful when imaginative responses and student creativity is called for.

Cooperative Learning

In a classroom using **cooperative learning,** students work on activities in small, heterogeneous groups, and they often receive rewards or recognition based on the overall group performance. Although cooperative learning can be traced back to the 1920s, it seems startling or new because the typical classroom environment is frequently competitive. For example, when grading is done on a curve, one student's success is often detrimental to others. This competitive structure produces clear winners and losers, and only a limited number of *As* are possible. But a cooperative learning structure differs from competitive practices, because students depend on one another and work together to reach shared goals.

According to researchers, cooperative learning groups work best when they meet the following criteria.[32] Groups should be *heterogeneous* and, at least at the beginning, should be *small,* perhaps limited to two to six members. Since face-to-face interaction is important, the groups should be *circular* to permit easy conversation. Positive *interdependence* among group members can be fostered by a *shared group goal, shared division of labor,* and *shared materials,* all contributing to a sense that the group sinks or swims together.

Robert Slavin, a pioneer in cooperative learning techniques, developed student team learning methods in which a team's work is not completed until all students on the team understand the material being studied.[33] Rewards are earned only when the entire team achieves the goals set by the teacher. Students tutor one another, so that everyone can succeed on individual quizzes, and each member of the group is accountable for learning. Since students contribute to their teams by improving prior scores, it does not matter whether the student is a high, average, or low achiever. Increased achievement by an individual student at any level contributes to the overall performance of the group, resulting in equal opportunity for success.

Research shows that cooperative learning promotes both intellectual and emotional growth:

- Students make higher achievement gains; this is especially true for math in the elementary grades.
- Students have higher levels of self-esteem and greater motivation to learn.
- Students have a stronger sense that classmates have positive regard for one another.
- Understanding and cooperation among students from different racial and ethnic backgrounds are enhanced.[34]

Yet the practical realities of cooperative learning are not all commendable. Some students, accustomed to starring roles in full class instruction, continue to dominate the small groups. Accurate grading requires an analysis of both the individual and group performance. And, even the most committed practitioners acknowledge that cooperative learning may take more time than direct teaching. Still, as ability grouping becomes more controversial, educators are growing increasingly interested in cooperative learning as a strategy for working successfully with mixed-ability groups and diverse classroom populations.

Mastery Learning

Based on Benjamin Bloom's Learning for Mastery model developed in 1968, **mastery learning** programs are committed to the credo that, given the right tools, all children can learn. Stemming from an individualized reward structure, these programs can be used in individual classrooms or throughout a school, from early childhood to graduate school. For example, after years of dismal test scores and lack of student motivation, the Chugach School District in Alaska adopted a student-centered, mastery learning approach. Unlike the standard grade-level system where students worry about passing into the next grade, with schoolwide mastery learning, each student moves at an individual pace and focuses on becoming proficient in 10 specific academic areas, like reading, mathematics, and service learning, as well as nonacademic subjects such as cultural awareness and career development. Some students achieve proficiency and graduate at age 14; some do not get there until 21. Not only are test scores and attendance greatly improved, students report feeling motivated to learn.[35]

Mastery learning programs require specific and carefully sequenced learning objectives. The first step is to identify a **behavioral objective,** a specific skill or academic task to be mastered. Students are taught the skill or material in the objective; then they are tested to determine if the objective has been reached. Students who complete the test successfully go on for acceleration or enrichment, while the students who fail to demonstrate mastery of the objective receive corrective instruction and are retested. The success of mastery learning rests on the *instructional alignment*, which is a close match between what is taught and what is tested.[36]

In mastery learning, students typically work at their own pace, perhaps at a computer terminal or with individualized written materials. The teacher provides assistance and facilitates student efforts, but mastery still remains a student responsibility. Since studies have shown that many students, particularly younger ones, find it hard to take charge of their own instruction, mastery learning programs highlight the role of the teacher as instructional leader, motivator, and guide. Mastery learning is often geared for large groups, and it can benefit from technology, since computers and appropriate software can be particularly effective in self-paced mastery of skills and knowledge.

Studies suggest that mastery learning can be beneficial across grade levels and subject areas. In mastery learning:

- Teachers have more positive attitudes toward teaching and higher expectations for their students.

- In general, students have more positive attitudes about learning and their ability to learn.

- Students achieve more and remember what they have learned longer.[37]

Problem-Based Learning

Focusing on authentic or real-life problems that often go beyond traditional subject areas is at the heart of **problem-based learning (PBL).** As you might imagine, real problems are not bound by a single subject field or even by the school building. This emphasis is apparent in the other terms used to describe PBL: *experience-based education, project-based instruction,* and *anchored instruction* (because it is "anchored" in the real world). In this instructional model, a crucial aspect of the teacher's role is to identify activities that fuel students' interest, such as

- Design a plan for protecting a specific endangered species.

- Formulate solutions that might have kept the United States from plunging into a Civil War.

- How can we stop bullying and harassment in this school?

- How can pollution in a local river or bay or the ocean be checked, or even reversed?

- Develop a set of urban policies to halt the deterioration of a central city.

- How can the racism and sexism in this community be eliminated?

Finding scintillating questions and projects to excite and motivate students is critical, but it is only one aspect of PBL. Other characteristics include

- *Learner cooperation.* Similar to cooperative learning, PBL depends on small groups or pairs of students collaborating as they explore and investigate various issues. This approach de-emphasizes competition. For teachers, the goal is to guide and challenge a dozen such small groups simultaneously.

- *Higher-order thinking.* Exploring real and complex issues requires students to analyze, synthesize, and evaluate material.

- *Cross-disciplinary work.* PBL encourages students to investigate how different academic subjects shed light on each other. In exploring ecological issues, for example, students touch not only on biology and chemistry but also on economics, history, sociology, and political science.

- *Artifacts and exhibits.* Students involved in PBL demonstrate what they learn in a very tangible way. Students may produce a traditional report or may create a video, a physical model, a computer program, a portfolio of artifacts, or even a presentation, such as a play or a debate. Teachers might organize a class or schoolwide exhibit to share the progress made by PBL students.

A veteran of the classroom for nearly five decades, Larry Cuban has examined America's schools from varying perspectives. He has been a professor at Stanford University and a teacher in an inner-city social studies classroom. But it was when Cuban was appointed superintendent in Arlington, Virginia, that Sharon Steindam first met him, and discovered some remarkable traits. Steindam, now Assistant Director of the National Study of School Evaluation, was a newly appointed school principal, and quite nervous about being evaluated by the new superintendent. But as she remembers, "He was the only superintendent that I worked for who truly used a variety of information about the school to help him determine how I was doing. He wanted to know why I felt certain students were doing well and others were not. And he was the most human superintendent I ever worked with. He would greet you in the grocery store and ask about your family. Cuban was a true leader, holding high expectations, providing meaningful feedback, and personally engaging."[1]

Cuban has witnessed many exciting efforts to reform and change America's schools. And yet, after sorting out nearly a century of change, he came to a fascinating insight: Teaching remains strikingly similar year in and year out. In *How Teachers Taught: Constancy and Change in American Classrooms, 1890–1980,* Cuban explores why.

Historically, schools have been built around teachers, not students. Not just philosophically, but physically as well. Classrooms featured desks all facing front, bolted to the floor, physically reinforcing the notion that the teacher is the center of instruction. As if the nuts and bolts were not strong enough, the curriculum proved the clincher. To survive instructing very large classes in eight or ten subjects, teachers became dependent on reading and dictating assignments directly from the text. Uniformity and standardization were emphasized. Principals told teachers what to do, and teachers told students what to do. The organizational climate did not nurture new teaching techniques.

As if all these in-school barriers were not enough to defeat change, teacher training all but guaranteed that the status quo would be maintained. New teachers were brought into the profession through a modeling or an apprenticeship program, doing their student teaching under the tutelage of veteran, often conventional, older teachers. It was a system geared to the passing down of traditional approaches and conservative attitudes from one generation of teachers to the next.

Cuban also believes that the suppression of student-based instruction was no accident. Schools were designed to mold a compliant workforce; student-centered instruction was viewed as rebellious, dangerous, and threatening to educational and economic stability.

To Cuban, technology is another phony revolution. In studying effective classrooms, he notes that teachers are very concerned with choosing electronic tools that are efficient. Teachers ask: How much time and energy do I have to invest in learning to use the technology versus the return it will have for my students? When students use the technology, will there be disruption? Will it bolster or compromise my authority to maintain order and cultivate learning? Even teachers eager to make use of new technologies face a serious stumbling block, given the pressures to design curriculum around standardized tests. And comprehensive teacher training to use technology effectively is still lacking. Only a small fraction of teachers find the new technologies efficient. The result: "Computers become merely souped-up typewriters and classrooms continue to run much as they did a generation ago."[2]

While Cuban recognizes that classrooms have undergone a few minor reforms—experimenting with online learning, greater informality between teacher and student, and even movable chairs—he concludes that instruction at the dawn of the twenty-first century looks strikingly similar to classroom instruction nearly 100 years ago.

[1] Sharon Steindam, personal communication (June 26, 2001). [2] Larry Cuban, *Oversold and Underused: Computers in Classrooms 1980–2000* (Cambridge: Harvard University Press, 2001).

> **REFLECTION:** Think of a few teaching reforms that are currently taking place in a school, district, or state. Which reforms do you think will stick? Why? Which instructional practices have remained constant? What factors contribute to their persistence?

www.mhhe.com/ sadker8e

To learn more about Larry Cuban, click on *Profiles in Education.*

- *Authentic learning.* Students pursue an actual unresolved issue. They are expected to define the problem, develop a hypothesis, collect information, analyze that information, and suggest a conclusion, one that might work in the real world.[38]

Technology as a Tool for Effective Teaching

Today's technological wonders are impacting the ways we teach and the ways students learn, transporting students around the world via virtual field trips, providing tutorials or drill-and-practice, and instantly and inexpensively adding millions of books and articles to a teacher's curriculum. Many educators believe that technology will reshape education, and currently more than 20 states require teachers to take at least one technology course or pass a technology test to receive an initial teaching license. Forty-seven states and the District of Columbia have established academic standards for student technology knowledge and skills.[39] Educators typically use computers to:[40]

- *Increase basic skills* in math, reading, and writing, as well as content areas, through sample quizzes, drill-and-practice, and additional course-related information. This reason becomes particularly attractive in this time of standardized testing.

- *Motivate students* through multimedia materials that capture their interest.

- *Promote higher order thinking* by introducing simulations, problem-based learning, Internet research, collaborative work, and student authoring programs.

- *Increase academic resources* by bringing the unlimited written and visual assets of the Internet into local schools.

- *Increase responsiveness to different learning styles* including special needs children, or students for whom the typical classroom culture means academic and/or social distress.

Typically, computers are used for drill and practice, simple programming, and educational games.

- *Improve workplace preparation* as students learn keyboarding skills, software applications, and technological operations common to future employment.

- *Save work for teachers* by creating a class Web page. A great deal of administrative time can be saved: Homework assignments, worksheets, notes, and exam dates can be posted on the Web page, and parent communication accomplished through e-mail. In fact, grading software can track attendance, average grades, and chart the results while even more cutting-edge programs use artificial intelligence, such as the Intelligent Essay Assessor (IEA), to grade essays.

- *Strengthen teacher performance* by adding resources, such as a PowerPoint presentation or a video clip, to create more dramatic and effective teacher presentations.

- *Make testing easier for teachers* by having computers create and grade tests, and maintain student records.

- *Modernize the school culture* by reshaping American education for the twenty-first century, moving beyond pencil and paper, chalk and chalkboards, into instant access to the world's digital resources.

www.mhhe.com/ sadker8e

INTERACTIVE ACTIVITY

Using Technology in Education. See examples of how technology is used in the classroom.

It's the Teaching, Not the Technology

Perspective is too often lost in the glitz surrounding exciting new technologies. "New" can be exhilarating; "new" can also disappoint. Software developer and educator George Brackett reminds us, "Thoughtful, caring, capable people change schools, sometimes with the help of technology, sometimes not, and sometimes even despite it. Too often we focus on the technology rather than the reform."[41]

Technology should be seen as a teacher's tool, and not the other way around. The first step is deciding how best to use that tool.[42] The following descriptions offer specific examples of how technology can enhance many of the effective teaching strategies discussed in this chapter. Since technology can also short-circuit learning, we note potential pitfalls as well. (Visit the Online Learning Center Appendix C for additional software and technology tools designed for specific subject areas.)

Problem–Based Learning

David Williamson Schaffer, a lecturer at the Harvard Graduate School of Education, points out that the current information age brings us back to John Dewey. Thanks to technology, teachers can now guide students in real-world problem solving, often through collaborations with government or business.[43] The Internet can facilitate problem-based learning by providing a wealth of resources and an avenue for sharing information. The federally funded Challenge 2000 Multimedia Project has assisted many teachers in creating successful problem-based learning (PBL) experiences. For example, in Belmont, California, elementary school students produced a multimedia presentation that documented the 150-year history of their town. The students used HyperStudio, a student-authoring tool, to create an interactive history with video

Teachers face numerous tech challenges: inaccurate or weak educational software, Web sites that young children should not be visiting—but do, and increased student plagiarism. Here are some of these common problems and possible solutions for you to consider.

Unsound Software. Much of the software out there is made for profit, not children, and is not based on sound pedagogy. Seek endorsements and objective evaluations from respected colleagues. Often software developed in a university setting is more likely to be academically sound.

Stereotypes and Violence. The forms of bias discussed in Chapter 6 apply to technology as well. Stereotyping, omission, and unreality, for example, thrive in software and on the Internet. And many computer games, even for the very young, are filled with violence. Evaluating materials for bias and violence is not only recommended, it is pretty much required.

Screen Potato Syndrome. Americans love technology, and have grown up in a media-rich environment, so it is not surprising that computer-generated images can mesmerize teachers and students, and lull them into an apathetic, non-active learning role. Variety is still important, so get yourself and your students away from the computer screen and into role-plays, manipulatives, and, "low-tech" learning options.

Information Overload. The wealth of technological imagery and video possibilities, not to mention overheads, slides, or simulations, can short-circuit learning. Make certain that students have enough time to digest and process what they have learned.

Internet Junk. While journals have editorial boards and libraries carefully evaluate acquisitions based on budgetary and other criteria, the Internet furnishes no such safeguards. Wonderful resources are provided along with propaganda, political advocacy, and hate literature. Most schools use filters to censor student access to inappropriate Internet material. Filters are not perfect, however, and teachers still should monitor what material students are accessing. You would be wise to teach your students how to evaluate Internet material. For example, have them ask: Who is providing this material? Is it an objective source? Does this group have a particular agenda? Is the material fact, or opinion? (Or opinion, disguised as fact?) Is the material current?

Internet Cheating. More than 50 percent of students report using the Internet to cheat, but there are resources to detect cheating.[1] Check the Plagiarism Resource Center at The University of Virginia for free software and links to related sites at www.plagiarism.phys.virginia.edu. Working with students on their papers, from the draft stage to final product, will minimize plagiarism and the downloading of student papers provided on the Internet. By the way, there are also Web sites that provide answers to the problems or tests found in your students' textbooks, so you may want to supplement published homework activities and tests with your own.

[1] Don McCabe, "Levels of Cheating and Plagiarism Remain High," *Center for Academic Integrity* (June 2005). Available at www.academicintegrity.org/cai_research.asp.

> **REFLECTION:** Which of these tech-tips do you find particularly helpful—or troubling? Can you add one of your own?

clips, digital pictures, and animated photographs. The students interviewed and videotaped members of the community, and conferred with the curator of a local museum. The "Belmont Then and Now Project" was not just a skill-building effort, for ultimately it taught the community and visitors about the area's history, and became an exhibit in the Belmont Historical Society.[44] (See also pblmm.k12.ca.us.)

Digital storytelling is another problem-based learning method that allows students to express their creativity and to capture real-life experiences through words and images. One example is the Neighborhood Story Project at John McDonough Senior High School in New Orleans, where teachers work with high school students and their families to write about their lives and neighborhoods. Students learn to write creative non-fiction, conduct in-depth interviews of family members and neighbors, and take digital photographs. The Project has published five best-selling books that celebrated the city from different perspectives. When Hurricane Katrina devastated New Orleans, some of the area's rich cultural history and memories were preserved thanks to the Neighborhood Story Project.[45] (Visit www.neighborhoodstoryproject.org/ for information.)

Teachers need to be concerned about hazards associated with problem-based learning. Whenever students are involved with the real world, inappropriate comments or behaviors can be amplified and cause problems for students, teachers, and the school. Moreover, collaboration with private companies raises the specter of inappropriate commercialism and improper business influence in education. Both dangers call for careful planning and constant monitoring when using problem-based learning.

Cooperative Learning and Scaffolding

Educators become concerned when technology isolates and alienates students, but academic learning can be enhanced by online learning and technology. The Web site Knowledge Forum allows participants to share information on the Internet, consider questions and ideas, and work together to solve problems. For example, students who are trying to develop a theory enter information in appropriate stages of the Theory Building feature: "My Theory, I Need to Understand, New Information, This Theory Cannot Explain, Much Better Theory, Putting Our Knowledge Together." Students are able to comment on each other's findings and connect ideas graphically. (For more information, visit www.knowledgeforum.com.) Wireless sensing systems, such as ImagiProbe and Palm, allow students to work through handheld computers, transforming the common lab experience of one student dominating an experiment to many hands-on participants. Let's say students are studying velocity. With ImagiProbe or Palm, one student can be in charge of attaching the sensor to a remote control car, another for driving the car, and yet another student can monitor the data being collected on the handheld computer. Or imagine a lesson on water pollution. Students with handheld computers and accompanying probes and thermometers can collect water samples and then instantly measure and graph pH, temperature, or oxygen levels. As more students are actively involved, learning becomes more meaningful.[46] (Learn more at www.imagiworks.com) As in any cooperative or independent learning activities, effective teachers monitor student work and interactions to ensure that they are making progress and working well with one another.

Mastery Learning

Many software products and Web sites build on the concepts of mastery learning. Working at their own pace, students can master concepts about Newtonian mechanics (ThinkerTools software) or develop mathematical skills (see www.renlearn.com/am). Tutorials can also support mastery learning, and are used across disciplines. Unlike drill and practice, tutorials present skills or concepts, check for understanding throughout the process, and evaluate student understanding once the program is completed. Tutorials allow teachers flexibility to individualize instruction and monitor student progress.

When mastery learning software is matched with traditional in-class learning, the result is called an integrated learning system (ILS). In Metrotech High School in Phoenix, Arizona, students attend classes to prepare for careers in areas as disparate as auto mechanics and television production, but they use software outside of class to refine their math and reading skills. The software diagnoses their levels of academic proficiency and then offers individualized programs designed to improve students' academic skills—all outside of class time, yet critical for in-class

Computers in Education *Enable* Us to . . .

TEACH MORE EFFECTIVELY

With computers we can individualize instruction, grant students autonomy, and empower students to learn at their own pace, rather than wait for the teacher's personal attention. Each learner benefits from having an omnipresent tutor to individually tailor schoolwork.

REACH AND TEACH MORE STUDENTS

Computers and Internet access can expand the educational horizons of children in isolated rural communities, children with limited community resources, or those children who are homebound because of disability or illness.

MAKE THE WORLD OUR CLASSROOM

Students with Internet access can directly tap resources in their communities or venture beyond their neighborhoods to other regions, nations, or cultures. Students can draw from limitless books, articles, pictures, and sound clips; follow links to experts or virtual field trips; and participate in real-time communications across the globe.

TURN LATCHKEY KIDS INTO CONNECTED KIDS

Too many youngsters have no one to talk to and are hesitant to ask questions of adults or teachers. The Internet offers a homework helper, a companion at the end of the school day, or a chat room of friends so that no one needs be home alone.

GET READY FOR THE FUTURE

Technology encourages interdisciplinary and collaborative work, facilitates problem-based learning, and provides an outlet for students to express their creativity. Students at ease with technology will be assets to future employers.

Computers in Education *Disable* Us Because . . .

EFFECTIVE TEACHING ALL BUT DISAPPEARS

Good teaching requires a personal connection. A teacher gazing at a student who is gazing at a computer screen is not teaching effectively. The Internet is unmonitored, filled with erroneous information, political propaganda, and phony research.

THE DIGITAL WORLD REMAINS DIVIDED

Technology amplifies economic disparities, awarding clear advantage to children from wealthy, high-tech homes attending wealthy, high-tech schools. Poor students soon discover technology's unwelcome mat tripping them up at the door of most career options.

STUDENTS RISK BECOMING ANTISOCIAL

Too many of today's youngsters can surf the Internet, but are unable to form personal connections. The Internet is home to countless narrow-interest groups that fragment society instead of unifying it. Technology can magnify antisocial behaviors, as children send destructive e-mails, organize sinister chat rooms, or create computer viruses.

COMPUTERS ARE A HEALTH RISK

Computer use is associated with increased eyestrain, repetitive motion injury, and the obesity that comes from a sedentary life style. Furthermore, how "healthy" is it for students to have easy access (via the Internet) to bombmaking information or pornographic material?

FUNDAMENTAL SKILLS ARE SIDELINED

As spelling and grammar tools correct student writing and computer screens replace engagement with books, real learning is compromised. Tomorrow's workers may become powerless automatons.

www.mhhe.com/
sadker8e

YOU DECIDE . . .

Do you believe that computers are an educational asset or a liability? In what ways has your education been enriched—or diminished—by technology? How might you plan to safeguard your students against dangers listed above?

progress and success. Teachers need to carefully monitor all aspects of the ILS to verify that the program meets students' individual needs and that appropriate progress is being made, and to supply additional instruction as needed.

Classroom Interactions and Teacher Feedback

The sometimes hectic pace of classroom interaction can make it difficult for teachers to engage all students in class discussions. Technology encourages student participation and allows for quality teacher feedback. For example, teachers can use a hand-held computer with random-name-generation software to ensure equitable student participation during class discussions. Teachers using such devices report that along with increasing participation, students are more attentive and better prepared.[47]

The TI-Navigator enables students to communicate instantly during class time with the teacher through an individual wireless terminal. The teacher can ask a question and each student takes the time needed to punch in a private response. Students instantly learn whether their answers are correct, and teachers can adjust instruction accordingly. The TI-Navigator ensures that each student has time to respond, and that each student does in fact respond. Classroom interaction becomes both more thoughtful, and more equitable. What are the downsides? For one, a false sense of security may develop as teachers get to know the electronic student at the cost of personal connection. Students also need the opportunity to develop interpersonal skills, such as speaking and listening in public settings, skills that could be lost with an overreliance on this sort of technology.

Direct Teaching

Traditional teacher-centered approaches can be enhanced by technology. Direct teaching and lecturing, for example, rely on effective presentations, and one of the more ubiquitous technological products in and beyond schools is the PowerPoint™ presentation. These computer-projected images are clear, organized, and appear like a "published" page for all the class to see. But savvy teachers tap other technology as well. DVDs, graphing calculators, computer graphics, and digital microscopes can provide effective visuals. Even guest speakers can be transported to class via a Web camera. RADVISION can provide a camera for the speaker, and another in the class, facilitating a two-way exchange carried over the Internet. Videoconferencing and teleconferencing with other teachers and with subject matter experts is yet another possibility with RADVISION. (To find out more, visit www.globalschoolhouse.org/cu.)

Effective and Reflective Teaching

Teaching is hard. Teaching well is fiercely so. Often confronted by too many students, a schedule without breaks, a pile of papers that regenerates daily, and incessant demands from every educational stakeholder, teachers can become predictable and mundane in their practices. Nevertheless, innovative, engaged, and reflective teaching is the path to effective teaching. Here are some ideas for you to consider.

"Less is more," is an aphorism attributed to education reformer Ted Sizer. According to Sizer, today's schools are misguided in their emphasis on "covering" material. The goal seems to be teaching and learning a vast body of information, in order to have a sense of accomplishment, or to score well on the ever-growing number of standardized tests. But international tests in science, for example, show that, although U.S. students have studied more science topics than have students in other countries, they have not studied them in depth, and their lower test scores reflect this superficiality. In Sizer's vision of effective instruction, good teachers limit the amount of content they introduce but develop it sufficiently for students to gain in-depth understanding.

This direction for teaching and schooling marks a radical departure from the current emphasis on uniform standards, test performance, and competition. In marked contrast to the superficial nature of such test-centered curriculum, Sizer advocates deep teaching. In **deep teaching,** teachers work to organize their content around a limited set of key principles and powerful ideas and then engage students in discussing these concepts. The emphasis is on problem solving and critical thinking, rather than on memorizing.[48]

Deeper teaching of the subject also suggests a deeper understanding of students. **Differentiated instruction** swims against the tide of standardization by organizing instructional activities not around content standards, but in response to individual differences. Teachers are asked to carefully consider each student's needs, learning style, life experience, and readiness to learn. Teachers are trained to develop learning activities that recognize these differences, because students learn best when they make connections between the curriculum and their interests and life experiences. While some see the current emphasis on standards-based instruction as quite the opposite of differentiated instruction, Carol Ann Tomlinson, a pioneer in the field does not. She advocates that standards-based curriculum tells us *what* curriculum to teach; differentiation tells us *how* to teach any curriculum well. In other words, differentiation can show us how to teach the same standards to diverse learners by employing a variety of teaching and learning modes.[49]

The idea of the classroom as a "learning community" conceives of the teacher as someone who helps students activate their prior knowledge of some subject and become intellectually engaged with one another.

What Teachers Should Know and Be Able to Do

The National Board for Professional Teaching Standards has described effective teachers with five core propositions.

1. TEACHERS ARE COMMITTED TO STUDENTS AND THEIR LEARNING

Accomplished teachers are dedicated to making knowledge accessible to all students. They act on the belief that all students can learn. They treat students equitably, recognizing the individual differences that distinguish one student from another and take account of these differences in their practice. They adjust their practice based on observation and knowledge of their students' interests, abilities, skills, knowledge, family circumstances, and peer relationships. Equally important, they foster students' self-esteem, motivation, character, civic responsibility, and their respect for individual, cultural, religious, and racial differences.

2. TEACHERS KNOW THE SUBJECTS THEY TEACH AND HOW TO TEACH THOSE SUBJECTS TO STUDENTS

Accomplished teachers have a rich understanding of the subject(s) they teach and appreciate how knowledge in their subject is created, organized, linked to other disciplines, and applied to real-world settings. Their instructional repertoire allows them to create multiple paths to the subjects they teach, and they are adept at teaching students how to pose and solve their own problems.

3. TEACHERS ARE RESPONSIBLE FOR MANAGING AND MONITORING STUDENT LEARNING

Accomplished teachers create, enrich, maintain, and alter instructional settings to capture and sustain the interest of their students and to make the most effective use of time. They are as aware of ineffectual or damaging practice as they are devoted to elegant practice. They know how to engage groups of students to ensure a disciplined learning environment, and how to organize instruction to allow the schools' goals for students to be met. They are adept at setting norms for social interaction among students and between students and teachers. Accomplished teachers can assess the progress of individual students as well as that of the class as a whole.

4. TEACHERS THINK SYSTEMATICALLY ABOUT THEIR PRACTICE AND LEARN FROM EXPERIENCE

Accomplished teachers are models of educated persons, exemplifying the virtues they seek to inspire in students—curiosity, tolerance, honesty, fairness, respect for diversity, and appreciation of cultural differences. They draw on their knowledge of human development, subject matter and instruction, and their understanding of their students to make principled judgments about sound practice. Their decisions are grounded not only in the literature, but also in their experience.

5. TEACHERS ARE MEMBERS OF LEARNING COMMUNITIES

Accomplished teachers contribute to the effectiveness of the school by working collaboratively with other professionals on instructional policy, curriculum development, and staff development. They can evaluate school progress and the allocation of school resources in light of their understanding of state and local educational objectives. Accomplished teachers find ways to work collaboratively and creatively with parents, engaging them productively in the work of the school.

SOURCE: www.nbpts.org/ABOUT/coreprops.cfm. Adapted from © 2006, National Board for Professional Teaching Standards.

REFLECTION: Can you demonstrate your understanding of each proposition with a classroom example from your past? If your schooling offers little to brag about (or your memories are faded), let your imagination give credence to the task. Envision an example from the five areas to confirm you comprehend each concept.

This vision of deep teaching and differentiated instruction highlights the social nature of learning and of the classroom. As the builder of a classroom **learning community,** the teacher is called on to be a guide or facilitator, skillful in conducting discussions, group work, debates, and dialogues. In this way, the teacher empowers the students to talk with one another and to rehearse the terminology and concepts involved in each discipline. Learning becomes a community effort, not an individual competition.[50]

It is not surprising, therefore, that educators are reconceptualizing schools to create more nurturing learning communities. When learning communities work well, students and teachers get to know each other well and they can develop shared academic goals. Learning communities can be encouraged through several strategies, including looping and block scheduling. In **looping,** schools "promote" teachers along with their students, a process that allows the teacher an extra year or more to get to know students in depth, to diagnose and meet their learning needs, and to develop more meaningful communication with their parents and families. Looping offers students an increased sense of stability and community. Similarly, **block scheduling** increases teacher-student contact by increasing the length of class periods. The longer periods allow teachers to get to know these students better, while the students benefit from an uninterrupted and in-depth academic study. If you were to teach in a school with block scheduling, you might have 75 students on any given day or in a particular semester, instead of 150.

This notion of a learning community contrasts sharply with many current practices that emphasize state- and school-mandated curriculum followed by standardized testing. It points to a more thoughtful classroom, one in which the teacher is the critical decision maker, and a reflective practitioner. Good teachers are expected to continually and intensely analyze their own practices, and to use their analysis to improve performance. "In order to tap the rich potential of our past to inform our judgment, we must move backward, reflect on our experiences, then face each new encounter with a broader repertoire of content-specific information, skills, and techniques."[51] When teachers engage in **reflective teaching,** they ask themselves such questions as:

- What teaching strategies did I use today? How effective were they? What might have been even more effective?

- Were my students engaged with the material? What seemed to motivate them the most? If I were to reteach today's class, how could I get even more students involved?

- How did I assess my students' learning today? Would there have been a better way to measure their learning? How well did the students grasp the main points of today's lesson? Do I need to reteach some of these concepts?

- Can I fine-tune tomorrow's or next week's lessons to capitalize on the gains made today?

Going far beyond the rhetorical, these questions are designed to raise consciousness, engender self-scrutiny, and result in effective teaching.[52]

SUMMARY

www.mhhe.com/ sadker8e

CHAPTER REVIEW

Go to the Online Learning Center to take a chapter self-quiz, practice with key terms, and review concepts from the chapter.

1. **Are teachers born, or made?**

   While the debate has raged for decades, most people agree that effective teaching can result from natural artistry as well as focused training.

2. **How is class time organized and what is academic learning time?**

   Teachers vary dramatically in the efficient use of time. Wise distribution of classroom time—defined as allocated, engaged, and academic learning time—is a predictor of student achievement.

3. **What classroom management skills foster academic achievement?**

Student achievement is also associated with effective classroom management. A well-managed classroom includes reasonable rules for students to follow, and teachers who can keep students on task through group alerting, smooth transitions, and similar skills.

4. **What are the roles of teachers and students in the pedagogical cycle?**

The pedagogical cycle consists of four stages: (1) structure, (2) question, (3) respond, and (4) react. The student's role is typically limited to responding, while teachers usually direct classroom discourse through structure, question, and reaction.

5. **How can teachers set a stage for learning?**

Most cycles of instruction begin by connecting prior learning to current objectives. Effective teachers motivate students, offer meaningful examples, give accurate directions, display enthusiasm, and present a brief closure to the lesson.

6. **What questioning strategies increase student achievement?**

Questioning is at the very foundation of effective teaching. Although teachers rely most heavily on lower-order questions, higher-order questions are associated with critical thinking and should be an important part of classroom instruction. Effective teachers use intentional strategies, such as proper wait time, to allocate questions fairly among all students. When providing feedback, teachers typically use neutral acceptance, while praise, remediation, and criticism are more precise and helpful reactions.

7. **How can teachers best tap into different student learning styles?**

Effective teachers provide variety. From discussions and debates to simulations and spot quizzes, teachers increase academic success by responding to the different learning styles in the class.

8. **What are several salient models of instruction?**

Four models of instruction include (1) direct teaching, (2) cooperative learning, (3) mastery learning, and (4) problem-based learning. Direct teaching includes teacher presentation, guided practice, teacher feedback, independent practice, and regular reviews. In a cooperative learning classroom, students work in small groups and appraisals often reflect the entire group's performance. In mastery learning, students work at their own pace to reach specific objectives. Problem-based learning stimulates students to explore authentic issues.

9. **How can teachers use technology to support effective instruction?**

Hardware, software, and Web sites can tie into effective teaching strategies such as problem-based, cooperative, and mastery learning, as well as direct teaching and teacher-student interactions. Technology raises some serious concerns for teachers, including monitoring the accuracy and biases of Internet material.

10. **What are the future directions of effective teaching research?**

Differentiated instruction is responsive to individual student differences, unlike the current emphasis on standardized instruction and testing. Deep teaching promotes meaningful instruction around essential content, while covering fewer topics. Looping and block scheduling foster classroom communities. The best of today's educators engage in reflective practice, continually analyzing the effectiveness of their instruction.

THE *TEACHERS, SCHOOLS, AND SOCIETY* READER WITH CLASSROOM OBSERVATION VIDEO CLIPS

Go to your *Teachers, Schools, and Society* Reader CD-ROM to:

READ CURRENT AND HISTORICAL ARTICLES

11.1 **The Engaged Classroom,** Sam M. Intrator, *Educational Leadership,* September 2004.

11.2 **Mapping a Route Toward Differentiated Instruction,** Carol Ann Tomlinsen, *Educational Leadership*, September 1999.

11.3 **Good Teachers Plural,** Donald R. Cruickshank and Donald Haefele, *Educational Leadership*, 58, no. 5 (2001).

ANALYZE CASE STUDIES

11.1 **Ken Kelly:** A teacher having trouble with questioning and with discussion teaching visits a teacher who is holding a Socratic discussion with a fourth-grade class. He questions the applicability of her methods to his situation.

11.2 **Judith Kent:** A teacher engages her students in whole-class discussion, and then the students work with partners on an assignment. She explains the planning process she went through to reteach the lesson after it had not worked the previous class.

OBSERVE TEACHERS, STUDENTS, AND CLASSROOMS IN ACTION

Classroom Observation: Effective Teaching

Part of being an effective teacher is creating a positive learning community. In this observation you will observe classroom teachers explaining how they use different strategies to create exciting learning communities.

KEY TERMS AND PEOPLE

DISCUSSION QUESTIONS AND ACTIVITIES

1. Do you think teachers are born, or made? Debate a classmate who holds the opposite point of view. Interview elementary and secondary teachers and ask them what they think about this question. Do some of them say that it is a combination of both? If so, why? Which part is art, which part skill?

2. Why do you think there is so much variation in how different teachers and schools use time for learning? Observe in your own college classrooms to determine how much time is wasted. For each class observed, keep a fairly detailed record of how time is lost (students six minutes late, class ends fifteen minutes early, PowerPoint presentation takes four minutes to set up, and so on).

3. Research suggests that, in order to achieve, students should be functioning at a very high success rate. Do you agree that this is likely to lead to higher achievement? Or do you think that students need to cope with failure and be "stretched" in order to achieve? Defend your position.

4. Analyze teacher reactions to student answers in elementary and secondary classrooms where you are an observer and in the college classrooms where you are a student. Are most of these classrooms "okay" classrooms? Why do you think some teacher reactions are vague and diffuse? What observations can you make about the use of praise, remediation, and criticism?

5. In an interview for a teaching position, you are asked your opinion of educational technology and your plans, if any, for incorporating technology into your teaching. How would you answer? Include at least five reasons to support your position.

WEB-*TIVITIES*
Go to the Online Learning Center to do the following activities:

1. Classroom Management: What Is in a Name?
2. Cooperative Learning
3. Problem-Based Learning
4. Is Computer Technology Worth the Effort?
5. Wiring Up Schools, Charging Up Teachers?

REEL TO REAL TEACHING

DEAD POETS SOCIETY (1989)
Run Time: 128 minutes

Synopsis: "Carpe diem! Seize the day boys, make your lives extraordinary," advises educator John Keating to his class of young men at an all boys boarding school. These words guide his unorthodox lessons that will change their young lives forever.

Reflection:

1. Do John Keating's instructional techniques mirror any of the effective teaching characteristics discussed in this chapter? What additional attributes of an effective teacher did you discover in the film that are not described in this chapter? Is Keating's teaching an art, a skill, or both? Recall scenes from the film to support your answer.

2. Questioning is not just about teachers: Students are also partners in the questioning process. Creating an environment that welcomes student-initiated questions is important to engaged learning time. How did Mr. Keating teach his students to ask questions? How did these questions deepen student understanding?

465

3. Consider how the character of the student body created a community. How might the story-line change in an all girls school or a historically black school?

Follow-up Activity: You've read about effective questioning and seen "on screen" effective questioning in action. Now take a turn at practicing these techniques. Compose a classroom discussion of *Dead Poet's Society*. Write out a sequence of questions, one each from the six levels of Bloom's taxonomy.

www.mhhe.com/ sadker8e

How do you rate this film? Go to *Reel to Real Teaching* on the Online Learning Center to review this film.

FOR FURTHER READING

Classroom Teaching Skills, by James Cooper (Editor) (8th edition) (2006). A self-instructional book designed to help teachers acquire basic teaching skills for classroom management, questioning, higher-order thinking, and cooperative learning.

Discipline in the Secondary Classroom: A Positive Approach to Behavior Management, by Randall S. Sprick (2nd edition) (2006). Discipline and lack of motivation are two of the most vexing problems facing teachers today. This book gives high school teachers step-by-step guidance for designing a behavior-management plan that will help prevent misbehavior and increase student motivation. This hands-on resource contains easy-to-implement strategies that are proactive, instructional, and effective.

Elementary Classroom Management: Lessons from Research and Practice, by Carol Simon Weinstein and Andrew Mignano, Jr. (4th edition) (2006). Written in conversational style, this book combines what research has to say about effective classroom management with knowledge culled from practice. The text shows how four teachers in very different school settings create classrooms that are orderly and productive, yet humane and caring.

Inside Mrs. B's Classroom, by Leslie Baldacci (2003). This book is reporter-turned-teacher Leslie Baldacci's extraordinary memoir of life in the trenches of inner-city teaching. She takes us inside the classroom and introduces a colorful cast of characters—both students and teachers alike. Developing strong (and absolutely essential) bonds with her fellow teachers proves to be her saving grace, but surprisingly, her students become her greatest inspiration. An entertaining and motivating story of success that reveals how one person *can* make a difference in the lives of students.

Looking in Classrooms, by Thomas Good and Jere Brophy (9th edition) (2003). Devoting particular attention to current issues, such as integrating traditional methods with constructivist, cooperative, and culturally diverse learning styles, this book provides teachers with the latest research and concrete skills to observe and interpret the classroom behavior of both teachers and students.

Teaching with Fire: Poetry that Sustains the Courage to Teach, by Sam Intrator and Megan Scribner (editors) (2003). A wonderful collection of 88 poems from such well-loved poets as Walt Whitman, Langston Hughes, Billy Collins, Emily Dickinson, and Pablo Neruda. Each of these evocative poems is accompanied by a brief story from a teacher explaining the significance of the poem in his or her life's work. Suggestions for how poetry can be used to grow both personally and professionally are also included.

Your First Classroom

12

FOCUS QUESTIONS

1. What are the stages of teacher development?
2. What resources do school districts provide for a teacher's first year in the classroom?
3. How do school districts, states, and the National Board for Professional Teaching Standards recognize and reward teachers?
4. What are the differences between the National Education Association and the American Federation of Teachers?
5. Are America's schools a secret success story, doing better than the press and the public believe?

www.mhhe.com/
sadker8e

WHAT DO YOU THINK? **What teaching skills are of most value?** Check off the teaching skills you believe are most important. See how your criteria compare to those of your colleagues.

CHAPTER PREVIEW

It looks so small: the distance between the students' chairs and the teacher's desk. But traveling from a student's desk to a teacher's desk represents an enormous journey. This chapter is intended to prepare you for that transformation, from student to teacher.

As you enter your first classroom, chances are that you will focus on lesson planning, classroom management, and preparing for those visits by your supervisor. In short, you will be all about classroom survival. With time and experience, you will begin to refine your teaching strategies and focus less on survival skills and more on ways to enhance student learning. While we would love to serve up some ready-to-use answers to help you meet these first year classroom challenges, truth is, there are many questions that only you will be able to answer. Here are just a few for you to consider: Where should I teach? How can I win that ideal (at least satisfying) teaching position? What will my first year be like? Should I join a teachers' association? Should I stay in teaching long term? If so, what are the routes to advancement? And with all the negative press I read about schools, is this something that I want to do? This chapter provides you with some insights and practical advice about making that first year of teaching a successful one, and perhaps the beginning of many rewarding years.

CHAPTER

Stages of Teacher Development

> Will I be able to manage this class? Can I get through the curriculum? Do I know my subject well enough? Will the other teachers like me? Will the administrators rehire me? Am I going to be a good teacher? Will I like this life in the classroom?

When you begin teaching, the questions that occupy you are mostly about your ability, about visits by supervisors, and about managing students. By the second year, teachers are more experienced (and confident), and they usually move beyond these questions, shifting the focus of their attention to improving instruction and student performance. For example, experienced teachers might spend time analyzing the needs of individual students, exploring a new curriculum strategy, and asking such questions as: How can I help this shy child? and Why is this student encountering learning problems? If a colleague is achieving success using a new teaching strategy, an experienced teacher might observe, then adapt that strategy. As talented and experienced teachers mature, their interests and vision extend beyond their own classrooms. At this more advanced stage, they work to develop programs that could benefit large numbers of students. The chart in Figure 12.1 suggests stages that teachers pass through as they become more skilled in their craft.[1]

Attempts to reform education and improve student achievement are dependent on our ability to move teachers through these developmental stages. Although earlier studies by James Coleman and others seemed to call into question the educational impact of teachers, comprehensive studies in the 1990s found that teacher performance is critical. Every dollar spent to increase teacher qualifications (as measured by teacher test scores, number of graduate degrees, professional training, etc.) improves students' academic performance more than money invested in most other areas. Although efforts to reduce class size or provide schools with up-to-date computer technology are critical, research reveals that teacher expertise is more important. In fact, *teacher qualifications and skills are among the MOST important factors in improving student performance.*[2]

What do we mean by a qualified and skillful teacher? The most effective teachers not only demonstrate mastery of the subjects they teach but also are adept in the methods of teaching and understand student development. Unfortunately, too many teachers receive little support, make little progress in their subject area or their teaching skills, and never grow to the more sophisticated levels of teaching. Some teachers struggle to master the initial survival level. That is why a growing number of districts are investing resources to ensure that, when you step into your first classroom, you will not be alone.

Your First Year: Induction into the Profession

We wish we could relive the excitement and intensity of our first year in the classroom. Okay, it was not always wonderful, and yes, it was often tough, but truth is, it was magical. Your first year could also be a magical time of learning and growing—or it could be quite the opposite. The quality of support you receive once you begin teaching may be the difference. Many schools understand this challenge and have created supportive climates to not only recruit, but retain teachers. A growing number of educators believe that there is no "teacher shortage" in America; rather there is a teacher retention problem. One out of three teachers

FIGURE 12.1
Stages of teacher development

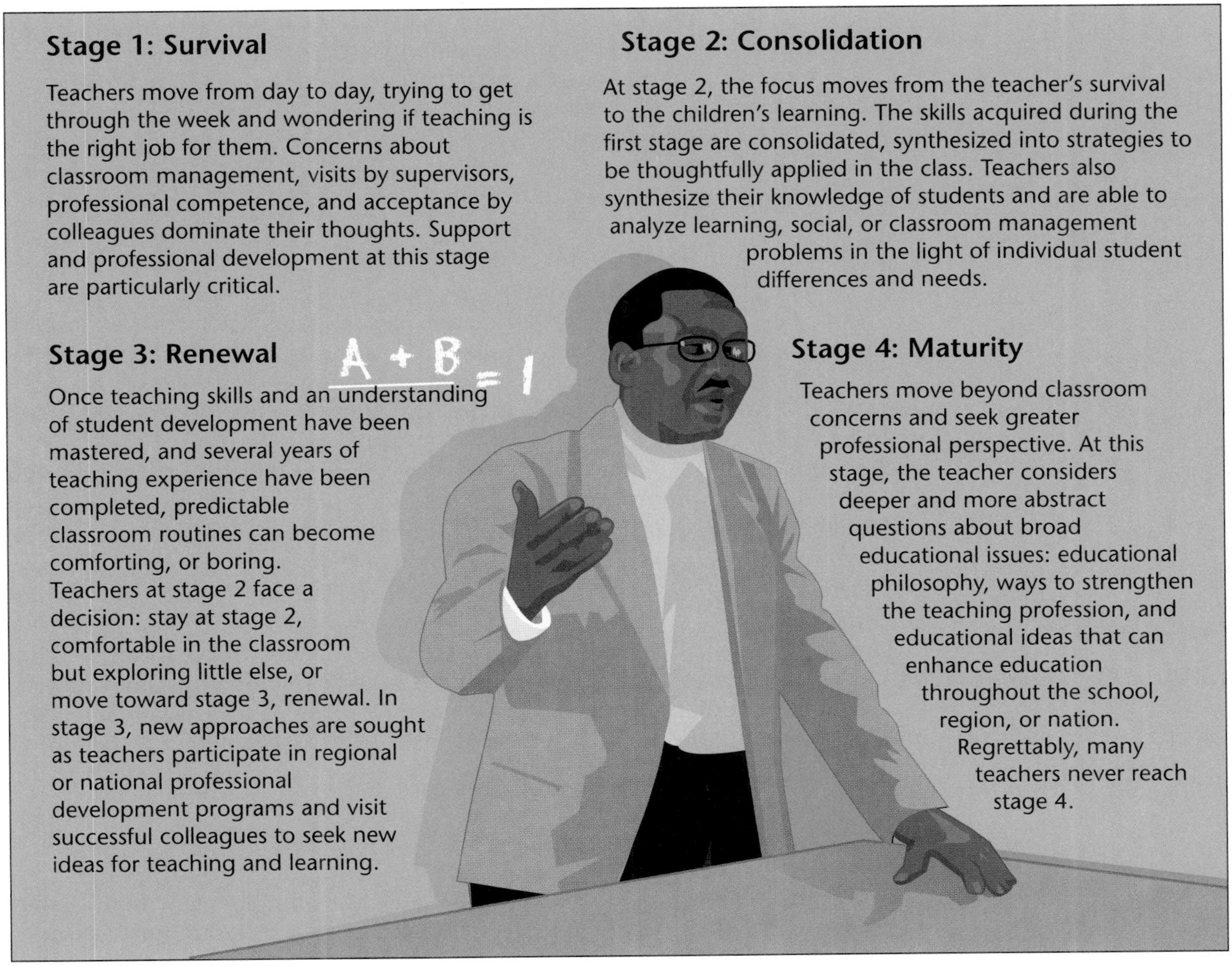

Stage 1: Survival

Teachers move from day to day, trying to get through the week and wondering if teaching is the right job for them. Concerns about classroom management, visits by supervisors, professional competence, and acceptance by colleagues dominate their thoughts. Support and professional development at this stage are particularly critical.

Stage 2: Consolidation

At stage 2, the focus moves from the teacher's survival to the children's learning. The skills acquired during the first stage are consolidated, synthesized into strategies to be thoughtfully applied in the class. Teachers also synthesize their knowledge of students and are able to analyze learning, social, or classroom management problems in the light of individual student differences and needs.

Stage 3: Renewal

Once teaching skills and an understanding of student development have been mastered, and several years of teaching experience have been completed, predictable classroom routines can become comforting, or boring. Teachers at stage 2 face a decision: stay at stage 2, comfortable in the classroom but exploring little else, or move toward stage 3, renewal. In stage 3, new approaches are sought as teachers participate in regional or national professional development programs and visit successful colleagues to seek new ideas for teaching and learning.

$$A + B = 1$$

Stage 4: Maturity

Teachers move beyond classroom concerns and seek greater professional perspective. At this stage, the teacher considers deeper and more abstract questions about broad educational issues: educational philosophy, ways to strengthen the teaching profession, and educational ideas that can enhance education throughout the school, region, or nation. Regrettably, many teachers never reach stage 4.

SOURCE: Based on the work of Lillian Katz.

REFLECTION: Have you been taught by teachers representing each of these four developmental stages? Describe behaviors at each of the four levels. If you were to build in strategies to take you from Stage 1 to Stage 4, what might they be?

leave the classroom within three years, and half leave within five years.[3] **Induction programs** "provide some systematic and sustained assistance to beginning teachers for at least one school year," in the hope that such support will create the first of many magical years.[4] Induction programs typically match new teachers, called **intern teachers,** with an experienced instructor, sometimes called a consulting teacher or mentor.

Mentors

Mentors are experienced teachers selected to guide intern teachers through the school culture and norms, shedding light on the *official* and *hidden* school culture (which memos need a quick response, which do not; who keeps the key to the supply room; where the best DVD players are hidden, and offering a shoulder to lean on during those very difficult days). Mentors offer insights on how best to use curricular materials, hints on teaching strategies, advice on scheduling problems and suggestions on smoothing out stressful communication with a student, parent, administrator, or colleague (no minor feat during a year filled with new faces). They can observe a class to analyze how you might improve your teaching or actually teach a class to model a skill for you to use.[5] Effective mentors offer a bridge for new teachers to become skilled professionals, but unfortunately, not all mentoring programs are successful. A weak mentor or inadequate time to work with a mentor can sabotage any program.[6] Some schools, unable to provide live mentors, resort to tele-mentors, also called **e-mentors,** who offer advice and support over the Internet. (Visit teaching.com).[7]

If having a mentor sounds appealing, and you find yourself in a school district that does not provide official mentors, you can certainly try to recruit an unofficial mentor to guide you through that first year. You might want to ask colleagues or administrators about teachers known for creative lessons or effective management or who generally might lend a helpful hand to a rookie such as yourself.

In many programs, mentors provide more than friendly support; they have an official responsibility to assess new teachers and to file reports to school supervisors. A poor performance report from a mentor can result in a recommendation for extra training for an intern teacher, which could be absolutely wonderful in solving a persistent problem.

Observation

Whether new teachers are assigned a mentor, find a mentor, or are mentorless, they are likely to have their classroom performance observed. It is not unusual for teachers to be observed three or four times in their first year and, in some districts, much more frequently. Observations come in two varieties: *diagnostic,* designed to help the teachers, and *evaluative,* intended to be used for employment decisions. Sometimes the same observation serves both purposes.

Observations may be conducted by your mentor, an administrator, or a veteran teacher. This last option, called **peer review,** has become popular in a number of school districts.[8] These districts, sometimes in cooperation with local teacher associations, identify their strongest teachers to evaluate and assist others, an approach that recognizes the movement toward greater teacher professionalism and autonomy.

What do observers look for during classroom observations of beginning teachers? It is wise for beginning teachers to ask a mentor or colleague about which skills and qualities are particularly valued in these observations. Some teachers find it useful (if a bit disconcerting) to arrange to be videotaped, so they can pinpoint strategies to improve their instruction. An evaluation framework, used by the

Toledo Public Schools, offers insight into the typical skills and attributes considered worth evaluating. (See Figure 12.2.)

Observations, whether official or informal, are usually followed by a conference in which the mentor or supervisor shares the high points and "not-as-high-as-we-would-like" points of your teaching. Take notes and carefully consider these comments. You may find the comments to be useful, even insightful, offering you wise counsel on how to improve. Your attitude and openness in these conferences indicates your willingness to analyze your teaching and refine your teaching skills.

Professional Development Programs

School systems sponsor an amazing variety of professional training options, for new and veteran teachers, both during the summer and throughout the school year. Through these programs, teachers might satisfy state requirements for renewal of teacher licensure, work toward an endorsement or a license in a second teaching field, attend a summer institute to master new skills, obtain an advanced degree, or earn a higher salary.

Most teacher pay schedules are connected to professional development. Sometimes salaries are linked to the number of hours invested in courses and training programs, so that a teacher who takes 30 graduate credits at a college or 30 training hours offered by a school district would get a certain salary raise. In other districts, salary increases are tied to evaluations of teacher performance.

School districts vary greatly in their approaches to professional training. Sometimes districts identify a topic (e.g., student portfolio development or emotional intelligence), invite in one or more speakers to make a presentation on that topic, and require the whole faculty to participate. These professional development efforts are scheduled before, during, and at the end of the academic year. Teachers call them **in-service** days, while students are more likely to consider them vacation days. Many have criticized these one-time programs as "dog and pony" shows, charging that brief presentations given to a large group of educators lack long-term impact.

Other staff development strategies require more time and offer greater focus on a specific subject or skill area. Examples of this more in-depth approach include meetings and workshops over the course of a year to improve the science program and weekly sessions on relevant software. Recent research has underscored the value of teacher-designed programs, closely tied to practical classroom skills. Educational reformers suggest that the best **professional development** programs

- Connect directly to the teacher's work with students
- Link subject content with teaching skills
- Use a problem-solving approach
- Reflect research findings
- Are sustained and supported over time[9]

How can professional development programs incorporate these characteristics? One way is to ask teachers to prepare portfolios for board certification or merit review. Portfolio construction encourages teachers to develop insight and reflection about their instruction by creating tangible examples of their competence. Hopefully, over time, these examples will document their progress and development. Some school districts create a "teaching academy" that offers courses directly linked to particular teacher needs. Over the period of a semester, summer, or year, teachers might enroll

FIGURE 12.2

Intern assessment form.

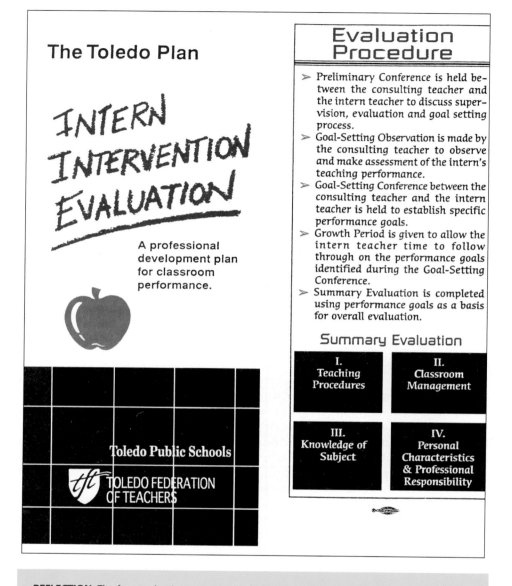

The Toledo Plan

INTERN INTERVENTION EVALUATION

A professional development plan for classroom performance.

Toledo Public Schools

TOLEDO FEDERATION OF TEACHERS

Evaluation Procedure

➤ Preliminary Conference is held between the consulting teacher and the intern teacher to discuss supervision, evaluation and goal setting process.
➤ Goal-Setting Observation is made by the consulting teacher to observe and make assessment of the intern's teaching performance.
➤ Goal-Setting Conference between the consulting teacher and the intern teacher is held to establish specific performance goals.
➤ Growth Period is given to allow the intern teacher time to follow through on the performance goals identified during the Goal-Setting Conference.
➤ Summary Evaluation is completed using performance goals as a basis for overall evaluation.

Summary Evaluation

| I. Teaching Procedures | II. Classroom Management |
| III. Knowledge of Subject | IV. Personal Characteristics & Professional Responsibility |

REFLECTION: The four evaluation areas on this form (I. Teaching Procedures, II. Classroom Management, III. Knowledge of Subject, IV. Personal Characteristics and Professional Responsibility) have been discussed in this text. As you glance over the form, which skills do you see as your strengths? Which ones need more study and practice? What specific steps in your teacher education program will prepare you to successfully pass this evaluation?

in these courses to improve their questioning skills, create more equitable classroom participation, establish effective management strategies, or implement a new curriculum. Many programs tie course assignments to daily instructional activities, providing a useful link between professional development and real-world application.

Collaborative action research (CAR) also connects daily teaching responsibilities with professional growth, but in this case through the use of research.

FIGURE 12.2
(concluded)

TEACHER SUMMARY EVALUATION REPORT

Name _____

College _____

School _____ Date _____

Grade or
Subject _____

Period of
Sept.-Dec. ☐

Period of
Jan.-March ☐

Period of
Apr.-Dec. ☐

Certification _____

Number of Observations and Time _____ Conference Time _____

Intern semester completed _____

Check on March and Dec Report	Check on March Report Only	Contract Status
☐ Outstanding	☐ Recommended for first one-year contract	☐ First year contract
☐ Satisfactory	☐ Recommended for a second one-year contract	☐ Second year contract
☐ Unsatisfactory		☐ Four-year contract
☐ Written comment only	☐ Recommended for initial four-year contract	☐ One-year contract
☐ Irregular term		☐ Continuing contract
☐ Recommended for 2nd semester intern program	☐ Recommended for third one-year contract	☐ Long-term substitute (60 or more days)
	☐ Not recommended for reappointment	

* OUTSTANDING: Performance shows exceptional professional qualities and growth.
  SATISFACTORY: Performance at expected and desired professional qualities and growth.
* UNSATISFACTORY: Performance shows serious weaknesses or deficiencies.
* For more complete definition refer to page 10 in the Toledo Plan.
* Unsatisfactory and/or outstandings must have a written supportive statement.

	Out-standing	Satis-factory	Unsatis-factory
I. TEACHING PROCEDURES			
A. Skill in planning			
B. Skill in assessment and evaluation			
C. Skill in making assignments			
D. Skill in developing good work-study habits			
E. Resourceful use of instructional material			
F. Skill in using motivating techniques			
G. Skill in questioning techniques			
H. Ability to recognize and provide for individual differences			
I. Oral and written communication skills			
J. Speech, articulation and voice quality			
II. CLASSROOM MANAGEMENT			
A. Effective classroom facilitation and control			
B. Effective interaction with pupils			
C. Efficient classroom routine			
D. Instructional leadership			
E. Is reasonable, fair and impartial in dealing with students			
III. KNOWLEDGE OF SUBJECT–ACADEMIC PREPARATION			
IV. PERSONAL CHARACTERISTICS AND PROFESSIONAL RESPONSIBILITY			
A. Shows a genuine interest in teaching			
B. Personal appearance			
C. Skill in adapting to change			
D. Adheres to accepted policies and procedures of Toledo Public Schools			
E. Accepts responsibility both inside and outside the classroom			
F. Has a cooperative approach toward parents and school personnel			
G. Is punctual and regular in attendance			

Evaluator's Signature
(when required)

Teacher's Signature

Principal's Signature
(when required)

Evaluator's Position

Date of Conference _____

DIRECTIONS

1. Rate all categories, bold face and subcategories.
2. Attach all supporting documents that have been signed or initialed.

A CLASSROOM CHALLENGE I JUST HAD TO TAKE

By Mathina Carkci

Mathina Carkci, who wrote about education as a reporter for suburban Maryland newspapers for three years, became a fourth-grade teacher at Bailey's Elementary School in Fairfax County, Virginia.

The most surprising thing about being a teacher is how often I feel like a failure. I knew that teaching fourth grade would be hard, but I expected to be able to keep up with everything and to succeed. So it's disheartening, just two months into my first job, to feel the weight of things left undone, questionable decisions made and professional duties unmet.

My teacher friends say they used to feel the same way. Some admit they still do. My student-teaching supervisor sympathetically cautions that the first two years are so unlike the "real thing" that they don't count. The teacher across the hall reminds me to take baby steps. My mom, a university professor, promises it will get better. I'm too hard on myself, a former professor tells me; it takes time to grow into the teacher I want to be.

I take some comfort from the fact that friends who were in the same one-year master's certification program at the University of Maryland last year have found it hard from the word go. I called Natalie the evening of her first day, a week before I started.

"If you told me I didn't have to go tomorrow," she said, "I wouldn't."

I called Al on his second day. "After the kids left today, I shut the door and cried," he said.

My friends and family told me I'd be a great teacher. They said they imagined a group of children gazing up at me, accompanying me on exciting journeys that would fill their minds with wonder. "You're such a good person," my husband told me. "The kids are going to love you." It gave me the chills, the way good classical music does, to think of myself and my merry band of students, gallivanting through the curriculum.

So it's difficult to admit now how hard it is to be a first-year teacher: how every single day I feel as if I am drowning; how I spend 12 hours at school each day working and four hours at home worrying; how each evening as I leave school, I have to decide which of 100 equally important things I should leave undone; how I feel so far behind that I will never catch up until Christmas, when I have 10 days "off."

When I get to school, anywhere from an hour and a half to two hours before the kids, a list of tasks swims through my head, and, as the minutes tick away until 8:40 arrives, I run through my priorities. With any luck, I'll have put up the day's schedule, written the daily message to the students and created the math warm-up exercise the night before. I might respond to kids' journals but change my mind when I realize the math lesson I had planned misses an important element. (Half my mind, all this time, is wondering what the best way is to teach kids to determine the volume of solid shapes.) I might walk to the copier, see the line of other teachers and decide instead to swing by the library to schedule a block of time for my students. Or I might run into the guidance counselor and discuss ways to help a student who's been misbehaving.

Then I notice a student's desk that seems to be exploding papers and books, and wonder how best to help the child get organized: Does she need me to go through the pile with her, paper by paper? (And when would I do that?) Or should I write her a note and carve out a chunk of the day for her to organize things herself? Or do I need to have a talk with the whole class about keeping things straight?

It isn't as if I wasn't well prepared or don't have support. My year-long internship, including 12 weeks of student teaching, gave me a taste of the challenges I'd face. A mentor at my school, Bailey's Elementary, meets with me regularly, and Fairfax County bends over backward to provide new teachers with help. Bailey's teems with kind, helpful colleagues. Volunteers, including my mom who comes in every Friday, offer assistance of all sorts. Short of having a personal assistant 12 hours a day, I don't think there's anything more anyone could do to ease my transition.

Idealistic grad school conversations about pedagogy and democracy in the classroom made me surer than ever that I was right to go into teaching, that here was where I would make my impact on a part of the world that mattered to me. The master's program helped me build a solid educational philosophy based on wanting children to discover for themselves how rewarding learning can be.

I never thought my career switch would be easy. I had covered education when I was a newspaper reporter, so I'd seen the kinds of tightropes that many teachers walk. But I wanted to do something more active than writing about them. As a teacher, I could be with students every day and show them in tangible ways that their ideas mattered.

I try to make this happen in the classroom, but as we all know, theory and practice don't always overlap. I spend more time thinking up ways to get students to hand in homework than I do thinking about how to help them to pursue their own questions, or promoting their curiosity. Despite having vowed not to use rewards and punishments as a method of controlling the class, I have found myself giving kids extra recess for walking quietly in line or sending them back to their seats if they seem disruptive. My interactions with kids are less positive than I once hoped they would be, and I say "No," without explanation, far more often than I would like. Instead of designing creative, hands-on lessons in every subject, I sometimes teach straight from the book in science and social studies classes.

But, in the end, I don't think I'm really a failure. We have meetings, where my whole class tries to solve problems anyone puts on the agenda. I play with the kids at recess, which might make me seem more like another kid than like a teacher, but I think it also helps them to see me as someone worth following. I've managed to avoid being ruled by the lesson plan. The other day, two boys invented their own way of conducting a science project that involved analyzing rocks, and, when I realized their way was better, I encouraged the rest of the class to go with it instead of following the instructions.

I may not be on the same social studies textbook chapter as the other fourth-grade teachers, and I'll probably be late returning standardized tests to the assistant principal, but I think my kids know they're important to me. I see it in tiny, fleeting moments. I see it when a student says, "Mrs. Carkci, I wish you could come to my house for the weekend. That would be fun." I see it when a boy writes to me to ask if I will take him to the movies, or when a girl gives me a goofy smile after I've led the class down the hall taking giant, silly steps. I'm proud that a girl believes it is okay to ask "Why in America do people speak lots of languages, while in Vietnam, they only speak one language?" Or that a boy knows I will encourage him to pursue his question, "Who invented the planets?"

Once or twice, early on, I considered quitting. But no longer. I like helping my 21 students learn about the four regions of Virginia; I enjoy encouraging them to write and to use new paragraphs for new ideas; and I thrive on watching them become mathematical thinkers. Just the other day a student told me, out of the blue, that he'd noticed how the desks in our classroom were like intersecting lines. It was our geometry unit made real.

I can't imagine what it will be like in two years, when I have figured out a good response to tattling and when I have prepared a classroom set of spelling games. I don't love teaching yet, but I am beginning to catch glimpses of what it will be like when I do.

SOURCE: Copyright 1998, Mathina Carkci, published in *The Washington Post* Company, Sunday, November 8, 1998, C3.

> **REFLECTION:** What insights and clues suggest that Mathina will succeed as a teacher? Do you share any of her attributes? Which teaching skills might you need to further refine?

Typically, a group of teachers identifies a genuine problem in the school or classes, designs ways to address the problem, and then evaluates their success. If the teachers are concerned about the poor performance of girls in high school science courses, for example, they might decide to experiment with new methods to improve that performance. One teacher might try cooperative learning strategies in her science class, while a second teacher develops techniques to involve parents in their daughters' science work. A third teacher might initiate a new science curriculum designed to motivate female students. Each of these approaches would be evaluated and the most effective selected for use by all teachers. CAR encourages thoughtful, objective analysis of real teacher concerns.

Professional development takes many forms: graduate degree programs, collaborative action research projects, and teaching academies or in-service days. A quick glance at Figure 12.3 should convince you of the wide range of professional development programs. These descriptions are adapted from *Education Week*, a weekly newspaper and Internet publication that covers national education events, so they reflect realistic opportunities available to teachers.

Personalizing Schools

From a new teacher's perspective, what were once familiar school surroundings soon become strange. Teachers and students see school very differently. As a teacher, you will likely be shocked by the endless stream of paperwork that engulfs you, and you

FIGURE 12.3

These announcements provide a taste of the continuous learning opportunities available to educators.

Professional Development
Once a Teacher, Always a Learner

What Works in Schools—Increasing Student Achievement Through Research-Based Practices, Alexandria, VA

The Role of the Arts in the Transformation of School Culture, Cambridge, MA

Learning & the Brain: Using Brain Research as the Pathway to Student Memory, Motivation, and Achievement, Cambridge, MA

No Teacher Left Behind: Technology Across the Curriculum, Smithtown, NY

Making Algebra Child's Play, Buffalo, NY

Hands-on Science workshop by the American Association for the Advancement of Science, K–6, Washington, DC

Teacher Training Sessions: National Foundation for Teaching Entrepreneurship, San Francisco, CA

Annual Conference for Year-Round Education, Waikiki, HI

Educational Theatre Association: Lighting for Musicals, Orlando, FL

Disciplined-Based Theatre Education, Austin, TX

Teachers' Symposium, American Montessori Society, Albuquerque, NM

Urban Education, Atlanta, GA

Learning Disabilities: Attention Deficit/Hyperactivity Disorder teachers grades 1–6, NYC

Six Traits, Methods of Assessing Student Writing, 2-day immersion, McCook, NE

Rap, Rhythm, and Rhyme, Transforming Teaching, KIPP Academy, Bronx, NY

Reaching All Students: Assessment in a Standards-Based Environment, Worcester, MA

Shape the Future of Technological Literacy by Opening Communication Lines Between Educators and Engineers, by the Institute of Electrical and Electronic Engineers, Baltimore, MD

The Nuts and Bolts of Operating a Local Teacher Organization by the National Association of Catholic School Teachers, Philadelphia, PA

Character Education Training and Information Conference, Baltimore, MD

Success, Standards, and Struggling Secondary Students: K–12 educators who work with at-risk youth, Renton, WA

National 1 Day Conference for Substitute Teachers, Petersburg, VA

Making Sense of Looping: Non-Graded Primary and Multi-age Classrooms, Cleveland, OH

Raising Standards in Rural Education, Fort Collins, CO

International Conference on Computers in Education, Beijing, China

Integrating the Curriculum with Multiple Intelligences: The Balancing Act, Bloomington, IN

Council of School Attorneys' Advocacy Seminar and School Law Retreat, San Antonio, TX

SOURCE: Adapted from *Education Week on the Web;* and *Teacher Magazine,* 2001, 2003.

REFLECTION: Which of these opportunities do you find most interesting? Why? (You might need to consider numerous factors from geography to finances.)

will struggle to learn the names of the students in your classes, as many as 150 students or more at the secondary level. You will work even harder getting to know the people behind the names. Typically, you will have only three to five scheduled hours a week to prepare your lessons or coordinate with your colleagues. You will find little time to meet with individual students, much less their parents. Much of your professional day will be spent trying to manage students in a world of adult isolation.[10] This school organization is at least a century old, and new teachers, as well as experienced ones, often find it both dehumanizing and inadequate.

It is not surprising, therefore, that educators are reconceptualizing schools in order to make them more responsive to the intellectual and emotional needs of both teachers and students. As you contemplate where you want to begin your teaching career, you may want to consider how school organization will affect your life in the classroom.

One major school reorganization effort is intended to nurture learning communities, an effort to create a more intimate and goal-oriented environment. When **learning communities** are established, students and teachers get to know each other both personally and intellectually as they develop shared academic goals and values. Reducing class size and lengthening school periods are two of several organizational changes that can reduce student alienation and build learning communities.

In other nations, teachers assume a greater number of responsibilities; as a result, they work more intensively with each student. In Japan, Germany, Switzerland, and Sweden, for example, teachers serve as counselors as well as instructors and have a greater range of interactions with their students. To meet their expanded responsibilities, teachers are given additional time to confer with their colleagues and plan their lessons. There are fewer support staff and administrators in these countries, and greater emphasis is placed on the teacher-student connection. While teachers constitute 60 to 80 percent of the school staff in European and Asian countries, they represent only 43 percent of the education staff in the United States. In fact, in the United States, the number of administrators and nonteaching staff members has more than doubled over the past three decades. Reformers believe student performance will not improve unless we reverse this trend.[11] (See Figure 12.4 for an international comparison of staffing patterns.)

Finding That First Teaching Position

The U.S. Department of Education projects that more than three million teachers will be needed over the next decade.[12] (See Figure 12.5 for the projected change in regional K–12 enrollments over the next few years.) With teachers in short supply, and many veteran teachers retiring, new teachers are in the driver's seat—sort of. If you are licensed or have an endorsement in certain fields, such as special education, bilingual education, chemistry, math, and physics, you are indeed in the driver's seat. You may find yourself courted by many school districts. (Isn't that nice!) Several districts now recruit teachers from abroad for these difficult-to-fill positions. As one Houston recruiter explained, "We saw more physics teachers in one week in Moscow than we see here in two or three years."[13] Also, if you want to teach in an urban or rural school district, you will most likely have an easy time finding a position.

But the teacher shortage is no guarantee that you will find a teaching position anywhere you want. Districts with high salary schedules and positive teacher morale, often located in popular locations with education-friendly communities, have little need to lure candidates. Since candidates flock to these districts, you will

FIGURE 12.4

International comparisons of teacher staffing patterns.

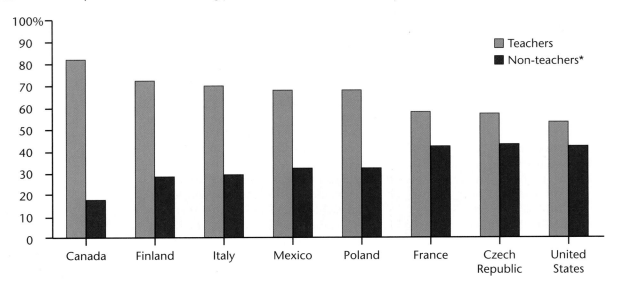

*Non-teachers include administrators, professional support, and maintenance.

SOURCE: Organization for Economic Cooperation Development (OECD), *Education at a Glance*, 2003. Teaching Staff and Non-Teaching Staff Employment in Public and Private Institutions.

REFLECTION: Why do you believe that U.S. schools are staffed so differently from other nations? Do you have a suggestion for an ideal or preferred teacher-staff ratio? In your years of schooling, have you been aware of the non-instructional staff and how they have contributed to your education? Explain.

have a tougher time competing for one of these positions. And something else to keep in mind is that while many new teachers are fresh out of college, others are more mature and experienced workers. Termed "career switchers," these new recruits have left other occupations to become teachers, bringing years of skills and experiences to the classroom. They are changing our image of "new" teachers.[14] You can research the ever-changing market for teaching positions online, at Web sites such as Education Job Openings (www.nationjob.com/education) and Recruiting New Teachers (www.rnt.org).

Where to Teach?

When pondering where to apply for your first teaching position, the community and your colleagues are just some factors to consider. You may want to make a list of other issues that matter to you:

What subject or grade level do I prefer? What kind of community and students do I want to serve? What part of the country appeals to me? Is there a particular school organization I like? What educational philosophy and school culture am I most comfortable with? How important to me are incentives for superior teaching? What salary

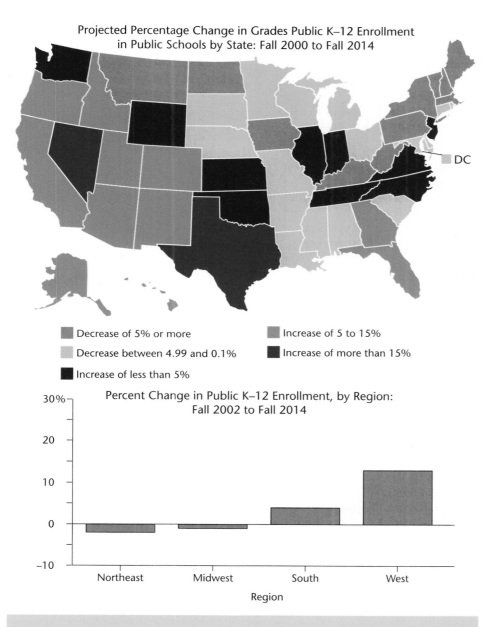

Projected Percentage Change in Grades Public K–12 Enrollment
in Public Schools by State: Fall 2000 to Fall 2014

Decrease of 5% or more

Decrease between 4.99 and 0.1%

Increase of less than 5%

Increase of 5 to 15%

Increase of more than 15%

Percent Change in Public K–12 Enrollment, by Region:
Fall 2002 to Fall 2014

FIGURE 12.5

Where the students are. As you consider where to teach, you may want to know where enrollments are likely to increase.

SOURCE: U.S. Department of Education, National Center for Education Statistics: Common Core of Data (CCD). "State Nonfiscal Survey of Public Elementary/Secondary Education," 2002–2003.

SOURCE: U.S. Department of Education, National Center for Education Statistics 2003, Common Core of Data surveys; and State Public Elementary and Secondary Enrollment Model.

REFLECTION: Do national trends like these influence your career decisions? Why or why not?

and benefits am I seeking? Am I more interested in a private or public school, or perhaps a charter or magnet school? Am I flexible and open to different options or focused in my preferences?

Many of the activities in this book, including the *You Be the Judge* in the first chapter, the inventory of your educational philosophy in Chapter 8, and the *RAPs*, will help you answer these questions. Once you sort out your priorities and identify the schools that are right for you, the next task is to get that first job.

Education World asked second-year teachers to reflect on their first year in the classroom, their successes and failures, and offer advice for new teachers:

- *Take charge.* Have a clear management plan, with well-defined rewards and consequences. Explain it to the students, send it home to the parents, and ask for signatures on the plan.
- *Keep students busy and engaged.* Have a number of potential class activities available. Bored kids get into trouble; busy kids stay out of trouble.
- *Get peer support.* If you are not assigned an official mentor, find an unofficial one.
- *Get parental support.* From extra supplies to celebration plans, parents are a hidden teacher resource, but only if they are pulled into class activities.
- *Organize yourself.* Develop a system that will keep you organized. There is a lot going on in teaching, grading, and monitoring dozens of children for hours each day.

- *Organize your students.* Teach students how to organize their homework, notebooks, etc.
- *Write and reflect.* Keep a journal to help you reflect on your first year, and become a stronger teacher your second year.
- *Have fun.* Teaching is not only stressful; it is joyful. Get into it and have fun!

SOURCE: *Education World* (www.educationworld.com

REFLECTION: Compare this advice with the more formal areas of teacher effectiveness cited in the research and by the National Board for Professional Teacher Standards described in Chapter 11. What are the similarities and differences?

Résumés, Portfolios, Online Assessments, and Interviews

The most crucial documents in your job search may well be your résumé and your portfolio. A résumé presents a concise description of your strengths and competencies, while a portfolio offers a more comprehensive profile, which might include videotapes of your teaching; sample lesson plans; journals; supervisor's observations; letters from parents, students, and administrators; and examples of student work. The *RAPs* in this text have put you on the road to creating your own portfolio.

If the résumé and portfolio do their job, you will be invited for an interview, but you may not be traveling anywhere for the interview. Some school districts are now experimenting with a short, online assessment to screen candidates. This electronic interview reduces the time and cost of an in-person interview.[15] The questions are standardized and meant to identify early the promising teacher candidates that the system wants to attract. Presenting well on an electronic or in-person interview can quickly move a candidate to the top of the "let's hire" list, and as you might guess, doing poorly can convert a promising candidate into an "also-ran." Knowing how to diagnose and respond to interview questions makes all the difference. Since résumés, portfolios, and interviews are important steps on your career road, we have pulled together some pointers for you to consider in the next chapter, "Question and Answer Guide to Entering the Teaching Profession."

 ## Teacher Recognition

Project yourself into the future. You have worked hard in your school, and you are widely acclaimed as a terrific teacher (congratulations!). After some wonderful years in the classroom, you begin to think about what lies ahead. Having parents, students, and colleagues sing your praises is wonderful, but is there more than that? How are dedicated and excellent teachers recognized and rewarded? Without formal and meaningful recognition, frustration may well follow, a sentiment captured in all-too-typical teacher comments, such as the following:

> How would I describe my teaching? Well, let me put it this way—I work hard. Free time is a thing of the past. My students are really important to me, and I'm willing to go the extra mile to give them feedback, organize field trips and projects, meet with them or their parents, and give them a stimulating classroom. In fact, most Saturdays I'm working on grades or new projects. And I think it pays off—my kids are blossoming! That's a great feeling. But sometimes I wonder if it's all worth it. Is anyone ever going to notice my hard work? Brad down the hall just comes in and does his job without a second thought, and his paycheck looks just like mine. It doesn't seem fair. Teachers who deserve it should be able to earn something more—more money, more respect.

This view is held by thousands of teachers struggling for professional recognition. Working hard in a demanding profession, teachers often do not feel valued or appreciated, and many leave the field each year as a result.

While not a comprehensive solution to the problem, North Carolina has made a grand gesture in response to teacher burnout. The state opened a mountain lodge dedicated to pampering teachers. Over the course of a school year, nearly two thousand teachers, about 2 percent of the state's teachers, are invited to spend five days in the combination spa and mini-university. Sumptuous meals, outdoor walks, and quiet contemplation recharge a teacher's batteries, and are a way of saying thanks for their efforts. Although in-service courses are a part of the week's schedule, they are kept to a minimum and the focus is on relaxation. As one teacher remarked, "This is the closest teachers get to being treated like the corporate world."[16] Perhaps the future will bring more teacher spas, but for now, we will focus on three more common approaches to teacher recognition: board certification, merit pay, and career ladders.

Part of the effort to assess, train, and reward qualified teachers involves direct observation of classroom teaching performance.

The National Board for Professional Teaching Standards

In 1987, the **National Board for Professional Teaching Standards (NBPTS)** was formed to promote teaching excellence through recognition of superior teachers. The NBPTS awards **board certification** to experienced teachers based on superior performance. It is available to all licensed teachers who hold a baccalaureate degree and have taught (in either public or private school) for a minimum of three years. In a few years, you may want to join the growing number of teachers participating in this effort. In January 1995, 86 National Board Certified Teachers were recognized; by 2006, more than 30,000 teachers had achieved board status.[17] When the NBPTS was launched, former North Carolina governor James Hunt, Jr., proclaimed,

> For once in this country, we are working out standards for measuring excellence rather than minimum competency. The certification process has the potential to transform the current educational system, leverage current investment in teaching, and build a national consensus for increased support of schools.[18]

Interview procedures vary by school and district—a meeting with the principal; a formal review by a panel of administrators, faculty, and school parents; a roundtable discussion with potential colleagues—any or all could await you. How might you prepare for each of these situations? Would you be more comfortable in one rather than another setting? Why?

Deciding who will be board certified is the task of the independent, nonpartisan NBPTS, comprising classroom teachers, school administrators, state political leaders, university officials, representatives from professional organizations, and business and community leaders.[19] Imagine yourself as a newly appointed board member responsible for determining what skills and behaviors identify truly excellent teachers, teachers who will be known as board certified. How would you begin? The board began by identifying five criteria: mastery of subject area, commitment to students, ability to effectively manage a classroom, continuous analysis of teaching performance, and a commitment to learning and self-improvement (see Chapter 11, "Teacher Effectiveness," for additional information about these five criteria).[20]

To demonstrate expertise to the NBPTS, teachers must complete a series of performance-based assessments, including written exercises that reflect mastery of their subject and understanding of the most effective teaching methods. Board candidates must also submit student work samples, videotapes of their teaching, and participate in simulations and interviews held at special assessment centers.[21]

Perhaps the biggest question is: What does board certification mean? Clearly, being recognized as exceptional is psychologically rewarding. Considering that there are literally millions of teachers in the United States, to be among a selected few is a major boost. Board certification has become a catalyst for rewarding superior teachers with salary increases and new job responsibilities. Several hundred local school districts and forty states provide some incentive for teachers who are board certified. However, such recognition is not universal. When funds are in short supply or a school district's organizational structure is inflexible, board-certified teachers may receive few tangible rewards or new responsibilities, despite their excellence. As you enter the teaching profession, you will want to stay abreast of the activities concerning the national board and determine if you want to work toward board certification. (For a current update of NBPTS activities, visit www.nbpts.org.)

Merit Pay

To understand merit pay, we need to understand non-merit pay. Typically, all teachers receive standard raises each year. The longer you teach, the more you earn. Teachers can also add to their salary by attending graduate school. But teachers are not given more money for being good at teaching. Merit pay is a major departure from this system. **Merit pay** sounds incredibly fair; tying teacher performance to salary and paying more productive teachers more money. The challenge, of course, is determining who is more productive. Supporters argue that merit pay makes teaching more accountable and more financially rewarding for talented teachers. Principal and superintendent organizations as well as the National Commission on Excellence in Education all support merit pay. But others are more skeptical.[22] Let's listen in on a hypothetical (but incredibly realistic) faculty meeting to hear both sides of the argument.

Dr. Moore faced her staff and began, "As you may have heard, several states and cities have recently adopted merit plans, and our school board wants us to consider our own merit plan. To help us, I have outlined some of the different plans, and then I'd like to hear your reactions."[23] Dr. Moore turns to her Power-Point presentation. "Here are four different approaches. Merit pay can be based on:

- *Student Performance.* This plan rewards teachers whose students make gains on standardized tests, and testing has become very important to the school board.

- *Teacher Performance.* This plan sends observers into your classroom to measure your teaching effectiveness, and merit is based on these observations.

- *Individualized Productivity.* Do you remember the professional goals each of you wrote for this school year? This plan would ask you to write more detailed goals for what you would like to accomplish each academic year, including new skills you will be working on, or any additional assignments you agree to take on. You would receive financial bonuses based on how much of your plan school administrators believe you have accomplished.

- *Teaching Assignment.* With this plan, compensation is related to market demands. Our math, science, and special education teachers would probably receive the greatest bonuses if we were to adopt this plan.

As the PowerPoint shuts down, the teachers jump in:

"This sounds great! I can finally get that bonus I deserve for all my extra hours."

"Does only the teacher with all the smart kids get merit when they do well on tests?"

"I don't think I'd feel comfortable if other people found out that I was getting extra money. Teaching is supposed to mean working as a team, not competing for bonuses."

"Dr. Moore, you try to be fair, but not everyone does. What about supervisors who give merit pay to their friends."

"Why can't we all get merit pay?"

"I don't think we all deserve merit pay. I think some of us are stronger teachers than others, and it is well past time that we recognize that."

As you can hear from these comments, merit pay can strain relationships among teachers, raise serious questions about measuring classroom success, fan the fear of "playing politics," and create a sense of being manipulated by outside forces. While some teachers are excited about the possibility of a higher salary and feel that too many weak teachers are paid the same as stronger ones, others see merit pay as a "bribe." Teacher organizations are cautious, but are more likely to support such plans if the merit is not based solely on test scores, if local teachers are involved in planning, and if the plan does not penalize teachers who work in under-resourced schools.[24] History does not suggest that merit pay is a successful long-term strategy. In fact, although merit pay is touted as a new, bold initiative, it actually began in England in 1710 when teacher salaries were tied to student test scores. You can probably predict the results: schools became all about test preparation.[25] Historians David Tyack and Larry Cuban write: "The history of merit performance-based salary plans has been a merry-go-round" as districts initially embrace such plans, only to drop them after a brief trial. But in spite of these failures, school officials keep "proposing merit pay again and again."[26]

Career Ladder Programs

Career ladder programs offer another teacher recognition strategy. The career ladder is designed to create different levels for teachers by creating a "ladder" that one can climb to receive increased pay through increased work responsibility and status.[27] Some critics argue that career ladders have the same drawbacks as merit pay—a lack of clear standards or appropriate evaluation tools—but others claim that career ladders can be more effective because they are rooted in professionalism. The distinguishing characteristic of the career ladder is the increased responsibility given to the teacher. The Rochester, New York, *Career in Teaching* plan is a good example. Here, an outstanding teacher has the opportunity to become a "master" or "mentor teacher," write curricula, select textbooks, or plan staff development programs while continuing to teach in the classroom.[28] Thus, good teachers are not removed from the classroom, yet they earn increased responsibility and salary.

All teacher recognition plans share the goal of making the teaching profession more attractive and more rewarding, whether through professional recognition, financial compensation, or increased responsibility. As you enter the teaching profession, you will want to consider which incentives appeal to you. But many districts are less responsive to treating teachers as professionals. Teachers' opinions and insights are not always sought, and sometimes they are kept far from policy-making circles. When Andy Baumgartner, National Teacher of the Year in 2000, criticized the lack of significant teacher representation on a commission to reform education in his home state of Georgia, he quickly became *persona non grata*. The governor would not have his photo taken with him, and several politicians roundly criticized him for his audacity.[29] This is precisely the sort of attitude that has led teachers to establish organizations dedicated to protecting their rights and promoting professional growth. When you take your first teaching position, you may want to join such a teacher organization, perhaps one affiliated with the NEA or the AFT. What's the difference between the two? Glad you asked.

 # Educational Associations

Today, teaching is one of the most organized occupations in the nation, and teachers typically belong to one of two major teacher organizations, the **National Education Association (NEA),** created in 1857, or the **American Federation of Teachers (AFT),** created in 1916 and affiliated with the American labor movement. The NEA and the AFT work to improve the salaries and the working conditions of teachers through **collective bargaining** (that is, all the teachers in a school system bargaining as one group through a chosen representative), organized actions (including strikes), and influencing education policy. In your first few years as a teacher, you will find yourself in a new environment and without the protection of tenure. Teacher associations, such as the NEA and the AFT, can help alleviate that sense of vulnerability by providing you with collegial support, opportunities for professional growth, and the security that one derives from participating in a large and influential group. Nine out of ten teachers belong to either the NEA or AFT, and six out of ten teachers are represented by one or the other in collective bargaining. It is not too early for you to start thinking about which may best represent you. So let's attend a faculty meeting here in Mediumtown and find out.

The NEA and the AFT

You have been a teacher in Mediumtown for all of two weeks, and you know about five faces and three names of other faculty members. You have just learned that there will be a teachers' meeting about the services provided by the National Education Association (NEA) and the American Federation of Teachers (AFT). Although you hear about these two organizations all the time, you know next to nothing about either. So to get to meet some of your new colleagues, and to find out about these organizations, you decide to attend.

At the meeting, you flip through the NEA brochure. You learn that the NEA is the largest professional and employee organization in the nation, with nearly three million members. If you join the NEA, you will benefit from publications like *NEA Today,* free legal services, and training opportunities on issues from technology to academic freedom. The NEA is a political force as well, and it works to elect pro-education candidates and to promote legislation beneficial to teachers and students. (See www.nea.org.) You like political involvement and the NEA seems like a perfect fit. But then a speaker from the AFT takes the floor.

IMAGINE . . .

Of Wives and Porcupines

Be ready for some unusual student insights during your first year in the classroom. Here are some actual student answers to teacher questions. While the answers were more than a little off base, they do offer a humorous insight into student thinking.

1. Ancient Egypt was inhabited by mummies and they all wrote in Hydraulics. They lived in the Sarah Dessert and traveled by Camelot. The climate of the Sarah is such that the inhabitants have to live elsewhere.
2. Solomon had three hundred wives and seven hundred porcupines.
3. Actually, Homer was not written by Homer but by another man of that name.
4. Socrates was a famous Greek teacher who went around giving people advice. They killed him. Socrates died from an overdose of wedlock. After his death his career suffered a dramatic decline.
5. The greatest writer of the Renaissance was William Shakespeare. He was born in the year 1564, supposedly on his birthday. He never made much money and is famous only because of his plays. He wrote tragedies, comedies, and hysterectomies, all in Islamic pentameter. Romeo and Juliet are an example of a heroic couplet.
6. Writing at the same time as Shakespeare was Miguel Cervantes. He wrote Donkey Hote. The next great author was John Milton. Milton wrote Paradise Lost. Then his wife died and he wrote Paradise Regained.
7. One of the causes of the revolutionary war was the English put tacks in their tea . . . Ben Franklin died in 1790 and is still dead.
8. The nineteenth century was a time of a great many thoughts and inventions. People stopped reproducing by hand and started reproducing by machine. The invention of the steam boat caused a network of rivers to spring up.

SOURCE: Teachers First, www.teachersfirst.com/humor.shtml.

Often marked by acrimony and bitterness, strikes changed the traditional image of teachers as meek and passive public servants.

"When John Dewey became our first member back in 1916, he recognized that teachers need their own organization. That is why the AFT will continue to be exclusively of teachers, by teachers, and for teachers.

It was the AFT that backed school desegregation years before the 1954 Supreme Court decision that established the principle that separate is not equal. We ran freedom schools for Southern black students, and we have a strong record on academic freedom and civil rights.

It was the AFT that demanded and fought for the teacher's right to bargain collectively. It was the AFT leaders who went to jail to show the nation their determination that teachers would no longer stand for second-class status.

And, as part of the great labor movement, the AFL-CIO, the AFT continues to show the nation that through the power of the union the voice of America's teachers will be heard."

You take a look at the AFT brochure. With over a million members, the AFT has significant influence. The AFT's image as a streetwise, scrappy union has shifted since the 1970s and today the AFT takes a leadership role in education reform. The AFT supported national standards for teachers, charter schools, and induction programs that enable new teachers to work with master teachers and the active recruitment of people of color into the teaching profession.[30] The AFT provides services similar to the NEA, although on a smaller scale. (See www.aft.org.)

As you weigh the relative merits of the two organizations, you overhear some teachers muttering that they don't care to join either group and that in their opinion the NEA and AFT put the salaries of teachers above the needs of children. Listening more closely, you hear these teachers claim that teacher associations have pitted administrators against teachers, and teachers against the public, creating needless hostility. Even worse, these critics charge, unions too often protect incompetent teachers who should be removed from the classroom.

Still, you are intrigued by the promise of collective action. In fact, you cannot help but speculate about a merger of these two professional organizations, a merger

"America is on trial," declared Margaret Haley, standing before the National Education Association convention. Poor salaries, overcrowded classrooms, and the lack of teacher voice in school policy and curricular decisions, she argued, all undermine teachers' effectiveness.

Though Haley's charges sound disquietingly current, she was not critiquing today's curricular standards created by nonteachers, or the growing dependence on standardized tests to measure both students and teachers, or even the top-down management style of some current school administrators. In fact, Margaret Haley gave this speech a century ago. In 1904, she became the first woman and the first teacher to speak from the floor of an NEA convention. Her speech, "Why Teachers Should Organize," condemned as undemocratic the practice of treating a teacher as an "automaton, a mere factory hand whose duty it is to carry out mechanically and unquestioningly the ideas and orders of those clothed with the authority."[1]

Haley was born in 1851 in Joliet, Illinois, to Irish immigrant parents who valued education and fairness. Haley learned to read from her mother, who used the Bible and a pictorial history of Ireland to educate her daughter. Her father was an active member of local stone quarry and construction unions, who shared accounts of heated union rallies with young Margaret as bedtime stories. Her father also championed the rights and talents of women, and taught Margaret about suffragette Susan B. Anthony and America's first woman physician, Elizabeth Blackwell. Such lessons planted the seeds for Margaret Haley's later efforts to empower women teachers.

At Cook County Normal School, Haley eagerly studied the progressive ideas set forth by John Dewey, embracing the school as a democratic training ground for students and teachers. But when she entered the classroom in Chicago's poor stockyard district, she encountered a vastly different reality. The curriculum she used was uninspiring and imposed by educational bureaucrats, and she was expected to teach it to 50 or 60 sixth graders. In the warm months, swarms of bugs visited her classroom, and in the winter, Haley shivered along with her students. Working in such deplorable conditions, she increasingly understood that teachers needed to fight the factory mentality of schools.

After 20 years of teaching in Chicago schools, Haley left the classroom to devote herself full-time to educational reform efforts through unions. As vice president and business agent for the Chicago Teachers' Federation (CTF), Haley transformed the fledgling organization into a national voice fighting for, "the right for the teacher to call her soul her own."[2]

Haley's first action for the CTF was to force the Illinois Supreme Court to wrest unpaid taxes from five public utility companies—money that was earmarked for teachers' salaries. For Haley, now known as the "Lady Labor Slugger," the victory was one for both education and democracy: Teachers were given a raise and Chicago businesses were forced to uphold their civic responsibility.

Unlike other teacher associations of the time, Haley deliberately limited the CTF to elementary school teachers. Women consequently dominated the organization, challenging the prevailing wisdom that women should remain quiet, confined to their classrooms. Through the CTF, teachers could become social activists. Under Haley's leadership, Chicago teachers won a tenure law, a pension plan, and were given power over curriculum and discipline. Haley also engineered a successful campaign to affiliate her union with the Chicago Federation of Labor. The status of teachers, in Haley's mind, was little more than that of a white-collar proletariat, strikingly similar to blue-collar manual workers. Although the CTF's alliance with labor shocked many teachers, the union ultimately helped the CTF gain political power. Though women could not yet vote, they worked with male labor workers to support a range of progressive issues: child labor laws, women's suffrage, and equal wages for men and women.

A century ago, Margaret Haley called for teachers "to save the schools for democracy and to save democracy in the schools."[3] Her tireless efforts and astute political skills helped create more humane schools for both teachers and students. Haley died in 1939.

[1] Nancy Hoffman, *Woman's "True" Profession: Voices from the History of Teaching* (Old Westbury, NY: The Feminist Press, 1981), p. 291.
[2] David Neiman (Producer), *Only a Teacher*, Part 2: *Those Who Can . . . Teach* (Princeton: Films for the Humanities and Sciences, 2000). [3] Ibid.

REFLECTION: Had you heard of Margaret Haley before reading this profile? If not, you are not alone. Why do we know so few of education's heroes, teachers whose efforts have improved the lives of teachers?

www.mhhe.com/ sadker8e

To learn more about Margaret Haley, click on *Profiles in Education.*

Milestones in the birth and growth of teacher associations.

1794 The Society of Associated Teachers of New York City becomes the country's first teacher association.

1840–1861 Thirty state teacher associations form.

1857 The first National Teachers' Association is formed. In the late 1870s, this group merges with the National Association of School Superintendents and the American Normal School Association to become the National Education Association (NEA).

1902 A group of teachers from San Antonio, Texas, becomes the first to join a labor union, the American Federation of Labor (AFL).

1916 The American Federation of Teachers (AFT) is formed.

1920s The AFT has more than 10,000 members.

1940s More than 200,000 teachers belong to the NEA (up from about 7,000 in 1910). More than 30,000 teachers belong to the AFT.

1940s–1950s More than 100 strike threats are carried out.

1960s–1970s The AFT and then the NEA take up militant tactics, including even more frequent strikes.

1980s–1990s Teacher organizations are involved in political action and show growing concern for increased professionalism.

1998 NEA members reject AFT merger plan. Talks for a future merger continue.

REFLECTION: Predict the future of teacher organizations and speculate when and what the next two or three entries might be.

that has been under discussion for several years.[31] A combined NEA–AFT could wield enormous national leverage, potentially gaining significant benefits for education in general and teachers in particular.

Professional Associations and Resources

In addition to the NEA and the AFT, you will find many resources that can help you in your professional development. Publications such as *Education Week* keep teachers abreast of educational developments. (The online version is available at www.edweek.org.) Journals, professional training, university courses, and professional associations can help you not only in those critical first few years, but throughout your teaching career as you refine your teaching techniques and adapt curricular resources. The Internet is a great source of classroom ideas and practical advice. Teacher-Zone (www.teacher-zone.com) and Beginning Teacher's Tool Box (www.inspiringteachers.com) are typical of the online resources now available. And sometimes, just talking to others and learning about techniques for stress reduction can make all the difference in that first job, which is the idea behind Education World (www.education-world.com).

Here are a few organizations that you may find helpful:

- *The Association for Supervision and Curriculum Development* is an international, nonprofit, nonpartisan association of professional educators whose jobs cross all grade levels and subject areas. (www.ascd.org)

- *National Middle School Association* works to improve the educational experiences afforded young adolescents, ages 10–15 years. (www.nmsa.org)
- *National Association for the Education of Young People* pulls together preschools, child care, primary schools, cooperatives, and kindergarten educators and parents in projects to improve the quality and certification of these schools. (www.naeyc.org)
- *National Association for Gifted Children* advances the opportunities and school programs for gifted students. (www.nagc.org)
- *The Council for Exceptional Children* is the largest international professional organization dedicated to improving educational outcomes for individuals with exceptionalities, students with disabilities, and the gifted. (www.cec.sped.org)

If you are interested in subject matter specialties, many organizations, journals, and Web sites can meet your needs. Here is a brief sample:

- *American Alliance for Health, Physical Education, Recreation and Dance* (www.aahperd.org)
- *National Council for Teachers of English* (www.ncte.org)
- *National Council for the Social Studies* (www.ncss.org)
- *National Science Teachers Association* (www.nsta.org)
- *Teachers of Speakers of Other Languages* (www.tesol.org)
- *National Council for the Teachers of Mathematics* (www.nctm.org)

As a teacher, you will find yourself in a learning community, not only teaching students, but continually improving your own knowledge and skills. We hope that these resources and others in this text will set you on that path of continuous learning and improvement. You may not have decided on whether teaching is right for you and you may still have a question or two left unanswered. That is what the final chapter is all about. In our last chapter, we share some of the frequent questions that students ask us about teaching. But before we get to that last chapter, there is one central (really irksome) question that we want to address now: Are America's schools failing? It is discouraging for teachers to invest their talent and energy only to be told by politicians and journalists that our schools are doing poorly. We would like to offer a platform to another side of the story, presenting a perspective we rarely hear.

American Schools: Better Than We Think?

School bashing is nothing new; it is as American as apple pie. In fact, some educators believe not only that the current wave of criticism is old hat, but that it is terribly misguided, because today's schools are doing as well as they ever have—maybe, just maybe, they are doing better.

Critics decry the low performance by U.S. students on international tests. But school advocates point out that test results may reflect cultural and curricular differences, not a failing educational system. Consider that Japanese middle school students score significantly higher than U.S. students on algebra tests, but most Japanese students take algebra a year or two earlier than U.S. students do. Moreover, most Japanese children attend private academies, called *Juku* schools, after school and on weekends. By 16 years of age, the typical Japanese student has

American Schools Have Failed Society Because . . .

INTERNATIONAL TESTS DOCUMENT POOR STUDENT PERFORMANCE

How embarrassing for the students in the richest, most powerful nation in the world to do so miserably on tests. Our students typically trail students in Korea, Japan, and most of Western Europe.

TOO MANY STUDENTS DROP OUT OR ACT OUT

The lack of discipline, decorum, and control in America's schools is a sign that basic values are missing, poor management is commonplace, and school violence and dropouts are rampant.

WORKERS LACK BASIC SKILLS

America does not produce enough scientists, engineers, and mathematicians, and our workers lack not only key technical skills, but basic reading and writing competencies as well. American companies are now forced to provide remedial instruction to our ill-prepared workers.

SCHOOLS HAVE BECOME A MONOPOLY

The power of teacher unions and the inertia of the school bureaucracies have robbed schools of initiative and creativity. Competition through vouchers and charter schools is the answer.

American Schools Have Served Society Well Because . . .

INTERNATIONAL TEST SCORES MISS THE POINT

Americans value individuality and creativity, characteristics absent from these tests. Lower scores are due to the high number of American poor taking these tests, a sign of our society's failure, not school failure.

STUDENT SUCCESS IS REAL

Graduation rates are up for the poor, for non-English speakers, and for special education students. And incidences of violence have actually been reduced.

WORKERS ARE AMONG THE BEST IN THE WORLD

Many Americans are unaware of the fact that our colleges produce a higher percentage of engineers and scientists than any other nation in the world, and our workers are among the most educated and skilled in the world. America is an economic superpower because of our worker productivity.

THEY REPRESENT THE DEMOCRATIC IDEAL

Jefferson and Mann were right: The nation's future rests on public schools. Vouchers and privatization take money from already underfunded public schools and hurt free, democratic education.

www.mhhe.com/
sadker8e

YOU DECIDE . . .

Why do Americans struggle over such a basic question? Do arguments about school effectiveness influence your decision to teach? Do school critics serve a useful purpose by prodding the public to create more effective schools, or are they more likely to mislead the public and discourage teachers?

attended at least two more years of classes than has a U.S. student. Yet because of the greater comparative effectiveness of U.S. colleges in relation to Japanese colleges, many of these differences evaporate on later tests. (Perhaps there are two lessons here: (1) U.S. students should spend more time in school and (2) the Japanese need to improve the quality of their colleges.)

Student selection also affects test scores. In other countries, students who do not speak the dominant language are routinely excluded. In some nations, only a small percentage of the most talented students are selected or encouraged to continue their education and go on to high school. As one might imagine, a highly selective population does quite well on international tests. In the United States, the full range of students is tested: strong and weak, English-speaking and non-English-speaking students. A larger number of American test-takers are likely to be poor. Comparing all of America's students with another nation's best is an unfair comparison.

Americans value a comprehensive education, one in which students are involved in a wide array of activities, from theater to sports to community service. The U.S. public typically values spontaneity, social responsibility, and independence in their children, values that are not assessed in international tests. Consider the way a South Korean teacher identifies the students selected for the International Assessment of Education Progress (IAEP).

> The math teacher . . . calls the names of the 13-year-olds in the room who have been selected as part of the IAEP sample. As each name is called, the student stands at attention at his or her desk until the list is complete. Then, to the supportive and encouraging applause of their colleagues, the chosen ones leave to [take the assessment test.][32]

U.S. students taking international exams do not engender cheers from their classmates and do not view such tests as a matter of national honor, as do the South Korean students. Too often, our culture belittles intellectuals and mocks gifted students.

Despite these obstacles, on several key tests the nation's students are doing quite well. For example, by the mid-1990s, American students had achieved the second-highest average score among thirty-one nations on international comparisons of reading. The proportion of students scoring above 650 on the SAT mathematics tests had reached an all-time high. The number of students taking Advanced Placement (AP) tests soared, a sign that far more students are in the race for advanced college standing. Improvements have been documented on the California Achievement Test, the Iowa Test of Basic Skills, and the Metropolitan Achievement Test, tests used across the nation to measure student learning. One of the most encouraging signs has been the performance of students of color, whose scores have risen dramatically. Among 17-year-old African American students, average reading scores on the NAEP tests rose dramatically.[33] Decades ago, many of these students probably would not have even been in school, much less taking tests. In 1940, the overall high school graduation rate in the United States was only 38 percent; by the 2000s, it approached 90 percent. Other indicators reflect that students are not only staying in school longer but also are enrolling in more advanced math and science classes. U.S. schools are teaching more students, students are staying in school for longer periods of time, and children are studying more challenging courses than ever before. According to the 2006 Lemelson-MIT Invention Index, teenagers reported that they are pleased with the problem-solving and leadership skills, teamwork and creativity they learned in school.[34] (See Figure 12.6.)

Then why is there a national upheaval about education—why all the furor about our failing schools and why the demands for radical school reform? Educators have advanced a number of possible explanations:[35]

- Journalists and politicians have been critiquing schools since the founding of our nation.
- Adults tend to romanticize what schools were like when they attended as children, for they always studied harder and learned more than their children do

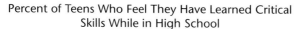

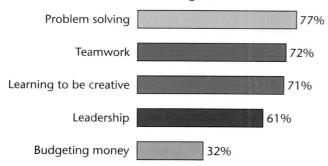

Percent of Teens Who Feel They Have Learned Critical
Skills While in High School

Problem solving	77%
Teamwork	72%
Learning to be creative	71%
Leadership	61%
Budgeting money	32%

FIGURE 12.6
Percent of teens who feel they have learned critical skills while in high school.

SOURCE: The Lemelson-MIT Invention Index 2006 http://web.mit.edu/newsoffice/2006/lemelson-teens.html.

REFLECTION: Why do so few reports about U.S. schooling examine topics like these?

(and when they went to school, they had to walk through four feet of snow, uphill, in both directions!).

- Americans hold unrealistic expectations. They want schools to conquer all sorts of social and academic ills, from illiteracy to teenage pregnancy, and to accomplish everything from teaching advanced math to preventing AIDS.

- Schools today work with tremendous numbers of poor students, non-English-speaking children, and special education students who just a few years ago would not be attending school as long or, in some cases, would not be attending school at all.

- In *The Manufactured Crisis,* David Berliner and Bruce Biddle put much of the blame for the current criticism on neoconservative policies of the 1990s supporting private schools, business interests, and vouchers. These policies marked the beginning of a major assault on public education, on federal involvement in schools, and on equal education programs targeting minority groups and women.

- Berliner and Biddle also finger the press, which has been all too willing to publish negative stories about schools—stories based on questionable sources. Sloppy, biased reporting has damaged the public's perception of schools.

It is helpful to remember two points. First, criticism can be fruitful. If additional attention and even criticism help shape stronger schools, then the current furor will have at least some positive impact. Second, there are countless students in all parts of the country who work diligently every day and perform with excellence. The United States continues to produce leaders in fields as diverse as medicine and sports, business and entertainment. To a great extent, these success stories are also the stories of talented and dedicated teachers. Although their quiet daily contributions rarely reach the headlines, teachers do make a difference. You represent the next generation of teachers who will, no doubt, weather difficult times and sometimes adverse circumstances to touch the lives of students and to shape a better America.

www.mhhe.com/ sadker8e

INTERACTIVE ACTIVITY
Edspeak. Do you know what these education-related terms mean?

SUMMARY

www.mhhe.com/
sadker8e

CHAPTER REVIEW

Go to the Online Learning
Center to take a quiz,
practice with key terms,
and review concepts from
the chapter.

1. What are the stages of teacher development?

Teachers provided with sufficient support can move through a series of stages: survival, consolidation, renewal, and maturity, growing from personal concerns (such as classroom management) to broader educational issues (school strategies that could enhance student learning). Studies underscore that, dollar for dollar, investments in teacher qualifications and training translate into improved student achievement.

2. What resources do school districts provide for a teacher's first year in the classroom?

Mentors, or consulting teachers, provide both personal and professional support, and sometimes evaluate new teachers. Effective professional development links subject content with teaching skills, uses problem solving, and is research-based and supported over time. Collaborative action research investigates real classroom problems in an effort to improve the quality of student learning.

3. How do school districts, states, and the National Board for Professional Teaching Standards recognize and reward teachers?

Established in 1987, the National Board for Professional Teaching Standards (NBPTS) seeks to identify and assess experienced teachers performing at a superior level. Most states and many school districts offer additional incentives for board certification, including salary bonuses and supplementary responsibilities. Merit pay offers teachers more money based on various criteria, including gains in student performance, typically measured by standardized tests; teacher performance, as measured by outside evaluators; individualized plans, in which teachers have a voice in setting their own goals; and the nature of the teaching assignment. Career ladders allow teachers to increase their responsibilities and salary as they advance. Merit pay and career ladders offer additional money for superior performance, but critics charge that these programs are compromised and do not improve education.

4. What are the differences between the National Education Association (NEA) and the American Federation of Teachers (AFT)?

The NEA is the largest professional and employee association in the nation. Formed during the second half of the 1800s, initially it was slow to work for the needs of its members, but by the 1960s and 1970s, the NEA became a strong teacher rights advocate. While significantly smaller, the AFT has historically taken a more militant position, demonstrated by its early support of teacher strikes. Today both the NEA and the AFT offer a range of services, including magazines, journals, and other professional communications; legal assistance; workshops and conferences; assistance in collective bargaining; and political activism. The NEA and AFT continue to explore a possible merger.

5. Are America's schools a secret success story, doing better than the press and the public believe?

The lower performance of American students on international tests may be attributed to curricular and cultural differences, not necessarily to educational deficiencies. Many indicators, from SAT scores to high school graduation rates, reflect an improvement in American schools. According to Berliner and Biddle, school bashing reflects an old tradition of journalists and a popular activity of today's neoconservative politicians. Despite all this, America's schools may be doing far better than we realize.

Go to your *Teachers, Schools, and Society* Reader CD-ROM to:

READ CURRENT AND HISTORICAL ARTICLES

12.1 **All Teachers Are Not The Same: A Multiple Approach to Teacher Compensation,** Julia E. Koppich, *Education Next,* Winter 2005.

12.2 **What Helps Beginning Teachers,** Linda Gilbert, *Educational Leadership,* May 2005.

12.3 **Autobiography of a Teacher: A Journey Toward Critical Multiculturalism,** Sarah J. Ramsey, *Scholar-Practitioner Quarterly* 2, no. 3, 2004.

12.4 **Lessons of a First-Year Teacher,** Molly Ness, *Phi Delta Kappan,* May 2001.

ANALYZE CASE STUDIES

12.1 **Christie Raymond:** A mature woman in the first month of her first full-time position teaching music in an elementary school loves the work as long as the children are singing, but dislikes the school's emphasis on and her part in disciplining the students. The case describes Christie's classroom teaching in detail as well as her after-school bus duty.

12.2 **Melissa Reid:** An enthusiastic young student teacher struggles to gain the respect and improve the behavior of her senior-level composition class and is devastated by one of her student's papers which is full of vindictiveness and hatred toward her.

OBSERVE TEACHERS, STUDENTS, AND CLASSROOMS IN ACTION

Beverly High School Teachers
Beverly, MA

Classroom Observation: Respect and Salary for Teachers

The public views teachers as important, but seems unwilling to pay them accordingly. The segment explores some reasons for this by noting a connection between the feminization of teaching and persistent negative stereotypes. In addition, the segment recognizes the "psychic" salary for teachers who love what they do.

KEY TERMS AND PEOPLE

American Federation of Teachers (AFT), 486

board certification, 481

collaborative action research (CAR), 472

collective bargaining, 486

e-mentors, 470

Margaret Haley, 488

induction program, 469

in-service, 471

intern teachers, 469

learning communities, 477

mentors, 470

merit pay, 484

National Board for Professional Teaching Standards (NBPTS), 481

National Education Association (NEA), 486

peer review, 470

professional development, 471

stages of teacher development, 469

DISCUSSION QUESTIONS AND ACTIVITIES

www.mhhe.com/
sadker8e

WEB-*TIVITIES*
Go to the Online
Learning Center to
do the following
activities:
1. Observation: Peer
   Review
2. Finding That First
   Teaching Position
3. The National Board for
   Professional Teaching
   Standards
4. Teacher Recognition:
   Merit Pay
5. Teacher Associations:
   the NEA and AFT

1. How might you redefine or modify any of the stages of teacher development? Can these stages be applied to other careers? Think of teachers you have observed. What are the specific behaviors and skills that place a teacher at each of these stages?

2. Survey local school districts and analyze their first-year induction programs. What resources do they provide new teachers to assist them in making a successful transition into teaching? Will this affect your decision as to where to teach? You might want to research first-year teacher induction programs in the library or on the Internet to get a sense of the range of resources offered to first-year teachers.

3. What do you look for in a mentor? What strategies can you use to recruit such a mentor in your first teaching job?

4. In order to get a sense of the breadth of professional opportunities available to you, add to the list started in this book. Pull together notices of professional service courses, workshops, and other opportunities available to teachers. To do this, you may want to review professional journals and also contact local school districts, professional associations, state department of education, and colleges.

5. Develop some potential topics for a collaborative action research project. Consider undertaking this project as a research activity during your teaching education program.

REEL TO REAL TEACHING: IT'S YOUR TURN

You've been invited to watch films and reflect and respond to *Reel to Reals* throughout this book. It is now time to switch roles! As future teachers, you will be challenged to develop assignments that are clear and promote meaningful learning. It is also common to use media in the classroom to inspire and inform students who are accustomed to *edutainment*. So, we are inviting you to apply your skills and creativity to write this chapter's *Reel to Real Teaching.*

Activity: Choose a film or television show with an educational theme. Here are a few suggestions:

- A new film that has just burst onto the movie scene.

- A film about education that has not been reviewed in earlier chapters. Browse your favorite video stores, educational resource center, or online listings for some ideas.

- A film suitable to your subject area and grade level. For example, the *Luzhin Defence* for mathematics, *Gandhi* for social studies, *Amadeus* for music, *Billy Elliot* for character education. Visit Teach with Movies at www.teachwithmovies.org for additional movie titles.

- A film mentioned in this text that you haven't yet seen.

Now, design an original *Reel to Real Teaching,* using the template presented in previous chapters.

1. Write a brief synopsis of the film.

2. Develop three or four reflection questions that encourage readers to connect the film's story with chapter content and with personal experiences.

3. Create a follow-up activity that applies themes from the film to real first-year classroom experiences, effective teaching, or your teaching interests.

Reflection: Add a brief, special paragraph that examines your development of the Reel to Real. How did it feel to change roles and create an activity? What did you learn from the process? Were you able to integrate content from the textbook? Did you enjoy initiating an activity versus responding to someone else's assignment? Was creativity the toughest part? Did you struggle with clear and concise directions?

Click on *Reel to Real Teaching* to submit your own film activity. Be sure to include a synopsis, reflection questions, and a follow-up activity.

www.mhhe.com/ sadker8e

FOR FURTHER READING

The Courage to Teach: Exploring the Inner Landscape of a Teacher's Life, by Parker Palmer (1998). Teachers choose their vocation for reasons of the heart, because they care deeply about their students and about their subject. But the demands of teaching cause too many educators to lose heart. In this book, Parker Palmer takes readers on an inner journey toward (re)connecting with their vocation and their students—and strengthening their passion for one of the most difficult and important of human endeavors.

Educating Esme: Diary of a Teacher's First Year, by Esme Raji Codell (2001). Do you want to know what teachers delight in, what teachers struggle with, and what teachers learn from themselves? This book will enlighten you. A funny, hip diary filled with honesty and unadorned thoughts that speak volumes about the raw, emotional life of a first-year teacher.

Handbook for the Beginning Teacher, by Courtney Moffatt and Thomas Moffatt (2003). Filled with teaching ideas, tips, and checklists for classroom success, including instructional techniques for students with different learning styles, with special needs, and from diverse cultural backgrounds. The many charts, outlines, and teacher materials are readily available for teacher use across the curriculum and grade level.

They Led by Teaching, by Sherry L. Field and Michael J. Berson (eds.) (2003). This inspirational collection of essays provides insights into the lives and careers of some influential educators, including Myra Sadker, co-author of this textbook.

Why We Teach, by Sonia Nieto (2005). Why teach? Listen to the voices of both veteran and new teachers as they share their most heartfelt and thoughtful replies to this simple but important question. This inspirational book focuses on the value of teaching; challenges current notions that focus on only accountability, testing, and standardization; and provides a compelling message of hope for public education.

13

CHAPTER

Q and A Guide to Entering the Teaching Profession

FOCUS QUESTIONS

1. What does the education job market look like? (or, put another way, will I be able to find a satisfying teaching position?)
2. Can I make a decent salary as a teacher?
3. How can new teachers increase their chances of working in a school of their choice?
4. What do I need in order to teach—a license or certification? (and how do I get one!)
5. What teacher competency tests do I need to take?
6. Why do teachers seek tenure? (and should I?)
7. Are there jobs in education outside of the classroom?

**www.mhhe.com/
sadker8e**

WHAT DO YOU THINK? **What Questions Do You Have?** Click on Ask the Author to submit any questions you still have. See what questions others have asked and the author's responses.

CHAPTER PREVIEW

Beyond questions concerning education as a field of study, students often have personal and practical questions about teaching, the kinds of questions that are more likely to be asked after class or during office hours. Students considering an education career want to know everything from where the jobs are to how to land a teaching position, from how teachers are licensed to what kinds of education careers are available beyond the classroom. We trust that this chapter will answer some of the questions you are asking, and even some you never thought to raise.

What are my chances of finding a teaching position?

This is a practical and quite natural question for you to be asking right now. After all, you are thinking about investing time, energy, money, and talent in preparing yourself to become a teacher, so it makes sense to ask whether you will be able to land a position when you graduate. Here is a shortcut to sorting out your employment possibilities, the *"four Ws"*: *when, what, where,* and *who.* Let's begin with *when.*

Although you may not have planned when you would enter teaching, the good news is that this is a terrific time to be looking for a position in education. While there are few guarantees when it comes to predicting national labor needs, several factors suggest that there will be a significant number of teaching positions available into the next decade. Perhaps we can appreciate the current situation better if we take a look at "the bad old days."

Historically, the demand for new teachers has resembled a roller coaster ride. In the 1950s and 1960s, a teaching shortage meant virtually anyone would be hired as a teacher, with or without the proper credentials. Back then, new graduates of teacher education programs enjoyed the view from the roller coaster as it soared. By the 1970s, the teacher employment roller coaster had begun to descend. Shrinking school budgets and the end of the baby boom had led to far more teachers than there were positions; as more teachers were licensed than positions existed, teacher oversupply became part of the educational lexicon, and teacher unemployment was common. By the 1980s and 1990s, the roller coaster was back on the ascent, as teacher retirements increased and student enrollments began to climb. Strong demand for new teachers continues due to an increasing student population, calls for smaller class sizes, and ongoing teacher retirements.

Let's consider the second *W: what* subject and grade level you plan to teach. Teachers of certain subjects, such as science and math, are in short supply. Science, computer science, and math are "hot" fields; in many districts, so are bilingual and special education.[1] One way to make yourself more marketable is to consider course work and school experiences in subjects and skills that are in demand.

Population shifts and political actions affect teacher demand, and they contribute to the third *w, where.* Recently, teacher shortages were felt in western and southwestern states (Arizona, California, Alaska, and Hawaii), while the need for new teachers was generally lower in the Northeast, Great Lakes, and Middle Atlantic areas.[2] But, despite these general trends, there are notable exceptions; for example, population increases in some communities in New Jersey and New Hampshire created local teacher shortages. Large cities, one of the more challenging classroom environs, also continue to experience shortages. In high-poverty urban and rural districts, more than 700,000 new teachers will be needed in the next decade.[3]

As we discussed earlier in the text, local and state governments are experimenting with new methods of school organization, changes that may impact the job market and go beyond the traditional four Ws. *Privatization* (the movement to turn over school management to private companies), voucher systems, and even charter schools challenge traditional employment practices by introducing productivity measures, individual school decision making, and the participation of parents and others in personnel actions. Many schools now monitor teacher competence through tests, requirements of *No Child Left Behind,* and even merit plans that link pay increments to student achievement. These changes may affect teacher supply and demand in particular regions and schools in the years ahead.

States and local communities also differ in their resources and priorities. Wealthier districts are more likely to sponsor a greater variety of programs and course offerings and to establish smaller average class sizes, actions that translate into a need for more teachers, while many urban areas struggle to find qualified teachers and adequate resources. School districts from Dallas to Detroit to Washington, DC, offer an ever-increasing array of incentives, including thousands of dollars in signing bonuses. Sometimes housing assistance and student loan forgiveness are offered to recruit teachers to urban schools.[4]

Q

A

Who are my teaching colleagues? What are the demographics of today's teachers?

There are more than three million teachers in America. Although 17 percent of students are African American, fewer than 8 percent of all teachers are African American; while 19 percent of students are Hispanic, only 6 percent of teachers are Hispanic. About three out of four teachers are women, and recruiting men and people of color to teaching remains a challenge.[5] (See Figure 13.1.)

You will not be alone as a new teacher: Nearly one in four of your colleagues will have begun teaching within the past five years. Your next few years may also mirror their activities, as more than half of your colleagues have earned a master's degree, and three out of four participate in annual professional development activities.[6]

Q

A

What are my chances for earning a decent salary?

The truth is that teaching offers incredible rewards, and these rewards go beyond salary. If you love teaching, as we do, it will be a joy to go to work, and a worthy way to invest your life. That joy, however, does not appear on your pay stub, and we are not alone in our belief that teachers are not paid what they deserve.

FIGURE 13.1

New K–12 teachers by race/ethnicity and by gender.

SOURCE: *Characteristics of Schools, Districts, Teachers, Principals and School Librarians 2003–04,* NCES, U.S. Department of Education, April 2006.

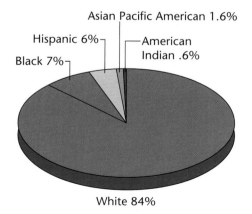

Racial/Ethnic Distribution of New K–12 Teachers

Asian Pacific American 1.6%

Hispanic 6%

Black 7%

American Indian .6%

White 84%

REFLECTION: How can teacher education programs recruit more students of color?

Starting teachers now average over $30,000 a year, and experienced teachers average about $50,000. But these are only averages. Some school districts pay teachers six figures, while others barely pay $20,000 a year. It would be wise to contact specific school districts of interest for a copy of their salary schedule.

Do private schools pay less than public schools?

Yes, most (but not all) private schools pay less than public schools. While the salaries are lower, many private (also called independent) schools offer teachers a different set of benefits—smaller classes, motivated students, supportive parents, a sense of community, a sense of teacher autonomy, a shorter school year, a more challenging curriculum, and sometimes, housing and meals. Many extraordinary teachers work in private schools, although as a group, private school teachers have less professional preparation, less experience, and participate less in professional development than do public school teachers—differences that some cite to explain their lower salaries. Private schools, like their public counterparts, vary significantly in their academic standing, salaries, and employment practices. While some private schools are incredibly strong academically and compete with local public schools in terms of employment benefits, others do not fare as well.[7] If you are interested in teaching in a private school, remember that each school needs to be evaluated on an individual basis.

How do I apply for a teaching job? Do I need a résumé or a portfolio?

The first step is to prepare a résumé to submit to prospective employers. When your résumé is strong, school districts will want a closer look, and that's when a portfolio or an interview will be requested. Résumés and portfolios open doors, so let's take a closer look at how best to construct them.

At the top of your résumé, list your contact information: name, address, telephone, and e-mail address. But the heart of the **résumé** is your relevant education and experience. Indicate your formal education background—your college and university, your major and your minor (if you have one), and describe your student teaching experience, as well as other educational accomplishments. Summarize relevant work experiences. If you offered private instruction, worked as a camp counselor or at a religious school, or volunteered at a day care center or in a recreation program for the elderly, include these and note dates of employment, salient responsibilities, and accomplishments. Many candidates include professional objectives and a brief educational philosophy at the beginning of a résumé. If you take this approach, you might write an employment objective that details the type of teaching position you are seeking. You could also include some of the reasons that propel you to teach and perhaps a brief statement about your educational philosophy and beliefs. Your résumé should be typed in a clear and readable format; there are software templates available to help you. Check if the school districts you are interested in prefer hard copy or e-mail.

Employers rely on references and recommendations to get a clearer picture of applicants. Remember, as you list professors, supervisors, previous employers, and cooperating teachers as references, you need to ask their permission and give them a "heads up" that they may be contacted. This is not only a basic courtesy, but also a way to measure their willingness to recommend you. Consider supplying them with "talking points" to aid them in preparing your recommendation.

Today, many school districts are going beyond résumés and recommendations, and are asking for a more in-depth view of you and your skills. A **portfolio** is a collection of materials that demonstrates your knowledge, competencies, and accomplishments as a teacher candidate. A portfolio does more than document your qualifications for a prospective teaching job (as a résumé does); it is a purposeful and reflective presentation of your professional development as a teacher.

People have different views concerning portfolios. Some see them as elaborate and lengthy presentations, while others consider an enhanced résumé with a few attachments to be a portfolio. Typically, portfolios include:[8]

I. Statement of Teaching Philosophy

II. Teaching Credentials

  A. Résumé

  B. Transcripts

  C. Letters of Reference

  D. Teaching Certificate/License

  E. Endorsement(s)

III. Teaching-Related Experiences

  A. Student Teaching

  1. Evaluations by University Supervisor

  2. Evaluations by Cooperating/Mentor Teacher

  3. Letters from Students and Parents

  4. Sample Lesson Plans

  5. Sample Classroom Floor Plans/Management Plans

  6. Reflective Teaching Journal

  7. Examples of Student Work

  8. Photographs of Students/Classrooms

  9. Videotape of Teaching

  B. Employment in Child-Related Fields

  C. Volunteer Work with Children

This text is designed to start you on the road to building a portfolio. The *RAP* activities guide your portfolio development. The reflection questions and *You Be the Judge* features infused throughout the text are intended to help you consider relevant issues and form your own educational views and beliefs. In organizing the contents of your portfolio, consider using national standards (such as the INTASC standards identified in the *RAP*s) or the state or local standards of the school district to which you are applying for a job. Many teaching candidates rely on a loose-leaf type notebook to organize their portfolio work, allowing for flexibility incorporating and removing material. More recently, digital formats, such as a CD-ROM or a Web page, have become popular. With a digital or **e-portfolio,** you can simultaneously present your qualifications and demonstrate your technological proficiency. In developing your portfolio, ask for input from university supervisors and cooperating teachers; and it is a good idea to practice presenting your portfolio to them as well.

How do I prepare for a successful interview?

Interviews take two forms these days: electronic or in person. A number of districts do their initial screening through an online series of questions. Candidates who successfully respond to these questions advance to the next step and are considered for employment. The questions are usually developed by a company specializing in online interviews and assess one's teaching philosophy, approach to a subject, and the like. The best way to prepare for such an online interview is to thoughtfully consider your educational philosophy, your approach to teaching, your long-term educational goals, your strategies for managing a class, and your plans to further develop your teaching skills. Reviewing the *RAP*s that you have prepared in this text as well as your portfolio can assist in this process.

In-person interviews may be conducted by one or more administrators, a panel of teachers, or a combination of teachers and parents, and the average interview usually lasts thirty minutes to an hour.[9] So how can these precious minutes work for you?

When you walk in for your interview, the first thing that will strike an interviewer is appearance. Your prospective interviewer (or interview team) will be looking not only for appropriate professional attire, but also for such qualities as poise, enthusiasm, self-confidence, and an ability to think quickly and effectively on your feet. Appropriate grammar, a well-developed vocabulary, and clear speech and diction are important. You should be focused about your teaching philosophy and goals if you want to appear confident and purposeful in the interview. If you have developed a portfolio of teaching materials or other information that you are particularly proud of, you should take it to the interview. It cannot hurt to have it present, and it might help win the day.

It is important to be prepared for likely questions. Common interview topics include your personal philosophy of teaching, your teaching strengths and weaknesses, professional goals, employment history, teaching style, and your approach to classroom management. Interviewers commonly look for: enthusiasm, warmth, caring, leadership skills, willingness to learn new things, and confidence.[10] You may also want to note what questions cannot legally be asked—for example, questions about your religion or marital or parental status. Such questions do not relate to your qualifications as a teacher. The Office for Civil Rights is one of several agencies that you can contact if you are victimized by such queries.

Do your homework: Find out as much as possible about both the particular school and the community. Talk to friends involved in the school or community, check local newspapers, try the local library or the Internet, or, better yet, stop by the school to talk with the students and others, scour the bulletin boards, and pick up available literature. Once you obtain information about a school or school system, you can begin matching your particular interests and skills with the school district's programs and needs.

As important as such preparatory work is, the most important way of learning what an interviewer is looking for is to listen. Sometimes interviewers state their needs openly, such as "We're looking for a teacher who is fluent in both Spanish and English." In other cases, interviewers merely imply their needs—for example, "Many of the children who attend our school are Hispanic." In this case, you have first to interpret the interviewer's remark and then to check your interpretation with a statement such as "Are you looking for someone who is fluent in both Spanish and English?" Or "Are you looking for someone who has experience in working with Spanish-speaking children?"

After interviewing, it is wise to send the interviewer a brief follow-up note, reminding her or him of how your qualifications meet the school system's needs. The interviewer may have talked with dozens of candidates, and under such circumstances it is easy to be forgotten in a sea of faces—your job is to make sure you stand out.

One word of caution: When a job offer comes your way, analyze the school system to make sure that you really want to teach there before signing on the dotted line. Try to find out

- If teachers in the district view it as a good place to work
- If there have been personnel problems recently and, if so, for what reasons
- What are the benefits and potential problems in the teachers' contract
- Typical class size
- What kind of support services are available
- If the school is adopting organizational changes to personalize the school climate.

If the answers do not please you, you may want to look elsewhere. It is unwise to accept a position with the notion that you will leave as soon as a better offer is made. That attitude can quickly lead to a job-hopping profile that may stigmatize you as someone who is either irresponsible or unable to work well with others. In short, do not simply jump at the first available job offer. If your credentials are good and you know how to market yourself, you will get other teaching offers.

Q **What do I need in order to teach—a license or certification? By the way, what's the difference?**

Project yourself a few years into the future. You have just completed your teacher preparation program. You stop by your local public school office and make a belated inquiry into teacher openings. The school secretary looks up from a cluttered desk, smiles kindly, and says, "We may have an opening this fall. Are you certified? Do you have a license?"

Oops! Certified? License? Now I remember. It's that paperwork thing. . . . I should have filled out that application back at school. I should have gone to that teacher licensure meeting. And I definitely should have read that Sadker and Zittleman textbook more carefully. I knew I forgot something. Now I'm in trouble. All that work and I will not be allowed to teach. What a nightmare!

And then you wake up.

A Many people use the terms *teacher certification* and *teaching license* interchangeably (as in "She has her teacher certification" while really meaning "She has her teaching license"). But it is important for you to be able to distinguish between a professional certification and a legal license, so we make the distinction in this book. **Teacher certification** confers professional standing; a **teacher's license** is a legal document. Teacher certification indicates that a professional group recognizes (certifies) that a teacher is competent and has met certain standards. A teacher's license, issued by the state government, grants the legal right to teach, not unlike a driver's license grants the legal right to drive. Both licenses mean that the "minimum" state requirements have been met. If you have been out on the roads recently, you know that meeting these minimum requirements to drive is not an indication that a person can, in fact, drive very well. It is the same with a teacher's license: Not all holders can teach well, especially if they are teaching a subject without adequate training in that field, a sad but not uncommon practice. Nevertheless, the intent of certification and licensure is to maintain high standards for teachers.

Who awards licenses, and how do I get one?

Teaching licenses are awarded by each of the 50 states and the District of Columbia. In a similar way, states are involved with the licensure of doctors, lawyers, and other professionals and nonprofessionals. When you meet the state's requirements, you can apply for and receive your teacher's license.

You should not assume that your teacher's license will automatically be issued to you when you graduate from your teacher education program, since state departments of education, not colleges and universities, issue teacher's licenses. Some colleges will apply to a designated state department in your name and request a license; others will not. In most states, filling out an application and passing the required national or state tests are all that is needed if you have graduated from an approved, accredited program. But not all teacher education programs are accredited (see the accreditation section of this chapter for more information). Regardless of your program, remember that you will probably need to apply to the state for a teacher's license. (See Appendix 2 for the contact information for the department of education in every state.)

You should also know that each state has its own requirements for teacher licensure. States have different policies concerning what courses teachers should take, what kinds of teacher's licenses should be offered, and even the length of time for which a teacher's license is valid. You may meet the standards in one state, but, if you decide to teach in another, you may find yourself unqualified for its license. Since the courses and experiences you need vary from state to state, it is useful to understand the major areas of preparation relevant to certification and licensure. Joseph Cronin, writing in the *Handbook of Teaching and Policy,* suggests three categories: knowledge of subject matter, knowledge of pedagogy, and practice teaching.[11] Chances are that your course work will fit within these categories.

When you have questions about obtaining a license, consult immediately with your college instructor, adviser, or teacher education placement office, or contact the appropriate state department of education. Do not depend on friends, whose well-intentioned advice may not be accurate.

What type of license do I need? (You mean, there's more than one?)

Most states issue more than one kind of license in order to differentiate among the applicants' qualifications and career goals. Although the specific names of these licenses (sometimes called certificates, now how's that for confusing!) vary from state to state, there are four common types:

1. An **initial,** or **provisional, license**—also called a *probationary certificate*—is the type frequently issued to beginning teachers and is generally nonrenewable. If you are awarded a provisional license, it means that you have

completed most, but not all, of the state's legal requirements to teach. It may also mean that you need to complete some additional course work or that you need to teach for several years before you qualify for a higher or more permanent license. You may find yourself first getting a provisional license, giving you some breathing room as you work to complete all of the state's requirements for a standard, or professional, license.

2. The **standard, or professional, license** is issued by the state after you have completed all the requirements to teach in that state. These requirements may include a specified number of courses beyond the bachelor's degree or one or more years of teaching experience.

3. A **special license** is a nonteaching license designed for specialized educational careers, including those in administration, counseling, library science, school social work, and school psychology. If after teaching for several years you decide that you want a career in school counseling (or administration, library science, and so forth), you will have to meet the requirements for this license.

4. A **conditional, or emergency, license** is a substandard license that is issued on a temporary basis to meet the needs of communities that do not have licensed teachers available. For example, a small high school in a rural community may not be able to attract a qualified teacher in physics. Faced with the unattractive prospect of not offering its students physics courses, the community may petition the state to award an emergency license to someone who does not meet current licensure standards.

Conditional licenses become commonplace when a shortage of teachers forces states to hire uncertified teachers. Historically, this has even included people who had never completed college. It is an unfortunate fact of life that, even today, when shortages in certain fields or geographic areas arise, substandard teaching licenses are issued.

What is an endorsement?

In some cases, a candidate may be licensed to teach in an additional area through what is termed an **endorsement.** For many teachers, especially those teaching in areas that have a large supply of candidates, endorsements can give you the edge over other applicants. You may want to give some consideration to this option. Carefully planning your courses can help you get a second teaching area. So can practical experience. For instance, a teacher may have a standard or professional license in U.S. history but finds herself teaching biology courses as well. Or perhaps she has taken a number of college courses in biology and decides she wants to be recognized as a biology teacher as well as a history teacher. Since she already has a standard or professional license (in history), she need not apply for a new license. Instead, she applies to the state for an *endorsement* in biology. Although she did not take biology methods or student teach in biology, her teaching experience and background are considered for her endorsement in biology. The endorsement means that the state has approved her teaching both history and biology. Sometimes the subjects are more closely related than these. A teacher licensed in bilingual education, for example, with a number of courses in English as a Second Language (ESL), may seek an endorsement in ESL as well.

If I want to teach in another state, do I need another teacher's license?

Each state issues its own teaching license. If you have a license in one state but want to teach in another, you must reapply for a license there. Although this sounds like a pain, states have created several procedures for making this process less onerous. Let's begin with your teacher education program. If your college or university has a *state-approved* teacher education program, then it has been evaluated and meets state standards. If you are in such a program (check with your college or with your state department of education to find out), then you will receive a state teacher's license when you graduate and be able to teach in that state.

But what if you are graduating from a program in one state, and want to teach in another state? If your teacher education program has also been approved by the **National Association for the Accreditation of Teacher Education (NCATE),** then it has met a set of standards widely accepted by educators and most states. If you graduate from such an NCATE-approved program, you will find that when you apply to most other states, you will receive at least a probationary license to begin teaching. You may be given a year or two while you are teaching to take additional courses or exams, but at least you can receive a teacher's license fairly quickly. So the second question you should ask: Is your teacher education program NCATE approved?

Moving beyond teacher preparation, states themselves have entered agreements in which they recognize each other's teaching licenses. State Departments of Education have such agreements with other states, which some call reciprocity agreements and others call compacts. So, for example, if you have a license in Missouri, then thirty or forty other states might say "show me" your Missouri teacher's license and we will issue you one from our state. Sometimes additional courses or tests may be required, while other times they are not. The **National Association of State Directors of Teacher Education and Certification (NASDTEC)** is working to make such interstate compacts widely accepted.

Interested in teaching in another state? First check to see if your teacher education program is state approved or NCATE approved, and see how your new state recognizes such programs. Once you have a license from one state, you can always check to see if the new state where you want to teach has an agreement whereby it recognizes your teacher license.

What are "alternative routes" to getting a teacher's license?

Few innovations in American education have created more controversy and debate than the alternative teacher certification. What officially began in the early 1980s as a way to ward off projected shortages of teachers has become part of the teacher education landscape. The term "alternative teacher certification" refers to nontraditional avenues for acquiring teacher training and licensure. Alternative programs are designed to attract individuals who have not gone through traditional teacher preparation programs in college. Although these candidates have not earned a teaching degree, they typically hold a bachelor's degree, bring nonteaching experiences to the classroom, and are willing to learn how to teach while they teach (which some believe to be a tricky proposition). These new teachers typically receive some summer training and begin teaching while enrolled in course work needed for their license. In essence, they are teaching as they are learning. One of the best known of these alternative approaches is *Teach for America (TFA),* which recruits motivated applicants who want to make a positive contribution to society by teaching in an under-resourced inner-city or rural school. The altruism of many *TFA* Corps members is reminiscent of Peace Corps volunteers, and their academic backgrounds are typically quite strong.[12] *Troops to Teachers* is another alternative program offering veterans a way to continue to serve their country and their communities as they pursue second careers. Many believe that these programs create a healthy competition with the more traditional approaches, and welcome their emphasis on the practical. In 2005, 47 states, plus the District of Columbia, reported 122 alternative routes to teacher certification, and an estimated 250,000 persons have received training and their teaching license through alternative paths since the mid-1980s. Approximately 35,000 individuals enter teaching this way annually, and this figure is on the rise.[13]

While it is no surprise that older and more life-experienced people enter teaching through this nontraditional route, it is interesting to note that a higher percentage of men and nonwhites are drawn to teaching through these programs. The National Center for Education Information (NCEI) has found that alternative prepared teaching candidates have the following characteristics:

- 70 percent are older than 30 years of age, 38 percent are male and 30 percent are nonwhite.
- 46 percent are teaching in a large city.
- Nearly half were working in a noneducation occupation the year prior to entering an alternative route program.
- "Being able to teach while getting certified" and "receiving a teacher's salary and benefits" were the most important variables in their choosing an alternate route to teaching.
- "Teaching full time as a teacher of record during the program" far outranked any other variable as the most helpful component of the alternate route program in developing competence to teach.
- On average, 97 percent of those entering teaching through alternate routes say they feel competent in several aspects of teaching.
- Nearly half say they would not have become a teacher if the alternate route to certification had not been available. An additional 25 percent said they weren't sure.[14]

Not everyone views alternative routes to teacher preparation as a terrific innovation. For one, the attrition rate for these programs is quite high: Many who volunteer to join also volunteer to leave. With limited preparation, these rookies wade into challenging teaching situations in some of the nation's most troubled and impoverished communities. Some studies of alternative licensure preparation suggest that graduates of alternative programs are more of a "quick fix" for teacher shortages than a permanent solution. Some fear that their not-yet-honed teaching skills are unlikely to be improved because graduates of alternative programs are less committed to staying in teaching or to pursuing graduate studies than are students from traditional teacher education programs. Although alternative preparation programs attract older, more experienced Americans to a teaching career, more than half of those enrolled are fresh out of college. Many teacher educators are concerned that this approach is a step back in time when anyone who wanted to teach was hired. They fear that the alternative preparation of teachers signals a retreat from efforts toward full teacher professionalism. Some also worry about the elementary and secondary students who will be in classrooms with these new and not well-prepared teachers.

Studies of the effectiveness of these programs will undoubtedly continue in the years ahead. For now they offer an interesting comparison to traditional programs, and while growing, still only prepare relatively few teachers.[15]

What are teacher competency tests?

People who want to teach today spend some of their time filling in the bubbles on teacher competency tests now mandated by most states.[16] These tests assess "basic skills" such as reading and mathematics, or pedagogical skills related to teaching practices, or subject matter knowledge. Sometimes the tests measure all three areas. Why are such tests required (and are they a good idea)?

The current teacher testing craze began in 1983, when California imposed a basic reading, writing, and math test called CBEST as a condition for entry to a teacher credential program. Today, most states have followed California's lead and require prospective teachers to pass one or more tests. These tests are administered not only after individuals complete their teacher education programs to see if they are ready to teach, but even before they are admitted to teacher education, to make certain they have minimum academic skills. While most people sail through these exams, not all do. You should realize that such exams are high-stakes gatekeepers used to restrict *entry* to professional training and to a career in teaching. Unlike the Graduate Record Exams and other tests required by many professional and graduate schools, these teacher tests carry the force of law. Results on this single test override all other state requirements in receiving a teacher's license.

Praxis Assessment for Beginning Teachers is a three-part teacher assessment. The *Praxis I: Preprofessional Skills Test* consists of hour-long academic skills tests in reading, writing, and mathematics. These basic tests apply to prospective teachers in all fields and all grades, and are required in most states for admission into teacher education, or to obtain an initial teacher license.[17] *Praxis I* can be taken in the standard paper-and-pencil format on specified dates around the country or by means of a more costly computer version, with far more flexible timing, widespread availability, and immediate scoring.

The *Praxis II* assesses subject area, pedagogy, and professional education knowledge, offering more than 100 exams in subjects ranging from art to social studies. *Praxis III* is a classroom performance assessment of teaching skills, covering classroom management, instructional planning, and assessment of student learning. While *Praxis III* is the most authentic assessment of beginning teachers, it is also the most challenging and costly test to implement, and it has not yet gained the widespread popularity of *Praxis I* and *II*.

Educators differ as to whether the Praxis series or other competency tests are necessary. Those who support competency exams maintain that the exams lend greater credibility and professionalism to the process of becoming a teacher. They claim that such tests identify well-educated applicants who can apply their knowledge in the classroom. They cite examples of teachers who cannot spell, write, or perform basic mathematical computations, and they plead persuasively that students must be protected from such incompetent teachers.

Some critics of the teacher exams argue that they are incredibly easy and not a real measure of competence. Other critics believe that such tests are more a political gesture than a way of improving education.[18] Part of the problem is the lack of evidence supporting the idea that teacher testing predicts teacher performance.[19] Some believe that the current process of state licensure and the period of assessment prior to tenure are sufficient to filter out incompetent teachers. Still others worry that we do not really know what makes good teachers, and we know even less about how to create tests to separate the good from the bad. We don't have tests that can measure enthusiasm, dedication, caring, and sensitivity—qualities that students associate with great teachers. Test makers are constantly working to respond to these charges, and to create more effective tests.

Another provocative and controversial problem is the impact of standardized competency tests on diversity. Historically, when African American teachers were systematically paid less, such tests were used as a vehicle for teachers of color to attain salary equity with whites. More recently, however, test results in states across the nation document the problems African American and Hispanic teacher candidates are having in passing such exams, problems that have been attributed to reasons ranging from test bias to social and educational differences. The continued use of such exams may deter people of color from becoming teachers. And the pipeline of nonwhite teaching candidates, already only a trickle, is in danger of dwindling further.[20] Nevertheless, the courts have ruled that such tests are an acceptable means of screening teacher candidates.[21] And with strong public sentiment favoring such tests, they are likely to be a part of the teacher education landscape for the foreseeable future.

Q
A

How do teaching contracts work?

Congratulations! You have been hired by the school system of your choice, and a contract is placed before you. Before you sign it, there are a few things you should know about teacher contracts. This contract represents a binding agreement between you and the school district. It will be signed by you as the teacher being hired and by an agent of the board of education, often the superintendent. The contract usually sets the conditions of your work, perhaps including specific language detailing your instructional duties, and, of course, your salary.

If you do not have tenure, you will receive a new contract each year. Once you earn tenure, you will be working under a continuing contract and will probably be asked to notify the school district each year as to whether you plan to teach for the district the following year.

Q
A

What are some advantages of tenure?

A teacher was once asked to leave his teaching position in Kentucky because he was leading an "un-Christian" personal life. He was Jewish.

A second-grade teacher was dismissed from her teaching assignment in Utah because of her dress. She wore miniskirts.

In Massachusetts, a teacher was fired because of his physical appearance. He had grown a beard.

Fortunately, these teachers all had one thing in common: **tenure.** And tenure prevented their school districts from following through on dismissal proceedings.

A vast majority of states currently have tenure laws. A newly hired teacher is considered to be in a probationary period. The probationary teaching period can be two, three, or even five years for public school teachers and about six years for college professors. After demonstrating teaching competence for the specific period, the teacher is awarded tenure, which provides a substantial degree of job security. Generally, a tenured teacher can be fired only for gross incompetence, insubordination, or immoral acts or because of budget cuts stemming from declining enrollments. In practice, public schools rarely fire a tenured teacher.

Most of America's public school teachers (58 percent) believe tenure protects teachers from district politics, favoritism, and the threat of losing their jobs to newcomers who would earn less.[22] Without tenure, hundreds, perhaps thousands, of financially pressed school systems could respond to pressure from taxpayers by firing their experienced teachers and replacing them with lower-paid, less experienced teachers. This would significantly reduce school budgets, usually the largest cost item in the local tax structure. After two or three more years, these teachers would also face the financial ax. In short, teachers would once again become an itinerant, poorly paid profession. Would anyone really benefit?

Without tenure, the fear of dismissal would cause thousands of teachers to avoid controversial topics, large and small. Many teachers would simply become a mirror of their communities, fearing to stir intellectual debate or to teach unsettling ideas because job security had become their prime objective. Classrooms would become quiet and mundane places, devoid of the excitement that comes from open discussion of controversial ideas.

Without tenure, many teachers would have to modify their personal lifestyles. In some communities, they would have to avoid places where liquor is served; in others, their clothing or hairstyles would have to be altered. Any behavior that differed from the norms of the community would be potentially dangerous, for such behavior could provide the spark that would trigger public clamor for dismissal. A conformist philosophy would spread from the classroom to teachers' personal lives.

In short, without some protection such as tenure, teaching would take a giant step backward. Tenure provides teachers with the fundamental security that allows them to develop and practice their profession without fear of undue pressure or intimidation. Unfortunately, not all teachers have respected the academic freedom provided by tenure, as we shall see in the next section.

What are some disadvantages of tenure?

Over the years, it has become apparent that the protection of academic freedom through the tenure process has entailed serious drawbacks. One such drawback is the reality that ineffective teachers are protected from dismissal. Many of these ineffective teachers view tenure as a right to job security without acknowledging a corresponding responsibility to continue professional growth. Feeling that they are no longer subject to serious scrutiny, such teachers fail to keep up with new developments in their field, and each year they drag out old lesson plans and fading lecture notes for yet another outdated performance. Who pays the price for such ineffective teaching? The students, of course. Think back a moment. How many ineffective, tenure-protected teachers were you subjected to during your total school experience? How many do you face at present?

In fact, a majority (58 percent) of teachers believe that tenure does not necessarily recognize good teaching and acknowledge that some tenured teachers "fail to do a good job and are simply going through the motions." About a third of teachers believe that it is extremely difficult to fire a tenured teacher. Nevertheless, some communities are taking a tougher look at tenure.[23] Some school districts have extended the amount of time it takes to be awarded tenure. In Florida, a recent law reduced the time that poor-performing teachers are given to improve from one year to ninety days. A special Colorado task force has been formed to explore ways to limit tenure. One reason for these attempts is the cost involved in dismissing a tenured teacher. A New York School Boards Association Study showed that, in that state in the mid-1990s, it took an average of 455 days and $177,000 to dismiss a teacher. If the teacher appealed, the average price rose to $317,000.[24] Removing a tenured teacher was costly back then, and is likely to be even more costly today.

As you can see, tenure is a double-edged sword. It serves the extremely important function of preserving academic freedom and protecting teachers from arbitrary and unjust dismissal. But it also provides job security for ineffective teachers, bad news for the students of these teachers or for the new and more competent teachers trying to enter the profession.

Q
A

Are untenured teachers protected?

Many believe that, until tenure is granted, they are extremely vulnerable, virtually without security. This is not true. During the 1970s, in *Goldberg* v. *Kelly, Board of Regents* v. *Roth,* and *Perry* v. *Sinderman,* the United States Supreme Court outlined several of the rights that are enjoyed by nontenured teachers. In many circumstances, these rights include advance notice of the intention to dismiss a teacher, clearly stated reasons for termination, and a fair and open hearing. In addition, teacher organizations, such as the National Education Association (NEA) and the American Federation of Teachers (AFT), provide legal assistance for teachers who might be subjected to the arbitrary and unjust action of a school system. If the AFT and the NEA ever merge, one result may be even greater legal protection for teachers.

If, during your probationary years, you feel that you have been unfairly victimized by the school administration, you should seek legal advice. Even nontenured teachers possess rights, but these rights are effective only if they are exercised.

Q
A

Can principals be tenured?

Although about a dozen states still grant tenure or equivalent rights to principals, this protection has all but disappeared. Historically, a satisfactory probationary period of one to five years would result in principals earning tenure, as teachers do. Not anymore. Many of the same arguments used against granting teachers tenure (a shield for mediocrity or even incompetence, a lengthy process to remove poor performers, and so on) have been successfully used to rescind tenure for principals. The crux of the argument seems to be how one views principals. Those who see them as managers believe that, if they are not managing well, they should be fired. Others view principals as master teachers (from the term "principal teacher"), who should be afforded the same protections from arbitrary political pressures and inappropriate personnel decisions as other teachers. The management view is clearly winning out.[25]

What kinds of educational careers are available beyond classroom teaching?

The assumption that your education degree has prepared you only for a teaching career is a widespread myth. Actually, there are dozens of education-related careers, although tunnel vision often keeps them from view. (See *Frame of Reference:* Education Want Ads.) Obviously, if you are interested in school administration or a counseling career, starting as a classroom teacher makes a lot of sense and gives you an important perspective that will serve you well in these other school careers. But beyond administration and counseling lie many other options. The following list is intended to give you some idea of the less typical but potentially quite rewarding **nontraditional educational careers** available to you.[26]

Early Childhood Education.   If you want to stay in touch with teaching but prefer a climate other than the typical classroom, you may want to explore such options as day care centers. Early childhood education is a vital component of the nation's educational system. Working parents seek quality options, not only for child care but for child education and development as well.

Although day care rarely offers much pay or status, a number of talented educators find early childhood education incredibly satisfying. If you are creative and flexible, you might even be able to develop your own facility. For example, some department stores advertise a day care service for shopping parents. You might consider opening a similar early childhood program and marketing your "children's center" to other stores, shopping malls, or businesses. (Check out your state's laws regarding operating standards, building restrictions, number of children permitted, and so on.) If you enjoy working with young children, you will find opportunities galore in this growing field.

Adult Education.   If you prefer to work with a mature population, you might be attracted to adult (continuing) education programs. These programs are offered through city and county governments, local school systems, and nearby colleges and universities. In addition, some private businesses now sponsor courses that are related to their products—recreation, crafts, cooking, technical training, and so forth. As the ranks of the retired swell with baby boomers, you can expect this field to grow rapidly. Older Americans often have the time, interest, and income to pursue education in topics, skills, and hobbies that have long eluded them. Elder hostels around the world are responding to the educational demand created by retirees. Researching available programs may take time, but you are apt to discover a variety of adult learning programs that can provide nontraditional teaching opportunities.

Pupil Service Professionals.   Service professionals—school social workers, counselors, and psychologists—typically work as a team, assisting teachers in creating more effective learning environments. These professionals receive special training and education to meet the unique needs that frequently emerge in schools. Social workers, for example, work to improve the relationship between home and school. School psychologists, prepared in education and mental health, are responsible for coordinating and evaluating special learning and behavior problems.

Colleges and Universities.   You will find many nonteaching, yet education-related, jobs in colleges and universities. To name a few, academic advisers work primarily on a one-to-one basis with students, discussing courses of study; admissions

You may find your education niche beyond the traditional classroom. Here are some authentic employment opportunities printed in the "want ads" of newspapers.

CAN YOU TEACH?

The largest computer software and network training company in the world is looking for additional full-time instructors to teach classes. Candidates must possess excellent presentation skills. Computer experience is helpful but not necessary; we will train you.

EDUCATIONAL CONSULTANT

We are seeking an experienced Education Consultant with classroom teaching background for per diem contracted and long-term assignments, with expertise in one or more of the following: dimensions of learning, performance assessments, state learning standards, early literacy, cooperative learning, differentiated instruction.

PRIVATE GIRLS' HIGH SCHOOL

seeks Director of Technology/Computer Teacher, Classroom Experience Necessary.

ELEMENTARY ZOO INSTRUCTOR

The Education Department of the Zoo, one of the country's foremost institutions of informal science teaching, is seeking a dynamic instructor for its elementary-level programs. A highly interactive teaching approach, creativity, and a theatrical background will be helpful. This position involves program development for parents and teachers in addition to direct instruction of children ages 4–12. Excellent oral and written communication skills required.

EDITOR/WRITER

Familiar with higher edu. issues needed for Publications Dept. Will work with campus colleagues and assoc. staff to develop a natl. quarterly newsletter for faculty & administrators. Must know curriculum development, have solid editorial and publications mgmt. skills, research aptitude, & good writing skills.

Major nonprofit YOUTH SERVICE AGENCY seeks to fill the following positions (Bilingual, Spanish/English preferred): YOUTH COUNSELOR: B.A. 2 years experience in social service setting, PROGRAM COORDINATOR: B.A. 3–5 years experience, strong supervisory/communication skills necessary.

EDUCATIONAL RESEARCHER

Research and develop abstracts for www-based project about science and math education. Writing skills, attention to detail, ability to synthesize information quickly, and confident phone skills. Background in education helpful.

EDUCATIONAL COORDINATOR

The Historical Society seeks a creative, self-motivated team player to plan, implement, & promote educational programs for schools, families, & adults. Responsibilities incl.: organizing public programs & tours: coordinating National History Day, providing services for schools.

CHILD CARE DIRECTOR

Join our management team! Nonprofit corporate-sponsored child care management co., looking for a talented director to manage our state-of-the-art center. Must have ECE experience and have been through NAEYC accred. process.

LEARNING CENTERS offering individualized diagnostic and prescriptive programs are looking for dynamic PT cert. teachers to instruct students of all ages in reading, writing, math, and algebra.

SUBSTANCE ABUSE PREVENTION INTERVENTION SPECIALISTS

Seeking experienced professionals to provide services to students in substance abuse prevention and intervention. Will provide both group and individual counseling and conduct peer leadership groups for students at risk at various schools.

AMERICAN INTERNATIONAL SCHOOLS

Seeking excellent candidates. June interview in major cities. Two years of experience reqd.

WORKSITE TEACHER

Conduct worksite visits & act as liaison between worksite & classroom instruction, BA plus 2 yrs. teaching experience with adults req'd.

LOVE TO TEACH?

Are you considering a career change where you can continue to use your teaching ability? Call.

PROGRAM ASSISTANT

New vision in schools seeks a program assistant to provide support to a major school reform initiative. Must be meticulous with details & be able to write well, handle multiple projects, & and meet deadlines. Interest in public schools is preferred.

EDITOR

One of the most progressive and respected names in children's publishing is currently seeking an editor for a supplement on early childhood. In addition to a degree, editorial/publishing experience, and early childhood classroom experience, you must be highly creative and possess a strong knowledge of early childhood issues.

COLLEGE GRAD

Prestigious sports program for children sks highly motivated coaches. Sports background & a love for children a must. Education majors a +.

EDUCATIONAL SALES REPS

See our ad in the SALES section under "Education."

VIOLENCE PREVENTION PROGRAM

(Peace Games) seeks F/T director to create curricula & resources for students, parents, & teachers.

TEACH ENGLISH ABROAD

BA/BS required. Interested in education. No exp nec.

SPECIAL EDUCATION

The Learning Center, a place for emotionally disturbed children, has the following possible positions: Resource Counselor, Cert. Teacher, Music Teacher, Level III Secretary, Therapist Assistant.

REFLECTION: Which of these careers do you find most appealing? Which is least appealing? Have you ever explored nonteaching education careers? Why or why not?

officers respond to the needs of students; alumni relations personnel conduct fund-raising campaigns, organize alumni events, and maintain job placement services; and student services personnel do psychological and vocational counseling, advise international students, and administer residential programs. Most colleges offer their employees tuition benefits, so, if you want to pursue graduate studies, this may be a good way to gain both experience and an advanced degree.

Community Organizations.   Think of a community group. Chances are, that group has an educational mission. Churches, synagogues, and nursing homes can use creative instructors and program planners. For example, a former English teacher, disturbed by the demeaning, artsy-craftsy programs in a local nursing home, inspired the residents to write their life histories, an experience they found very stimulating. Recreation and community centers hire instructors, program planners, and directors for their numerous programs. Hospitals and health clinics need people to plan and deliver training to their professional and administrative staffs. Some of the large municipal zoos conduct programs to protect endangered animal species and to interact with school groups. Libraries and media centers require personnel to maintain and catalog resources and equipment, as well as to train others in their use. Art galleries and museums hire staff to coordinate educational programs for school and civic groups and to conduct tours of their facilities.

The Media.   The publishing and broadcasting industries hire people with education backgrounds to help write and promote their educational products. For example, large newspapers, such as *The Washington Post,* maintain staff writers whose job is to cover education, just as other reporters cover crime, politics, and finance. Some newspapers even publish a special edition of their paper for use in schools. Likewise, textbook publishers, educational journals, the Internet service providers, and television talk shows need people familiar with educational principles to help develop their programs.

Private Industry and Public Utilities.   Large public and private corporations often rely on education graduates in their programs to train their staffs in areas such as organizational effectiveness, new technology training, civil rights and safety laws, and basic company policies and practices. Sometimes client needs come into play, as many of these firms need people with well-developed instructional skills to demonstrate the use of their sophisticated equipment or products to potential customers. Some education-related companies maintain permanent learning centers and seek persons with education backgrounds to plan and run them. If you like writing, you may want to work on pamphlets, brochures, curricula, and other materials describing a company's services and products, often written by education graduates.

Computer Software Development.   With the dramatic increase in the use of educational software in the classroom, many companies are soliciting people with experience in education as consultants to help develop new programs. Creativity, familiarity with child psychology, and knowledge of the principles of learning are important resources for developing software that will appeal to a diverse and competitive market.

Technology.   The blossoming of the computer age, with its software, e-mail, Web sites, and Internet resources, has divided the population into those who are computer literate and those who are computer challenged (sometimes called technophobic). Those who are not yet citizens of cyberworld represent a ready population of potential students. If you enjoy programming, surfing the Net, or designing Web sites, you may want to become a tech-teacher, teaching these skills in either formal or informal settings. You may consider a position as a technology consultant for schools, helping design Web sites, create networks, or select software. You may choose to work outside a school organization, as a company representative providing educational services and equipment.

Educational Associations.   National, state, and regional educational associations hire writers, editors, research specialists, administrators, lobbyists, and educators for a host of education-related jobs, from research and writing to public relations. There are hundreds of these associations, from the NEA to the American Association of Teachers of French. Check the *National Trade and Professional Associations of the United States and Canada* (Columbia Books, Inc.) for listings and descriptions of positions, or use the *Encyclopedia of Associations* (Gale Research) or the Internet to contact the associations directly.

Government Agencies.   A host of local, state, and federal government agencies hire education graduates for training, policy planning, management, research, and so on. Various directories can help you through the maze of the federal bureaucracy. Among these is the *United States Government Manual* (Office of the Federal Register, National Archives and Records Service), which describes the various programs within the federal government, including their purposes and top-level staffs. The Internet is another useful source for exploring career opportunities in government-related education programs.

Global Opportunities.   Want an international experience? Consider Department of Defense schools, private international schools, religious and international organizations, military bases offering high school and college courses to armed forces personnel, and the Peace Corps. A number of foreign companies now hire U.S. college graduates to teach English to their workers, positions that are sometimes very well paid. No matter the wages, high or low, the excitement of teaching in another culture (while learning about that culture) is hard to match.

As we indicated (more than once!), we love classroom teaching, but you should know there are many ways that you can serve society with an education background. You may want to explore one or more of these nonclassroom careers, even as an intern or volunteer at first, to see if these career paths appeal to you.

In this chapter—and in this text—we have tried to answer your questions about teaching. (If we missed one, we invite you to submit it to the Web site using the OLC Ask the Author button.) We hope that you have found this text chock-full of useful and interesting information, and that you have enjoyed reading this book. In fact, we hope that you enjoyed it so much that you choose to keep the book as a useful reference in the future (and do not resell it to the used bookstore!). But more than that, we hope that you are gaining greater clarity on your decision about whether teaching is for you, and whatever that decision turns out to be, we wish you the best of luck!

www.mhhe.com/
sadker8e

INTERACTIVE ACTIVITY

Ask the Author. Ask us any questions you still have for us about teaching!

SUMMARY

1. **What does the education job market look like? (or, put another way, will I be able to find a satisfying teaching position?)**

   Growth in the student population, efforts to reduce class size, and ongoing teacher retirements have increased the demand for teachers, while budget shortfalls have curtailed hiring in some areas. It is predicted that more than two million teachers will be needed in the next decade, and certain areas, such as math, science, and bilingual and special education are experiencing a serious teacher shortage. Urban school districts and the federal government are offering signing bonuses, housing assistance, and loan forgiveness to attract teachers, but rural areas also face a teacher shortage. While students of color constitute nearly 40 percent of the school population, only about 15 percent of new teachers are of color.

2. **Can I make a decent salary as a teacher?**

   Teacher salaries have steadily improved in the last twenty years, although increases have been more modest in the last ten years. Beginning teachers average above $30,000, the average teacher earns nearly $50,000, yet some school districts pay considerably more.

3. **How can new teachers increase their chances of working in a school of their choice?**

   A strong résumé provides prospective employers with critical information. A portfolio goes beyond a résumé by providing actual artifacts of a candidate's qualifications. Some portfolios, called e-portfolios, can be constructed and transferred electronically. Exploring a teaching position takes careful planning, as do interviews. Teaching candidates need to learn about the schools and faculties they are considering joining, and give careful consideration to questions such as: Do other teachers enjoy working in this school? Are benefits satisfactory? What are the children like? What kind of support do teachers receive? Does the community support its school system?

4. **What do I need in order to teach—a license or certification? (and how do I get one!)**

   Teacher certification indicates that a professional group recognizes or certifies that a teacher is competent and has met certain standards. A teacher's license, issued by the state government, grants the legal right to teach. Teacher certification is a professional designation; a teacher's license is a legal document. Requirements for teacher licensure differ from state to state. A teacher's license in one state may not be valid in another, unless the states have entered into a compact or reciprocity agreement. Accreditation of college-level teacher education programs can facilitate new graduates becoming eligible for multistate teacher licenses.

   States issue various types of teaching licenses, from initial or probationary to special licenses for administration and counseling. Endorsements enable experienced teachers to gain additional licensure in a second subject area.

5. **What teacher competency tests do I need to take?**

   Teacher competency tests are used for admission into teacher education programs, for certification, and for licensure. Teacher competency tests are required in most states. (See Appendix 1 for more specific details.) *Praxis I* focuses on basic literacy, *Praxis II* on pedagogy and subject area competence, and the less used *Praxis III* on classroom performance. Many states have designed their own competency tests, which they require prospective teachers to take before being licensed. The purpose, use, and appropriateness of teacher tests is intensely debated by educators and politicians. Despite these controversies, there is strong support from the public and from politicians for testing teachers and their students.

**www.mhhe.com/
sadker8e**

CHAPTER REVIEW

Go to the Online Learning Center to take a quiz, practice with key terms, and review concepts from the chapter.

6. **Why do teachers seek tenure? (and should I?)**

   After demonstrating teaching competence for the specified period (usually 2–5 years), a teacher may be awarded tenure, which provides a substantial degree of job security. While tenure preserves academic freedom and protects teachers from arbitrary and unjust dismissal, it can also provide job security for ineffective teachers.

7. **Are there jobs in education outside of the classroom?**

   An education degree prepares you not only for a teaching career, but for many education-related careers as well, in areas such as early childhood education, adult education, counseling and advising, and distance learning, and in organizations such as nonprofits, educational associations, private corporations, government agencies, and the media.

KEY TERMS AND PEOPLE

conditional (emergency) license, 506

e-portfolio, 502

endorsement, 506

initial (provisional) license, 505

National Association of State Directors of Teacher Education and Certification (NASDTEC), 507

National Council for the Accreditation of Teacher Education (NCATE), 507

nontraditional educational careers, 513

portfolio, 502

Praxis Assessment for Beginning Teachers, 509

résumé, 501

special license, 506

standard (professional) license, 506

teacher certification, 504

teacher's license, 504

tenure, 510

The Courage to Teach: A Final Word

In this text, we have tried mightily to include relevant information, witty insights, useful studies, and engaging chapters about education law, history, and other topics to offer you a balanced and objective view of teaching. In short, we wanted you to understand the fundamentals of teaching and schooling in the United States. We also constructed several features to encourage reflection and help you decide if teaching is the right career for you. But objective information, balanced debates, and even personal examples have their limits. Now we suggest that you explore something even more critical than objective insights: subjective feelings.

In this brief, last section we are doing what textbook authors rarely do: asking you to take a moment and listen to your heart. For in the end, all the chapters and all the objective information are far less important than the answer to one question, a question only you can answer: is teaching right for you? For some, teaching will be the perfect life work; for others, it will not. Either answer is correct; the trick is knowing which answer applies to you. Take a moment to listen to your heart, to hear that inner voice, to *feel* what it is like to be a teacher.

We borrowed the title of this last section, *The Courage to Teach,* from a wonderful book by Parker Palmer.[1] Why does Palmer link teaching and courage? Palmer believes that good teaching is far more than mastering a subject, far more than strategies and techniques, and certainly more than raising student test scores. Palmer believes that powerful teachers must first make an inner journey to discover who they are as people, to be open and honest with themselves and with their students. This means looking beyond the safe conventions of curriculum and schools, and looking deeply into your beliefs and values, and taking some risks.

Teaching takes courage because good teachers remove the protective barriers defined by the roles that separate teacher and student. Good teachers teach from the heart in a society consumed by hierarchies and materialism. We all know of the power and influence our culture gives to a person's wealth, status, and material acquisitions. Most of us have been taught to compete and to acquire more material wealth, although few of us ever acquire enough things to be satisfied. And without this inner satisfaction, we can never feel fulfilled. Author and teacher Marianne Williamson explains it this way: "Meaning does not lie in things. Meaning lies in us."[2]

Learning itself has been shaped (some would argue misshaped) by our society's materialistic value system. Math and the hard sciences are prized more than social sciences and the arts, computer technology and personal electronics are considered a mark of modern excellence, and student test scores are equated with their education. We prepare teachers to work with testing and technology, but we do not help teachers learn how, as Parker Palmer puts it, "to engage students' souls." In our contemporary culture, engaging souls is seen as little more than romantic fantasy, but it is precisely this invisible engagement that is the heart of teaching and learning. Parker pleads for more teachers to honor this hidden world of the heart. In our materialistic world, honoring the heart takes courage.

Never underestimate the power of this unseen personal energy. Vaclav Havel, the first President of the Czech Republic, spent years in prison as a "guest" of the Soviet occupation of his country. Even though he was physically restrained, he never abandoned his belief in the inherent power of the individual. Havel's faith in freedom not only sustained him during his long ordeal, but eventually contributed to the downfall of a powerful, oppressive Soviet regime. Havel reminded the Czech people that they were not victims of the physical might of an occupying nation unless they agreed to the victim role; they possessed an inner power that could not be taken from them. As he described it, "the salvation of this human world lies nowhere else than in the human heart."[3] Havel's inner strength proved decisive: the Soviet's were forced to leave Czechoslovakia in what was called, "The Velvet Revolution." The unseen power of the individual in the physical world has been demonstrated by Gandhi in India, Nelson Mandela in South Africa, Aung San Sui Kyi in Burma, and the Reverend Martin Luther King Jr. right here in the United States. They have all taught us this same lesson: the power that each of us possesses. Yet we always seem to need constant reminding. As one insightful individual pointed out: "Our deepest fear is not that we are inadequate. Our deepest fear is that we are powerful beyond measure. It is our light, not our darkness that most frightens us."[4]

So the purpose of this last, brief section is simple enough: to remind us to listen to that powerful voice within, for that is where an authentic call to a profession originates. Such a call invites you to honor your true nature. A person's true vocation is "the place where your deep gladness and the world's deep hunger meet."[5] If teaching is the place of that meeting, you are fortunate indeed.

Beginning Teacher Diary

One of our students, Maria Moser, has taught for two years in a challenging inner-city middle school, recording her experiences and her thoughts in her diary. She has shared her diary with us, and has allowed us to share it with you. As you read through some of her entries, consider not only the challenges she faced, but how she translated these challenges into positive learning for herself and others. In Maria's diary you learn not only about teaching, but how her "deep gladness and the world's deep hunger meet" in her classroom.

AUGUST 28, 2004

Not since the threat of leaving behind my mother and my favorite stuffed animal for the jungle of kindergarten has the prospect of starting a new school year terrified me so. I think of keywords from the training I received over the summer: significant gains, demanding excellence, teaching responsibility. As I steel myself for the 13-year-olds behind my classroom door, I remind myself of the things I think I know about education. It is the key to success. It is not distributed equally in this country. Students in inner-city schools are likely to be 2–3 grade levels behind their suburban peers. This is why I am teaching. Lesson 1: Know why you're doing it. Try not to forget.

SEPTEMBER 3, 2004

Today, for the first time, a student asked me a question that I definitively knew the answer to. In that glorious moment, I became *An Educator*. The bright-eyed, smiling child asked me what time school started the next day. With authority in my voice and confidence in my heart, I stated, "tomorrow is Saturday." Lesson 2: Be grateful for the times when you know the right answer.

MARCH 7, 2005

Today I spoke to one of my friends about the challenges that my school faces, from serious material shortages to violence in the surrounding community. I attempted to illustrate the inequities in our educational system by comparing DCPS (District of Columbia Public Schools) to the suburban schools that he and I attended. He asked a question that I found quite insightful: "Is making inner-city schools more like suburban schools our goal?"

After a good deal of reflection, I decide that the answer is no. The failure of our inner-city schools cannot be taken as an independent phenomenon from the oppressive homogeny of the suburbs. Our students' inability to envision a successful future goes hand in hand with the inability of suburban students to imagine the realities of poverty, racism, and classism. A true revolution in education requires all of our schools to be equally invested in opportunities for all. Lesson #3: Know what your objective is.

APRIL 4, 2005

Today I spent an hour walking one of my students through the process of calling Planned Parenthood. She is a 15-year-old 8th grader with two children. I am confused and conflicted, but I listen to her and give her the help she asks for. I think of what I know about poverty: It is crushing. It is hard to escape from. Sometimes, all of your choices are bad. I think of what I know about education: if we do not let our children know that we are there for the things that are scary, for the things that are hard, for the things that confuse us too, then our advice, our lessons, and our efforts will not be received. Lesson #4: Sometimes, being an educator requires being a mentor and a leader. Other times, it requires being a shoulder to cry on.

SEPTEMBER 21, 2005

After spending my summer reading *The Art of Teaching Reading,* I decided to implement a Readers Workshop in my ESL English classes. It is successful beyond my wildest hopes. I watch students argue over who gets to have a new Walter Dean Myers book first. I hear them discuss the pros and cons of reading nonfiction. I begin each lesson with the phrase "good readers . . ." and I remind them that this is our job and our work. We are a community of readers, sharing advice, helping one another.

The most amazing thing about my students is their ability to accept differences. My reading workshop has 35 students, from newcomers who speak no English and cannot read in Spanish, to students born in the United States who can read chapter books in English. Yet they sit alongside one another, and support each others' efforts. As I watch a Jamaican girl and a Salvadoran student read *The Little Prince* in respective English and Spanish, I think of what I know about classrooms: everyone, children and adults alike, wants to be a contributing member of a community. Lesson #5: If you are truly successful in building a classroom community, students can learn more from each other than they ever could from only you.

JANUARY 8, 2006

My students are being attacked in the cafeteria nearly every day. There is tremendous racial tension at our school between African American and Latino students, and our principal refuses to acknowledge it. Instead, when ESL children are missing from school, I am told that I am making my students afraid. I recall a Teach for America class on working within the boundaries of your school community. "Remember to ask yourself," they advised us, "if this is the hill that you're willing to die on." When Juan returns crying from lunch for the second day in a row, I have found my hill. I do battle with the administration and with other teachers, making a few enemies, but ultimately reclaiming the cafeteria for the terrified newcomers. A student's mother calls me in tears to thank me. This is why I teach. Lesson #6: Never forget Maslow's hierarchy of needs, and remember that teachers must care for the whole person that they are working with.

MARCH 28, 2006

Today, I take the bus to Columbia Heights with a student after school. We are looking into daycare for her baby, to be born in July. We talk to the admissions counselors at B_____ M_____ School [a multicultural school that focuses on the needs of these students] and my eyes well up as I realize that in this place, she will have a chance to succeed. It is so important to know that there are other people in the same struggle that we are, to know that we can pass these children safely into the hands of others who will treasure them in the same way that we have. Lesson #7: Find allies and value them, and remember that none of us can do this work alone.

APRIL 5, 2006

Today we kept our students in lockdown after two high school kids were shot in front of our building. I teach all day, spending hours with the students. I am proud of myself for keeping it together amidst the chaos that is happening. Then, when I get home, as soon as I speak to my mother on the phone, I break down in tears. I can hardly breathe, I am crying so hard. I try to articulate what I am feeling. "You just . . . love them . . . and want them to be safe, and then you realize, you can't protect them." I care about them so much that it hurts. This is why I teach. Lesson #8: Loving and caring about people is difficult, important work.

APRIL 7, 2006

At parent-teacher conferences today, one of my students comes up with his mother and tells me that I am the best teacher he has had. The truth is, he is one of the best students I have had, learning disabled but with a drive to work that has brought him to the top of my class. He asks if I will return to our school next year, and I dodge the question, knowing that the answer is no. I am moving to Chicago and I will teach there. When he realizes there is a chance that I am changing schools, he asks me to come work at the high school he plans to attend. "I'm serious, Ms. Moser," he mumbles, "you showed me how to do so much stuff." This is why I teach. Lesson #9: It's all about the kids.

APRIL 30, 2006

I am reflecting on so many experiences, trying to summarize what I have learned, and felt, and done, and I realize that there is not enough room to express all the ways that I have grown and changed in the last two years. I think of a day last year when the power went out. An emotionally disturbed child in my room began to attack another student with a pencil, and no security would come from the school. When the power finally returned, an hour later, and the students were able to move to their next classes, I put my head down on my desk in exhaustion. My students surrounded me and began a barrage of, "Who did this? Why are you so upset? Do I need to go whup somebody's @#$%? I ain't about to let somebody talk to my teacher like that." I put my head up and smiled at the sudden show of support from these fierce pre-teens. This is why I teach. Lesson #10: You will get back more than you give, no matter how much you give.

We hope that Maria's diary speaks to you, but more than that, we hope that whatever path you choose, you too find yourself both giving and receiving loving energy.

Part IV: Your Classroom

4:1 Teaching Is Learning

INTASC PRINCIPLE 1
Knowledge of
Subject Matter

Purpose: Teachers know a secret: If you really want to learn a subject, teach it. Planning to teach, reviewing key points, and considering unexpected student questions while you are teaching all help you to learn a subject in far greater depth than simply reading about it. The purpose of this activity is to help you master a subject area just this way, by teaching it, initially as a tutor.

Activity: This activity can be used with students of all ages and requires that you work in a tutoring setting. Your teacher education program might offer you the opportunity to tutor or assist in local schools. If not, you will need to find a situation where you can volunteer to tutor. You may find it useful to audiotape or videotape your sessions for at least fifteen minutes each time. (You may need to get permission from the student or parent as well as the school before taping.)

The feedback teachers give students also provides useful insights into the subject matter mastery. Chapter 11 covers four feedback reactions to student answers: praise, acceptance, remediation, and criticism. Using these four types of feedback effectively is a challenge. Think about it. If a teacher is using only or predominantly acceptance reactions, that suggests that the topic is challenging, or that everyone is sharing ideas and not being evaluated, or maybe that the teacher is not listening. If remediation predominates, that means the teacher is working hard to correct errors and improve understanding. Teachers who use praise, criticism and remediation typically are involved in more precise and active instruction than teachers who use a great deal of acceptance. In this tutoring session, we ask you to monitor and interpret your feedback.

Artifact: Use the chart below to record your teacher feedback from the audiotape or videotape, or from a colleague who can observe your class. You may find it helpful to review the criteria for each type of feedback. Work with a partner if you are unsure about particular comments.

Feedback (Sample Entries)	Number of Responses
Praise: *Good job!*	II
Acceptance: *Okay.*	III
Remediation: *Now read all the word parts together.*	I
Criticism: *No, that's not the way to pronounce it.*	I

www.mhhe.com/
sadker8e

FORM:
Teacher Feedback

Reflection: As you prepared to tutor, what did you learn about your own knowledge of your subject? Did preparing to teach serve as a review, or did you need to relearn much of this material? Did teaching offer you greater insights into your subject?

What did you notice about the type and frequency of your feedback? How did your use of feedback compare to the typical teacher who uses acceptance more than half the time? If you used acceptance, what form did your acceptance comments take (okay, aha, silence)? Did your use of praise represent the attributes identified in Chapter 11? Was criticism clear and appropriate? Was remediation specific enough to allow the student to improve? (By the way, did you use ample wait time?) How would you assess your use of these feedback skills? What activity can you devise to help you practice and improve your feedback?

What inferences can you make about your knowledge of the subject—and your student's knowledge of the subject—from the types and frequency of feedback? Can you see a connection between using praise, remediation, and criticism and subject matter mastery? Describe that connection? (Include this chart and reflection in your portfolio.)

4.2 Understanding the Developmental and Psychosocial Stages of Students You Wish to Teach

INTASC PRINCIPLE 2
Human Development and Learning

Purpose: Who is the average 5-year-old? 10-year-old? 15-year-old? What can they do academically? How do they behave in class? What can a teacher do to help them grow and succeed? One of the traditional ways we organize schools, by age, requires teachers to understand the progressive patterns of children's growth. An understanding of student developmental patterns will help you to develop objective, plan activities, and assess classroom behaviors. Do you know the typical psychosocial issues of the students you plan to teach?

Activity: According to psychologist Erik H. Erikson, each individual passes through eight developmental stages during a lifetime. He calls them "psychosocial stages." Your task will be to observe evidence of these stages in the students you wish to instruct. First, gain an understanding of Erikson's work. A psychosocial or developmental psychology text is a good source of information about your students' development patterns. The Web is another great source. Type into a search engine "psychosocial" and "Erik H. Erikson."

Next, arrange to observe students in one of the following ranges Erikson identified:

- Stage 3: Early Childhood (ages 2–6)
- Stage 4: Elementary and Middle School Years (ages 6–12)
- Stage 5: Adolescence (ages 12–18)

Finally, use the chart below to document the traits and characteristics Erikson identified. Here is an example of how your chart might look:

Example

Artifact: "Developmental and Psychosocial Stages"
Stage: 2—Early Childhood (ages 2–6)

Description: Children have newfound power at this stage as they develop motor skills and social interest with people around them. They now must learn to achieve a balance between eagerness for more adventure and more responsibility, and learning to control impulses and childish fantasies.

Evidence Observed: I observed a kindergarten class and the students would listen to the teacher's every word, but then a moment later, they would be talking to the person next to them. The students seemed keen to handle scissors and other tools of the classroom. Some of the students would hold hands with friends whenever they would venture around the room. The kids were generally very polite to each other, though one child shed tears because of a disagreement with another student.

Developmental and Psychosocial Stages

Stage:

Characteristics of this Stage:

Evidence Observed:

Reflection: What did you learn from this activity? Any surprises? Has this activity influenced your decision about teaching at a particular grade level? What more would you like to learn about the students? How can "average" or "typical" get in the way of your teaching?

4:3 Observing Different Teaching Strategies

INTASC PRINCIPLE 3
Diversity in
Learning

Purpose: Teachers report that observing other teachers is one of the most useful activities for improving their own teaching. Reading about different teaching styles and strategies is informative, but seeing these styles in action brings these ideas to life. The purpose of this activity is to encourage you to observe what you have read: different teaching strategies at work in real classrooms.

Activity: The first (and perhaps toughest) challenge in this activity is to find classrooms that reflect a variety of teaching styles. Plan on observing teachers at the grade level or in the subject area of your choice. If you want to teach lower elementary grades, visit some local elementary schools, meet with the principal at each school, and share with them your interest in observing some diverse teaching styles. Hopefully, the principal will have some recommendations and help you schedule some observations. Same is true at the secondary school. If you want to teach English, ask the principal or department head if you can visit some English instructors who use different teaching styles. This will probably work for you, but if you strike out, you can always ask friends, teachers, or other students to recommend teachers they know who use diverse styles and make your own arrangement to observe. Your own campus may also provide some interesting teaching variety.

Once you have your list of teachers to visit, you can begin your observations and record your impressions on the observations form below. (If you want to learn more about observation techniques, visit the Classroom Observations section on the Online Learning Center.)

Artifact: Spend the first few minutes getting a feel for the classroom. When you are ready, begin to fill out the form below which is intended to help you organize your reactions. Write down the teaching style (cooperative learning, mastery learning, direct teaching—or you may want to create your own title to capture the essence of this style). Then record specific examples of this strategy to make the approach and the activities clear. Once the examples are clear, make your own assessment. Feel free to write down what you see as the assets and liabilities of this strategy, as well as whether this strategy appeals to you. Try to enrich your insights by speaking with the teacher or with some students about the teaching style after class. Finally, consider what student learning styles are best matched with this teaching strategy. Record your reactions on the form below.

www.mhhe.com/
sadker8e

FORM:
Teaching Strategies
Observation Form

Teaching Strategies Observation Form
Teaching Style: _____
Class: _____
Examples:
Assets:
Downside:
What appealed to you?
What student learning style does this build on?

Reflection: Visiting and observing other teachers can provide rich insights into teaching methods and strategies. What insights did you take away from your observations? Did any of the observations surprise you? Which strategies did you find appealing? Will you try some of these styles and strategies in your own classroom? Which styles did not appeal to you? What do your preferences tell you about your own approach to teaching and learning?

4:4 Memories of a Teacher

Purpose: Many of us choose education because of a special teacher—someone who may have inspired us to bring a special "style" to the field. This individual was probably good because he or she modeled the best of effective instruction. You may not have been consciously aware of these skills and traits when you were a student, but you knew the class was interesting, challenging, productive, and maybe even arduous. Perhaps you had friends in the class and you accomplished projects in meaningful ways. Possibly you were the star, the standout who could grasp the material and help others understand. You may have been the kid who didn't connect with others, but this teacher made your year better. Whatever the story, we suspect you have one (and hope you have many). Connecting your memories with the research on effective teaching should help you be a more purposeful, and successful, educator.

INTASC PRINCIPLE 4
Variety of
Instructional
Strategies

Activity: Consider one terrific educator from your past. First, brainstorm memories from that class. On the left side of a piece of paper, list each item. See what you can generate at this point without reading farther (it's tempting to peek but worth the effort to wait).

After your first and open response, use the following cues to generate even more memories. Think about the way lessons began, about the subject matter, and about the use of resources or even gimmicks.

- How was the room arranged?
- Where did the teacher "hang out"?
- Do you recall big field trips or perhaps small adventures?
- How were you engaged in academic learning?
- What management techniques or rules do you remember?
- Were transitions from one activity to another handled smoothly?
- What about questioning opportunities and teacher feedback? Did you raise your hand and were you called on? Were others?
- Can you recall anything about tests (their kind, frequency, and resultant anxiety level)?
- Were term papers, major projects, special event days, or assemblies part of the curriculum?
- What else made this teacher the one who made a difference for you?

Artifact: You may want to entitle your description "My Student Memories of a Special Teacher," or some related title. You will never be closer to these memories than right now. The longer you teach, the further from these memories you will find yourself. These memories can become a touchstone, a place to return and read and reflect on what mattered to you when you sat on the other side of the desk.

Extra Artifact: If you are still in contact with this terrific teacher, you might want to write a letter explaining the assignment and why you chose him or her as a subject. Teachers don't receive enough of this sort of recognition for their time and talent. Receiving such a letter will probably be quite meaningful. Someday you may find yourself on the receiving end of such a letter, or perhaps teaching just down the hall from that special teacher you remembered.

Reflection: Now, read your terrific teacher memories and meander back through Chapter 11, "Teacher Effectiveness." Consider each point you describe. What connections can you make between the research on instructional quality and your memorable teacher? What insights about effective instruction did you acquire? This reflection should be included with your artifact.

4:5 Rules, Rituals, and Routines

INTASC PRINCIPLE 5
Motivation and Management

Purpose: Most teachers struggle to balance motivating students with managing them. Sometimes, in an attempt to keep it "all together and in control" teachers overregulate a class. At other times, they wait too long to rein in exuberant students. Consider behavior techniques along with your study of school, because as a prospective teacher, it is never too early to begin sorting out how you will manage your classroom.

Activity: Arrange to visit a few classrooms of the age of children you want to teach. Use the chart below to record your observations. You may find it helpful to review the section on classroom management and the findings of classroom management expert Jacob Kounin prior to your observations.

Artifact:

Management/Motivation Observation
Examples
Group alerting
Withitness
Overlapping
Least intervention
Flip-flops
Overdwelling
Fragmentation
Thrusts
Dangles

www.mhhe.com/
sadker8e

FORM:

Management/
Motivation
Observation

Reflection: Were you able to find evidence/examples of all the categories on the chart? What successful management and motivation strategies and techniques did you see? How might you employ what you learned from this teacher in your own classroom? What, if any, evidence of the hidden or implicit curriculum did you witness? If you observed a teacher struggling with management and motivation, what lessons did you take from this experience? What do you believe is the most difficult aspect of motivation? What do you believe is the most difficult aspect of management? Attach your artifact to your reflection and include in your portfolio.

4:6 Class Comedy Club

Purpose: For all the crises in classrooms and children at risk, humor in the educational workplace survives and even thrives. Thank goodness! Healthful humor (as opposed to targeted humor and sarcasm) can motivate students to participate and learn. Student humor, often unintentional, can be a major factor in keeping you happy and in the business of teaching. While you may never aspire to be a comic, sharing a funny teaching story with your students will help you practice setting a positive and welcoming learning climate.

INTASC PRINCIPLE 6
Communications
Skills

Activity: While there are books about kids who say and do the darnedest things, as well as e-mail and magazine features filled with funny stories, there is nothing like oral history and the stories of your peers to tickle a funny bone. Begin by freewriting answers to the following questions:

- The funniest teacher I recall from school . . .
- The funniest student happening was . . .
- It sure was funny in school when . . . and she/he/they really did (or didn't) get in trouble . . .
- A teacher walks into a staff lounge . . .
- How many teachers does it take to . . .

www.mhhe.com/
sadker8e

FORM:

Class Comedy Club

Practice and dramatically deliver your funny stories. Encourage your peers to help you embroider them with colorful commentary, body language, and well-timed punch-lines. Hone your presentation until you have a tight 5- to 10-minute routine.

Artifact: Videotape or record your "Teaching and Humor" in a comfortable environment. If you feel emboldened, present your education comedy sketch to your classmates.

Reflection: How hard was this activity for you? Can you picture yourself using your "material" in the classroom? What did you learn about yourself from this activity? Be sure to save both your notes and taping for use in your first classroom. Include your taping and reflection in your portfolio.

4:7 Technology in the Classroom: Bane or Boom?

INTASC PRINCIPLE 7
Instructional
Planning Skills

Purpose: Technology can be a wonderful teaching tool, or a disappointing distraction. Much of technology's effectiveness relies on your instructional planning. This exercise will help you incorporate the assets that technology offers as well as avoid the pitfalls.

Activity: Consider what you have read about and explored in educational technology and generate a balance sheet that both supports and refutes the place of technology in education. (For a model, consider any of the *You Be the Judge* features throughout the textbook that take contrasting views on timely educational topics.) Select a very specific theme, especially one that is related to your subject area or grade level. Generate a title that polarizes opinions such as the following suggestions:

- Word Processing—Helping or Hurting Writing Skills
- Computers in Kindergarten—Absolutely Not or For Sure
- Our Technology Dollars—Classes for the Arts or for Computers
- Computers—One per Classroom or One per Child
- The Internet—Amazing Research Tool or Ticket to Plagiarism

For a more challenging activity, cite research studies to support both positions.

Artifact: "You be the Judge: Technology." Develop and present "You Be the Judge: Technology" through a PowerPoint presentation.

Reflection: Did your views on technology change as you developed positions on each side of the debate? What did you learn about how you will plan for technology in your teaching? What types of technology are you likely to use in your teaching, and which ones will you avoid? Why?

4:8 Pruning Your Portfolio

INTASC PRINCIPLE 8
Assessment

Purpose: Earlier *RAP* activities, reflections, and artifacts helped you create a *working* portfolio. Now is the time to assess your portfolio and decide what is worth keeping or upgrading.

Activity: Evaluate your *working* portfolio. Use the following portfolio assessment rubric below to chart the status of your collection. Score your portfolio according to how well it meets the criteria listed, on a scale of 1 to 5. Provide verbal or written evidence to support your position. Select a partner (or two) and set aside ten minutes to discuss and share your *working* portfolios and the assessment charts.

Artifact:

Portfolio Assessment					
Not at All **1**	**2**	**3**	**4**	**Very** **5**	**Not Applicable**

Item

Purposeful:

Selective:

Diverse:

Ongoing:

Reflective:

Collaborative:

Other: _____

Overall Appraisal:

Reflection: What have you learned about your portfolio, including both its strengths and weaknesses, from this exercise? What did your discussion with your partners teach you? How could your portfolio be improved? How do you see this portfolio helping you become an effective instructor? How do you see this portfolio helping you attain employment? Attach this reflection to the artifact and include in your portfolio.

www.mhhe.com/
sadker8e

FORM:
Portfolio Assessment

4:9 Web Site of the Month

Purpose: Web sites and Internet sources may prove to be of extraordinary benefit to your professional growth. However, quality control does not exist on the Internet, so, to be a reflective and responsible practitioner, you must learn to evaluate Internet sources. Plus you will find it extremely helpful to compile a bank of useful educational Web sites that you can draw on at any time.

INTASC PRINCIPLE 9
Reflection and
Responsibility

Activity: Select three educational Web sites. (Links from the Online Learning Center are certainly a good starting place.) Choose one that is relevant to a subject matter area; another that is interactive, featuring bulletin boards or opportunities to chat with colleagues; and a third that is monitored or sponsored by a professional organization such as the NEA or AFT. Use the rubric below to evaluate each of these sites.

Artifact: "Assessing the Internet"

	Need to Improve			Did This Well	
	1	2	3	4	5
Frequency of Updates					
Ease of Navigation					
Accuracy					
Clarity of Content					
Value of Content					
_____ (Your criterion)					
_____ (Your criterion)					
Overall Appraisal:					

Reflection: What other criteria can you use to decide which Web sites and Internet resources are reliable? Are there techniques and shortcuts to *surfing* educational sites? What Web addresses might offer lesson plans, emotional support for new teachers, factual materials for curriculum planning, and colleagues for an issue-based dialogue? Attach your reflection to the artifact and include in your portfolio.

4:10 Showtime: Go on an Information Interview

Purpose: Interviewing for employment can be a daunting experience. As with all new and difficult endeavors, the more experience you gain the easier the task becomes. You will find it easier to begin the interviewing process by participating in a series of information interviews. This type of interview is pretty low stress and revolves around the interviewee simply learning about the employer, job, and the employer's needs without the pressure to "land" a job.

Activity: Armed with what you have learned in this class and other education courses and experiences, set up at least one information interview with an official from a school or grade level that you could envision yourself teaching at. Use the questions below as a guide for the interview. What other questions might you add? Record both the questions and answers for future interviews.

Artifact: "Information Interview"

www.mhhe.com/
sadker8e

FORM:
Information Interview

1. What is the school district looking for in a teacher-candidate?
2. Are there any special training or experience beyond state certification that the district looks for or requires?
3. In what subject areas and at what grade levels does the district have the greatest need?
4. What should a teacher-candidate know about the students and families in this district?
5. How are teachers evaluated in this district?
6. What emphasis does this district place on standardized tests?
7. What is the average class in this district?
8. Does the district have a mentor program for new teachers, and if so how does it work?
9. What is the process for applying to this district?
10. Are there any additional suggestions for gaining employment in this district?

Reflection: How did the interview go? Were you nervous? What did you learn? What might you do differently next time? Did anything surprise you? Would you want to work in this district? Do you now feel more comfortable about future interviews? Attach your reflection to your artifact and include in your portfolio.

APPENDICES

Text Appendices

1. Teacher Competency Exams and Praxis™ Sample Test Questions
2. State Offices for Teacher Certification and Licensure

Online Appendices

www.mhhe.com/sadker8e

Online Appendix A: Curricular Tension Points and Trends
Online Appendix B: Classroom Observation Guidelines
Online Appendix C: Software by Subject Area
Online Appendix D: Summary of Selected Reports on Education Reform
Online Appendix E: State Offices of Teacher Certification and Licensure

A

Teacher Competency Exams and Praxis™ Sample Test Questions

National Evaluation Systems, Inc. (NES), and Educational Testing Service (ETS)—developers of Praxis™—are two of the largest companies to provide tests and other services for states to use as part of their teacher licensure process. Some colleges and universities use these assessments to qualify individuals for entry into teacher education programs. And since some states choose to develop their own teacher competency exams, be sure to check with your specific teacher education program or state department of education for information on your particular testing requirements.

National Evaluation Systems

While the Praxis™ assessments from ETS have received a great deal of attention, assessing more than half a million aspiring teachers, National Evaluation Systems, Inc., assesses almost as many prospective teachers, but is less well known. The reason is that NES customizes its exams for individual states. Some states use both NES and Praxis™ exams to assess their teachers. Specific information about NES-created tests is available directly from teacher licensure departments in:

California

Colorado

Illinois

Massachusetts

Michigan

New York

Oklahoma

Texas

Praxis™

The Praxis Series™ is the choice of most states that include common tests as part of their teacher licensure process. You will take The Praxis Series™ if you want to teach public school in one of these states or if you want to enter a teacher education program at a college or university that uses Praxis I™: Academic Skills

Assessments. Different states and institutions require different tests in The Praxis Series™, so be sure you know which tests you need before you register.

The three categories of assessments in The Praxis Series™ correspond to the three milestones in teacher development.

Praxis I:™ Academic Skills Assessment. These assessments are designed to be taken early in the student's college career to measure reading, writing, and mathematics skills vital to all teacher candidates. The assessments are available in two formats, paper-based and computer-based. Both measure similar academic skills, but the computer-based tests (CBTs) are tailored to each candidate's performance. CBTs also offer a wider range of question types, provide an immediate score in reading and math, and are available on demand throughout the year by appointment, eliminating the need to register in advance. The paper-based tests, called the PPST or Pre-Professional Skills Tests, are given approximately six to seven times a year.

Praxis II:™ Principles of Learning and Teaching and Subject Assessments. The Principles of Learning and Teaching exam assesses aspiring teachers' pedagogy-related knowledge and skills. The subject assessments measure candidates' knowledge of the content areas they will teach, as well as how much they know about teaching that subject. More than 120 content tests are available. These performance-based items allow test-takers to demonstrate in-depth knowledge and reinforce the importance of writing in the teaching profession.

Praxis III:™ Classroom Performance Assessments. These assessments are used at the beginning teaching level to evaluate all aspects of a beginning teacher's classroom performance. Designed to assist in making licensure decisions, these comprehensive assessments are conducted in the classroom by trained local assessors who use a set of consistent, reliable, nationally validated criteria.

If you are planning to take one or more of these tests, you need a copy of *The Praxis Series:™ Professional Assessments for Beginning Teachers, Registration Bulletin.* The bulletin is free and provides complete test information plus test registration instructions. It's available online at www.ets.org/praxis. *Tests at a Glance* and *Praxis*™ *Study Guides* are other Praxis™ "must have" resources. These booklets include detailed descriptions of topics covered, test-taking strategies, sample tests, and scoring guides, and are also available online at www.ets.org/praxis or by calling 1–800–772–9476.

The states and territories listed next use The Praxis Series™ tests as part of their teacher licensure process. You should check with each state to find out which tests are required, what passing scores are, and other information.

Alabama	New Hampshire
Alaska	New Jersey
Arkansas	New Mexico
California	New York
Colorado	North Carolina
Connecticut	North Dakota
Delaware	Ohio
District of Columbia	Oklahoma
Georgia	Oregon
Guam	Pennsylvania
Hawaii	Rhode Island
Idaho	South Carolina
Indiana	South Dakota
Kansas	Tennessee
Kentucky	Texas
Louisiana	U.S. Virgin Islands
Maine	Utah
Maryland	Vermont
Minnesota	Virginia
Mississippi	Washington
Missouri	West Virginia
Nebraska	Wisconsin
Nevada	Wyoming

Praxis™ Sample Test Questions

The following sample test questions are from Praxis II:™ Principles of Learning and Teaching. For additional items visit the Praxis™ Web site at www.ets.org/praxis and download *Tests at a Glance*. Good luck!

Principles of Learning and Teaching: Grades 7–12

The sample questions that follow illustrate the kinds of questions in the test. They are not, however, representative of the entire scope of the test in either content or difficulty. Answers with explanations follow the questions.

CASE HISTORY: 7–12

Directions: The case history is followed by two short answer questions.

Mr. Payton

Scenario

Mr. Payton teaches world history to a class of thirty heterogeneously grouped students ages 14 to 16. He is working with his supervisor, planning for his self-evaluation to be completed in the spring. At the beginning of the third week of school, he begins gathering material that might be helpful for the self-evaluation. He has selected one class and three students from this class to focus on.

Mr. Payton's first impression of the three students

Jimmy has attended school in the district for ten years. He repeated fifth and seventh grades. Two years older than most of the other students in class and having failed twice, Jimmy is neither dejected nor hostile. He is an outgoing boy who, on the first day of class, offered to help me with "the young kids" in the class. He said, "Don't worry about me remembering a lot of dates and stuff. I know it's going to be hard, and I'll probably flunk again anyway, so don't spend your time thinking about me."

Burns is a highly motivated student who comes from a family of world travelers. He has been to Europe and Asia. These experiences have influenced his career choice, international law. He appears quiet and serious. He has done extremely well on written assignments and appears to prefer to work alone or with one or two equally bright, motivated students. He has a childhood friend, one of the slowest students in the class.

Pauline is a withdrawn student whose grades for the previous two years have been mostly C's and D's. Although Pauline displays no behavior problems when left alone, she appears not to be popular with the other students. She often stares out the window when she should be working. When I speak to Pauline about completing assignments, she becomes hostile. She has completed few of the assignments so far with any success. When I spoke to her counselor, Pauline yelled at me, "Now I'm in trouble with my counselor too, all because you couldn't keep your mouth shut!"

Mr. Payton's initial self-analysis, written for his supervisor

I attend workshops whenever I can and consider myself a creative teacher. I often divide the students into groups for cooperative projects, but they fall apart and are far from "cooperative." The better-performing students, like Burns, complain about the groups, claiming that small-group work is boring and that they learn more working alone or with students like themselves. I try to stimulate all the students' interest through class discussions. In these discussions, the high-achieving students seem more interested in impressing me than in listening and responding to what other students have to say. The low-achieving students seem content to be silent. Although I try most of the strategies I learn in workshops, I usually find myself returning to a modified lecture and the textbook as my instructional mainstays.

Background information on lesson to be observed by supervisor

Goals:

- To introduce students to important facts and theories about Catherine the Great
- To link students' textbook reading to other sources of information
- To give students practice in combining information from written and oral material
- To give students experience in note taking

I assigned a chapter on Catherine the Great in the textbook as homework on Tuesday. Students are to take notes on their reading. I gave Jimmy a book on Catherine the Great with a narrative treatment rather than the factual approach taken by the textbook. I told him the only important date is the date Catherine began her reign. The book has more pictures and somewhat larger print than the textbook.

I made no adaptation for Burns, since he's doing fine. I offered to create a study guide for Pauline, but she angrily said not to bother. I hope that Wednesday's lecture will make up for any difficulties she might experience in reading the textbook.

Supervisor's notes on Wednesday's lesson

Mr. Payton gives a lecture on Catherine the Great. First he says, "It is important that you take careful notes because I will be including information that is not contained in the chapter you read as homework last night. The test I will give on Friday will include both the lecture and the textbook information."

He tape records the lecture to supplement Pauline's notes but does not tell Pauline about the tape until the period is over because he wants her to do the best note taking she can manage. During the lecture, he speaks slowly, watching the class as they take notes. In addition, he walks about the classroom and glances at the students' notes.

Mr. Payton's follow-up and reflection

Tomorrow the students will use the class period to study for the test. I will offer Pauline earphones to listen to the tape-recorded lecture. On Friday, we will have a short-answer and essay test covering the week's work.

Class notes seem incomplete and inaccurate, and I'm not satisfied with this test as an assessment of student performance. Is that a fair measure of all they do?

Sample Questions

This section presents two short-answer questions and sample responses along with the standards used in scoring these responses. When you read these sample responses, keep in mind that they are less polished than if they had been developed at home, edited, and carefully presented. Examinees do not know what questions will be asked and must decide, on the spot, how to respond. Readers assign scores based on the following scoring guide.

GENERAL SCORING GUIDE

A response that receives a score of 2:

- Demonstrates a thorough understanding of the aspects of the case that are relevant to the question
- Responds appropriately to all parts of the question
- If an explanation is required, provides a strong explanation that is well supported by relevant evidence
- Demonstrates a strong knowledge of pedagogical concepts, theories, facts, procedures, or methodologies relevant to the question

A response that receives a score of 1:

- Demonstrates a basic understanding of the aspects of the case that are relevant to the question
- Responds appropriately to one portion of the question
- If an explanation is required, provides a weak explanation that is supported by relevant evidence
- Demonstrates some knowledge of pedagogical concepts, theories, facts, procedures, or methodologies relevant to the question

A response that receives a score of 0:

- Demonstrates misunderstanding of the aspects of the case that are relevant to the question
- Fails to respond appropriately to the question
- Is not supported by relevant evidence
- Demonstrates little knowledge of pedagogical concepts, theories, facts, procedures, or methodologies relevant to the question

No credit is given for a blank or off-topic response.

<u>Directions:</u> Questions 1 and 2 require you to write short answers. You are not expected to cite specific theories or texts in your answers; however, your responses to the questions will be evaluated with respect to professionally accepted principles and practices in teaching and learning. Be sure to answer all parts of the questions. Write your answers in the spaces indicated in the response book.

<u>Question 1</u>

In his self-analysis, Mr. Payton says that the better-performing students say small-group work is boring and that they learn more working alone or only with students like themselves. Assume that Mr. Payton wants to continue using cooperative learning groups because he believes they have value for all students.

- Describe TWO strategies he could use to address the concerns of the students who have complained.
- Explain how each strategy suggested could provide an opportunity to improve the functioning of cooperative learning groups. Base your response on principles of effective instructional strategies.

Sample response that received a score of 2:
Mr. Payton has to be creative to find strategies that will address the concerns of the students who have

complained and still support the strengths of cooperative learning. One way he can do that is to assign these students a variety of roles in which they can share their insights and knowledge with others in a way that will provide them recognition and will help other students. He can also build specific requirements that provide for individual work into the cooperative work, either before the groups meet or as the groups are working. This individual work provides the more able or motivated students with an opportunity to demonstrate their insights and knowledge and be given appropriate credit for them. The individual work can also serve as a basis for the group work.

Sample response that received a score of 1:
I understand why these students are concerned. But Mr. Payton shouldn't just give up on cooperative learning groups. I had a situation like this, when four really bright and eager kids just didn't want to work with students who were less able or less motivated. One thing he could do would be to assign his groups very carefully, so that one of the complaining kids is in each group. He could then use a system where he begins the cooperative work by regrouping, numbering the kids in each group 1, 2, 3, 4. First, all the "1's" work together, all the "2's" work together, and so forth. All the kids who complained would have the same number. After they have had the opportunity to work together on an advanced level, the groups would reform. The "1's" could go back to their own groups and share with them what the "1" group came up with. In this way, they have the intellectual stimulation of working together first, and then the status of sharing with other kids.

Sample response that received a score of 0:
Probably the best thing he can do is to let the complaining kids work individually. They are only going to resent the less able kids and will probably end up insulting them. The kids who are complaining will learn more if they work individually and can push themselves to their limits. The other kids can work at a level more appropriate to their ability.

<u>Question 2</u>

In the introduction to the lesson to be observed, Mr. Payton briefly mentions the modification he has or has not made for some students. Review his comments about modifications for Jimmy and Burns.

- For each of these two students, describe ONE different way Mr. Payton might have provided a modification to offer a better learning situation for each.
- Explain how each modification could offer a better learning situation. Base your explanation on principles of varied instruction for different kinds of learners.

Sample response that received a score of 2:
For Burns who is a bright, independent learner, providing him the opportunity to take extra responsibility for mastering challenging material and figuring out how to help his classmates understand it might help him to be more open and positive in his classroom behavior. For example, he might use more complex materials to access information, or might create a program using technology to share his knowledge and insights with others. For Jimmy, Mr. Payton might have a conference with him to find out how he was expected to learn social studies in the past and why he is so accepting of failing social studies. This conference may lead to a strategy such as the use of information presented visually or orally, or the use of graphic organizers to access information, or an alternate means of demonstrating his understanding if written assessments are part of the problem.

Sample response that received a score of 1:
Jimmy is a very interesting student to consider. He has a history of failure, and seems to accept the fact that he may fail again. However, he seems quite outgoing so he might be willing to try if approached right. I think the first thing Mr. Payton could do would be to sit down and talk with him. He needs to try to figure out why Jimmy failed in the past. He might ask him if he has any ideas about how he learns best—and things teachers have had him do that don't help him. Then, with this information, Mr. Payton might be able to come up with some approaches based on Jimmy's learning style. If Jimmy says he hates to read, Mr. Payton needs to find a way for him to access the information other than reading! Another thing Mr. Payton might do is adjust what he expects Jimmy to learn. Jimmy says he has problems with "a lot of dates and stuff." But he may be interested in other aspects of history—why people did the things they did, for example. By tailoring the study of history to aspects that might be more appropriate for Jimmy, Mr. Payton might have a better chance of helping Jimmy succeed.

Sample response that received a score of 0:
I think the modification he should make for both students is to be much clearer about what the expectations of the course are. Sometimes students are tuned out or bored because they just don't know what is expected of them. Maybe Mr. Payton needs to post his expectations prominently in the room so that both of these students can see what is expected. The expectations also need to indicate what is required for passing, so that Jimmy and Burns will know what the limits are.

Discrete Multiple-Choice Questions

Directions: Questions 3–5 are not related to the previous case. For each question, select the best answer and mark the corresponding space on your answer sheet.

3. A teacher gives his students a list of terms to use in an essay and intends the list to serve as a kind of learning support called a scaffold. If the students use the list effectively, which of the following would be an appropriate next step for the teacher to take when assigning the students their next essay?

   (A) Asking the students to come up with their own list of terms to use in the new assignment
   (B) Giving the students a longer list of terms to use in the new assignment
   (C) Giving the students a list of terms and asking them to write down a definition of each before beginning the new assignment
   (D) Asking the students to use the same terms in the new assignment

4. The concept of the placement of students in the "least restrictive" educational environment developed as a result of efforts to

   (A) equalize educational opportunities for females and minorities
   (B) normalize the lives of those children with disabilities who were being educated in isolation from their peers
   (C) obtain increased federal funding for the non-educational support of children living in poverty
   (D) reduce the overall costs of educating students with special needs

5. A teacher would get better information from a criterion-referenced test than from a norm-referenced test about which of the following?

(A) How much each individual student has learned about a particular aspect of the curriculum

(B) How each individual student's knowledge of a particular aspect of the curriculum compares to that of students across the school district and state

(C) How each individual student's knowledge of a particular aspect of the curriculum compares to that of a national sample of students at the same age level

(D) How much of what each student knows about a particular aspect of the curriculum is based on prior knowledge

Questions 6–7 are based on the following passages. *The following passages are taken from a debate about the advantages and disadvantages of a constructivist approach to teaching.*

Why constructivist approaches are effective

The point of constructivist instruction is to have students reflect on their questions about new concepts in order to uncover their misconceptions. If a student cannot reason out the answer, this indicates a conceptual problem that the teacher needs to address. It takes more than content-related professional expertise to be a "guide on the side" in this process. Constructivist teaching focuses not on what the teacher knows, but on what and how the student learns. Expertise is focused on teaching students how to derive answers, not on giving them the answers. This means that a constructivist approach to teaching must respond to multiple different learning methods and use multiple approaches to content. It is a myth that constructivist teaching never requires students to memorize, to drill, to listen to a teacher explain, or to watch a teacher model problem-solving of various kinds. What constructivist approaches take advantage of is a basic truth about human cognition: we all make sense of new information in terms of what we already know or think we know. And each of us must process new information in our own context and experience to make it part of what we really know.

Why constructivist approaches are misguided

The theory of constructivism is appealing for a variety of reasons—-especially for its emphasis on direct student engagement in learning. However, as they are implemented, constructivist approaches to teaching often treat memorization, direct instruction, or even open expression of teacher expertise as forbidden. This demotion of the teacher to some sort of friendly facilitator is dangerous, especially in an era in which there is an unprecedented number of teachers teaching out of their fields of expertise. The focus of attention needs to be on how much teachers know about the content being taught.

Students need someone to lead them through the quagmire of propaganda and misinformation that they confront daily. Students need a teacher who loves the subject and has enough knowledge to act as an intellectual authority when a little direction is needed. Students need a teacher who does not settle for minimal effort but encourages original thinking and provides substantive intellectual challenge.

6. The first passage suggests that reflection on which of the following after a lesson is an essential element in constructivist teaching?

(A) The extent to which the teacher's knowledge of the content of the lesson was adequate to meet students' curiosity about the topic

(B) The differences between what actually took place and what the teacher planned

(C) The variety of misconceptions and barriers to understanding revealed by students' responses to the lesson

(D) The range of cognitive processes activated by the activities included in the lesson design and implementation

7. The author of the second passage would regard which of the following teacher behaviors as essential for supporting student learning?

(A) Avoiding lecture and memorization

(B) Allowing students to figure out complex problems without the teacher's intervention

(C) Emphasizing process rather than content knowledge

(D) Directly guiding students' thinking on particular topics

Answers

1. See sample responses on page A–4.

2. See sample responses on page A–5.

3. The best answer is A. A scaffold is a temporary learning aid, designed to help the student to grow in independence as a learner; thus, once the skill

the scaffold is intended to help teach has been mastered, the scaffold should be withdrawn. Asking the students to come up with their own list of terms to use in the new assignment in effect withdraws the scaffold and encourages independence. None of the actions described in the other answer choices does these things.

4. The best answer is B. The concept of "least restrictive" stems from P.L. 94-142 and subsequent legislation regarding the education of students with disabilities and implies that special students are not to be classified by disability and given permanent special placement on the basis of these classifications. Rather, they are to be moved to special settings only if necessary and only for as long as necessary.

5. The best answer is A. Criterion-referenced tests are developed to assess knowledge and understanding of specified standards for learning particular content. They are designed to enable individual students or groups of students who have studied the same material to assess how much they have learned as compared to the criterion, or standard. A norm-group performance is not required for a criterion-referenced test, since the goal is to measure knowledge against a predefined knowledge standard. Whether a person passes a criterion-referenced test is not judged in relation to how other applicants performed (which would be norm-referenced) but in relation to an established standard for minimum number correct.

6. The best answer is C. Constructivist teaching depends on the connection of new information to already learned information or understandings, whether or not they are accurate. The passage says, "The point of constructivist instruction is to have students reflect on their questions about new concepts in order to uncover their misconceptions. If a student cannot reason out the answer, this indicates a conceptual problem that the teacher needs to address." Thus, a consideration of barriers and/or misconceptions in response to the presentation of new material is an essential follow-up to a constructivist lesson.

7. The best answer is D. The second author maintains that students require teacher guidance and a direct expression of the teacher's expert content knowledge in order to learn most effectively. Choices A (avoiding lecturing), B (learning without teacher intervention), and C (de-emphasis on content knowledge) are not consistent with this approach to teaching. Direct guidance of students' thinking is consistent with the second author's approach.

APPENDIX 2

State Offices for Teacher Certification and Licensure

ALABAMA
Alabama Department of Education
Teacher Education and Certification
5201 Gordon Persons Building
P.O. Box 302101
Montgomery, Alabama 36130-2101
Telephone: (334) 242-9977
Fax: (334) 242-0498
www.alsde.edu

ALASKA
Alaska Department of Education
Teacher Education and Certification
801 West 10th Street, Suite 200
P.O. Box 110500
Juneau, AK 99811-0500
Telephone: (907) 465-2831
Fax: (907) 465-2441
www.educ.state.ak.us

ARIZONA
Arizona Department of Education
P.O. Box 6490
Phoenix, Arizona 85005-6490
1535 West Jefferson Street
Phoenix, Arizona 85007
Telephone: (602) 542-4367
http://ade.state.az.us

ARKANSAS
Arkansas Department of Education
Office of Professional Licensure
#4 State Capitol Mall
Room 106B or Room 107B
Little Rock, AR 72201
Telephone: (501) 682-4342
Fax: (501) 682-4898
http://arkedu.state.ar.us/

CALIFORNIA
California Commission on Teacher
Credentialing
P.O. Box 944270
Sacramento, CA 94244-2700
1900 Capitol Avenue
Sacramento, CA 95814
Telephone: (916) 445-7254
Toll Free: (888) 921-2682
Fax: (916) 327-3166
E-mail: credentials@ctc.ca.gov
www.ctc.ca.gov/contact.html

COLORADO
Colorado Department of Education
Educator Licensing

201 East Colfax Avenue, Room 105
Denver, CO 80203
Telephone: (303) 866-6628
Fax: (303) 866-6866
www.cde.state.co.us

CONNECTICUT
Connecticut State Department
of Education
Bureau of Educator Preparation,
Certification, Support and Assessment
P.O. Box 150471—Room 243
Hartford, Connecticut 06115-0471
Telephone: (860) 713-6969
Fax: (860) 713-7017
E-mail: teacher.cert@po.state.ct.us
www.state.ct.us/sde/

DELAWARE
Delaware Department of Education
Licensure/Certification Office
401 Federal Street, Suite 2
Dover, DE 19901
Telephone: (302) 735-4120
Toll Free: (888) 759-9133
http://deeds.doe.k12.de.us/

DISTRICT OF COLUMBIA
District of Columbia Board
of Education
Office of Academic Credentials
and Standards
825 North Capitol Street, NE,
Sixth Floor
Washington, D.C. 20002-4232
Telephone: (202) 442-5377
Fax: (202) 442-5311
www.k12.dc.us

FLORIDA
Florida Department of Education
Bureau of Educator Certification
Suite 201, Turlington Building
325 West Gaines Street
Tallahassee, Florida 32399-0400
Telephone: (800) 445-6739
Outside U.S.: (850) 245-5049
www.fldoe.org/edcert

GEORGIA
Georgia Department of Education
Georgia Professional Standards
Commission
Two Peachtree Street
Suite 6000

Atlanta, GA 30303
Telephone: (404) 232-2500
Toll Free: (800) 869-7775
Fax: (404) 232-2560
www.gapsc.com

HAWAII
Hawaii State Department
of Education
Hawaii Teacher Standards Board
650 Iwilei Rd. #201
Honolulu, HI 96817
Telephone: (808) 586-2600
Fax: (808) 586-2606
www.htsb.org/contact.html

IDAHO
Idaho State Department of Education
Bureau of Certification
P.O. Box 83720
650 W. State Street, Room 251
Boise, ID 83720-0027
Telephone: (208) 332-6880
www.sde.state.id.us/

ILLINOIS
Illinois State Board of Education
100 North First Street
Springfield, IL 62777-0001
Telephone: (217) 782-4321
Toll Free: (866) 262-6663
Fax: (217) 524-4928
www.isbe.net

INDIANA
Indiana Department of Education
Division of Professional Standards
101 W. Ohio St., Suite 300
Indianapolis, IN 46204
Telephone: (317) 232-9010
Toll Free: (866) 542-3672
Fax: (317) 232-9023
www.doe.state.in.us

IOWA
Iowa Department of Education
Board of Educational Examiners
Licensure
Grimes State Office Building
400 East 14th Street
Des Moines, IA 50319-0146
Telephone: (515) 281-5294
Fax: (515) 242-5988
www.state.ia.us/educate

KANSAS
Kansas State Department
of Education
Teacher Education and Licensure Team
120 SE 10th Avenue
Topeka, KS 66612-1182
Telephone: (785) 291-3678
www.ksde.org/

KENTUCKY
Kentucky Department of Education
Education Professional Standards
Board
100 Airport Road, 3rd Floor
Frankfort, KY 40601
Phone: (502) 564-4606
Toll Free: (888) 598-7667
Fax: (502) 564-7092
www.education.ky.gov/

LOUISIANA
Louisiana State Department of
Education
Certification and Higher Education
1201 N. Third Street, Claiborne
Building, 3rd Floor
P.O. Box 94064
Baton Rouge, LA 70804-9064
Telephone: (225) 342-3490
Toll Free: (877) 453-2721
E-mail: Customerservice@la.gov
www.teachlouisiana.net

MAINE
State of Maine Department of
Education
Certification Office
23 State House Station
Augusta, ME 04333-0023
Telephone: (207) 624-6603
Fax: (207) 624-6604
E-mail: cert.doe@maine.gov
www.maine.gov/education/
index.shtml

MARYLAND
Maryland State Department of
Education
200 West Baltimore Street
Baltimore, MD 21201
Telephone: (410) 767-0412
www.marylandpublicschools.org/

MASSACHUSETTS
Massachusetts Department of
Education
350 Main Street
Malden, MA 02148-5023
Telephone: (781) 338-3000
www.doe.mass.edu/educators

MICHIGAN
Michigan Department of Education
608 W. Allegan Street
P.O. Box 30008
Lansing, MI 48909
Telephone: (517) 373-3324
E-mail: MDEweb@michigan.gov
www.michigan.gov/mde

MINNESOTA
Minnesota Department of Education
Educator Licensing
1500 Highway 36 West
Roseville, MN 55113
E-mail: mde.educator-licensing
@state.mn.us
http://education.state.mn.us/mde/
index.html

MISSISSIPPI
Mississippi Department of Education
Office of Educator Licensure
Central High School Building
P.O. Box 771
Jackson, MS 39205-0771
Telephone: (601) 359-3483
Fax: (601) 359-2778
E-mail: cchester@mde.k12.ms.us
www.mde.k12.ms.us/

MISSOURI
Missouri Department of Elementary
and Secondary Education
Educator Certification
P.O. Box 480
205 Jefferson Street
Jefferson City, MO 65102
Telephone: (573) 751-0051 or
(573) 751-3847
Fax: (573) 522-8314
http://dese.mo.gov/

MONTANA
Montana Office of Public Instruction
Montana Educator Licensure
Program
P.O. Box 202501
Helena, MT 59620-2501
Telephone: (406) 444-3150
E-mail: cert@mt.gov
www.opi.state.mt.us/cert/

NEBRASKA
Nebraska Department of Education
Teacher Certification
301 Centennial Mall South
P.O. Box 94987
Lincoln, NE 68509
Telephone: (402) 471-0739
www.nde.state.ne.us/

NEVADA
Nevada Department of Education
Teacher Licensing Office
1820 East Sahara Avenue, Suite 205
Las Vegas, NV 89104
Telephone: (702) 486-6457
Fax: (702) 486-6450
Teacher Licensing Office
700 East Fifth Street
Carson City, NV 89701
Telephone: (775) 687-9115
Fax: (775) 687-9101
E-mail: license@doe.nv.gov
www.doe.nv.gov/

NEW HAMPSHIRE
New Hampshire Department
of Education
101 Pleasant Street
Concord, NH 03301-3860
Telephone: (603) 271-3494
Fax: (603) 271-1953
www.ed.state.nh.us/education/

NEW JERSEY
New Jersey Department of Education
Office of Licensure & Credentials
P.O. Box 500
Trenton, NJ 08625-0500
Telephone: (609) 292-2070
Fax: (609) 292-3768
www.state.nj.us/education/

NEW MEXICO
New Mexico Public Education
Department
Professional Licensure Bureau
300 Don Gaspar
Santa Fe, NM 87501-2786
Telephone: (505) 827-5800
www.sde.state.nm.us/

NEW YORK
New York State Education Department
89 Washington Avenue
Albany, New York 12234
Certification Unit
New York State Education Department
5N Education Building
Albany, NY 12234
Telephone: (518) 474-3901
E-mail: tcert@mail.nysed.gov
www.highered.nysed.gov/

NORTH CAROLINA
North Carolina Department of
Public Instruction
301 N. Wilmington St.
Raleigh, NC 27601
Telephone: (919) 807-3300
www.ncpublicschools.org/

NORTH DAKOTA
North Dakota Education Standards
and Practices Board
2718 Gateway Avenue, Suite 303
Bismarck, ND 58503-0585
Telephone: (701) 328-9641
Fax: (701) 328-9647
E-mail: espbinfo@nd.gov
www.nd.gov/espb/

OHIO
Ohio Department of Education
Office of Educator Licensure
25 South Front St., Mail Stop 105
Columbus, OH 43215-4183
Telephone: (614) 466-3593
www.ode.state.oh.us/

OKLAHOMA
Oklahoma State Department
of Education
Professional Standards Section
Hodge Education Building—Room 212
2500 North Lincoln Boulevard
Oklahoma City, OK 73105-4599
Telephone: (405) 521-3337
http://sde.state.ok.us

OREGON
Oregon Department of Education
The Teacher Standards and Practices
Commission
465 Commercial St., NE
Salem, OR 97301
Telephone: (503) 378-3586
www.ode.state.or.us/

PENNSYLVANIA
Pennsylvania Department of
Education
Bureau of Teacher Certification and
Preparation
Division of Candidate Evaluation
Services
333 Market Street
Harrisburg, PA 17126-0333
Telephone: (717) 787-3356
Hearing Impaired TDD#:
(717) 772-2864
Fax: (717) 783-6736
E-mail: ra-teachercert@state.pa.us
www.pde.state.pa.us/

RHODE ISLAND
Rhode Island Department of
Elementary and Secondary Education
Room 400
The Shepard Building

255 Westminster Street
Providence, RI 02903-3400
Telephone: (401) 222-4600
www.ridoe.net/

SOUTH CAROLINA
South Carolina Department
of Education
Office of Educator Certification
Landmark II Office Building, Suite 500
3700 Forest Drive
Columbia, SC 29204
Telephone: (803) 734-8466
Toll Free: (877) 885-5280
Fax: (803) 734-2873
www.scteachers.org/
www.myscschools.com/

SOUTH DAKOTA
South Dakota Department
of Education
Office of Accreditation and
Teacher Quality
700 Governors Drive
Pierre, SD 57501
Telephone: (605) 773-3134
Fax: (605) 773-6139
E-mail: certification@state.sd.us
http://doe.sd.gov/

TENNESSEE
Tennessee Department of Education
Office of Teacher Licensing
4th Floor, Andrew Johnson Tower
710 James Robertson Parkway
Nashville, TN 37243-0377
Telephone: (615) 532-4885
Fax: (615) 532-1448
E-mail: Education.Licensing@state.tn.us
www.tennessee.gov/education/lic

TEXAS
Texas Education Agency
Educator Certification & Standards
1701 North Congress Avenue
WBT 5-100
Austin, TX 78701-1494
Telephone: (512) 936-8400
Toll Free: (888) 863-5880
www.sbec.state.tx.us/

UTAH
State of Utah Office of Education
250 East 500 South
P.O. Box 144200
Salt Lake City, UT 84114-4200
Telephone: (801) 538-7740
www.usoe.k12.ut.us

VERMONT
Vermont Department of Education
120 State Street
Montpelier, VT 05620-2501
Phone: (802) 828-2445
E-mail: licensinginfo@education.
state.vt.us
www.state.vt.us/educ

VIRGINIA
Virginia Department of Education
P.O. Box 2120
Richmond, VA 23218
Telephone: (800) 292-3820
www.pen.k12.va.us

WASHINGTON
Office of Superintendent of
Public Instruction
Old Capitol Building
P.O. Box 47200
Olympia, WA 98504-7200
Telephone: (360) 725-6000
www.k12.wa.us/certification/

WEST VIRGINIA
West Virginia Department
of Education
1900 Kanawha Boulevard East
Charleston, WV 25305
Telephone: (800) 982-2378
E-mail: mfmiller@access.k12.wv.us
http://access.k12.wv.us

WISCONSIN
Wisconsin Department of Public
Instruction
125 S. Webster Street
P.O. Box 7841
Madison, WI 53707-7841
Telephone: (800) 441-4563
www.dpi.state.wi.us/

WYOMING
Wyoming Department of Education
2300 Capitol Avenue
Hathaway Building, 2nd Floor
Cheyenne, WY 82002-0050
Telephone: (307) 777-7291
Toll free: (800) 675-6893
www.k12.wy.us

GLOSSARY

A

ability grouping   The assignment of pupils to homogeneous groups according to intellectual ability or level for instructional purposes.

academic freedom   The opportunity for teachers and students to learn, teach, study, research, and question without censorship, coercion, or external political and other restrictive influences.

academic learning time   The time a student is actively engaged with the subject matter and experiencing a high success rate.

academy   A classical secondary school in colonial America that emphasized elements of Latin and English grammar schools and by the nineteenth century became more of a college preparatory school. Also the name of the ancient Greek school founded by Plato.

accelerated program   The more rapid promotion of gifted students through school.

accountability   Holding schools and teachers responsible for student performance.

accreditation   Certification of an education program or a school that has met professional standards of an outside agency.

acculturation   The acquisition of the dominant culture's norms by a member of the nondominant culture. The nondominant culture typically loses its own culture, language, and sometimes religion in this process.

achievement tests   Examinations of the knowledge and skills acquired, usually as a result of specific instruction.

adequate education   Provides a legal approach for ensuring educational opportunities for poorer students based on state constitution guarantees for an efficient, thorough, or uniform education. Calls for adequate education have replaced previous calls for equal educational expenditures.

adequate yearly progress (AYP)   Under the *No Child Left Behind Act,* each state establishes annual criteria to determine school district and school achievement. Schools that fail to meet the AYP criteria (often determined by standardized tests) are held accountable and may be closed.

adult education   Courses and programs offered to high school graduates by colleges, business, industry, and governmental and private organizations that lead to academic degrees, occupational preparation, and the like.

advanced placement   Courses and programs in which younger students can earn college credit.

aesthetics   The branch of philosophy that examines the nature of beauty and judgments about it.

affective domain   The area of learning that involves attitudes, values, and emotions.

affirmative action   A plan by which personnel policies and hiring practices reflect positive steps in the recruiting and hiring of women and people of color.

allocated time   The amount of time a school or an individual teacher schedules for a subject.

alternative families   Family units that differ from the traditional image; examples include foster care children, single parents, central role of grandparents, and gay couples.

alternative licensure   A procedure for acquiring a teacher's license for those who have not graduated from a traditional state approved teacher education program.

alternative school   A private or public school that provides religious, academic, or other alternatives to the regular public school.

American Federation of Teachers (AFT)   A national organization of teachers that is primarily concerned with improving educational conditions and protecting teachers' rights.

Americanization   The acculturation of American norms and values.

assertive discipline   A behavior modification program developed by Lee and Marlene Canter designed to "catch" and reward students being good, while discouraging off-task and inappropriate behavior.

assimilation   (See enculturation)

assistive (adaptive) technology   Devices that help the disabled to perform and learn more effectively, from voice-activated keyboards and mechanical wheelchairs to laptops for class note taking and personal scheduling.

asynchronous   Nonsimultaneous students enrolled in an Internet course need not participate at the same time, and may take the course although they live in different time zones.

authentic assessment   A type of evaluation that represents actual performance, encourages students to reflect on their own work, and is integrated into the student's whole learning process. Such tests usually require that students synthesize knowledge from different areas and use that knowledge actively.

B

back to basics   During the 1980s, a revival of the back-to-basics movement evolved out of concern for declining test scores in math, science, reading, and other areas. Although there is not a precise definition of back to basics, many consider it to include increased emphasis on reading, writing, and arithmetic, fewer electives, and more rigorous grading.

behavioral objective   A specific statement of what a learner must accomplish in order to demonstrate mastery.

behaviorism   A psychological theory that interprets human behavior in terms of stimuli-response.

behavior modification   A strategy to alter behavior in a desired direction through the use of rewards.

bilingual education   Educational programs in which students of limited or no English-speaking ability attend classes taught in English, as well as in their native language. There is great variability in these programs in terms of goals, instructional opportunity, and balance between English and a student's native language.

block grants   Federal dollars provided to the states, with limited federal restrictions, for educational aid and program funding.

block scheduling   Using longer "blocks" of time to schedule classes results in fewer but longer periods given to each subject. It is designed to promote greater in-depth study.

Bloom's taxonomy   A classification system in which each lower level is subsumed in the next higher level. The Bloom's taxonomy describes simple to more complex mental processes, and usually is used to classify educational objectives or classroom questions.

board certification   Recognition of advanced teaching competence, awarded to teachers who demonstrate high levels of knowledge, commitment, and professionalism through a competitive review process administered by the National Board for Professional Teaching Standards.

board of education   Constituted at the state and local levels, this agency is responsible for formulating educational policy. Members are sometimes appointed but, more frequently, are elected at the local level.

bond   A certificate of debt issued by a government guaranteeing payment of the original investment plus interest by a specified future date. Bonds are used by local communities to raise the funds they need to build or repair schools.

Brown v. Board of Education of Topeka   U.S. Supreme Court ruling that reversed an earlier "separate but equal" ruling and declared that segrated schooling was inherently unequal and therefore unlawful.

Buckley Amendment   The 1974 Family Educational Rights and Privacy Act granting parents of students under 18, and students 18 or over the right to examine their school records.

busing   A method for remedying segregation by transporting students to create more ethnically or racially balanced schools. Before busing and desegregation were linked, busing was not a controversial issue, and, in fact, the vast majority of students riding school buses are not involved in desegregation programs.

C

canon   The collection of literature and other works that typically reflects a white, Euro-centered view of the world.

career technical education   A program to teach elementary and secondary students about the world of work by integrating career awareness and exploration across the school curriculum.

career ladder   A system designed to create different status levels for teachers by developing steps one can climb to receive increased pay through increased responsibility or experience.

Carnegie unit   A credit awarded to a student for successfully completing a high school course. It is used in determining graduation requirements and college admissions.

categorical grant   Financial aid to local school districts from state or federal agencies for specific purposes.

certification   State government or professional association's evaluation and approval of an applicant's competencies.

character education   A model comprised of various strategies that promote a defined set of core values to students.

charter school   A group of teachers, parents, and even businesses may petition a local school board, or state government, to form a charter school which is exempt from many state and local regulations. Designed to promote creative new schools, the charter represents legal permission to try new approaches to educate students. The first charter legislation was passed in Minnesota in 1991.

chief state school officer   The executive head of a state department of education. The chief state school officer is responsible for carrying out the mandates of the state board of education and enforcing educational laws and regulations. This position is also referred to as *state superintendent.*

child abuse   Physical, sexual, or emotional violation of a child's health and well-being.

child advocacy movement   A movement dedicated to defining and protecting the rights of children. Child advocates recognize that children are not yet ready to assume all the rights and privileges of adults, but they are firmly committed to expanding the rights currently enjoyed by children and to no longer treating children as objects or of the property of others.

child-centered instruction (individual instruction)   Teaching that is designed to meet the interests and needs of individual students.

classroom climate   The physical, emotional, and aesthetic characteristics, as well as the learning resources, of a school classroom.

Coalition of Essential Schools (CES)   This was founded by Theodore Sizer and is a reform effort that creates smaller schools, learning communities and more in-depth study of the curriculum.

cognitive domain   The area of learning that involves knowledge, information, and intellectual skills.

Coleman report   A study commissioned by President Johnson (1964) to analyze the factors that influence the academic achievement of students. One of the major findings of James Coleman's report was that schools in general have relatively little impact on learning. Family and peers were found to have more impact on a child's education than the school itself did.

collaborative action research   Connects teaching and professional growth through the use of research relevant to classroom responsibilities.

collective bargaining   A negotiating procedure between employer and employees for resolving disagreements on salaries, work schedules, and other conditions of employment. In collective bargaining, all teachers in a school system bargain as one group through chosen representatives.

Comer model   James Comer of Yale has created and disseminated a program that incorporates a team of educational and mental health professionals to assist children at risk by working with their parents and attending to social, educational, and psychological needs.

Committee of Ten   In 1892, the National Education Association formed the committee, influenced by college presidents, to reform the nation's high schools. The result was an academically oriented curriculum geared for colleges, and the creation of the Carnegie unit as a measure of progress through the high school curriculum.

common school A public, tax-supported school. First established in Massachusetts, the school's purpose was to create a common basis of knowledge for children. It usually refers to a public elementary school.

community schools Schools connected with a local community to provide for the educational needs of that community.

compensatory education Educational experiences and opportunities designed to overcome or compensate for difficulties associated with a student's disadvantaged background.

competency The ability to perform a particular skill or to demonstrate a specified level of knowledge.

comprehensive high school A public secondary school that offers a variety of curricula, including vocational, academic, and general education programs.

compulsory attendance A state law requiring that children and adolescents attend school until reaching a specified age.

computer-assisted instruction (CAI) Individualized instruction between a student and programmed instructional material stored in a computer.

computer-managed instruction (CMI) A recordkeeping procedure for tracking student performance using a computer.

conditional teacher's license Sometimes called an emergency license, a substandard license that is issued on a temporary basis to meet a pressing need.

consolidation The trend toward combining small or rural school districts into larger ones.

constructivism With roots in cognitive psychology, this educational approach is built on the idea that people construct their understanding of the world. Constructivist teachers gauge a student's prior knowledge, then carefully orchestrate cues, classroom activities, and penetrating questions to push students to higher levels of understanding.

content standards The knowledge, skills, and dispositions that students should master in each subject. These standards are often linked to broader themes and sometimes to testing programs.

cooperative learning In classrooms using cooperative learning, students work on activities in small groups, and they receive rewards based on the overall group performance.

Copyright Act A federal law that protects intellectual property, including copyrighted material. Teachers can use such material in classrooms only with permission, or under specific guidelines.

core curriculum A central body of knowledge that schools require all students to study.

core knowledge Awareness of the central ideas, beliefs, personalities, writings, events, etc. of a culture. Also termed "cultural literacy."

corporal punishment Disciplining students through physical punishment by a school employee.

Creationism The position that God created the universe, the earth, and living things on the earth in precisely the manner described in the Old Testament, in six, 24-hour periods.

critical pedagogy An education philosophy that unites the theory of critical thinking with actual practice in real-world settings. The purpose is to eliminate the cultural and educational control of the dominant group, to have students apply critical thinking skills to the real world and become agents for social change.

cultural difference theory This theory asserts that academic problems can be overcome if educators study and mediate the cultural gap separating school and home.

cultural literacy Knowledge of the people, places, events, and concepts central to the standard literate culture.

cultural pluralism Acceptance and encouragement of cultural diversity.

culturally responsive teaching Recognizes that students learn in different ways, and that effective teachers recognize and respond to these differences. This approach focuses on the learning strengths of students, as well as mediates the frequent mismatch between home and school cultures.

culture A set of learned beliefs, values, and behaviors; a way of life shared by members of a society.

curriculum (formal, explicit) Planned content of instruction that enables the school to meet its aims.

curriculum development The processes of assessing needs, formulating objectives, and developing instructional opportunities and evaluation.

D

dame schools Primary schools in colonial and other early periods in which students were taught by untrained women in the women's own homes.

day care centers Facilities charged with caring for children. The quality of care varies dramatically and may range from well-planned educational programs to little more than custodial supervision.

decentralization The trend of dividing large school districts into smaller and, it is hoped, more responsive units.

deductive reasoning Working from a general rule to identify particular examples and applications to that rule.

de facto segregation The segregation of racial or other groups resulting from circumstances, such as housing patterns, rather than from official policy or law.

deficit theory A theory that asserts that the values, language patterns, and behaviors that children from certain racial and ethnic groups bring to school put them at an educational disadvantage.

de jure segregation The segregation of racial or other groups on the basis of law, policy, or a practice designed to accomplish such separation.

delegate representative Form of representative government in which the interests of a particular geographic region are represented through an individual or "delegate." Some school boards are organized so that members act as delegates of a neighborhood or region.

demographic forecasting The study and predictions of people and their vital statistics.

Department of Education U.S. cabinet-level department in charge of federal educational policy and the promotion of programs to carry out policies.

descriptive data Information that provides an objective depiction of various aspects of school or classroom life.

desegregation   The process of correcting past practices of racial or other illegal segregation.

detrack   The movement to eliminate school tracking practices, which often have racial, ethnic, and class implications.

differentiated instruction   Instructional activities are organized in response to individual differences rather than content standards. Teachers are asked to carefully consider each student's needs, learning style, life experience, and readiness to learn.

digital divide   A term used to describe the technological gap between the "haves" and "have nots." Race, gender, class, and geography are some of the demographic factors influencing technological access and achievement.

direct teaching   A model of instruction in which the teacher is a strong leader who structures the classroom and sequences subject matter to reflect a clear academic focus. This model emphasizes the importance of a structured lesson in which presentation of new information is followed by student practice and teacher feedback.

disability   A learning or physical condition, a behavior, or an emotional problem that impedes education. Educators now prefer to speak of "students with disabilities," not "handicapped students," emphasizing the person, not the disability.

distance learning   Courses, programs, and training provided to students over long distances through television, the Internet, and other technologies.

dot.kids   An adult-supervised Internet domain designed to protect children from inappropriate Internet content.

dual-track system   The European traditional practice of separate primary schools for most children and secondary schools for the upper class.

due process   The procedural requirements that must be followed in such areas as student and teacher discipline and placement in special education programs. Due process exists to safeguard individuals from arbitrary, capricious, or unreasonable policies, practices, or actions. The essential elements of due process are (1) a notice of the charge or actions to be taken, (2) the opportunity to be heard, (3) and the right to a defense that reflects the particular circumstances and nature of the case.

E

e-mentor   Mentors who work over the Internet to advise, counsel, and support others. Some schools use e-mentors for beginning teachers.

early childhood education   Learning undertaken by young children in the home, in nursery schools, in preschools, and in kindergartens.

eclecticism   In this text, the drawing on of elements from several educational philosophies or methods.

Edison Schools (Edison Project)   An educational company that contracts with local school districts, promising to improve student achievement while making a profit in the process.

educable child   A mentally retarded child who is capable of achieving only a limited basic learning and usually must be instructed in a special class.

educational malpractice   A new experimental line of litigation similar to the concept of medical malpractice. Educational malpractice is concerned with assessing liability for students who graduate from school without fundamental skills. Unlike medical malpractice, many courts have rejected the notion that schools or educators be held liable for this problem.

educational park   A large, campuslike facility often including many grade levels and several schools and often surrounded by a variety of cultural resources.

educational television programming   Television programs that promote learning.

educational vouchers   Flat grants or payments representing the cost of educating a student at a school. Awarded to the parent or child to enable free choice of a school—public or private—the voucher payment is made to the school that accepts the child.

Eight-Year Study   Educator Ralph Tyler's study in the 1930s that indicated the effectiveness of progressive education.

elementary school   An educational institution for children in grades 1 through 5, 6, or 8, often including kindergarten.

emergency license   A substandard license that recognizes teachers who have not met all the requirements for licensure. It is issued on a temporary basis to meet the needs of communities that do not have licensed teachers available.

EMO (Educational Maintenance Organization)   The term is borrowed from Health Maintenance Organizations (HMOs) and refers to the growing number of profit-driven companies in the business of public education.

emotional intelligence (EQ)   Personality characteristics, such as persistence, can be measured as part of a new human dimension referred to as EQ. Some believe that EQ scores may be better predictors of future success than IQ scores.

empiricism   The philosophy that maintains that sensory experiences, such as seeing, hearing, and touching, are the ultimate sources of all human knowledge. Empiricists believe that we experience the external world by sensory perception; then, through reflection, we conceptualize ideas that help us interpret the world.

enculturation   The process of acquiring a culture; a child's acquisition of the cultural heritage through both formal and informal educational means.

endorsement   Having a license extended through additional work to include a second teaching field.

engaged time   The part of time that a teacher schedules for a subject in which the students are actively involved with academic subject matter. Listening to a lecture, participating in a class discussion, and working on math problems all constitute engaged time.

English grammar school   The demand for a more practical education in eighteenth-century America led to the creation of these private schools that taught commerce, navigation, engineering, and other vocational skills.

English language learners (ELL)   (Also referred to as limited English proficiency or LEP.) Students whose native language is not English and are learning to speak and write English.

environmental education   The study and analysis of the conditions and causes of pollution, overpopulation, and waste of natural resources, and of the ways to preserve Earth's intricate ecology.

epistemology   The branch of philosophy that examines the nature of knowledge and learning.

e-portfolio   A digital version of the teacher's professional portfolio.

equal educational opportunity   Refers to giving every student the educational opportunity to develop fully whatever talents, interests, and abilities he or she may have, without regard to race, color, national origin, sex, disability, or economic status.

equity   Educational policy and practice that are just, fair, and free from bias and discrimination.

essentialism   An educational philosophy that emphasizes basic skills of reading, writing, mathematics, science, history, geography, and language.

establishment clause   A section of the First Amendment of the U.S. Constitution that says that Congress shall make no law respecting the establishment of religion. This clause prohibits nonparochial schools from teaching religion.

ethics   The branch of philosophy that examines questions of right and wrong, good and bad.

ethnic group   A group of people with a distinctive culture and history.

ethnicity   Refers to shared common cultural traits such as language, religion, and dress. A Latino or Hispanic, for example, belongs to an ethnic group, but might belong to the Black, Caucasian, or Asian race.

ethnocentrism   The tendency to view one's own culture as superior to others, or to fail to consider other cultures in a fair or equitable manner.

evaluation   Assessment of learning and instruction.

evolution   As put forth by Charles Darwin, a keystone of modern biological theory and postulates that animals and plants have their origin in other preexisting types and that there are modifications in successive generations.

exceptional learners   Students who require special education and related services in order to realize their full potential. Categories of exceptionality include retarded, gifted, learning disabled, emotionally disturbed, and physically disabled.

existentialism   A philosophy that emphasizes the ability of an individual to determine the course and nature of his or her life and the importance of personal decision making.

expectation theory   First made popular by Rosenthal and Jacobson, this theory holds that a student's academic performance can be improved if a teacher's attitudes and beliefs about that student's academic potential are modified.

expulsion   Dismissal of a student from school for a lengthy period, ranging from one semester to permanently.

extracurriculum   The part of school life that comprises activities, such as sports, academic and social clubs, band, chorus, orchestra, and theater. Many educators think that the extracurriculum develops important skills and values, including leadership, teamwork, creativity, and diligence.

F

failing school   The term given to a school when a large proportion of its students do not do well on standardized tests or other academic measures. Critics charge that students attending such schools are not receiving their constitutionally guaranteed adequate education.

fair use   A legal principle allowing limited use of copyrighted materials. Teachers must observe three criteria: brevity, spontaneity, and cumulative effect.

five factor theory   School effectiveness research emphasizes five factors, including effective leadership, monitoring student progress, safety, a clear vision, and high expectations.

Flanders Interaction Analysis   An instrument developed by Ned Flanders for categorizing student and teacher verbal behavior. It is used to interpret the nature of classroom verbal interaction.

flexible scheduling   A technique for organizing time more effectively in order to meet the needs of instruction by dividing the school day into smaller time modules that can be combined to fit a task.

foundation program   Program for distribution of state funds designed to guarantee a specified minimum level of educational support for each child.

Franklin Academy   A colonial high school founded by Benjamin Franklin that accepted females as students and promoted a less classical, more practical curriculum.

full service school   These schools provide a network of social services from nutrition and health care to parental education and transportation, all designed to support the comprehensive educational needs of children.

future shock   Term coined by Alvin Toffler. It refers to the extraordinarily accelerated rate of change and the disorientation of those unable to adapt to rapidly altered norms, institutions, and values.

futurism   The activity of forecasting and planning for future developments.

G

gender bias (see sex discrimination)   The degree to which an individual's beliefs and behavior are unduly influenced on the basis of gender.

gendered career   A term applied to the gender stereotyping of career and occupational fields. Teaching, for example, was initially gendered male, and today is gendered female, particularly at the elementary school level.

generalizations   Broad statements about a group that offer information, clues, and insights that can help a teacher plan more effectively. Generalizations are a good starting point, but as the teacher learns more about the students, individual differences become more educationally significant.

gifted learner   There is great variance in definitions and categorizations of the "gifted." The term is most frequently applied to those with exceptional intellectual ability, but it may also refer to learners with outstanding ability in athletics, leadership, music, creativity, and so forth.

global education   Because economics, politics, scientific innovation, and societal developments in different countries have an enormous impact on children in the United States, the goals of global education include increased knowledge about the peoples of the world, resolution of global problems, increased fluency in foreign languages, and the development of more tolerant attitudes toward other cultures and peoples.

Great Books The heart of the perennialists' curriculum that includes great works of the past in literature, philosophy, science, and other areas.

guaranteed tax base program Adds state funds to local tax revenues, especially in poorer communities in order to enhance local educational expenditures.

Gun-free Schools Act Enacted in Congress in 1994, schools can lose federal funds if they do not have a zero-tolerance policy mandating one-year expulsions for students bringing firearms to schools. The vast majority of schools report zero-tolerance policies for firearms.

H

Head Start Federally funded pre-elementary school program to provide learning opportunities for disadvantaged students.

heterogeneous grouping A group or class consisting of students who show normal variation in ability or performance. It differs from homogeneous grouping, in which criteria, such as grades or scores on standardized tests, are used to group students similar in ability or achievement.

heteronormativity A view point that denies lesbian, gay, bisexual, and transgendered individuals and sees all people as heterosexual.

hidden (implicit) curriculum What students learn, other than academic content, from what they do or are expected to do in school; incidental learnings.

hidden government The unofficial power structure within a school. It cannot be identified by the official title, position, or functions of individuals. For example, it reflects the potential influence of a school secretary or custodian.

higher-order questions Questions that require students to go beyond memory in formulating a response. These questions require students to analyze, synthesize, evaluate, and so on.

home schooling A growing trend (but a longtime practice) of parents educating their children at home, for religious or philosophical reasons.

homogeneous grouping The classification of pupils for the purpose of forming instructional groups having a relatively high degree of intellectual similarity.

hornbook A single sheet of parchment containing the Lord's Prayer and letters of the alphabet. It was protected by a thin sheath from the flattened horn of a cow and fastened to a wooden board—hence, the name. It was used during the colonial era in primary schools.

humanistic education A curriculum that stresses personal student growth; self-actualizing, moral, and aesthetic issues are explored.

I

idealism A doctrine holding that knowledge is derived from ideas and emphasizing moral and spiritual reality as a preeminent source of explanation.

ideologues Home school advocates focused on avoiding public schools in order to impart their own set of values.

inclusion The practice of educating and integrating children with disabilities into regular classroom settings.

immersion This bilingual education model teaches students with limited English by using a "sheltered" or simplified English vocabulary, but teaching in English and not in the other language.

independent school A nonpublic school unaffiliated with any church or other agency.

individualized education program (IEP) The mechanism through which a disabled child's special needs are identified, objectives and services are described, and evaluation is designed.

individualized instruction Curriculum content and instructional materials, media, and activities designed for individual learning. The pace, interests, and abilities of the learner determine the curriculum.

Individuals with Disabilities Education Act (IDEA) Federal law passed in 1990, which extends full education services and provisions to people identified with disabilities.

induction A formal program assisting new teachers to successfully adjust to their role in the classroom.

inductive reasoning Drawing generalizations based on the observation of specific examples.

informal education In many cultures, augments or takes the place of formal schooling as children learn adult roles through observation, conversation, assisting, and imitating.

infrastructure The basic installations and facilities on which the continuance and growth of a community depend.

in loco parentis Latin term meaning "in place of the parents"; that is, a teacher or school administrator assumes the duties and responsibilities of the parents during the hours the child attends school.

instruction The process of implementing a curriculum.

INTASC The Interstate New Teachers Assessment and Support Consortium, an organization that has identified competency standards for new teachers.

integrated curriculum (interdisciplinary curriculum) Subject matter from two or more areas combined into thematic units (i.e., literature and history resources to study civil rights laws).

integration The process of educating different racial and ethnic groups together, and developing positive interracial contacts.

Intelligent Design The argument that instances in nature cannot be explained by Darwinian evolution, but instead are consistent with the notion of an intelligent involvement in the design of life.

interest centers Usually associated with an open classroom, such centers provide independent student activities related to a specific subject.

Internet The worldwide computer network that rapidly facilitates information dissemination.

J

junior high school A two- or three-year school between elementary and high school for students in their early adolescent years, commonly grades 7 and 8 or 7 through 9.

K

Kalamazoo, Michigan, case A 1874 U.S. Supreme Court decision that upheld the right of states to tax citizens in order to provide public secondary education.

kindergarten A preschool, early childhood educational environment first designed by Froebel in the mid-nineteenth century.

L

labeling Categorizing or classifying students for the purposes of educational placement. One unfortunate consequence may be that of stigmatizing students and inhibiting them from reaching their full potential.

laboratory schools Schools often associated with a teacher preparation institution for practice teaching, demonstration, research, or innovation.

land grant colleges State colleges or universities offering agricultural and mechanical curricula, funded originally by the Morrill Act of 1862.

language submersion This bilingual education model teaches students in classes where only English is spoken, the teacher does not know the language of the student, and the student either learns English as the academic work progresses or pays the consequences. This has been called a "sink or swim" approach.

last mile problem Geography contributes to a digital divide, in part because running fiber optic cables to rural schools is often an expense that telecommunications companies avoid.

latchkey (self-care) kids A term used to describe children who go home after school to an empty house; their parents or guardians are usually working and not home.

Latin grammar school A classical secondary school with a Latin and Greek curriculum preparing students for college.

learning communities The creation of more personal collaboration between teachers and students to promote similar academic goals and values.

learning disability An educationally significant language and/or learning deficit.

learning styles Students learn in different ways and have different preferences, ranging from preferred light and noise levels to independent or group learning formats.

least-restrictive environment The program best suited to meeting a disabled student's special needs without segregating the student from the regular educational program.

license Official approval of a government agency for an individual to perform certain work, such as a teacher's license granted by a state.

limited English proficiency (LEP) A student who has a limited ability to understand, speak, or read English and who has a native language other than English.

locus of control Learners may attribute success or failure to external or internal factors. "The teacher didn't review the material well," is an example of attribution to an external factor and represents an external locus of control. In this case, the learner avoids responsibility for behavior. When students have an internal locus of control, they believe that they control their fate and take responsibility for events.

logic The branch of philosophy that deals with reasoning. Logic defines the rules of reasoning, focuses on how to move from one set of assumptions to valid conclusions, and examines the rules of inference that enable us to frame our propositions and arguments.

looping The practice of teaching the same class for several years, over two or even more grades. The purpose is to build stronger teacher-student connections.

lower-order questions Questions that require the retrieval of memorized information and do not require more complex intellectual processes.

M

magnet school A specialized school open to all students in a district on a competitive or lottery basis. It provides a method of drawing children away from segregated neighborhood schools while affording unique educational specialties, such as science, math, and the performing arts.

mainstreaming The inclusion of special education students in the regular education program. The nature and extent of this inclusion should be based on meeting the special needs of the child.

maintenance approach (or developmental approach) A bilingual model that emphasizes the importance of acquiring English while maintaining competence in the native language.

malfeasance Deliberately acting improperly and causing harm to someone.

mastery learning An educational practice in which an individual demonstrates mastery of one task before moving on to the next.

McGuffey Reader For almost 100 years, this reading series promoted moral and patriotic messages and set the practice of reading levels leading toward graded elementary schools.

mentor A guide or an adviser, and a component of some first-year school induction programs designed to assist new teachers.

merit pay A salary system that periodically evaluates teacher performance and uses these evaluations in determining salary.

metacognition Self-awareness of our thinking process as we perform various tasks and operations. For example, when students articulate how they think about academic tasks, it enhances their thinking and enables teachers to target assistance and remediation.

metaphysics The area of philosophy that examines the nature of reality.

microteaching A clinical approach to teacher training in which the teacher candidate teaches a small group of students for a brief time while concentrating on a specific teaching skill.

middle schools Two- to four-year schools of the middle grades, often grades 6 through 8, between elementary school and high school.

minimum competency tests Exit-level tests designed to ascertain whether students have achieved basic levels of performance in such areas as reading, writing, and computation. Some states require that a secondary student pass a minimum competency test in order to receive a high school diploma.

misfeasance Failure to act in a proper manner to prevent harm.

moral stages   Promoted by Lawrence Kohlberg as a model of moral development in which individuals progress from simple moral concerns, such as avoiding punishment, to more sophisticated ethical beliefs and actions.

Morrill Act   Federal legislation (1862) granting federal lands to states to establish colleges to promote more effective and efficient agriculture and industry. A second Morrill Act, passed in 1890, provided federal support for "separate but equal" colleges for African Americans.

multicultural education   Educational policies and practices that not only recognize but also affirm human differences and similarities associated with gender, race, ethnicity, nationality, disability, and class.

multiple intelligences   A theory developed by Howard Gardner to expand the concept of human intelligence to include such areas as logical-mathematical, linguistic, bodily-kinesthetic, musical, spatial, interpersonal, intrapersonal, and naturalist.

N

National Assessment of Educational Progress (NAEP)   Program to ascertain the effectiveness of U.S. schools and student achievement.

National Association of State Directors of Teacher Education and Certification (NASDTEC)   An organization, comprising participating state departments of education, that evaluates teacher education programs in higher education.

National Board for Professional Teaching Standards (NBPTS)   A professional organization charged with establishing voluntary standards for recognizing superior teachers as board certified.

National Council for the Accreditation of Teacher Education (NCATE)   An organization that evaluates teacher education programs in many colleges and universities. Graduates of programs approved by the NCATE receive licenses in over half the states, pending the successful completion of required state exams.

national curricular standards   Nationally prescribed or recommended standards, content skills, and testing.

National Defense Education Act (NDEA)   Federally sponsored programs (1958) to improve science, math, and foreign language instruction in schools.

National Education Association (NEA)   The largest organization of educators, the NEA is concerned with the overall improvement of education and of the conditions of educators. It is organized at the national, state, and local levels.

networking   The term used to describe the intentional effort to develop personal connections with individuals who could be helpful in finding positions or gaining professional advancement.

New England Primer   One of the first textbooks in colonial America, teaching reading and moral messages.

nondiscriminatory education   The principle of nondiscriminatory education, based on the Fifth and Fourteenth Amendments of the U.S. Constitution, mandates that children with disabilities be fairly assessed, so that they can be protected from inappropriate classification and tracking.

nonfeasance   Failure to exercise appropriate responsibility that results in someone's being harmed.

nongraded school   A school organization in which grade levels are eliminated for two or more years.

nonverbal communication   The act of transmitting and/or receiving messages through means not having to do with oral or written language, such as eye contact, facial expressions, and body language.

normal school   A two-year teacher education institution popular in the nineteenth century, many of which were expanded to become today's state colleges and universities.

norm-referenced tests   Tests that compare individual students with others in a designated norm group.

Northwest Ordinance (1785, 1787)   Provided for the sale of federal lands in the Northwest territory to support public schools.

null curriculum   The curriculum that is not taught in schools.

O

objective   The purpose of a lesson expressed in a statement.

objective-referenced tests   Tests that measure whether students have mastered a designated body of knowledge rather than how they compare with other students in a norm group.

observation techniques   Structured methods for observing various aspects of school or classroom activities.

Old Deluder Satan Law (1647)   Massachusetts colony law requiring teachers in towns of fifty families or more and that schools be built in towns of one hundred families or more. Communities must teach children to read so that they can read the Bible and thwart Satan.

open classroom   Based on the British model, it refers not only to an informal classroom environment but also to a philosophy of education. Students pursue individual interests with the guidance and support of the teacher; interest centers are created to promote this individualized instruction. Students may also have a significant influence in determining the nature and sequence of the curriculum. It is sometimes referred to as *open education*.

open enrollment   The practice of permitting students to attend the school of their choice within their school system. It is sometimes associated with magnet schools and desegregation efforts.

open-space school   A school building without interior walls. Although it may be designed to promote the concept of the open classroom, the open-space school is an architectural concept rather than an educational one.

opportunity to learn standards (also called delivery standards)   These standards attempt to recognize and respond to individual differences and circumstances. Poorer students learning in schools with fewer resources should receive more appropriate and adequate learning opportunities, and if some students need more time to take tests, additional time should be provided.

oral tradition   Spoken language is the primary method for instruction in several cultures around the world. Word problems are used to teach reasoning, proverbs to instill wisdom, and stories to teach lessons about nature, history, religion, and social customs.

outcome based education (OBE) An educational approach that emphasizes setting learning outcomes and assessing student progress toward attaining those goals, rather than focusing on curricular topics.

P

paraprofessional A lay person who serves as an aide, assisting the teacher in the classroom.

parochial school An institution operated and controlled by a religious denomination.

peace studies The study and analysis of the conditions of and need for peace, the causes of war, and the mechanisms for the nonviolent resolution of conflict. It is also referred to as *peace education.*

pedagogical cycle A system of teacher-student interaction that includes four steps: structure—teacher introduces the topic; question—teacher asks questions; respond—student answers or tries to answer questions; and react—teacher reacts to student's answers and provides feedback.

pedagogues Term given to home school advocates motivated by humanistic rather than religious goals.

pedagogy The science of teaching.

peer review The practice of having colleagues observe and assess teaching, as opposed to administrators.

perennialism The philosophy that emphasizes rationality as the major purpose of education. It asserts that the essential truths are recurring and universally true; it stresses Great Books.

performance standards Statements that describe what teachers or students should be able to do, and how well they should do it.

permanent license Although there is some variation from state to state, a permanent license is issued after a candidate has completed all the requirements for full recognition as a teacher. Requirements may include a specified number of courses beyond the bachelor's degree or a specified number of years of teaching.

philosophy The love of or search for wisdom; the quest to understand the meaning of life.

phonics An approach to reading instruction that emphasizes decoding words by sounding out letters and combinations of letters (as contrasted with the whole language approach).

Plessey v. Ferguson An 1896 Supreme Court decision that upheld that "separate but equal" was legal and that the races could be segregated. It was overturned in 1954 by *Brown* v. *The Board of Education of Topeka.*

political philosophy An approach to analyzing how past and present societies are arranged and governed and how better societies may be created in the future.

portfolio Compilations of work (such as papers, projects, videotapes) assembled to demonstrate growth, creativity, and competence. Often advocated as a more comprehensive assessment than test scores.

pragmatism A philosophical belief that asserts truth is what works and rejects other views of reality.

Praxis series of tests Developed by ETS to assess teachers' competence in various areas: reading, writing, math, professional and subject area knowledge. Praxis test requirements differ among states (see the Appendix).

primary school A separately organized and administered elementary school for students in the lower elementary grades, usually grades 1 through 3, and sometimes including preprimary years.

private school A school controlled by an individual or agency other than the government, usually supported by other than public funds. Most private schools are parochial.

privatization The movement toward increased private sector, for-profit involvement in the management of public agencies, including schools.

probationary teaching period A specified period of time in which a newly hired teacher must demonstrate teaching competence. This period is usually three years for public school teachers and six years for college professors. Generally, on satisfactory completion of the probationary period, a teacher is granted tenure.

problem-based learning An approach that builds a curriculum around intriguing real-life problems and asks students to work cooperatively to develop and demonstrate their solutions.

procedural due process The right of children with disabilities and their parents to be notified of school actions and decisions; to challenge those decisions before an impartial tribunal, using counsel and expert witnesses; to examine the school records on which a decision is based; and to appeal whatever decision is reached.

professional development School district efforts to improve knowledge, skills and performance of its professional staff.

progressive education (progressivism) An educational philosophy emphasizing democracy, student needs, practical activities, and school-community relationships.

property tax Local real estate taxes (also cars and personal property) historically used to fund local schools.

provisional license Also referred to as a *probationary license,* a provisional license is frequently issued to beginning teachers. It may mean that a person has completed most, but not all, of the state requirements for permanent licensure. Or it may mean that the state requires several years of teaching experience before it will qualify the teacher for permanent licensure.

R

race Refers to a group of individuals sharing common genetic attributes, physical appearance, and ancestry.

racial discrimination Actions that limit or deny a person or group any privileges, roles, or rewards on the basis of race.

racism Attitudes, beliefs, and behavior based on the notion that one race is superior to other races.

rationalism The philosophy that emphasizes the power of reason and the principles of logic to derive statements about the world. Rationalists encourage schools to emphasize teaching mathematics, because mathematics involves reason and logic.

readability formulas Formulas that use objective, quantitative measures to determine the reading level of textbooks.

reciprocity States recognize and honor another state's actions, such as recognizing a teacher's license in one state as valid in another.

reconstructionism (reconstructionist)   Also called social reconstructionism, this is a view of education as a way to improve the quality of life, to reduce the chances of conflict, and to create a more humane world.

reflective teaching   Predicated on a broad and in-depth understanding of what is happening in the classroom, reflective teaching promotes thoughtful consideration and dialogue about classroom events.

regular education initiative   The attempt to reduce the complications and expense of segregated special education efforts by teaching special needs students in the standard educational program through collaborative consultation, curricular modifications, and environment adaptations.

relational aggression   Refers to subtle, unhealthy peer dynamics used to gain social power (examples include spreading rumors and gossip, excluding peers, teasing, covert bullying).

résumé   A summary of a person's education and experiences, often used for application to school or employment.

revenue sharing   The distribution of federal money to state and local governments to use as they decide.

Robin Hood laws   As a result of court actions, many states are redistributing revenue from wealthier to poorer communities to equalize educational funding, a process not unlike the efforts of the hero of Sherwood Forest.

romantic critics   Critics such as Paul Goodman, Herbert Kohl, and John Holt who believed that schools were stifling the cognitive and affective development of children. Individual critics stressed different problems or solutions, but they all agreed that schools were producing alienated, uncreative, and unfulfilled students.

rubric   A scoring guide that describes what must be done, and often describes performance levels ranging from novice to expert, or from a failing grade to excellence.

S

sabbatical   A leave usually granted with full or partial pay after a teacher has taught for a specified period of time (for example, six years). Typically, it is to encourage research and professional development. While common at the university level, it is rare for K–12 teachers.

scaffolding   Taking from the construction field, scaffolding provides support to help a student build understanding. The teacher might use cues or encouragement or well-formulated questions to assist a student in solving a problem or mastering a concept.

school-based management   The recent trend in education reform that stresses decision making on the school level. In the past, school policies were set by the state and the districts. Now the trend is for individual schools to make their own decisions and policies.

school choice   The name given to several programs in which parents choose what school their child will attend.

school financing   Refers to the ways in which monies are raised and allocated to schools. The methods differ widely from state to state, and many challenges are being made in courts today because of the unequal distribution of funds within a state or among states.

school infrastructure   The basic facilities and structures that underpin a school plant, such as plumbing, sewage, heat, electricity, roof, masonry, and carpentry.

school superintendent   The chief administrator of a school system, responsible for implementing and enforcing the school board's policies, rules, and regulations, as well as state and federal requirements. The superintendent is directly responsible to the school board and is the formal representative of the school community to outside individuals and agencies.

School to Work Opportunities Act   Programs that link school learning to job settings, often developed in partnerships between school and industry.

schools without walls   An alternative education program that involves the total community as a learning resource.

secondary school   A program of study that follows elementary school and includes junior, middle, and high school.

second-generation segregation   When a school's multiracial populations are separated through tracking, extracurricular activities, and even in informal social events, the school is considered to be in second-generation segregation.

secular humanism   The belief that people can live ethically without faith in a supernatural or supreme being. Some critics have alleged that secular humanism is a form of religion and that publishers are promoting secular humanism in their books.

self-censorship (also called stealth censorship)   In order to avoid possible problems and parental complaints, some educators quietly remove a book from a library shelf or a course of study. Teachers practice the same sort of self-censorship when they choose not to teach a topic or not to discuss a difficult issue.

separate but equal   A legal doctrine that holds that equality of treatment is accorded when the races are provided substantially equal facilities, even though those facilities are separate. This doctrine was ruled unconstitutional in regard to race.

service credit   By volunteering in a variety of community settings, from nursing homes to child care facilities, students are encouraged to develop a sense of community and meet what is now a high school graduation requirement in some states.

sex discrimination   Any action that limits or denies a person or group of persons opportunities, privileges, roles, or rewards on the basis of sex.

sexism   The collection of attitudes, beliefs, and behavior that results from the assumption that one sex is superior to the other.

sex-role stereotyping   Attributing behavior, abilities, interests, values, and roles to a person or group of persons on the basis of sex. This process ignores individual differences.

sexual harassment   Unwanted, repeated, and unreturned sexual words, behaviors, or gestures prohibited by federal and some state laws.

simulation   A role-playing technique in which students take part in re-created, life-like situations.

social reconstructionism (see **reconstructionism**)

sociogram   A diagram that is constructed to record social interactions, such as which children interact frequently and which are isolates.

Socratic method   An educational strategy attributed to Socrates in which a teacher encourages a student's discovery of truth by questions.

special education   Programs and instruction for children with physical, mental, emotional, or learning disabilities or gifted students who need special educational services in order to achieve at their ability level.

special license   A nonteaching license that is designed for specialized educational careers, such as counseling, library science, and administration.

spirituality   A personal and pluralistic view of life's meaning, broader than any particular religion, but encompassing many ideas common to all religions. It includes beliefs and activities which renew, lift up, comfort, heal, and inspire both ourselves and others.

standards-based education   Education that specifies precisely what students should learn, focuses the curriculum and instruction (and perhaps much more) on meeting these standards, and provides continual testing to see if the standards are achieved.

state adoption   The process by which members of a textbook adoption committee review and select the books used throughout a state. Advocates of this process say that it results in a common statewide curriculum that unites educators on similar issues and makes school life easier for students who move within the state. Critics charge that it gives too much influence to large states and results in a "dumbed down" curriculum.

state board of education   The state education agency that regulates policies necessary to implement legislative acts related to education.

state department of education   An agency that operates under the direction of the state board of education, accrediting schools, certifying teachers, appropriating state school funds, and so on.

stepfamilies   These relationships are created when divorced or widowed parents remarry, creating a whole set of new relationships, including stepchildren, stepgrandparents, and stepparents.

stereotypes   Absolute statements applied to all members of a group, suggesting that members of a group have a fixed, often inherited set of characteristics.

stereotype threat   A measure of how social context, such as self-image, trust in others, and a sense of belonging, can influence academic performance.

street academies   Alternative schools designed to bring dropouts and potential dropouts, often inner-city youths, back into the educational mainstream.

student-initiated questions   These are content-related questions originating from the student, yet comprising only a small percentage of the questions asked in class.

superintendent of schools   The executive officer of the local school district.

T

taxonomy   A classification system of organizing information and translating aims into instructional objectives.

teacher centers   Sites to provide training to improve teaching skills, inform teachers of current educational research, and develop new curricular programs.

teacher flexibility   Adapting a variety of skills, abilities, characteristics, and approaches, according to the demands of each situation and the needs of each student.

Teach for America   A program that places unlicensed college graduates in districts with critical teacher shortages as they work toward attaining a teacher license.

tenure   A system of employment in which teachers, having served a probationary period, acquire an expectancy of continued employment. The majority of states have tenure laws.

Tesseract   Formerly Educational Alternatives, this private company works in the public school sector, attempting to improve school efficiency and student achievement, while making a profit.

textbook adoption states   States, most often those in the South and West, that have a formal process for assessing, choosing, and approving textbooks for school use.

Title I   Section of the Elementary and Secondary Education Act that provides federal funds to supplement local education resources for students from low-income families.

Title IX   A provision of the 1972 Educational Amendments that prohibits sex discrimination in any educational program receiving federal financial assistance.

tracking   The method of placing students according to their ability level in homogeneous classes or learning experiences. Once a student is placed, it may be very difficult to move up from one track to another. The placements may reflect racism, classism, or sexism.

transitional bilingual education   A bilingual education program in which students are taught for a limited time in their own language as well as English. The goal is to move students into English-only speaking classrooms.

trustee representatives   This conception of a school board member's role differs from the delegate approach, as members are viewed as representatives of the entire community, rather than representing the narrower interests of a particular group or neighborhood.

tuition tax credits   Tax reductions for parents or guardians of children attending public or private schools.

U

unobtrusive measurement   A method of observing a situation without altering it.

unremarked revolution   The unheralded but persistent move of schools away from formal tracking programs.

V

values clarification   A model, comprising various strategies, that encourages students to express and clarify their values on different topics.

virtual field trip   Visiting distant sites and events via the computer and the Internet.

vouchers   A voucher is like a coupon, and it represents money targeted for schools. In a voucher system, parents use educational vouchers to "shop" for a school. Schools receive part or all of their per-pupil funding from these vouchers. In theory, good schools would thrive and poor ones would close for lack of students.

W

wait time   The amount of time a teacher waits for a student's response after a question is asked and the amount of time following a student's response before the teacher reacts.

whole language approach   Teaching reading through an integration of language arts skills and knowledge, with a heavy emphasis on literature (as contrasted with a phonics approach).

women's studies   Originally created during the 1970s to study the history, literature, psychology, and experiences of women, topics typically missing from the traditional curriculum.

World Wide Web   Most common connection to the Internet; contains numerous sites which can be accessed by a Web browser.

Z

zero reject   The principle that no child with disabilities may be denied a free and appropriate public education.

zero-tolerance policies   Such rigorous rules offer schools little or no flexibility in responding to student infractions related to alcohol, drugs, tobacco, violence, and weapons. These policies have been developed by both local school districts and a number of state legislatures, and in most cases, students who violate such policies must be expelled.

zone of proximal development   The area where students can move from what they know to new learning, a zone where real learning is possible.

CHAPTER 1 BECOMING A TEACHER

1. National Education Association, *Status of the American Public School Teacher,* 2000–2001 (Washington, DC: NEA, 2003).
2. Amy DePaul, *What to Expect Your First Year of Teaching* (Washington, DC: U.S. Department of Education, September 1998), p. 28.
3. Quoted in Ann Lieberman and Lynn Miller, *Teachers, Their World and Their Work* (Alexandria, VA: Association for Supervision and Curriculum Development, 1984), p. 22.
4. Louis Harris and Associates, *The Metropolitan Life Survey of the American Teacher 2001* (New York: Metropolitan Life Insurance Company, 2001).
5. Lieberman and Miller, *Teachers, Their World and Their Work,* p. 47.
6. William Lyon Phelps, quoted in Oliver Ikenberry, *American Education Foundations* (Columbus, OH: Merrill, 1974), p. 389.
7. Quoted in Myron Brenton, *What's Happened to Teacher?* (New York: Coward, McCann & Geoghegan, 1970), p. 164.
8. Stephen Gordon quoted in "What Keeps Teachers Going?," *Educational Leadership 60,* no. 8 (May 2003), p. 18.
9. Steve Twomey and Richard Morin, "Teachers: Besieged, Delighted," *The Washington Post,* July 4, 1999, pp. A1, A12.
10. American Federation of Teachers, "Survey and Analysis of Teacher Salary Trends 2004" (Washington, DC: AFT), retrieved on February 8, 2006, from www.aft.org.
11. Quoted in Brenton, *What's Happened to Teacher?* p. 97.
12. Ibid., p. 94.
13. National Commission on Teaching and America's Future, "No Dream Denied: A Pledge to America's Children" (Washington, DC: NCTAF, 2003).
14. Carol Davis quote from "Are You Treated Like a Professional? Or a Tall Child?" *NEA Today,* December 1988, p. 4.
15. Jillian N. Lederhouse, "Show Me the Power" Education Week, June 13, 2001; National Education Association, *Status of the American Public School Teacher,* 2000–2001 (Washington, DC: NEA, 2003).
16. Ron Brandt, "On Teacher Empowerment: A Conversation with Ann Lieberman," *Educational Leadership* 46, no. 8 (May 1989), pp. 23–24.
17. Adopted from Robert Howsam et al., *Educating a Profession, Report on the Bicentennial Commission of Education for Profession of Teaching* (Washington, DC: American Association of Colleges for Teacher Education, 1976), pp. 6–7.
18. Ibid., pp. 8–9.
19. *Tomorrow's Teachers: A Report of the Holmes Group* (East Lansing, MI: Holmes Group, 1986).
20. Carnegie Forum on Education and the Economy, Task Force on Teaching as a Profession, *A Nation Prepared: Teachers for the Twenty-First Century* (New York: Forum, 1986).
21. John Goodlad, "A Study of the Education of Educators: One Year Later," *Phi Delta Kappan* 73, no. 4 (December 1991), pp. 311–16.
22. "Quality Counts 2006" (Bethesda, MD: Editorial Projects in Education, January 5, 2006), vol. 25, issue 17.
23. Michael Podgursky, "Should States Subsidize National Certification?" *Education Week on the Web,* April 11, 2001.
24. Linda Darling-Hammond, "Who Will Speak for the Children?: How 'Teach for America' Hurts Urban Schools and Students," *Phi Delta Kappan* 76, no. 1 (September 1994), pp. 21–34; Linda Darling-Hammond, "Teacher Quality and Student Achievement," *Education Policy Analysis,* vol. 8, no. 1 (January 2000), retrieved from http://epaa.asu.edu/epaa/v8n1; For the other side of this debate, see Wendy Kopp, "Ten Years of Teach for America" in *Education Week on the Web,* June 21, 2000, and Wendy Kopp, *One Day All Children Will Triumph: The Unlikely Story of Teach for America and What I Learned Along the Way* (New York, PublicAffairs, 2003).
25. Linda Darling-Hammond, "The Futures of Teaching," *Educational Leadership* 46, no. 3 (November 1988), p. 6; Linda Darling-Hammond, Ruth Chung, and Fred Frelow, "Variation in Teacher Preparation: How Well Do Different Pathways Prepare Teachers to Teach?" *Journal of Teacher Education* 53, no. 4 (September/October 2002), p. 286.
26. Idiko Laczko-Kerr and David Berliner, "In Harm's Way: How Uncertified Teachers Hurt Their Students," *Educational Leadership 60,* no. 8 (May 2003), pp. 34–39.
27. Linda Darling-Hammond, "Keeping Good Teachers: Why It Matters What Leaders Can Do, "*Educational Leadership 60,* no. 8 (May 2003), pp. 7–13.
28. Susan Moore Johnson and Sarah Birkeland, "Fast-Track Certification: Can We Prepare Teachers Both Quickly and Well?" *Education Week* 25, issue 23, pp. 37, 48 (Bethesda, MD: Editorial Projects, February 15, 2006); "Research-Based Characteristics of High-Quality Teacher Preparation," *ASCD SmartBrief 1,* no. 4 (February 19, 2003); Linda Darling-Hammond, Deborah J. Holtzman, Su Jin Gatlin, and Julian Vasquez Heilig, *Does Teacher Preparation Matter? Evidence about Teacher Certification, Teach for America, and Teacher Effectiveness.* Paper presented at the American Educational Association Annual Meeting, Montreal, April 2005. Retrieved on July 19, 2005 from www.schoolredesign.net/srn/binaries/teachercert.pdf; Marilyn Cochran-Smith and Kenneth Zeichner (eds.), *Studying Teacher Education: The Report of the AERA Panel on Research and Teacher Education* (Mahwah, NJ: Lawrence Erlbaum, 2005).
29. *Different Drummers: How Teachers of Teachers View Public Education* (New York: Public Agenda, 1997).
30. Peter D. Hart and Robert M. Teeter, *A National Priority: Americans Speak on Teacher Quality* (Princeton, NJ: Educational Testing Service, 2002); Leslie Kaplan and William Owning, "No Child Left Behind: The Politics of Teacher Quality," *Phi Delta Kappan 84,* no. 9 (2003), pp. 687–692.
31. Linda Darling-Hammond, "Keeping Good Teachers: Why It Matters What Leaders Can Do," *Educational Leadership 60,* no. 8 (May 2003), pp. 7–13.

32. David C. Berliner, "A Personal Response to Those Who Bash Teacher Education," *Journal of Teacher Education* 51, no. 5 (November/December 2000), pp. 358–71; Suzanne M. Wilson, Robert E. Floden, and Joan Ferrini-Mundy, "Teacher Preparation Research: An Insider's View from the Outside," *Journal of Teacher Education 53,* no. 3 (May/June 2002), pp. 190–204.

33. Ibid., p. 363. See also College Board, "2005 College-Bound Seniors" retrieved on February 11, 2006, from www.collegeboard.com/prod_downloads/about/news_info/cbsenior/yr2005/2005-college-bound-seniors.pdf.

34. Lowell Rose and Alec Gallup, "The 33rd Phi Delta Kappa Poll of the Public's Attitudes Toward the Public Schools," retrieved on February 12, 2006, from www.pdkintl.org/kappan/kimages/kpoll83.pdf; For other public reaction to education issues, follow the annual Phi Delta Kappa/Gallup Poll report on the Public's Attitudes toward the Public Schools at www.pdkintl.org/kappan/kpollpdf.htm.

35. Arthur E. Wise, "What's Wrong with Teacher Certification?" *Education Week 22,* no. 30 (April 9, 2003), pp. 56, 42; and Susan Moore Johnson and Sarah Birkeland, "Fast-Track Certification: Can We Prepare Teachers Both Quickly and Well?" *Education Week* 25, issue 23, (February 15, 2006), pp. 37, 48.

36. Andy Baumgartner, "A Teacher Speaks Out: Insights from the National Teacher of the Year," *The Washington Post,* March 26, 2000, p. B4.

37. Robert Gates, "Questions Every Teacher Should Answer," *Classroom Leadership* (August 1999), pp. 1–3; Kevin and Jackie Freiberg, *Nuts!* (New York: Broadway Books, 1996), pp. 320–327.

CHAPTER 2　DIFFERENT WAYS OF LEARNING

1. Kenneth Dunn and Rita Dunn, "Dispelling Outmoded Beliefs About Student Learning," *Educational Leadership* 45, no. 7 (March 1987), pp. 55–63.

2. James Keefe, *Learning Style Theory and Practice* (Reston, VA: National Association of Secondary School Principals, 1987); Paul Zielbauer, "Considering a Later Bell for Connecticut's Sleepy Children," *The New York Times,* February 20, 2001 (www.nytimes.com); Tamara Henry, "Open Up Schools, Let Sun Shine In: Creature Comforts Can Aid Learning," *USA Today,* 22 March 2001, p. 8D.

3. Dunn and Dunn, "Dispelling Outmoded Beliefs About Student Learning"; see also G. Price, "Which Learning Style Elements Are Stable and Which Tend to Change?" *Learning Styles Network Newsletter* 4, no. 2 (1980), pp. 38–40; J. Vitrostko, *An Analysis of the Relationship Among Academic Achievement in Mathematics and Reading, Assigned Instructional Schedules and the Learning Style Time Preferences of Third-, Fourth-, Fifth-, and Sixth-Grade Students,* unpublished doctoral dissertation, St. John's University, Jamaica, New York, 1983.

4. Gay, Lesbian, and Straight Education Network, www.glsen.com.

5. Jason Cianciotto and Sean Cahill, *Education Policy: Issues Affecting Lesbian, Gay, Bisexual and Transgender Youth* (New York: The National Gay and Lesbian Task Force Policy Institute, 2003).

6. Ian K. Macgillivray, *Gay-Straight Alliances: A Handbook for Students, Educators, and Parents* (Binghampton: Haworth Press, 2007).

7. Howard Gardner and Thomas Hatch, "Multiple Intelligences Go to School: Educational Implications of the Theory of Multiple Intelligences," *Educational Researcher* 18, no. 8 (November 1989), p. 5.

8. Kathy Checkley, "The First Seven . . . and the Eighth: A Conversation with Howard Gardner," *Educational Leadership* 55, no. 1 (September 1997), pp. 8–13; Howard Gardner, "Beyond the I.Q.: Education and Human Development," *Harvard Educational Review* 57, no. 2 (Spring 1987), pp. 187–93.

9. Thomas Armstrong, "Multiple Intelligences: Seven Ways to Approach Curriculum," *Educational Leadership* 52 (November 1994), pp. 26–28; see also Howard Gardner, *Intelligence Reframed: Multiple Intelligences for the 21st Century* (New York: Basic Books, 1999).

10. Howard Gardner, "Can Technology Exploit the Many Ways of Knowing?" in David T. Gordon, ed., *The Digital Classroom* (Cambridge, MA: Harvard College, 2000), pp. 32–35.

11. Howard Gardner, "Reflections on Multiple Intelligences: Myths and Messages," *Phi Delta Kappan 77,* no. 3 (November 1995), pp. 200–9; Veronica Borruso Emig, "A Multiple Intelligence Inventory," *Educational Leadership* 55, no. 1 (September 1997), pp. 47–50.

12. Thomas R. Hoerr, "How the New City School Applies the Multiple Intelligences," *Educational Leadership* 52 (November 1994), pp. 29–33.

13. Nancy Gibbs, "The E.Q. Factor," *Time* 146, no. 14 (October 2, 1995), pp. 60–68.

14. Ibid. See also Kevin R. Kelly and Sidney M. Moon, "Personal and Social Talents," *Phi Delta Kappan* 79, no. 10 (June 1998), pp. 743–46.

15. Daniel Goleman, "Emotional Intelligence: Why It Can Matter More Than IQ," *Learning* (May/June 1996), pp. 49–50; see a sample application of EQ in Emily Wax, "Educating More Than the Mind," *The Washington Post,* October 4, 2000, p. B3.

16. These categories build on the ones described by William Heward and Rodney A. Cavanaugh, "Educational Equality for Students with Disabilities," in James Banks and Cherry Banks (eds.), *Multicultural Education,* 5th edition (San Francisco: Jossey Bass, 2004), pp. 317–349.

17. Gene I. Maeroff, "The Unfavored Gifted Few," *New York Times Magazine,* August 21, 1977, reprinted in Celeste Toriero (ed.), *Readings in Education 78/79* (Guilford, CT: Dushkin, 1978); Michael Janofsky, "Some New Help for the Extremely Gifted," *The New York Times* (October 26, 2005). Retrieved from www.nytimes.com.

18. Valerie Strauss, "Looking for a Few Wise Children," *The Washington Post,* September 17, 2002, p. A11.

19. John F. Feldhusen, "Programs for the Gifted Few or Talent Development for the Many?" *Phi Delta Kappan* 79, no. 10 (June 1998), pp. 735–38; Dona J. Matthews and Joanne F. Foster, "Mystery to Mastery: Shifting Paradigms in Gifted Education," *Roeper Review,* vol. 28, Iss. 2 (Winter 2006), pp. 64–69.

20. Judy Galbraith, "Gifted Youth and Self-Concept," *Gifted Education* 15, no. 2 (May 1989), pp. 15–17.
21. Ibid., p. 16.
22. Diana Jean Schemo, "Schools, Facing Tight Budgets, Leave Gifted Students Behind," *The New York Times* (March 2, 2004). Retrieved from www.nytimes.com.
23. Robert Morris, "Educating Gifted for the 1990s," *Gifted Education* 15, no. 2 (May 1989), pp. 50–52; for more information about gender bias, *see Gender Gaps: Where Schools Still Fail Our Children* (Washington, DC: American Association of University Women Educational Foundation, 1998); Dona J. Matthews and Joanne F. Foster, "Mystery to Mastery: Shifting Paradigms in Gifted Education," *Roeper Review,* vol. 28, Iss. 2 (Winter 2006), pp. 64–69.
24. Susan Winebrenner, "Gifted Students Need an Education, Too," *Educational Leadership* 58, no. 1 (September 2000), pp. 52–56.
25. John Feldhusen, "Synthesis of Research on Gifted Youth," *Educational Leadership* 46, no. 6 (March 1989), pp. 6–11.
26. Quoted in Galbraith, "Gifted Youth and Self-Concept," p. 17.
27. Marie Killilea, *Karen* (New York: Dell, 1952), p. 171.
28. Ed Martin, quoted in "PL 94–142," *Instructor* 87, no. 9 (1978), p. 63.
29. Michael D. Simpson, "Rights Watch: Who's Paying for Special Ed?" *NEA Today* 15, no. 9 (May 1997), p. 20; Linda Greenhouse, "Parents Now Have the Burden of Proof in School Cases, Court Rules, *The New York Times* (November 15, 2005). Retrieved from www.nytimes.com.
30. United States Department of Education, Office of Special Education Programs. Twenty-fifth Annual Report to Congress on the Implementation of the Individuals with Disabilities Education Act, Washington, DC (2003).
31. Sandra Blakeslee, "Study Shows Increase in Autism," *The New York Times,* January 1, 2003, online.
32. "Disproportionate Identification of Students with Learning Disabilities," *ASCD SmartBrief 1,* no. 3 (February 5, 2003); Shari Rudavsky, "Report Targets Special Needs: Limits Urged on Enrollment," *Boston Globe,* December 29, 2002, p. A27.
33. "Special Report/Racial Inequities in Special Education," *Education Leadership 60,* no. 4 (December 2002/January 2003), p. 91; Jay Mathews, "Study Finds Racial Bias in Special Ed," *The Washington Post,* 3 March 2001, p. A1.
34. Katherine Seligman, "Hyperactive Girls Escape Detection," *San Francisco Chronicle,* October 1, 2002, p. A-1; Anand Vaishnav and Bill Dedman, "Special Ed Gender Gap Stirs Worry," *Boston Globe,* July 8, 2002, p. A1.
35. Suzy Ruder, "We Teach All," *Educational Leadership 58,* no. 1 (September 2000), pp. 49–51; Mary Beth Doyle, "Transition Plans for Students with Disabilities," *Educational Leadership 58,* no. 1 (September 2000), pp. 46–48.
36. Condition of Education 2005, "Inclusion of Students with Disabilities in Regular Classrooms" (Washington, DC: National Center for Educational Statistics, 2005). Retrieved from http://nces.ed.gov/pubs2005/2005094.pdf, p. 35.
37. Quoted in David Milofsky, "Schooling the Kid No One Wants," *The New York Times Magazine,* January 2, 1977, pp. 24–29.
38. Charles A. MacArthur, "Using Technology to Enhance the Writing Processes of Students with Learning Disabilities," *Journal of Learning Disabilities* 29, no. 4 (1996), pp. 344–54; Debra K. Bauder, "Assistive Technology: Learning Devices for Special Needs Students," *Media & Methods* 32, no. 3 (1996), pp. 16, 18; Nancy Trejos, "Handheld PCs Put to the Test," *The Washington Post,* September 4, 2001, pp. B1, B2; Jennifer Medina, "Technology Eases the Way for the Visually Impaired," *The New York Times,* July 3, 2002, www.nytimes.com; Michael P. Bruno, "High-Tech Help for Disabled Children," Washtech.com, May 10, 2002, p. 5.
39. Solomon Moore, "Special Ed Joins the Mainstream," *Los Angeles Times,* October 2002, online.

CHAPTER 3 CULTURALLY RESPONSIVE TEACHING

1. *Do We Still Need Public Schools?* (Washington, DC: Center on National Educational Policy and Phi Delta Kappa, 1996), p. 14; Maxine Schwartz Seller, "Immigrants in the Schools—Again: Historical and Contemporary Perspectives on the Education of Post 1965 Immigrants in the United States," *Educational Foundations* 3, no. 1 (Spring 1989), pp. 53–75.
2. The demographic information in the following section is based on the following: "Overview of Race and Hispanic Origin," *Census 2000 Brief* (Washington, DC: U.S. Census Bureau, March 2001); "Projections of the Resident Population by Race, Hispanic Origin, and Nativity: 2025 to 2045," *Census 2000 Brief* (Washington, DC: U.S. Census Bureau, March 2001); "Profiles of General Demographic Characteristics," *Census 2000* (Washington, DC: U.S. Census Bureau, March 2001); William Branigin, "Nearly 1 in 10 in U.S. Is Foreign Born, Census Says," *The Washington Post,* April 9, 1997, p. A18; Jessica I. Sandham, "Graduates Growing More Diverse, Study Finds," *Education Week on the Web,* April 1, 1998; *Statistical Abstract of the United States, 1997* (Washington, DC: U.S. Department of Commerce, Bureau of the Census, 1996); *Youth Indicators* (Washington DC: National Center for Education Statistics, Department of Education, 1996).
3. Christopher B. Swanson, *The Real Truth about Low Graduation Rates, An Evidenced Based Commentary* (Washington, D.C.: The Urban Institute, 2004); Debra Viadero and Robert Johnson, "Lifting Minority Achievement: Complex Answers," *Education Week* 19, no. 30 (April 5, 2000), pp. 14–16.
4. Lowell C. Rose and Alec M. Gallup, "The 33rd Annual Phi Delta Kappa/Gallup Poll of the Public's Attitude Toward the Public Schools," *Phi Delta Kappan* 83, no. 1 (September 2001), pp. 41–58.
5. Lowell C. Rose and Alec M. Gallup, "The 37th Annual Phi Delta Kappa/Gallup Poll of the Public's Attitude Toward the Public Schools," *Phi Delta Kappan* 87, no. 1 (September 2005), pp. 41–57.

6. Robert Evans, "Reframing the Achievement Gap," *Phi Delta Kappan 86*, no. 8 (April 2005), pp. 582–589.

7. Andrew Hacker, *Two Nations: Black, White, Separate, Hostile, Unequal* (New York: Charles Scribner's, 1992), pp. 31–32.

8. Ana Maria Villegas, "Culturally Responsive Pedagogy for the 1990s and Beyond," Washington, DC: ERIC Clearinghouse on Teacher Education, American Association of Colleges for Teacher Education, 1991.

9. Israel Zangwill, *The Melting Pot* (play), 1909; cited in Pamela Tiedt and Iris Tiedt, *Multicultural Education* (Needham Heights, MA: Allyn and Bacon, 1999), p. 2.

10. James Crawford, ed., *Language Loyalties: A Source Book on the Official English Controversy* (Chicago: University of Chicago Press, 1992); see also Jonathon Zimmerman, "A Babel of Tongues," *U.S. News & World Report*, 24 November 1997, p. 39.

11. Diane Ravitch, "Politicization and the Schools: The Case of Bilingual Education," in *Taking Sides*, James W. Noll (ed.) (Guilford, CT: Dushkin, 1997), pp. 232–40.

12. James Lyon, "Legal Responsibilities of Education Agencies Serving National Origin Language Minority Students" (Chevy Chase, MD: Mid-Atlantic Equity Center, 1992). Available at www.maec.org/lyons/contents.html#return.

13. *The Condition of Education, 2005* (Washington, DC: National Center for Educational Statistics, 2005). Available at www.nces.ed.gov/programs/coe/2005/section1/indicator05.asp.

14. Christine Bennett, *Comprehensive Multicultural Education: Theory and Practice,* 5th ed. (Boston: Allyn & Bacon, 2003).

15. D. Hugo Lopez and Merle T. Mora, "Bilingual Education and the Labor Market Earnings Among Hispanics: Evidence Using High School and Beyond," *READ Perspectives* (Amherst, MA: Institute for Research in English Acquisition and Development), 1998.

16. Jorge Amselle, "Adios, Bilingual Ed," *Policy Review* no. 86, November 1997 (Washington, DC: Heritage Foundation), pp. 52–55; Charles B. Swanson, *The Real Truth about Low Graduation Rates: An Evidence-Based Commentary* (Washington, DC: The Urban Institute, 2004).

17. Rene Sanchez and William Booth, "California Rejection: A Big Blow to Bilingualism: Decisive Vote Could Set Pace for Rest of Nation," *The Washington Post,* June 4, 1998, p. A16; Peter Baker, "Education Dept Faults Anti-Bilingual Measure," *The Washington Post,* April 28, 1998, p. A3; Lisa Anderson, "Bilingual Debate Reaches Boiling Point: Battle Wages with Ballots, Initiatives, Studies, Placards," *Tribune on the Web,* May 29, 2001; Tyche Hendricks, "No Benefit Found in English-Only Instruction," *San Francisco Chronicle* (February 22, 2006), p. A1; *Effects of the Implementation of Proposition 227 on the Education of English Learners, K–12* (Washington, DC: American Institutes of Research and WestEd, 2006), retrieved from www.wested.org/online_pubs/227YR5_Report.pdf.

18. Yilu Zhao, "Wave of Pupils Lacking English Strains Schools," *The New York Times,* August 5, 2002, online.

19. James Crawford, *Hold Your Tongue: Bilingualism and the Politics of "English Only"* (New York: Addison-Wesley, 1992), pp. 111–12.

20. Gary A. Cziko, "The Evaluation of Bilingual Education: From Necessity and Probability to Possibility," *Educational Researcher* 21, no. 2 (March 1992), p. 24; J. David Ramirez, "Executive Summary," *Bilingual Research Journal* 16 (Winter/Spring, 1992), pp. 1–245.

21. Rosalie Pedalino Porter, New York City Study. *READ Perspectives* 12 (2), 1995, quoted in Robert F. McNergney and Joanne M. Herbert, *Foundations of Education* (Needham Heights, MA: Allyn & Bacon, 1998), p. 311.

22. Peter Schmidt, "Three Types of Bilingual Education Effective, E.D. Study Concludes," *Education Week,* February 20, 1991, pp. 1, 23.

23. Wayne Thomas and Virginia Collier, "Two Languages Are Better Than One," *Educational Leadership* 55, no. 4 (December 1997/January 1998), pp. 23–26; Kenneth J. Cooper, "Riley Endorses Two-Way Bilingual Education," *The Washington Post,* March 26, 2000, p. A2; Cara Simmon, "School Puts New Accent on Learning Two Languages," *Seattle Times,* April 1, 2003, online.

24. Frederick M. Hess, "Schools of Reeducation," *The Washington Post*, February 5, 2006, p. B7.

25. Christopher B. Swanson, *The Real Truth about Low Graduation Rates, An Evidenced-Based Commentary* (Washington, D.C.: The Urban Institute, 2004); Phillip Kaufman, Martha Naomi Alt, and Christopher Chapman, *Dropout Rates in the United States: 2000* (Washington, D.C.: National Center for Educational Statistics, 2001); M. F. Riche, "American Diversity and Growth: Signposts for the 21st Century," *Population Bulletin* (Washington, D.C.: Population Reference Bureau, 2000), vol. 55, no. 2, pp. 3–38; and Gary Orfield and Chungmei Lee, *Racial Transformation and the Changing Nature of Segregation* (Cambridge, MA: The Civil Rights Project, Harvard University, 2006).

26. Christine Sleeter, "Curriculum Controversies in Multicultural Education," in *Issues in the Curriculum: A Selection of Chapters from Past NSSE Yearbooks, Ninety-eighth Yearbook of the National Society for the Study of Education,* Margaret Early and Kenneth Rehage, eds. (Chicago: University of Chicago Press, 1999), p. 261.

27. James Banks, "Multicultural Education: Characteristics and Goals," in James A. Banks and Cherry A. McGee Banks (eds.), *Multicultural Education: Issues and Perspectives,* 4th ed. (Boston: Allyn & Bacon, 2001), pp. 3–30.

28. James Banks, "Approaches to Multicultural Curriculum Reform," in Banks and Banks, *Multicultural Education,* 4th ed., pp. 225–46.

29. Peter Schmidt, "New Survey Discerns Deep Divisions Among U.S. Youths on Race Relations," *Education Week,* March 25, 1992, p. 5.

30. Christine I. Bennett, *Comprehensive Multicultural Education: Theory and Practice,* 4th ed. (Needham Heights, MA: Allyn & Bacon, 1999), pp. 255–256; and Gloria Ladson-Billings, "But That's Just Good Teaching," *Theory Into Practice* 34, no. 3 (Summer 1995), pp.159–165.

31. Geneva Gay, "Achieving Educational Equality Through Curriculum Desegregation," *Phi Delta Kappan* 72, no. 1 (September 1990), pp. 56–62.

32. Carol Gilligan, *In a Different Voice: Psychological Theory and Women's Development* (Cambridge, MA: Harvard

University Press, 1982). See also Mary Field Belenky, Blythe McVicker Clinchy, Nancy Rule Goldberger, and Jill Mattuck Tarule, *Women's Ways of Knowing: The Development of Self, Voice, and Mind* (New York: Basic Books, 1986).

33. Julie Chlebo, "There Is Not Rose Garden: A Second Generation Rural Head Start Program," unpublished doctoral dissertation, 1999, quoted in Christine I. Bennett, *Comprehensive Multicultural Education: Theory and Practice,* 4th ed. (Needham Heights, MA: Allyn & Bacon, 1999), pp. 259.

34. Joshua Aronson, "The Threat of Stereotype," *Educational Leadership* 62, no. 3 (November 2004), pp. 14–19.

35. Joshua Aronson, "The Effects of Conceiving Ability as Fixed or Improvable on Responses to Stereotype Threat," unpublished manuscript, New York University, 2004.

36. Carol Dweck, *Self Theories: Their Role in Motivation, Personality and Development* (Philadelphia: Taylor & Francis, 1999).

37. Carlos Cortes, *The Children Are Watching: How the Media Teach About Diversity* (New York: Teachers College Press, 2000), pp. 149–150; Barbara J. Shade, Cynthia Kelly, and Mary Oberg, *Creating Culturally Responsive Classrooms* (Washington, DC: American Psychological Association, 1997).

38. "Common Core Data, 2003–04 (Washington, DC: U.S. Department of Education, NCES). Found online March 8, 2006 at http://nces.ed.gov/ccd/; Children's Defense Fund www.childrensdefense.org/. . . childpoverty/default.aspx, modified on March 5, 2006, and retrieved March 9, 2006; www.census.gov/; and Ian K. Macgillivray, *Sexual Orientation and School Policy: A Practical Guide for Teachers, Administrators, and Community Activists* (Lanham, MD: Rowman & Littlefield, 2004).

39. The information about generalizations and different group learning styles is drawn from a variety of sources, including Bobby Ann Starnes, "What We Don't Know Can Hurt Them: White Teachers, Indian Children," *Phi Delta Kappan* 87, no 5 (January 2006); pp. 384–392; Christine Bennett, *Comprehensive Multicultural Education: Theory and Practice* 5th ed. (Boston: Pearson Education Inc., 2003); Kenneth Cushner, *Human Diversity in Action: Developing Multicultural Competencies for the Classroom* (New York: McGraw-Hill, 2006); Gary A. Davis & Sylvia Rimm, *Cultural Diversity and Children from Low Socioeconomic Backgrounds* (Boston: Allyn & Bacon, 1997); K. M. Evenson Worthley, "Learning Style Factor of Field Dependence/Independence and Problem Solving Strategies of Hmong Refugee Students," master's thesis, University of Wisconsin–Stout, July 1987 (cited in Christine I. Bennett, *Comprehensive Multicultural Education: Theory and Practice,* 4th ed. (Needham Heights, MA: Allyn & Bacon, 1999); Norene Dresser, *Multicultural Manners: New Rules of Etiquette for a Changing Society* (New York: John Wiley & Sons, 1996); Education Alliance at Brown University, *The Diversity Kit: An Introductory Resource for Social Change in Education* (Providence, RI: Northeast and Islands Regional Educational Laboratory–LAB at Brown University, 2002); Rowena Fong, Sharlene Furuto, and Sharlene B. Furuto, *Culturally*

Competent Practice: Skills, Interventions, and Evaluations (Needham Heights, MA: Allyn & Bacon, 2001); Eleanor W. Lynch (ed), and Marci J. Hanson, *Developing Cross-Cultural Competence: A Guide for Working with Children and Their Families* (Baltimore, MD: Paul H. Brookes Publishing Company, 2004); and Ian K. Macgillivray, *Sexual Orientation and School Policy: A Practical Guide for Teachers, Administrators, and Community Activists* (Rowman & Littlefield, 2004).

40. We thank Louise Wilkinson for this poignant quote. We couldn't have said it better.

41. Kent L. Koppelman with R. Lee Goodhart, *Understanding Human Differences: Multicultural Education for Diverse America* (Boston: Pearson Education, 2005), p. 344.

42. Nancy P. Gallavan, "I, Too, Am an American: Preservice Teachers Reflect upon National Identity," *Multicultural Teaching*, Spring 2002, pp. 8–12.

CHAPTER 4   SCHOOLS: CHOICES AND CHALLENGES

1. James Shaver and William Strong, *Facing Value Decisions: Rationale Building for Teachers* (Belmont, CA: Wadsworth, 1976).

2. Sara Neufeld, "Photos Reveal Decrepit State of City Schools," (February 24, 2006), retrieved from www.baltimoresun.com.

3. Ernest L. Boyer, *High School: A Report on Secondary Education in America* (New York: Harper & Row, 1983), pp. 209–10.

4. Linda Perlstein, "'Serving' the Community Without Leaving School," *The Washington Post,* June 28, 1999, pp. A1, A6.

5. *The Condition of Education 2001,* U.S. Department of Education, NCES, Indicator 16: Social and Cultural Outcomes, Community Service Participation in Grades 6–12, p. 142, http://nces.ed.gov/pubs2001/2001072_2.pdf.

6. Bill Bigelow, "The Human Lives Behind the Labels: The Global Sweatshop, Nike, and the Race to the Bottom," *Phi Delta Kappan* 79, no. 2 (October 1997), pp. 112–19.

7. Paulo Freire, *The Pedagogy of the Oppressed* (New York: Herder & Herder, 1970).

8. John Goodlad, *A Place Called School* (New York: McGraw-Hill, 1984), pp. 35–39.

9. Arthur Eugene Bestor, *Educational Wastelands: The Retreat from Learning in Our Public Schools* (Urbana: University of Illinois Press, 1953), p. 75.

10. Boyer, *High School,* p. 5.

11. National Commission on Excellence in Education, *A Nation at Risk: The Imperative for Educational Reform* (Washington, DC: U.S. Government Printing Office, 1983), p. 1.

12. David Hill, "Fixing the System from the Top Down," *Teacher Magazine* (September/October 1989), pp. 50–55.

13. David L. Clark and Terry A. Astuto, "Reconstructing Reform: Challenges to Popular Perceptions About Teachers and Students," *Phi Delta Kappan* 75, no. 7 (March 1994), pp. 512–20.

14. Donald C. Ohlrich, "Education Reforms: Mistakes, Misconceptions, Miscues," *Phi Delta Kappan* 170, no. 7 (March 1989), pp. 512–17.

15. Clinton Boutwell, "People Without People," *Phi Delta Kappan* 79, no. 2 (October 1997), pp. 104–11.

16. Valerie Strauss, "When Success Doesn't Add Up," *The Washington Post on the Web,* December 2000.

17. Joy Dryfoos, "Full Service Schools," *Educational Leadership* 53, no. 7 (April 1996), pp. 18–23.

18. Henry J. Perkinson, *The Imperfect Panacea: American Faith in Education* (New York: McGraw-Hill, 1995), p. 191.

19. Debra Viadero, "Students Learn More in Magnets Than Other, Study Finds," *Education Week,* March 6, 1996, p. 6; Caroline Hendrie, "Magnets Value in Desegregating Schools Is Found to Be Limited," *Education Week on the Web,* November 13, 1996; "Research Notes," *Education Week on the Web,* September 16, 1998.

20. A. S. Byrk, Valerie Lee, and P. B. Holland, *Catholic Schools and the Common Good* (London: Harvard University Press, 1993); Public School Review, "What Is a Magnet School?" retrieved on March 22, 2006 from www. publicschoolreview.com/magnet-schools.php.

21. "Another Round on Vouchers," *The Washington Post,* December 18, 2000, p. A26; Terry Moe, "The Public Revolution Private Money Might Bring," *The Washington Post,* May 9, 1999, p. B3. For more on the legal dispute, see *Jackson v. Benson* (1998), which held that vouchers used for religious school tuition did not violate the Wisconsin State Constitution; Sam Dillon, "For Parents Seeking a Choice, Charter Schools Prove More Popular than Vouchers," (July 23, 2005); retrieved from www. nytimes.com.

22. David Stout, "Public Money Can Pay Religious-School Tuition, Court Rules," *The New York Times,* June 27, 2002, online.

23. Kavan Peterson, "School Vouchers Slow to Spread," www.Stateline.org, May 5, 2005; National Education Association, "Florida High Court Rules Against Vouchers," (January 5, 2006), retrieved from www.nea.org/ vouchers/flvouchers1-06.html.

24. Timothy McDonald, "The False Promise of Voucher," *Education Leadership* 59, no. 7 (April 2002), pp. 33–37; Kaleem M. S. Caire, "The Truth about Vouchers," *Education Leadership* 59, no. 7 (April 2002), pp. 33–37; Joseph P. Viteritti, "Coming Around on School Choice," *Education Leadership* 59, no. 7 (April 2002), pp. 44–48; National Education Association, "Vouchers" (March 22, 2006), retrieved from www.nea.org/vouchers/index.html.

25. Sam Dillon, "For Parents Seeking a Choice, Charter Schools Prove More Popular than Vouchers" (July 23, 2005), retrieved from www.nytimes.com; U.S. Charter Schools, "Frequently Asked Questions" (March 22, 2006), retrieved from www.uscharterschools.org/pub/uscs_docs/ o/faq.html; Center for Education Reform, "Charter Schools" (March 22, 2006), retrieved from www.edreform. com/index.cfm?fuseAction=stateStats&pSectionID= 15&cSectionID=44; "New CER Report Gives Evidence of Charters' Impact," *Charter Schools Today,* Washington, DC, May 5, 2004.

26. Bruno V. Manno, Chester E. Finn, Louann A. Bierlein, and Gregg Vanurek, "How Charter Schools Are Different: Lessons and Implications from a National Study," *Phi Delta Kappan* 79, no. 7 (March 1998), pp. 489–98.

27. Thomas L. Good and Jennifer Braden, "Charter Schools: Another Reform Failure or a Worthwhile Investment?" *Phi Delta Kappan* 81, no. 10 (June 2000), pp. 745–50.

28. Michael Winerip, "When It Goes Wrong at a Charter," *The New York Times,* March 5, 2003, online.

29. Meredith May, "Report Critical of Charter Schools: Un-credentialed Teachers, Funding Shortage, Racial Isolation Cited," *San Francisco Chronicle,* April 8, 2003.

30. Molnar, "Charter Schools," p. 10; Chuck Sudetic, "Reading, Writing, and Revenue," *Mother Jones,* May–June 2001, pp. 84–95.

31. Amanda Paulson, "Virtual Schools, Real Concerns," *The Christian Science Monitor,* www.csmonitor.com, May 4, 2004; U.S. Department of Education, National Center for Education Statistics, Fast Response Survey System (FRSS), "Distance Education Courses for Public School Elementary and Secondary School Students: 2002–03," Washington, DC; Kate Moser, "Online Courses Aren't Just for Home-Schoolers Anymore," *Christian Science Monitor* (March 30, 2006), retrieved from www.csmonitor.com/2006/ 0330/p14s02-legn.html.

32. Moser, "Online Courses Aren't Just for Home-Schoolers Anymore"; Michelle Galley, "Despite Concerns, Online Elementary Schools Grow," *Education Week* 22, no. 16 (January 8, 2003), pp. 1, 12.

33. Joel Spring, *American Education* (New York: McGraw-Hill, 1996), pp. 184–85.

34. Diana B. Henriques, "Edison Schools' Founder to Take It Private," *New York Times,* July 15, 2003, www.nytimes.com; Gerald Bracey, "The 12th Bracey Report on the Condition of Public Education," *Phi Delta Kappan* 84, no. 2 (October 2002), pp. 135–50; Chris Brennan, "Ex-Edison Official: Company Lacks Integrity," *Phillynews.com,* July 24, 2002; Michael Fletcher, "Private Enterprise, Public Woes in Phila School," *The Washington Post,* September 17, 2002, p. A1; Brian Gill, Laura S. Hamilton, J. R. Lockwood, Julie A. Marsh, Ron Zimmer, Deanna Hill, and Shana Pribesh, *Inspiration, Perspiration, and Time: Operations and Achievements in Edison Schools* (October 2005), RAND Corporation, retrieved on March 13, 2006 from www.rand.org/pubs/monographs/ MG351/index.html.

35. Katrina E. Bulkley, *Recentralizing Decentralization? Educational Management Organizations and Charter Schools' Educational Programs* (National Center for the Study of the Privatization of Education, Columbia Teachers College, 2003), available at www.ncspe.org/; For additional studies on the privatization of schools and school choice, see the National Center for the Study of the Privatization of Education, www.ncspe.org/; Bill Brubaker, "Sylvan Learning Systems Renamed Laureate to Focus on Universities," *The Washington Post,* May 18, 2004, p. E04; Jamie Smith Hopkins, "Sylvan, LeapFrog Plan to Tutor Kids in Big Stores: Parents Might Soon Be Able to Shop While Their Children Are Being Tutored a Few Aisles Away," *Baltimore Sun*, December 22, 2004.

36. Pedro Noguerar, "More Democracy Not Less: Confronting the Challenge of Privatization in Public Education," *Journal of Negro Education* 623, no. 2 (1994), p. 238.

37. Justin Blum and Jay Mathews, "Quality Uneven, Despite Popularity," *The Washington Post,* June 19, 2003, pp. A1, A12.

38. Jane H. Holloway, "Research Link," *Educational Leadership* 39, no. 7 (April 2002), pp. 84–85.

39. "Study Finds that Nation's Charter Schools Are Places of Racial Isolation," The Harvard Civil Rights Project, July 10, 2003, www.civilrightsproject.harvard.edu/research/deseg/CharterSchools.php.

40. Alex Molnar interviewed in "Giving Kids the Business, an Interview with Alex Molnar," *The Education Industry: The Corporate Takeover of Public Schools,* www.corpwatch.org/feature/education/; see also Alex Molnar, *Giving Kids the Business: The Commercialization of America's Schools* (Boulder, CO: Westview Press, 1996); see also Majorie Coeyman, "Vouchers Get a Boost from Black Alliance."

41. Tamar Lewin, "In Public Schools, the Name Game as a Donor Lure" (January 26, 2006), retrieved from www.nytimes.com; Pam Belluck, "And for Perfect Attendance, Johnny Gets . . . a Car" (February 5, 2006), retrieved from www.nytimes.com; Alex Molnar and David Garia, "The Battle Over Commercialized Schools," *Educational Leadership* 63, no.7 (April 2006), pp. 78–82.

42. Neil Buckley, "Obesity Campaign Eyes School Drinks," *Financial Times.com,* MSNBC News Online (June 2003); Alex Molnar, "The Corporate Branding of Our Schools," *Educational Leadership* 60, no. 2 (October 2002), pp. 74–78.

43. Alfie Kohn, "The 500–Pound Gorilla," *Phi Delta Kappan* 84, no. 2 (October 2002), p. 117; Molnar and Garia, "The Battle Over Commercialized Schools."

44. Molnar, "The Corporate Branding of Our Schools," p. 76.

45. "Live and Learn," *Harper's Bazaar* (September 1994), pp. 268–70.

46. National Center for Education Statistics, "Homeschooling in the United States: 2003" (February 2006), retrieved from http://nces.ed.gov/pubs2006/2006042.pdf.

47. Ibid.

48. J. A. Van Galen, "Schooling in Private: A Study of Home Education," doctoral dissertation, University of North Carolina, Chapel Hill, 1986.

49. Barbara Kantrowitz and Pat Wingert, "Learning at Home: Does It Pass the Test?" *Newsweek,* October 5, 1998, pp. 64–71; "Charter 'Profit': Will Michigan Heap Money on an Electronic Charter School?" *The American School Board Journal* 181, no. 9 (September 1994), pp. 27–28; "The Dawn of Home Schooling," *Newsweek,* October 10, 1994, p. 67; see also, Nancy Trejos, "Home Schooling's Net Effect," *The Washington Post,* July 16, 2000, pp. C1, C9.

50. Brian Ray, "Customization through Homeschooling," *Education Leadership* 59, no. 7 (April 2002), p. 50.

51. Rob Reich, "The Civic Perils of Home Schooling" *Education Leadership* 59, no. 7 (April 2002), pp. 56–59.

52. George Weber, *Inner-City Children Can Be Taught to Read: Four Successful Schools* (Washington, DC: D.C. Council for Basic Books, 1971); Ronald Edmonds, "Some Schools Work and More Can," *Social Policy* 9 (1979), pp. 28–32; Barbara Taylor and Daniel Levine, "Effective Schools Projects and School-Based Management," *Phi Delta Kappan* 72, no. 5 (January 1991), pp. 394–97. See also Herman Meyers, "Roots, Trees, and the Forest: An Effective Schools Development Sequence," Paper delivered at the American Educational Research Association, San Francisco, April 1992.

53. Sara Lawrence Lightfoot, *The Good High School* (New York: Basic Books, 1983).

54. Ibid., p. 67.

55. David Clark, Linda Lotto, and Mary McCarthy, "Factors Associated with Success in Urban Elementary Schools," *Phi Delta Kappan* 61, no. 7 (March 1980), pp. 467–70. See also David Gordon, "The Symbolic Dimension of Administration for Effective Schools." Paper delivered at the American Educational Research Association, San Francisco, April 1992.

56. William Rutherford, "School Principals as Effective Leaders," *Phi Delta Kappan* 67, no. 1 (September 1985), pp. 31–34. See also R. McClure, "Stages and Phases of School-Based Renewal Efforts." Paper presented at the annual meeting of the American Educational Research Association, New Orleans, 1988.

57. Steven C. Schlozman, "The Shrink in the Classroom: Fighting School Violence," *Ed Leadership* 60, no. 2 (October 2002). pp. 89–90; Harris Interactive & Gay, Lesbian and Straight Education Network, "From Teasing to Torment: School Climate in America—A Survey of Students and Teachers" (New York: Harris Interactive, Inc., 2005), Retrieved from www.glsen.org/binary-data/GLSEN_ATTACHMENTS/file/499-1.pdf.

58. *The Metropolitan Life Survey of the American Teacher 1999* (New York: Harris Interactive, Inc., 2001), pp. 39, 42.

59. Lowell C. Rose and Alec M. Gallup, "The 37th Annual Gallup Poll of the Public's Attitudes Toward the Public Schools," *Phi Delta Kappan* 87, no. 1 (September 2005), p. 44.

60. Lightfoot, *The Good High School;* Kevin Dwyer and D. Osher, *Safeguarding Our Children: An Action Guide* (Washington, DC: U.S. Department of Education, August 2000).

61. Wilbur Brookover, Laurence Beamer, Helen Efthim, Douglas Hathaway, Lawrence Lezotte, Stephen Miller, Joseph Passalacqua, and Louis Tornatzky, *Creating Effective Schools* (Holmes Beach, FL: Learning Publications, 1982).

62. Herbert Walberg, Rosanne Paschal, and Thomas Weinstein, "Homework's Powerful Effects on Learning," *Educational Leadership* 42 (1985), pp. 76–79.

63. Robert Rosenthal and Lenore Jacobson, *Pygmalion in the Classroom* (New York: Holt, Rinehart & Winston, 1968).

64. Patrick Proctor, "Teacher Expectations: A Model for School Improvement," *Elementary School Journal* (March 1984), pp. 469–81; William Wayson, "The Politics of Violence in Schools: Double Speak and Disruptions in Public Confidence," *Phi Delta Kappan* 67, no. 2 (October 1985), pp. 127–32.

65. *Metropolitan Life Survey of the American Teacher 2001* (New York: Harris Interactive, Inc., 2001), p. 61.

66. Larry Cuban, "Effective Schools: A Friendly but Cautionary Note," *Phi Delta Kappan* 64, no. 10

(June 1983), pp. 695–96; Daniel Levine, "Creating Effective Schools: Findings and Implications from Research and Practice," *Phi Delta Kappan* 72, no. 5 (January 1991), pp. 389–93.

67. Anne T. Henderson, *A New Wave of Evidence: The Impact of School, Family, and Community Connections on Student Achievement,* Southwest Educational Development Laboratory, 2002, available at www.sedl.org/pubs/catalog/items/fam33.html; Mary Anne Raywid, "Synthesis of Research: Small Schools: A Reform That Works," *Educational Leadership* (December 1997–January 1998), pp. 34–39; Kenneth J. Cooper, "9 Schools Show How to Make the Grade," *The Washington Post,* January 13, 2000, p. A17; Ann Marie Moriarity, "Just Right: School Size Matters," *The Washington Post* (August 7, 2002), p. H9; Alan B. Kruger, "Smaller Classes Help Many," *USA Today* (August 2, 2002), p. 8A; "The Effect of Classroom Practice on Student Achievement," *ASCD SmartBrief* 1, no. 11 (May 27, 2003), online; Catherine Gewertz, "'Trusting' School Community Linked to Student Gains," *Education Week,* October 16, 2002, online; Michael Dobbs, "Big Schools Reborn in Small World in N.Y., Six Are Better Than One," *The Washington Post* (November 28, 2003), p. A01.

CHAPTER 5:   STUDENT LIFE IN SCHOOL AND AT HOME

1. Philip W. Jackson, *Life in Classrooms* (New York: Holt, Rinehart & Winston, 1968).

2. Ibid.

3. Manuel Justiz, "It's Time to Make Every Minute Count," *Phi Delta Kappan* 65, no. 7 (March 1984), pp. 483–85; see also Herbert Walberg, "Families as Partners in Educational Productivity," *Phi Delta Kappan* 65, no. 6 (February 1984), pp. 397–400.

4. John Goodlad, *A Place Called School* (New York: McGraw-Hill, 1984).

5. Quoted in Ernest L. Boyer, *High School* (New York: Harper & Row, 1983); C. Fisher, N. Filby, E. Mariliave, L. Cohen, M. Dishaw, J. Moore, and D. Berliner, *Teacher Behaviors, Academic Learning Time, and Student Achievement,* Final Report of Phase III-B, Beginning Teacher Evaluation Study (San Francisco: Far West Laboratory for Educational Research and Development, 1978).

6. G. Madaus et al., *School Effectiveness: A Reassessment of the Evidence* (New York: McGraw-Hill, 1980).

7. Jackson, *Life in Classrooms.*

8. Ned Flanders, "Intent, Action, and Feedback: A Preparation for Teaching," *Journal of Teacher Education* 14, no. 3 (September 1963), pp. 251–60.

9. Arno Bellack, *The Language of the Classroom* (New York: Teachers College Press, 1965).

10. Romiett Stevens, "The Question as a Measure of Classroom Practice," in *Teachers College Contributions to Education* (New York: Teachers College Press, 1912).

11. W. D. Floyd, *An Analysis of the Oral Questioning Activity in Selected Colorado Primary Classrooms.* Unpublished doctoral dissertation, Colorado State College, 1960.

12. Myra Sadker and David Sadker, "Questioning Skills," in James Cooper (ed.), *Classroom Teaching Skills,* 8th ed. (Boston: Houghton Mifflin, 2006).

13. Mary Budd Rowe, "Wait Time: Slowing Down May Be a Way of Speeding Up!" *Journal of Teacher Education* 37 (1986), pp. 43–50.

14. Goodlad, *A Place Called School.*

15. Talcott Parsons, "The School as a Social System: Some of Its Functions in Society," in Robert Havinghurst and Bernice Neugarten, (eds.), *Society and Education* (Boston: Allyn & Bacon, 1967), pp. 191–214.

16. Robert Lynd and Helen Lynd, *Middletown: A Study in American Culture* (New York: Harcourt Brace Jovanovich, 1929).

17. W. Lloyd Warner, Robert Havinghurst, and Martin Loeb, *Who Shall Be Educated?* (New York: Harper & Row, 1944).

18. August Hollingshead, *Elmtown's Youth* (New York: Wiley, 1949).

19. Robert Havinghurst et al., *Growing Up in River City* (New York: Wiley, 1962).

20. Ernest L. Boyer, *High Schools: A Report on Secondary Education in America* (New York: Harper & Row, 1983).

21. Shirl Gilbert and Geneva Gay, "Improving the Success in School of Poor Black Children," *Phi Delta Kappan* 67, no. 2 (October 1985), pp. 133–38.

22. Ray Rist, "Student Social Class and Teacher Expectations. The Self-Fulfilling Prophecy of Ghetto Education," *Harvard Education Review* 40, no. 3 (1970), pp. 411–51.

23. Jeannie Oakes, "Two Cities' Tracking and Within-School Segregation," *Teachers College Record* 96, no. 4 (Summer 1995), pp. 681–90.

24. Jeannie Oakes and Martin Lipton, "Detracking Schools: Early Lessons from the Field," *Phi Delta Kappan* 73, no. 6 (February 1992), pp. 448–54.

25. James Rosenbaum, "If Tracking Is Bad, Is Detracking Better?", *American Educator.* Washington, DC: American Federation of Teachers (Winter 1999–2000), pp. 24–29, 47.

26. Samuel Lucas, *Tracking Inequality: Stratification and Mobility in American High Schools* (New York: Teachers College Press, 1999).

27. Rebecca Gordon and Libero Della Piana, *Testing, Tracking, and Students of Color in U.S. Public Schools* (Oakland, CA: Applied Research Center, 1999).

28. Jeannie Oakes, *Multiplying Inequalities: The Effects of Race, Social Class, and Tracking on Opportunities to Learn Mathematics and Sciences* (Santa Monica, CA: RAND, 1990), (ED329615).

29. Carol Ascher, "Successful Detracking in Middle and Senior High Schools," *ERICICUE Digest* 82 (New York: ERIC Clearinghouse on Urban Education, October 10, 1992). (ED351426); Gary Burnett, "Alternatives to Ability Grouping: Still Unanswered Questions," *ERICICUE Digest* 111 (New York: ERIC Clearinghouse on Urban Education, December 1995), (ED390947).

30. Quoted in "Tracking," *Education Week on the Web,* October 14, 1998; see also Susan Allan, "Ability Grouping Research Reviews: What Do They Say About Grouping and the Gifted?" *Educational Leadership* 48, no. 6 (March 1991), pp. 60–65; Adam Gamoran, "Alternative

Use of Ability Grouping in Secondary Schools: Can We Bring High-Quality Instruction to Low-Ability Classes?" *American Journal of Education* 102 (1993), pp. 1–22; Robert E. Slavin, "Achievement Effects of Ability Grouping in Secondary Schools: A Best-Evidence Synthesis," *Review of Educational Research* 60 (1990), pp. 471–99.

31. Quoted in Raphaela Best, *We've All Got Scars* (Blooming-ton: Indiana University Press, 1983), p. 9.

32. Ibid., p. 162.

33. "Unpopular Children," *The Harvard Education Letter,* Harvard Graduate School of Education in association with Harvard University Press, January/February 1989, pp. 1–3. See also Lisa Wolcott, "Relationships: The Fourth 'R,'" *Teacher* (April 1991), pp. 26–27.

34. Quoted from a student letter in the *Arlingtonian,* May 13, 1993.

35. Jaana Juvonen, et al., *Focus on the Wonder Years: Challenges Facing the American Middle School* (Santa Monica, CA: RAND Corporations, 2004). Retrieved on February 19, 2006, from www.rand.org/pubs/monographs/2004/RAND_MG139.pdf.

36. Jay Matthews, "Traditional Social Focus Yielding to Academics," *The Washington Post* (October 4, 2005), p. A04.

37. Karen Zittleman, *Title IX and Gender: A Study of the Knowledge, Perceptions, and Experiences of Middle and Junior High School Teachers and Students.* Dissertation Abstracts International 66 (11) (UMI No. 3194815, 2005).

38. Zappa, Coleman, Friedenberg, Vonnegut, and Ford are quoted in Ralph Keyes, *Is There Life After High School?* (Boston: Little, Brown, 1976).

39. James Coleman, *The Adolescent Society* (New York: Free Press, 1961).

40. Goodlad, *A Place Called School.*

41. Quoted in Boyer, *High School,* p. 202.

42. Ibid., p. 206.

43. David Owen, *High School* (New York: Viking Press, 1981).

44. Keyes, *Is There Life After High School?*

45. Lloyd Temme, quoted in Keyes, *Is There Life After High School?*

46. Mel Brooks and Dustin Hoffman are quoted in Keyes, *Is There Life After High School?*

47. Quoted in Boyer, *High School.*

48. Patricia Hersch, *A Tribe Apart: A Journey Into the Heart of American Adolescence* (New York: Random House, 1999).

49. U.S. Census Bureau, Statistical Abstracts of the United States, *Current Population Survey 2002: Household by Size* (Washington, DC: U.S. Census Bureau, 2002).

50. Pat Wingert, "I do, I do—Maybe," *Newsweek,* November 2, 1998; Karen S. Peterson, "Cohabitation Is Increasing, Census Data Confirm," *USA Today,* August 13, 2001 (www.usatoday.com/news/census/2001–05–15–cohabitate.htm); Federal Interagency Forum on Child and Family Statistics, *America's Children: Key National Indicators of Well-Being, 2005.* Available at www.childstats.gov/americaschildren/.

51. "Divorce Detrimental to Kids' Academics," *USA Today,* June 4, 2002, p. A2.

52. U.S. Department of Labor, Bureau of Labor Statistics, "Employment Status of Population by Sex, Marital Status, and Presence and Age of Own Children, 2001–2002," Table 5 (Washington, DC: U.S. Department of Labor, 2003).

53. Phyllis Moen, "Couples and Careers Study," *Cornell Employment and Family Institute* (Cornell University Ithaca, NY: 1999), www.blcc.cornell.edu/cci/current.html.

54. Eitzen, "Problem Students"; Lizette Peterson-Homer, "Latchkey Children," *Gale Encyclopedia of Childhood & Adolescence.* Gale Research, 1998; Sandra L. Hofferth and Zita Januniene, "Life After School," *Educational Leadership* 58, no. 7 (April 2001), pp. 10–23; Sue Shellenbarger, "Home Alone After School Is OK for Some Children," *The Wall Street Journal,* November 14, 2002, www.wsj.com.

55. Federal Interagency Forum on Child and Family Statistics, *America's Children: Key National Indicators of Well-Being, 2005.* Available at www.childstats.gov/americaschildren/.

56. Candy Carlile, "Children of Divorce," *Childhood Education* 64, no. 4 (1991), pp. 232–34.

57. Beverly Bliss, *Step Families,* Parenthood in America Proceedings of the conference held in Madison, Wisconsin (1998). http://parehthood.library.wisc.edu/Bliss/Bliss.html.

58. Michael A. Fletcher, "Interracial Marriages Eroding Barriers," *The Washington Post,* December 29, 1998, p. A-1; Michael A. Fletcher, "The Myth of the Melting Pot, America's Racial and Ethnic Divide," *The Washington Post,* December 28, 1998, p. A1. www.washingtonpost.com/wpsrv/national/daily/dec98/melt29.htm.

59. Quoted in John O'Neil, "A Generation Adrift?" *Educational Leadership* 49, no. 2 (September 1991), pp. 4–10.

60. Children's Defense Fund, *Key Facts: Children's Health Coverage,* Retrieved on March 28, 2006, from www.childrensdefense.org/childhealth/chip/key_facts.aspx; United States Census Bureau, "Current Population Survey 2005" (Washington, DC: U.S. Census Bureau).

61. Ruby Payne, *Framework for Understanding Poverty* (Highlands, TX: Aha Process Inc, 2001).

62. Ibid.

63. This anecdote is based on information in Children's Defense Fund, *A Vision for America's Future,* pp. 27–36. Washington, DC, 1989.

64. John Holloway, "Research Link: Addressing the Needs of Homeless Students," *Educational Leadership* 60, no. 4 (December 2002/January 2003), pp. 89–90; Linda Jacobson, "ESEA Includes New Requirements on Educating Homeless Students," *Education Week,* August 7, 2002, www.edweek.com.

65. "Schools Dropouts: Home and School Effects," ASCD *RESEARCH BRIEFS 1,* no. 9, April 29, 2003, www.ascd.org.

66. Christopher B. Swanson, *The Real Truth about Low Graduation Rates, An Evidenced Based Commentary* (Washington, D.C.: The Urban Institute, 2004). Available at www.urban.org/publications/411050.html.

67. Amanda Paulson, "Dropout Rates High, But Fixes on the Way," *Christian Science Monitor,* (March 3, 2006). Available at www.csmonitor.com/2006/0303/p01s02-legn.html.

68. Paulson, "Dropout Rates High, But Fixes on the Way"; National Dropout Prevention Center Network, *Effective Strategies* (Clemson University, South Carolina, 2006). Available at www.dropoutprevention.org/effstrat/effstrat.htm.

69. Sexuality Information and Education Council of the United States. *Policy Updates, 2006.* Available at www.siecus.org/.

70. Rebecca Vesely, "Some States Rejecting Abstinence-Only Sex Ed," *Women's E News,* March 11, 2002, www.womensenews.org; Ceci Connolly, "Texas Teaches Abstinence, with Mixed Grades," *The Washington Post,* January 21, 2003, p. A1; Brigid McKeon, *Effective Sex Education* (Washington, DC: Advocates for Youth, 2006). Available at www.advocatesforyouth.org/publications/factsheet/fssexcur.htm; Vaishali Honawar, "Study: Pledgers of Sex Abstinence Still at Risk for STD's," *Education Week,* 24, issue 29 (Bethesda, MD: Editorial Projects in Education, March 30, 2005), p. 5.

71. The National Center on Addiction and Substance Abuse at Columbia University, *CASA National Survey of American Attitudes on Substance Abuse X: Teens and Parents* (August 2005). Available at www.casacolumbia.org/.

72. Lloyd Johnston, Patrick O'Malley, Jerald Bachman, and John Schulenberg, *Monitoring the Future: National Results on Adolescent Drug Use: Overview of Key Findings, 2005* (Bethesda, MD: National Institute on Drug Abuse, 2006). Available at www.monitoringthefuture.org/.

73. Ibid.

74. The National Center on Addiction and Substance Abuse at Columbia University, *CASA National Survey of American Attitudes on Substance Abuse X: Teens and Parents.*

75. Substance Abuse and Mental Health Services Administration, *2004 National Survey on Drug Use and Health. Substance Abuse and Mental Health Services Administration* (Washington, DC: U.S. Department of Health and Human Services, 2005). Available at www.samhsa.gov.

76. S. Schlozman, "The Shrink in the Classroom: Why 'Just Say No' Isn't Enough," *Educational Leadership,* 59, no. 7 (2002), pp. 87–89; Matthew Rees, "Neither Safe nor Drug-Free," *New Directions: Federal Education Policy in the 21st Century* (Washington, DC: The Thomas B. Fordham Institute, 1999). Available at www.edexcellence.net/institute/publication/publication.cfm?id=38&pubsubid=610#610.

77. Centers for Disease Control and Prevention, National Center for Injury Prevention and Control, *Suicide Data Page, 2004.* Available at www.cdc.gov/ncipc/factsheets/suifacts.htm

78. Jeanne Wright, "Treating the Depressed Child," *The Washington Post,* December 2, 1996, p. C-5.

79. Amy Milsom and Laura L. Gallo, "Bullying in Middle Schools: Prevention and Intervention," *Middle School Journal,* 37, no. 3 (January 2006), pp. 12–19.

80. KidsHealth Poll, *Bullying* (2004). Available at www.nahec.org/KidsPoll/archive/ and http://kidshealth.org/parent/emotions/behavior/bullies.html; Harris Interactive and GLSEN, *From Teasing to Torment: School Climate in America. A Survey of Students and Teachers* (New York:

GLSEN, 2005). Available at www.glsen.org/binary-data/GLSEN_ATTACHMENTS/file/499-1.pdf; Marcelle Fischler, *Confronting Bullies Who Wound with Words* (www.nytimes.com, October 16, 2005).

81. Doug Cooper and Jennie L. Snell, "Bullying—Not Just a Kid Thing," *Educational Leadership* 60, no. 6 (March 2003), pp. 22–25; Dan Olweis, "A Profile of Bullying at School," *Educational Leadership* 60, no. 6 (March 2003), pp. 12–17; Milsom and Gallo, "Bullying in Middle Schools: Prevention and Intervention"; Ian Shapira, "Peacemakers in Training," *The Washington Post* (February 28, 2006), pp. B1, B4.

82. The Metropolitan Life Survey of the American Teacher 2000. *Are We Preparing Students for the 21st Century?* (New York: Harris Interactive, Inc., 2000).

83. Quoted in Ernest L. Boyer, "What Teachers Say About Children in America," *Educational Leadership* 46, no. 8 (May 1989), p. 73.

84. Ibid.

85. Ibid., p. 74.

86. Frances Ianni, "Providing a Structure for Adolescent Development," *Phi Delta Kappan* 70, no. 9 (May 1989), p. 677.

87. Urie Bronfenbrenner, "Alienation and the Four Worlds of Childhood," *Phi Delta Kappan* 67, no. 6 (February 1986), pp. 430–35.

88. Lightfoot, *The Good High School.*

89. Quoted in Ianni, "Providing a Structure for Adolescent Development," p. 680.

90. Alfie Kohn, "Caring Kids: The Role of Schools," *Phi Delta Kappan* 72, no. 7 (March 1991), pp. 496–506.

91. Anthony Jackson and Gayle Davis, *Turning Points: Educating Adolescents in the 21st Century* (New York: Teachers College Press, 2000).

92. Carnegie Council on Adolescent Development, *Turning Points: Preparing American Youth for the 21st Century,* excerpted in "The American Adolescent: Facing a Vortex of New Risks," *Education Week,* June 21, 1989, p. 22.

CHAPTER 6: CURRICULUM, STANDARDS, AND TESTING

1. Hilda Taba, *Curriculum Development: Theory and Practice* (New York: Harcourt Brace Jovanovich, 1962).

2. Stephen Hamilton, "Synthesis of Research on the Social Side of Schooling," *Educational Leadership* 40, no. 5 (February 1983), pp. 65–72.

3. National Center for Education Statistics, *The Condition of Education 1995.* Indicator 43, Extracurricular Activities (Washington, DC: U.S. Department of Education); Feminist Majority Foundation, *Empowering Women in Sports,* Washington, DC, 1995; Susan Black, "The Well Rounded Student," *American School Board Journal* 189, no. 6 (June 20, 2002), pp. 33–35.

4. Jan Sokol-Katz and Jomills Braddock, "Interscholastic Sports Participation and School Engagement: Do They Deter Dropouts?" Paper presented at the annual meeting of the American Educational Research Association, New Orleans, April 2000.

5. Ben Feller, "Bowling Rolls into High Schools," *Seattle Times,* December 29, 2005, www.Seattletimes.com.

6. Donna Lopiano, "Equity in Women's Sports—A Health and Fairness Perspective," Women's Sports Foundation, www.womenssportsfoundation.org; John Holloway, "Extracurricular Activities: The Path to Academic Success? *Educational Leadership* 57, no. 4 (December 1999–January 2000); Theodore Coladarci and C. Cobb, "Extracurricular Participation, School Size, and Achievement and Self-Esteem among High School Students: A National Look," *Journal of Research in Rural Education* 12 (1996), pp. 92–103; J. Mahoney and R. Cairns. "Do Extracurricular Activities Protect against Early School Dropout?" *Developmental Psychology* 33, no. 2 (1997), pp. 241–53.

7. National Center for Education Statistics, *Trends Among High School Seniors, 1972–1992* (Washington, DC: U.S Department of Education, 1995); American Association of University Women, *Gender Gaps: Where Schools Still Fail Our Children,* (Washington, DC: AAUW, 1998); National Center for Educational Statistics. *Trends in Educational Equity for Girls and Women,* Indicator 20, Washington DC, 2000.

8. B. Bradford Brown, "The Vital Agenda for Research on Extracurricular Influences: A Reply to Holland and Andre," *Review of Educational Research* 58, no. 1 (Spring 1988), pp. 107–11; T. Coladarci and C. Cobb, "Extracurricular Participation, School Size, and Achievement and Self-Esteem among High School Students," pp. 92–103; W. Jordan and S. Nettles, *How Students Invest Their Time Out of School: Effects on School Engagement, Perceptions of Life Chances, and Achievement* (Baltimore: Center for Research on the Education of Students Placed at Risk, 1999); National Center for Education Statistics, *The Condition of Education, 1995;* Indicator 43, Extracurricular Activities. Washington, DC, July 1995.

9. Sean Cavanaugh, "Electives Getting the Boot? It Depends on Where and What," *Education Week, 35* (issue 2), April 19, 2006, p. 7.

10. Paul Barry, "Interview: A Talk with A. Bartlett Giamatti," *College Review Board* (Spring 1982), p. 48.

11. Todd Oppenheimer, "The Computer Delusion," *The Atlantic Monthly* (July 1997), pp. 45–48, 50–56, 61–62.

12. Cara Branigan, "Study Probes Technology's Effect on Math and Science," *eSchool News,* January 8, 2003, eschoolnews.com; John Clare, "Pupils Make More Progress in 3 Rs 'Without Aid of Computers,'" *Daily Telegraph*, March 21, 2005, www.telegraph.co.uk/.

13. Kevin Bushweller, "Beyond Machines," *Education Week* 20, no. 35 (2001), p. 34.

14. "The Effects of Computers on Student Writing: What the Research Tells Us," *ASCD SmartBrief* 1, no. 7 (April 1, 2003), www.ascd.org; Jennifer Lee, "Nu Shortcuts in School R 2 Much 4 Teachers," *The New York Times,* September 19, 2002, www.nytimes.com; Victoria Irwin, "Hop, Skip . . . and Software?" *The Christian Science Monitor,* March 11, 2003, www.csmonitor.com.

15. Kelly Heyboer, "Cut-and-Paste Turn It In—You Call That Cheating?" *New Jersey Star Ledger,* August 28, 2003, www.NJ.com.

16. *Computer Technology in the Public School Classroom: Teacher Perspectives*, U.S. Department of Education, Institute of Educational Science, March 2005.

17. Jeffrey Selingo, "Students and Teachers, From K to 12, Hit the Podcasts," *The New York Times*, January 25, 2006, www.nytimes.com.

18. Andrew Trotter, "A Question of Effectiveness," *Education Week on the Web,* October 1, 1998; Larry Cuban, *Teachers and Machines: The Classroom Use of Technology since 1920* (New York: Teachers College Press, 1986).

19. Andrew Trotter, "Closing the Digital Divide," *Education Week* 20, no. 35 (2001), pp. 37–38, 40; Maisie McAdoo, "The Real Digital Divide: Quality Not Quantity," in David T. Gordon, ed., *The Digital Classroom* (Cambridge: Harvard College, 2000), pp. 143–51; American Association of University Women, *Gender Gaps: Where School Still Fails Our Children* (Washington, DC: American Association of University Women, 1998); "Dividing Lines," *Education Week* 20, no. 35 (2001), p. 12.

20. Michel Marriott, "Digital Divide Closing as Blacks Turn to Internet," *The New York Times,* March 31, 2006, www.nytimes.com; "Researchers Find Internet Use Has Pros and Cons," *Consumer Affairs*, April 30, 2006, www.consumeraffairs.com.

21. American Association of University Women, *Gender Gaps: Where Schools Still Fail Our Children*; John Gehring, "Not Enough Girls," *Education Week* 10, no. 35 (2001), pp. 18–19; www.electronic-school.com, e-wire (June 1999); Margaret Riel, "A Title IX for the Technology Divide?" in David T. Gordon, ed., *The Digital Class-room* (Cambridge: Harvard College, 2000), pp. 161–170; Ellen McCarthy, "Where Girls and Tech Make a Match," *The Washington Post,* March 20, 2003, p. E1; Jane Margolis, "The Computer World Could Use More IT Girls," *The Los Angeles Times,* May 21, 2003, www.latimes.com.

22. Robert C. Johnson, "Money Matters," *Education Week* 20, no. 35 (2001), p. 14; "Internet Access in U.S. Public Schools and Classrooms: 1994–2000," National Center for Education Statistics, U.S. Department of Education, 2002.

23. Mary Ann Zehr, "Rural Connections," *Education Week* 10, no. 35 (2001), pp. 24–25.

24. Ibid.

25. Ansell and Park, "Tracking Tech Trends"; Andy Sullivan, "'Digital Divide' Shrinks Among Children—Study," Reuters, March 19, 2003.

26. Tamar Lewin, "Children's Computer Use Grows, but Gaps Persist, Study Says," *The New York Times*, January 22, 2001, p. A11.

27. Rebecca Jones, "Textbook Troubles," *American School Board Journal,* December 2000, pp. 18–21; Richard Venezky, "Textbooks in School and Society," in P. Jackson (ed.), *Handbook of Research on Curriculum* (New York: Macmillan, 1992); G. Morrison, *Contemporary Curriculum K-8* (Boston: Allyn & Bacon, 1993).

28. Harriet Tyson Bernstein, *A Conspiracy of Good Intentions: America's Textbook Fiasco* (Washington, DC: The Council for Basic Education, 1988), p. 2.

29. Ibid., p. 20.

30. Gilbert Sewall, "Textbook Publishing," *Phi Delta Kappan* 48 (no. 1), March 2005, pp. 498–502.

31. Quoted in David Elliott, Kathleen Carter Nagel, and Arthur Woodward, "Do Textbooks Belong in Elementary School Studies?" *Educational Leadership* 42, no. 7 (April 1985),

pp. 21–25; see also Rebecca Jones, "Textbook Troubles," *American School Board Journal,* V187 (December 2000).

32. Jean Osborn, Beau Fly Jones, and Marcy Stein, "The Case for Improving Textbooks," *Educational Leadership* 42, no. 7 (April 1985), pp. 9–16; see also Michael Apple, "Regulating the Text: The Social Historical Roots of State Control." Paper delivered at the American Educational Research Association, San Francisco, April 1992.

33. M. Pittman and Jeff Frykholm, "Turning Points: Curriculum Materials as a Catalyst for Change," Paper presented at the annual meeting of the American Educational Research Association, Seattle WA, April 2002.

34. John Merrow, "Undermining Standards," *Phi Delta Kappan* 82, no. 9 (May 2001), pp. 653–59.

35. "Setting Standards in Our Schools: What Can We Expect?" *Education World,* www.educationworld.com, retrieved April 22, 2006.

36. John Elson, "History, the Sequel," *Time,* November 7, 1994, p. 53; see also Von Wiener, "History Lesson," *The New Republic,* January 2, 1995, pp. 9–11.

37. Joel Spring, *American Education* (New York: McGraw-Hill, 1996), pp. 237–41.

38. Lyn Nell Hancock with Nina Archer Biddle, "Red, White—and Blue," *Newsweek,* November 7, 1994, p. 54.

39. Christopher T. Cross, "The Standards Wars: Some Lessons Learned," *Education Week on the Web,* October 21, 1998, pp. 1–4.

40. "Seeking Stability for Standards Based Education," *Education Week on the Web,* Quality Counts 2001 Survey in 2001 Editorial Projects in Education 20, no. 17 (January 11, 2001), pp. 8, 9.

41. L. Hardy, "A New Federal Role," *American School Board Journal,* 189, no 9 (September 2002), pp. 20–24.

42. Teresa Mendez, "Reading Choices Narrow for Schools with Federal Aid," *The Christian Science Monitor,* January 22, 2004 at www.csmonmitor.com.

43. O. L. Davis, "New Policies and New Directions: Be Aware of the Foolprints! Notice to Nightmares!" *Journal of Curriculum and Supervision* 18, no. 2, (Winter 2003), pp. 103–109; Gerald W. Bracey, "The 12th Bracey Report on the Condition of Public Education," *Phi Delta Kappan* 84, no. 2, October 2002, pp. 113–50; David Goodman, "No Child Left Unrecruited," *Mother Jones,* November/December 2002, www.MotherJones.com; Jay Mathews, "Inside the No Child Left Behind Law," *The Washington Post,* January 28, 2003, www.washingtonpost.com.

44. Sam Dillon, "New Law May Leave Rural Teachers Behind," *The New York Times,* June 23, 2003, www.nytimes.com; "Report: Nation Has Climb to Meet Teacher-Quality Requirement, *CNN Student News,* July 16, 2003, cnn.com; Gerald W. Bracey, "The 12th Bracey Report on the Condition of Public Education," *Phi Delta Kappan* 84, no. 2, October 2002, pp. 113–50; Leslie S. Kaplan and William A. Owings, "The Politics of Teacher Quality," *Phi Delta Kappan* 84, no. 9, May 2003, pp. 687–92.

45. "My School's on the List; Here's Why," *The Washington Post* Outlook section, March 12, 2006, pp. B1, B4, B5.

46. Lynn Olson and Linda Jacobson, "Analysis Finds Minority NCLB Scores Widely Excluded," *Education Week,* April 26, 2006.

47. Diana Jean Schemo, "New Federal Rule Tightens Demands on Schools," *The New York Times,* November 27, 2002, online; Michael A. Fletcher, "States Worry New Law Sets Schools Up to Fail," *The Washington Post,* January 2, 2003, p. A1.

48. Susan Saulny, "Meaning of 'Proficient' Varies for Schools Across Country," *The New York Times,* January 19, 2005; Michael Dobbs, "'No Child' Tests for Schools Relaxed English Learners Get Transition Time," *The Washington Post,* February 20, 2004, p. A1.

49. Kevin Kosar, "National Education Standards . . . They're Back!" March 13, 2006, at http://hnn.us/articles/22591.html; Rich Shea, "The Whattaya-Think-of-NCLB? Tour, Darwin at the Pupit, and Psyche Assessments: *Teachers Magazine*'s Take on the News from Around the Web," February 9–15, 2006.

50. Sam Dillon, "States Cut Test Standards to Avoid Sanctions," *The New York Times,* May 22, 2003, www.nytimes.com; David Hoff, "States Revise the Meaning of 'Proficient,'" *Education Week* 22, no. 6, October 9, 2002, pp. 1, 24, 25; Duke Helfand, "State Keeps Education Standards," *Los Angeles Times,* January 9, 2003, LATimes.com.

51. Erika Hayasaki, "Humor Not Left Behind in Attacks on Bush Law," *Los Angeles Times,* July 14, 2004.

52. Lynn Olson, "NCLB Choice Option Going Untapped, But Tutoring Picking Up," *Education Week*, March 16, 2005.

53. Susan Saulny, "Tutor Program Offered by Law Is Going Unused," *The New York Times,* February 12, 2006, www.nytimes.com.

54. Diana Jean Schemo, "Poor Rural Schools Try to Meet New Federal Rules," *The New York Times,* December 2, 2002, online; Don Joling, "Rural Schools in Alaska Lag Behind Federal Plan," *Seattle Times,* May 14, 2003, www.seattletimes.com; Diana Jean Schemo, "New Federal Rule Tightens Demands on Schools," *The New York Times,* November 27, 2002,www.nytimes.com; Rick Karlin, "Federal School Act a Possible Litigation Magnet," *Albany Times Union,* February 13, 2003, online; Jay Mathews, "Inside the No Child Left Behind Law," *The Washington Post,* January 28, 2003, www.washingtonpost.com.

55. Merrow, "Undermining Standards," p. 655.

56. Kate Zernike, "Scarsdale Mothers Succeed in First Boycott of 8th-Grade Test," *New York Times on the Web,* May 4, 2001.

57. Michael A. Fletcher, "High Stakes Rise, School Group Put Exam to Test," *The Washington Post,* July 9, 2001, p. A1; "Seeking Stability for Standards Based Education," *Education Week on the Web;* Mathew Pinzur, "Fear of Failure Leads to FCAT Rebellion," *Miami Herald,* May 13, 2003, www.miami.com; Michele Kurtz, "Berkshire District to Flout MCAS Rule," *Boston Globe,* February 21, 2003, p. B5; Rosalind Rossi," Chicago Refuses to Give Bad Exam," *Chicago Sun Times,* October 16, 2002, online; David Hoff, "Teacher Probed for Role in Anti-Testing Activity," *Education Week* 21, no. 36, May 15, 2002, p. 3.

58. Monty Neill, "The Dangers of Testing." *Educational Leadership* 60, no. 5, February 2003, pp. 43–46; Michael A. Fletcher, "Exit Exam Hurt At-Risk Students," *The Washington Post,* August 14, 2002, p. A7; Dan

DePasquale and Frank Adams, "Midland Voices: Beware the Risks of Statewide Testing," Snowbizz.com; Jennifer Medina, "Top-Performing School Teaches Art of Test-Taking," *The New York Times,* March 28, 2003, www.nytimes.com; Audrey L. Amrein and David C. Berliner "High-Stakes Testing, Uncertainty, and Student Learning" *Education Policy Analysis Archives* 10, no. 18 (March 2002), http://epaa.asu.edu/epaa/v10n18.

59. Diana Jean Schemo, "Education Secretary Defends School System He Once Led," *The New York Times,* July 26, 2003, www.nytimes.com; Jay Heubert and Robert Hauser, eds., *High Stakes: Testing for Tracking, Promotion, and Gradua-tion* (Washington, DC: National Research Council, 1998); Dan DePasquale and Frank Adams, "Midland Voices: Be-ware the Risks of Statewide Testing," Snowbizz.com; Alfie Kohn, *The Case Against Standardized Testing: Raising Scores and Ruining Schools* (Portsmouth, NH: Heine-mann, 2000); Linda McNeil, "Contradictions of School Reform: Educational Costs of Standardized Testing" *Phi Delta Kappan* 81, no. 10, (June 2000), pp. 729–34; "Only '50-50' Chance of High School Graduation for U.S. Minority Students, Weak Accountability Rules Found" (Washington, DC: The Civil Rights Project at Harvard and the Urban Institute, February 25, 2004).

60. Linda McNeil, "Creating New Inequities: Contradictions of Reform," *Phi Delta Kappan* 81, no. 10, (June 2000), pp. 729–34.

61. John Merrow, "Undermining Standards," *Phi Delta Kappan* 82, no. 9 (May 2001), pp. 653–59; James W. Popham, "Why Standardized Tests Don't Measure Quality Education," *Educational Leadership* 56, no 6, (1999); pp. 8–15; Alfie Kohn, *The Case Against Standardized Testing: Raising Scores and Ruining Schools,* (Portsmouth, NH: Heinemann, 2000); James Hoffman, Assaf Czop, Lori Paris, and Scott Paris, "High- Stakes Testing in Reading: Today in Texas, Tomorrow?" *The Reading Teacher* 54, no. 5 (February 2001), pp. 482–92; "Quality Counts 2001: A Better Balance." *Education Week* 20, no. 16 (Bethesda, MD: Editorial Projects); Audrey L. Amrein and David C. Berliner, "High-Stakes Testing, Uncertainty, and Student Learning" *Education Policy Analysis Archives* 10, no. 18 (March 2002), http://epaa.asu.edu/epaa/v10n18; Ben Feller, "Gaps Appear in State, Federal Test Scores," *The Boston Globe*, March 3, 2006, www.boston.com/news/globe/; Susan Saulny, "Meaning of 'Proficient' Varies for Schools Across Country," *The New York Times*, January 19, 2005, www.nytimes.com.

62. Connie Langland, "Tests No Help to Learning," *Philadel-phia Inquirer,* May 29, 2003, www.phillly.com.

63. Sam Dillon, "Schools Cut Back Subjects to Push Reading and Math," *The New York Times,* March 26, 2006, www.nytimes.com.

64. James Hoffman, Assaf Czop, Lori Paris, and Scott Paris, "High-Stakes Testing in Reading: Today in Texas, Tomorrow?" *The Reading Teacher* 54, no. 5 (February 2001), pp. 482–92.

65. James Traub, "The Test Mess," *The New York Times,* April 7, 2002, www.nytimes.com.

66. Nancy Kober, "Teaching to the Test: The Good, the Bad, and Who's Responsible," *TestTalk for Leaders,* Issue 1 (June 2002); Michele Kurtz and Anand Vaishnav, "Student's MCAS Answer Means 449 Others Pass," *Boston Globe,* December 5, 2002, p. A1.

67. Sam Dillon, "Before the Answer, the Question Must Be Correct," *The New York Times,* July 16, 2003, www. nytimes.com; Karen W. Arenson and Diana B. Henriques, "SAT Errors Raise New Questions About Testing," *The New York Times,* March 10, 2006, www.nytimes.com.

68. Diana B. Henriques and Jacques Steinberg, "Right Answer, Wrong Score: Test Flaws Take Toll," *New York Times on the Web,* May 20, 2001; Norman Draper, "Testing Firm to Pay Students $7 Million for Grading Goof," *Minneapolis-St. Paul Star Tribune,* November 26, 2002, startribune.com; Tamara Henry, "Results Are in for States' Student Tests," *USA Today,* June 19, 2002, p. 7D.

69. Kevin Rothstein, "Instructors: Testing Hurts Teaching," *Boston Herald,* March 5, 2003, online; Michele Kurtz, "Teachers' Views Mixed on Testing," *Boston Globe,* March 5, 2003, p. B5.

70. Kathleen Kennedy Manzo, "Protests Over State Testing Widespread," *Education Week on the Web,* May 16, 2001.

71. Abby Goodnough, "Strains of Fourth-Grade Tests Drive Off Veteran Teachers," *New York Times on the Web,* June 14, 2001; Liz Seymour, "SOL Tests Create New Dropouts," *The Washington Post,* July 17, 2001, pp. A1, A8.

72. Tana Thomson, "105-year-old Saline County Test in Nation's Spotlight," *The Salina Journal,* July 9, 2000.

73. Richard Elmore, "Testing Trap," adapted from *Education Next* 105, September–October 2002, p. 35; Barbara Gleason, "ASCD Adopts Positions in High-Stakes Testing and the Achievement Gap," *ASCD Conference News*, March 20–22, 2004.

74. Grant Wiggins, "Teaching to the (Authentic) Test," *Educational Leadership* 46, no. 7 (April 1989), pp. 41–47. See also Rieneke Zessoules and Howard Gardner, "Authentic Assessment: Beyond the Buzzword and into the Classroom," in Vito Perrone (ed.), *Expanding Student Assessment* (Alexandria, VA: Association for Supervision and Curriculum Development, 1991); Grant Wiggins, "Healthier Testing Made Easier," EDUTOPIQ George Lucas Educational Foundation, April 6, 2006, www. edutopia.org/magazine/.

75. Gene I. Maeroff, "Assessing Alternative Assessment," *Phi Delta Kappan* 73, no. 4 (December 1991), pp. 272–81.

76. Theodore Sizer, *Horace's School: Redesigning the American High School* (New York: Houghton Mifflin, 1992).

77. Craig Timberg, "Bible's Second Coming," *The Washington Post,* June 4, 2000, p. A1.

78. "Public School Drops Christian Textbooks," *The Washington Post,* September 17, 1999, p. 2.

79. Mark Sappenfield and Mary Beth McCauley, "God or Science?" *Christian Science Monitor,* November 23, 2004; Lisa Anderson, "Darwin's Theory Evolves into Culture War Kansas Curriculum Is Focal Point of Wider Struggle Across Nation," *Chicago Tribune,* May 22, 2005; Scott Stephens, "Panel OKs Disputed 10th-grade Biology Plan," *Cleveland Plain Dealer*, March 10, 2004.

80. Steve Olson, "An Argument's Mutating Terms," *The Washington Post*, March 20, 2005, p. B01.

81. Anthony Podesta, "For Full Discussion of Religion in the Schools," *The Wall Street Journal,* November 12, 1986, p. 32. See also Perry Glanzer, "Religion in Public Schools: In Search of Fairness," *Phi Delta Kappan* 80, no. 3 (November 1998), pp. 219–22; G. Jeffrey MacDonald, "Now Evolving in Biology Classes: A Testier Climate," *The Christian Science Monitor*, May 3, 2005.

82. "Religion in Class: More Needed, Report Says," *The Washington Post,* December 5, 2000, p. A-22.

83. Debra Viadero, "Christian Movement Seen Trying to Influence Schools," *Education Week,* April 15, 1992, p. 8.

84. Liz Leyden, "Story Hour Didn't Have a Happy Ending," *The Washington Post,* December 3, 1998, p. A3.

85. L. Adler, *Curriculum Challenges in California: Third statewide survey of challenges to curriculum materials and services* (Fullerton: California State University, ERIC Document Reproduction Service, 1993), (No. 375 475).

86. Myra Sadker and David Sadker, *Now upon a Time: A Contemporary View of Children's Literature* (New York: Harper & Row, 1977).

87. American Library Association, "Challenged and Banned Books," retrieved from www.ala.org on July 25, 2006.

88. Suzanne Fisher Staples, "Why Johnny Can't Read: Censorship in American Libraries," *Digital Library and Archives,* Virginia Tech University on the Web (Winter 1996).

89. *Attacks on the Freedom to Learn,* People for the American Way, 1995–1996 report.

90. *The Most Frequently Challenged Books of 2005,* Office for Intellectual Freedom, American Library Association, www.ala.org/ala/oif/bannedbooksweek/challengedbanned/challengedbanned.htm.

91. Kathleen Kennedy Manzo, "Despite Flap, Seattle to Keep Grant for Books About Homosexuality," *Education Week on the Web,* May 28, 1997.

92. Quoted in Lynne Cheney, *Humanities in America: A Report to the President, Congress and the American People* (Washington, DC: National Endowment for the Humanities, 1988), p. 17.

93. Quoted in William Bennett, *American Education: Making It Work* (Washington, DC: U.S. Department of Education, 1988).

94. Allan Bloom, *The Closing of the American Mind* (New York: Simon & Schuster, 1987), p. 63.

95. E. D. Hirsch, Jr., *What Your First Grader Needs to Know, and What Your Second Grader Needs to Know* (New York: Doubleday, 1991).

96. James Banks, "Multicultural Education: For Freedom's Sake," *Educational Leadership* 49, no. 4 (December 1991/January 1992), pp. 32–36.

97. Abner Peddiwell (Harold Benjamin), *The Saber-Tooth Curriculum* (New York: McGraw-Hill, 1939).

98. Louis Raths, Selma Wasserman, Arthur Jones, and Arnold Rothstein, *Teaching for Thinking: Theory and Application* (Columbus, OH: Merrill, 1966.) See also Selma Wasserman, "Teaching for Thinking: Louis E. Raths Revisited," *Phi Delta Kappan* 68, no. 6 (February 1987), pp. 460–66.

99. J. Wink, *Critical Pedagogy: Notes from the Real World* (New York: Addison Wesley Longman, 1999), pp. 28–45.

CHAPTER 7   THE HISTORY OF AMERICAN EDUCATION

1. Sheldon Cohen, *A History of Colonial Education, 1607–1776* (New York: Wiley, 1974).

2. Nathaniel Shurtlett, ed., *Records of the Governor and Company of the Massachusetts Bay in New England, II* (Boston: Order of the Legislature, 1853); see also H. Warren Button and Eugene F. Provenzo, Jr., *History of Education and Culture in America* (Englewood Cliffs, NJ: Prentice Hall, 1983).

3. James Hendricks, "Be Still and Know! Quaker Silence and Dissenting Educational Ideals, 1740–1812," *Journal of the Midwest History of Education Society,* Annual Proceedings, 1975; R. Freeman Butts and Lawrence A. Cremin, *A History of Education in American Culture* (New York: Holt, 1953).

4. Lawrence A. Cremin, *American Education: The Colonial Experience, 1607–1783* (New York: Harper & Row, 1970); see also Button and Provenzo, *History of Education and Culture in America.*

5. James C. Klotter, "The Black South and White Appalachia," *Journal of American History* (March 1980), pp. 832–49.

6. John H. Best, *Benjamin Franklin on Education* (New York: Teachers College Press, 1962).

7. Jonathon Messerli, *Horace Mann: A Biography* (New York: Alfred A. Knopf, 1972); Steven Tozer, Paul Violas, and Guy Senese, *School and Society* (Boston: McGraw-Hill, 1998).

8. Lawrence Cremin, *The Transformation of the School: Progressivism in American Education, 1876–1957* (New York: Alfred A. Knopf, 1961).

9. Wilbur R. Jacobs, "The Tip of an Iceberg: Pre-Columbian Indian Demography and Some Implications for Revisionism," *William and Mary Quarterly,* 3rd Ser., 31, no. 1 (January 1974), pp. 123–132.

10. Much of the earlier educational history discussion of Native Americans, African Americans, and Latinos is based on Meyer Weinberg, *A Chance to Learn: A History of Race and Education in the United States* (New York: Cambridge University Press, 1977).

11. Robert S. Catterill, *The Southern Indians: The Story of the Civilized Tribes Before Removal* (1954; reprinted, Norman: University of Oklahoma Press, 1966).

12. William Denmert, "Indian Education: Where and Whither?" *Education Digest* 42 (December 1976). See also Ron Holt, "Fighting for Equality: Breaking with the Past," *NEA Today*, March 1989, pp. 10–11; NEA Ethnic Report, *Focus on American Indian/Alaska Natives,* October 1991; Mary Ann Zehr, "Indian Tribes Decry Plan to Privatize BIA-Run Schools," *Education Week* 21, no. 30, April 10, 2002, pp. 20, 23.

13. Lee Little Soldier, "Is There an 'Indian' in Your Classroom?" *Phi Delta Kappan* 78, no. 8 (April 1997), pp. 650–53.

14. Jackie M. Blount, "Spinsters, Bachelors and Other Gender Transgressors in School Employment, 1850–1990," *Review of Educational Research* 70, no. 1 (Spring 2000), pp. 83–101.

15. E. Marcus, *Making History: The Struggle for Gay and Lesbian Equal Rights, 1945–1990, An Oral History* (New York: Harper Collins Publishers, 1992).

16. Blount, "Spinsters, Bachelors and Other Gender Transgressors in School Employment, 1850–1990," p. 94.

17. Edward A. Krug, *The Shaping of the American High School, 1880–1920,* I (New York: Harper & Row, 1964); see also John D. Pulliam, *History of Education in America,* 4th ed. (Columbus, OH: Merrill, 1987); Joel Spring, *The American School, 1642–1985* (New York: Longman, 1986).

18. M. Lee Manning, "A Brief History of the Middle School," *The Clearing House* 73, no. 4, March–April 2000, p. 192.

19. National Education Association, *Report of the Committee on Secondary School Studies* (Washington, DC: U.S. Government Printing Office, 1893).

20. Susie King Taylor, *Reminiscences of My Life in Camp with the 33rd U.S. Colored Troop Late First S.C. Volunteers* (1902; reprinted, New York: Amo Press, 1968).

21. W. E. B. Du Bois, "The United States and the Negro," *Freedomways* (1971), quoted in Weinberg, *A Chance to Learn.*

22. Joel Spring, *American Education* (Boston: McGraw-Hill, 2002), p. 110.

23. National Advisory Commission on Civil Disorders, *Report of the National Advisory Commission on Civil Disorders* (Washington, DC: U.S. Government Printing Office, 1968), p. 369. See also Andrew Hacker, *Two Nations Black and White, Separate, Hostile, Unequal* (New York: Charles Scribner's, 1992).

24. Louis Fischer, David Schimmel, and Cynthia Kelly, *Teachers and the Law* (New York: Addison Wesley Longman, 1999), p. 352; "Narrow Use of Affirmative Action Preserved in College Admissions," CNN.COM, June 25, 2003; Greg Winter, "Schools Resegregate, Study Finds," *The New York Times,* January 21, 2003, nytimes.com.

25. Gary Orfield, Erica D. Franenberg, and Chungmei Lee, "The Resurgence of School Segregation," *Educational Leadership* 60, no. 4 (December 2002/January 2003), pp. 16–20; Darryl Fears, "Schools Racial Isolation Growing," *The Washington Post*, July 18, 2001, p. A3; Richard Morin and Claudia Deane, "Defending Desegregation," *The Washington Post*, July 24, 2001, p. A19.

26. James Comer, "All Our Children," *School Safety*, Winter 1989, p. 19.

27. Genaro C. Arms, "Hispanics Outnumber Blacks in U.S.," Associated Press, January 21, 2003, www.chicagotribune.com; "Hispanics: A People in Motion," Pew Hispanic Center, January 2005 http://pewhispanic.org/files/reports/40.pdf; "Current Population Survey, Annual Social and Economic Supplement, 2004," Ethnicity and Ancestry Statistics Branch, Population Division, U.S. Census Bureau, December 6, 2005.

28. "Hispanics: A People in Motion," Pew Hispanic Center, January 2005 http://pewhispanic.org/files/reports/40.pdf

29. "Dropout Rates in the United States: 2001," National Center for Education Statistics NCES, Institute of Education Sciences, U.S. Department of Education November 2004, NCES 2005-046; "Hispanics: A People in Motion," Pew Hispanic Center, January 2005, http://pewhispanic. org/files/reports/40.pdf; Gary Orfield, "Losing Our Future: How Minority Youths Are Being Left Behind by the Graduation Rate Crises" (Washington DC: Urban Institute, February 25, 2004), available at www.urban.org; Anne Turnbaugh Lockwood and Patricia Anne DiCerbo, eds. "Transforming Education for Hispanic Youth: Broad Recommendations for Policy and Practice," *Issues Brief*, National Clearinghouse for Bilingual Education, no. 1 (January 2000).

30. Quoted in Weinberg, *A Chance to Learn.*

31. National Center for Education Statistics, *Condition of Excellence 2003* (Washington, DC: U.S. Department of Education, 2003).

32. *Puerto Rico Herald,* May 10, 2001. www.puertorico-herald.org/issues/2001/vol5n19/Media1-en.shtml.

33. President's Advisory Commission on Educational Excellence for Hispanic Americans, *Our Nation on the Fault Line: Hispanic American Education.*

34. "Nation's Population One-Third Minority" U.S. Census Bureau, May 10, 2006, www.census.gov/Press-Release/www/releases/archives/population/006808.html.

35. Much of the information on the history of Asian Americans is adapted from James Banks, *Teaching Ethnic Studies* (Boston: Allyn & Bacon 1996).

36. National Center for Education Statistics, *Early Child Longitudinal Study, Kindergarten Class of 1998–99* (Washington, DC: U.S. Department of Education, 1999).

37. U.S. Department of Education, National Center for Education Statistics, Recent College Graduates Surveys (1977) and 1993 Baccalaureate and Beyond Longitudinal Study, First Follow-up (B&B: 93/94); *The Condition of Education 1996*, Supplemental Table 35–90; U.S. Bureau of the Census, Statistical Abstract of the United States (1998); findings from *Statistical Abstract of the United States,* (Washington, DC: U.S. Census Bureau, 2000).

38. Carlos Ovando, "Interrogating Stereotypes: The Case of the Asian 'Model Minority,' " *Newsletter of the Asian Culture Center* (Indiana University, Fall 2001). www.modelminority.com/academia/interrogating.htm.

39. Fred Cordova, *Filipinos: Forgotten Asian-Americans* (Dubuque, IA: Kendall/Hunt, 1983), pp. 9–57; Brian Ascalon Roley, "Filipinos—The Hidden Majority," *San Francisco Chronicles*, August 20, 2001, p. A-17.

40. Arthur W. Helweg and Usha M. Helweg, *Immigrant Success Story—East Indians in America* (Philadelphia, PA: University of Pennsylvania Press, 1990). See also Srirajasekhar Bobby Koritala, "A Historical Perspective of Americans of Asian India Origin, 1790–1997," www.tiac.net/users/koritala/india/history.htm.

41. Laurie Olsen, "Crossing the Schoolhouse Border: Immigrant Children in California," *Phi Delta Kappan* 70, no. 3 (November 1988), p. 213.

42. J. Shaheen, *The TV Arab* (Bowling Green, OH: Bowling Green State University, 1984).

43. For more information about Arab Americans, visit the website of the American-Arab Anti-Discrimination Committee at www.adc.org.

44. Patty Adeed and G. Pritchy Smith, "Arab Americans: Concepts and Materials," in James Banks (ed), *Teaching Ethnic Studies* (Boston: Allyn and Bacon, 1997), pp. 489–510.

45. Myra Sadker and David Sadker, "Sexism in the Classroom of the 80s," *Psychology Today* (March 1986). See also Myra Sadker, David Sadker, and Susan Klein, "The Issue of Gender in Elementary and Secondary Education," in Gerald Grant, ed., *Review of Research in Education* (Washington, DC: American Educational Research Association, 1991), pp. 269–334; American Association of University Women, *How Schools Shortchange Girls* (Washington, DC: American Association of University Women, 1992). See also Myra Sadker and David Sadker, *Failing at Fairness: How Our Schools Cheat Girls* (New York: Touchstone Press, 1995).

46. M. Carey Thomas, "Present Tendencies in Women's Education," *Education Review* 25 (1908), pp. 64–85. Quoted in David Tyack and Elisabeth Hansot, *Learning Together: A History of Coeducation in American Schools* (New Haven: Yale University Press, 1990), p. 68.

47. Adapted from "Through the Back Door: The History of Women's Education" and "Higher Education: Colder by Degrees," Myra Sadker and David Sadker, *Failing at Fairness: How Our Schools Cheat Girls*; Michael Kimmel, *The Gendered Society* (New York: Oxford University Press, 2000); Susan Faludi, *Stiffed: The Betrayal of American Men* (New York: William Morrow & Company, 2000); William Pollack, *Real Boys: Rescuing Our Sons from the Myths of Boyhood* (New York: Random House, 1998).

48. Special thanks to Kate Volker for developing the Crandall and Ashton-Warner biographies.

CHAPTER 8   PHILOSOPHY OF EDUCATION

1. William Bagley, "The Case for Essentialism in Education," *National Education Association Journal 30*, no. 7 (1941), pp. 202–20.

2. Robert M. Hutchins, *The Higher Learning in America* (New Haven, CT: Yale University Press, 1962), p. 78.

3. Mortimer Adler, *Reforming Education* (Boulder, CO: Westview Press, 1977), pp. 84–85.

4. John Dewey, *Experience and Education* (New York: Macmillan, 1963).

5. Larry Cuban, *How Teachers Taught*, 2nd ed. (New York: Teachers College Press, 1993).

6. Paulo Freire, *Pedagogy of the Oppressed* (New York: Continuum Press, 1989).

7. Maxine Greene, *Landscapes of Learning* (New York: Teachers College Press, 1978); See also Maxine Greene, "Reflections on Teacher as Stranger" in C. Kridel (ed.) *Books of the Century Catalog* (Columbia, SC: University of South Carolina, Museum of Education, 2000).

8. Danna Harman, "This Is School?" *The Christian Science Monitor*, May 18, 2004, p. 11; Nick Anderson "Learning on Their Own Terms: Md. School With No Curriculum Challenges Conventions of Modern Education," *The Washington Post*, April 24, 2006, p. A01.

9. Jay Mathews, "Educators Blend Divergent Schools of Thought," *The Washington Post*, May 9, 2006, p. A12.

10. Lee Canter, "Assertive Discipline: More Than Names on a Board and Marbles in a Jar," *Phi Delta Kappan,* 71, 1989, pp. 57–61.

11. Timothy Reagan, *Non-Western Educational Traditions: Alternative Approaches to Educational Thought and Practice* (Mahwah, NJ: Lawrence Earlbaum Associates, 1996).

12. *Aristotle, Politics*, trans. and intro. by T. A. Sinclair (Middlesex, England: Penguin, 1978).

CHAPTER 9:   FINANCING AND GOVERNING AMERICA'S SCHOOLS

1. Mark G. Yudof, David L. Kip, Betsy Levin, *Educational Policy and the Law*, 3rd ed. (St. Paul: West, 1992), p. 658; Betsy Levin, Thomas Muller, and Corazon Sandoval, *The High Cost of Education in Cities* (Washington, DC: The Urban Institute, 1973).

2. Barry Siegel, "Parents Get a Lesson in Equality," *Los Angeles Times* (Washington edition), April 13, 1992, pp. A-1, A-18–A-19.

3. *Robinson* v. *Cahill*, 69 N.J. 133 (1973); *Abbott* v. *Burke*, 119 N.J. 287 (1990) (known as *Abbott I*); *Abbott* v. *Burke*, 153 N. J. 480 (1998) (known as *Abbott V*).

4. Peter Enrich, "Leaving Equality Behind: New Directions in School Finance Reform," *Vanderbilt Law Review* 48 (1995), pp. 101–194; for a description of this movement to adequacy arguments, visit nces.ed.gov/edfin/litigation/Contents.asp. For a discussion of the impact in Wisconsin, see Daniel W. Hildebrand, "2000 Significant Court Decisions," *Wisconsin Lawyer* 74, no. 6 (June 2001). Similar analyses are available in other such law updates.

5. Joshua Benton, "One District Reaps the Benefit of Another's Belt-tightening," *The Dallas Morning News,* December 12, 2002, www.dallasnews.com; David Mace, "Act 60 Reform Likely," *Rutland Herald,* January 6, 2003, online; "Tennessee's School Funding Declared Unconstitutional Again," *Associated Press,* October 9, 2002, CNN.COM.

6. "Financing Better Schools: Too Often, Traditional Methods of Paying for Schools Come Up Short," *Education Week* 24, Issue 17 (January 6, 2005), p. 7.

7. Richard Rothstein, "Equalizing Education Resources on Behalf of Disadvantaged Children," *A Nation at Risk: Preserving Public Education as an Engine for Social Mobility,* Richard D. Kahlenberg, editor (New York: The Century Foundation Press, 2000), p. 74.

8. W. E. Thro, "The Third Wave: The Impact of the Montana, Kentucky and Texas Decisions on the Future of Public School Finance Reform Litigation," *Journal of Law and Education* 199, no. 2 (Spring 1990), pp. 219–50; Robert F. McNergney and Joanne M. Herbert, *Foundations of Education: The Challenge of Professional Practice* (Boston: Allyn & Bacon, 1995), pp. 475–78; Chris Pipho, "Stateline: The Scent of the Future," *Phi Delta Kappan* 76 (September 1994), pp. 10–11; Greg Kocher, "Group Says Education Not Getting Enough Money Due It by Law," *Lexington Herald-Leader,* June 25, 2003, www.kentucky.com.

9. Cited in *Campaign for Fiscal Equality* v. *New York,* 86 N.Y. 2d 307 (1995); see also Bess Keller, "School Finance Case Draws to Close in N.Y.," *Education Week,* August 2, 2000.

10. Lori Montgomery, "Maryland Seeks 'Adequacy,' Recasting School Debate," *The Washington Post,* April 22, 2002, p. A1.

11. Robert Slavin, "How Can Funding Equity Ensure Enhanced Achievement?" *Journal of Educational Finance* 24, no. 4 (Spring 1999), pp. 519–28.

12. Bruce J. Biddle and David C. Berliner, "Unequal School Funding in the United States," *Education Leadership* 59, no. 8 (May 2002), pp. 48–59; Diana Jean Schemo, "Neediest Schools Receive Less Money, Report Finds," *The New York Times,* August 9, 2002, www.nytimes.com.

13. Amanda Paulson, "Does Money Transform Schools?" *Christian Science Monitor,* August 9, 2005, www.csmonitor.com.

14. Rebecca Sausner, "How Do You Spend Your Money*?*" *District Administration*, September 2005, www.districtadministration.com.

15. Thomas Toch, "Separate but Not Equal," *Agenda* 1 (Spring 1991), pp. 15–17.

16. Peter Keating, "How to Keep Your State and Local Taxes Down," *Money* 24, no. 1 (January 1995), pp. 86–92.

17. Bill Norris, "Losing Ticket in Lotteries," *Times Educational Supplement,* March 19, 1993, p. 17.

18. Joetta L. Sack, "Priorities Emerging for ESEA Reauthorization," *Education Week on the Web,* September 30, 1998; Anne C. Lewis, "Washington Report: House Democrats Criticize (in Unison) the Education Block Grant: Republicans Sing a Different Tune," *Phi Delta Kappan* 65, no. 6 (February 1984), pp. 379–80.

19. Kris Axtman, "Schools Bend under Tight Budgets," *The Christian Science Monitor,* November 20, 2002, online; "Schools Cut Costs With 4–Day Weeks," September 11, 2002, CNN.COM; Richard Rothstein, "Raising School Standards and Cutting Budget: Huh?" *The New York Times,* July 10, 2002, www.nytimes.com.

20. Jay Matthews, "More Public Schools Using Private Dollars," *The Washington Post,* August 28, 1995, pp. A-1, A-8; Justin Blum, "PTAs Give Some D.C. Schools an Edge," *The Washington Post,* April 17, 2000, p. B1; Nancy Trejos, "Schools Turning to No-Fuss Fundraising Online," *The Washington Post,* May 23, 2000, p. A1.

21. Anne Lewis, "Washington Seen: Buildings in Disrepair," *Education Digest* 60, no. 8 (April 1995); p. 71; Jacques Steinberg and John Sullivan, "In Disrepair for Years, Many Schools Pose a Risk," *The New York Times,* February 2, 1998, p. A-21; "Educator's Wish List: Infrastructure Tops High-Tech," *The Washington Post,* October 24, 2000, p. A-13; "Fast Response Survey System, Survey on the Conditions of Public School Facilities," U.S. Department of Education, National Center for Education Statistics, Washington, DC, 1999.

22. Frederick M. Hess, *School Boards at the Dawn of the 21st Century* (Arlington, VA.: National School Boards Association, 2002).

23. For an insightful discussion of school boards, see Joel Spring, *American Education* (New York: McGraw-Hill, 2002), pp. 178–82.

24. Chester Finn, "Reinventing Local Control," in Patricia First and Herbert Walberg (eds.), *School Boards: Changing Local Control* (Berkeley: McCutchan, 1992); Emily Feistritzer, "A Profile of School Board Presidents," in *School Boards: Changing Local Control;* Neal Pierce, "School Boards Get Failing Grades, in Both the Cities and the Suburbs," *Philadelphia Inquirer,* April 27, 1992, p. 11; Mary Jordan, "School Boards Need Overhaul, Educators Say," *The Washington Post,* April 5, 1992, p. A-51.

25. Jay Mathews, "Playing Politics in Urban City Schools," *The Washington Post,* September 11, 2002, www.washingtonpost.com.

26. Catherine Gewertz, "Race, Gender, and the Superintendency," *Education Week* 26, issue 24 (February 17, 2006), pp. 1, 22, 24.

27. Cited in Joel Spring, *American Education* (New York: McGraw-Hill, 2002), pp. 180–81.

28. Jay Mathews, "Nontraditional Thinking in Central Office," The School Administrator Web Edition, *The Washington Post,* June 2001; Tamar Lewin, "Leaders from Other Professions Reshape America's Schools, from Top to Bottom," *The New York Times,* June 8, 2000; Nancy Mitchell, "Nontraditional School Bosses," *Denver Rocky Mountain News,* April 16, 2001; Abby Goodnough, "Retired General Takes on New Mission: Schools," *New York Times,* November 6, 2002, www.nytimes.com; Jennifer Steinhauer, "Bloomberg Picks a Lawyer to Run New York Schools," *The New York Times,* July 30, 2002, www.nytimes.com.

29. Joanna Richardson, "Contracts Put Superintendents to Performance Test," *Education Week,* September 14, 1994, pp. 1, 12.

30. Emily Wax, "A Tough Time at the Head of the Classes," *The Washington Post,* June 18, 2002, p. A9.

31. Vincent L. Ferrandino, "Challenges for 21st-Century Elementary School Principals," *Phi Delta Kappan* 82, no. 6 (February 2001), pp. 440–42; Linda Borg, "The Principal Dilemma Facing Schools in R.I.," *The Providence Journal,* www.projo.com/education (August 26, 2001); Jacques Steinberg, "One Principal's World (The Unscripted Version)," *The New York Times,* January 1, 2003, www.nytimes.com.

32. "Seeing the Big Picture" in Education Vital Signs, *American School Board Journal,* December 1999.

33. Ferrandino, "Challenges for 21st-Century Elementary School Principals."

34. Edmund Janko, "The Untouchables: There Are Some People You Don't Mess With, and Many of Them Work in Schools," *Teacher Magazine* 16, issue 6 (May 1, 2005), pp. 50–51.

35. James G. Cibula, "Two Eras of Urban Schooling: The Decline of Law and Order and the Emergence of New Organizational Forms," *Education and Urban Society,* 29, no. 3 (May 1997), pp. 317–41.

36. Quoted in "Building Better Business Alliances," *Instructor* (Winter 1986); (special issue), p. 21; see also Brian Dumaine, "Making Education Work," *Fortune,* Spring 1990 (special issue), pp. 12–22.

37. For a good overview of school consolidation, see Karen Irmsher, "School Size." *ERIC Digest,* no. 113 (Eugene, OR: ERIC Clearinghouse on Educational Management, July 1997) (ED414615).

38. Catherine Gewertz, "The Breakup: Suburbs Try Smaller High Schools," *Education Week on the Web,* May 2, 2001; Craig Howley and Marty Strange and Robert Bickel, "Research about School Size and School Performance in Impoverished Communities," (Charleston, WV:

ERIC Clearinghouse on Rural Education and Small Schools, December 2000); William Ayers, Gerald Bracey, and Greg Smith, "The Ultimate Education Reform? Make Schools Smaller," (Milwaukee: Center for Education Research, Analysis, and Innovation, University of Wisconsin-Milwaukee, December 14, 2000).

39. Elissa Gootman, "New York City Plans to Open Small Secondary Schools," *The New York Times*, March 12, 2004, www.nytimes.com.

40. See Marianne Perle and David Baker, *Job Satisfaction Among America's Teachers: Effects of Workplace Conditions, Background Characteristics, and Teacher Compensation* (Washington, DC: National Center for Education Statistics, U.S. Department of Health, Education and Welfare, August 1997), pp. 41–42; See also John Lane and Edgar Epps (eds.), *Restructuring the Schools: Problems and Prospects* (Berkeley: McCutchan, 1992); Jeff Archer, "New Roles Tap Expertise of Teachers," *Education Week,* May 30, 2001.

41. Fern Shen, "New Strategy for School Management," *The Washington Post,* February 17, 1998, pp. B-1, B-7; Patrick McCloskey, "Vocal Arrangement," *Teacher Magazine* 17, issue 1 (September 1, 2005), pp. 30–35, www.edweek.org; Jeff Archer, "S.F. School Councils Help Chart Improvement Course," *Education Week* 25, issue 31 (April 12, 2006), p. 10.

42. Ann Bradley and Lynn Olson, "The Balance of Power: Shifting the Lines of Authority in an Effort to Improve Schools," *Education Week,* February 24, 1993, p. 10.

CHAPTER 10   SCHOOL LAW AND ETHICS

1. Julius Menacker and Ernest Pascarella, "How Aware Are Educators of Supreme Court Decisions That Affect Them?" *Phi Delta Kappan* 64, no. 6 (February 1983), pp. 424–26; Louis Fischer, David Schimmel, and Leslie Stellman, *Teachers and the Law* (New York: Longman, 2006); Karen Zittleman, "Title IX and Gender: A Study of the Knowledge, Perceptions, and Experiences of Middle and Junior High School Teachers and Students," *Dissertation Abstracts International* 66, no.11 (2005) (UMI No. 3194815); Gerry Doyle, "Study: Americans Know Bart Better than 1st Amendment," *Chicago Tribune* (February 28, 2006), available at www.chicagotribune.com.

2. Louis Fischer and David Schimmel, *The Civil Rights of Teachers* (New York: Harper & Row, 1973).

3. The legal situations and interpretations included in this text are adapted from a variety of sources, including Myra Sadker and David Sadker, *Sex Equity Handbook for Schools* (New York: Longman, 1982); Fischer and Schimmel, *The Civil Rights of Teachers,* and *Your Legal Rights and Responsibilities: A Guide for Public School Students* (Washington, DC: U.S. Department of Health, Education and Welfare, n.d.); Fischer, Schimmel, and Kelly, *Teachers and the Law;* Michael LaMorte, *School Law: Cases and Concepts* (Boston: Allyn & Bacon, 2004).

4. Sadker and Sadker, *Sex Equity Handbook for Schools.*

5. *Gebser* v. *Lago Vista Independent School District* (96 U.S. 1866 (1998); Greg Henderson, "Court Says Compensatory Damages Available Under Title IX," UPI, February 26, 1992; *North Haven Board of Education* v. *Bell,* 456 U.S. 512 (1982); *Franklin* v. *Gwinnett County Schools,* 503 U.S. 60 (1992).

6. *Thompson* v. *Southwest School District,* 483 F. Supp. 1170 (W.D.M.W. 1980). See also *Board of Trustees* v. *Stubblefield,* 94 Cal. Rptr. 318, 321 [1971]; *Morrison* v. *State Board of Education,* 461 P. 2d 375 [1969]; *Pettit* v. *State Board of Education,* 513 P. 2nd 889 [Cal. 1973]; *Blodgett* v. *Board of Trustees, Tamalpais Union High School District,* 97 Cal. Rptr. 406 (1970); Fischer, Schimmel, and Kelly, *Teachers and the Law;* Human Rights Campaign Foundation, "Discrimination in the Workplace" (August 7, 2003). Available online at www.hrc.org/worknet/nd/nd_facts.asp#2.

7. *Kingsville Independent School District* v. *Cooper,* 611 F. 2d 1109 (5th Cir. 1980); *Parducci* v. *Rutland,* 316 F. Supp. 352 (M.D. Ala. 1979); *Brubaker* v. *Board of Education, School District 149, Cook County, Illinois,* 502 F. 2d 973 (7th Cir. 1974). See also Martha McCarthy and Nelda Cambron, *Public School Law: Teachers' and Students' Rights* (Boston: Allyn & Bacon, 2003).

8. *Pickering* v. *Board of Education of Township High School District 205, Will County,* 391 U.S. 563 (1968); *Givhan* v. *Western Line Consolidated School District,* 439 U.S. 410 (1979); Nathan L. Essex, *School Law and the Public Schools: A Practical Guide for School Leaders* (Boston: Allyn & Bacon, 2004).

9. *Basic Books* v. *Kinko's Graphics Corp.,* 758 F. Supp. 1522 (S.D.N.Y.1991); Miriam R. Krasno, "Copyright and You," *Update,* Winter 1983; Thomas J. Flygare, "Photocopying and Videotaping for Educational Purposes: The Doctrine of Fair Use," *Phi Delta Kappan* 65, no. 8 (April 1984), pp. 568–69; Gary Becker, "Copyright in a Digital Age: How to Comply with the Law and Set a Good Example for Students," *American School Board Journal* 187, no. 6 (June 2000), pp. 26–27; Constance S. Hawke, *Computer and Internet Use on Campus: A Legal Guide to Issues of Intellectual Property, Free Speech, and Privacy* (San Francisco: Jossey-Bass, 2001); Hall Davidson, "The Educators' Guide to Copyright and Fair Use," *Technology & Learning* 23, no. 3 (October 2002), pp. 26–32.

10. 115 ILCS 5/13 (1993 State Bar Edition); Ind. Code Ann 20–7.5–1–14 (West 1995); Nev. Rev. State 288.260 (1995); see also Michael La Morte, *School Law: Cases and Concepts* (Boston: Allyn & Bacon, 2004); *Hortonville Joint School District No. 1* v. *Hortonville Education Association,* 426 U.S. 482 (1976).

11. Fisher, Schimmel, and Stellman, *Teachers and the Law;* Karen Zittleman, "Teachers, Students, and Title IX: A Promise for Fairness," in *Gender in the Classroom: Foundations, Skills, Methods and Strategies across the Curriculum,* David Sadker and Ellen Silber, eds. (Mahwah, NJ: Lawrence Erlbaum, 2007).

12. See Fischer, Schimmel, and Stellman, *Teachers and the Law, Owasso Independent School District* v. *Falvo* 534 U.S. 426 (2002).

13. Sadker and Sadker, *Sex Equity Handbook for Schools;* Fischer, Schimmel, and Stellman, *Teachers and the Law.*

14. *Goss* v. *Lopez,* 419 U.S. 565 (1975); *Wood* v. *Strickland,* 420 U.S. 308 (1975); *Ingraham* v. *Wright,* 430 U.S. 651 (1977); Martha McCarthy and Dean Webb, "Balancing

Duties and Rights," *Principal Leadership* 1, no. 1 (September 2000), pp. 16–21; Michael Martin, "Does Zero Mean Zero? Balancing Policy with Procedure in the Fight Against Weapons at School," *American School Board Journal* 187, no. 3 (March 2000), pp. 39–41; *James v. Unified School District No. 512,* 899 F. Supp. 530 (1995); Stacy Teicher, "To Paddle or Not to Paddle? It's Still Not Clear in U.S. Schools," *Christian Science Monitor* (March 17, 2005), available at www.csmonitor.com/2005/0317/p01s04-legn.html.

15. Howard Fischer, "Court: Schools Can Ban Hurtful T-Shirt Slogans," *Arizona Daily Star* (April 21, 2006), available at www.azstarnet.com/news/125690.

16. *Tinker* v. *Des Moines Independent Community School District,* 393 U.S. 503 (1969); *Beussink* v. *Woodland R-IV School District,* 30 F. Supp. 2d 1175 (1998); Jamin Raskin, *We the Students: Supreme Court Cases for and about Students* (Washington, DC: CQ Press, 2000).

17. *Bethel School District No. 403* v. *Fraser,* 478 U.S. 675 (1986); *J. S.* v. *Bethlehem Area School District,* 757A. 2d 412 (2000); Kathleen Conn, "Offensive Student Web Sites: What Should Schools Do?" *Educational Leadership* 50, no. 5 (February 2001), pp. 74–77.

18. Benjamin Sendor, "Guidance on Graduation Prayer," *The American School Board Journal* (April 1997), pp. 17–18; Benjamin Sendor, "When May School Clubs Meet?" *The American School Board Journal* (August 1997), pp. 14–15; Ralph D. Mawdsley, "Religion in the Schools: Walking a Fine Legal Line," *School Business Affairs* 63, no. 5 (May 1997), pp. 5–10; *Engel* v. *Vitale,* 370 U.S. 421 (1962); *School District of Abington Township* v. *Schempp and Murray* v. *Curlett,* 373 U.S. 203 (1963); *Lee* v. *Weisman,* 112 U.S. 2649, (1992); *Good News Club* v. *Milford Central Schools,* 99 U.S. 2036 (2001); *Santa Fe Independent School District* v. *Doe,* 99 U.S. 62 (2000); John Sank, "Patriotism Push: New Laws Require Kids to Say the Pledge, Pass Civics Course." *Rocky Mountain News* (August 4, 2003). Available online at www.rockymountainnews.com; United States Department of Education, *No Child Left Behind Guidance on Constitutionally Protected Prayer in Public Elementary and Secondary Schools* (February 7, 2003). Available online at www.ed.gov/inits/religionandschools/ prayer_guidance.html.

19. *Bellnier* v. *Lund,* 438 F. Supp. 47 (N.Y. 1977); *Doe* v. *Renfrou,* 635 F. 2d 582 (7th Cir. 1980), *cert. denied,* 101 S. Ct. 3015 (1981); *Veronia School District* v. *Acton,* 115 U.S. 2386 (1995); *New Jersey* v. *T.L.O.,* 105 U.S. 733 (1985); *Board of Education of Independent School District No. 92 of Pottawatomie County* v. *Earls,* no. 01–3332 (2002).

20. *Hazelwood School District* v. *Kuhlmeier,* 108 S. Ct. 562 (1988); *Shanley* v. *Northeast Independent School District,* 462 F. 2d 960 (5th Cir. 1972); *Gambino* v. *Fairfax County School Board,* 564 F. 2d 157 (4th Cir. 1977).

21. Fischer, Schimmel, and Stellman, *Teachers and the Law.*

22. "U.S. Supreme Court Decision on Teacher-Student Sexual Harassment Changing Legal Landscape," *Educator's Guide to Controlling Sexual Harassment* 5, no. 12 (September 1998), pp. 1, 3, 4–5; Joel Spring, *American Education,*

12th ed. (New York: McGraw-Hill, 2006); *Davis* v. *Monroe County Board of Education,* 97 U.S. 843 (1999).

23. Harris Interactive Poll, *Hostile Hallways: Bullying, Teasing, and Sexual Harassment in School* (Washington, DC: American Association of University Women, 2001); Raskin, *We the Students: Supreme Court Cases for and about Students;* Gay, Lesbian and Straight Education Network, "State of the States" (August 26, 2002). Available online at www.glsen.org; National Center for Lesbian Rights, "Victory in School Discrimination Case" (April 4, 2003). Available online at www.nclrights.org/releases/massey040303.htm; United States Department of Education, Office of Civil Rights (1997). *Sexual Harassment: It's Not Academic.* Available online at www.ed.gov.

24. Millicent Lawson, "False Accusations Turn Dream into Nightmare in Chicago," *Education Week,* August 2, 1994, p. 16; Harris Interactive Poll, *Hostile Hallways: Bullying, Teasing, and Sexual Harassment in School;* Mark Walsh, "High Court Addresses Harassment," *Education Week,* July 8, 1999, pp. 1, 30–31.

25. Lynn Thompson, "Educators Blame Internet for Rise in Student Cheating," *The Seattle Times* (January 16, 2005), available at www.seattletimes.nwsource.com; Don McCabe, "Levels of Cheating and Plagiarism Remain High," *Center for Academic Integrity* (June 2005), available at www.academicintegrity.org/cai_research.asp.

26. "Poll: Student Cheating Prevalent," *Detroit News,* April 30, 2004, www.detnews.com.

27. Fred Hechinger, *Fateful Choices: Healthy Youth for the 21st Century* (New York: Carnegie Council on Adolescent Development, 1992); Administration on Children, Youth, and Families U.S. Department of Health and Human Services, *Child Maltreatment* (2004), available online at www.acf.hhs.gov/programs/cb/pubs/cm04/index.htm.

28. Character Education Partnership Online, "Public Support for Character Education," www.character.org (May 18, 2006).

29. Bates, "A Textbook of Virtues": Irene McHenry, "Conflict in Schools: Fertile Ground for Moral Growth," *Phi Delta Kappan* 82, no. 3 (November 2000), pp. 223–27; Meg Lundstrom, "Character Makes a Comeback," *Instructor* 109, no. 3 (October 1999), pp. 25–28.

30. David Carr, "Moral Formation, Cultural Attachment or Social Control: What's the Point of Values Education?" *Educational Theory* 50, no. 1 (Winter 2000), pp. 49–62; Susan Gilbert, "Scientists Explore the Molding of Children's Morals." *The New York Times* (March 18, 2003), section F, p. 5; Kathleen Kennedy Manzo, "Educators Urge Broad View on How to Build Character," *Education Week* 25, issue 15 (December 14, 2005), pp. 1, 16.

31. Joan F. Goodman, "Objections (and Responses) to Moral Education," *Education Week* 20, no. 38 (May 30, 2001), pp. 32, 35; Debra Viadero, "Nice Work." *Education Week* 22, no. 33 (April 30, 2003), pp. 38–41.

32. Alfie Kohn, "How Not to Teach Values," *Phi Delta Kappan* 78, no. 8 (April 1997), pp. 428–37; Goodman, "Objections (and Responses) to Moral Education."

33. Howard Kirschenbaum, "A Comprehensive Model for Values Education and Moral Education," *Phi Delta Kappan* 73, no. 10 (June 1992), pp. 771–76.

34. Diane Berreth and Sheldon Berman, "The Moral Dimensions of Schools," *Educational Leadership* 54, no. 8 (May 1997), pp. 24–27; Karl Hostetler, *Ethical Judgment in Teaching* (Boston: Allyn & Bacon, 1997); Katherine Simon, "Making Room for Moral Questions in the Classroom," *Education Week* 21, no. 10 (November 7, 2001), pp. 51, 68.

CHAPTER 11: BECOMING AN EFFECTIVE TEACHER

1. Among the resources on teacher effectiveness that you may want to consult are the *Journal of Teacher Education, Handbook of Research on Teaching, The Review of Research in Education* and *Educational Leadership.*

2. N. Filby Fisher, E. Marleave, L. Cahen, M. Dishaw, M. Moore, and D. Berliner, *Teaching Behaviors, Academic Learning Time, and Student Achievement: Final Report of Beginning Teacher Evaluation Study* (San Francisco: Far West Laboratory, 1978).

3. John Goodlad, *A Place Called School* (New York: McGraw-Hill, 1984).

4. Barbara M. Taylor, David P. Pearson, Kathleen F. Clark, and Sharon Walpole, "Effective Schools/Accomplished Teachers," *Reading Teacher* 53 (1999), pp. 156–59; Susan Black, "Time for Learning." *American School Board Journal* 189, no. 9 (September 2002), pp. 58, 60, 62, available at www.asbj.com/2002/09/0902research.html; Chip Wood, "Changing the Pace of School: Slowing Down the Day to Improve the Quality of Learning." *Phi Delta Kappan* 83, no. 7 (March 2002), pp. 545–50; WestEd, "Making Time Count," *Policy Brief* (2001), available at http://web.wested.org/online_pubs/making_time_count.pdf.

5. Herbert Walberg, Richard Niemiec, and Wayne Frederick, "Productive Curriculum Time," *The Peabody Journal of Education* 69, no. 3 (1994), pp. 86–100; Steve Nelson, *Instructional Time as a Factor in Increasing Student Achievement* (Portland, OR: Northwest Regional Lab, 1990); David Berliner, "The Half-Full Glass: A Review of Research on Teaching," in Philip Hosferd (ed.), *Using What We Know About Teaching* (Alexandria, VA: Association for Supervision and Curriculum Development, 1984); Geoffrey Borman, "Academic Resilience in Mathematics Among Poor and Minority Students," in *Elementary School Journal* 104, no. 3 (2004), pp. 177–195; WestEd, "Making Time Count." *Policy Brief* (2001), available at http://web.wested.org/online_pubs/making_time_count.pdf; Cori Brewster and Jennifer Fager, *Increasing Student Engagement and Motivation: From Time on Task to Homework* (Portland, OR: Northwest Regional Educational Laboratory, 2000), online: www.nwrel.org/request/oct00/textonly.html.

6. Jacob Kounin, *Discipline and Group Management in Classrooms* (New York: Holt, Rinehart & Winston, 1970).

7. C. M. Evertson, E. T. Emmer, and M. E. Worsham, *Classroom Management for Elementary Teachers,* 7th ed. (Boston: Allyn & Bacon, 2006). See also Carolyn Evertson and Alene Harris, "What We Know About Managing Classrooms," *Educational Leadership* 49, no. 7 (April 1992), pp. 74–78.

8. Robert Slavin, "Classroom Management and Discipline," in *Educational Psychology: Theory into Practice* (Englewood Cliffs, NJ: Prentice Hall, 1986); Vernon F. Jones and Louise S. Jones, *Comprehensive Classroom Management: Creating Communities of Support and Solving Problems* (Needham Heights, MA: Allyn & Bacon, 2001), pp. 251–55.

9. E. T. Emmer, C. M. Evertson, and M. E. Worsham, *Classroom Management for Secondary Teachers,* 7th ed. (Boston: Allyn & Bacon, 2006); B. Malone, D. Bonitz, and M. Rickett, "Teacher Perceptions of Disruptive Behavior: Maintaining Instructional Focus," *Educational Horizons* 76, no. 4 (1998), pp. 189–94.

10. Thomas L. Good and Jere E. Brophy, *Looking in Classrooms,* 9th ed. (Boston: Allyn & Bacon, 2003).

11. Marilyn E. Gootman, *The Caring Teacher's Guide to Discipline: Helping Young Students Learn Self-Control, Responsibility, and Respect* (Thousand Oaks, CA: Corwin Press, 1997).

12. Kathleen Cushman, *Fires in the Bathroom: Advice for Teachers from High School Students* (New York: The New Press, 2003).

13. David Berliner, "What Do We Know About Well-Managed Classrooms? Putting Research to Work," *Instructor* 94, no. 6 (February 1985), p. 15; Carol Cummings, *Winning Strategies for Classroom Management* (Alexandria, VA: Association for Supervision and Curriculum Development, 2000).

14. Arno Bellack, *The Language of the Classroom* (New York: Teachers College Press, 1966).

15. Several of the sections on the pedagogical cycle are adopted from Myra Sadker and David Sadker, *Principal Effectiveness—Pupil Achievement (PEPA) Training Manual* (Washington, DC: American University, 1986).

16. Donald Cruickshank, "Applying Research on Teacher Clarity," *Journal of Teacher Education* 36 (1985), pp. 44–48.

17. Myra Sadker and David Sadker, "Questioning Skills" in James M. Cooper (ed.), *Classroom Teaching Skills,* 8th ed. (Boston: Houghton Mifflin, 2006); P. Smagoinsky, "The Social Construction of Data: Methodological Problems of Investigation Learning in the Zone of Proximal Development," *Review of Educational Research* 65, no. 3 (1995), pp. 191–212.

18. John Dewey, *How We Think,* rev. ed. (Boston: D. C. Heath, 1933), p. 266.

19. Myra Sadker and David Sadker, "Sexism in the Schoolroom of the 80s," *Psychology Today* 19 (March 1985), pp. 54–57.

20. Benjamin Bloom (ed.), *Taxonomy of Educational Objectives, Handbook I: Cognitive Domain* (New York: David McKay, 1956).

21. Myra Sadker and David Sadker, "Questioning Skills" in James Cooper (ed.), *Classroom Teaching Skills;* Trevor Kerry, "Classroom Questions in England," *Questioning Exchange* 1, no. 1, (1987), p. 33; Arthur C. Grassier and Natalie K. Person, "Question Asking During Tutoring," *American Educational Research Journal* 31 (1994), pp. 104–37; William S. Carlsen, "Questioning in Classrooms: A Sociolinguistic Perspective," *Review of Educational Research* 61 (1991), pp. 157–78; David Berliner, "The Half-Full Glass: A Review of Research on

Teaching," in Philip L. Hosford (ed.), *Using What We Know About Teaching,* pp. 51–84; L. M. Barden, "Effective Questions and the Ever-Elusive Higher-Order Question," *American Biology Teacher* 57, no. 7 (1995), pp. 423–26; Meredith D. Gall and T. Rhody, "Review of Research on Questioning Techniques," in William W. Wilen (ed.), *Questions, Questioning Techniques, and Effective Teaching* (Washington, DC: National Education Association, 1987), pp. 23–48.

22. Adapted from Myra Sadker and David Sadker, "Questioning Skills" in James M. Cooper (ed.), *Classroom Teaching Skills.*

23. Mary Budd Rowe, "Wait Time: Slowing Down May Be a Way of Speeding Up!" *Journal of Teacher Education* 37 (January/February 1986), pp. 43–50; Mary Budd Rowe, "Science, Silence, and Sanctions," *Science and Children* 34 (September 1996), pp. 35–37; Jim B. Mansfield, "The Effects of Wait-time on Issues of Gender Equity, Academic Achievement, and Attitude Toward a Course," *Teacher Education and Practice* 12, no. 1 (Spring/Summer 1996), pp. 86–93.

24. D. Bridges, "A Philosophical Analysis of Discussion" in J. Dillion (ed.), *Questioning and Discussion: A Multidisciplinary Study* (Norwood, NJ: Alblex, 1988), p. 26; A. E. Edwards and D. G. P. Westgate, *Investigating Classroom Talk,* Social Research and Educational Studies Series: 4 (London and Philadelphia: Falmer, 1987), p. 170.

25. Myra Sadker, David Sadker, and Susan Klein, "The Issue of Gender in Elementary and Secondary Education," *Review of Research in Education* 17 (1991), pp. 269–334.

26. Goodlad, *A Place Called School.*

27. Martha McCarthy, *High School Survey of Student Engagement* (Bloomington, IN: University of Indiana Press, 2005), retrieved on May 21, 2005, from www.iub.edu/~nsse/hssse.

28. Jere E. Brophy, "Teacher Praise: A Functional Analysis," *Review of Educational Research* 51 (1981), pp. 5–32; Dan Laitsch, "Student Behaviors and Teacher Use of Approval versus Disapproval," *ASCD Research Brief* 4, no. 3 (March 27, 2006).

29. Gary Davis and Margaret Thomas, *Effective Schools and Effective Teachers* (Boston: Allyn & Bacon, 1989); Charles A. Dana Center, University of Texas at Austin, *Hope for Urban Education: A Study of Nine High-Performing, High-Poverty, Urban Elementary Schools* (Washington, DC: U.S. Department of Education, Planning and Evaluation Service, 1999), www.ed.gov./pubs/urbanhope/execsumm.html.

30. Susan Black, "Stretching Students Minds: Effective Teaching Is about What Students Will Learn, Not Just What They Will Do," *American School Board Journal* (June 2001), www.asbj.com/current/research.html; Metropolitan Life Inc., *The American Teacher* (New York: Metropolitan Life Company, 2001), pp. 13–15.

31. Bruce R. Joyce and Emily F. Calhoun, *Learning Experiences: The Role of Instructional Theory and Research* (Alexandria, VA: Association for Curriculum and Supervision, 1996); Barak Rosenshine, "Synthesis of Research on Explicit Teaching," *Educational Leadership* 43, no. 4 (May 1986),

pp. 60–69. See also Davis and Thomas, *Effective Schools and Effective Teachers.*

32. David Johnson and Roger Johnson, *Learning Together and Alone: Cooperative, Competitive, and Individualistic Learning,* 5th ed. (Boston: Allyn and Bacon, 1999); Robert Slavin, "Research on Cooperative Learning: Consensus and Controversy," *Educational Leadership* 47, no. 4 (December 1989–January 1990), pp. 52–54.

33. Robert E. Slavin, "Cooperative Learning in Middle and Secondary Schools," *Clearinghouse* 69, no. 4 (March–April 1996), pp. 200–2004; Robert E. Slavin, "Cooperative Learning," *Review of Educational Research* 50 (Summer 1980), pp. 315–42. See also Robert Slavin, *Cooperative Learning: Student Teams* (Washington, DC: National Education Association, 1987).

34. Robert E. Slavin, *Cooperative Learning: Theory, Research, and Practice* (Boston: Allyn & Bacon, 1995); Roger Johnson and David Johnson, "Student Interaction: Ignored but Powerful." *Journal of Teacher Education* 36 (July–August 1985), p. 24. See also Robert Slavin, "Synthesis of Research on Cooperative Learning," *Educational Leadership* 48, no. 5 (February 1991), pp. 71–82; Susan Ellis and Susan Whalen, "Keys to Cooperative Learning," *Instructor* 101, no. 6 (February 1992), pp. 34–37.

35. Jay Matthews, "Students Move at Own Pace Toward Proficiency," *The Washington Post,* June 13, 2006, p. A8.

36. David Meichenbaum and Andrew Biemiller, *Nurturing Independent Learners: Helping Students Take Charge of Their Learning* (Cambridge, MA: Brookline Books, 1998); Joan S. Hyman and S. Alan Cohen, "Learning for Mastery: Ten Conclusions After 15 Years and 3000 Schools," *Educational Leadership* 36 (November 1979), pp. 104–9.

37. Glenn Hymel, "Harnessing the Mastery Learning Literature: Past Efforts, Current Status, and Future Directions," Paper presented at the annual meeting of the American Educational Research Association, Boston, MA, 1990; Thomas Guskey and Sally Gates, "Synthesis of Research on the Effects of Mastery Learning in Elementary and Secondary Classrooms," *Educational Leadership* 43 (May 1986), pp. 73–80; J. Ronald Gentile, "Assessing Fundamentals in Every Course through Mastery Learning," *New Directions in Teaching & Learning* 100 (December 2004), pp. 15–20; Helen Patrick and Caroline Yoon, "Early Adolescents' Motivation During Science Investigation," *Journal of Educational Research,* 97, no. 6, (July–August 2004), pp. 317–318.

38. Diane Curtis, "The Power of Projects," *Educational Leadership* 60, no. 1 (September 2002), pp. 50–53; Linda Torp and Sara Sage, *Problems as Possibilities: Problem-Based Learning for K–12 Education* (Alexandria, VA: Association for Supervision and Curriculum Development, 1998); Robert Delisle, *How to Use Problem-Based Learning in the Classroom* (Alexandria, VA: Association for Supervision and Curriculum Development, 1997).

39. *Education Week,* "The Information Age: Using Data to Accelerate Achievement," *Technology Counts 2006* 25, no. 35 (May 4, 2006), available at www.edweek.org/ew/toc/2006/05/04/index.html

40. Margaret Roblyer, *Integrating Educational Technology into Teaching,* 4th ed. (Upper Saddle River, NJ: Merrill/ Prentice Hall, 2006).

41. George Brackett, "Technologies Don't Change Schools— Caring, Capable People Do," in David T. Gordon, ed., *The Digital Classroom* (Cambridge: Harvard College, 2000), pp. 29–30.

42. Peter W. Foltz, Darrel Laham, and Thomas K. Landauer, "Automated Essay Scoring: Applications to Educational Technology." Paper presented at the ED-Media/ED-Telecom '99, World Conference on Educational Multimedia/Hypermedia & Educational Telecommunications, Seattle, WA, June 19–24, 1999; "Tech's Answer to Testing," *Education Week,* May 8, 2003, www.edweek.org; Michelle Galley, "The Teacher's New Test," *Education Week,* May 8, 2003, www.edweek.org.

43. David Williamson Schaffer, "This Is Dewey's Vision Revisited," in David T. Gordon, ed., *The Digital Classroom,* (Cambridge: Harvard College, 2000), pp. 176–178.

44. William R. Penuel, Barbara Means, and Michael Simkins, "The Multimedia Challenge," *Educational Leadership* 58, no. 2 (October 2000), p. 34.

45. *The Neighborhood Story Project* (June 9, 2006), available at www.neighborhoodstoryproject.org/. Ann Jones and Kim Issroff, "Learning Technologies: Affective and Social Issues in Computer-Supported Collaborative Learning," *Computers & Education* 44, no. 4 (May 2005), pp. 395–409.

46. ImagiProbe Wireless Sensing System (September 20, 2005), available at www.imagiworks.com/Pages/News/ PR092005.html.

47. "Bias-Busting Tech Keeps Kids Focused," *eSchool News. com* (June 2, 2006), available at www.eschoolnews.com/ news/showStory.cfm?ArticleID=6341.

48. Jere Brophy, "Probing the Subtleties of Subject-Matter Teaching," *Educational Leadership* 49, no. 7 (April 1992), pp. 4–8; Jay McTighe, Elliott Seif, and Grant Wiggins, "You Can Teach for Meaning," *Educational Leadership* 62, no. 1 (September 2004), pp. 26–30.

49. Carol Ann Tomlinson, "Reconcilable Differences? Standards-Based Teaching and Differentiation," *Educational Leadership* 58, no. 1 (September 2000), pp. 6–11; Carol Ann Tomlinson, "Differentiating Instruction for Academic Diversity," in James M. Cooper (ed.), *Classroom Teaching Skills,* 8th ed. (Boston: Houghton Mifflin, 2006).

50. Richard Prawat, "From Individual Differences to Learning Communities—Our Changing Focus," *Educational Leadership* 49, no. 7 (April 1992), pp. 9–13; Jonathan Supovitz and Jolley Bruce Christman, "Small Learning Communities That Actually Learn: Lessons for School Leaders," *Phi Delta Kappan* 86, no. 9 (May 2005), pp. 649–51; Robert Blum, "A Case for Connectedness," *Educational Leadership* 62, no. 7 (April 2005), pp. 16–20.

51. Joellen Killion and Guy Todnem, "A Process for Personal Theory Building," *Educational Leadership* 48, no. 6 (March 1991), pp. 14–16.

52. Bud Wellington, "The Promise of Reflective Practice," *Educational Leadership* 48, no. 6 (March 1991), pp. 4–5; Melody J. Shank, "Common Space, Common Time, Common Work," *Educational Leadership* 62, no. 8 (May 2005), pp. 16–19; Lynn McAlpine, Danis Berthiaume, and Gail Fairbank-Roch, "Reflection on Teaching: Types and Goals of Reflection," *Educational Research & Evaluation* 10, nos. 4–6 (December 2004), pp. 337–64; John Ward and Suzanne McCotter, "Reflection as a Visible Outcome for Preservice Teachers," *Teaching & Teacher Education* 20, no. 3 (April 2004), pp. 243–58; Carol Rodgers, "Seeing Student Learning: Teacher Changes and the Role of Reflection," *Harvard Educational Review* 72 (2002), pp. 230–53.

CHAPTER 12　YOUR FIRST CLASSROOM

1. Lilian Katz, "The Development of Preschool Teachers," *The Elementary School Journal* 73, no. 1 (October 1972), pp. 50–54; John L. Watzke, "Longitudinal Study of Stages of Beginning Teacher Development in a Field-Based Teacher Education Program," *Teacher Educator* 38, no. 3 (Winter 2003), pp. 209–29.

2. Linda Darling-Hammond, "Teachers and Teaching: Testing Policy Hypothesis from a National Commission Report," *Educational Researcher* 27, no. 1 (January– February 1998), pp. 5–15; Debra Viadero, "Studies Say Students Learn More from Licensed Teachers," *Education Week* 22, no. 3 (September 18, 2002), p. 7; Linda Darling-Hammond, "Keeping Good Teachers: Why It Matters, What Leaders Can Do," *Educational Leadership* (May 2003) pp. 6–13.

3. *Status of the American Public School Teacher* (Washington, DC: National Education Association, 2003); Mary Patterson, "Hazed," *Educational Leadership* 62, no. 8 (May 2005), pp. 20–23; Susan Moore Johnson, Susan Kardos, and Edward Liu, "New Teachers' Experiences of Hiring and Professional Culture: A Four State Survey Study," The Project on the Next Generation of Teachers, Harvard Graduate School of Education (Cambridge, MA, 2003); Ben Feller, "Teacher Shortage Misdiagnosed, Group Says," *Minneapolis Star Tribune,* January 29, 2003, www.startribune.com; Association of Curriculum and Supervision, "Teaching Out of the Field: An Overlooked Factor in Unqualified Teaching," *ASCD SmartBriefs* 1, no. 5, March 5, 2003.

4. L. Huling-Austin, "Research on Learning to Teach: Implications for Teacher Induction and Mentoring," *Journal of Teacher Education* 43, no. 3 (May/June 1992), pp. 173–78; Andrew J. Wayne, Peter Youngs, and Steve Fleischman, "Improving Teacher Induction," *Educational Leadership* 62, no. 8 (May 2005), pp. 76–77; Mary C. Clement, "My Mother's Teaching Career—What It Can Tell Us About Teachers Who Are Not Certified," *Phi Delta Kappan* 87, no. 10 (June 2006), pp. 772–776.

5. Melody J. Shank, "Common Space, Common Time, Common Work," *Educational Leadership* 62, no. 8 (May 2005), pp. 16–19.

6. Thomas M. McCann, Larry R. Johannessen, and Bernard Ricca, "Responding to New Teachers' Concerns," *Educational Leadership* 62, no. 8 (May 2005), pp. 30–34; Juliet Williams, "Higher Pay No Longer Enough to Make New Teachers Stay," *Contra Costa Times,* February 15, 2006, www.contracostatimes.com/mld/cctimes/.

7. Rhea Borja, "E-Mentors' Offer Online Support, Information for Novice Instructors," *Education Week* 21, no. 29

(April 3, 2002), p. 12; "Induction and Teacher Turnover," *Teaching Quality RESEARCH MATTERS,* The Southeast Center for Teaching Quality, Issue 5, May 2003, p. 1.

8. Ellen Nakashima, "Montgomery Teachers May Face Peer Review," *The Washington Post,* January 2, 1999, pp. B-1, B-6.

9. Judith W. Little, "Teachers' Professional Development in a Climate of Educational Reform," *Educational Evaluation and Policy Analysis* 15 (1993), pp. 129–51; Linda Darling-Hammond and Milbrey W. McLaughlin, "Policies That Support Professional Development in an Era of Reform," in Milbrey W. McLaughlin and Ida Oberman, eds., *Teaching and Learning: New Policies, New Practices* (New York: Teachers College Press, 1996), pp. 208–18.

10. National Education Association, *Status of the American Public School Teacher, 1995–1996* (Washington, DC: National Education Association, 1997).

11. Organization for Economic Cooperation and Development (OECD), *Education at a Glance, OECD Indicators* (Paris: OECD, 1995), pp. 176–77.

12. *Condition of Education,* National Center for Education Statistics, NCES (Washington, D.C.: U.S. Department of Education, 2003).

13. Jeff Archer, "Recruitment Pinch Fuels Global Trade in K–12 Teachers," *Education Week* 20, no. 22 (February 14, 2001), p. 8; Lynette Holloway, "Foreign Teachers Receive a Short Course on the City," *The New York Times on the Web,* August 14, 2001.

14. Susan Moore Johnson, Susan Kardos, and Christine Sanni, "Research on New Teaching Shows a Changing Profession: 43% of New Teachers in New Jersey Plan to Leave Classroom Teaching; Nearly Half Are Mid-Career Entrants," *Harvard Graduate School of Education on the Web,* August 27, 2001; Lee Foster, "New Teachers Relish Mid-Life Career Change," *The Hartford Courant on the Web,* October 23, 2000.

15. Bess Keller, "Schools Employing Online Talent Tests to Screen Prospects," *Education Week* 23, no. 37 (May 19, 2004), pp. 1, 22.

16. Jacques Steinberg, "Giving the Teacher Balm for Burnout," *The New York Times on the Web,* January 7, 2001.

17. National Board for Professional Teaching Standards, 2006, www.nbpts.org/nbct/nbctdir_byyear.cfm.

18. Quoted in "Forging a Profession," *Teacher* (September/October 1989), pp. 12, 16.

19. National Board for Professional Teaching Standards Web site (www.nbpts.org).

20. "National Certification Picks Up Steam," *American Teacher* 76, no. 6 (May/June 1992), p. 3.

21. National Board for Professional Teaching Standards Web site (www.nbpts.org).

22. Briant Farnsworth, Jerry Debenham, and Gerald Smith, "Designing and Implementing a Successful Merit Pay Program for Teachers," *Phi Delta Kappan* 73, no. 4 (December 1991), pp. 320–25.

23. Juan A. Lozano, "Houston to Link Teachers' Pay, Test Scores," *The Guardian,* January 11, 2006, www.guardian.co.uk; Jocelyn Wiener, "Governor's Merit Pay Program for Teachers Is Risky in Big State, Kirst Says," *Sacramento Bee,* January 18, 2005; Holly K. Hatcher and Terrence

Stutz, "Incentive Pay Enters Classroom; Other States Watching as Texas Ties Teacher Bonuses to Test Scores," *The Dallas Morning News,* June 12, 2006, www.dallasnews.com.

24. "Teachers Willing to Talk About Merit Pay," *Chicago Daily Herald,* June 7, 2006, www.asq.org.

25. Vivian Truen and Katherine C. Boles, "How 'Merit Pay' Squelches Teaching," *The Boston Globe,* September 28, 2005, www.boston.com/news/globe/.

26. Kenneth J. Cooper, "Performance Pay for Teachers Catches On," *The Washington Post,* February 26, 2000, p. A4; Alfie Kohn, "The Folly of Merit Pay," *Education Week* 23, no. 3 (September 17, 2003), pp. 44, 31.

27. *Is "Paying for Performance" Changing Schools?* The SREB Career Ladder Clearinghouse Report 1988 (Atlanta: Southern Regional Education Board), p. 8.

28. Adam Urbanski, "The Rochester Contract: A Status Report," *Educational Leadership* 46, no. 3 (November 1988), pp. 48–52.

29. Andy Baumgartner, "A Teacher Speaks Out: Insights from the National Teacher of the Year," *The Washington Post,* March 26, 2000, p. B4.

30. Albert Shanker, "Where We Stand: Is It Time for National Standards and Exams?" *American Teacher* 76, no. 6 (May/June 1992), p. 5.

31. Jeff Archer, "NEA Board Approves AFT 'Partnership' Pact," *Education Week on the Web,* February 21, 2001.

32. Lapointe quoted in Gerald W. Bracey, "The Second Bracey Report on the Condition of Public Education," *Phi Delta Kappan* (October 1992), pp. 104–17, cited in David C. Berliner and Bruce J. Biddle, *The Manufactured Crisis,* (Reading, MA: Addison Wesley, 1995), p. 54.

33. Gerald W. Bracey, "U.S. Students: Better Than Ever," *The Washington Post,* December 22, 1995, p. A-9; and Robert J. Samuelson, "Three Cheers for Schools," *Newsweek,* December 4, 1995, p. 61. See also Berliner and Biddle, *The Manufactured Crisis,* pp. 13–64.

34. "Survey Gauges Teens' View of Tech Future," *Lemelsin-MIT Invention Index,* Massachusetts Institute of Technology, January 12, 2006, web.mit.edu.

35. Berliner and Biddle, *The Manufactured Crisis,* p. 146; see also Richard Rothstein, *The Way We Were? The Myths and Realities of America's Student Achievement* (Washington, DC: Century Fund, 1998).

CHAPTER 13 Q AND A GUIDE TO ENTERING THE TEACHING PROFESSION

1. *Teachers—Preschool, Kindergarten, Elementary, Middle, and Secondary, Occupational Handbook, 2006–07 Edition* (Washington DC: U.S. Department of Labor, Bureau of Labor Statistics, 2006).

2. American Association for Employment in Education, *Educator Supply and Demand in the United States, 1999* (Columbus, OH: AAEE, 2001).

3. National Education Association (NEA), *Fact Sheet on Teacher Shortages* (Washington, DC: NEA, 2001).

4. Barbara Kantrowitz and Pat Wingert, "Teachers Wanted," *Newsweek,* October 2000, pp. 37–42; Julie Blair, "Districts Wooing Teachers with Bonuses, Incentives" in *Education Week on the Web,* August 2, 2000.

5. National Center for Education Statistics (NCES), *Digest of Education Statistics, 2002* (Washington, DC: U.S. Department of Education, 2002).

6. NEA, *Status of the American Public School Teacher,* Washington, DC, 2003.

7. Martha Naomi Alt and Katharin Peter, *Private Schools: A Brief Portrait,* (Washington DC: U.S. Department of Education, National Center for Education Statistics, 2002).

8. Patricia L. Rieman, *Teaching Portfolios: Presenting Your Professional Best* (New York: McGraw-Hill Companies, 2000).

9. Maria Mihalik, "Thirty Minutes to Sell Yourself," *Teacher,* April 1991, p. 32d.

10. Ibid., p. 32e.

11. Joseph Cronin, "State Regulations of Teacher Preparation," in Lee Shulman and Gary Sykes (eds.), *Handbook of Teaching and Policy* (New York: Longman, 1983), p. 174.

12. NEA, *Status of the American Public School Teacher.*

13. "Alternative Routes to Teacher Certification: An Overview" (Washington, DC: The National Center for Education Information, 2005), www.ncei.com.

14. Ibid.

15. Jessica Sandman, "Study Finds Alternative Teachers Less Qualified, But Meeting Needs," *Education Week on the Web,* September 10, 1997.

16. Brenda Freeman and Ann Schopen, "Quality Reform in Teacher Education: A Brief Look at the Admissions Testing Movement," *Contemporary Education,* 62(4), p. 279; Educational Testing Service (ETS), *The Praxis Exam: State by State Requirements.*

17. Educational Testing Service (ETS), *The Praxis Exam: State by State Requirements* (Princeton, NJ: ETS, 2001).

18. Thomas Toch, *In the Name of Excellence* (New York: Oxford University Press, 1991), p. 164.

19. National Research Council, *Testing Teacher Candidates: The Role of Licensure Tests in Improving Teacher Quality* (Washington, DC: National Academy Press, 2001); Harold Berlak, *Testing Teachers to Raise Standards: Does It Work?* (*Milwaukee:* Center for Education Research, Analysis, and Innovation, School of Education, University of Wisconsin—Milwaukee, May 23, 2000), www.asu.edu/educ/epsl/EPRU/point_of_view_essays/cerai-00-12.htm#3.

20. National Center for Education Statistics (NCES), *Condition of Education, 2001* (Washington, DC: U.S. Department of Education, 2001); National Center for Education Statistics (NCES), *America's Teachers: Profile of a Profession, 1993–1994* (Washington, DC: U.S. Department of Education, 1997).

21. Freeman and Schopen, "Quality Reform in Teacher Education: A Brief Look at the Admissions Testing Movement"; National Research Council, *Testing Teacher Candidates: The Role of Licensure Tests in Improving Teacher Quality* (Washington, DC: National Academy Press, 2001).

22. George A. Clowes, "Teachers Like Tenure But Admit Its Flaws: New Teachers Left with Most Difficult Students," (Chicago: The Heartland Institute, July 1, 2003), www.heartland.org.

23. Steve Farkas, Jean Johnson and Ann Duffett with Leslie Moye and Jackie Vine., *Stand by Me: What Teachers Really Think About Unions, Merit Pay and Other Professional Matter, Public Agenda,* 2003, www.publicagenda.org; Ari Kaufman and Aaron Hanscom, *Extending Teacher Tenure,* January 10, 2006, www.OpinionEditorials.com.

24. Kerry White, "In a Push for Accountability, Tenure Becomes a Target," *Education Week on the Web,* June 25, 1997.

25. Caroline Hendrie, "Principals Losing Tenure," *Teacher Magazine on the Web,* April 1998.

26. Special thanks to Diana Coleman, Kevin Dwyer, Phyllis Lerner, and Kathryn McNerney for their assistance in preparing this section.

THE COURAGE TO TEACH: A FINAL WORD

1. Parker Palmer, *The Courage to Teach* (New York: Jossey-Bass, 1998).

2. Marianne Williamson, *A Return to Love, Reflections on the Principles of "A Course in Miracles"* (New York: Harper Paperback, 1996).

3. Vaclav Havel, speech delivered to a joint meeting of the U.S. Congress quoted in *Time* magazine, March 5, 1990, pp. 14–15.

4. The origin of this quote is in some doubt. Some attribute it to Nelson Mandela and others to author Marianne Williamson.

5. Frederick Buechner, *Wishful Thinking: A Seeker's ABC* (San Francisco: HarperSanFrancisco, 1993), p. 119.

CREDITS

TEXT AND LINE ART CREDITS

CHAPTER 1

Figure 1.2: E. Muir, F. H. Nelson, & A. Baldaro (2005). "Survey and Analysis of Teacher Salary Trends," 2005, Washington, D.C.: American Federation of Teachers. Used with permission. **pp. 12, 13:** Robert Howsam et al., "Criteria for a Profession" and "Criteria for a Semi-Profession" from *Educating a Profession Report on the Bicentennial Commission of Education for Profession of Teaching.* Copyright © 1978. Reprinted with the permission of American Association of Colleges for Teacher Education. **Figure 1.3:** National Education Association, "Status of the American Public School Teacher," 2000–2001. © 2003 National Education Association. Used with permission. **Figure 1.4:** "America's Priorities" from Public Agenda 2005. Public Agenda data: Gallup 2005. Used by permission. **p. 16:** Reprinted courtesy of the *Chicago Tribune,* September 28, 1975, Section 1. **p. 26:** "Profile in Education" by Jamie Escalante. From *Educational Leadership* 46, no. 5 (February 1989), pp. 46–47. Reprinted by permission. The Association for Supervision and Curriculum Development is a worldwide community of educators advocating sound policies and sharing best practices to achieve the success of each learner. To learn more, visit ASCD at www.ascd.org.

CHAPTER 2

p. 47: From *All I Really Need to Know I Learned in Kindergarten* by Robert L. Fulghum. Copyright © 1986, 1988 by Robert Fulghum. Used by permission of Villard Books, a division of Random House, Inc.

CHAPTER 3

p. 87: Virginia Nolan, excerpt from "The Song in His Heart" from *Instructor* 101.8 (1992). Copyright (1992 by Scholastic, Inc. Reprinted with the permission of Scholastic, Inc. **p. 90:** From "There is No Rose Garden: A Second Generation Rural Head Start Program" by Julie Chlebo. Unpublished doctoral dissertation, 1999. Used with permission by the author. **p. 96:** Text adapted from Jacqueline Jordan and Beverley Jean Armento, *Culturally Responsive Teaching: Lesson Planning for Elementary and Middle Grades.* Copyright © 2001.Adapted with permission by The McGraw-Hill Companies. **p. 104:** Courtesy of Lacey Rosenbaum. **p. 104:** Courtesy of John Burns. **Figure 3.2:** National Clearinghouse for English Language Acquisition, Washington DC, December 2005. **Figure 3.3:** "Reaching Students' Families on Their Terms" by Lori Pratani from *The Washington Post,* January 24, 2006, p. B3. © 2006, The Washington Post, reprinted with permission. **Figure 3.4:** "States with Official Language" from U.S. English, Inc. (2002). Reprinted with permission. **Figure 3.5:** Data from Orfield and Lee, "Racial Transformation and the Changing Nature of Segregation," Civil Rights Project, Harvard University, January 2006.

CHAPTER 4

p. 125: From Marta I. Cruz-Janzen, "Culturally Authentic Bias," *Rethinking Schools* 13.1 (Fall 1998): 5. Reprinted by permission. **Figure 4.2:** In order to improve public education in America, some people think the focus should be on reforming the existing pubic school system. Others believe the focus should be on finding an alternative to the existing public school system. Which approach do you think is preferable—reforming the existing school system or finding an alternative to the existing public school system? © 2000, 2003, 2005 The Gallup Organization/Phi Delta Kappa. Used with permission. **Figure 4.3:** Do you favor or oppose allowing students and parents to choose a private school to attend at public expense? © 2005 The Gallup Organization/Phi Delta Kappa. Used with permission. **p. 146:** From Jonathan Kozol, *Educational Leadership* 50.3 (November 1992). Copyright © 1992 by the Association for Supervision & Curriculum Development. Reprinted by permission. The Association for Supervision and Curriculum Development is a worldwide community of educators advocating sound policies and sharing best practices to achieve the success of each learner. To learn more, visit ASCD at www.ascd.org.

CHAPTER 5

Figure 5.1 and p. 177: From Joseph Goodlad, *A Place Called School.* Copyright © 1984. Reprinted with permission by The McGraw-Hill Companies. **pp. 182–183:** Letter to *The Arlingtonian* school newspaper. Reprinted by permission. **p. 195:** Ruby K. Payne, Ph.D., *A Framework for Understanding Poverty,* Highlands, TX: aha! Process, Inc. (Rev. 2005). Used with permission.

CHAPTER 6

p. 230: "Selected State Content Standards" from Education World, www.educationworld.com/standards. Reprinted with the permission of Education World. **Figure 6.5:** Drawing by a female high-school English teacher from a rural unified school district. From the collection of Tirupalavanam G. Ganesh (2002), Educators images of high-stakes testing: An exploratory analysis of the value of visual methods. Paper presented at the Annual Meeting of the American Educational Research Association, April 1–5, 2002, New Orleans, LA. Reprinted by permission. **pp. 248–249:** From J. Abner Peddiwell, *Saber-Tooth Curriculum.* Copyright © 1939, 1972 The McGraw-Hill Companies. Reprinted with permission from The McGraw-Hill Companies. **p. 232:** From Reginald Ballard in "My School's on the List: Here's Why," *The Washington Post* Outlook section, March 12, 2006, pp. B1, B4, B5. **p. 232:** From Rhonda Pitts, "My School's on the List: Here's Why," *The Washington Post* Outlook section, March 12, 2006, pp. B1, B4, B5. Used with permission by Rhonda Pitts. **p. 233:** From Rodney Henderson, "My School's on the List: Here's Why," *The Washington Post* Outlook section, March 12, 2006, pp. B1, B4, B5. Used with permission by Rodney Henderson. **p. 233:** From Sue Dziedzic, "My School's on the List: Here's Why," *The Washington Post* Outlook section, March 12, 2006, pp. B1, B4, B5.

PART III

p. 265: John Solomon Otto, "Class Act." Used with permission.

PART IV

p. 427: Melissa Steel, "Class Act." Reprinted with permission.

CHAPTER 11

Figure 11.4: The MetLife Survey of The American Teacher, 2001: Key Elements of Quality Schools (Harris Interactive, Inc., 2001). Used with permission.

CHAPTER 12

Figure 12.6: © 2006 Lemelson-MIT Invention Index. Used with permission. http://mit.edu/invent/n-pressreleases/n-press-06index.html. **pp. 474–475:** Marthina Carkci, *The Washington Post,* November 8, 1998, p. C3. Used by permission.

PHOTO CREDITS

PART I

p. 2: Bob Daemmrich/The Image Works

CHAPTER 1

p. 11: Bonnie Kamin Photography; **p. 15:** Library of Congress; **p. 19:** Butch Martin/Getty Images Inc.; **p. 26:** AP Wide World Photos

CHAPTER 2

p. 36 (top): Bob Daemmrich/The Image Works; **p. 36 (bottom):** Jack Hollingsworth/Getty Images Inc.; **p. 37 (top):**, Ariel Skelley/Corbis; **p. 37 (bottom):** Masterfile Royalty Free; **p. 40:** Mary Kate Denny; **p. 41:** Bob Daemmrich/The Image Works; **p. 43:** Robin Samper Image Services; **p. 45:** Lori Adamski Peek/Getty Images Inc.; **p. 55:** Courtesy of Sally Smith; **p. 56:** AP Wide World Photo/Joe Raymond; **p. 59:** Bob Daemmrich/PhotoEdit Inc.

CHAPTER 3

p. 69: Thinkstock Images/Jupiter Images; **p. 71:** Kevin Dodge/Corbis; **p. 75:** Woodfin Camp/Woodfin Camp & Associates; **p. 76:** Florida State Archive; **p. 84 (top):** Bettmann/Corbis; **p. 84 (bottom):** Rhonda Sidney/PhotoEdit; **p. 90:** Charles Gupton/Corbis; **p. 94:** Erin Patrice O'Brien/Getty Images Inc.; **p. 95 (top):** Comstock/PictureQuest; **p. 95 (bottom):** Dynamic Graphics Group/Creatas/Alamy; **p. 96:** Michael Newman/PhotoEdit; **p. 97 (top):** David Young-Wolff; **p. 97 (bottom):** Bruce Ando/Index Stock Imagery; **p. 98 (top):** David Young-Wolff; **p. 98 (bottom):** Digital Vision/PunchStock; **p. 102:** BananaStock/PunchStock

INDEX